The Random House International Encyclopedia of

GOLF

THE RANDOM HOUSE INTERNATIONAL ENCYCLOPEDIA OF GOLF

THE DEFINITIVE GUIDE TO THE GAME

MALCOLM CAMPBELL

FOREWORD BY TOM WATSON

PHOTOGRAPHY BY BRIAN D. MORGAN

RANDOM HOUSE
NEW YORK

To my parents . . . for what they gave that I might have

SPECIAL CONTRIBUTORS
Bobby Burnet
Alick A. Watt

PROJECT EDITOR Roger Smoothy
ART EDITOR Brian Rust

EDITORS Reg Grant, Jon Kirkwood
DESIGNERS Emma Ainsworth, Mark Johnson Davies, Heather McCarry

SENIOR ART EDITOR Caroline Murray
MANAGING EDITOR Carolyn King
MANAGING ART EDITOR Nick Harris

 PUBLISHED IN THE UNITED STATES BY RANDOM HOUSE, INC., NEW YORK.

ORIGINALLY PUBLISHED IN GREAT BRITAIN BY DORLING KINDERSLEY

LIBRARY OF CONGRESS CARD CATALOGUE NUMBER 91-52661
ISBN 0-394-58893-2

MANUFACTURED IN ITALY

24689753
FIRST U.S. EDITION

Half-title (page 1) *Bronze statuette of J.H. Taylor*

Title (pages 2–3) *Panoramic view of Royal County Down, Northern Ireland; and Seve Ballesteros after driving*

CONTENTS

Foreword / Introduction 6

1
THE EARLY GAME: 8

Misty Origins 10
The Playclub Era 20
The Clubmaker Professional 22
The Golf Revolution 24
Featheries and Gutties 26
Bulgers, Brassies, and Baffies 28
Tees / Carrying the Clubs 30
Taking Golf to the World 32

A Willie Park, Sr. putter of 1875 and feathery ball contrast with their modern counterparts of a century later (top)

2
THE MODERN GAME: 38

Competing for Glory 40
Women in Golf 46
The Rise of the Rubber-core Ball 48
Modern Club Design 50
The Full Set of Clubs 52
Golf Accessories 54
Course Architects 56

3
CHAMPIONSHIP COURSES OF THE WORLD: 58

The World of Golf 60
Augusta National 62
Ballybunion 66
Baltusrol 68

Sunrise over the 16th hole at Oakland Hills, Michigan, U.S.A.

Carnoustie 70
Chantilly 74
Club zur Vahr 76
Colonial 78
Cypress Point 80
Desert Highlands 82
Falsterbo 84
Ganton 86
Glen Abbey 88
Harbour Town 90
Lindrick 92
Mariya 94
Medinah 96
Merion 98
Muirfield 102
Muirfield Village 106
The National 110
Oakland Hills 114
Oakmont 116
Pebble Beach 118
Pevero 120
Pine Valley 122
Pinehurst 124
Portmarnock 128
Riviera 132
Royal Birkdale 134
Royal Cape 136
Royal County Down 138

Royal Dornoch 140
Royal Liverpool 144
Royal Lytham and St. Annes 148
Royal Melbourne 150
Royal North Devon 152
Royal Portrush 156
Royal St. George's 158
Royal Sydney 160
Royal Troon 162
Rye 166
St. Andrews 168
El Saler 174
Shinnecock Hills 176
Sunningdale 180
Tryall 184
Turnberry 186
Valderrama 190
Wentworth 192
Winged Foot 194
World Directory of Courses 196

4
The Hall of Fame: 214

Amy Alcott, Peter Alliss, Isao Aoki 216
Seve Ballesteros 218
John Ball, Miller Barber 220
Patty Berg, Tommy Bolt, Michael Bonallack 222
James Braid 224
Jack Burke, Sir Guy Campbell, JoAnne Carner 226
Joe Carr, Billy Casper, Bob Charles 228
Henry Cotton 230
Ben Crenshaw, Bernard Darwin 232
Laura Davies, Bruce Devlin, Flory Van Donck 234
George Duncan, Willie Dunn, Jr. 236
Nick Faldo 238
Max Faulkner, Ray Floyd, Ed Furgol 240
David Graham, Hubert Green, Ralph Guldahl, Sandy Herd 242
Walter Hagen 244
Ben Hogan 246
Harold Hilton, Horace Hutchinson, Hale Irwin 248
Tony Jacklin 250
Bobby Jones 252
Andrew Kirkaldy, Tom Kite 254
Johnny Laidlay, Bernhard Langer 256
Tony Lema, Gene Littler 258
Bobby Locke, Henry Longhurst 260
Nancy Lopez 262
Sandy Lyle 264

Image of a golfer in a whisky advertisement of about 1905

Alister Mackenzie, Graham Marsh, Gerald Micklem 266
Cary Middlecoff, Johnny Miller, Abe Mitchell 268
Old Tom Morris, Young Tom Morris 270
Kel Nagle, Tommy Nakajima, Byron Nelson 272
Larry Nelson, Jack Newton, Norman Von Nida 274
Jack Nicklaus 276
Greg Norman 278
Andy North, Christy O'Connor, Christy O'Connor, Jr. 280
Ayako Okamoto, Francis Ouimet, Alf Padgham 282
Arnold Palmer 284
Willie Park, Jr., Gary Player 286
Ted Ray, Dai Rees 288
Allan Robertson 290
Doug Sanders, Gene Sarazen 292
Sam Snead 294
Craig Stadler, Jan Stephenson, Curtis Strange 296
Freddie Tait, J.H. Taylor 298
Lee Trevino 300
Peter Thomson, Jessie Valentine, Roberto de Vicenzo 302
Harry Vardon 304
Glenna Collett Vare, Tom Watson 306
Tom Weiskopf, Joyce Wethered 308
Kathy Whitworth, Ian Woosnam 310
Mickey Wright, Charlie Yates, Fuzzy Zoeller 312
Babe Zaharias 314

5
Records and Reference: 316

Official souvenir program from the Ryder Cup of 1933, hosted at Southport and Ainsdale, the fourth match played between the United States and Great Britain and Ireland

Glossary: 330
Index: 332
Acknowledgments: 336

Foreword

When I was approached to write a foreword to *The Random House International Encyclopedia of Golf*, I examined the book and was honestly delighted with what I read and saw. More than most, this volume truly covers not only the history and traditions of our game, but in its enormous scope and range will bring home to every reader the magnitude and majesty of the sport.

For me to aver that I love the game and what it stands for is, naturally, hardly a surprise. However, I must emphasize that I love *all* things that are Golf – the history and tradition, the places we golfers travel to, the courses and links on which we play, the code of honesty and self-discipline under which the game is played and, most importantly of all, the people I have met and the friends I have made from the sport.

While the courses in the United States are magnificent, it is the world scope of the game that intrigues me most. I love playing golf any place there is a course and an opportunity. I have played and won in Asia, Australia, the United States, and Europe. I have won five British Opens in Scotland and England, where playing the game is wonderful. But please, let us not forget Ireland, which is also very special. I play Ballybunion and some of the other great Irish links almost every year during the week prior to the British Open. To me, playing the British Isles is always a memorable experience. What could be closer to heaven on earth than to sit in a pub after a round and lift a glass of single malt with people for whom golf is a national sport?

Enjoy this encyclopedia. It carries you back in time to the fascinating origins of the sport, portrays the current state of the international game, and transports you to the most challenging and most beautiful courses in the world.

Tom Watson

Introduction

"Golf is a wonderful game. It is more than a game to me: it is a life's work, a career, a profession. Whether it is a science or an art I do not know – it is probably half and half – but it is a noble occupation all the same."

This was how the late Sir Henry Cotton, three times winner of the British Open, once explained how he felt about the royal and ancient game of golf. In his later years, when he had finished with playing and the implements of his profession had long been consigned to the locker room, golf still ruled his life and set the standards by which he lived during his retirement years.

Noble occupation
The author (left) hands Henry Cotton a club at the 1982 Open.

It was not just the game that was important to him; it was the friendship, the people and the traditions. So it is with most of us who love and cherish this golfing life. There are few other fields of human endeavor in which so many are held together by a common bond, for golf commands wide appeal and is truly an international sport.

Golf offers a dignified and honest lifestyle because the essence of fine manners, humor and good taste are at the heart of its traditions. More than any other game, it is the ultimate test of character for the individual. To cheat at golf is to cheat no one but oneself, but to strike the ball honestly on the center of the clubface and watch it soar from an elevated tee against a backdrop of blue sky to a green fairway below is to experience a sense of euphoria.

Golf is also a great leveller. While it is inconceivable that a once-a-week tennis player could ever play on the Centre Court at Wimbledon, it is perfectly feasible for a novice to stand on the first tee of the Old

Dressing the part
Golf and fashion have always gone together, but manners and sportsmanship define the true golfer.

course at St. Andrews and embark upon an enjoyable and reasonably competitive game with a professional player. The ability to close the gap and make a competitive match possible is due to golf's sometimes abused but largely equitable handicap system, which is unique to the game. For the professional, a combination of ability and endless practice provides the means to make a living – in many cases a very good living indeed – from the sport, while for the rest of us, blessed with less golfing dexterity, golf is simply a pastime of immense pleasure.

It was the Scots who took the game from their famous links courses to the far corners of the earth. Yet it matters not whether golfers gather around the long table at Prestwick or at golf clubs in the U.S. or the Far East. Wherever they meet they share a rich experience and enjoy the best of the great traditions and spirit of the game's origins. These values are understood in golf clubs throughout the world, and long may this heritage continue.

The ease of travel today has allowed the professional variation of the game to flourish throughout the world. No longer do the great champions have to spend weeks traveling from one event to another in the way that Bobby Jones, Walter Hagen, and Henry Cotton had to at the height of their careers.

For those who wish to explore the world of golf outside their own country, the horizons are now limitless. I have been fortunate in the course of my profession to travel to a wide and varied assortment of golf courses around the world. The common factor in those thousands of miles traveled has been the friendship and hospitality of fellow golf lovers. Unlike so many other games which, when exposed to international attention have become abused or corrupted, golf has resisted any efforts to change the legacy of its historic past. Today golf remains much the same as it was when the first players put club to ball on a wind-swept stretch of linksland on the east coast of Scotland.

The aim stays the same (right)
Despite materials from the space-age, a modern American, graphite-shafted metal wood (top) does not differ greatly from the Scottish, lancewood-shafted, aluminium-headed driver of 100 years ago.

Time-honored traditions
Standing majestically at the edge of one of the world's oldest courses, the Royal & Ancient clubhouse at St. Andrews embodies the spirit and traditions of golf.

The preservation of such values and traditions is a responsibility for all of us who call ourselves golfers, and one we must hand on to future generations. By so doing we will retain what Sir Henry Cotton rightly described as something that is "more than a game." In this volume I have tried to give a flavor of what this game is about, its history, the people who have made it what it is, and the great courses upon which it is played. If I have succeeded in some small measure I shall feel the effort spent on such a wonderful subject to have been entirely worthwhile.

Malcolm Campbell
Auchinloch, Scotland

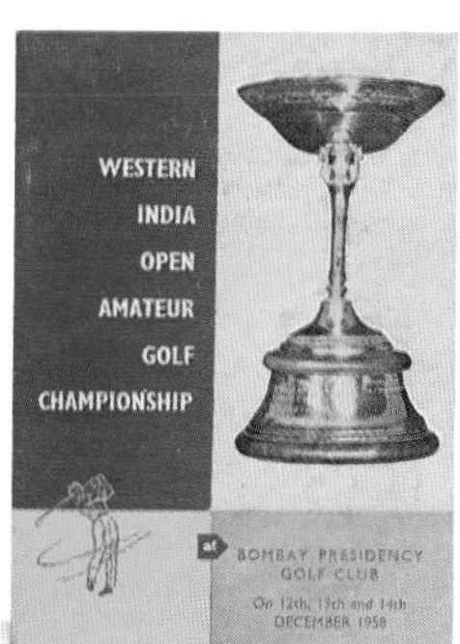

International sport
The brotherhood of golf has expanded swiftly throughout the world. This program for the Western India Open Amateur at Bombay bears witness to the universality of the appreciation of golf.

Satisfying scene
Great course design combines beautiful surroundings with challenging playing conditions, as at Baltusrol. To strike the ball accurately and see it safely reach its target is a sublime experience.

CHAPTER 1

The Early Game

There is no dispute that golf, or a pastime similar to the game we know today, has been played for centuries, but exactly how and when this game of club and ball first arrived to test and frustrate the human soul remains a matter of speculation. Some trace golf's origins back to the game of paganica, played in the time of the Roman Empire, while others see it as evolving from the French jeu de mail or the Dutch game of kolven.

A 1920s Doulton jug showing a Jacobean golfer

Whatever the truth of these speculations, the pioneers of golf were undoubtedly the Scots. It was the Scots who developed the game on their seaside links and transported it with them all over the world. Inspired by their passion for the game, they taught other nations to play. But just as importantly, they provided the first implements for golf and the courses to play on, and they laid down the standards and basic rules that still, to a large degree, prevail today.

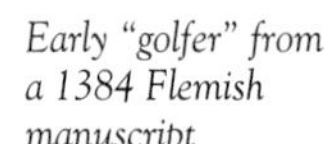

Early "golfer" from a 1384 Flemish manuscript

Kolven in Holland, 1668 (left)
A painting by Adriaen van de Velde shows this early club-and-ball game being played on ice near Haarlem.

MISTY ORIGINS

Set the ball rolling
Although the first golf ball was probably made of beechwood, there was no lack of design experimentation. This early relative of the golf ball is made of animal hair and thread in a linen pouch.

Hours of pleasure
A Flemish Book of Hours *from 1530, illustrated under the supervision of the famous miniaturist Simon Bennink, displays perhaps the first true image of golf.*

LIKE SO MANY *other forms of human activity, golf has no clear recorded origins. With little solid evidence available, accounts of the early history of the game often depend heavily on the writer's imagination. Accepting that, as Voltaire sagely observed, the ancient histories are but fables that have been agreed upon, there are many mythological starting points from which to embark on an account of the game.*

The danger of fable is that it is too readily confused with fact. Quite simply, there is no documentary evidence of golf, as we know it today, prior to the middle of the fifteenth century, and there is no hard evidence to disprove the most obvious and well-documented theory that the game began on the east coast of Scotland. But the quest to find earlier evidence of the game in its present form has taxed the minds of eminent men over many decades.

QUEST FOR ORIGINS

Most research has centered on establishing the relationship between golf and other pastimes in Europe, and seeking support for the theory that one or another of them was the forerunner of golf. There have been so many different types of club-and-ball game throughout the course of history that speculation knows almost no limit. Although the lack of solid facts frustrates attempts to reach a substantial conclusion, it is both illuminating and fascinating to compare other club-and-ball games with golf, consider any areas of overlap between them, and judge their possible influence on the development of the game.

ROMAN COUNTRY SPORT

Some historians have gone back as far as ancient Rome and forged a link between golf and paganica, a game that was popular with country folk in the early days of the Roman Empire. Little is known about the rules of the game, but legend has it that paganica was played with a bent stick and a ball made from leather filled with feathers. The interesting connection here is that early golf balls were also made with feathers stuffed into leather covers (see page 26), although the paganica ball is believed to have been about 4–7 inches (10–18cm) in diameter, so its resemblance to a "feathery" is not that close.

The expansion of the Roman Empire north and west from the Mediterranean could well have carried paganica across Europe. The legions who supported the Roman governors were recruited from the country districts, and it would have been natural for the occupying forces to have indulged their rural pastimes in foreign lands as they did at home.

This theory suggests that paganica was at the root of the later development of various other club-and-ball games in northern Europe, particularly in France and the Low Countries, which have also been proposed as the forerunners of golf. The principal

candidates among them are cambuca, jeu de mail, chole, crosse, kolven, and pell mell. Cambuca (or cambuta) was played in England in the mid-fourteenth century during the reign of Edward III. There are close similarities with paganica: cambuca players used a curved club and a ball that was made from feathers which, it is thought, was propelled toward a mark set in the ground. In 1363 a royal proclamation was issued banning able-bodied men from all games on feast days. The list ranged from cockfighting to football and "other vain games," but also included cambuca and club ball, which was a form of hockey. Instead, the men were urged, on penalty of imprisonment, to practice shooting with bow and arrow. Less than 100 years later, a Scottish Act of Parliament was to ban golf for the same reasons and threaten the same penalty of imprisonment for those caught playing it.

In the Great East Window of Gloucester Cathedral in the west of England, also dating from the mid-fourteenth century, a headless figure in stained glass is depicted swinging a curved club. The object of his attention is a yellow ball on a green background. Although the figure is known as the "golf player," it is more likely the game in question was cambuca, as the window is contemporary with the game and the ban that went with it.

Mail shot
Lauthier's Nouveaux Règles pour le Jeu de Mail *of 1717 shows the wooden mallet swung by a player of the game.*

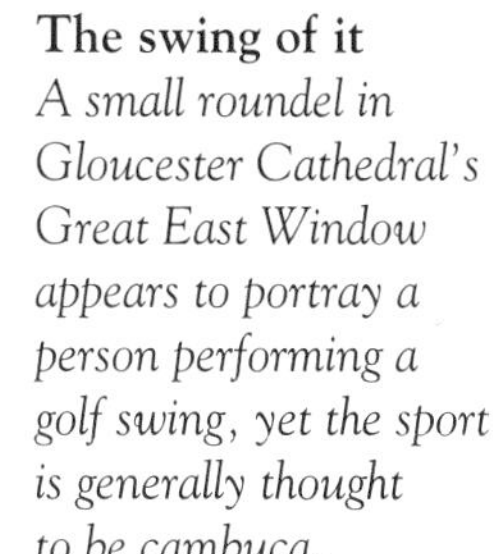

The swing of it
A small roundel in Gloucester Cathedral's Great East Window appears to portray a person performing a golf swing, yet the sport is generally thought to be cambuca.

The Games of France

Another game that appears to have owed much in its origins to the Roman game of paganica was the southern French sport of jeu de mail. The game was played with a *mail* (wooden mallet) and a wooden ball. The mallet was quite flexible and the ball could be struck substantial distances.

The object of the game was to play the ball along a designated course about a half a mile long to a fixed point. Jeu de mail seems to have resembled golf in being an individual game, with each player retaining the use of his own ball throughout the game. The

Players at pell mell
An engraving from the Stuart period depicts pell mell being played in St. James's Park, London. Golf evolved either from or alongside the other club-and-ball games of Europe.

Art and craft
In this painting, dated 1624, Flemish painter Paul Bril provides a fascinating visual record of the cross-country game of jeu de mail. In the lower right corner of the oil painting, a clubmaker, surrounded by his products, can be seen crafting a wooden ball.

***Choleurs* in action**
Unlike golfers, chole players shared a single ball, as seen in the Duchess of Burgundy's 1450 *Book of Hours. Opponents hit the ball in different directions.*

winner of jeu de mail was the player who required the least number of strokes to reach the designated mark, which is obviously not unlike the basic concept of scoring in golf. A game in most respects similar to the ancient form of jeu de mail was still being played at Montpellier in the south of France around the start of the twentieth century. In his *Historical Gossip about Golf and Golfers*, published in 1863, A. Robb offers an interesting account of jeu de mail, describing it as strikingly similar to the game of golf. "The club is made in the shape of a hammer," Robb writes. "The handle is rather longer than that of a golf club, of the same size and thickness, and having a good deal of spring in it." The *mail* club was even designed to cope with a bad lie: "One end of the club is nearly flat, like the flat end of a hammer, with which the ball is usually hit, while the other is more sloped, so as to give a facility for striking the ball when it gets into a position of difficulty. Both ends are strongly bound with iron, which is necessary to give weight to the club as well as prevent the wood from breaking." The ball was also not unlike a golf ball, being "solid and round, made of the root of the box tree, about two inches [5cm] in diameter."

Chole and Crosse

A later version of jeu de mail was chole, which dates back to the mid-fourteenth century in Belgium and France. Chole was played cross-country, using clubs with long wooden shafts and balls that were made of either beechwood or leather, stuffed with whatever material was readily available. The ball was teed up for the first stroke and spare clubs and balls were probably carried around for the players.

The game itself was played in open fields with the object of reaching a fixed point, often some considerable distance away, and touching it with the ball in a specified number of strokes. However, unlike golf, there was only one ball, which all players, including opponents, played. Three members of the striking side each played strokes to advance the ball towards their objective. Then a member of the opposing team was allowed to strike the ball back from where it had come, or towards any hazard that would impair the progress of the striking team. This backward stroke was called a *decholade*, after which the striking team was allowed another three strokes. Crosse seems to have been just another version of chole. The name for the game is derived from the French word for a hooked stick. It is known that the heads of the clubs were made of iron, similar to golf clubs, but like chole, the game seems actually to have had more resemblance to hockey than to golf.

Kolven and the Case for Holland

Those who believe that the origins of golf are to be found in Holland present kolven (or kolf) as the basis of their case. Quite a lot is known about the game (in fact, it is still played in Friesland and north Holland), but its similarity to golf is limited.

Although occasionally played outside on ice, kolven is essentially an indoor game played on a wooden floor, or in kolf courts built specifically for the purpose. In *The Statistical Account of Scotland in 1795*, there is a graphic account of the Dutch game that reinforces the view that kolf and golf are separated by more than their initial letter.

In this account by the Rev. Walker, one of the ministers at the Canongate Church in Edinburgh, there is confirmation that kolven was played in a confined area of about 20 by 60 feet (6 by 18m) and indoors. The reverend gentleman's recollection of the game comes from a period when he was resident in Holland and can therefore be assumed to be close to the mark. He writes: "The floor, which is composed of sand, clay and pitch, is made as level as a billiard table, and the inclosing walls are, for 2 ft. [60cm] above the floor, faced either with polished stone or sheet lead, that they may cause the ball to rebound with accuracy. At about 8 to 10 ft. [2.5 to 5.5m] from each end wall, a circular post of about 5 in. [13cm] diameter is placed precisely in the middle of the area with regard to breadth, consequently opposite the one to the other, at the distance of 40 ft. [12m] or thereby."

Neither the balls nor the clubs were close to their golf equivalents in design: "The balls used in the game are about the size of cricket balls, made perfectly round and elastic, covered with soft leather and sewed with fine wire. The clubs

From pillar to post
The sport that appears on this early Delft tile is certainly the Dutch game of kolven, in which the players took their aim at fixed marks, such as posts. It was sometimes played indoors, and at other times in open country or even on ice.

Dutch winter scene
In winter, a version of kolven was played outside on Holland's frozen rivers and canals.

Kolf in Amsterdam
The limited dimensions of an outdoors kolf court are clearly shown in N.M. Aartman's engraving of kolven players behind the Stadlander Inn in the Amsterdam of 1755.

are from 3 to 4 ft. [1 to 1.2m] long, with stiff shafts. The heads are of brass, and the face, with which the ball is struck, is perfectly smooth, having no inclination, such as might have a tendency to raise the ball from the ground." The target in kolven was two posts: "The game may be played by any number, either in parties against each other, or each person for himself; and the contest is who shall hit the two posts in the fewest strokes and make his ball retreat from the last one with such an accurate length as that it shall lie nearest to the opposite wall of the area."

It seems kolven bears only a limited resemblance to golf. It is more likely to have influenced hockey and, by its transfer on to frozen canals in winter, ice hockey.

Pell mell was another ball-and-mallet game played in a restricted area with palisades, but nonetheless similar in concept to jeu de mail. In the sixteenth century, the game was introduced to Scotland from France, and Mary Queen of Scots is recorded as having played pell mell. But since it is separately recorded that the Scottish queen also played golf, the two games can hardly have been confused in anybody's mind.

The kolf club
Kolven was played with sturdy, heavy wooden clubs with brass plates to reinforce the head. Sixteenth-century examples of the fearsome-looking weapons used in this particular Dutch pastime are rare, but a few survive.

Magic of the Hole

There is a single, simple element missing from these various club-and-ball pastimes that separates them from the game of golf as we know it today: the hole. All use targets of one sort or another, but all are above ground. Golf is unique in that the object of the exercise is to propel a ball across a course, which is liberally littered with obstacles designed to prevent that accomplishment, from a point where it is balanced in midair to another point where it finishes underneath the ground.

It may be a fiendish game, the aim of which is, as Sir Winston Churchill allegedly remarked, "to hit a very small ball into an even smaller hole, with weapons singularly ill designed for the purpose," but the hole is the vital factor. It is the existence of the hole that locates the game's origins firmly in Scotland. In effect, the history of golf is contained within the record of Scottish golf. Golf has been a Scottish national pastime since long before the Scots' ignominious defeat at the hands of the English in 1513, when they lost their king and the flower of their noble families at the Battle of Flodden Field.

Hole change (right)
It is the hole, the unique feature of golf, that has taxed the skill and patience of countless generations of golfers. A lighthearted look at Jacobean golfers on this 1920s Doulton Seriesware Trophy shows a caddie directing the ball in the direction of the ever-tricky hole with a helpful puff of breath.

Prohibition
In the middle of the fifteenth century, James II decreed that "golfe be utterly cryed downe, and not to be used," in order to return the priority to archery, jousting, and allied martial activities crucial to the defense of the Scottish realm.

The Banning of "Golfe"

It is not too difficult to make the case that golf was at least one contributing factor in that merciless defeat. The Scots were no match for the English archers in the first assault and were eventually defeated. It was only a matter of 50 years earlier that King James II of Scotland had been so concerned that golf was interfering with the practice of archery that he banned the game in the Scottish Act of Parliament of 1457 – the first documented reference to today's game. There is every evidence that the people of Scotland took little notice of the Act.

Subsequent bans were introduced, only to be as widely ignored; it can be fairly assumed that the nation's collective ability to put a club to a ball grew in equal proportion to the decline in their prowess with bow and arrow. Indeed, so determined were the Scots to pursue the "golfe" that the Act banning it was repealed just over 40 years later.

Even in Scotland, golf's origins remain obscure. However, it is thought that it was being played there as much as a century before James II ordered that "golfe be utterly cryed downe." It was, indeed, probably already a Scottish pastime as early as 1319, when the French authorities banned all ball games for the same reasons that had been given by the Scottish monarch – to encourage martial skills.

How golf actually originated will remain a mystery. One theory is that fishermen on the east coast of Scotland invented the game to amuse themselves as they returned home from their boats. What would be more natural than for a young fisherman, making his way across the rolling stretches of fine turf among the sand dunes, to pick up a stick of driftwood and aim a blow at a pebble? If he knocked the pebble forward, the competitive instinct inborn in man would demand that he hit it again to see if he could send it even farther.

Inventing the Bunker

If the pebble rolled into a hollow, where sheep had huddled for shelter and their hooves had broken through to the sand just below, then the first obstacle to forward progress of the pebble had been found: the player would then have experienced the frustration that guarantees further attempts. It does not require a great leap of the imagination to develop that scene into a game between competing fishermen played across the links from boat to village, finishing at the same point each time, perhaps close to the local hostelry. If the pebble fell into a rabbit hole then the game of golf had almost been "invented." There are copious links at St. Andrews, and the Old course there is probably the most ancient stretch of land in the world in continuous use for the pursuit of golf. It is the classic links formed by nature, with the hand of man having played little part in its development over the centuries.

As to where the game was first played in Scotland, there can only be conjecture. King James II would not have banned golf in 1457, had it not been widely popular by then and probably much earlier. There is good evidence that it was played at Leith at this time and possibly earlier.

Those who claim that Leith predated St. Andrews as a golf links point to what was then called the German Ocean to uphold the claim, maintaining that St. Andrews could not have been used because the links was then covered by the sea at high tide. However, the links at St. Andrews was almost certainly further inland than it is now because the sea has receded. There is no doubt that golf was played at St. Andrews early in the sixteenth century. The citizens of the town were given the rights to use the links for "golf, futball,

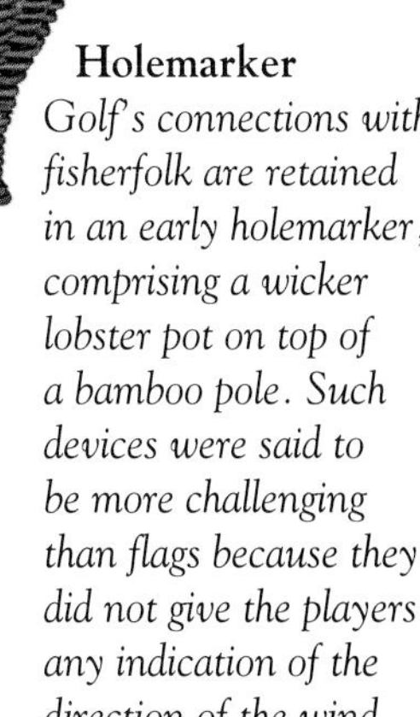

Holemarker
Golf's connections with fisherfolk are retained in an early holemarker, comprising a wicker lobster pot on top of a bamboo pole. Such devices were said to be more challenging than flags because they did not give the players any indication of the direction of the wind.

St. Andrews (left)
The east coast of Scotland was the birthplace of golf, and St. Andrews was probably one of the first courses there. This detail from an anonymous oil painting shows golfers on the Old course, in front of the distinctive St. Andrews skyline. The painting dates from around 1720 and is thought to be the earliest image of golf in Scotland.

shuteing at all times with all other manner of pastimes" by a charter dated January 15, 1552. And it is almost certain that golf was played there a century before that. Much of the other evidence about early golf is found in Kirk Session (church court) records in the sixteenth and seventeenth centuries. In many parts of the east coast of Scotland, parishioners were being punished for playing golf "at the time of the preaching of the Sermon." At St. Andrews in 1599, miscreants were fined small sums for the first two offenses, before the more ominous use of "the repentance pillar." After that, the culprits were "deprived of office" – excommunicated! Had there been as keen an appreciation of art in Britain as there was in the Low Countries at that time, more pictorial evidence might have survived of the early courses. But, as golf historian Robert Browning states: "The fact that the Flemish pictures of chole and the Dutch picture of kolven have no parallel of similarly early date in English or Scottish pictures of golf, is evidence of nothing except the superior artistic sense of the Continent, for it is a remarkable fact that up to the middle of the seventeenth century the art of painting made no appeal to the English taste."

Sabbath-breakers *Two children suffer the wrath of the Church for indulging in golf on the Sabbath. Habitual offenders who "passis to play at the goufe" on Sundays faced a series of fines – and eventual excommunication – for their passion for the burgeoning game.*

Royal Patronage

During the sixteenth century, the game became firmly established on the east coast of Scotland and began to spread farther afield. By this time, golf had gained respectability among the highest levels of society and was certainly played by James VI of Scotland before he acceded to the English throne, as James I, in 1603. His mother, Mary Queen of Scots, was also a notable player. We know that she played golf with one of her attendants, Mary Seton, because the queen lost a match against her and presented her conqueror with a still famous necklace. She also fell foul of the Church for playing golf only a few days after the murder of her husband, Lord Darnley, in 1567. But royal interest in the game in Scotland went back further than this. We know that golf was played as far north as Montrose and had moved inland to Perth by the beginning of the sixteenth century, probably taken there by King James IV. Grandson of the Scottish king who had first tried to ban the game, James IV had in his turn tried to stop the Scots from playing golf, but eventually he was converted to the

Golf royalty (right) *Mary Queen of Scots was one of the first known devotees of golf.*

King of clubs (left) *James VI of Scotland is said to have taken his clubs with him when he acceded to the English throne as James I in 1603. Its court connections gave golf a firm foothold in its progress.*

game himself. By 1502, the king's treasurer had paid 14 shillings to a bowmaker in Perth to supply clubs. From then onwards there was a series of bills paid from the royal coffers for golf balls, and even for lost bets incurred at the game. There is one account of the royal treasurer having to pay the Earl of Bothwell 14 shillings that the king had lost in a wager on a golfing combat somewhere out on the links.

Golf Spreads across Scotland

It was this royal interest in golf that contributed greatly to its spread throughout Scotland and, ultimately, to its export farther afield. The earliest centers of golf all had associations with royalty or, in the case of St. Andrews, with two other influential pillars of Scots society – education and the Church. St. Andrews is Scotland's oldest seat of learning and it was also a powerful Church stronghold.

Scotland's capital, Edinburgh, was the headquarters of the court, and golf blossomed around the city, aided by royal patronage. The same was true in other towns, such as Dunfermline and Perth, where there were royal palaces. The Bishop of Galloway became a player, possibly through court connections, and was probably responsible for the spread of the game to the southwest of the country. The Marquis of Montrose was another keen player, which may well account for that town having a connection with early golf. By the start of the seventeenth century, golf was pursued from the southeast of the country to as far north as the remote and windswept Orkney Islands, where it is believed to have been taken by two men, David Monteith and James Dickson.

Despite golf's popularity, it would be another 150 years before efforts were made to bring an organized structure to the game. But there was no lack of space for the enthusiasts to play. From as far north as Wick

Golf in Edinburgh
One of the first English watercolorists, Paul Sandby, painted soldiers' golf on the links at Bruntsfield in the mid-eighteenth century. Edinburgh Castle, once home to the Scottish court which did so much to spread golf, dominates the scene.

Matching pairs
The Scottish painter Charles Lees completed his Summer Evening at Musselburgh *in 1859. As Edinburgh expanded, the seaside links at Musselburgh superseded Bruntsfield and Leith as the chief local course for the city's golfers, becoming the leading center of golf until eclipsed by St. Andrews in the 1890s.*

Sand tees (right)
On the earliest courses, there were no separate teeing-grounds. A handful of sand was excavated from the previous hole and then molded into a cone on which to set the ball.

Classic ground
The gently undulating terrain of east Scotland is covered in beautifully springy turf and coarse, hazardous gorse and heather. Allied to a fickle climate – prone to rapid changes of wind direction – this land remains the classic environment for golf.

in Caithness to well south of Edinburgh, the east coast of Scotland is blessed with mile upon mile of linksland, quite unsuitable for the growing of crops, but perfect terrain for the leisurely pursuit of golf.

The links evolved from great tracts of unsheltered sand, left by the sea as it receded over the centuries; in confirmation of the fact that they were once covered by the ocean, many courses around Britain are still peppered with seashells. Rivers running through this sandy wasteland to the sea deposited silt and seeds. Offshore breezes blew the sand into great dunes that constantly moved until wild grasses took root and made them stable, permanent features. Fertilizer was supplied by the birds and water by the Scottish climate, to encourage the grasses further. The links was land just waiting for golf to be invented.

Golf's Natural Landscape

The humps and hollows left by the shifting sand and sea and the tight turf cropped short by rabbits and grazing sheep were perfect for the game. The championship courses of Great Britain and Ireland stand as testimony to this truth. All the courses

currently on the Open Championship schedule in Britain, from St. Andrews, currently the farthest north, to Royal St. George's in southeast England, have evolved from linksland. And there are dozens of other links courses in the British Isles – from Royal Dornoch in the far northeast of Scotland to the marvelous links of Ireland, such as Portmarnock, Royal Portrush, and Ballybunion. There are also examples of this terrain in courses in France, Belgium, and the Netherlands, as well as a particularly fine example at Falsterbo in southern Sweden.

However, the early courses were not like those of today. There were no putting greens or tees as such; the courses were rough and received little or no attention. The hole was a crude affair and served not only as the ultimate resting place for the ball but also as a continuous supply of sand for the building of a tee from which to play the next drive.

Pinch of Sand

The player took a handful of damp sand from the hole when he removed his ball and pinched it together to form a small mound. The tee was right beside the hole, which became progressively deeper as more sand was removed. Finally, it was dug so deep that a player could hardly retrieve his ball, at which point a new hole was started.

The areas between the sandhills developed into smooth stretches of turf, probably as a result of continual tracking over the decades by animals such as rabbits and foxes, and by the men who hunted them. These tracks developed into the fairways, and the areas around the holes, worn out by continual play, were expanded to form greens that were allocated exclusively for the delicate task of putting. This meant that eventually a separate, fresh area had to be set aside for teeing. Rabbits grazed the turf and kept it short; there was no machinery to do the job. Many of Britain's seaside links courses, such as

Saunton Sands in north Devon, relied exclusively on rabbits to keep their fairways tightly cropped until well into the second half of the twentieth century. Only recently, when the amount of play began to damage the turf faster than nature's ability to repair it, did science take a hand in golf's evolution with artificial fertilizer and irrigation.

Tradition of the Silver Clubs

During the eighteenth century, golf experienced the first stirrings of a desire for organization of the game, and clubs devoted exclusively to golf and the development of an accepted set of rules were formed.

The earliest club for which there is concrete evidence is the Gentlemen Golfers of Leith (later to become, as they are now known, the Honourable Company of Edinburgh Golfers), instituted in 1744. Royal Blackheath and Royal Burgess both declare they are older, but so far no evidence has been found to substantiate their claims. Blackheath has been entered in *The Golfer's Handbook* as "instituted traditionally in 1608," but the earliest evidence for its existence dates from 1766, when the first ball was attached to their silver club. It was common among eighteenth-century clubs to have a competition, the winner of which was declared captain for the ensuing year. A silver ball was attached to a silver club with the date and the captain's name inscribed on it.

The Society of St. Andrews Golfers (later awarded the title of "Royal and Ancient" by King William IV in 1834) purchased their silver club in 1754. It was stated in their minute-book that it was open for competition to all clubs in Great Britain and Ireland. But when looking around for more senior clubs with whom to play, they could only find the Gentlemen Golfers. It seems strange that if the Royal Burgess Golfing Society was formed in 1735, as they claim, they did not make contact.

The early clubs were as much a place to eat and drink vast quantities of claret as they were for the more healthy pursuit of golf. It is no coincidence that the trophy for the British Open is a claret jug. It would be hard to find an exception to the rule that the majority of golf clubs were formed by small groups of like-minded souls brought together in drinking and eating establishments of one sort or another. Once the clubs were formed, members could more easily combine their appetites for all three activities. Some may feel little has changed in the last 250 years.

As golf became more popular, it inevitably spread out from its beginnings on the east coast of Scotland. The Scots had strong trading links with the Low Countries and a diplomatic "Auld Alliance" with the French. In the same way that the Romans brought paganica to southern Europe, so the Scots took golf to the south and east and, ultimately, to virtually every country on the map of the world.

Captain of the Golf (left)
An oil painting by David Allan portrays William Inglis, captain of the Honourable Company of Edinburgh Golfers from 1782 to 1784. Behind him, on Leith links, drummers announce the procession of the annually contested silver club, for which the first set of formal rules was established.

Fact and figures
This 1908 pair of Staffordshire figurines, representing William Innes and his caddie, was modeled on the subjects of a 1790 painting by Lemuel Francis Abbott. Innes wears the captain's coat of the Blackheath club, which officially dates back to 1766 but claims a heritage from 1608.

The Playclub Era

A WEALTH OF equipment has survived from the early years of golf in Scotland, and the collecting of antique golf clubs is now a hobby that fascinates many golfing enthusiasts. From the start of the eighteenth century to well beyond the middle of the nineteenth, a golfer would head out to do battle on the links armed with some eight to twelve clubs. Typically, the essential implements comprise a couple of playclubs, a grassed driver, three or more spoons, a baffing spoon, a wooden niblick, and a wooden putter.

Set of 1850 clubs
Left to right: a playclub for tee shots; spoons for fairway strokes; a putter; two irons for escaping trouble.

It is assumed that the first clubs used in Scotland during the fifteenth century were fashioned from wood, comprising a sturdy shaft, a weighted head, and a padded handle, bound with hide from a sheep, pig, horse, or cow, or with chamois. Later, from around 1700, metal-headed clubs joined the player's set, initially as additional implements for special tasks, but eventually taking the place of some of the long-nosed wooden clubs.

Supple Drivers

It was the elegant playclubs that above all characterized this whole era of golf in the eighteenth and nineteenth centuries. They were long-nosed, long-shafted, supple driving clubs that gave distance from the tee. Straight in the face, they made the ball run on when hit off the tee with a flat swing. Playclubs could easily split and golfers usually carried two of them in case one broke.

Shorter than the playclub was the grassed driver. This club was used to lift the ball off good fairway lies or to give the ball height when hit downwind because of the loft on its clubface. Spoons (otherwise known as scrapers) came in long, middle, and short sizes for dealing with various fairway lies, the clubs differing in the length of shaft and the degree of loft of the clubface. The baffing spoon was a sturdy implement for taking turf with the ball to create maximum lift and minimum run. The wooden niblick was short and well-lofted, and was used to remove the ball from bunkers and deep rough.

Finally came the wooden putter. It was broader- and shorter-headed, and shorter-shafted, than the other woods. Upright in lie, the club was straight-faced and surprisingly heavy in the head. One might expect all of

Spliced Woods

Early woods were constructed from a strong, straight-grained shaft tapering to a long, flat wedge, which was joined to a taper on the socket of the clubhead. After being glued, the joint was bound with twine whipping to hold it in place and to prevent damage.

Shaft
Tapering splice
Spliced joint
Clubhead
Whipping

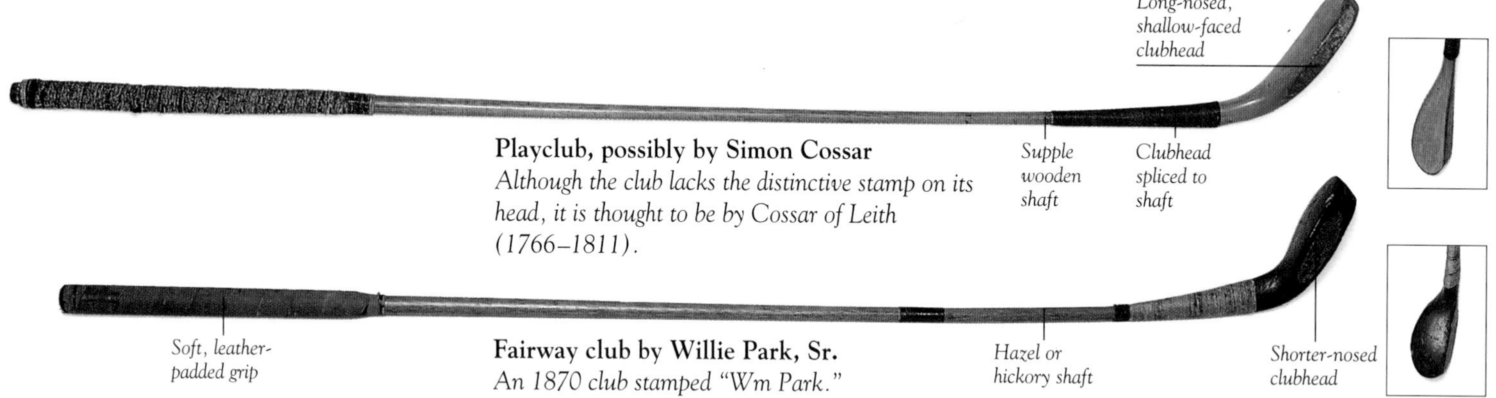

Playclub, possibly by Simon Cossar
Although the club lacks the distinctive stamp on its head, it is thought to be by Cossar of Leith (1766–1811).

Fairway club by Willie Park, Sr.
An 1870 club stamped "Wm Park."

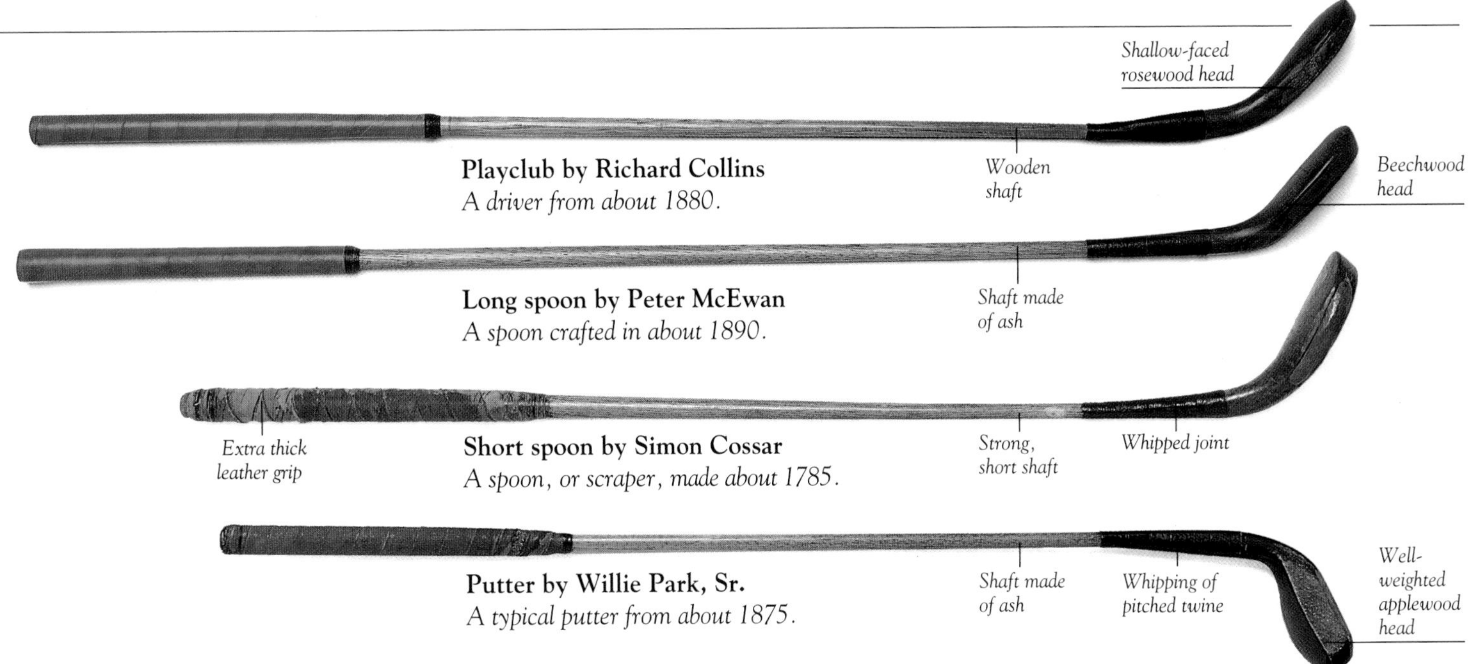

Playclub by Richard Collins
A driver from about 1880.

Long spoon by Peter McEwan
A spoon crafted in about 1890.

Short spoon by Simon Cossar
A spoon, or scraper, made about 1785.

Putter by Willie Park, Sr.
A typical putter from about 1875.

Club comparison
Club design varied little for over 100 years, with playclubs and spoons having long, slim heads.

these early clubs to be unwieldy, but they were not. Though differing in width, heads were elegantly shaped, nicely balanced, and attractively colored in ocher or a dark keel stain.

Choice of Wood

The timber chosen to fashion the wooden clubs varied greatly. Most of the fruit-woods, including apple, pear, plum, and cherry, were used for heads, along with hornbeam, dogwood, thornwood, beech, and eventually and most effectively, persimmon – a dense, straight-grained wood that was imported to Scotland from North America. The shafts, attached to the underside of the neck of the clubhead by a simple splice, were slender and finely tapered to ensure that the "spring" or "kick" was in the correct position. The integrity of the splice was maintained by whipping, a binding of pitched twine or cord that was wrapped around the joint. Shafts were made from ash, hazel, green-heart, lemonwood, or lancewood, until hickory was found to be vastly superior in strength and straightness of grain.

Hard on the heels of the wooden-headed clubs came the irons. The first ones looked like weapons of war. With square-toed blades, thick sockets, sturdy shafts, and well-padded grips, they were made for hard-hitting golfers.

Modifications to the heavy irons began in the mid-nineteenth century. The first was the track iron, a small, round-headed, well-weighted tool for removing the ball from cart tracks, hoof marks, and rabbit holes. Next came the cleek, a long-shafted, parallel-bladed iron with the loft of a middle spoon, for playing out of tight lies or light sand. The lofter, which vied with the baffing spoon, also became popular during this time.

Hand-forged Irons

Early iron heads were hand-forged with a socket, the opening of which was nicked with a cold chisel to grip the wooden shaft. The shaft of the club was filed to a slight taper to rest snugly in the socket before being driven into the clubhead to ensure a firm, secure fit.

Shaft
Slight taper
Socket
Iron head

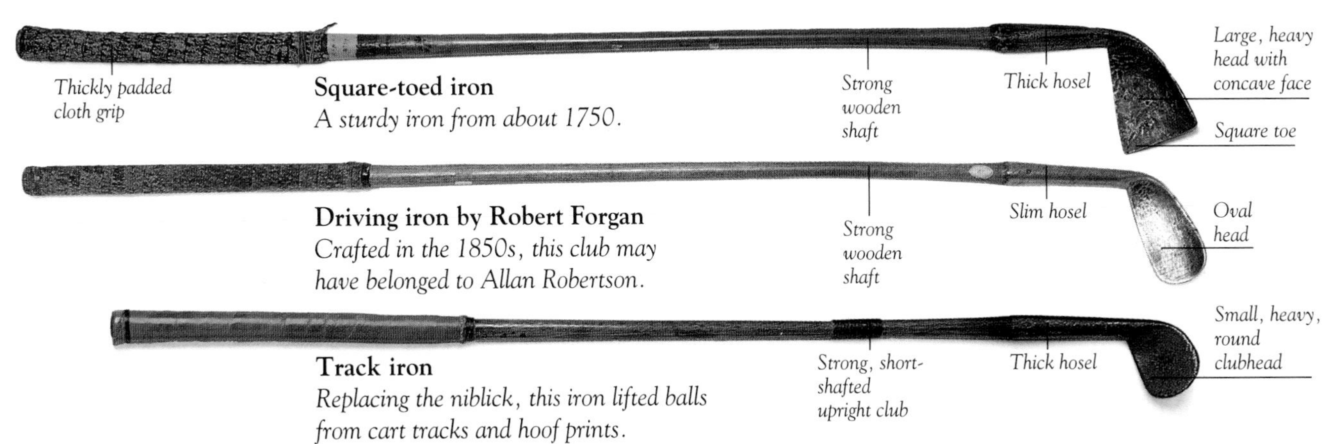

Square-toed iron
A sturdy iron from about 1750.

Driving iron by Robert Forgan
Crafted in the 1850s, this club may have belonged to Allan Robertson.

Track iron
Replacing the niblick, this iron lifted balls from cart tracks and hoof prints.

The Clubmaker Professional

THE CRAFTSMEN WHO *made golf clubs during the eighteenth and nineteenth centuries were a fascinating group of individuals who played a vital part in the history of the game. The earliest clubs were fashioned by bow-makers, wood-turners, and carpenters, and their clubmaking skills were passed from father to son. Their family businesses were often associated with individual courses such as Musselburgh, St. Andrews, or Leith. Many of the clubmakers were also among the leading golfers of their day – men such as Willie Park, Sr., winner of the first British Open in 1860, Willie Dunn, Jr., winner of the first, unofficial U.S. Open, and the legendary Old Tom Morris.*

The clubs these men produced were the long-nosed woods that predominated in golf until the 1880s. Before the arrival of machine tools, all the parts of a wooden club were made by hand. To make a playclub, for instance, the clubmaker had to form a rough block of wood into a shaped head with a curved socket that tapered into a splice to fit the shaft. He used a special vise fitted to his bench and supported by a rod fixed to the floor to give complete rigidity while he worked.

Many of his tools were typical of any carpenter – saws, hammers, screwdrivers, files, planes, and drills. A bunsen burner

Hammer

Screw-driver

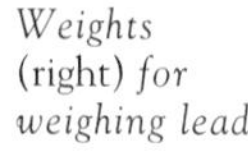

Weights (right) for weighing lead

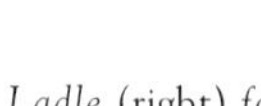

Ladle (right) for pouring lead

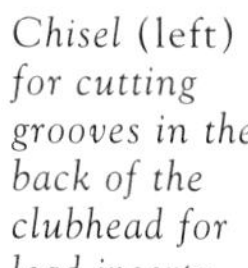

Chisel (left) for cutting grooves in the back of the clubhead for lead inserts

Tools of the trade
The essential tools of the clubmaker were the same as those used by any woodworker. The implements changed little during the period when the clubs were made by hand.

Varnish or shellac pot and brush

Glue pot

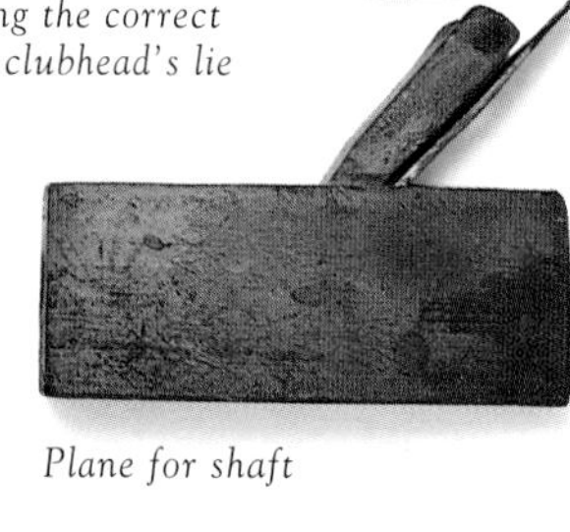

Wood block with template for measuring the correct angle of the clubhead's lie

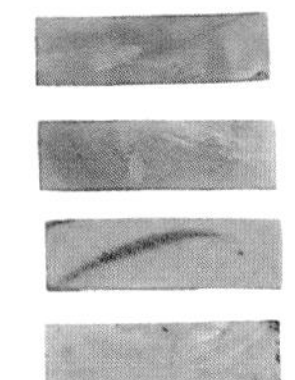

Protective ram's horn inserts for the leading edge of the clubhead

Plane for shaft

Spliced clubheads

Old Tom Morris
A famous clubmaker, Old Tom Morris for many years served as the professional at the R & A, where his duties included repairing members' clubs.

Oil can

Gouge

Bradawl

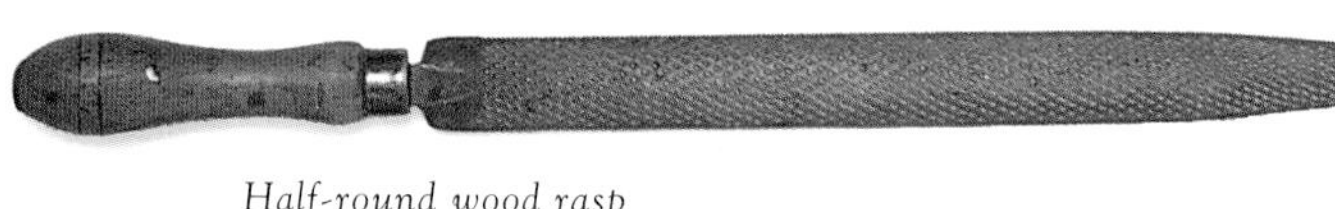

Half-round wood rasp

Half-round cabinet file

Stain pot and brush

was employed to melt lead, which was then ladled into a groove in the back of the club to give the head more balance, power, and "feel." Ram's horn was used as an insert in the sole and face of the clubhead to minimize damage from rocks and stones. Clubmakers also used name stamps to distinguish their output, which conveniently allows them to be identified today. Among the famous names from between the late eighteenth and late nineteenth centuries were the Dickson family of Leith; Simon Cossar, also of Leith; Hugh Philp of St. Andrews, the first clubmaker to concentrate on balancing and streamlining wooden clubs; Andrew Strath, also a noted player who won the 1865 British Open; and the Patrick family from Leven in Fife.

While some of these craftsmen were solely clubmakers, others were employed at the links as "rangers" or "keepers of the green," jacks-of-all-trades who could play golf, supervise the upkeep of the course, give tuition, collect fees, organize caddies, regulate play, and repair anything from a scythe to a sand-iron. This role evolved into that of the modern club professional.

Workplace (left)
This room, as set out for use by a club professional in 1904, shows the round-topped, flat-faced vise fixed to the workbench.

Hand-forging (right)
There were few early makers of irons due to a lack of forges, anvils, and tools. Here a blacksmith hand-forges heads for irons at the Premier Golf Company in 1909.

Tenon saw

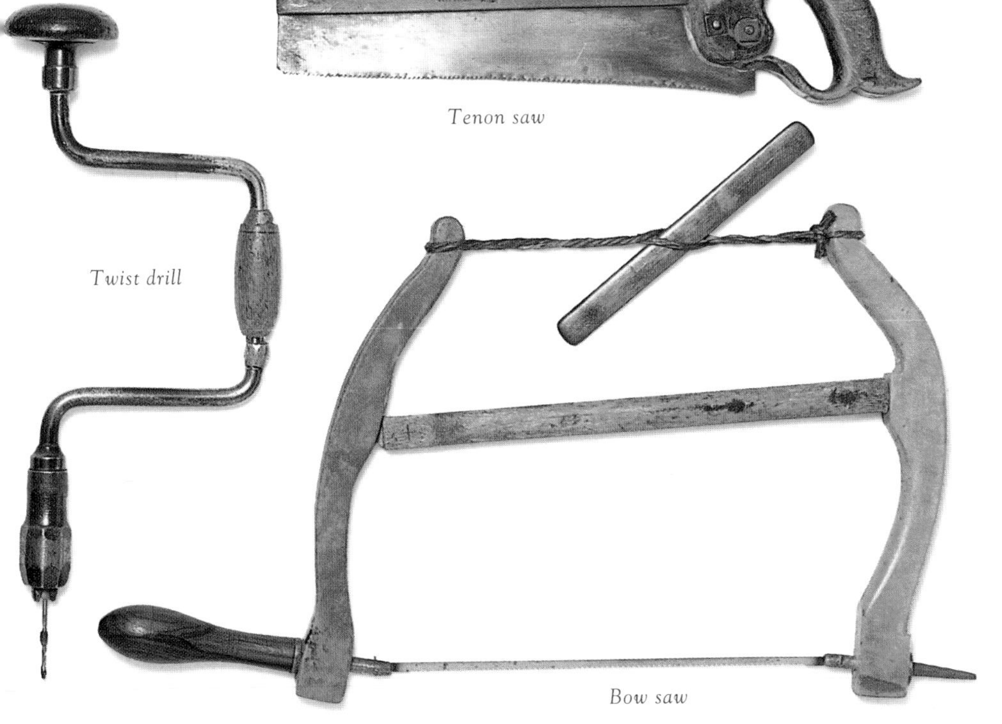

Twist drill

Bow saw

Irons were much less common than woods until the late nineteenth century. As golf gained in popularity, however, the range and variety of irons increased. Makers who hand-forged heads included Robert Brodie, James Anderson of Anstruther, the Carrick family, John Gray, Robert White, and Robert Wilson. Some early blade-and-socket irons were made from two pieces of metal, a process followed by drop-forging and cast-molding. The names of the "cleekmakers" appearing on such early clubs include those of Craigie, Brand, Nicholson, and Stewart.

Wooden shaft-former

Full-length shaft

THE GOLF REVOLUTION

SCOTTISH GOLF CLUBS numbered about 30 in 1864; in the same year there were just 3 English clubs – Royal Blackheath, Old Manchester and Westward Ho! But by 1900 there were over 2,000 clubs in Britain, and most of them were across the border, in England.

Golf coaches
A publicity photograph that appeared in the coaches of the London and North Eastern Railway around 1900 shows golfers on the Holy Island links. The coming of the railroad was a major factor in the rapid spread of golf around Britain.

This revolutionary growth of golf occurred as the industrial and imperial expansion of the Victorian era brought new prosperity to the English middle class. With increasing money and leisure time, many of these affluent Victorians imitated the royal family in their habit of vacationing in Scotland. There they discovered the delights of golf and became infused with a fascination for the game, which they then took back to England.

The golf boom was made possible by two major developments: the advent of the "guttie" ball and the expansion of the railroads. Balls made from gutta percha (see page 27) were introduced around the mid-nineteenth century and were about a quarter of the price of the short-lived feathery balls they replaced, bringing golf within the financial reach of the Scottish working man. As gutties could also be produced in greater quantity, there was a ready supply of balls to meet the exploding demand.

The great improvement in transportation provided by the expanding railroad system (the railroad reached St. Andrews in 1850) gave enthusiasts access to the existing courses and to the newly developed seaside resorts of England and Scotland. Toward the latter part of the century, seaside towns built courses as an attraction for their new visitors. Many links courses of Britain have had, or still have, railroad lines running along one of their boundaries. Inland courses were built within train distance of the cities to satisfy the craze for this newly popular sport.

BOOM IN BRITAIN

The number of clubs in Britain was thought to be about 60 in 1880; 387 in 1890; and 2,330 in 1900. There were fewer courses than clubs, since several clubs shared each course. But clearly the rise in the number of clubs points to a dramatic increase in both the popularity of golf and the number of courses.

The people who knew most about golf were the Scottish professionals. They were a hardy group of individuals who originally earned money making clubs and balls and acting as caddies for their more wealthy employers. They played in some of the earliest matches for money, and they counted among their number such

The golfing life
A calendar of the year 1913, advertising the Life Association Insurance Company, incorporates a watercolor by J. Michael Brown depicting Horace Hutchinson's approach to the 4th hole at Royal North Devon, one of England's first clubs.

Wind skill (right)
In the shadow of its famous windmill, Wimbledon Common was one of London's earliest golf courses.

THE DEVELOPMENT OF THE RULES OF GOLF

The first written rules of golf were formulated by the Gentlemen Golfers of Leith in 1744. The presentation of a valuable silver club by the City of Edinburgh as a prize necessitated a common agreement on the way the game should be played, so Leith drew up 13 "Articles & Laws in Playing at Golf." New clubs continued to draw up their own rules, but looked to Leith for guidance until the Society of St. Andrews Golfers became more influential in the mid-nineteenth century. In 1897 the Royal & Ancient Golf Club of St. Andrews (as it had then become) was invited by the leading clubs of the day to compile a uniform code of rules.

During the first half of this century the Royal & Ancient and the USGA, the governing body of American golf, both applied the same basic rules, but they made separate interpretations of decisions. These differences were largely resolved at a special conference in 1951, which was also attended by representatives from Canada and Australia. The only stumbling block was ball size, and some minor points on play. Importantly, the Royal & Ancient and the USGA agreed that they would meet every four years to review the rules, and they set up a Joint Decisions Committee to establish uniformity.

A book of *Decisions on the Rules* is now jointly published by the two organizations and revised annually. It first appeared in 1984, marking a breakthrough in cooperation.

Duncan Forbes (left) *The first captain of the Gentlemen Golfers of Leith, Duncan Forbes was instrumental in drawing up the first rules in 1744. Until then, golf had survived for about three centuries without a written set of rules.*

National Inter-club Championship, 1857 *Competitors in an early R & A championship, congregating from many different clubs, highlighted the need for a uniform set of rules.*

great names as Allan Robertson (see page 290) and Old Tom Morris (see page 270). Scottish professionals were imported south of the border to lay out courses, and were much in demand to teach how to play golf to the wealthy English at the new clubs that were being set up all over the country.

First English Links

The oldest existing seaside links in England, at Westward Ho! in north Devon, were created in 1864 when Old Tom Morris came down from Scotland to lay out the holes. Much of the early golfing history of England came out of the course at Westward Ho! and its Royal North Devon Club, along with many top players, including J. H. Taylor, the first Englishman to break the Scottish dominance of golf when he won the British Open in 1894.

As the game spread gradually throughout England more clubs were founded. All around the southeast coast of England, prospective golfers explored links land for its suitability for the game. Nearer the capital, the London Scottish Club was formed in 1865 when members of the London Scottish regiment were granted permission to play on Wimbledon Common. The civilian members broke away to form what is now the Royal Wimbledon Club, playing on a heath by the Common. Among other early clubs, the Royal Liverpool Club at Hoylake, founded in 1869, played a major role in the development of English golf, hosting the first Amateur Championship in 1885.

Whereas in Scotland golf was played by all levels of society, in England the game attracted the majority of its devotees from the middle and upper classes, and clubs tended to invoke traditions of exclusivity. Although Scots were largely responsible for spreading the game to the rest of the world, this English identification of the game as the preserve of the gentleman was to become a component of golf's image when it arrived in the United States.

Beer and bunkers *A 1910 poster for a Glasgow beer captures a significant image of Scottish culture. The Scots exported golf to England, marketing their professional expertise in the game.*

Featheries and Gutties

NO SINGLE ELEMENT has had greater influence on golf's development than the ball. The nature and effectiveness of the various types of ball have shaped the way that the game has evolved and greatly influenced club design. In the early seventeenth century, the "feathery" superseded the wooden missile, probably made of beech, that was the earliest known ball. Expensive and easily damaged, these feather-filled balls held sway until the momentous advent of the gutta percha ball in 1848.

Featheries (below)
Hard to make and easy to damage, featheries were expensive. They responded badly to poor weather, and if the leather or stitching was cut by a club, the ball became useless. The antique featheries shown here are from the Royal & Ancient Club at St. Andrews.

As well as being arduous, the task of crafting a feathery was detrimental to the maker's health. His lungs filled with feather dust, and his chest was weakened by the constant pressure of filling the ball, which was cupped in a wooden mold strapped against his body. Even the most experienced maker could only complete four balls a day; this accounted for their price of three to four shillings, often more than the price of a club. Despite its drawbacks, the feathery did noble service for

The Feathery Ball

The feathery cover was made from three specially shaped lobes of dampened horse- or bull-hide (below), which were sewn together with thin twine, leaving a small aperture, and then turned outside in. Wetted feathers were crammed into the hole with a special crutch-handled stuffing rod before it was stitched. On drying, the feathers expanded as the hide shrank, forming a hard ball. Its roundness depended on the skill of the cutting and stitching.

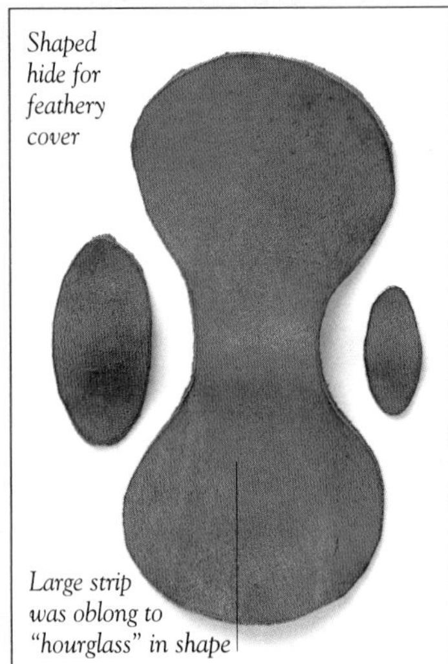

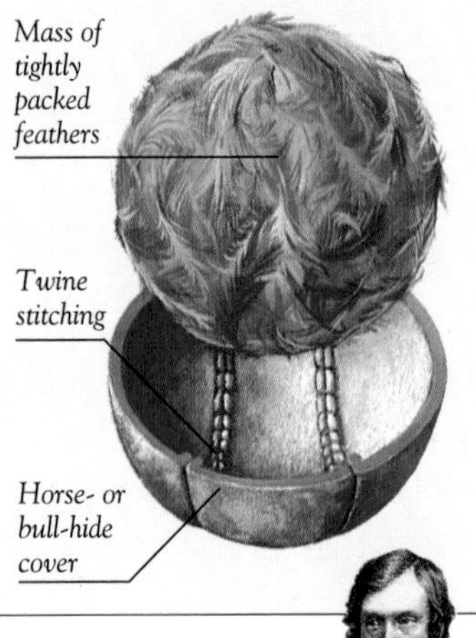

Feathery ball used by Allan Robertson in 1842 when playing the Old course at St. Andrews in 87 strokes

Allan Robertson feathery ball of 1843

Last feathery made by Robertson, in 1852

Feathery by Old Tom Morris, formerly Robertson's employee

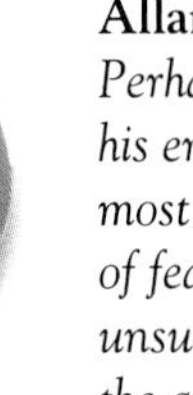

Allan Robertson (right)
Perhaps the finest golfer of his era, Robertson was the most famous of a family of feathery makers. He unsuccessfully resisted the arrival of the new gutta percha ball.

Red feather ball for use in snow

Feathery made by John Gourlay of Musselburgh around 1840

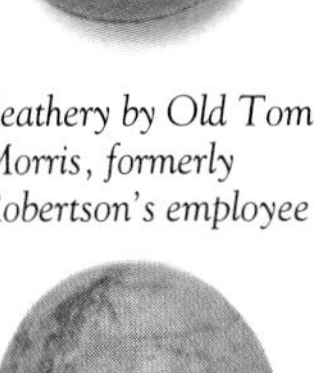
Feathery made by William Gourlay of Bruntsfield

Rare feathery owned by J.H. Taylor

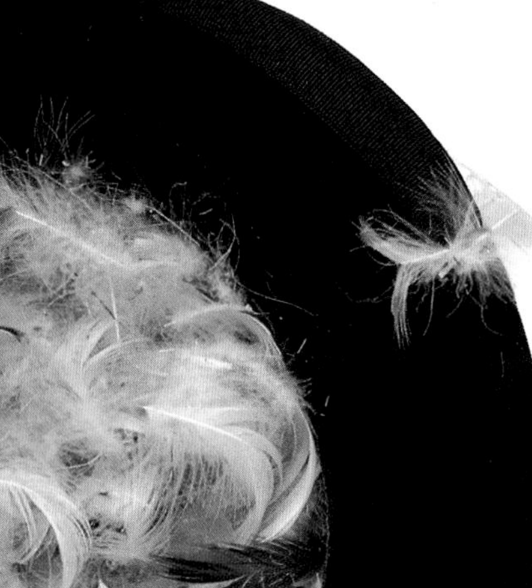

Top-hat rule (left)
Tradition had it that as many poultry feathers as it took to fill an entire top hat to the brim were needed to stuff a single feathery.

Old feathery, dated 1820 on the ball, by an unknown maker

Rare feather ball by Tom Alexander "famed on the Burntisland links"

Feather ball stamped "William" in Gothic script, date unknown

Undated ball with sprung seam that shows feather insides

over 200 years, until the middle of the nineteenth century. Of the early makers of featheries, the Gourlay and Robertson families are the best known.

In 1848, a dramatic change came with the arrival of gutta percha, a rubber-like substance from the tropical percha tree. It was found to be malleable when boiled in water, and was easily pressed into the shape of a ball, hardening as it cooled. Moreover, when misshapen or broken, the parts could be re-shaped after re-boiling. The new gutta percha ball (or "guttie") heralded the demise of the expensive feathery and brought the game within the reach of the less affluent. It made standardization easier, and detailed attention was given to ball size and weight. Makers stamped the weight, between 26 and 31 pennyweight, on each ball, along with their name. With golf's new popularity, more people became ballmakers and most tire and rubber companies were making balls before the end of the century. The reign of the guttie lasted until the introduction of the rubber-core Haskell ball at the start of the twentieth century (see page 48).

The Guttie Ball

The first gutta percha balls, shaped by gloved hand or by rolling the hot material between two flat boards, were smooth. Players discovered that the guttie flew better after it had been indented by mis-hit strokes, leading to the idea of marking the finished ball with a cold chisel or the claw end of a hammer. This hand-marking method was used until the introduction of the engraved iron or brass mold. Gutties made in a mold were more precisely round and had the flight-assisting marks built in.

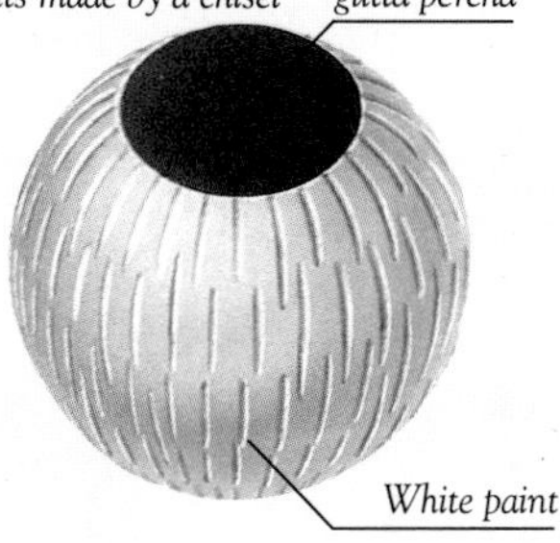

Hand-rolled guttie with indents made by a chisel

Pure black gutta percha

White paint

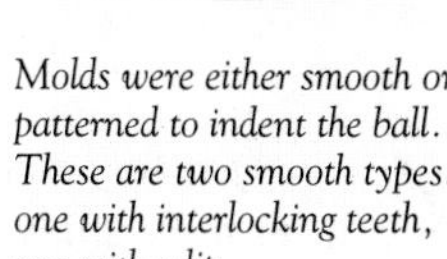

Molds were either smooth or patterned to indent the ball. These are two smooth types: one with interlocking teeth, one with a lip.

Composition ball with circle pattern created by a mold

Mixture of gutta and metal filings

White paint

Collecting gutta
Gutta percha was tapped from the base of tropical trees, such as the Malaysian Palaquium gutta. *Before tapping was introduced, the trees used to be cut down to extract their resin, each tree yielding 13 lb. (6 kg.) of gutta percha.*

Well-used black gutta percha ball

Badly marked, white-painted guttie

Gutta percha balls
The black gutta percha was painted white to make the ball more visible. "Composition" gutties had other materials mixed in, such as cork or metal filings.

Smooth ball made by Robertson in 1852

Hand-hammered Robertson guttie from the 1850s

Red, hand-hammered guttie for use in snow

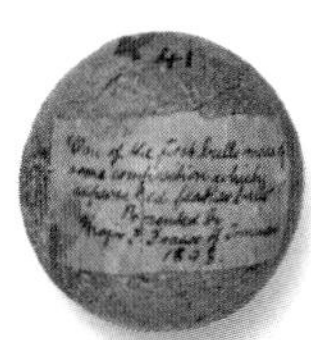

Composition guttie with smooth finish

Paterson's original "New Composite" guttie ball

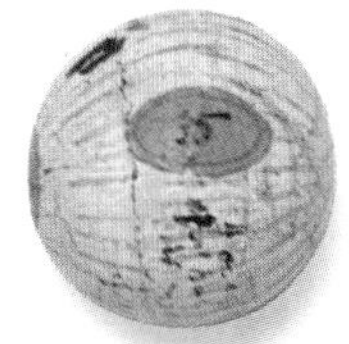

Guttie with which Robertson played the St. Andrews Old course in a record 79

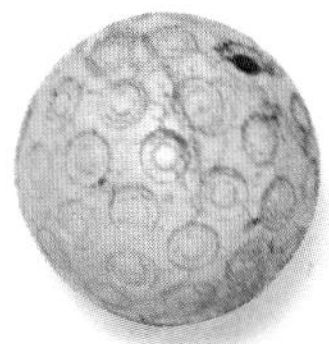

Guttie ball stamped with a distinctive circle marking

Black ball of about 1852 with mold-stamped marking

Gutta percha (right)
Once collected, the hardened sap of the gutta percha tree is wound in strips. It becomes malleable when it is boiled.

BULGERS, BRASSIES, AND BAFFIES

THE ARRIVAL OF *the guttie ball dramatically altered club design. The harder and heavier new ball was difficult to control with the slender, long-nosed woods and easily damaged them. Consequently, from 1880, wooden heads became shorter, broader, and deeper, leading to the introduction of the "bulger," a driver with a convex face, which was designed to minimize a sliced or hooked stroke.*

The bulger driver
The new clubhead shape focused the club weight in a small area.

Also toward the end of the nineteenth century, the spoons gradually disappeared from the set, being replaced by a baffy and a brassie, the heads of which were fitted with a brass striking plate on the sole. At the same time, the number of iron clubs increased, primarily because they were cheaper to manufacture and could not harm the guttie, as they had the feathery. Around 1900, the irons, each with a different degree of loft, consisted of a driving cleek, iron cleek, lofter, mashie, sand iron, niblick, and putting cleek.

HEADS AND JOINTS

The new shape of wooden heads allowed clubmakers to alter the way the shaft was attached to the head. The bulkier, wider head could accommodate a hole drilled to take a round, tapered shaft, typically of hickory, which was less "whippy." This method was superseded by the

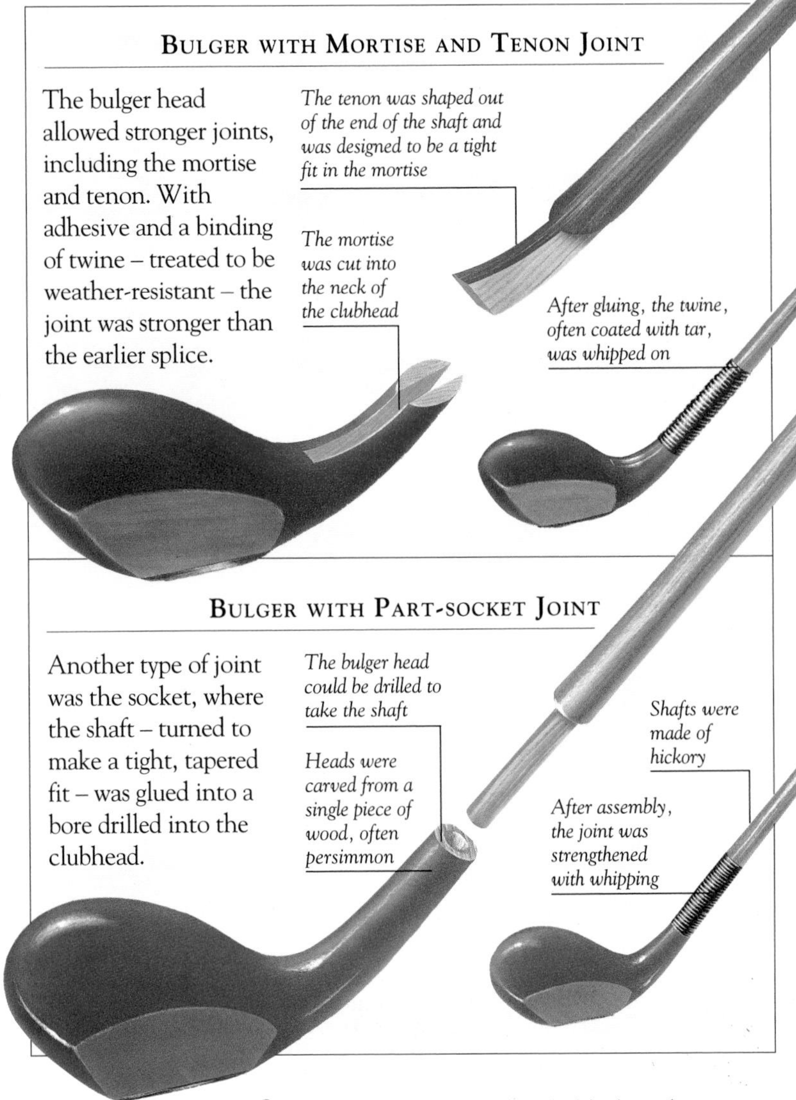

BULGER WITH MORTISE AND TENON JOINT

The bulger head allowed stronger joints, including the mortise and tenon. With adhesive and a binding of twine – treated to be weather-resistant – the joint was stronger than the earlier splice.

BULGER WITH PART-SOCKET JOINT

Another type of joint was the socket, where the shaft – turned to make a tight, tapered fit – was glued into a bore drilled into the clubhead.

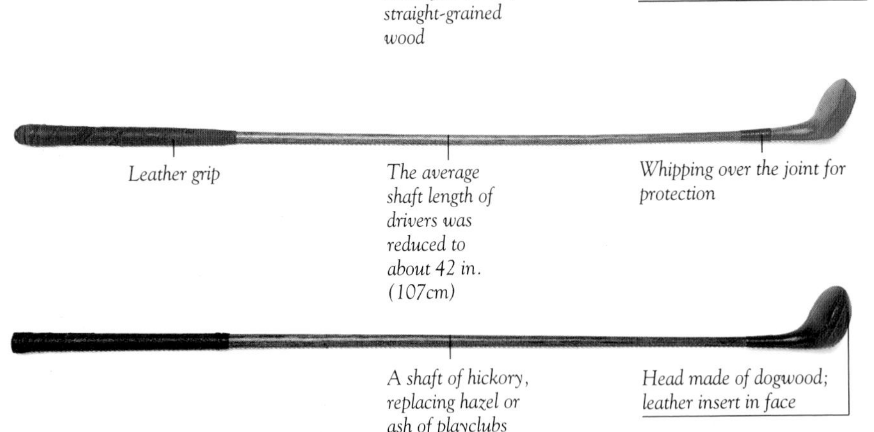

Socket-headed bulger driver
This club, made in 1903, is stamped "Jack White," the Open champion in 1904. The convex face gave a small striking area for accurate players.

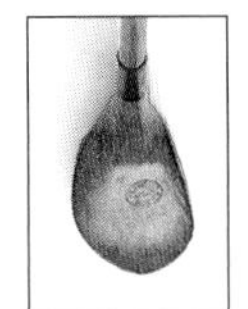

Mortise and tenon joint driver
This driver was made about 1900 by A.H. Scott of Elie, Fife. This joint was used locally before being displaced by the through socket.

Old Tom Morris baffy
The baffy replaced the longer-headed baffing spoon. This club was made in Tom Morris's shop in about 1905, three years before his death.

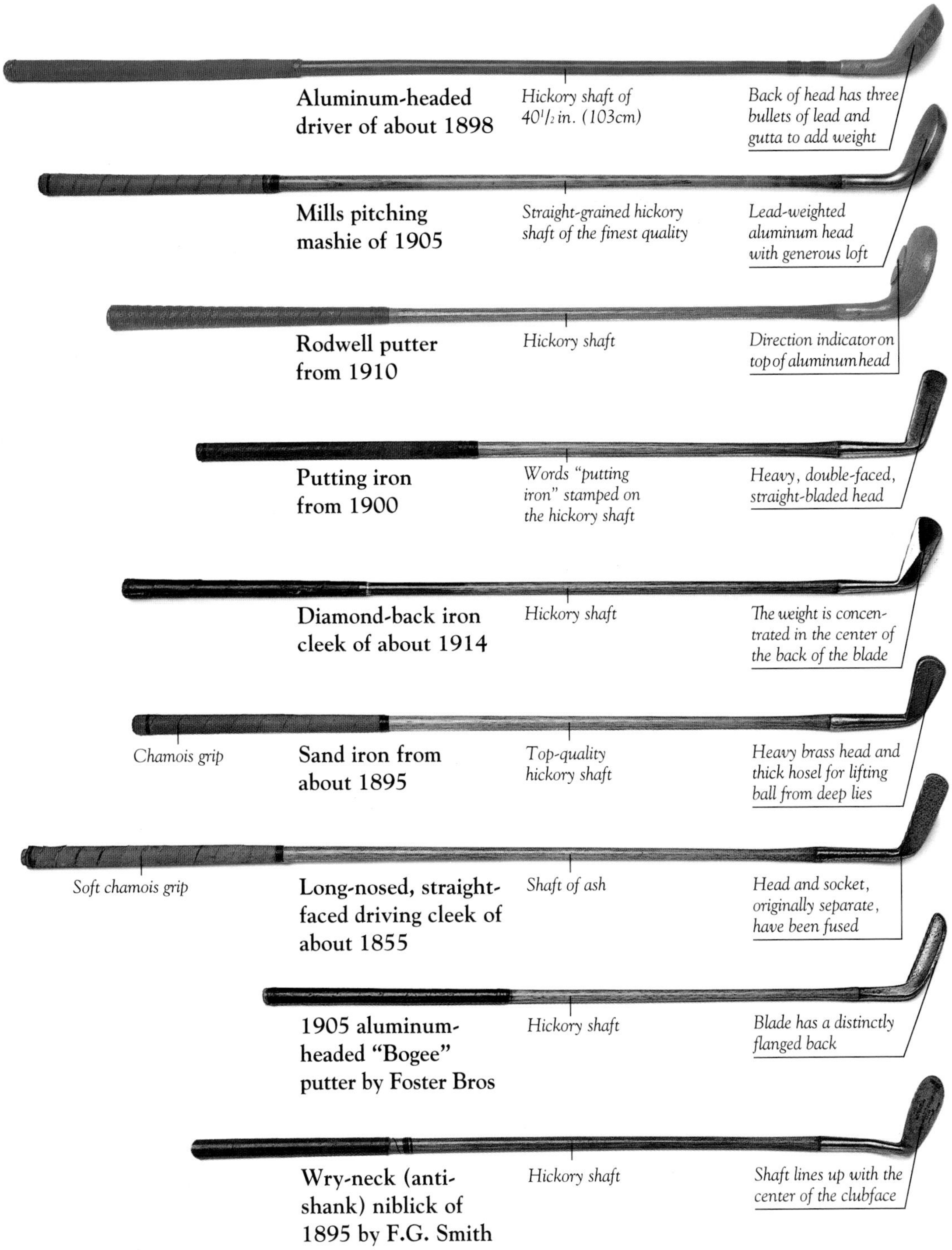

Aluminum-headed driver of about 1898
Hickory shaft of 40½ in. (103cm)
Back of head has three bullets of lead and gutta to add weight

Mills pitching mashie of 1905
Straight-grained hickory shaft of the finest quality
Lead-weighted aluminum head with generous loft

Rodwell putter from 1910
Hickory shaft
Direction indicator on top of aluminum head

Putting iron from 1900
Words "putting iron" stamped on the hickory shaft
Heavy, double-faced, straight-bladed head

Diamond-back iron cleek of about 1914
Hickory shaft
The weight is concentrated in the center of the back of the blade

Sand iron from about 1895
Chamois grip
Top-quality hickory shaft
Heavy brass head and thick hosel for lifting ball from deep lies

Long-nosed, straight-faced driving cleek of about 1855
Soft chamois grip
Shaft of ash
Head and socket, originally separate, have been fused

1905 aluminum-headed "Bogee" putter by Foster Bros
Hickory shaft
Blade has a distinctly flanged back

Wry-neck (anti-shank) niblick of 1895 by F.G. Smith
Hickory shaft
Shaft lines up with the center of the clubface

"through socket," where the shaft fitted in a hole drilled through to the sole of the head. Other techniques were the mortise and tenon, twin-splice, and V-insert.

Many curious variants found their way to the clubmaker's shop, including the "one-piece" club. It was made of ash, thornwood, or dogwood, usually fashioned from the root or thick lower branches of a mature shrub or small tree. The bulbous root formed the head, and the shaft was shaped from the slimmed-down branch.

Other oddities included the vast range of inserts used on driving and fairway clubs to protect the face from the impact with the tougher ball. These ranged from glass, rubber, and slate to rhinoceros and elephant hide and ivory. Also tried were small rollers fitted into driver soles. On the face of the club, a coil spring with a strip of metal, or with a ball bearing, was tested to speed the ball. Lead weights were placed in the heel and toe of the head to aid the player who was unable to strike his ball as intended. Most of these ambitious inventions failed to find a market, even though face inserts are still fitted today.

Clubs with aluminum heads also appeared on the scene. First came putters, with heads shaped in the style of a short, wooden-headed putter. These proved popular, and by 1895 the demand was sufficient for manufacturers to make a full range of clubs from this light metal, including drivers, cleeks, and mashies.

Up to about 1900 the clubface was left unmarked, reducing the amount of backspin that could be put on the ball. But it proved popular when manufacturers took to marking the center of the clubface by indenting or grooving its metal.

The Odd, the Banned, and the Ugly

Around the turn of the century there was an explosion of experimentation in club design. Alongside their mass-produced clubs, many leading manufacturers invested time and money in prototypes designed to aid convenience, improve performance, or keep abreast of changes in playing technique. From 1893 to 1906, the Urquhart family worked to perfect an iron with an adjustable blade (left) that enabled the loft to be varied as desired. J. Brown's rake mashie, "The Major" (center left), was useful when playing out of rye grass or fine sand bunkers. The small, mallet-headed dual-purpose club (center right) had varying lofts on each side. And in their spring-faced cleek (right), Spalding sandwiched a strip of gutta behind a scored steel face, which was riveted to an iron head. Many patented clubs were short-lived, either proving impractical or being banned.

TEES

GOLF HISTORIANS BELIEVE that the practice of using the green as a teeing ground to the next hole was phased out during the eighteenth century. Instead, after holing out, players moved a short distance from the green and teed up on a specially formed patch of turf. This meant that the green was spared the ravages of divot-digging playclubs and boot-stud scratches. More importantly, the game speeded up as players moved promptly off the green.

Along with the evolution of the teeing ground came the iron sand box. This contained dense sand, which enabled the caddie or player to form a cone or mound of sand for the ball to sit on. The box also marked the driving area.

Over the years the sand box became more sophisticated. First it was fitted with runners to enable greenskeepers to pull the heavy container to a new position on the teeing ground. Later, legs were added to bring the box up to waist height.

Even after the arrival of celluloid tees at the beginning of the 1900s, followed by others made of cardboard, wood, and rubber (for use on hard, frozen ground), a variety of molds and gadgets were patented to help form a sand tee. These "tee stamps" were usually made of brass in the shape of a miniature inverted bell.

Eventually, as the use of cheap ready-made tees became almost universal, sand boxes were used instead as receptacles for broken tees and other litter.

On the teeing ground
Golfers teed up their balls on small mounds of sand (above); a mold (left) was used to form sand cones.

This sand mold has two heights: one for teeing up with a driver, the shorter one for use with an iron

Paper tees (below)
A popular alternative to sand was the disposable tee cup, a ring of cardboard that lifted the ball off the turf. They were even sold in perforated booklets; the golfer had to tear off one of these along the perforation and shape it by rolling it between his fingers.

Colonel Bogey's brand from Illinois was designed to "eliminate bothersome sand tees"

Booklet of cardboard tees, "Novel-tees," from Chicago

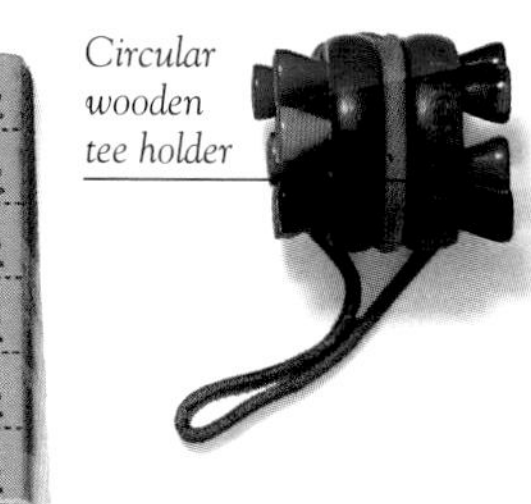

Circular wooden tee holder

Rubber ball support

"Perfect Golf Tee" for use on hard ground

Experimental tees (above)
Many innovative devices were marketed, including the tee holder. The "Perfect Golf Tee" of 1927 included a nail to anchor the support and stop it flying off when the ball was hit.

Rubber tees (below)
Rubber tees were introduced for use on hard ground or in snow. The tees are of different heights: the low one was employed with irons and the taller one with drivers.

Low tee for use with irons

Tall tee for shots with drivers

Cord to tie tees to bag or clothing

Canvas bag of 100 wooden tees for one shilling

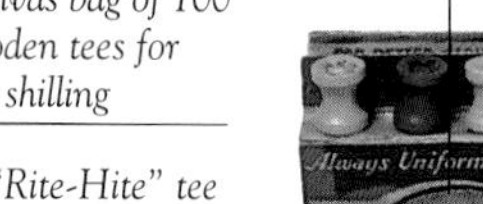

Tees advertising shops and services

"Rite-Hite" tee box from 1925

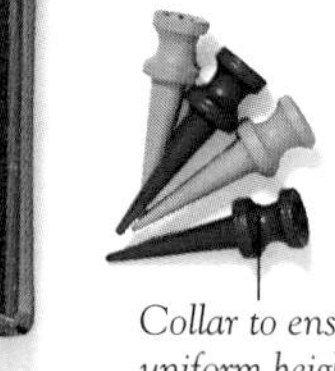

Collar to ensure uniform height

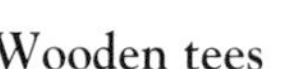

Wooden tees
The advantage of wooden tees was that they did not damage clubheads.

Bright finish for tees made them easier to find in the grass

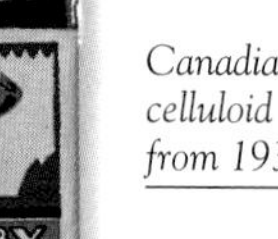

Canadian celluloid tees from 1932

Pack of tees with a book of matches

Plastic tees advertising Dewar's whisky in Scotland

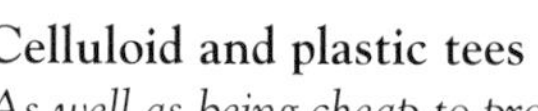

Celluloid and plastic tees
As well as being cheap to produce, plastic tees did not break easily.

Carrying the Clubs

The modifications and improvements made to clubs and balls during the latter half of the nineteenth century were accompanied by advances in ancillary equipment not directly related to play. One major leap forward was the introduction of the golf bag. Previously clubs had been carried about loose under the arm of the golfer or his caddie, and the bag was a welcome addition to their comfort.

Golf bags first appeared on the market between 1885 and 1895 in the style of a slender, tubular wicker basket, or of a wooden tripod supporting a canvas pocket, which could be carried by a single handle. The tripod was constructed so that the legs opened automatically when the base of the bag was placed on the ground. By the end of the century the golf bag had become an essential part of the golfer's equipment, enabling many accessories to be carried including a tee mold for sand tees, a pouch-shaped ball cleaner, finger tape for treating blisters, and multi-purpose tape for repairing damage to clubs.

Wooden dowel wrapped in American green cloth

Noosed leather straps for holding clubs

Aluminium rod to separate straps

Leather pouch for carrying balls

Rare club-carrier
To transport the clubs around the course, they were suspended between the two straps of this nineteenth-century club-carrier.

Before the bag (above)
Caddies used to carry a bundle of clubs under their arms before the introduction of golf bags. Caddying is almost as old as the game itself.

Caddies for Pennies

The word "caddie" derives from the French *cadet*, a title given to a youth serving in the armed forces or at court. Cadets were looked upon as page boys, porters, and bearers, and in local parlance "caddie" was applied to those who carried golfers' clubs. Mainly young boys, they were expected to select the correct clubs, tee up the ball, and attend to the flag stick on the green. They were also required to remain as silent as possible.

As golf has changed, so too have the fortunes of caddies. For a long time they were treated as mere club-carriers, given a few pennies for hours at the player's beck and call. In modern times, however, caddying has become a serious profession, with the best of them highly prized and paid, traveling around the world in the employ of professional golfers, many of whom began as caddies themselves.

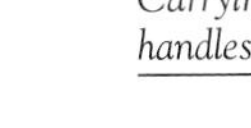

The Bussey (right)
This club-carrier had a club-retainer that could be adjusted according to the varying length of the clubs. The twin legs swung out on hinges every time the carrier was put on the ground.

Canvas ball pouch at top

Adjustable leather club-retainer

Bipod supporting legs

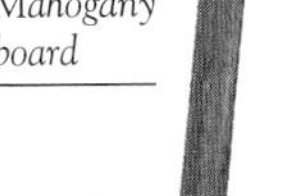

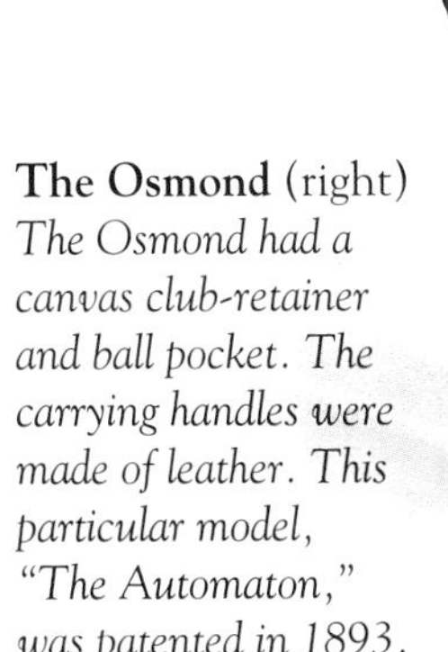

Canvas ball pocket

Leather handles

Canvas club-retainer

Supporting legs

The Osmond (right)
The Osmond had a canvas club-retainer and ball pocket. The carrying handles were made of leather. This particular model, "The Automaton," was patented in 1893.

Golfer and bag
The bag made it easier for golfers to manage their equipment on the course. Clubs could be kept dry and accessories could be carried.

Taking Golf to the World

THE SPREAD OF golf across the world since the late nineteenth century has been rapid but uneven. The game boomed in the United States long before its current explosion in Japan. The early apostles of golf were almost invariably Scots, who set up golf courses wherever they traveled, so that they could indulge in their favorite sporting pastime. They were largely responsible for establishing the game in the United States.

The pioneers (left) *The first photo of golf in the United States, dated 1888, shows play on the St. Andrew's cow-pasture course.*

John Reid (right) *U.S. golf's founder was president of the first club at St. Andrew's, Yonkers, New York.*

The men credited with much of the early pioneering effort in the United States were John Reid and Robert Lockhart, two expatriate Scottish school friends from Dunfermline in Fife, a town famous for its linen, and not far from St. Andrews itself. Reid, a resident of Yonkers, New York, and manager of an iron works, is now generally regarded as the "father of American golf," but Lockhart, a New York linen merchant, had a significant part to play as well. He was in the habit of bringing unusual gifts back from Scotland, which he visited in the course of his linen business. On one trip he brought back tennis rackets and balls, but failed to create much interest in that game among his acquaintances.

Farewell dinner *To celebrate leaving their course in the orchard on the Weston estate at the end of 1893, the members of the St. Andrew's club held a dinner. The "Apple Tree Gang" and their guests signed the menu for H. O. Tallmadge, later the first USGA secretary. Their new quarters were at Grey Oaks.*

Fateful Trip

In the summer of 1887, Lockhart visited Old Tom Morris's shop in St. Andrews and ordered six golf clubs and two dozen gutta percha balls, presumably with the intention of taking them back over the Atlantic. However, the order for the clubs was not completed in time for his departure, and his implements had to be dispatched by sea, reaching him some time later.

The clubs were ordered on behalf of John Reid, but before he passed them on, Lockhart, who had played as a youth on the Musselburgh links and at least knew the rudiments and basic rules of the game, decided to put the clubs to a test himself. There are several accounts of what happened that day in late autumn, 1887, including one which claims that Lockhart had to be bailed out by Reid after being arrested for playing golf in a public place. The most accurate description of the event is probably that given by Robert Lockhart's son, Sydney. He recalled accompanying his father and his brother Leslie one Sunday morning to "a place on the river which is now Riverside Drive." There his father selected a teeing ground, watched by a mounted policeman.

"Father teed up the first little white ball," Sydney Lockhart writes, "and, selecting one of the long wooden clubs, dispatched it far down the meadow. He tried all the clubs and then we boys were permitted to drive some balls too." Their efforts attracted the policeman's attention and he asked if he could join in. "The officer got down off his horse and went through the motions of teeing up, aping father in waggling and squaring off to the ball and other preliminaries. Then he let go and hit a beauty straight down the field which went fully as far as any that father had hit. Being greatly encouraged and proud of his natural ability at a game that involved a ball and stick, he tried again. This time he missed the ball completely and then in rapid succession he missed the little globe three more times; so with a look of disgust on his face he mounted his horse and rode away."

The Gift of Golf

Thus initiated, the products of the craft of Old Tom Morris, three woods and three irons acquired for about $2 each, were presented to Lockhart's friend, John Reid, who then embarked – although one suspects he did not know it at the time – on a mission that was to change the sporting future of his country forever. It was in mid-winter, on February 22, 1888, Washington's birthday, that Reid and five of his friends – John B. Upham, Henry O. Tallmadge, Harry Holbrook, Kingman H. Putman and Alexander P.W. Kinnan – took themselves to a cow pasture opposite Reid's home on Lake Avenue in Yonkers to lay out their course. They found it difficult to make six clubs serve the needs of so many players, but they played the first "round." That they were able to do so was only by the good fortune of the weather, however. Their pioneering efforts on their three-hole course lasted less than three weeks, for a blizzard left it under 3 feet of snow and the American golf revolution came to a temporary halt.

Champion of American golf
Charles Blair Macdonald was an important figure in the early years of golf in America, as player, administrator and architect. His Chicago design, the first 18-hole layout in the United States, influenced many subsequent courses.

The Six-club Club

Once the snow had cleared, however, Reid and his friends were back on the course, and soon were looking for another site to build a bigger one. They moved around the corner to a 30-acre field owned by a German butcher by the name of John C. Shotts. Reid and his friends had neither asked nor been given permission to use the land for their new course, but since they were among Mr. Shotts's best customers he felt it prudent not to make any complaint. The game had begun and the pioneering players persevered in their pastime.

Through the summer they played on, incurring in turn the ridicule of other local residents and the wrath of the clergy for playing on the Sabbath. But since the Scots had been ignoring clerical edicts on this subject for centuries, they were little concerned on that front. Indeed, such criticism strengthened their resolve to provide a more structured form to their activities. To this end Reid invited his golfing friends to his home after their round on November 14, 1888. There they formed the St. Andrew's Golf Club, named after the famous links course on the east coast of Scotland known throughout the world as the home of golf. The club was distinguished from its namesake in Scotland by the use of the apostrophe (St. Andrew's, not St. Andrews), but the same principles and traditions of the game were to apply to both. It was hoped that the name would help inspire and generate the same enthusiasm for the game in the United States as existed in Scotland. It turned out to be a propitious choice, as the subsequent history of golf in North America was to prove.

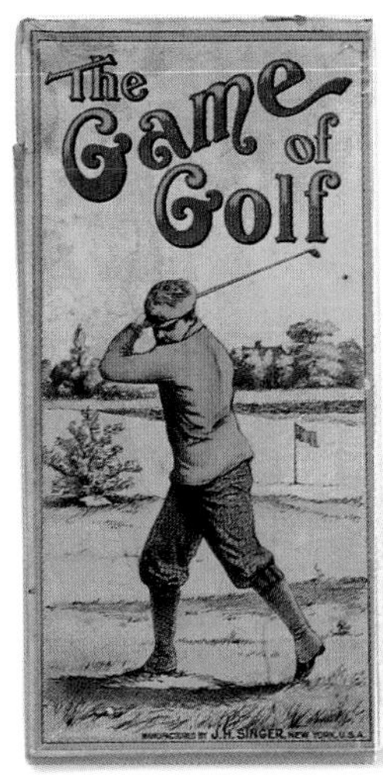

Home golf
There was such enthusiasm for golf in America in the early years of the twentieth century that many board games, such as this one made in 1910 in New York, were sold. They enabled would-be golfers to practice tactics away from crowded courses.

Following the example of their predecessors in St. Andrews, Scotland, more than a hundred years before, the founders then adjourned to dinner to celebrate their new club and to toast the future of golf in their country. Reid was elected president, with Upham as secretary and treasurer, and the game of golf had officially arrived in the United States.

President Havermeyer
The first president of the USGA, the ruling body of American golf, was Theodore Augustus Havermeyer, builder of the course at Newport, Rhode Island. The USGA was formed in 1894 by six golf clubs in the northeast.

The Apple Tree Gang

In 1892 the club moved to another site, set in an apple orchard on the Weston estate, with views over the Hudson River and Palisades in New Jersey. It took only a day to design the new layout, which was threaded between the apple trees, and when it was finished the St. Andrew's Club at Yonkers could boast six holes measuring a total of 1,500 yards. Reid and his colleagues became known as the "The Apple Tree Gang," after the tree under which they sat for shade while taking suitable refreshment following a round.

By that time a handful of other clubs had joined the St. Andrew's pioneers. Among them were Shinnecock Hills and Meadow Brook on Long Island, White Plains in Westchester, Richmond on Staten Island, Greenwich in Connecticut, and, across the river in New Jersey, Lakewood, New Brunswick, Montclair, Paterson and Baltusrol. From this trickle there started a flood, and by the turn of the century the United States had more than 1,000 golf clubs. The Apple Tree Gang could have had no idea, when they took their first tentative golf steps a little over a decade before, of what they were unleashing on the United States.

Golf cup
A drinking stein, made in the United States by O'Hara around 1899, carries a Harvard University crest on its lid. Many of the golf clubs that burgeoned in the U.S. at the turn of the century were created by groups of drinking companions.

Great as the influence of the St. Andrew's founders was, however, it should be noted that they were not the first people actually to play golf in America; neither was their club the first in the country. It is known that Scottish officers who fought during the American Revolution, which began in 1775, brought golf with them across the Atlantic. Four years later an advertisement appeared in *Rivington's Royal Gazette*, New York, which, under a heading "To the Golf Players," announced: "The season for this pleasant and healthy exercise now advancing Gentlemen may be furnished with excellent CLUBS and the veritable CALEDONIAN BALLS by enquiring at the Printer's." Charleston in South Carolina was the site of the formation of the South Carolina Golf Club in 1786, and the Savannah Golf Club was operating in Georgia in 1796. But although it is clear that there was a certain interest in the game over a century before John Reid and his friends first played in their cow pasture, it did not endure. Thus, it was not until the The Apple Tree Gang introduced the game to the northeastern United States that the American passion for golf began to take hold, and they are justly credited as the founding fathers of the American game.

Founding the USGA

Among the other early American golf pioneers was Theodore Havermeyer, who, despite some lack of enthusiasm among his contemporaries, built a course in Newport, Rhode Island, a resort for the wealthy. In 1894 Havermeyer was elected the first president of the United States Golf Association (USGA) when it was formed at a meeting of six of the newly established clubs: St. Andrew's, and the Country Clubs of Brookline, Newport, Southampton, Shinnecock Hills and Chicago. Newport was also selected as the site of the first official U.S. Open and U.S. Amateur Championships that were held the following year.

Other important figures of the game at that time were Henry O. Tallmadge, the first secretary of the association, and Charles Blair Macdonald, who became a golf addict while studying at St. Andrews, Scotland. Influenced by the Scottish links,

Macdonald built the Chicago Golf Club, which is credited with being the first 18-hole course in the United States. Macdonald's work affected much of the early thinking on courses in the United States, which explains why the first layouts on the eastern seaboard bear such a resemblance to Scottish courses.

Taking Root around the World

Canada had already been bitten by the golf bug as it spread from Scotland. The country's first club in Montreal, later to become the Royal Montreal, was founded in 1873, 15 years before The Apple Tree Gang first put club to ball. The Royal Quebec Club was formed in 1875, and these two clubs played the first inter-club match in Canada at Cove Fields in 1876. That year another club was formed in Toronto, but golf did not spread as quickly in Canada as in the United States. This was perhaps partly due to the smaller population north of the border, and partly to the colder climate, which made the golf season much shorter. Yet the influence of Canada on golf in North America has been considerable, and today there are more than 1,600 courses across the country.

It was not only to the other side of the Atlantic that the Scots took their game; they were responsible for its introduction to most of the countries in the expanding British Empire. In fact, the Royal Calcutta Club in India, formed in 1829, is among the oldest of all clubs; Royal Bombay dates back to 1842. Both clubs were founded by Scottish golfing enthusiasts engaged in trade with India. The Royal Calcutta Club inaugurated the Amateur Championship of India and the Far East in 1892, by which time there were clubs not only in India but in Ceylon (now Sri Lanka), Singapore, and Burma. The first amateur championship was played over 54 holes of the nine-hole layout, and until 1948 British players still dominated the event. As the standard of the home players' game improved, British influence faded. There are now about 150 golf courses in India.

Postcard from Pinehurst (right)
Pictures of famous holes made excellent greetings, as in this image of the 16th at Pinehurst's Number 2.

Gone golfing (below)
Golf was the great escape from everyday cares. Heading off to battle with bunkers had more appeal than tiresome toil on the treadmill.

Islands and Continents

The spread of golf to Australasia came somewhat later than its establishment in the Indian subcontinent. The Royal Christchurch Club in New Zealand dates back to 1867 and the Otago Club to 1871. In Australia there is some confusion over the origins of the game. It is thought that golf was played in some form as early as 1870 in Adelaide, although the Royal Adelaide Club officially dates back only to 1892. The Royal Melbourne Club was founded a year earlier, in 1891, and the Royal Sydney Club came along shortly afterward in 1893.

South Africa, which has produced many fine players over the decades, had pioneering clubs too, of which Royal Cape is generally accepted as the oldest, having come into existence in 1885. The island of Mauritius took to golf, by all accounts, in 1844 when the Mauritius Naval and Military Gymkhana Club is believed to have been formed, and Hong Kong has had a golf club, the Royal Hong Kong, since 1889. In continental Europe, the Golf Club de Pau in

Fowl stroke
A memento of the earlier days of golf in America: a ceramic figure of Walt Disney's Donald Duck takes a swing at a golf ball. He has learned the first lesson of keeping his eye on the ball.

Golf at Pau
The first golf club on the continent of Europe was at Pau in France, close to the border with Spain and in the gentle foothills of the Pyrenees. The club was founded in 1856 at the fashionable British holiday colony there. Golf had originally been played in the area by Scottish officers of the Duke of Wellington's army toward the end of the Napoleonic Wars.

southwest France is generally accepted as the oldest club, having been founded by British visitors in 1856, while the Royal Antwerp Club in Belgium was founded in 1888, the same year that The Apple Tree Gang was finding a new use for its cow pasture. Strangely, despite all the speculation over the origins of the game and its possible connections to the Low Countries (see page 13), the first golf club in the Netherlands did not appear until almost the end of the nineteenth century. This honor belongs to the Rosendaelsche Club in Arnhem, which was founded by Dutch golfing enthusiasts in 1896.

The twentieth century has seen golf develop all over the world on a major scale. The great boost to the game given by the United States at the turn of the century, when hundreds of clubs were formed, followed over the years by the development of resort golf courses to cater to holiday golf, has made the United States by far the biggest golfing nation in the world. But there have been major golf booms as significant in their own way elsewhere in the world, especially since the Second World War.

For instance, in the last 20 years there has been a massive expansion in golf on the European continent, particularly in France and Germany, where interest was stimulated by the emergence of such international stars as Catherine Lacoste and Bernhard Langer. In Spain and Portugal, the construction of golf courses has been largely to provide facilities for visiting players from further north in Europe escaping the winter weather, rather than to meet local demand. But the existence of these courses has encouraged the development of local talent, especially in Spain, which has produced such brilliantly gifted players as Seve Ballesteros and Jose-Maria Olazabal.

Come to Italy
An Italian state tourist department brochure of 1932 tempts British players to head south for golfing holidays. After the First World War, golf spread rapidly over the European continent.

Playing the Green Card

Sweden has been a major golfing nation for many years and has the largest number of active golfers in Europe outside the British Isles. The Swedes have made a significant impact on the game through their "green card" system, which requires newcomers to the game to pass a written and practical examination before they are allowed to play on a full-length course. The golfing authorities have an aggressive youth policy, and the country is already producing players capable of winning on the European Tour.

Golf was played in most of the countries of central and eastern Europe before the Second World War, including Hungary, Poland, Yugoslavia, Romania and Czechoslovakia. Today there remains a fine course at Bled in Yugoslavia, and there has been a resurgence of interest in the game in Czechoslovakia.

Africa has not been left out of the expansion of golf. In addition to the many fine courses in South Africa, of which the Royal Cape and the Royal Johannesburg are the most impressive, there are more than 70 courses in Zimbabwe (formerly Rhodesia), with the Bulawayo Club, founded in 1896, the oldest.

The expansion in the popularity of the game since the Second World War has been especially intense in the Far East. By 1987 Taiwan could boast 23 courses and 200,000 players. In Lu Liang Huan, the island produced a player capable of taking second place in the British Open in 1971 and of helping to win the World Cup for Taiwan the following year.

It is the Japanese, however, who have taken to golf with an enthusiasm unmatched by any other recent converts. The game was first played in Japan almost as early as the turn of the century, when a Scot named Arthur Groome built a few holes on top of Mount Rokko, near Kobe, for a group of English and Scottish expatriates. The Kobe Club soon had 18 holes, and other clubs followed in Yokohama and around Tokyo, but most of the early members were foreigners. Today the Japanese themselves flock to play golf. There were fewer than 30 clubs in Japan at the end of the Second World War, but today there are several hundred, despite the fact that the country has a severe shortage of suitable land on which to build courses.

Golf on the Range

It is estimated that there are nearly eight million Japanese golfing enthusiasts, but as few as 15 percent of them ever have the chance to play on a course. Instead, complete with a full set of clubs, bag, and other equipment, they set off for a driving range, which is often a multi-story construction and always a high-tech operation. The enormous Shiba Park in Tokyo is a three-story range where hundreds of golfers can practise at one time, shooting balls out 280 yards to a sloping rubber mat. There are well over 4,000 such ranges in Japan. Because of the shortage of space at home, many large Japanese companies have bought into golf in foreign countries. Japanese-owned courses abroad include the Riviera and Pebble Beach in the United States.

The premium on space means the few courses that do exist in Japan are exceedingly exclusive, with money and connections being the only passports to membership. It can cost a golfer as much as $400,000 to join a Japanese club, and the same amount again as an annual subscription.

There is no sign of an end to the expansion of golf as a world game. Arnold Palmer has designed a course in Beijing, the capital of mainland China, and a new course, complete with driving range, has opened in post-glasnost Moscow. Golf is now played regularly by an estimated 30 million people in 80 countries worldwide, and their numbers continue to increase.

Iberian golf
The dramatic setting for golf at Vale do Lobo, on the Portuguese Algarve, provides a stern challenge to tourists, who make use of one of the most popular resort courses built to cater to the needs of golfing vacationers.

Tobacco jar (left)
The famous ceramic works of Noritake in Japan made this golf-motif tobacco jar in the 1930s, showing that golf had some followers in Asia before the Second World War.

Big range (right)
At the huge Shiba Park range in Tokyo, hundreds of golfers practise their strokes. Such ranges have proliferated because there are not enough courses for would-be players.

CHAPTER

2

The Modern Game

The great golf-course building explosion of the late nineteenth century, coupled with the invention of the superior-quality rubber-core ball, which made golf altogether easier to play, set the game well on the way to becoming the mass-participation sport that it is today. The large number of clubs around the world celebrating their centenaries in the 1990s is a testament to the scale of the golf revolution a century ago. In the United States alone, 1,000 golf courses were built in the last decade of the nineteenth century.

With the new courses arrived players anxious to learn, and the professional golfer came into his own. New technology brought rapid advances in golfing equipment.

Today, golf is enjoying another boom around the world as the demand for the game rises, encouraged by the televised exploits of the superstar players of the international Tours.

French ceramic golfing figure from the 1950s

Popular spectator sport (left)
The 1988 U.S. Open is watched by a huge gallery of avid golf enthusiasts.

State-of-the-art, wide-bodied carbon graphite woods with boron-reinforced shafts

Competing for Glory

Model player
Enthusiasm for golf permeated other leisure areas. This lead toy is part of a board game from the beginning of the century.

Top trio
Clement Flower's 1913 portrait of the Triumvirate shows, left to right, Taylor, Braid, and Vardon (driving) at the 2nd tee on the Old course at St. Andrews.

G OLF HAS COME *a long way since its tentative beginnings five or six centuries ago on the east coast of Scotland. The pastime of the Scots has become the passion of millions of people, as well as being, for a celebrated few, a passport to wealth. It was around the turn of the century, as the game expanded and became better organized, that the professional golfer first rose to the status of popular hero.*

Until the end of the nineteenth century, golf was very much an amateur pursuit. Early in the development of the game, the job of the golf professional was to make clubs and balls, and to carry the clubs, and later the bags, of amateur players. Even in the late Victorian period, golf professionals were much less highly regarded than they are now.

Golf Professional or Professional Golfer

Essentially, the professional was there to provide a service for club players, although he played in occasional money matches, and increasingly in organized tournaments. Today, of course, golf professionals still aid their club members in much the same way. But no equivalent to the modern tournament players – professional golfers who play for a living on the various tours around the world – existed until the emergence of three masters of the game in the 1890s heralded a new era.

The British players Harry Vardon (see page 304), James Braid (see page 224), and J. H. Taylor (see page 298) dominated the game for two decades and were known as The Great Triumvirate. The trio, who between them won 16 British Opens from 1894 to 1914, became the first golfing superstars. Spectators flocked to see them, and they were in demand to open new courses and clubhouses. The combined impact of these three champions on the growth of golf cannot be overstated. Harry Vardon brought a new artistry to the game, while Braid made an outstanding contribution to course architecture. Taylor, despite his fabulous record of five British Open wins, is famed as much for improving the lot of the professional golfer as for his prowess as a player. It was largely due to him that the first Professional Golfers' Association was formed in 1901.

Challenge from the Americans

In the days of The Great Triumvirate, British players dominated the game of golf. But by building 1,000 courses between 1890 and 1900 and importing hundreds of Scottish professionals to teach the game, Americans soon started to catch up. In 1911 Johnny McDermott became the first home-bred American to

Cigarette-card hero (right)
Gene Sarazen dominated the game during the 1920s and 1930s, winning international fame.

On the way up (below)
Walter Hagen was instrumental in raising the status of professional golfers, winning them the right to use the clubhouse.

Magazine cover (left)
As the popularity of the game grew, the volume of golf-related literature swelled, particularly in the United States. A plethora of books and magazines with golfing themes was made available to an increasingly golf-mad general public.

Great year
America saluted Ben Hogan with a victory parade in New York after he won the British Open in 1953. With victories in the U.S. Open and Masters that year, Hogan became the player closest to winning the four professional Majors in a single season.

win the U.S. Open, but the real breakthrough followed two years later with the memorable victory of Francis Ouimet (see page 282), a 20-year-old amateur from Brookline. Taking time off work to play in the Open, which was being held that year on his local course, Ouimet defeated two experienced visiting British professionals, Harry Vardon and Ted Ray (see page 288), to take the title. It was an immensely popular triumph, and golf in the United States never looked back.

It was not until 1922 that an American defeated the British on their home ground, when the flamboyant Walter Hagen (see page 244) won the British Open. Following his victory, his fellow Americans Bobby Jones (see page 252), Gene Sarazen (see page 292), and Denny Shute held sway over the event for more than a decade. Henry Cotton (see page 230) restored British dominance at home by winning the Open in 1934 at St. George's, but the balance of power in the world of golf had shifted radically in the direction of the United States.

Tournament Play

The first three decades of the twentieth century witnessed the transition from a professional game dominated by challenge matches between individual players or teams of two, to modern tournament golf. The great days of head-to-head encounters were before the First World War. Although these matches continued into the 1920s and even later, tournament play now predominated.

Until the 1930s the amateur game still produced formidable players who were a match for the professionals. The four championships generally regarded as the major events were the U.S. and British Opens and the U.S. and British Amateur Championships – the four titles won by Bobby Jones in his "Grand Slam" of 1930. But with the advent of the U.S. Masters in 1934, all four of the championships now regarded as the Majors – the British and U.S. Open Championships, the Masters, and the USPGA Championship – were in place, and the professional game was establishing its preeminence.

Big-money Golf

After the Second World War the game blossomed in the United States. Between 1945 and 1970, the number of courses in the country more than doubled and the prize money available to the top U.S. professionals increased dramatically. Ben Hogan (see page 246) was the first dominant American in the postwar game. In 1953 he came closer than any other player to winning the four professional Majors in one year. All he missed was the USPGA

Top trophies
These glittering prizes are the trophies for the four Majors, the apex of achievement for professional golfers today: from left to right, the British Open, the USPGA Championship, the Masters, and the U.S. Open.

TV golf (right)
The arrival of television had a remarkable effect on golf. It brought millions of dollars to the professional game in the United States through advertising and sponsorship, and its influence quickly spread to Europe.

Championship, which he could not enter because it clashed with the British Open. Later in the 1950s Arnold Palmer (see page 284) seized center stage. Thanks to his manager, Mark McCormack, and to the emerging medium of television, Palmer became a legend first in the United States and then across the world. He was a hero whose exploits were viewed by millions on television, and he started a new international boom in the popularity of the game both as spectator and participant sport.

The great Palmer
An exciting player, Arnold Palmer breathed new life into the British Open, helping to restore it to its rightful place as the most prestigious of all golf events. He also promoted a new boom in golf's overall popularity.

Television changed the nature of professional golf in many ways. It was a major factor in the virtual disappearance of matchplay, which sets individual players against one another, from professional tournament play. The last of the Majors to abandon the matchplay formula was the USPGA Championship in 1958. Four rounds of strokeplay on separate days became the standard formula, players pitting their skills against the course rather than against individual opponents. Rare exceptions include the World Matchplay Championship and such hybrid events as the Dunhill Cup. The amateur game, however, retained its allegiance to matchplay, and the majority of ordinary players still compete in their club matches on a matchplay basis today.

Reviving the Open

Ben Hogan's decision to cross the Atlantic to play in the British Open in 1953 was not typical of its time. So great were the incentives to play in the United States that the leading American players ignored the British Open during much of the 1950s. Despite the absence of Americans, however, British professionals rarely won the championship after the Second World War. The end of hostilities heralded the emergence of new centers of golfing excellence, including most notably the British Dominions. Of the 12 British Opens between 1949 and 1960, South African and Australian players won 10, including four each for Bobby Locke (see page 260) and Peter Thomson (see page 302).

The world's greatest championship was, in effect, languishing through lack of the money that would produce a new breed of financially motivated professional players in Britain. The Royal & Ancient Golf Club, which runs the British Open, saw that investment was needed to attract top players to return the event to its former glory. For the Centenary Open in 1960, the prize money was increased, and the facilities at St. Andrews were

Major money (right)
The administration of major golf championships is big business. This tented village housing a network of sponsors, retailers, and exhibitors was set up at Turnberry for the 1986 British Open.

Golf in art (left) *American LeRoy Neiman's vivid golf paintings are famous.* The Eighteenth at Pebble Beach *shows the 1983 Bing Crosby Pro-Am. The players are ex-President Gerald Ford, Jack Nicklaus (putting), Tom Watson, and actor Clint Eastwood.*

renovated. Despite this, few top Americans came, but one of those who did was Arnold Palmer. His appearance revivified the championship, and he returned to win it in 1961 and 1962. His example was followed by Jack Nicklaus (see page 276), perhaps the greatest golfer ever, Lee Trevino (see page 300), and Tom Watson (see page 306). The Americans had returned to Britain with a vengeance.

In the 1960s Arnold Palmer, Jack Nicklaus, and the South African Gary Player (see page 286) were featured prominently in exhibition matches, usually staged for television. They became, in effect, a "Modern Triumvirate" and took golf into a new era in much the same way as Vardon, Braid, and Taylor had half a century before. They also became golf's first millionaires, confirming what Walter Hagen had realized decades before – that vast fortunes could be made by the world's best players.

The United States dominated the golf scene during the 1960s and 1970s with the reign of Palmer followed by that of Nicklaus, but a European revival was signaled in 1979 when Seve Ballesteros (see page 218) won the British Open at Royal Lytham and St. Annes; Ballesteros won the Open again in 1984. The following year Sandy Lyle (see page 264) became the first home-based Scot to win the Open since 1920.

The emergence of Germany's Bernhard Langer (see page 256), who won the Masters in 1985, and of promising professionals from Sweden, such as Anders Forsbrand, Magnus Persson and Ove Sellberg, and Spain, reflected the strength of European golf. The revival culminated in the victory of the European team in the Ryder Cup. This biennial event, instituted in 1927 between the professionals of Great Britain and the United States, had become such a one-sided affair

Out of this world *Golf is the only sport to have been played away from Earth. Apollo 14 astronaut Alan B. Shepard, Jr. used a 6-iron head on top of a soil sampler to hit a ball about 200 yards on February 6, 1971.*

Modern Triumvirate (left) *Jack Nicklaus, Gary Player, and Arnold Palmer became the three most popular and successful champions of the 1960s. In that decade alone, they won a total of 18 Majors between them.*

Masters record
Jack Nicklaus became the oldest winner of the Masters when he took the title in 1986 for a record sixth time, his twentieth Major win. Here, before an enthralled crowd at Augusta's 15th green, he sinks a crucial 12-foot putt for an eagle 3, on his way to a final round of 65. The unsurpassed record-holder of Majors, Nicklaus has also distinguished himself as a top course designer.

by the 1970s that its continued existence was in danger. In 1979, in order to make the matches more competitive, European players became eligible to play against the United States. Although the European team just failed to win in America in 1983, they triumphed in 1985, and retained the trophy with a win in 1987 and a tie in 1989.

The European Invasion

As well as playing on the expanding European Tour, which has been systematically built up since 1975, the best of the European players have had an increasing impact in the United States. Englishman Nick Faldo (see page 238) not only won the British Open twice, in 1987 and 1990, but also captured the Masters in two consecutive years, 1989 and 1990. Welshman Ian Woosnam (see page 311) won at Augusta in 1991, with Spaniard Jose-Maria Olazabal coming in second, confirming the resurgence of European players. Even before the 1991 Masters, Europeans were allotted the top three places in the Sony World Rankings.

Professional golf now has lucrative tours, not only in the U.S. and Europe, but also in Australia and Japan, and this has encouraged a new generation of top professionals from these countries. Although the Japanese are successful in their own country, where they beat many of the world's leading players, so far victory in the Majors has eluded them, but they are sure to make a breakthrough soon.

Separate divisions of the British PGA and the USPGA – the PGA European Tour in Britain and the PGA Tour in America – represent the

Jug logo (above)
The logo on this distinctive caddie's bib shows the British Open trophy, the famous claret jug. The first Open drew eight entrants; by 1990 there were 1,707.

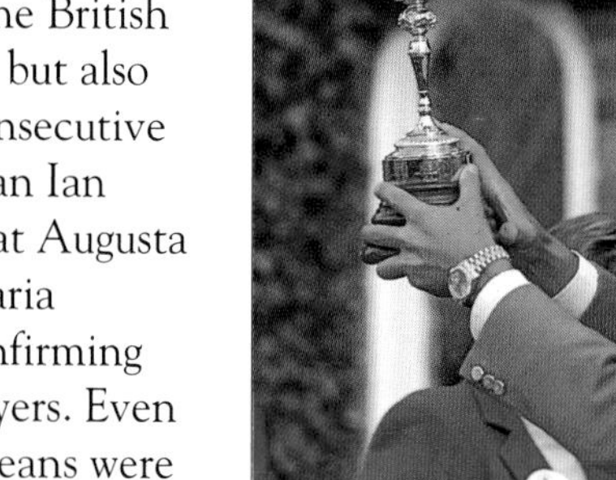

Ryder Cup triumph
Tony Jacklin lifts the Ryder Cup after the European win at The Belfry in 1985, having just led his team to the first victory over the United States in 28 years. When the Europeans beat the Americans for the first time on their home soil in 1987, the balance of power in world golf shifted.

tournament players on their various tours and organize and administer the many events in which they play. In addition, golf management has become a major business in the financially oriented environment of the modern professional game, where the top stars can command largee sums in "appearance money" – that is, by merely playing in an event.

Managing the Game

Back in the 1920s, Walter Hagen was assisted by Bob Harlow; they, along with another American, Fred Corcoran, were the first managers. Today the management role is filled by companies like Mark McCormack's International Management Group, which runs the affairs of leading players and organizes tournaments around the world, as well as conducting various other sporting interests.

The financial rewards of professional golf are now so great that the higher echelons of the amateur game have become little more than a breeding ground for would-be professionals. As a result, the best up-and-coming young players disappear from the amateur game in their early 20s, or even as teenagers.

Spanish stars (above) *In Ryder Cup partnership, Seve Ballesteros (right) advises fellow Spaniard Jose-Maria Olazabal. Spain is now providing the game with some of its finest players.*

Fewer and fewer players of real ability decide to retain their amateur status, although there have been notable exceptions, such as Jay Sigel, Michael Bonallack (see page 223) and Charlie Green.

The televised exploits of millionaire stars continue to attract new golf converts at the club and public-course level. This causes its own problems. Even in the U.S., where new courses have been built at a fantastic rate for several decades, capacity for new players is limited, and in Britain in the 1980s the number of club members was exceeded by those excluded because membership lists were full.

Ballesteros's ball
The amateur game supports a worldwide industry manufacturing clothing and equipment. Today's bewildering choices include several ranges endorsed by golf's top professionals.

Crazy for Golf

Well over one million golfers in Britain play on public courses, as green-fee-paying visitors to private clubs, or in an increasing number of societies. The overcrowding can only be eased by the building of some 700 new courses in the 1990s, according to research by the Royal & Ancient Golf Club. For golf-crazy Japan's eight million golfing fans, the situation is much worse (see page 37).

Unlike other sports, the amateur and professional elements of golf run in parallel and, by common consent, are kept carefully apart. The pastime that the Scots gave to the world will continue to earn fortunes for those who are able to exploit the huge financial sums now involved. But more important for the millions of ordinary people who play simply for the love of the game, golf will continue to flourish in much the same way, and with the same spirit, that it has for centuries.

Facing the future
One of the leading players of recent years, Nick Faldo, assisted by caddie Fanny Sunneson, has earned a fortune from his golfing triumphs.

WOMEN IN GOLF

Fashion victims
Conforming to the styles of the 1890s, women golfers were severely restricted by long, billowing skirts and corsets designed to shape a narrow waist at the expense of free body movement.

WOMEN'S GOLF HAS *changed dramatically since the Second World War, when the few women's professional tournaments barely paid enough to cover expenses. Today a leading international star such as Nancy Lopez or Laura Davies can expect to win money and fame on a scale to rival all but the greatest male players.*

Lady Scott (above)
Margaret Scott (second from the left) won the 1895 British Ladies' at Portrush, where the women's game was strong.

The first women's golf clubs came into existence in the second half of the nineteenth century, when golf was played by genteel ladies of leisure, but only as a glorified form of pitch-and-putt. It was considered indelicate to raise the club above shoulder height, and restrictive clothing severely limited movement. Voluminous full-length skirts were secured just above the ankle with elastic belts.

But such decorous and inhibiting behavior and attire were not to last long after the formation of the Ladies' Golf Union in 1893. The major influence behind this new group of golfing women was its secretary, Issette Pearson, runner-up to Lady Margaret Scott in the first British Ladies' Amateur Championship in that same year.

Required reading
Genevieve Hecker, twice U.S. Women's Amateur Champion, published this useful book for women golfers in 1904.

WOMEN TAKE THE LEAD

Also in 1893, across the Atlantic, American women were taking the initiative. Members of the newly formed Shinnecock Hills Club in New York, were persuaded by their wives to build them a separate nine-hole course. Where men refused to share or build a course, women created their own. By 1894, a group of female golfers had founded their own club and created a seven-hole course in Morristown, New Jersey. It would take only a few years for American women to match the level of British women's golfing activity.

The first superstar of British women's golf was Charlotte Cecilia Pitcairn Leitch, who reached the semifinals of the British Ladies' Amateur in 1908 at the age of 17. She shortened her name to Cecil Leitch in 1914 and went on to win 12 titles in Britain, France, and Canada. With her strong, flat swing, she dominated the game until finally overcome by Joyce Wethered (see page 309), who played an aggressively stylish and elegant game. Wethered was so effective that she captured eight titles in four years before retiring from competitive play in 1925. She made a comeback to win the British Ladies' Amateur for the fourth and last time at St. Andrews four years later.

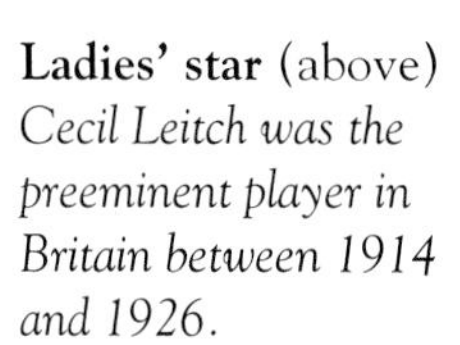

Ladies' star (above)
Cecil Leitch was the preeminent player in Britain between 1914 and 1926.

TRANSATLANTIC RIVALRY

Wethered's opponent in the final on that occasion was Glenna Collett (see page 306), who held an equal supremacy in golf in the United States and was to win the American Women's Amateur Championship six times. Women's international golf had begun when an American team traveled to Britain in 1905 to play in the British Ladies' Amateur. The first international women's trophy, the Curtis Cup, was donated by two American sisters, Harriot

Americans abroad (left)
The American women golfers who visited Britain in 1930 included Glenna Collett (standing, second from right) who that year lost in the final of the British Ladies' Amateur.

and Margaret Curtis, who had taken part in the original 1905 event. The Americans won the first Curtis Cup match in 1932, and were not beaten until 20 years later. The British amateurs won in 1952 and 1956, but the Americans regained their domination with 13 successive victories up to 1986. In that year, the British women recorded a historic victory at Prairie Dunes, and they won again in 1988. The Americans reasserted themselves at Somerset Hills in 1990.

Postwar Growth

Unlike the men's game, women's golf remained predominantly amateur until well after the Second World War. In 1949 a fledgling Ladies' Professional Golf Association (LPGA) was created in the United States, led by Patty Berg (see page 222) and Babe Zaharias (see page 314), but for some years tournaments remained sparse, and prize money was far below the levels available to male players.

Zaharias was the most successful female player of the immediate postwar period, winning 17 tournaments in 1946 alone. She dominated the early days of the LPGA Tour with her talent and enthusiasm. Her leading role was later taken over by Mickey Wright (see page 312), who emerged in the 1950s, and then by Kathy Whitworth (see page 310) and Nancy Lopez (see page 262). Only one European player of this period challenged American superiority – Catherine Lacoste of France. In 1967, at the age of 22, she became the youngest winner of the U.S. Women's Open, as well as being the first amateur and the first overseas player to take the title.

By the time the charismatic Lopez achieved superstar status in the late 1970s, women's professional golf in the United States had truly come of age, with extensive television coverage and annual prize money of millions of dollars. In Britain, by contrast, the professional game did not begin until 1979, and it struggled for years without arousing a great deal of public interest or attracting much financial sponsorship.

Yet with the emergence of a growing number of European competitors and a rise in playing standards, a regular Tour in Britain and Europe has eventually been established. One star of the Tour is Laura Davies (see page 234), who became the first British woman to win the U.S. Women's Open in 1987. Another, Marie Laure de Lorenzi of France, has become a multiple titleholder since turning professional in 1986. Other proven players such as Alison Nicholas, Kitrina Douglas, Jane Connachan, Dale Reid, Cathy Panton and Helen Alfredsson are adding to the progress of European women in the game.

After 70 years of the Ryder Cup, the women professionals at last established their own equivalent in 1990, the Solheim Cup, a mixture of foursomes, four-balls and singles. The first match was won by the American team, by the large margin of $11^{1}/_{2}$ to $4^{1}/_{2}$.

Women's golf has recently been enhanced by the increase of prize money on the professional circuit. The emergence of a band of talented young players in the amateur game seems likely to continue the success of the women's game.

THE HEEL OF ACHILLES by P.G. Wodehouse

Sporting heroine
P. G. Woodhouse's popular golfing stories were published in 1904.

Freer styles
This 1930s bronze statuette shows how comfort and elegance started to appear in women's attire to make golf easier to play.

True professional
Women golfers, such as Canada's Sandra Post, are now able to earn good prize money on the Tour.

THE RISE OF THE RUBBER-CORE BALL

THE INVENTION OF the wound, rubber-core Haskell ball at the turn of the century was a momentous event in golf history, ushering in the modern age of the game. Created by winding lengths of rubber around a solid core, the Haskell's added "spring" offered golfers greater distance since the new ball flew and bounced farther than its guttie predecessor, and performed better even when mis-hit.

THE RUBBER-CORE BALL

The rubber-core ball, developed by Coburn Haskell in 1898 and first made commercially in 1901, could be hit farther and faster than previous designs. It was made by winding great lengths of rubber yarn, stretched under tension, around a rubber core. The livelier core enabled golfers to exercise more control over the ball's spin and flight. Early models had a gutta percha covering, onto which was molded a flight-assisting pattern.

Rubber thread

Gutta percha cover

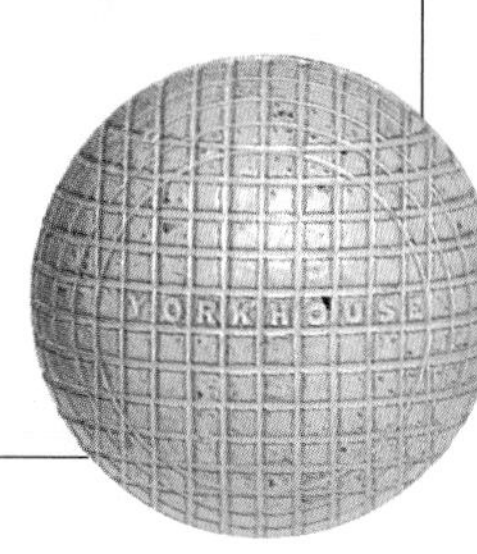

The rubber-core ball was invented by a wealthy American amateur golfer, Coburn Haskell, in collaboration with Bertram Work, an engineer at the Goodrich Rubber Company at Akron, Ohio. The earliest protoypes were not successful, because the hand-wound balls tended to duck and curve. However, the creation of an automatic winding machine, coupled with the use of a bramble cover, facilitated greater control, and Work's company began mass manufacturing. Walter J. Travis won the U.S. Amateur Championship with a Haskell in the autumn of 1901, and the following year, on the other side of the Atlantic, Sandy Herd won the British Open using a Haskell. The adoption of the new ball, with its much livelier feel and greater distance, led to a surge in the popularity of the game.

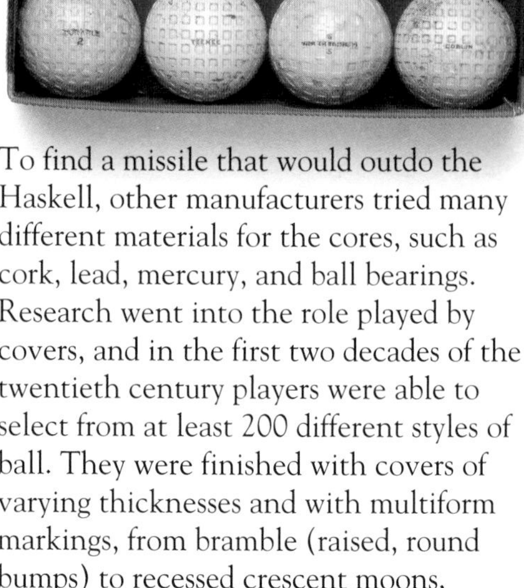

Mesh-marked balls
This collection of a dozen named rubber-core balls, with a variety of recessed mesh or lattice patterns, dates from the early 1930s.

To find a missile that would outdo the Haskell, other manufacturers tried many different materials for the cores, such as cork, lead, mercury, and ball bearings. Research went into the role played by covers, and in the first two decades of the twentieth century players were able to select from at least 200 different styles of ball. They were finished with covers of varying thicknesses and with multiform markings, from bramble (raised, round bumps) to recessed crescent moons, triangles, and squares (or "mesh"), each of which was claimed to outfly the others.

Box of Scottish rubber-core balls dating from about 1910

American rubber-core balls from about 1925, "guaranteed for 54 holes"

Non-floating dimpled balls; the first dimples appeared on balls in 1908

Box of repainted, recycled balls from the early 1930s, of practice quality for beginners

Cheap balls, numbered for identification, made by Dunlop Rubber in London about 1938

The 1940s Dunlop Warwick brand of ball, with recessed dimple marks

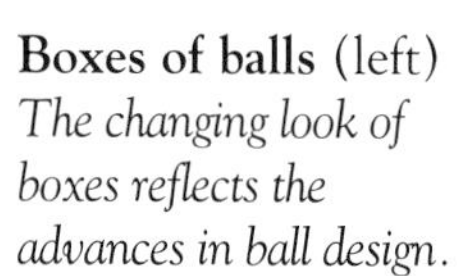

Boxes of balls (left)
The changing look of boxes reflects the advances in ball design.

High flyer (right)
The makers of the core-wound "Kite," with distinctive bramble markings, were sued by Haskell for breach of patent, but in vain.

The study of golf-ball aerodynamics and the laws governing a ball's trajectory has come a long way since then. Today the patterns have been replaced by dimples, which accentuate the effects of lift and minimize the amount of drag on the ball. Their exact shape and overall distribution is a continuing matter of intense study by manufacturers. In 1973, Titleist created the icosahedron pattern, dividing the ball surface into 20 identical triangles to achieve more consistent dimple coverage.

Modern technology and new materials have improved the performance of golf balls dramatically. Mass production made balls cheaper and enabled the establishment of a uniform size. In 1921, the USGA and the Royal & Ancient had decided on a uniform ball, 1.62 in. (41mm) in diameter. Ten years later, the USGA increased the ball size to 1.68 in. (43mm), and in 1987, the R & A decreed that the American size would become mandatory.

Golf Balls Today

Modern balls are of three different basic construction types. The one-piece ball is ideal for beginners and for driving ranges. The two-piece is most commonly used by club members because it combines durability with maximum length.

The three-piece ball has either a solid or liquid center; around this rubber is wound, over which is molded a cover of durable Surlyn or balata. It has a higher spin rate than a two-piece ball and is more controllable by good players.

Have a ball
This 1920s hand-painted, plaster-of-Paris statuette, 16 in. (40cm) tall, was distributed to pro shops to encourage sales of Dunlop balls.

1940s American balls, sold as adding "distance and accuracy"

English balls, with dimple markings, of the late 1950s

Bromford balls manufactured in Great Britain in the 1960s

Three-piece (Surlyn Cover)

This version of the three-piece wound ball has a solid rubber core over which rubber yarn is wound for good control. The cover is made from Surlyn, a thermoplastic resin that is harder than balata and is thus considerably more durable; it is virtually uncuttable.

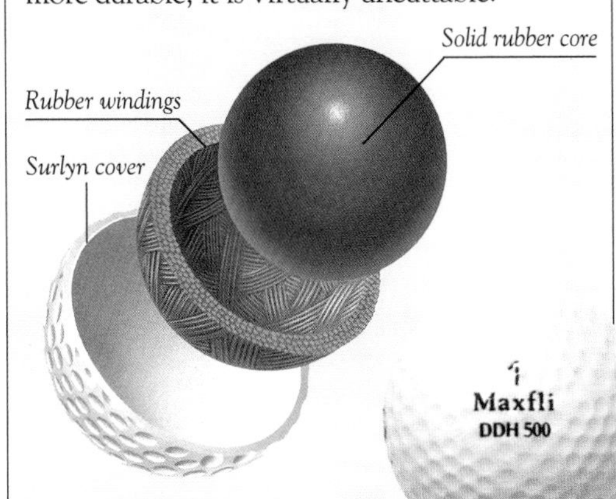

Two-piece

A high-energy acrylate or resin core with a tough, cut-proof, blended cover gives the two-piece more length than any other ball. It is also virtually indestructible, which, with its high roll distance, makes it by far the most popular ball among ordinary golfers. However, because it has a lower spin rate, it is less easy to control.

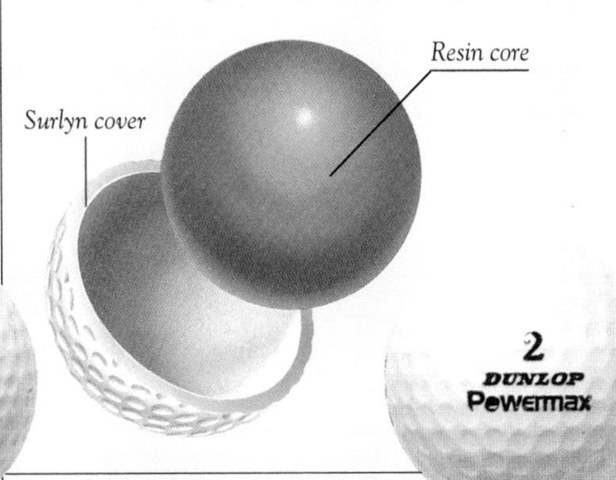

One-piece

Seldom used as a playing ball, the one-piece, made from a solid piece of Surlyn with dimples molded in, is usually found on practice grounds and driving ranges. It is the least expensive golf ball and is extremely durable, but it gives less distance because of its lower compression. The one-piece ball has a distinctly soft feel on impact with the clubface.

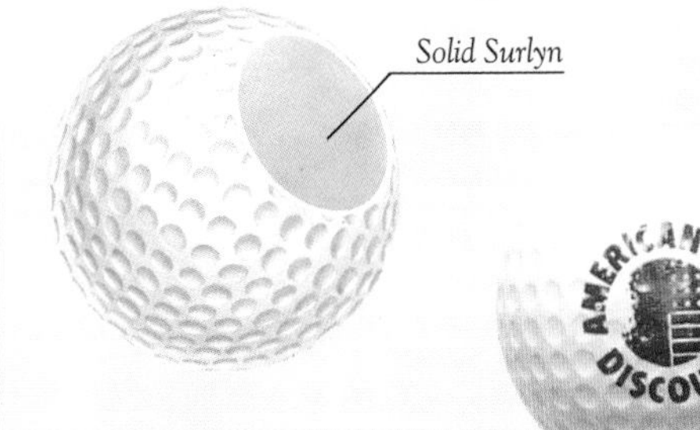

Three-piece (Balata Cover)

The balata-covered, liquid-centered, three-piece ball can fairly be described as the most advanced golf ball. The wound construction over a liquid center, combined with a soft, synthetic balata cover, produces the highest spin rate, providing maximum control and superb feel.

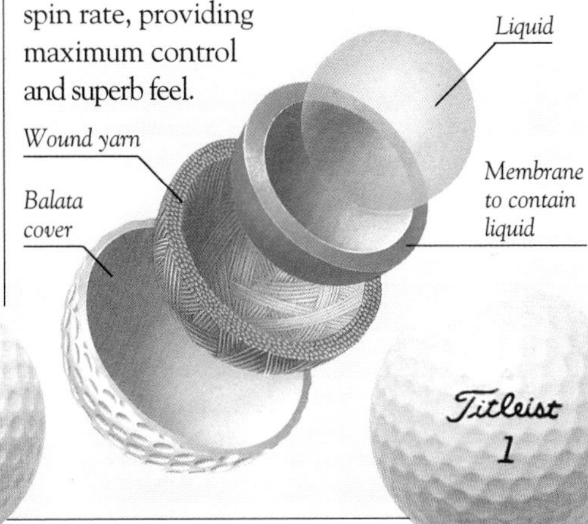

Modern Club Design

NEW MATERIALS AND advancing technology have always been the major influences in the development of golf clubs. Just as hickory shafts, introduced by the clubmaker Forgan, were a radical innovation, so modern designers have revolutionized the clubmaker's craft. The most significant advance in the first years of the twentieth century was the introduction of the steel shaft. Experiments with steel shafts began as early as the 1890s by blacksmith Thomas Horsburgh and by professional Willie Dunn, Jr. Horsburgh patented the idea but let the patent lapse. The first seamless steel shafts were made in Britain about 1912.

1890 aluminum-headed driver with hickory shaft

1990 steel-headed driver with steel shaft

Head to head
Metal-headed woods, increasingly popular, are not new, however. Aluminum-headed clubs have been available since before the turn of the century. The construction, materials, and details, such as the slim hosel, may have altered, but the modern club differs little in basic design.

Types of driver construction
Seventy per cent of today's woods are made of metal; hence the unusual term "metal woods." Traditionalists prefer persimmon, but the steel-headed driver is more forgiving to mis-hits. An offset-headed club encourages confidence.

Persimmon driver

Steel-headed driver

Offset-headed driver

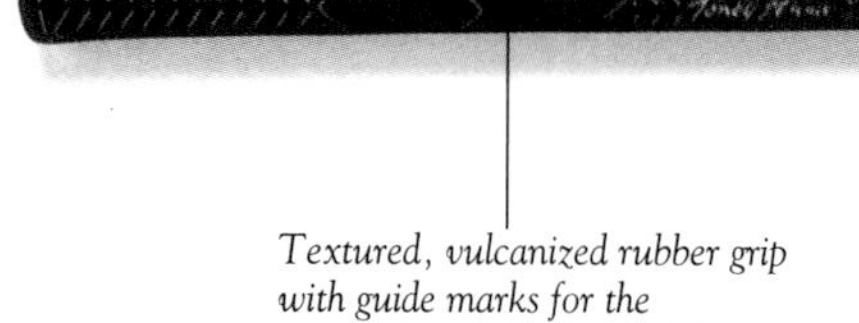
Textured, vulcanized rubber grip with guide marks for the positioning of thumbs and fingers

The steel shaft is thicker at the top than at the bottom; an average driver is about 43 in. (109cm) long

Range of modern iron clubs
Irons are either forged or cast: the traditional hand-forged blade is liked by good players because it has more feel at impact. Peripherally weighted cast-iron clubs offer a larger sweet spot. New fairway woods include this 7-wood, with the loft of a 5-iron.

Hand-forged 5-iron

Peripherally weighted 5-iron

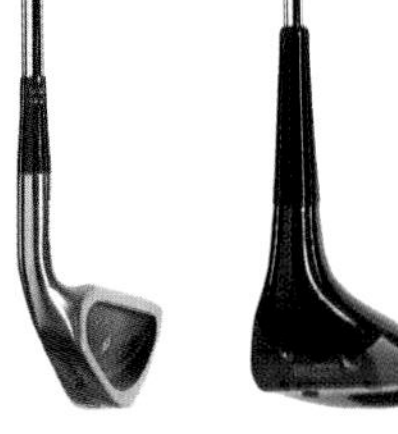
Fairway 7-wood

Most irons are made with steel shafts, and many come with a range of shaft flexes; a typical length is about 37½ in. (95cm)

Wedges and special-purpose irons
Wedges are used to loft the ball high over short distances. The sand wedge is used for escaping from bunkers, and the pitching wedge (or 10-iron) hits the ball onto the green with a spin that makes it hold there. The utility wedge serves both functions.

Sand wedge

Utility wedge

Pitching wedge

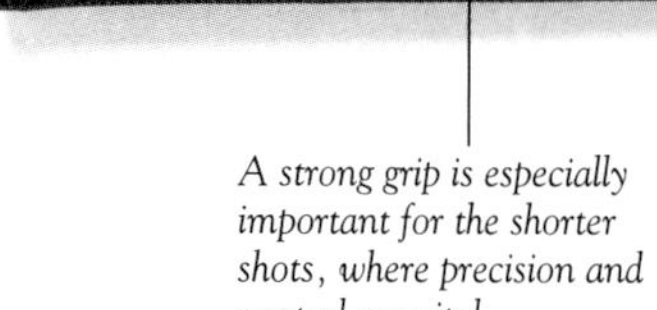
A strong grip is especially important for the shorter shots, where precision and control are vital

Wedges are rarely used when a full swing is required so the amount of flexibility of the shaft is less important; the average length is 35½ in. (90cm)

"Toe-and-heel" putters
Putters come in a larger variety of shapes than any other club. Many are peripherally weighted to maximize the size of the sweet spot. "Toe-and-heel" putters concentrate the weight at both ends of the head to reduce torque.

Straight-set toe-and-heel

Toe-and-heel with large head

Offset toe-and-heel

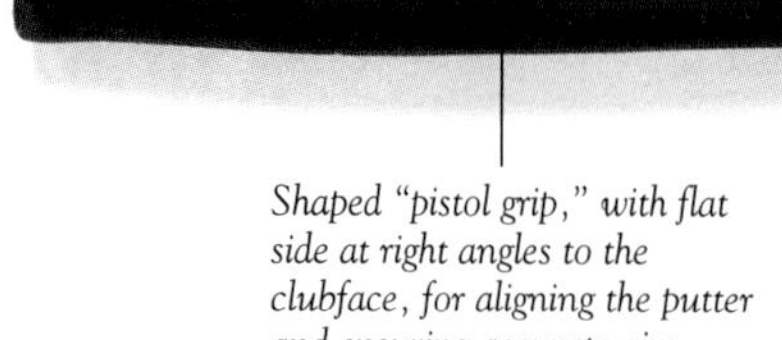
Shaped "pistol grip," with flat side at right angles to the clubface, for aligning the putter and ensuring accurate aim

Stainless steel shaft; putters are generally 32–35 in. (81–90cm) in length

Steel shaft | Graphite shaft | Boron-reinforced shaft | Colored graphite shaft | Titanium shaft

Shaft types
Major advances have been made in shaft construction since the days of hickory. Steel shafts revolutionized the game in the late 1920s, and steel is still the most common material for the modern golf club. But other materials are now being used, including graphite, which is light but very strong, as well as boron/graphite mixes and titanium.

By the late 1920s steel was being used freely in the United States, but it was not until 1929 that the Royal & Ancient Club legalized steel shafts when the Prince of Wales (the future Edward VIII) played with a set of steel-shafted clubs on the Old course at St. Andrews. It is said that the Royal & Ancient had either to legalize them or else disqualify the Prince.

Mass-produced clubs followed, and with them came matched sets with numbered, instead of named, clubs (see page 52). Steel is still the main shaft material for the irons, but carbon fiber (or graphite) in a range of flexes and colors, is becoming popular; so is, to a lesser extent, titanium. When persimmon, used to make wooden heads, became scarce, steel heads shaped like traditional wooden heads took over. As with shafts, steel is now being threatened by heads made from graphite. With its light weight and high strength it is ideal for use both in shafts and heads.

The majority of golf manufacturers' production is now geared to "game-improvement clubs" such as peripherally weighted irons. With new casting techniques, the mass of a clubhead can be redistributed around the outside edges of metal woods and irons. This minimizes the effects of poor shots. Customized clubs, tailored to fit individuals in terms of shaft length and flexibility, lie (the angle between head and shaft), and swingweight (weight distribution) are now available.

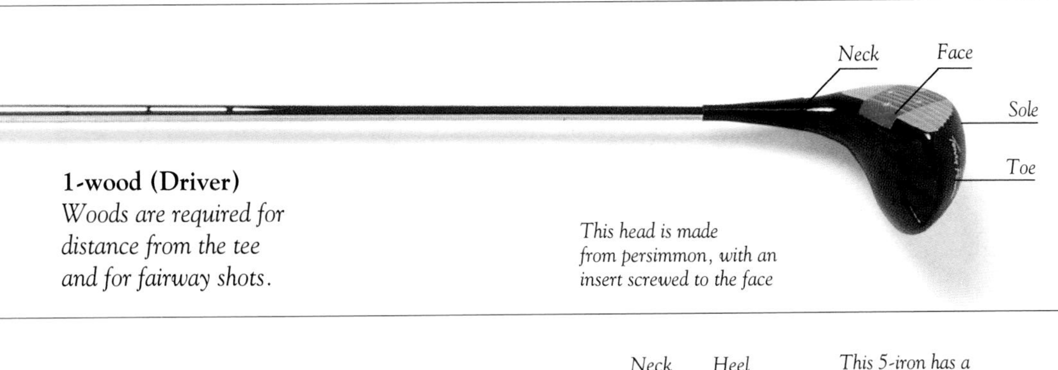

1-wood (Driver)
Woods are required for distance from the tee and for fairway shots.

This head is made from persimmon, with an insert screwed to the face

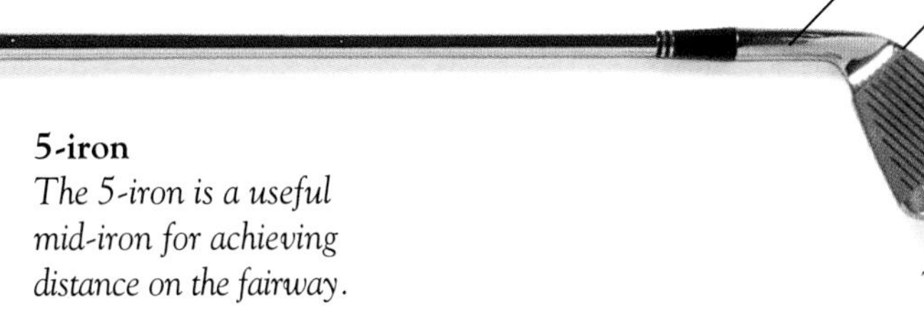

This 5-iron has a traditionally forged blade

5-iron
The 5-iron is a useful mid-iron for achieving distance on the fairway.

Heel | Neck | Sole | Toe

The sand wedge has a thick-flanged sole

Sand wedge
The sand wedge is designed to lift the ball out of sand traps.

Shape of soles and bounce
The sand wedge has a thick, rounded "bounce" on the sole to prevent it from digging into the sand. The medium bounce of the utility wedge suits its dual purpose. The pitching wedge has a narrower bounce since it is used for an approach shot.

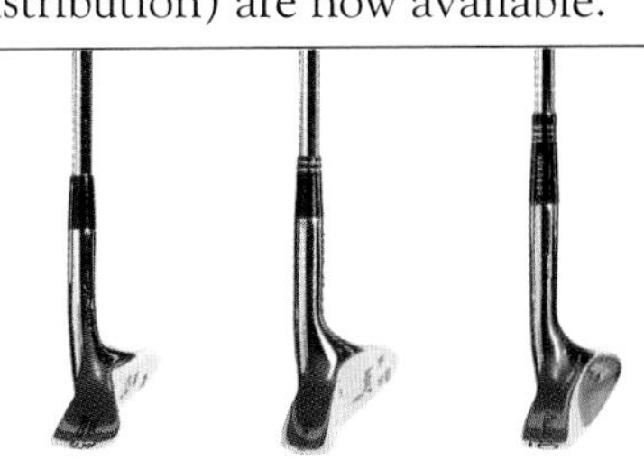

Sand wedge | Utility wedge | Pitching wedge

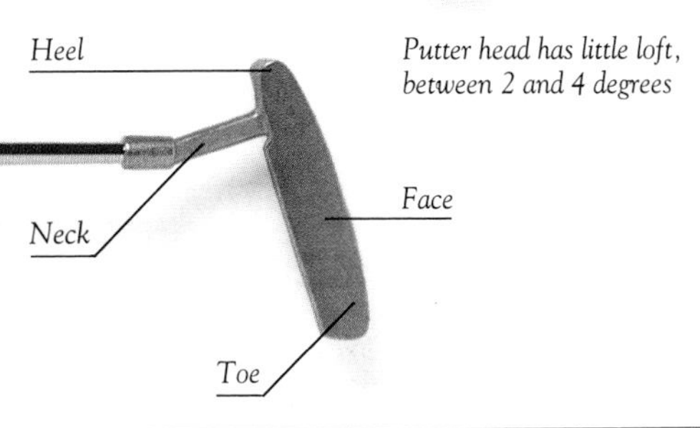

Putter head has little loft, between 2 and 4 degrees

Putter
Designed for precision play on the greens, the putter rolls the ball.

Wide variety of putter heads
The traditional, center-shafted putter with a straight head still has more adherents than the semicircular mallet head with its bent shaft, or the center-shafted putter with its onset head and long flange to focus the weight behind the sweet spot.

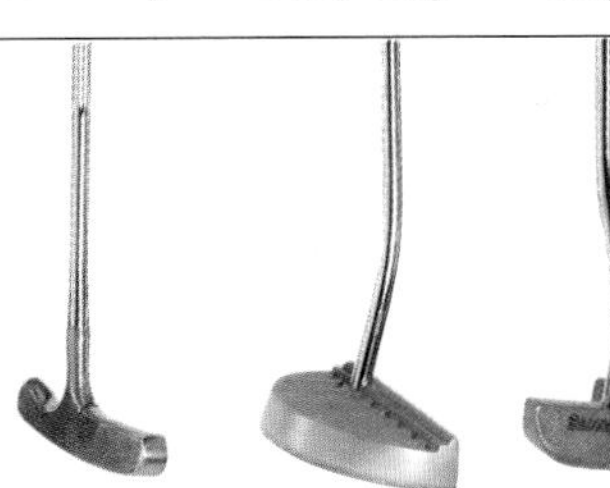

Center-shafted putter | Mallet-headed putter | Onset-headed putter

THE FULL SET OF CLUBS

WITH THE ADOPTION of steel shafts in the 1930s came the possibility of matched sets of clubs, produced to precise specifications in size, flex, and weight. Manufacturers devised special clubs for every conceivable eventuality, and some golfers carried as many as 20 or more clubs of various kinds. The USGA imposed a 14-club limit on January 1, 1938, and the Royal & Ancient followed suit the following year. The decision to limit the number was intended "to restore the making of individual shots, and increase the skill of the player."

Within this limit, however, there is scope to choose the club needed to deal with almost any circumstance. The driver and fairway woods are designed for striking the ball the farthest distances from tee or fairway. The iron clubs are divided into long, medium, and short, according to the distance they send the ball. Long irons send the ball farther than short ones, which are designed for accuracy or getting out of trouble. The putter is used almost

Whole in one (above)
An adjustable iron had all the range of a set by means of its variable loft.

Matched set
A classic set comprises a driver and two fairway woods; irons numbered from 2 to 9; a pitching wedge, sand iron and putter, making 14 clubs.

Driver

3-wood

5-wood

2-iron

3-iron

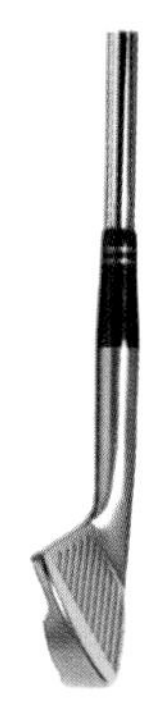

4-iron

5-iron

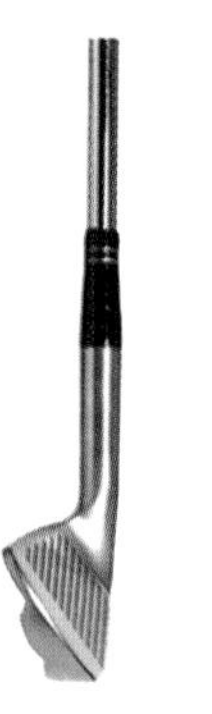

6-iron

7-iron

WOODEN CLUB CONSTRUCTION

Production of the traditional wooden head owes more to craftsmanship than to the pure engineering of stainless steel and graphite. There will always be a demand for the special skills of the experienced clubmaker. The construction of wooden-headed clubs has changed little over the decades. The shape of the head is marked out on a piece of close-grained wood, such as persimmon. The basic shape of the head is then cut out and worked to its final form, and a bore is drilled into the neck or hosel to receive the shaft.

Graphite clubs (right)
Despite retaining their traditional names, today woods and irons are often made from carbon fiber.

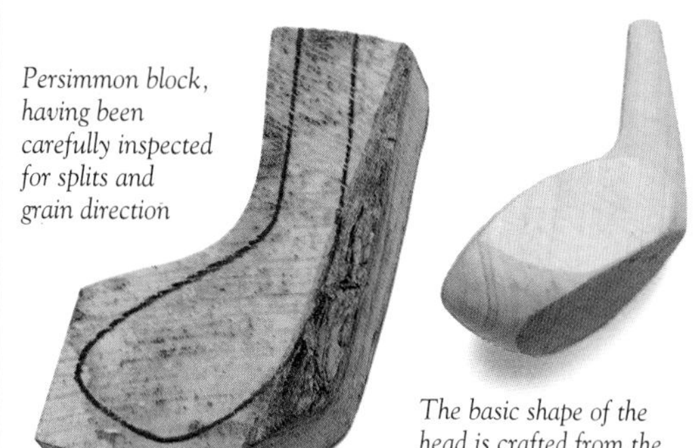

Persimmon block, having been carefully inspected for splits and grain direction

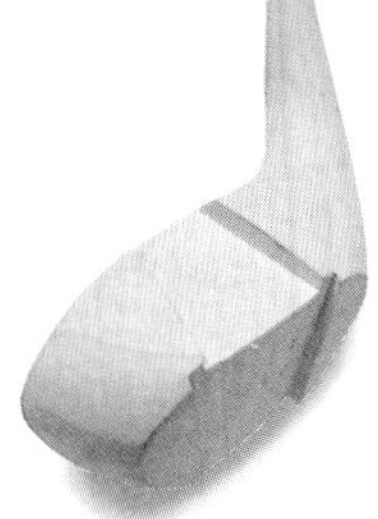

The basic shape of the head is crafted from the wooden block; the streamlined back of the head is all-important

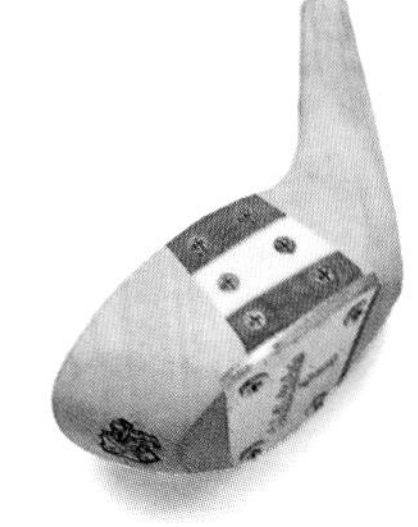

Slots are cut for a plastic insert in the face and for a metal plate on the bottom of the club to protect it from damage

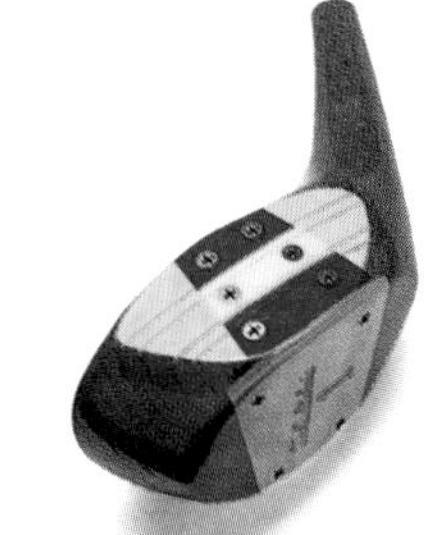

Weight can be added by pouring molten lead into a hole under the sole-plate, or by adding lead to the back of the head

After fine sanding, staining adds to the visual appeal, and varnishing seals the wood from the elements

Space-age profile
Carbon fibers bonded together in layers produce a strong, lightweight clubhead.

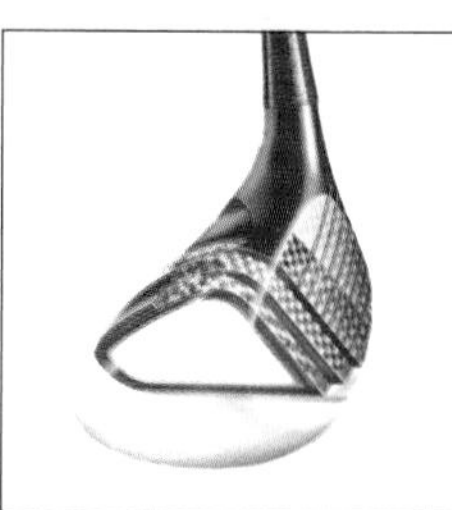

exclusively on the green or on its closely-cut fringes. Woods are usually numbered from 1 (the driver) to 5. A full set of irons normally ranges from 2 to 10. The loft on the face of the club (the angle that the clubface makes from the vertical), which heightens the trajectory of the ball, increases with the number, while the shaft length of the club decreases. Although 1-irons are also produced, these clubs are usually only available on special order from club manufacturers. This long iron is a specialist club for the better player and is not recommended for average golfers, who often find it easier to use a wood.

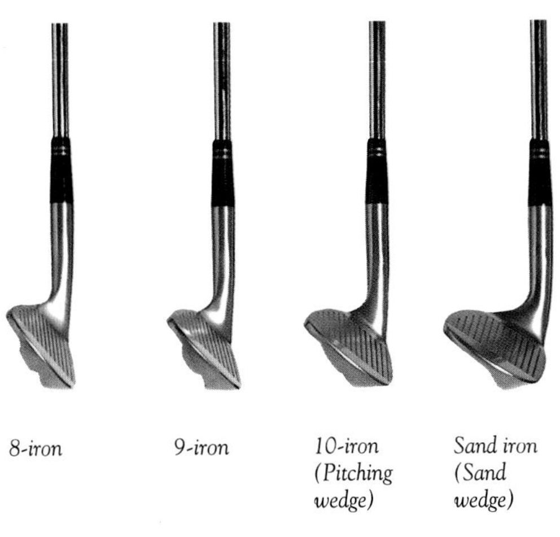

8-iron *9-iron* *10-iron (Pitching wedge)* *Sand iron (Sand wedge)*

Strong fiber (left) *Carbon fiber woven into a cloth strip and then coupled with bonding materials produces an incredibly strong material.*

Modern Materials

The most successful new material is carbon fiber or graphite, although other composite materials are gaining converts. The material is used for clubheads but is most commonly found in the production of a wide range of lightweight, variable-flex shafts. Early problems in poor resistance to twisting have now been overcome by improved production techniques and the addition of materials such as boron. The saving of weight in shafts allows the mass to be concentrated in the head, without increasing the overall weight.

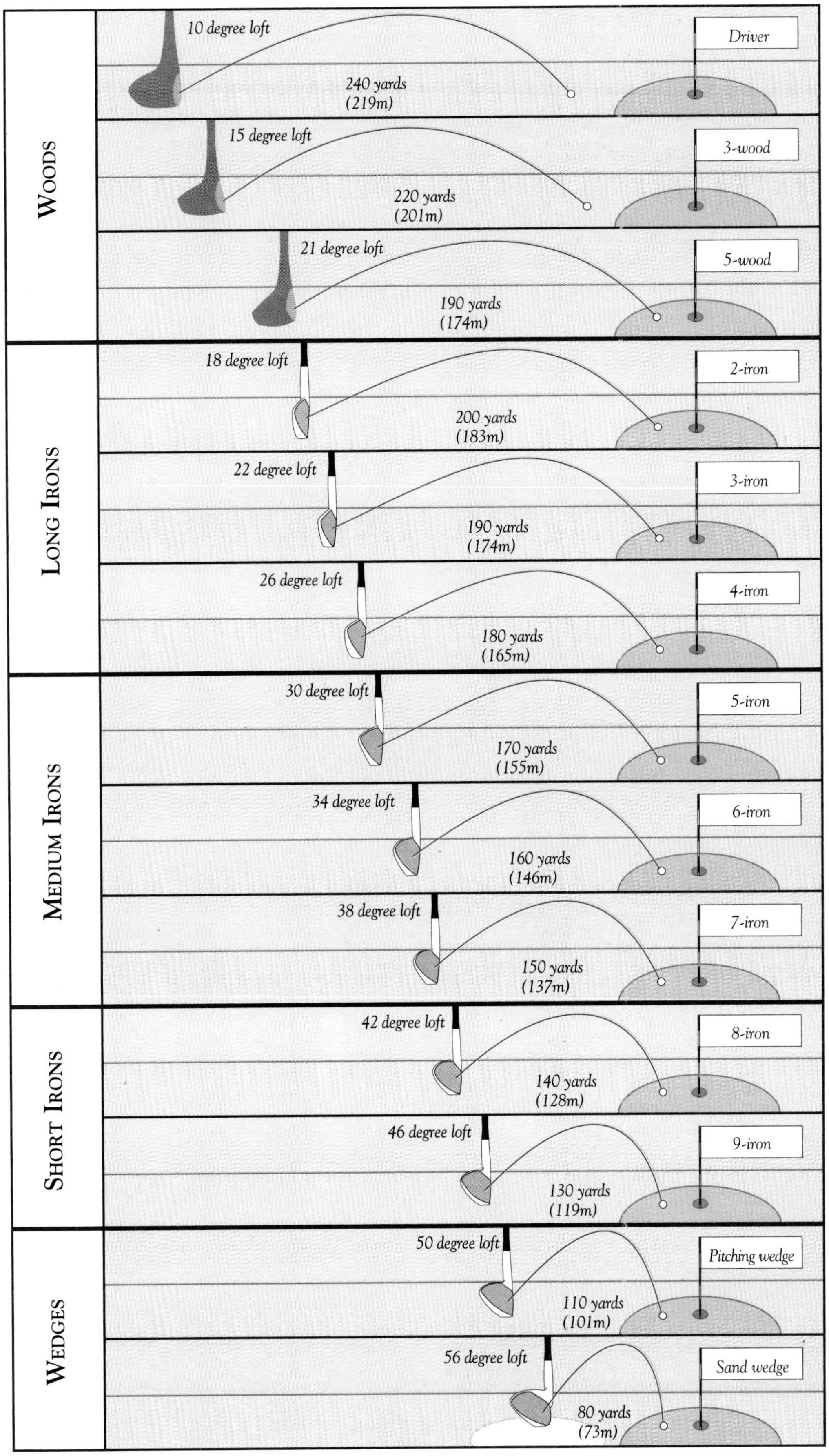

	Loft	Distance	Club
Woods	10 degree loft	240 yards (219m)	Driver
	15 degree loft	220 yards (201m)	3-wood
	21 degree loft	190 yards (174m)	5-wood
Long Irons	18 degree loft	200 yards (183m)	2-iron
	22 degree loft	190 yards (174m)	3-iron
	26 degree loft	180 yards (165m)	4-iron
Medium Irons	30 degree loft	170 yards (155m)	5-iron
	34 degree loft	160 yards (146m)	6-iron
	38 degree loft	150 yards (137m)	7-iron
Short Irons	42 degree loft	140 yards (128m)	8-iron
	46 degree loft	130 yards (119m)	9-iron
Wedges	50 degree loft	110 yards (101m)	Pitching wedge
	56 degree loft	80 yards (73m)	Sand wedge

Golf Accessories

IN THE EARLIEST days of golf, people went to the local links in their everyday clothes, casually carrying their clubs and unencumbered by bagfuls of ancillary equipment. But as interest in the game spread, special clothing and items designed to make life easier for the player began to appear.

The traditional red coats worn by the pioneers of the game, and retained today as ceremonial attire for the captains of several of the world's oldest clubs, were probably the first golfing fashion. They were worn for a practical reason: to warn fellow users of the commonly-held links-land who were not involved in the game that golfers were on the course. (It was a warning in many ways similar to the carrying of red flags in front of the first automobiles.) Through the twentieth century, golf has witnessed a remarkable revolution in fashion. The tweedy practicality of plus-fours and Norfolk jackets for men in the early part of the century has given way to the more comfortable clothing of the modern player. Women players have moved from crinolines to

Smart but casual
Pre–First World War golfers wore baggy plus-fours as standard dress. Woollen socks and sweaters have always been practical.

Golfing lady
This 1902 print shows how impractical women's fashions were at that time.

Clothing for the Course

Almost all clubs have rules governing what is permitted to be worn on the course. Denim is often barred, as are collarless shirts and untailored shorts. Fortunately there is a large range of fully acceptable practical clothing on the market from which to choose.

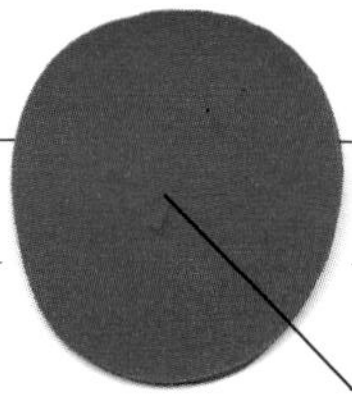

Men's sport shirt

Sun visor

Beret

Golf umbrella

Women's golf shirt

Rain suit

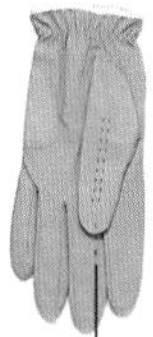

Leather left-hand glove (for right-handers)

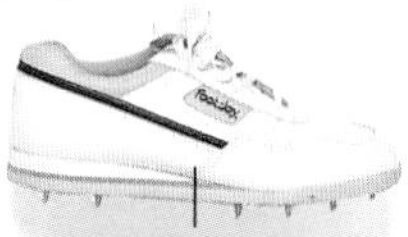

Men's pullover

Mid-length skirt

Lightweight shoe

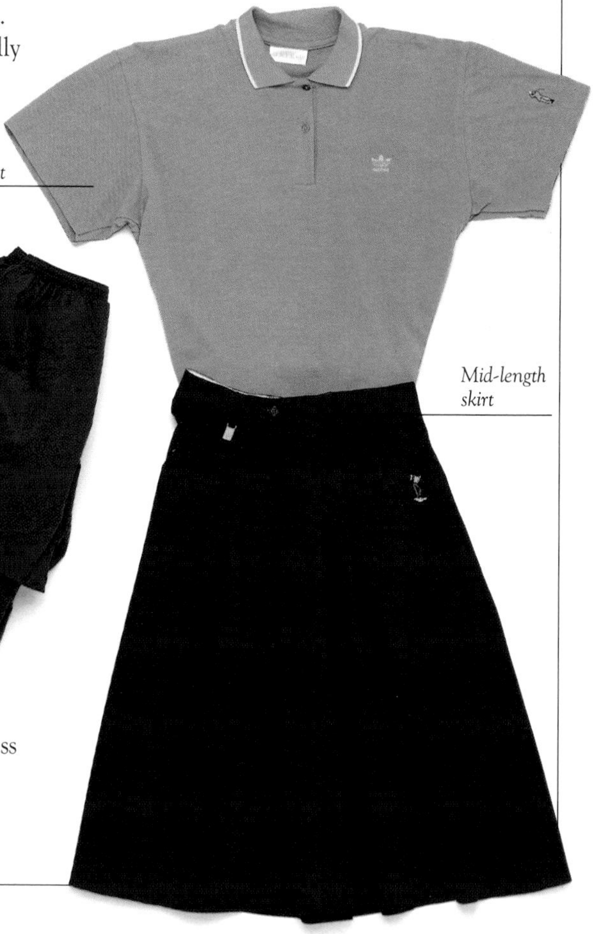

Men's trousers

Classic brogue shoe

Lightweight fabrics that repel water, while letting perspiration out, have made rain less of a problem. Spiked shoes give an improved grip, especially when the ground is wet underfoot.

The Golf Cart

The golf cart had its beginnings in the United States in the 1920s. Today the vehicle, otherwise known as a caddie cart, trolley, or trundler, has largely replaced the caddie. The cart, which is collapsible for compact storage, can take the strain out of carrying a full bag, which may weigh as much as 33 lb. (15kg), and is helpful to out-of-shape golfers.

the latest in designer labels. Golf clothing is now a multi-million-dollar industry, and many professionals accept large fees to endorse a particular line. Ancillary equipment has been added to the player's inventory, with everything from electric trolleys to solid-gold ballmarkers. Rain-wear for protection against the weather, and specialist footwear, are now carried or used by virtually all golfers.

The modern golf bag, often pulled on a trolley or carried on an electric cart, is a repository for all manner of equipment. Made from polyurethane, special lightweight bags can be transported on the shoulder, and while they lack the overall storage capacity and strength of the professional tour bag, they have room for clubs, balls, tees, shoes, additional clothing, and an umbrella.

Golf Bags

A carry bag (below left) is a lightweight bag slung over the shoulder by the golfer. It can hold a full set of clubs along with other equipment, such as clothing, balls, and tees, but it is smaller than the professional tour bag (below right). This contains everything the player might need, and has large pockets and a full hood to keep the clubs dry when it is raining.

Adjustable pull handle

Strong webbing straps

Clubhead cover

Lightweight tubular aluminum frame

Golf umbrella attached to golf bag

Towel for drying equipment

Small pocket for scorecard

Soft, wide wheels to prevent damage to the course

Ball pocket

Robust molded plastic base

Aboard the trolley
A trolley should be light yet strong, with large, wide wheels to cope with bumpy ground on the course. Many designs fold up to store in the trunk of a car.

The Bits in the Bag

Among items that golfers carry are tees, ballmarkers, a divot repairer, a scorecard and pencil, a ball cleaner, a towel, and a practice air ball. A towel is vital for drying grips and clubheads before making a stroke in the rain.

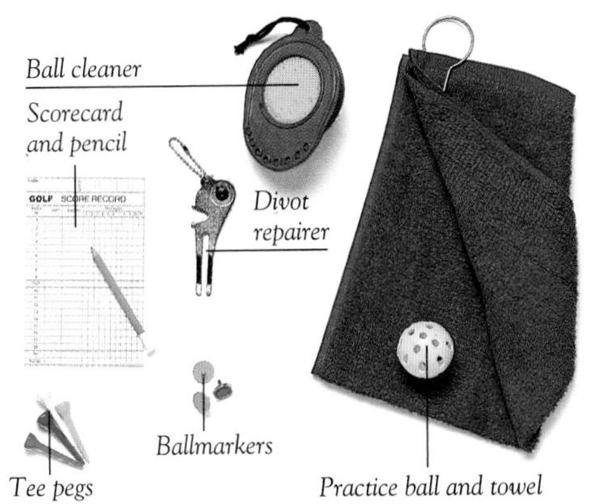

Course Architects

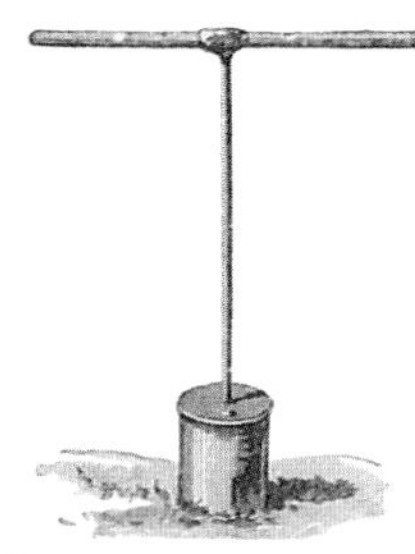

Neat cutter
One of the basic tools of the greenskeeper, and one of the first to be invented, was the hole cutter. It is used to remove a plug of turf and soil to create a neat hole of uniform size in the green.

NATURE WAS THE *first golf architect, shaping the links of eastern Scotland out of the undulating dunes along the shoreline. But as golf developed, leading professionals were called in to lay out courses, and the construction of tests for the player's skills became ever more elaborate.*

Initially the methods of the architects were simple in the extreme. They would pace the available ground, dotting the landscape with colored stakes to indicate tees and greens. The job would usually be completed in under a day, and when a mower had been run over the areas designated as greens, the course was deemed ready for play.

In 1894, Old Tom Morris, one of the leading course architects of his era, charged £1 per day, plus traveling expenses, to design a course. Ninety years later Jack Nicklaus could command $1million for the same task, but it would entail more than banging stakes into the ground.

Blasting out
Architects are not prepared to let a few tree roots stand in their way during the construction or improvement of a course. Explosives have long been used to clear the way, as at the St. George's Hill course in Surrey before the First World War.

Course architecture took a leap forward when the possibility of using inland sites was realized. The pioneer was Willie Park, Jr., who was largely responsible for moving golf away from its seaside origins. He discovered the potential of a sand-based heath to the west of London, where he laid out Sunningdale in the 1890s. Park was followed by five-times British Open champion James Braid, a prolific architect in the early years of the twentieth century, who designed the Gleneagles courses.

International Design

Sunningdale was later modified by its secretary, H. S. Colt, who then designed the more exposed New course at the club. He became one of Britain's finest designers in an era that produced courses such as Wentworth and The Berkshire, and talented architects like Tom Simpson, Charles Alison and Herbert Fowler, who also worked in the United States.

The Chicago golf-course architect Charles Blair Macdonald began researching British golf courses in 1902 to help create the first course of real quality in the United States, The National Golf Links. He also inspired George Crump, A. W. Tillinghast and Hugh Wilson to produce courses at Pine Valley, Baltusrol and Merion. Two Scots, Alister Mackenzie and Donald Ross, left a legacy of fine courses in the United States and around the world. Pinehurst Number 2 is the best of the Ross layouts, while Mackenzie partnered Bobby Jones in creating Augusta National. This creation, with its emphasis on strategic rather than penal design, revolutionized course design in the United States.

The renowned Robert Trent Jones first attracted attention and controversy when he adapted the Oakland Hills course in Birmingham, Michigan,

The Cutting Edge of Greenskeeping

Before grass-cutting machines, greenskeepers relied on hungry sheep and rabbits to graze on the fairways and keep them closely cropped. The mower's introduction meant that conditions for play improved dramatically, so that greenskeepers were not dependent on natural grass cutters.

Early model (above)
This motor mower, used on the Old course at St. Andrews in 1913, replaced the work done by sheep.

Latest design (left)
The triplex mower reduces the time spent cutting the green and leaves a perfect finish ready for play.

for the 1951 U.S. Open, with dramatic results (see page 114). He became by far the most prominent golf-course architect in the United States during the 1960s and 1970s, leaving his trademark of lakes and massive bunkers on an extraordinary number of courses across the breadth of the continent.

The Modern Layout

Course design has continued to evolve, and many would agree that it entered its modern phase in the late 1960s, when Pete Dye teamed up with Jack Nicklaus on the Harbour Town Golf Links in South Carolina. They combined different-textured grasses to demarcate areas of the course and used railroad-tie bulkheads as boundaries. Nicklaus and Dye went on to dominate the course-design business in the late 1970s and the 1980s.

Meanwhile, in Europe Dave Thomas and Peter Alliss came into golf-course architecture from the professional tour, joining men of vast experience such as C. K. Cotton, Charles Lawrie, Henry Cotton, Frank Pennink, John Harris, and Fred Hawtree.

By the 1980s, leading professionals had again begun to dominate the business, as they had almost a century earlier. Australian Peter Thomson, Arnold Palmer from the U.S., Seve Ballesteros from Spain, Bernhard Langer from Germany, Britain's Tony Jacklin, Neil Coles and Brian Huggett, and dozens more have all been involved in the worldwide demand for courses.

The power and scope of modern machinery and the development of irrigation techniques and new grass strains have produced some spectacular feats of course design and construction. For instance, in Florida, Georgia, and South Carolina, massive drainage and earth-filling operations have allowed courses to emerge out of swampland, leaving only an occasional alligator to remind golfers of what existed before. Also, such is the shortage of land in Japan that courses are constructed out of seemingly impossible hilly terrain. Some Japanese courses have installed escalators to transport golfers from one secluded valley hole up a steep incline to the next tee, ready to swoop down into an adjoining valley.

Where golfers in desert terrain were once content to play through scrubland to greens made from a stodgy mixture of sand and oil, at a golf course like Jack Nicklaus's Desert Highlands they now play on manicured grass fairways and perfect greens, kept alive by millions of gallons of water pumped out each night by computer-controlled irrigation systems.

But despite the technology that is now available to the course architect, the best courses are still those that fit easily and naturally into their surroundings. This is why the features of legendary links courses such as St. Andrews have so often been an inspiration to architects the world over.

Blueprint for success *The value of a layout depends on the course architect's ability to create challenges for players of every skill level, and to fit the holes into the existing landscape. Jack Nicklaus succeeded brilliantly at Desert Highlands in Arizona.*

Designer flair (left) *Gary Player teamed up with top course architect Pete Dye (right) at Sawgrass, Florida. The course displays a Dye trademark, an island green.*

Dual career (right) *Jack Nicklaus is also one of the most prolific golf-course designers. He created the popular Huis Ten Bosch course for Japanese clients in Nagasaki.*

CHAPTER 3

Championship Courses of the World

Any selection of 100 of the world's greatest championship courses has to be a subjective exercise. The choice that follows is not intended as a simple ranking of courses in terms of difficulty or quality. It is rather a worldwide voyage of discovery across a landscape of the game's outstanding venues. The courses featured include fabled old links of stunning beauty with wild, remote fairways, and cunningly crafted modern layouts created by the most influential of course architects, such as Robert Trent Jones, Pete Dye, and Jack Nicklaus. Along with world-famous championship venues, some lesser-known courses are profiled here, as well as many golf clubs that have a special story to relate. In addition, there are those courses built in the most unlikely and hostile of environments utilizing all the latest technology, fine examples of human ingenuity without which a comprehensive review of the world's golf courses would be sadly incomplete.

The centuries-old natural links of St. Andrews

An American silver brooch with a golf-course tableau, made in the early 1900s

Widening horizons (left)
An aerial view of Shinnecock Hills shows its splendid Long Island setting.

THE WORLD OF GOLF

SINCE THE NINETEENTH century, golf has spread from its traditional home on the east coast of Scotland to virtually every part of the planet, from New Zealand's South Island to the American northwest. Although the majority of the world's courses are located in either North America or the British Isles, the rest are scattered across the world. Indeed, such is the hold of golf on the sporting imagination that Antarctica is the only continent on which golf is not played. These maps show the locations of the 100 courses that are featured in this Championship Courses chapter.

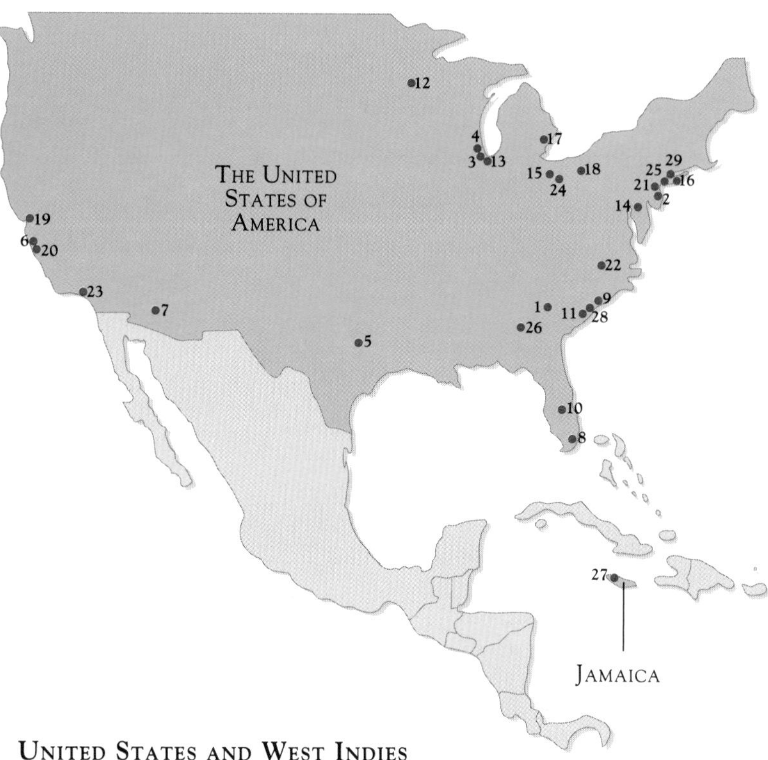

UNITED STATES AND WEST INDIES

1 AUGUSTA NATIONAL P.62
2 BALTUSROL P.68
3 BUTLER NATIONAL P.197
4 CHICAGO P.197
5 COLONIAL P.78
6 CYPRESS POINT P.80
7 DESERT HIGHLANDS P.82
8 DORAL P.199
9 THE DUNES P.199
10 GRAND CYPRESS P.201
11 HARBOUR TOWN P.90
12 HAZELTINE P.202
13 MEDINAH P.96
14 MERION P.98
15 MUIRFIELD VILLAGE P.106
16 NATIONAL GOLF LINKS OF AMERICA P.205
17 OAKLAND HILLS P.114
18 OAKMONT P.116
19 OLYMPIC P.207
20 PEBBLE BEACH P.118
21 PINE VALLEY P.122
22 PINEHURST P.124
23 RIVIERA P.132
24 SCIOTO P.211
25 SHINNECOCK HILLS P.176
26 SHOAL CREEK P.211
27 TRYALL P.184
28 WILD DUNES P.213
29 WINGED FOOT P.194

UNITED KINGDOM AND IRELAND

30 BALLYBUNION P.66
31 THE BELFRY P.196
32 CARNOUSTIE P.70
33 FORMBY P.200
34 GANTON P.86
35 GLENEAGLES P.200
36 GULLANE P.201
37 LINDRICK P.92
38 MUIRFIELD P.102
39 NAIRN P.205
40 PORTMARNOCK P.128
41 PRESTWICK P.208
42 ROYAL ABERDEEN P.209
43 ROYAL BIRKDALE P.134
44 ROYAL COUNTY DOWN P.138
45 ROYAL DORNOCH P.140
46 ROYAL LIVERPOOL P.144
47 ROYAL LYTHAM AND ST. ANNES P.148
48 ROYAL NORTH DEVON P.152
49 ROYAL PORTRUSH P.156
50 ROYAL ST. GEORGE'S P.158
51 ROYAL TROON P.162
52 RYE P.166
53 ST. ANDREWS P.168
54 SAUNTON P.210
55 SUNNINGDALE P.180
56 TURNBERRY P.186
57 WALTON HEATH P.212
58 WENTWORTH P.192
59 WOODHALL SPA P.213

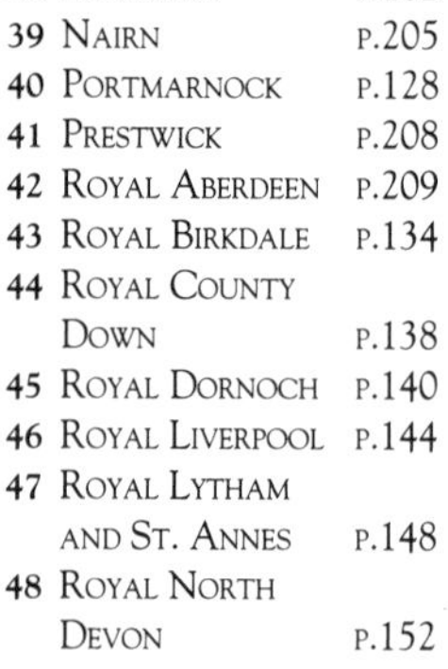

CANADA AND SOUTH AMERICA

60 BANFF P.196
61 GLEN ABBEY P.88
62 THE JOCKEY CLUB P.202
63 THE NATIONAL P.110

Europe

64 Las Brisas p.197
65 Chantilly p.74
66 Club zur Vahr p.76
67 Corfu p.198
68 Crans-sur-Sierre p.198
69 Estela p.200
70 Falsterbo p.84
71 Hamburg-Falkenstein p.201
72 Kennemer p.203
73 La Manga p.204
74 Olgiata p.206
75 Palmares p.207
76 Penina p.208
77 Pevero p.120
78 Rome p.208
79 Royal Belgique p.209
80 El Saler p.174
81 Seefeld-Wildmoos p.211
82 Valderrama p.190

The Netherlands
Belgium
Germany
Sweden
Switzerland
Austria
France
Italy
Portugal
Spain
Greece

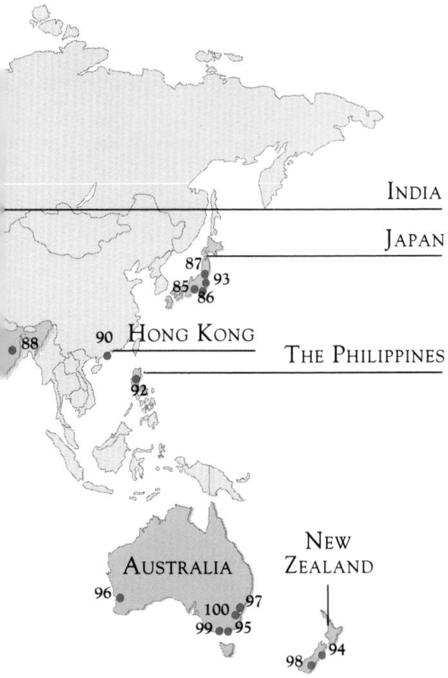

India
Japan
Hong Kong
The Philippines
Australia
New Zealand

Africa and Asia

83 Emirates p.199
84 Karen p.202
85 Kasugai p.203
86 Mariya p.94
87 New St. Andrews p.205
88 Royal Calcutta p.209
89 Royal Cape p.136
90 Royal Hong Kong p.210
91 Royal Johannesburg p.210
92 Wack Wack p.212
93 Yomiuri p.213

Australasia

94 Christchurch p.198
95 Kingston Heath p.203
96 Lake Karrinyup p.204
97 New South Wales p.206
98 Otago p.207
99 Royal Melbourne p.150
100 Royal Sydney p.160

Major Courses

Each of the 50 major courses covered in depth in the following pages is represented by a large-scale, computer-generated plan showing the layout of the holes in topographical detail. The plan indicates all the chief features of the course, including the clubhouse, trees, roads, bunkers, and water hazards. Each course entry also includes a panel showing the pars and lengths for the outbound and inbound nine holes of championship play, together with the course record for a competitive round. The pars and distances of individual holes from the championship tees are shown on the course plan. If the course has hosted any Major championships, the winners are listed (the † symbol indicates an amateur). Where the course has holes with famous names, these are detailed, along with a brief note on how such names were acquired.

Key to Course Plans

Ball trajectories

The red line shows the path and trajectory of the ball from tee to green. Once on the green, a player is expected to finish in two putts. Consequently on a par-5 hole, the map shows three fairway strokes to the green; on a par-4 hole two shots; on a par 3 one shot.

Scorecard data

Each hole has a flag giving its championship par and length. The length is generally in yards, although meters are used where the club itself employs a metric measurement. A 200-yard hole is about 185m and a 500-yard hole is approximately 460m.

A compass on each of the main maps is oriented to due north

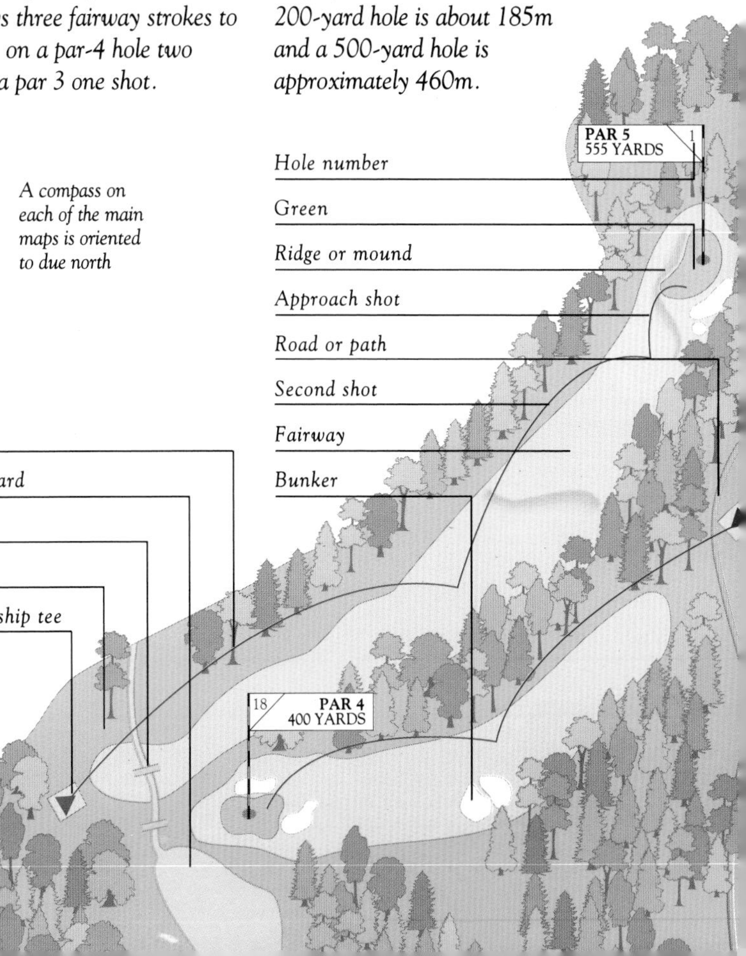

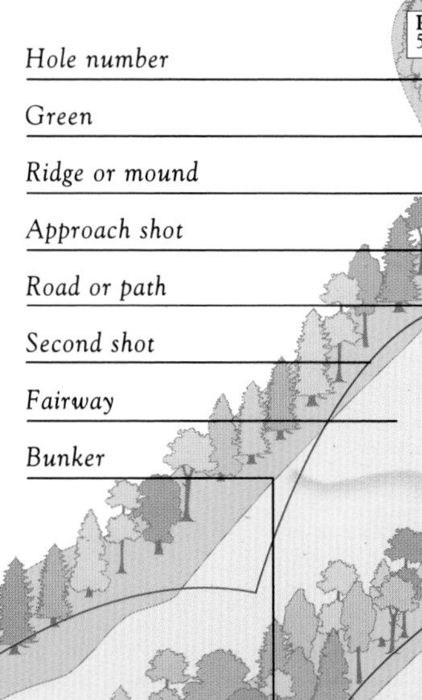

Augusta National

Augusta National Golf Club, Augusta, Georgia, U.S.A.

ONE OF THE few courses almost every golfer harbors dreams of playing is at Augusta National Golf Club, birthplace and home of the U.S. Masters tournament. The course's beauty and cunning design have played a great part in making the Masters – the first of the year's Majors – an attractive and testing event. But the course was originally made for one man's pleasure.

Course creator
Champion amateur Bobby Jones retired in 1930, aged just 28, with no worlds left to conquer.

Master guide (below)
Bobby Jones is the President in Perpetuity of Augusta National, and his spectators' guide is reproduced in the annual Masters program.

Soon after Bobby Jones's victories in the Open and Amateur Championships of Britain and the United States in the single triumphant year of 1930, he decided to retire and build a golf course of his own. It was to be a private place where he could play with friends, away from the attentions of the thousands of golf fans who followed him everywhere he went.

Jones set out to build his dream course in collaboration with a close friend, the wealthy New York financier Clifford Roberts. They chose Augusta because it was a favorite venue for Jones to play in the winter months. Lying in a valley near the South Carolina border, at its low point only 137 feet above sea level, it was much milder than his home town of Atlanta, which sits at an elevation of more than 1,000 feet. Roberts had also wintered there.

Ben Hogan Bridge
The span over Rae's Creek by the testing 12th commemorates the two-time Masters winner.

The site Jones and Roberts chose for the new course was a 365-acre property called Fruitlands Nursery, acquired on the recommendation of a mutual friend, Thomas Barrett, Jr. of Augusta. The land was already beautiful, as many trees and shrubs had been left behind after the nursery closed, including a splendid avenue of magnolia trees leading to the old colonial building that today forms the central part of the Augusta National clubhouse complex.

Winner's jacket
The presentation of the Green Jacket to the Masters champion by the previous year's winner is now the climax of the event. Here Sandy Lyle hands the jacket to Nick Faldo in 1989.

Partners in Design

To this magnificent setting Bobby Jones brought Dr. Alister Mackenzie, a Scotsman who had given up medicine and turned to the design of golf courses. Fruitlands Nursery provided Mackenzie with a piece of mildly rolling ground ideal for the style of course he had in mind – an inland version of his native Scottish links. Sadly, he died in 1934, just before the course opened for play, but with the knowledge that Augusta was his greatest creation. Almost as soon as the course was finished, Jones invited a band of amateur and professional players to a tournament, and the U.S. Masters was born. Today the course is still exclusive, as Jones had originally intended, being set aside for a select group of Augusta National members. It is shared, however, if only for a few days, by millions of viewers watching the Masters on television each April.

Masters trophy
The permanent trophy (above), *modeled on the colonial clubhouse* (right), *was introduced in 1961. A band of silver embraces the trophy and provides space to engrave the names of the winners and runners-up for a period of 54 years. The Masters winner is given a small replica.*

Augusta flag
The flag outside the clubhouse sports Augusta's distinctive map logo.

There have been many improvements to Augusta, but the layout has changed little in the last 60 years. The attractive flowering trees and shrubs and the carefully tended margins of the course are matched by the painstakingly manicured fairways and greens. Jones's basic idea was to create a course that made the most of the natural advantages of the site and that did not rely on man-made hazards or deep rough to make the test interesting. The fairways are inviting, the greens large and fast, and the bunkers sparingly distributed.

10 **On in two**
Before players hit the notorious Amen Corner they play the 10th, a deceptive 485 yard par 4. The 10th starts the second leg with a downhill drive from the tee near the clubhouse. There are few modern players who cannot reach the green in two.

Test of Strategy

The course is a prime example of strategic design, where the golfer is challenged to think each shot through carefully. There are several ways to play each hole, and players have to choose the route according to their ability. Strategic courses are constructed to lure golfers to get into trouble by attempting too much. They contrast to the penal design, where there are few options other than the correct line towards the green and mistakes are punished.

The Augusta National clubhouse stands at the top of the hill where Jones and Roberts first viewed the land that would become Jones's dream course. At the foot of the hill, through the pine trees in the bottom corner of the course, lurks a group of three holes, the 11th, 12th, and 13th, called Amen Corner. This is where the Masters has often been won and lost. At the 11th, a par 4 of 455 yards with a pond to the front and left of the green, Nick Faldo won play-offs for the Masters in consecutive years, 1989 and 1990.

There are some players, the great Jack Nicklaus among them, who believe that the 12th, a par 3 of 155 yards, is the most demanding of the holes, needing extreme care from the tee to avoid running into trouble. The dogleg 13th, which is a par 5 of 465 yards, is almost equally challenging. Many a player has been tempted to go for the green from too far out, only to land in the stream that crosses in front of the hole.

There is a similar problem at the par-5 15th. A player has to decide whether to try for the green and risk dropping short into the water. It was here that Gene Sarazen played one of the most famous shots in Masters history for a double eagle in 1935 (see page 293). The 18th hole ends the course in classic style – although it was originally the 9th, until Jones reversed the front and back nines in 1935.

Bobby Jones said of Augusta, "There isn't a single hole out there that can't be birdied if you just think. But there isn't one that can't be double-bogeyed if you ever stop thinking."

The Names of Augusta

1st Tea Olive	10th Camellia
2nd Pink Dogwood	11th White Dogwood
3rd Flowering Peach	12th Golden Bell
4th Flowering Crab Apple	13th Azalea
5th Magnolia	14th Chinese Fir
6th Juniper	15th Firethorn
7th Pampas	16th Redbud
8th Yellow Jasmine	17th Nandina
9th Carolina Cherry	18th Holly

Each hole is named after one of the many shrubs, trees, or flowers on the course. The 5th is named after the 21 magnolia trees that bloom in May alongside its fairway and green.

Augusta National championship course

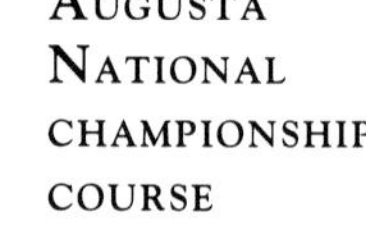

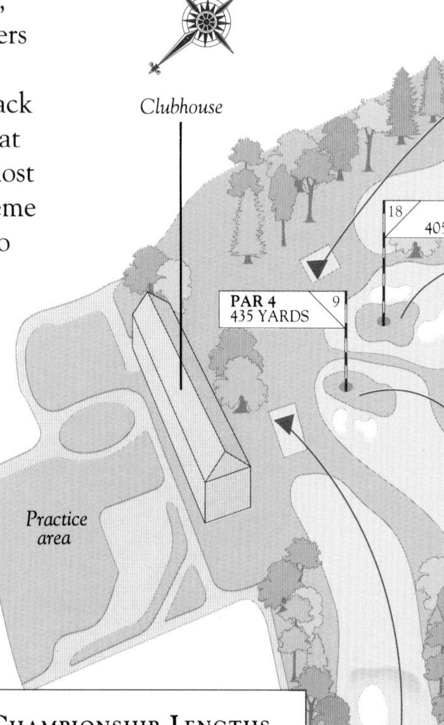

Championship Lengths

Out	3,465 Yards	Par 36
In	3,440 Yards	Par 36
Total	6,905 Yards	Par 72

Course Record

63 Nick Price, U.S. Masters 1986

U.S. Masters Champions at Augusta

See Page 321

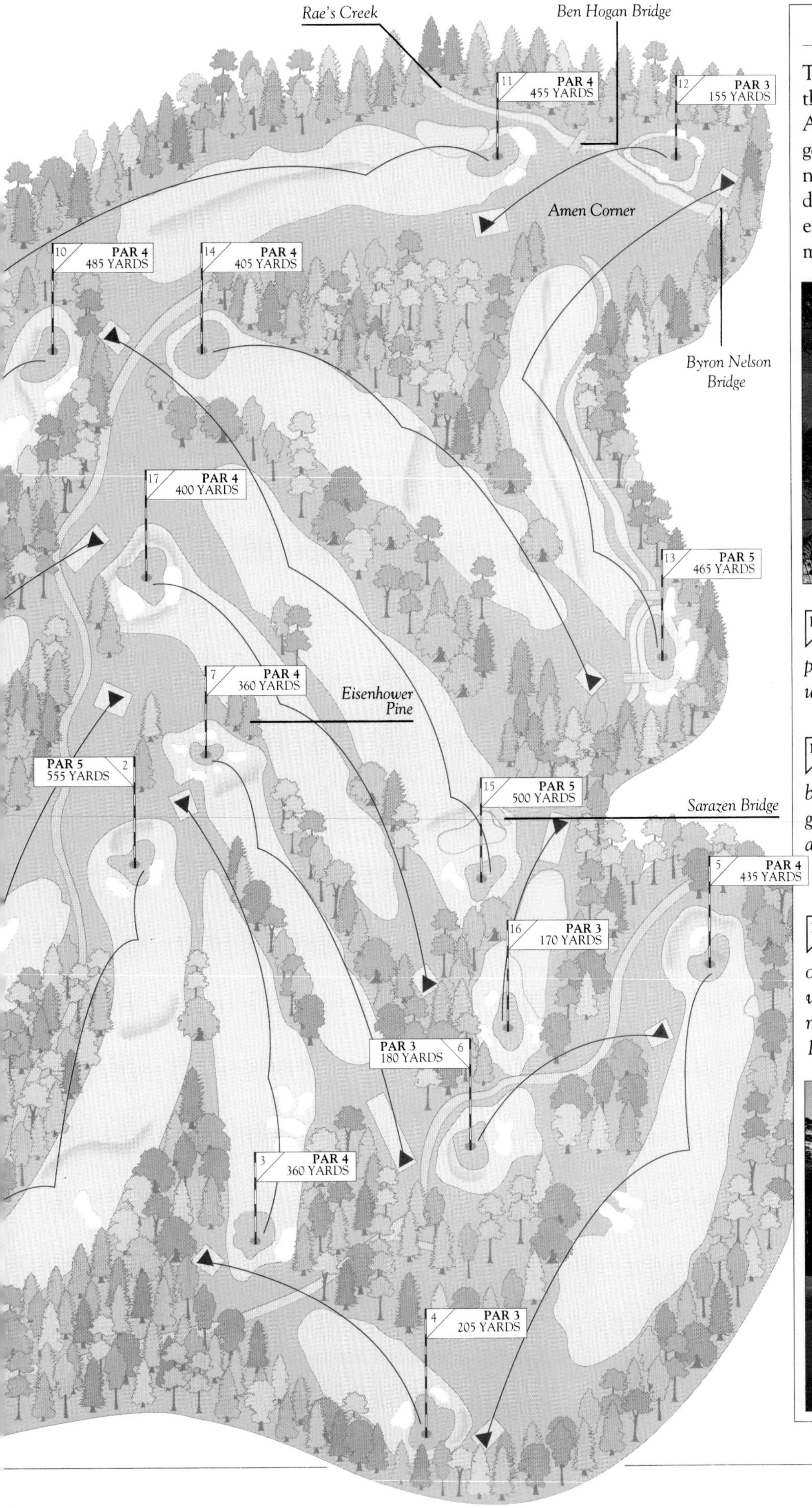

Rae's Creek
Ben Hogan Bridge
11 PAR 4 455 YARDS
12 PAR 3 155 YARDS
Amen Corner
10 PAR 4 485 YARDS
14 PAR 4 405 YARDS
Byron Nelson Bridge
17 PAR 4 400 YARDS
13 PAR 5 465 YARDS
7 PAR 4 360 YARDS
Eisenhower Pine
PAR 5 555 YARDS 2
15 PAR 5 500 YARDS
Sarazen Bridge
5 PAR 4 435 YARDS
16 PAR 3 170 YARDS
PAR 3 180 YARDS 6
3 PAR 4 360 YARDS
4 PAR 3 205 YARDS

AMEN CORNER

The 11th, 12th, and 13th holes are the vital key to playing the back nine at Augusta. They have become known as Amen Corner, first christened such by the great American golf writer, Herb Warren Wind, who thought prayers were needed to help get through them without disaster. The difficulty of the approach shots, combined with the extreme speed of the greens, which is typical of Augusta, make them a formidable test of golfing skills.

11 **Sand trap** *Bunkers and a pond ensnare the unwary at the 11th.*

12 **Tee shot** *Rae's Creek before the 12th green, bunkered front and back, demands a perfect tee shot.*

13 **Hit long** *Long hitters, or those who gamble with the stream, might get on the 13th green in two.*

BALLYBUNION

BALLYBUNION GOLF CLUB, BALLYBUNION, COUNTY KERRY, REPUBLIC OF IRELAND

TUCKED AWAY DEEP in the southwest of Ireland, in the county of Kerry, lies one of the truly great links golf courses of the world. It takes a little effort and determination to reach Ballybunion, but the rewards for persistence are great indeed. The course threads its way among huge dunes of sand, scattered at random along a shoreline of outstanding beauty and splendor. The natural features of the links have been exploited so effectively in the creation of the course that some respected critics have dubbed Ballybunion "the best golf course in the world."

The club had a checkered early history. It was originally founded in March, 1893 but five years later suffered a severe financial crisis. The first book of minutes has its final entry in August, 1898. It was only the fortuitous appearance of a retired Indian Army officer, Colonel Bartholomew, that led to a revival of Ballybunion's fortunes.

Together with a small group of his associates, the Colonel formed the club as it exists today in 1906. He brought in Lionel Hewson, the former editor of *Irish Golf*, to lay out nine holes. It was another 21 years before the course was extended to 18, but by 1937 Ballybunion had gained

15 **Testing target** (above)
The 15th is the toughest of the course's par 3s, particularly when the wind blows off the Atlantic. The green presents a tiny target below the tee with a huge sandhill on the left and punitive bunkering on the right.

18 **Emerald Isle desert** (left)
A wasteland of rough sand, known as the Sahara, has to be crossed at the 18th. The second shot is blind to the green, adding to the challenge of a fine finishing hole.

16 **In from the sea**
The drive must hit the fairway which slopes up from the ocean. The second shot is threatened by a bunker on the left and the green is guarded by two bunkers on the right.

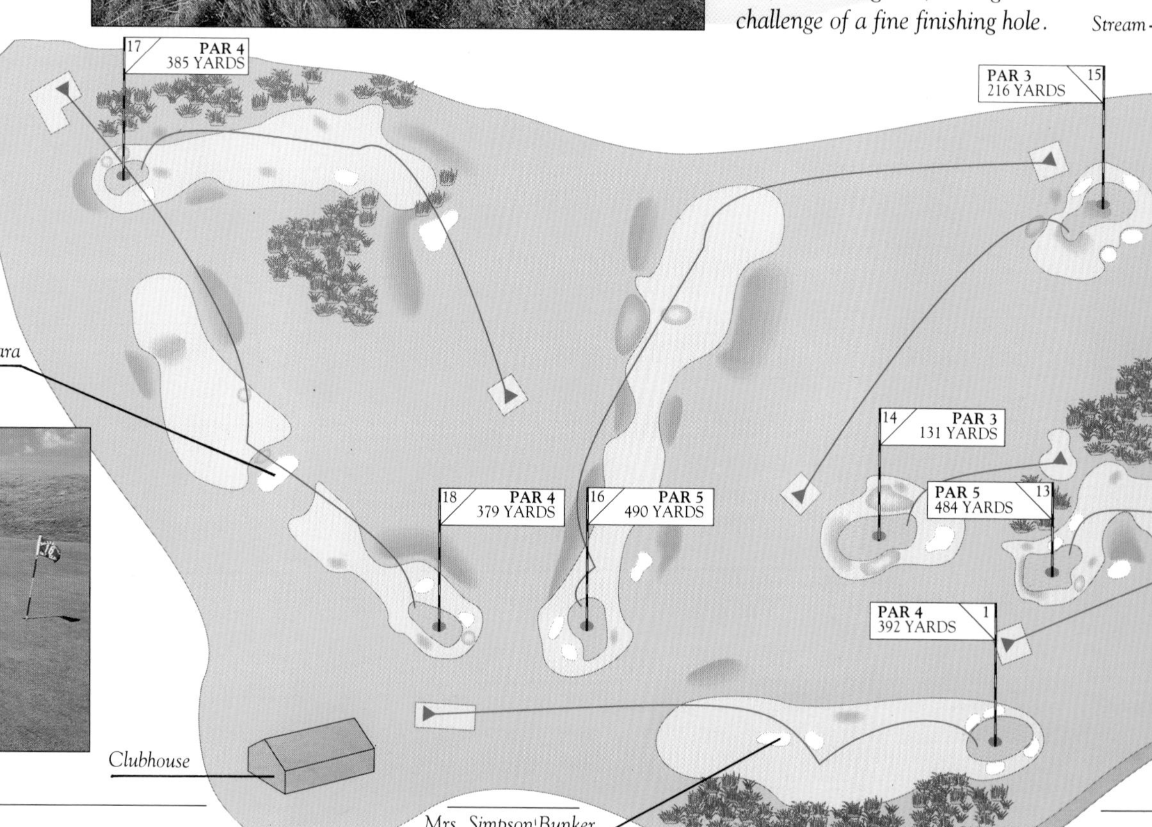

sufficient reputation to be chosen to host the Irish Men's Close Championship. English golf-course architect Tom Simpson was brought in before the 1937 Championship to suggest alterations to the course, but he found little that needed attention. He confined his labors to the re-siting of three greens and the addition of a controversial fairway bunker at the 14th hole. The order of the holes changed in 1971, when a new clubhouse was built, and the course now begins at the original 14th. But the bunker is still known as Mrs. Simpson – after the architect's wife, but appropriate for a feature that caused as much argument as the American who led Edward VIII to abdicate in 1936.

Saving Ballybunion

In the late 1970s a campaign had to be launched to save the course from erosion on the cliff face. "Friends of Ballybunion" raised more than £100,000 under the leadership of Jackie Hourigan, and the erosion was stopped. But the sea also gives the course its character; the links is virtually treeless and there are many sharp contours to the land. Despite the long grass that covers the rolling sandhills, the course is not unfair. Even on the blind shots there is usually at least some indication of the line of play.

But it is the contours that really create the challenge. The course is crammed with uphill, downhill, and sidehill lies. The greens, too, are heavily contoured. As a whole, the course is demanding enough to provide a serious test of the skill and patience of any golfer.

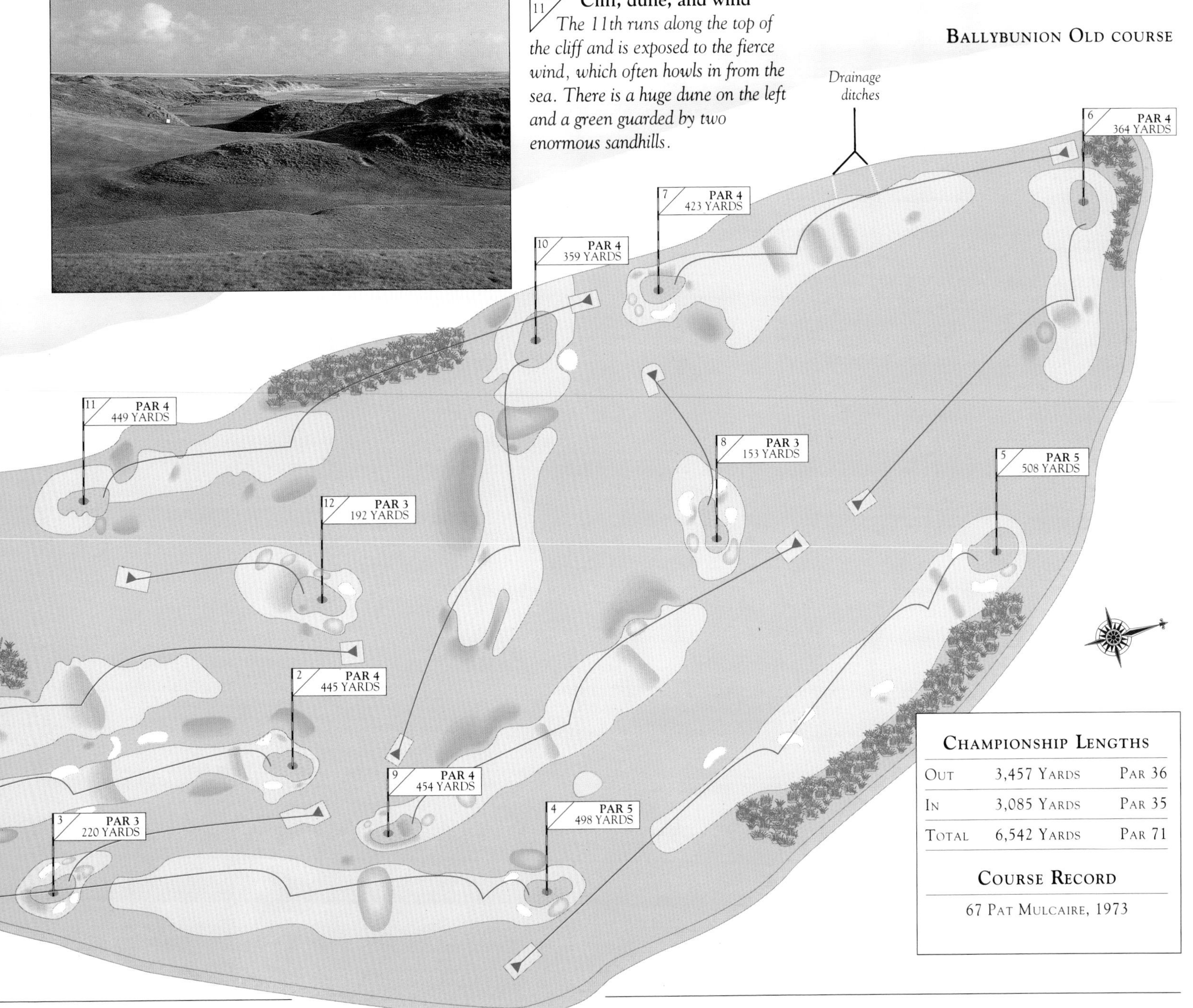

11 Cliff, dune, and wind
The 11th runs along the top of the cliff and is exposed to the fierce wind, which often howls in from the sea. There is a huge dune on the left and a green guarded by two enormous sandhills.

Championship Lengths

Out	3,457 Yards	Par 36
In	3,085 Yards	Par 35
Total	6,542 Yards	Par 71

Course Record

67 Pat Mulcaire, 1973

BALTUSROL

BALTUSROL GOLF CLUB, SPRINGFIELD, NEW JERSEY, U.S.A.

BALTUSROL GOLF CLUB has a special place in American golf history. Not only has it hosted a record six U.S. Opens, but it is one of the oldest clubs in the country: golf was first played there in 1895. Unlike most country clubs, Baltusrol remains dedicated to golf alone and does not have the usual fringe activities. In fact, the original constitution of the club states: "The object of this Club shall be the playing, cultivation, and advancement of the royal and ancient game of golf."

The course was laid out by Louis Keller, owner and publisher of the *New York Social Register*, on land he owned at the foot of Baltusrol Mountain, about 17 miles (27km) from the New York state line. He wrote inviting some of his friends to join, explaining that nine holes had been laid out "upon sandy hills, naturally adapted for the purpose, and now ready for use."

OPEN WINNER

In 1903 the USGA took the U.S. Open to Baltusrol for the first time, where it was won, appropriately, by Willie Anderson, whom Keller had appointed as the club's first professional. Little is known about Anderson, a shy and retiring man originally from North Berwick, Scotland. However, during his brief life – he died in his early thirties in 1910 – he won no fewer than four U.S. Opens, a record since matched only by Bobby Jones, Ben Hogan, and Jack Nicklaus. Anderson won his four titles within a space of five years, and he remains the only player in the history of the U.S. Open to win three in a row.

Baltusrol hosted its second U.S. Open in 1915, when the amateur Jerome Travers won with a score of 297. Shortly afterwards the members decided that a tougher Baltusrol was needed and they brought in A.W. Tillinghast to supervise the construction of two completely new 18-hole layouts. Additional land was acquired for the purpose, and work began

17 **High green**
This is the longest hole on any U.S. Open course. If the second shot avoids the "Sahara Desert," the hole needs a long third to the elevated green.

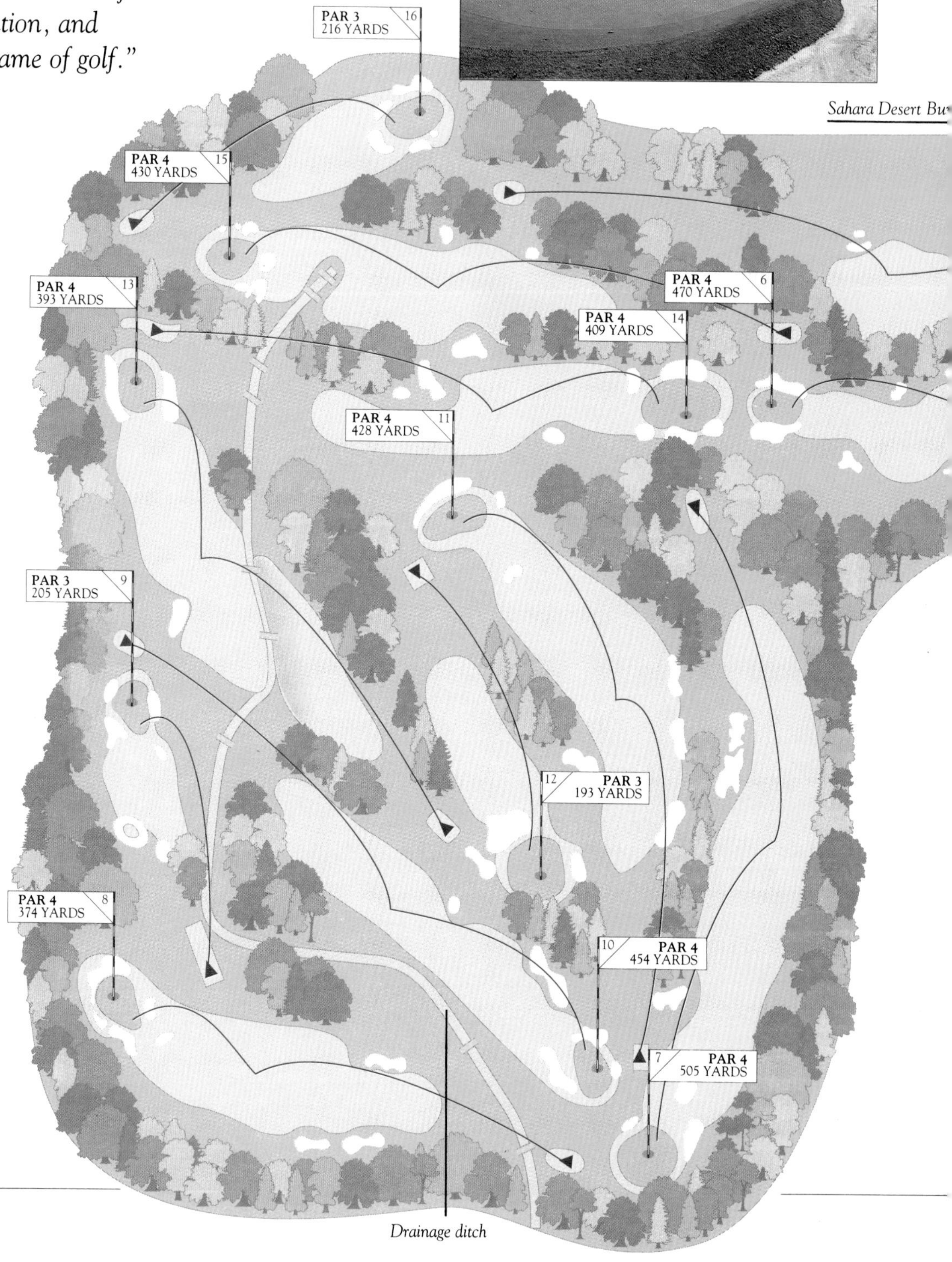

PAR 3 216 YARDS 16
Sahara Desert Bu
PAR 4 430 YARDS 15
PAR 4 393 YARDS 13
PAR 4 470 YARDS 6
PAR 4 409 YARDS 14
PAR 4 428 YARDS 11
PAR 3 205 YARDS 9
12 PAR 3 193 YARDS
PAR 4 374 YARDS 8
10 PAR 4 454 YARDS
7 PAR 4 505 YARDS
Drainage ditch

in 1920. The following year the Upper and Lower courses were opened for play. Although changes have been made to both courses over the years, notably by Robert Trent Jones on the Lower course before the 1954 U.S. Open, the layouts are essentially as Tillinghast created them.

The Lower course has been the scene of three U.S. Opens – in 1954, 1967, and 1980 – while the Upper course was used for the 1936 Championship. Baltusrol therefore has the unique distinction in the history of the U.S. Open of having hosted six of the championships on three different courses at the same club.

18 Tricky second shot
Although it is more than 540 yards long, the finishing par 5 plays shorter, because the tee shot is sharply downhill. This puts the green within reach of most professionals in two, but the second shot is extremely demanding. The hole doglegs left, with water crossing the fairway. A gaggle of bunkers protects the green; a long carry is needed to clear them and reach the green in two.

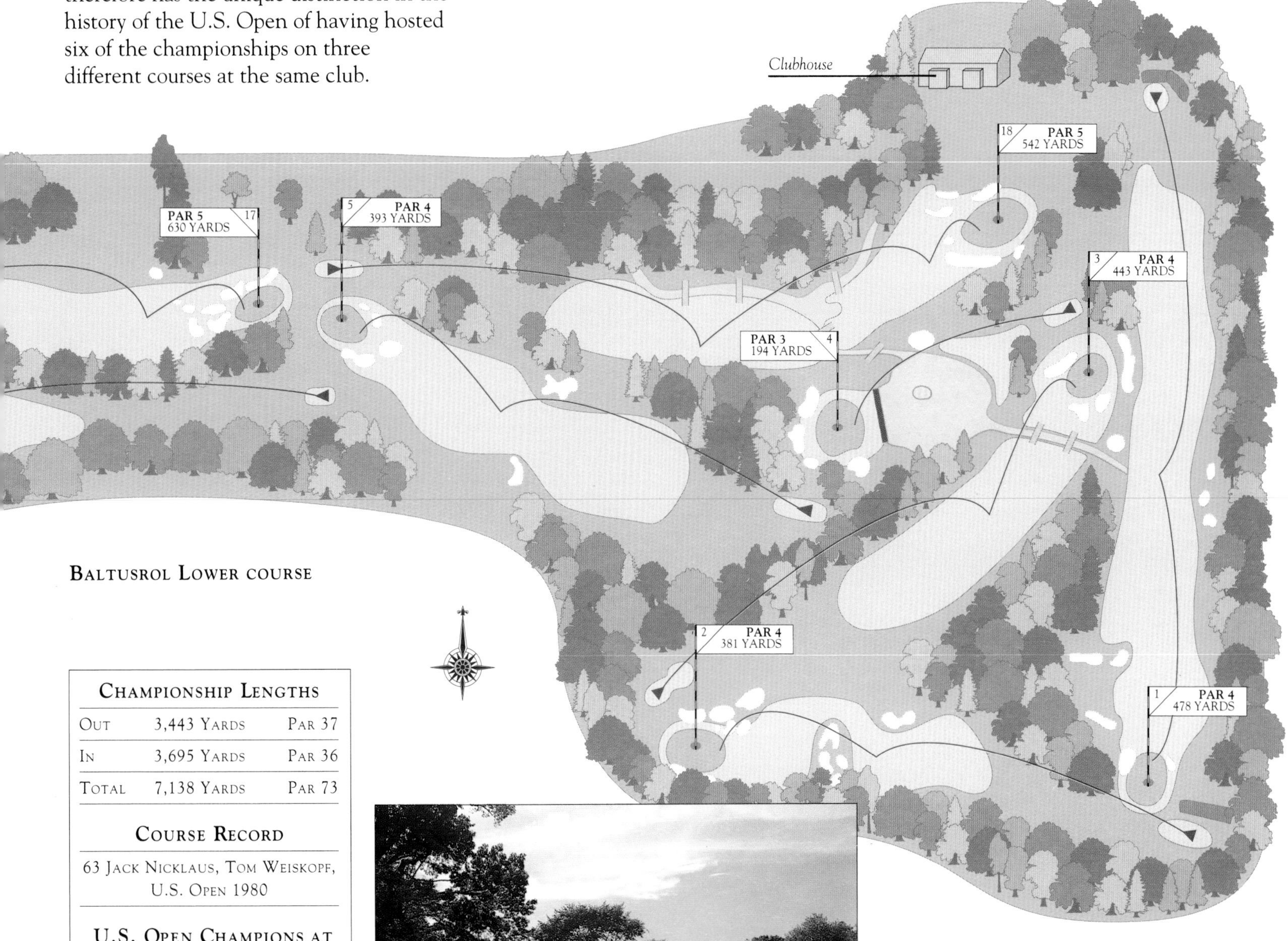

Clubhouse

PAR 5 630 YARDS 17

5 PAR 4 393 YARDS

18 PAR 5 542 YARDS

3 PAR 4 443 YARDS

PAR 3 194 YARDS 4

2 PAR 4 381 YARDS

1 PAR 4 478 YARDS

BALTUSROL LOWER COURSE

CHAMPIONSHIP LENGTHS		
OUT	3,443 YARDS	PAR 37
IN	3,695 YARDS	PAR 36
TOTAL	7,138 YARDS	PAR 73

COURSE RECORD

63 JACK NICKLAUS, TOM WEISKOPF, U.S. OPEN 1980

U.S. OPEN CHAMPIONS AT BALTUSROL

1903 WILLIE ANDERSON; 1915 JEROME TRAVERS †; 1936 TONY MANERO; 1954 ED FURGOL; 1967, 1980 JACK NICKLAUS

5 Tight drive
At the relatively short par-4 5th, the drive is the key to success. It must be threaded carefully between bunkers on both sides of the fairway, and the approach has to carry a group of dangerous bunkers just in front of the green.

CARNOUSTIE

CARNOUSTIE GOLF LINKS, CARNOUSTIE, ANGUS, TAYSIDE, SCOTLAND

THE CARNOUSTIE CHAMPIONSHIP course lies like a discarded string of pearls on links retreating from the ravages of the Tay estuary on the east coast of Scotland. Its 18 holes present one of the greatest challenges for any player at the top level of the game. In a world where the word "championship" has been devalued, Carnoustie remains a true test for those who would be real champions.

Birdie route (above)
The 6th is where Ben Hogan birdied twice on the last day of the 1953 Open. The route he took is now known as Hogan's Alley.

Crow crest
This region was once plagued with crows, and was thus named Craw's Nestie, later changed to Carnoustie.

Carnoustie players
Carnoustie has given many great players to the game, and none better than the three Smith brothers, Alex, Willie, and Macdonald. Alex Smith twice won the U.S. Open.

Carnoustie has been host to the British Open on five occasions since 1931, and the roll call of the winners there makes impressive reading: Tommy Armour, Henry Cotton, Ben Hogan, Gary Player, and Tom Watson. Between them, these five players have recorded championship-winning scores that average close to the nominal par of the course. At Carnoustie this is a standard that only the great players have any hope of matching over four hard rounds of tournament play.

WIND POWER

As with all the highest quality British links courses, part of the challenge of Carnoustie lies in the whim of the weather. The battle is always with the elements as much as with the course itself. It is the wind that really makes the difference; when it blows at Carnoustie, the course is not only unrelenting and unforgiving, but can even be virtually unplayable. The course is laid out in such a way that there are never more than two consecutive holes played in the same direction, and so it presents a constantly changing challenge to the players, who have to cope with the wind from all quarters.

There is no such thing as a simple hole at Carnoustie, and the difficult ones are among the fiercest to be found anywhere. The course has no chinks in its armor and it is no place for the faint of heart or for players with anything but the tightest control of their game. Fast-running streams are a notable hazard. Jockie's Burn comes into play on four of the first six holes, and the infamous Barry Burn, where so many players have come to grief in Carnoustie history – either playing into it or trying and failing to jump over it – gives this majestic course its famous finish.

East coast championship
The 1968 Open was the fourth hosted by Carnoustie.

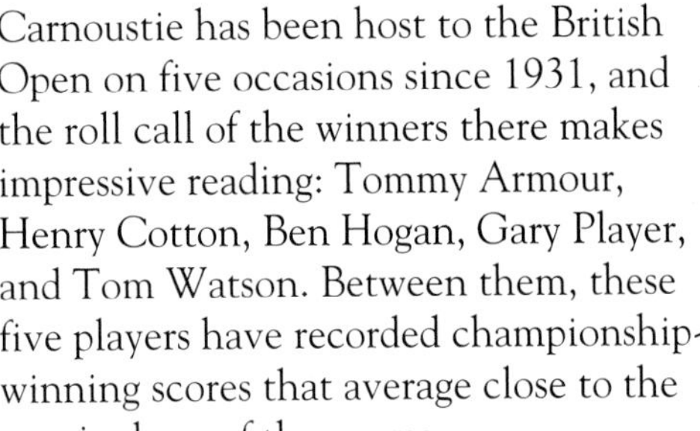

As with most of the courses that developed on the east coast of Scotland, Carnoustie has little recorded history relating to its origins. It is known that golf was played on the Barry links next to Carnoustie as early as the sixteenth century. Sir Robert Maule, whom history records as being one of the first players, is known to have enjoyed the "gouff" on the Barry links, and parish records confirm the existence of the game there in 1560.

Allan Robertson, the first of the great early professionals, laid out ten holes at Carnoustie around the time of the formation of the Carnoustie Club, which

Hogan hero (above)
Ben Hogan's victory in the 1953 British Open was a masterful display; he finished four shots ahead of his rivals.

The links (right)
Carnoustie is typical of the links on the east coast of Scotland in being shaped by wind and weather. Artificial additions to the natural hazards include this bunker at the 16th.

10 Avoid the Burn

A short distance before the green at the par-4 10th, the Barry Burn offers a watery threat, while farther down by the green and to the left, a pair of bunkers waits for shots played too short. To the right of the green lurks another bunker, not far from the site of the new 11th tee. The 10th is 452 yards long and the drive requires a solid hit. The shot is threatened by a number of bunkers both to the right and left sides of the fairway.

The Names of Carnoustie

1st Cup	10th South America
2nd Gulley	11th Dyke
3rd Jockie's Burn	12th Southward Ho!
4th Hillocks	13th Whins
5th Brae	14th Spectacles
6th Long	15th Luckyslap
7th Plantation	16th Barry Burn
8th Short	17th Island
9th Railway	18th Home

The name of the 10th recalls the story of a young caddie, the worse for drink, who set off to seek his fortune in South America one night, only to wake up the next morning by the 10th hole.

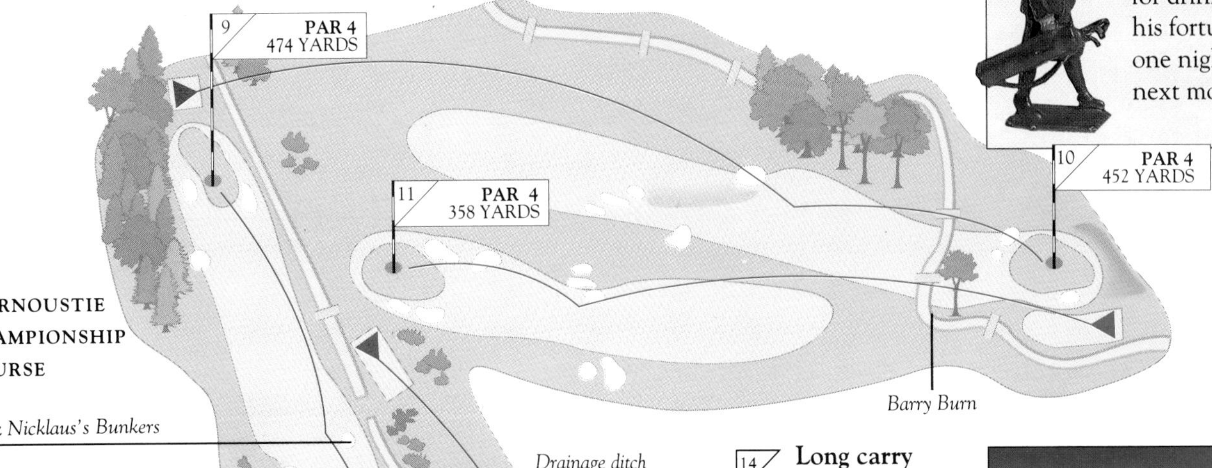

14 Long carry

The par-5 14th is a classic links hole and very tough for its length. The second shot must carry the famous Spectacles, a pair of bunkers cut out of a slope about 75 yards from the center of the double green, which is shared with the 4th.

is accepted as occurring between 1839 and 1842. The course was extended to 18 holes by Old Tom Morris in 1857, and he had the satisfaction of seeing his son, "Young Tom," win a tournament there the same year, when the lad was only 16.

James Braid was brought in to revamp the course in 1926, and five years later Tommy Armour, a Scot from Edinburgh who had emigrated to America, won the first British Open played at Carnoustie.

In 1937 Henry Cotton took on a field which included the entire United States Ryder Cup team and beat them all, ending with a round of 71 in appalling weather. But the most memorable Open victory at Carnoustie was unquestionably Ben Hogan's matchless triumph in 1953.

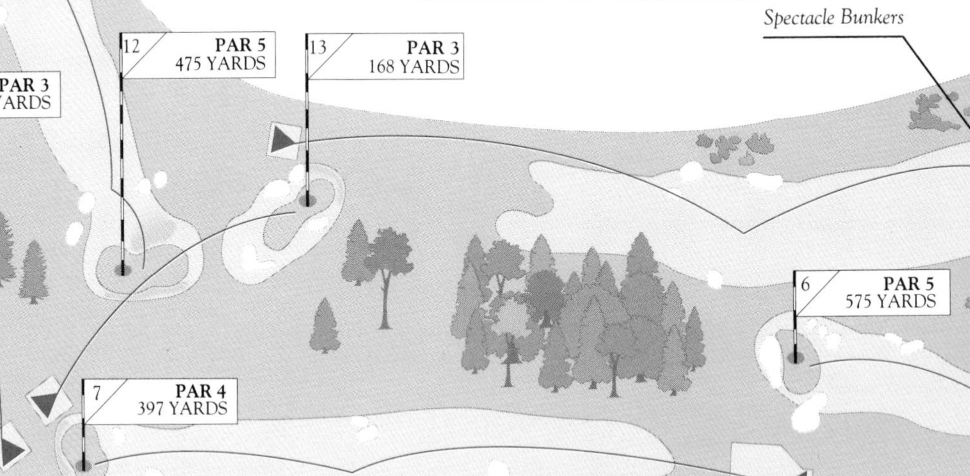

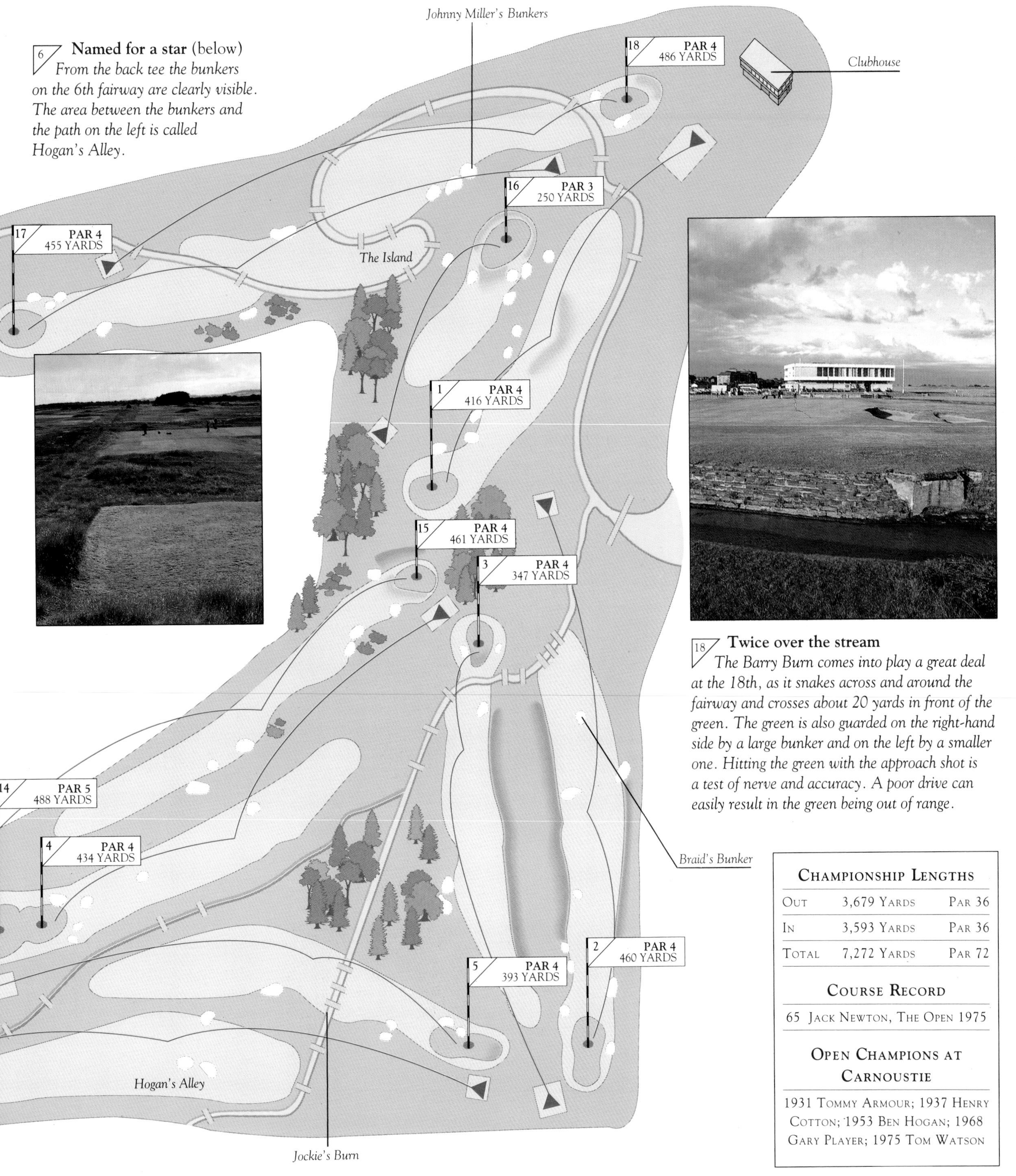

6 **Named for a star** (below)
From the back tee the bunkers on the 6th fairway are clearly visible. The area between the bunkers and the path on the left is called Hogan's Alley.

18 **Twice over the stream**
The Barry Burn comes into play a great deal at the 18th, as it snakes across and around the fairway and crosses about 20 yards in front of the green. The green is also guarded on the right-hand side by a large bunker and on the left by a smaller one. Hitting the green with the approach shot is a test of nerve and accuracy. A poor drive can easily result in the green being out of range.

Championship Lengths		
Out	3,679 Yards	Par 36
In	3,593 Yards	Par 36
Total	7,272 Yards	Par 72

Course Record

65 Jack Newton, The Open 1975

Open Champions at Carnoustie

1931 Tommy Armour; 1937 Henry Cotton; 1953 Ben Hogan; 1968 Gary Player; 1975 Tom Watson

CHANTILLY

GOLF DE CHANTILLY, VINEUIL-SAINT-FIRMIN, CHANTILLY, FRANCE

CHANTILLY IS WIDELY regarded as the finest course in France and is one of the oldest in the country. It dates back to 1908 and has hosted the French Open Championship many times. There are hints of some of the great heathland courses, such as Sunningdale and The Berkshire, in this beautiful setting only 25 miles north of Paris. Much of the course is relatively open, despite the surrounding woodland, and Chantilly's 6,597 meters are among the most testing in Europe.

13 **Hollow shot**
The 13th is one of the toughest of the course's long par 4s. A good drive is needed to open up the green on this sharp dogleg left, leaving a demanding second shot over a deep grassy hollow to a green surrounded by trees.

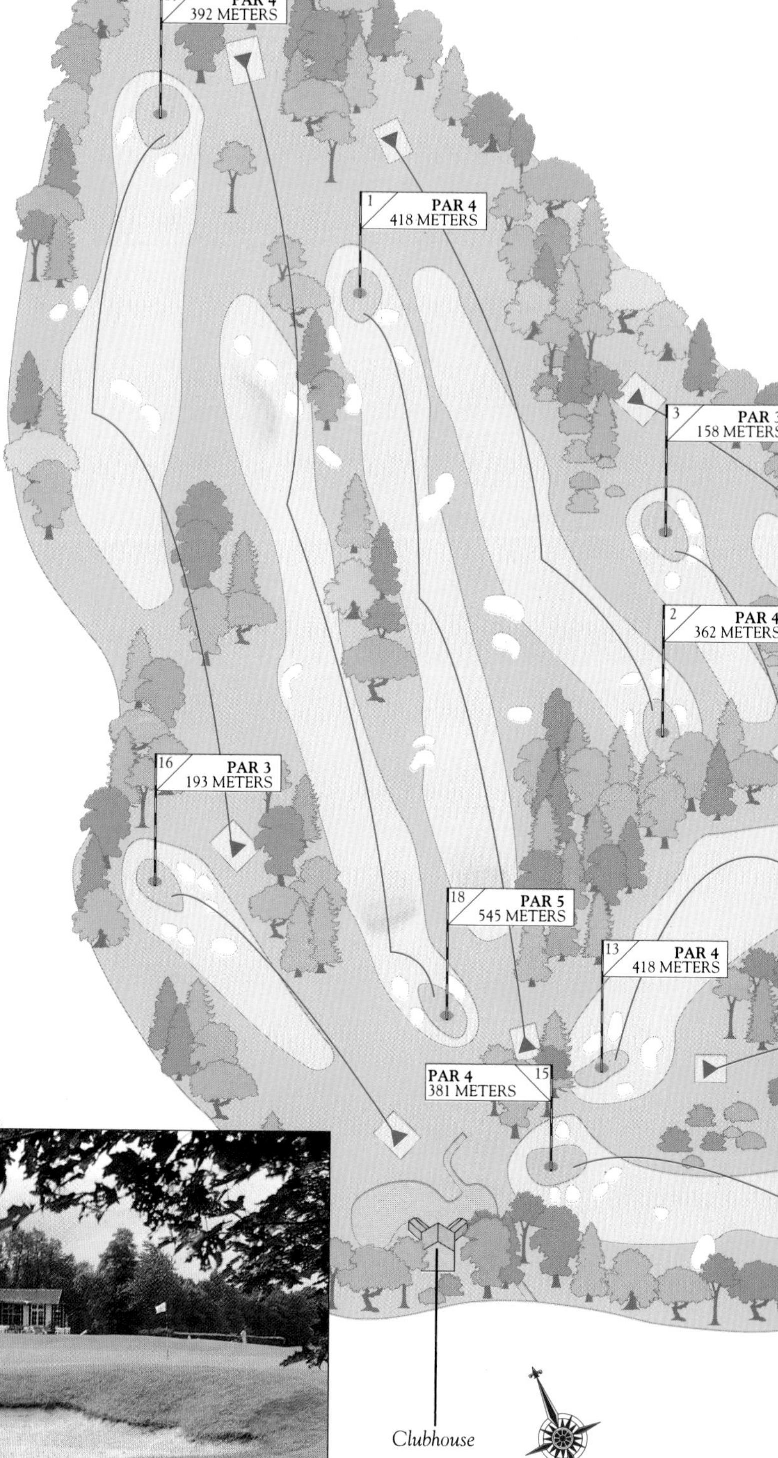

In the early part of the 1920s, Tom Simpson was commissioned to redesign the holes that make up today's championship course, and one of his acts was to remove many of the bunkers. His work was badly damaged in the Second World War, but the championship course retains much of his original design. It contains three uncompromising par 5s and four tough par 3s, three of them more than 190m long, to make up an overall par of 71. Of the par 4s, eight exceed 380m. Much of the bunkering is penal, and, particularly on the short holes, there is a premium on length combined with precision.

This peaceful course is set in beautiful woodland, and there is plenty of space to enjoy; the solemn calm of the surrounding forest shuts out the world, and the player's mind can focus on golf alone.

The list of French Open champions is an indication of the quality of the course. George Duncan won the first

15 **Testing trio**
The 15th is the third of a group of three holes, starting at the 13th, that present a stern test and are crucial to any round at Chantilly. The drive must be long and straight to open up a green well protected by deep bunkers.

Championship Lengths		
Out	3,278 Meters	Par 36
In	3,319 Meters	Par 35
Total	6,597 Meters	Par 71

Course Record

63 Peter McEvoy 1987

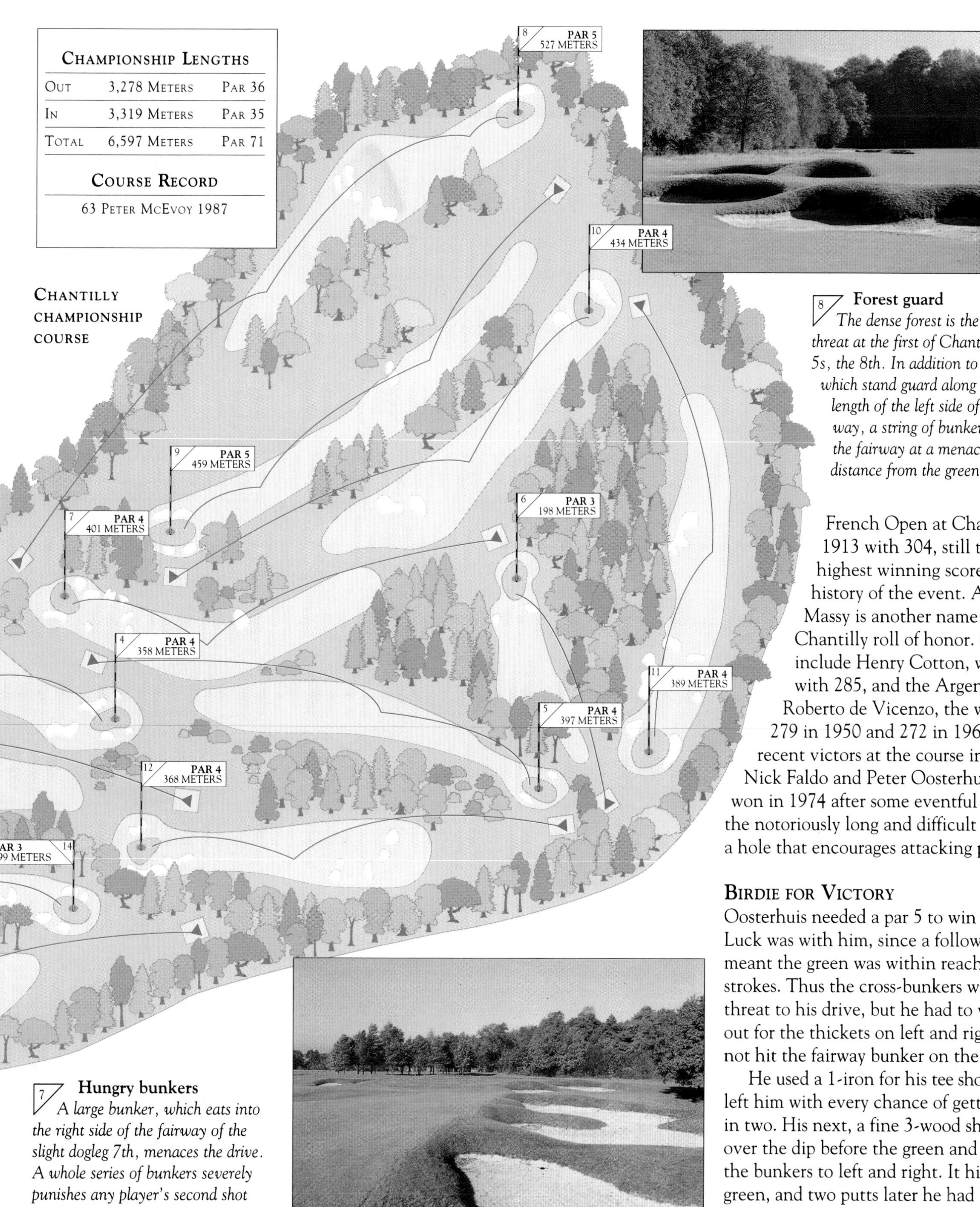

8 Forest guard

The dense forest is the main threat at the first of Chantilly's par 5s, the 8th. In addition to the trees, which stand guard along the whole length of the left side of the fairway, a string of bunkers crosses the fairway at a menacing distance from the green.

7 Hungry bunkers

A large bunker, which eats into the right side of the fairway of the slight dogleg 7th, menaces the drive. A whole series of bunkers severely punishes any player's second shot that is pushed or sliced off line.

French Open at Chantilly in 1913 with 304, still the highest winning score in the history of the event. Arnaud Massy is another name on the Chantilly roll of honor. Others include Henry Cotton, who won with 285, and the Argentinian Roberto de Vicenzo, the winner at 279 in 1950 and 272 in 1964. More recent victors at the course include Nick Faldo and Peter Oosterhuis, who won in 1974 after some eventful play on the notoriously long and difficult 18th, a hole that encourages attacking play.

Birdie for Victory

Oosterhuis needed a par 5 to win the title. Luck was with him, since a following wind meant the green was within reach in two strokes. Thus the cross-bunkers were no threat to his drive, but he had to watch out for the thickets on left and right and not hit the fairway bunker on the right.

He used a 1-iron for his tee shot, which left him with every chance of getting on in two. His next, a fine 3-wood shot, flew over the dip before the green and avoided the bunkers to left and right. It hit the green, and two putts later he had birdied, beating Peter Townsend by two strokes.

CLUB ZUR VAHR

CLUB ZUR VAHR, BREMEN, GERMANY

LONG AND ACCURATE shots from the tee are the key to good scores at the magnificent Garlstedter Heide course, part of the Club zur Vahr sports club, near Bremen. The site of the course is heavily forested and the design philosophy followed makes use of the abundant natural hazards. The 18-hole course is one part of a club complex also featuring a nine-hole course and other sports and leisure facilities. It has been rated as one of the finest championship courses in Europe.

Although there was a nine-hole course at Bremen from as early as 1895, the present layout dates back only to 1970. It was the brainchild of August Weyhausen, a former German junior champion. He chose a 220-acre site in undulating countryside 12 miles (20km) from Bremen. Weyhausen brought in course architect Dr. Bernhard von Limburger, a former German amateur champion.

Von Limburger created a course that could be enjoyed by ordinary club members but that would also be worthy of championship golf. When it is stretched to its full championship potential of 7,147 yards, it is a fearsome test for even the world's finest players. Trees dominate the course, and many of the holes are doglegs, demanding long and accurate

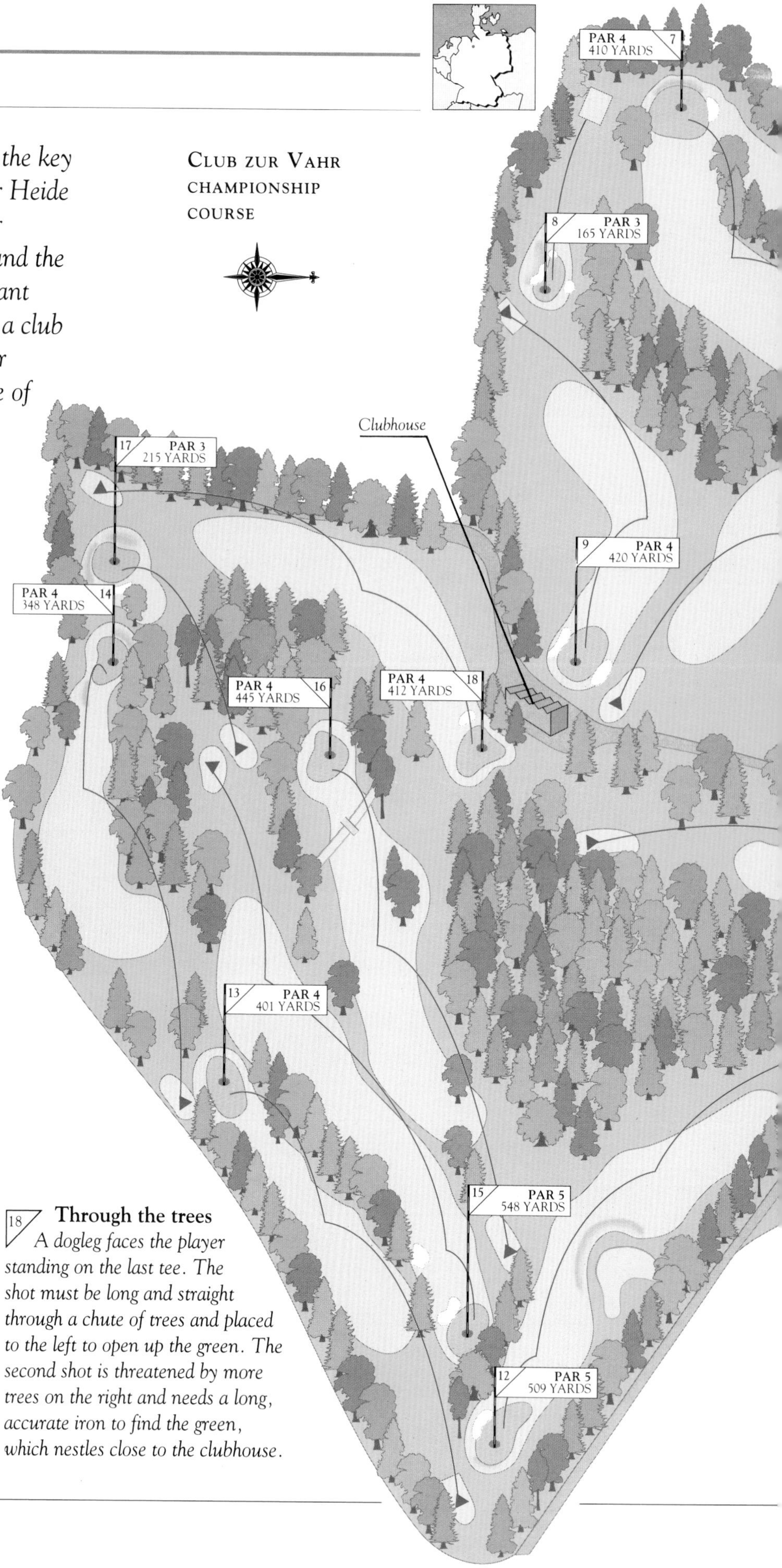

CLUB ZUR VAHR CHAMPIONSHIP COURSE

7 PAR 4 410 YARDS

8 PAR 3 165 YARDS

Clubhouse

9 PAR 4 420 YARDS

17 PAR 3 215 YARDS

14 PAR 4 348 YARDS

16 PAR 4 445 YARDS

18 PAR 4 412 YARDS

13 PAR 4 401 YARDS

15 PAR 5 548 YARDS

12 PAR 5 509 YARDS

18 Through the trees
A dogleg faces the player standing on the last tee. The shot must be long and straight through a chute of trees and placed to the left to open up the green. The second shot is threatened by more trees on the right and needs a long, accurate iron to find the green, which nestles close to the clubhouse.

3 Solid iron

As with most of the Club zur Vahr course, trees provide the main problems at the first of the short holes – the par-3, 206-yard 3rd. An extremely solid blow with a long iron is needed to reach the sanctuary of the green. Trees are a threat on both sides of a green that is also well protected by two strategically placed bunkers. Among the trees, which are predominantly silver birch and pines, there is extremely thick undergrowth in which it is only too easy to lose a stroke – or a ball.

driving to open up the green for the second shot. Decisive tactical thinking is needed, as there is usually a choice of paths. Wayward shots are punished harshly, running into the thick undergrowth between the pine trees bordering the fairways. Because of the trees, few artificial hazards, such as fairway bunkers, have been added to the terrain. There are less than 30 bunkers, with all but one sited near the greens.

Hosting the German Open

A year after it was officially opened, Club zur Vahr hosted the German Open with an outstanding field from more than 20 countries. A crowd of well over 6,000 people, a record for a German golf event, turned out to watch England's Neil Coles win with a remarkable score of 279, 17 under par. Coles rated the Bremen course as one of the best championship courses in Europe, and few would disagree.

The German Open has been played at Club zur Vahr on two subsequent occasions, in 1975 and 1985. Bernhard Langer won the 1985 event, which was hit by rain, forcing the organizers to reduce the championship to 54 holes.

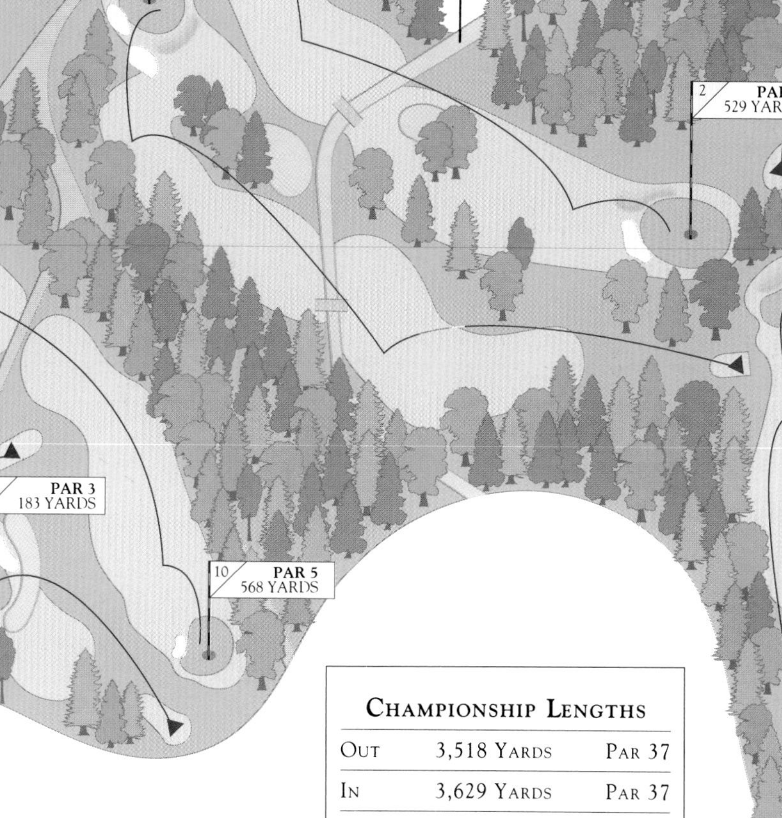

2 Tight down the left

Only a perfect drive tight down the left side – but avoiding the trees – gives any hope of reaching the green of this long par 5 in two strokes. A stream crosses the fairway some 300 yards from the tee, with a pond just beyond. A couple of trees stand sentinel in the center of the fairway.

Championship Lengths

Out	3,518 Yards	Par 37
In	3,629 Yards	Par 37
Total	7,147 Yards	Par 74

Course Record

68 Neil Coles, Peter Thomson, German Open 1971

COLONIAL

COLONIAL COUNTRY CLUB, FORT WORTH, TEXAS, U.S.A.

AT OVER 7,000 yards and with a par of only 70, the course where the great Ben Hogan learned his golf puts a premium on accurate driving. The Trinity River and the mass of trees through which the course is cut are supplemented by craftily strategic bunkering that makes tee shots extremely tight. This in turn creates demanding second shots on a course where only three of the 12 par-4 holes are less than 400 yards long.

Many people believe that Ben Hogan's success was due in large part to the fact that he played his early golf on this tough layout in Fort Worth, Texas. Every other course in the world, so the argument goes, was bound to seem simple by comparison.

Colonial was founded in 1935 by Marvin Leonard, a local golfing enthusiast. The original course was designed by John Bredemus, and Perry Maxwell was brought in to strengthen the 3rd, 4th, and 5th holes in preparation for the 1941 U.S. Open. This was the only time that Colonial staged the Open; it was won by Craig Wood, who beat his rival, Denny Shute, by three strokes.

Ben Hogan was for many years the dominant player at the Colonial course, winning the National

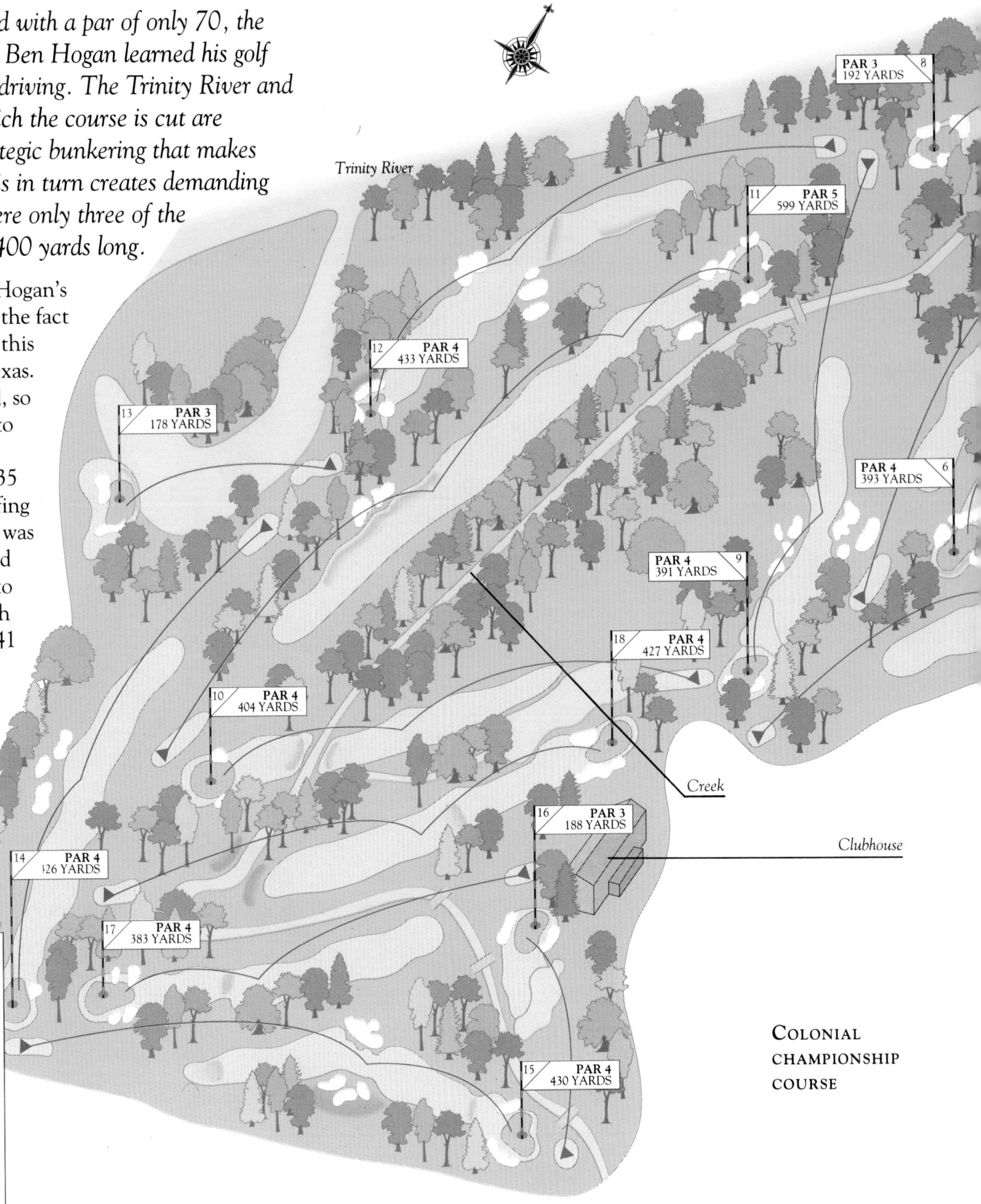

CHAMPIONSHIP LENGTHS		
OUT	3,542 YARDS	PAR 35
IN	3,468 YARDS	PAR 35
TOTAL	7,010 YARDS	PAR 70

COURSE RECORD

62 JOEY SINDELAR, NIT 1985; GENE SAUERS 1990

U.S. OPEN CHAMPIONS

1941 CRAIG WOOD

Trinity River
PAR 3 192 YARDS 8
11 PAR 5 599 YARDS
12 PAR 4 433 YARDS
13 PAR 3 178 YARDS
PAR 4 393 YARDS 6
PAR 4 391 YARDS 9
18 PAR 4 427 YARDS
10 PAR 4 404 YARDS
Creek
16 PAR 3 188 YARDS
Clubhouse
14 PAR 4 426 YARDS
17 PAR 4 383 YARDS
15 PAR 4 430 YARDS

COLONIAL CHAMPIONSHIP COURSE

5 Precision is the key
Only an accurate drive down the center of the fairway avoids trouble at the 5th. The river on the player's right, and rough and a ditch on his left, menace the tee shot.

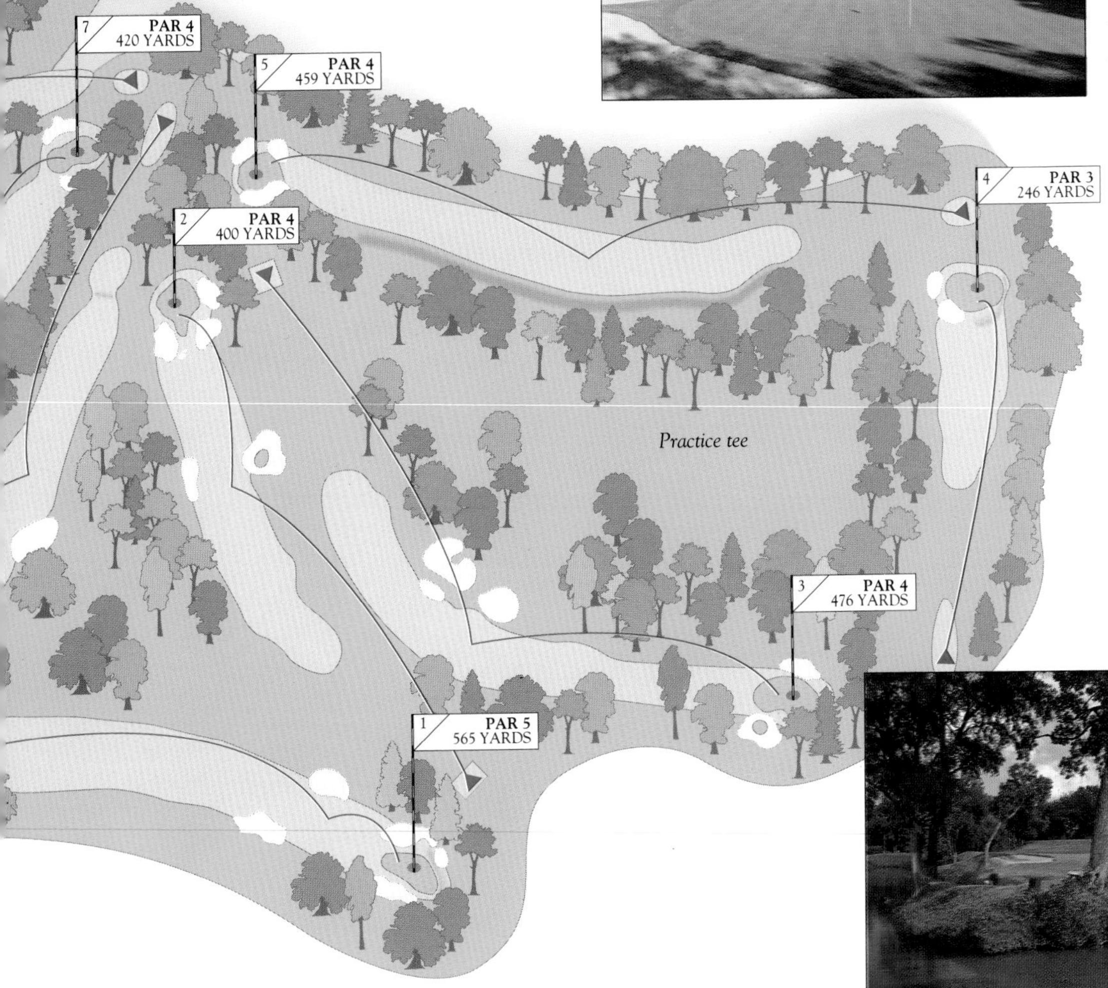

7 PAR 4 420 YARDS
5 PAR 4 459 YARDS
4 PAR 3 246 YARDS
2 PAR 4 400 YARDS
Practice tee
3 PAR 4 476 YARDS
1 PAR 5 565 YARDS

Invitation Tournament (NIT) there five times. Another player who apparently found a way to tame Colonial was Joey Sindelar. In 1985 he played the course in an incredible 62, a record that was equaled by Gene Sauers in the 1990 Southwestern Bell Colonial. Such a score could be achieved only through hitting that was both long and straight; players endowed with strength but without accuracy will not succeed at Colonial.

The Long and the Short

Despite being more than 7,000 yards, the course has only two par 5s, but both are monsters. The 1st, at 565 yards, is a prodigious enough beginning to a course. But the 11th, at 599 yards, is a genuine three-shotter for anyone, and apart from its length, there is the added hazard of trees down the length of the fairway on the right. By comparison the four short holes are modest in length, with only the 4th stretching to more than 200 yards, but all demand precision. There is no more obvious example of the need for supreme accuracy from the tee, however, than at the long par-4 5th.

The hole doglegs to the right, and those players favoring a bold fade shot from the tee to cut off part of the corner must be careful, because the Trinity River lurks dangerously behind the trees. On the left, thick trees and rough combine to threaten the tee shot struck too far through the dogleg. This leaves the player with no option but to strike a perfect drive to the center of the fairway in order to avoid getting into trouble.

18 Ending up
There is no letup at Colonial, right up to the finishing hole. The 18th is a tough par 4 which demands a long and accurate tee shot. Water to the left of the green and menacing greenside bunkers add to the challenge of the final approach shot.

16 Stage fright
The last of the par-3 holes, the 16th is not unduly long at 188 yards, but it demands an accurate tee shot over water to reach the green. Mistakes can be embarrassing since the green, guarded by some intrusive bunkers, is next to the clubhouse.

Cypress Point

Cypress Point Golf Club, Pebble Beach, California, U.S.A.

The southern tip of the Monterey Peninsula in California is home to Cypress Point, generally rated as one of the most spectacular courses in the world. The 1921 U.S. Women's Amateur Champion, Marion Hollins, fell in love with California after a visit to the state and bought the 175-acre clifftop site with the support of local businesspeople for $175,000. Here, high above the crashing waves of the Pacific, the great course architect Dr. Alister Mackenzie created a masterpiece.

The first course architect engaged to look at this stunning natural location was Seth Raynor, but he died unexpectedly and Mackenzie was appointed to continue the work. The Cypress Point Golf Club eventually opened in 1928.

The natural setting of the course, in the foothills of the Santa Lucia Mountains, is superb. Huge Monterey cypress trees brood quietly by the fairways and greens, and deer wander the course in the early morning and in the dusk.

The Mackenzie layout makes the best use of the landscape for golf. He resisted the temptation to create holes just to take advantage of the majestic views, and put the need for challenge by the course before everything else.

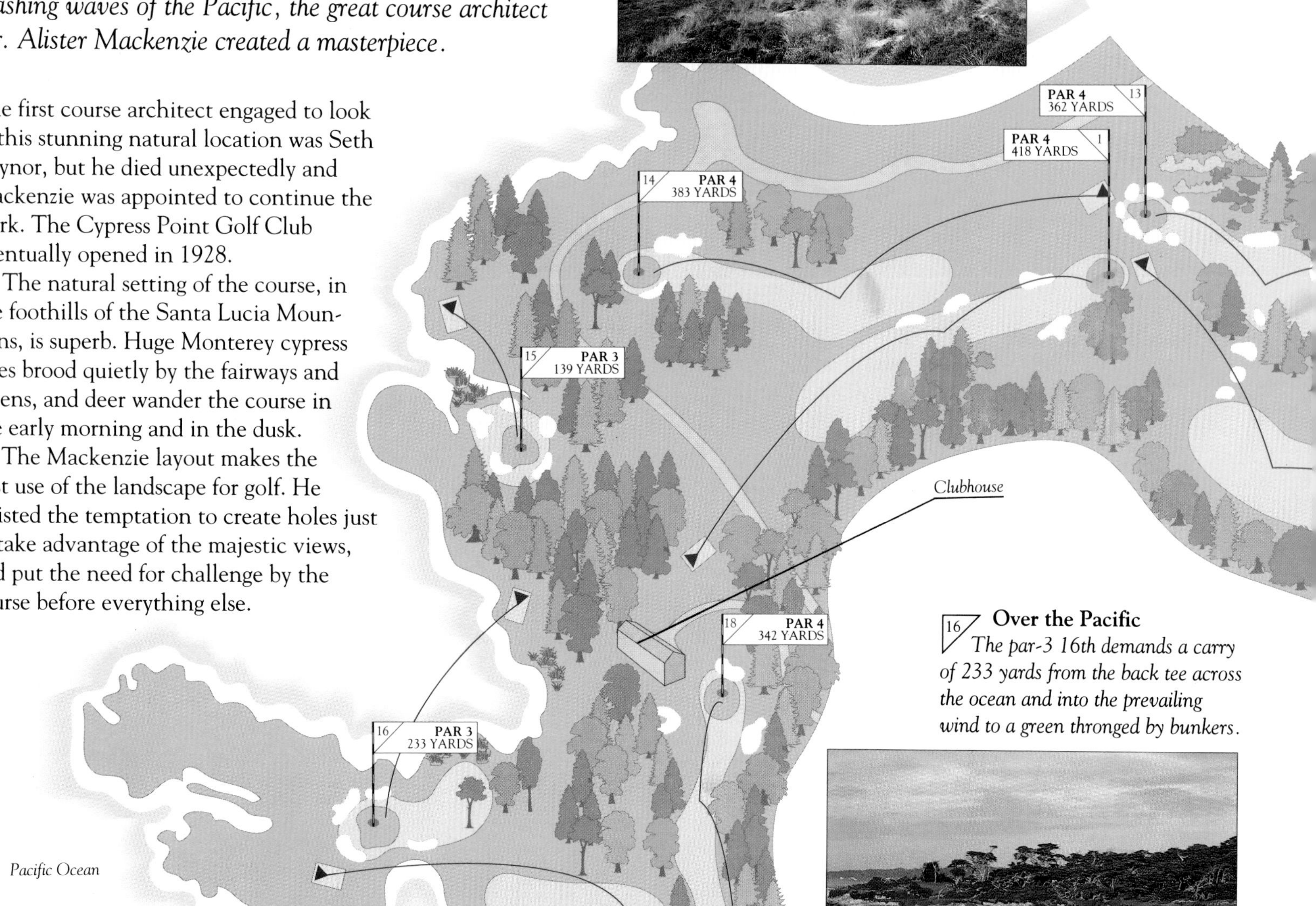

13 **Barred by sand**
The drive at the par-4 13th must carry a sandbar in the center of the narrowing fairway. The two-tiered green is defended by a necklace of bunkers.

13 PAR 4 362 YARDS

1 PAR 4 418 YARDS

14 PAR 4 383 YARDS

15 PAR 3 139 YARDS

Clubhouse

18 PAR 4 342 YARDS

16 PAR 3 233 YARDS

17 PAR 4 376 YARDS

Pacific Ocean

16 **Over the Pacific**
The par-3 16th demands a carry of 233 yards from the back tee across the ocean and into the prevailing wind to a green thronged by bunkers.

Cypress Point is most unusual among the world's greatest courses in having both consecutive par 5s and consecutive par 3s. It has all its par 5s in the first ten holes and two of the par 3s in the last four.

Mackenzie was careful to build plenty of contour and slope into the greens, in order to compensate for the course's modest length of 6,506 yards. The first green has a sharp slope, for instance, and the 5th has a two-tier green on a plateau at the end of a fairway that winds its way uphill through a pine forest. Mackenzie also emphasized the approach to the greens. At the 3rd, the challenge is to avoid bunkers of glittering sand on a short par 3. The green at the 6th is protected by five bunkers and a group of pines.

Clifftop Challenge

The high spots of the course come at the 15th, 16th, and 17th, a great trio of holes along the clifftop beside the Pacific. Some of the most exciting golf in the world takes place here, where breathtaking views and challenging play combine.

Cypress Point was once described by the fine American player Jimmy Demaret as "the best 17-hole golf course in the world." Demaret considered that the 18th hole, a modest 342-yard dogleg, lacked sufficient strength for a finishing hole on a major course, and many other players have agreed with him since.

Today, Cypress Point is one of the world's most exclusive clubs, with only 250 members, who come from all over the United States and abroad. Exclusivity takes its toll, however, and Cypress Point is a somewhat anonymous place, where members avoid publicity and guard their prerogatives jealously.

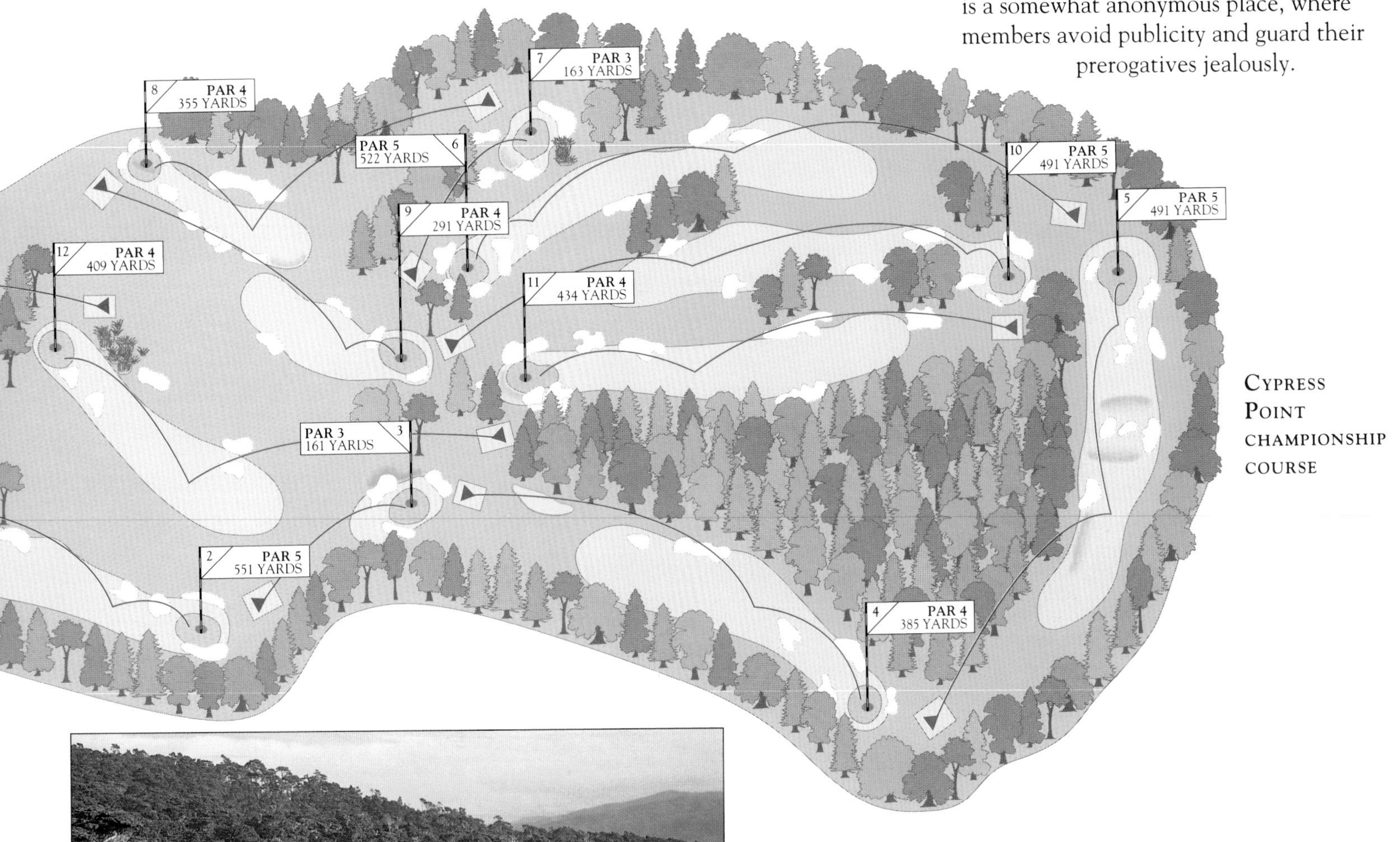

Cypress Point Championship Course

17 Tree trouble

The fairway at the 17th is wide along the clifftop, but the shot from the tee, high on a cliff, must carry a stretch of ocean and be placed left to give a clear shot to the green. Too far right brings a pine tree on the front right of the green into play. There are massive bunkers to the left and back of the green, and a knot of cypress trees has to be avoided.

Championship Lengths		
Out	3,337 Yards	Par 37
In	3,169 Yards	Par 35
Total	6,506 Yards	Par 72

Course Record

64 Craig Stadler, AT&T National Pro-Am 1982

Desert Highlands

Desert Highlands Golf Club, Scottsdale, Arizona, U.S.A.

A small part of the old and fabled land of the Arizona desert, where native American Indians lived, has been transformed into a new-style reservation for wealthy, upwardly mobile Americans. At the heart of the Desert Highlands community is a quite remarkable Jack Nicklaus golf course, like a series of green footprints in the desert. It is a supreme example of what technology and careful planning can do to balance the aspirations of man with sensitivity to the environment.

18 Jack's view
Only the brave try to get home in two at the 18th. Most players will play short of the narrow green, which is protected by a mound. It was from Clubhouse Rock, close to the 18th, that Nicklaus first surveyed the desert and planned his course.

The days are long past when the desert was regarded as a hostile wasteland, inimical to golf as to most other human activities. Today, golf architects realize that the warmth of the desert offers a near-perfect climate for spectacular courses, provided enough water can be supplied.

Protect and Conserve

It took Nicklaus two years of study and 20 visits to the site in the early 1980s to achieve what he was after at Desert Highlands. At the heart of all the design thinking was the need to protect the desert environment, its plants and wildlife. The conservation of water had the highest priority: only 80 acres of the course need irrigation and recycling ensures that every drop counts.

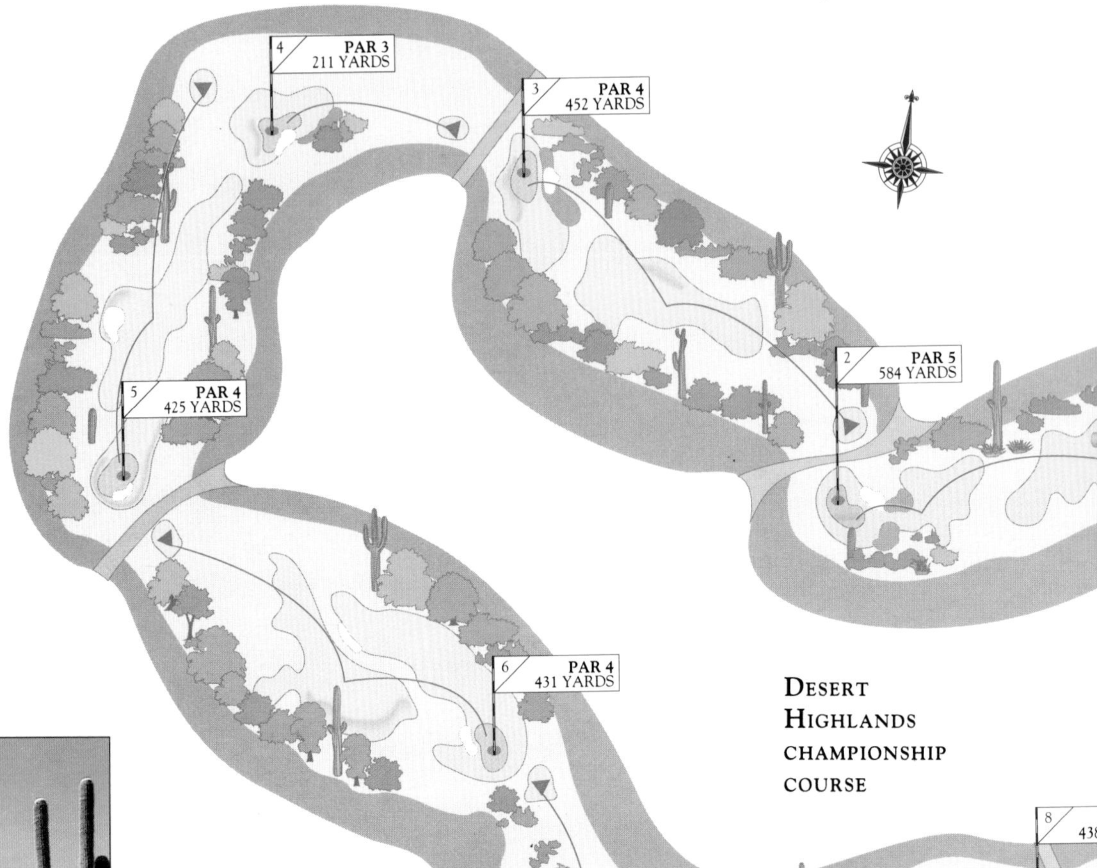

Desert Highlands championship course

9 To the peak
Pothole bunkers and grassy hollows are a feature of the long par-5 9th. This is a demanding three-shot hole curving to the left and played uphill toward Pinnacle Peak. Tall cacti constantly remind the golfer of the arid desert setting for the finely maintained greens and fairways.

Nicklaus has achieved a harmony between the course and the boulder-strewn desert terrain with its distinctive vegetation. The fairways are, in essence, landing areas. They have an edge of semi-rough that runs into what Nicklaus calls "transitional bunkers," meaning that they border the cultivated area on one side and merge into the desert itself on the other.

The course is 2,400 feet (730m) above sea level and is 7,099 yards at championship length. Nicklaus has used craggy mounds for the teeing areas, with the first hole a classic example; the drive is played out into space toward a green 120 feet (37m) below. There are bent grass greens, typical of Nicklaus with their undulating contours, and fiendish pot bunkers.

A unique feature of the Desert Highlands complex is the remarkable par-41 18-hole putting course, designed by architect Gary Panks. It is so hard that Jack Nicklaus managed only 45 on it.

16 **Long and low**
The long par-3 16th has a three-tiered green. It is best played with a long, low shot that can run up onto the green. A bunker on the left threatens wayward drives, and a series of the hostile humps and hollows that are characteristic of the course waits for short, off-line shots.

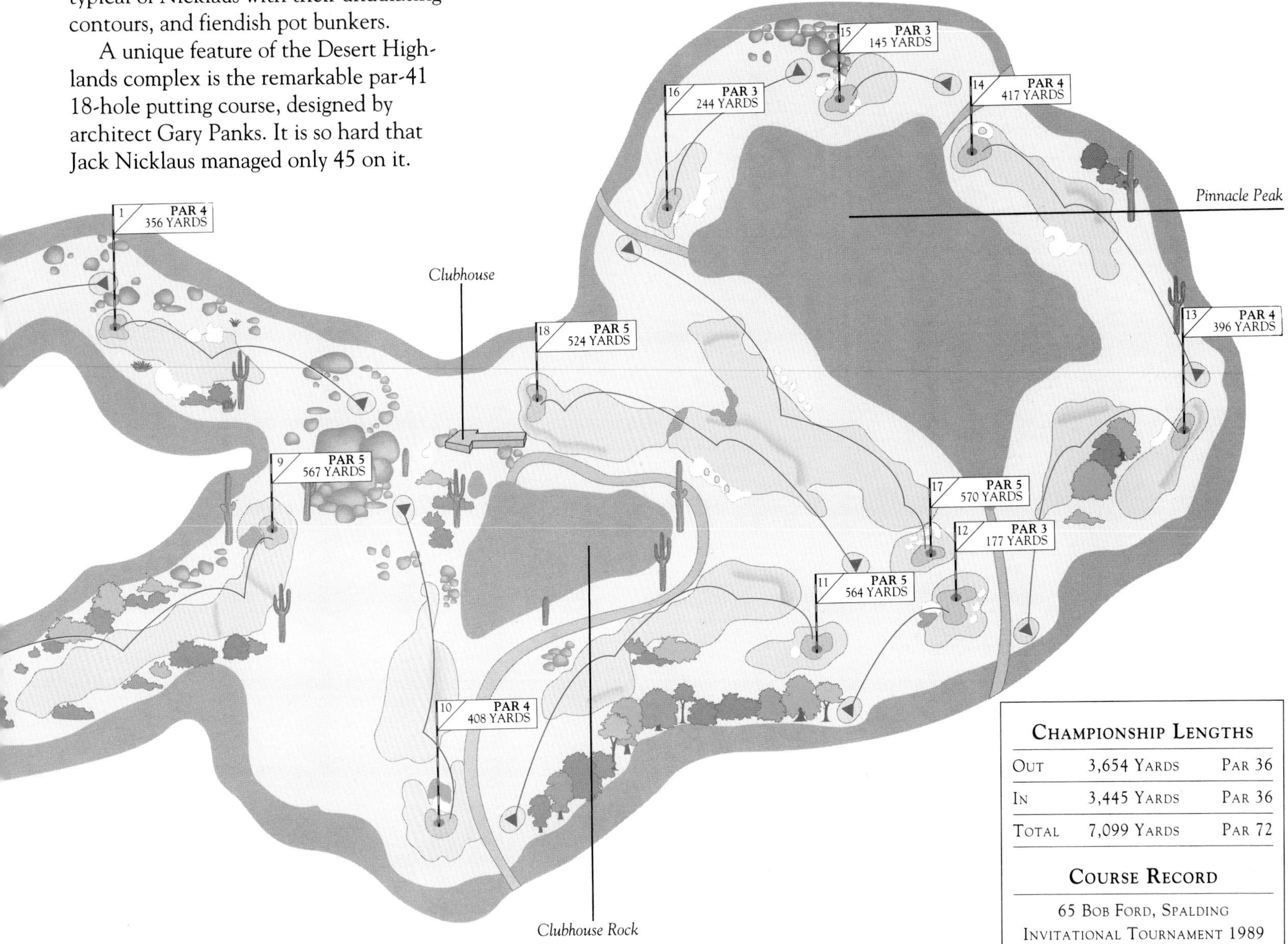

15 PAR 3 145 YARDS
16 PAR 3 244 YARDS
14 PAR 4 417 YARDS
Pinnacle Peak
1 PAR 4 356 YARDS
Clubhouse
18 PAR 5 524 YARDS
13 PAR 4 396 YARDS
9 PAR 5 567 YARDS
17 PAR 5 570 YARDS
12 PAR 3 177 YARDS
11 PAR 5 564 YARDS
10 PAR 4 408 YARDS
Clubhouse Rock

Championship Lengths

Out	3,654 Yards	Par 36
In	3,445 Yards	Par 36
Total	7,099 Yards	Par 72

Course Record

65 Bob Ford, Spalding Invitational Tournament 1989

FALSTERBO

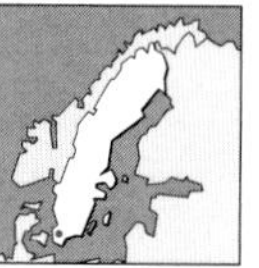

FALSTERBO GOLFKLUBB, FALSTERBO, SWEDEN

DOWN AT THE southernmost tip of Sweden, on a peninsula where the Baltic Sea and the waters of the Oresund meet, lies one of Europe's most dramatic courses, Falsterbo. It is a classic links course, one of the few fine examples of this type of golf to be found in continental Europe. Challenging to play, it is also a home to wildlife.

7 Bunker trouble
A drive well to the right on this sharp left dogleg opens up the green for a short approach. Set in a hollow, the green is severely bunkered, but a delicate pitch should avoid the sand and hold the green, which slopes from front to back.

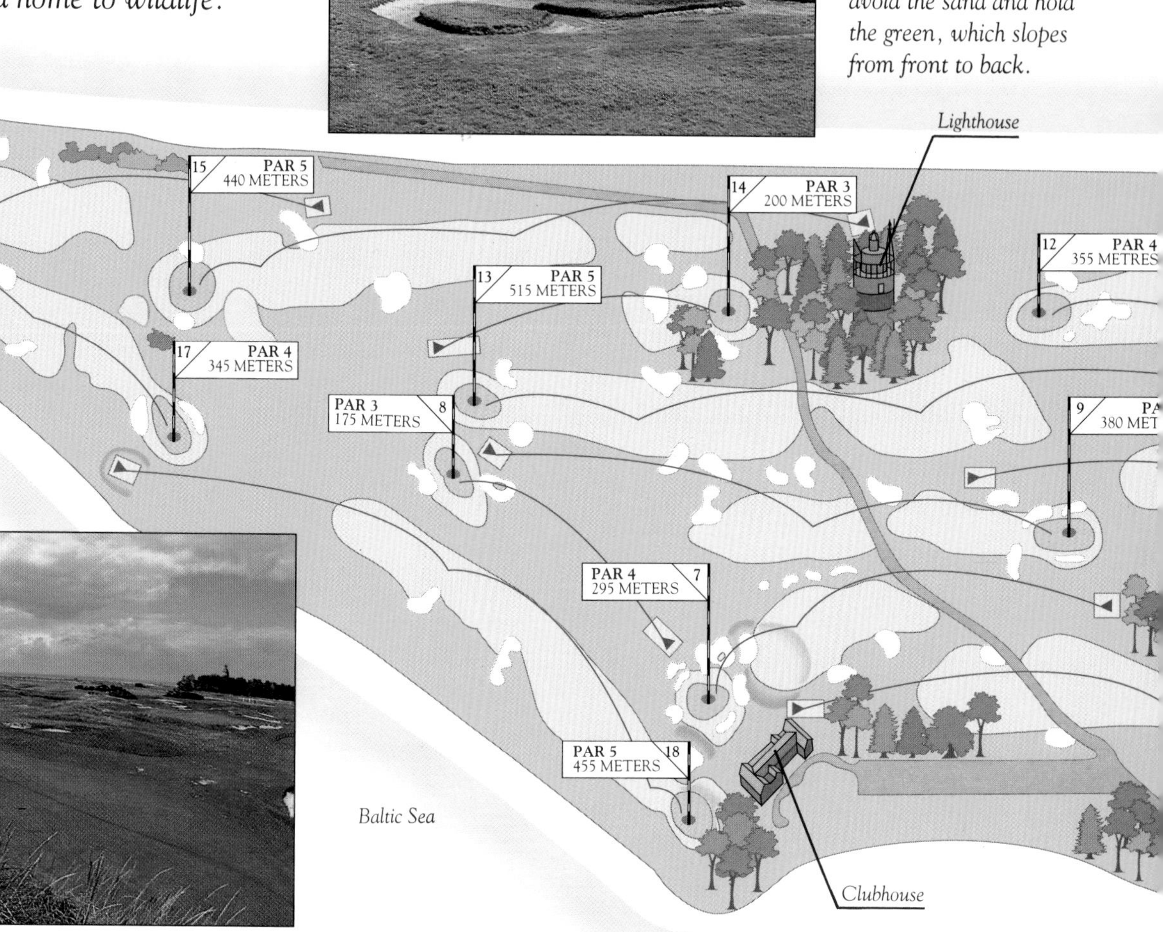

18 By the dunes
This hole doglegs to the right near giant sand dunes; bunkers guard the corner of the dogleg and the green, beside the clubhouse. Danger lurks in the rough to the left and even more in the grasses and sand of the dunes.

16 PAR 4 340 METERS
15 PAR 5 440 METERS
14 PAR 3 200 METERS
12 PAR 4 355 METRES
13 PAR 5 515 METERS
17 PAR 4 345 METERS
PAR 3 175 METERS 8
9 PA 380 MET
PAR 4 295 METERS 7
PAR 5 455 METERS 18
Lighthouse
Baltic Sea
Clubhouse

Though Falsterbo dates back to 1909, it is not the oldest club in Sweden. That distinction belongs to Hovas, near Gothenburg. But Falsterbo is the only true links course in the country, even though there are some that are partly links, such as Falsterbo's neighbor, Flommen.

Robert Turnbull, the professional at Copenhagen Golf Club, laid out the original nine holes of Falsterbo. The course was expanded to 18 holes in 1930 by Gunnar Bauer. A lighthouse stands in the middle of the course, which has fine turf and magnificent natural surroundings of a rare beauty to satisfy aesthetic sensibilities. Frequent changes in wind direction make the golf interesting.

The course is also an important nature reserve; the marshes at the northern end are a haven for bird life as well as a challenging set of golfing hazards. But the player cannot afford to let his concentration wander for too long over the natural surroundings. This links course demands the most careful attention.

The toughness of the course manifests itself right from the beginning. The tee shot at the 1st must avoid the out-of-bounds down the right side and the trees on the other side of the fairway, which swings slightly to the right. A par at this 400m hole is not a bad start, considering the toughness of the rest of the course. A shortish par 3 and a relatively benign par 5 follow, but when the player turns back alongside the marsh the going gets tougher.

Down by the Marsh

The uncompromising 360m par-4 4th is the first hole beside the marsh, and is usually played into the prevailing wind. The water hazard is clearly defined by tall reeds down the entire right side of the fairway; the green is tucked into a corner of the marsh. The second shot, which often requires a wood, must cross the corner of the marsh if it is to find sanctuary on the green. A single bunker protects the left side of the green; no other defense save the marsh is required.

The internal water hazards – natural here, but unusual on a links course – present a dangerous prospect on the next two holes. Further on, the holes around the central lighthouse are delightful in their variety, but from the 15th the golf is played alongside the great sand dunes that are the mark of this fine course.

The 16th, a beautiful 340m par 4, gently doglegs its way into the corner of the peninsula. Here the views to Denmark on the one side are spectacular, while on the other there is nothing but the Baltic between the player and the Soviet Union.

The Names of Falsterbo

1st Vågen	10th Kålhagen
2nd Dickens	11th Vattenhålet
3rd Tångvallen	12th Strandskatan
4th Flommen	13th Tipperary
5th Chicago	14th Fyrhålet
6th Vanningen	15th Öresund
7th 1911	16th Gunnar Bauer
8th Sahara	17th Nabben
9th Sydvästen	18th Klitterna

The holes at Falsterbo are named in a mixture of Swedish and English. The 5th hole was called Chicago in the gangster days of the 1920s, because it has dangers lurking at every turn. The name of the 15th refers to a geographical feature, the sound alongside Falsterbo, while the 16th celebrates the architect of the 18-hole course.

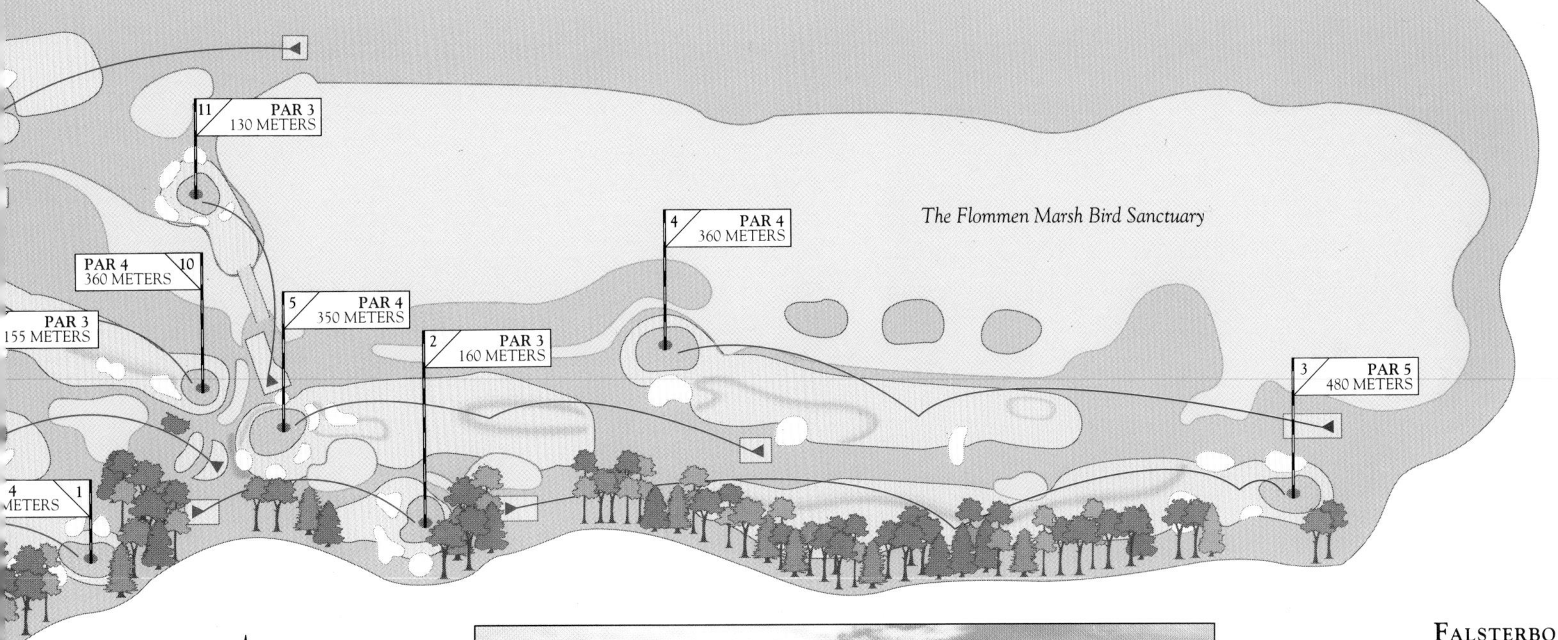

Falsterbo Championship Course

Championship Lengths

Out	2,755 Meters	Par 34
In	3,140 Meters	Par 37
Total	5,895 Meters	Par 71

Course Record

65 Peter Senior, PLM Open 1986

11 **Bridge over water trouble**
The fourth of Falsterbo's five par 3s is the most spectacular. The hole is a modest 130m long, but it is surrounded on three sides by water. It is death or glory here, particularly if, as so often, a brisk breeze is blowing from left to right across the hole. Access to the green is over a long footbridge that has been built across the middle of the inlet.

GANTON

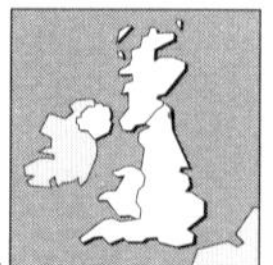

GANTON GOLF CLUB, GANTON, SCARBOROUGH, NORTH YORKSHIRE, ENGLAND

PURE HEATHLAND GOLF is the closest substitute for the classic links of the seaside, where the game was born and nurtured. There are numerous similarities, for in many cases the "inland" heath was at one stage covered by the sea and appeared to the light of day only as the ocean receded. This is almost certainly true of Ganton, which lies only a few miles from the sea and is a course of charm, challenge, and outstanding quality.

18 Over the road

The final green at Ganton is hemmed in by deep bunkers. This par-4 18th demands an accurate tee shot well to the right, across the diagonal, to avoid a huge sand dune on the left. The second shot to the green has to be played through an alley of pines and over a road, avoiding those dangerous bunkers.

CHAMPIONSHIP LENGTHS		
OUT	3,476 YARDS	PAR 36
IN	3,346 YARDS	PAR 35
TOTAL	6,822 YARDS	PAR 71

COURSE RECORD

65 NEIL COLES,
PGA CHAMPIONSHIP 1981

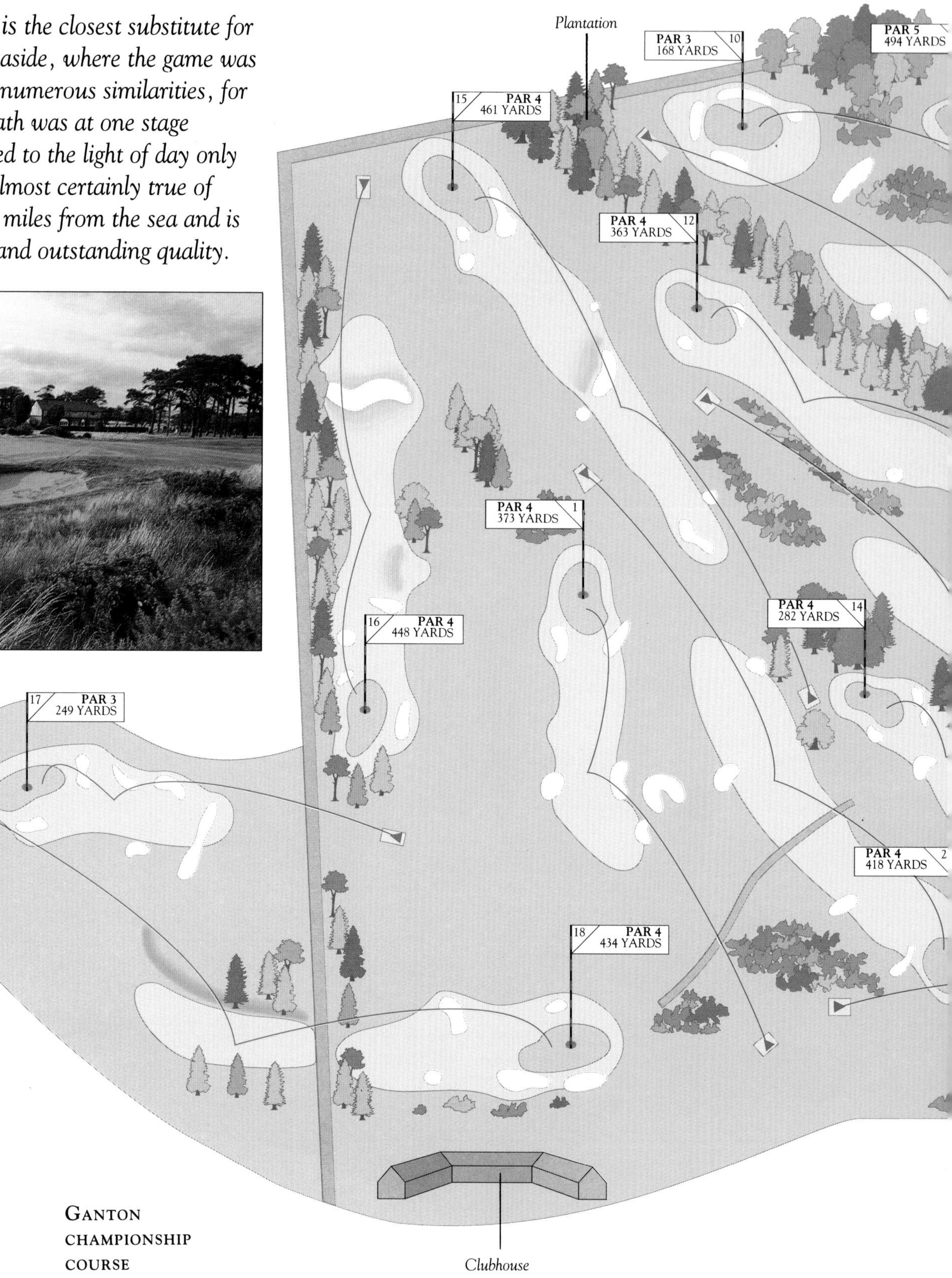

GANTON CHAMPIONSHIP COURSE

6 Demanding length
At more than 440 yards, the 6th hole is a challenging par 4 out of reach for all but the longest-hitting players. The initial problem for any player, however, is the long drive over the pond, which provides a water hazard in front of the tee.

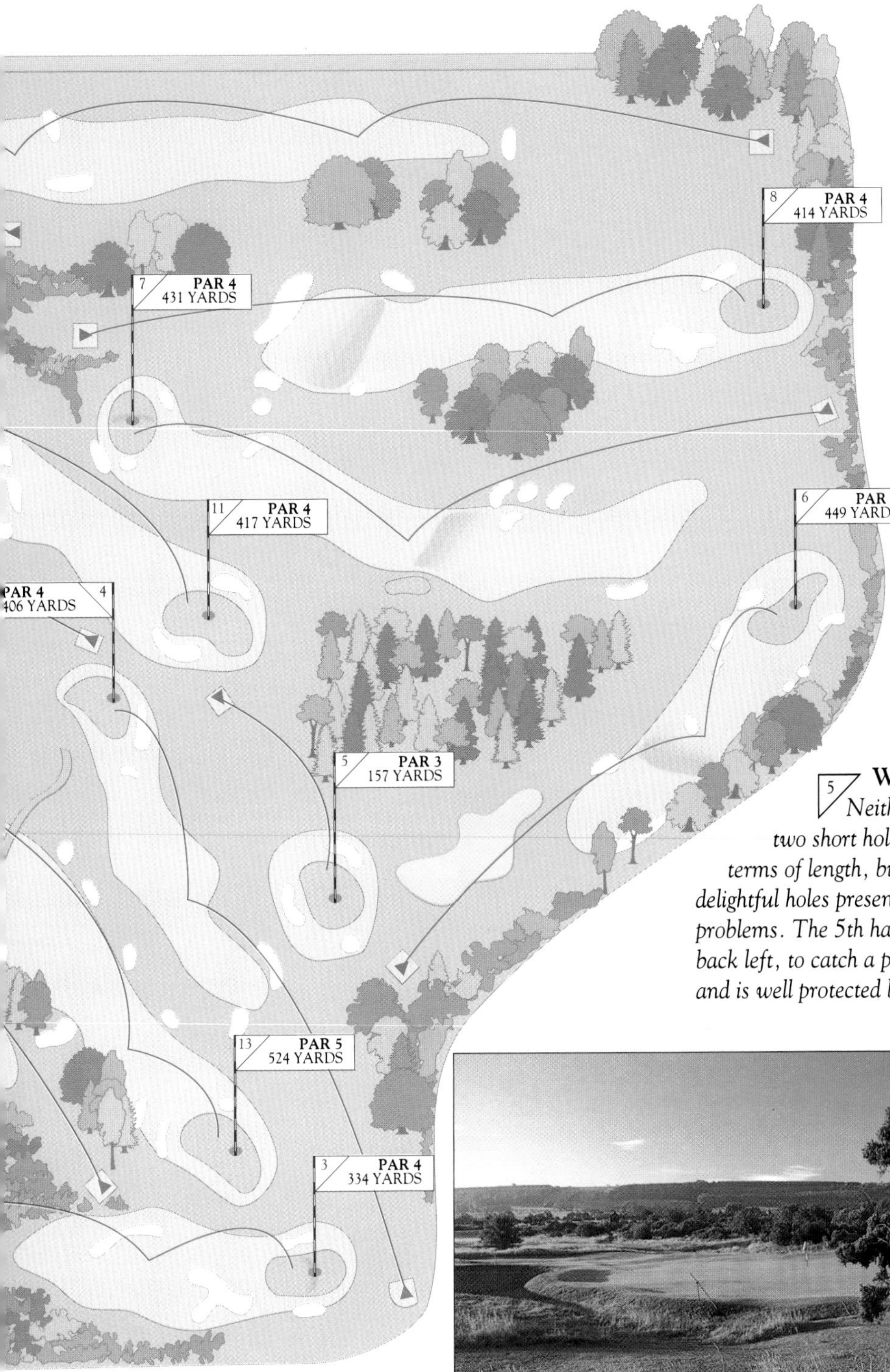

8 PAR 4 414 YARDS

7 PAR 4 431 YARDS

11 PAR 4 417 YARDS

6 PAR 4 449 YARDS

4 PAR 4 406 YARDS

5 PAR 3 157 YARDS

13 PAR 5 524 YARDS

3 PAR 4 334 YARDS

5 Water hole
Neither of Ganton's two short holes is testing in terms of length, but they are delightful holes presenting their own problems. The 5th has water to the back left, to catch a pull or hook, and is well protected by bunkers.

While on many courses of its period trees were introduced to define fairways and as a consequence the natural openness of the heath was destroyed, Ganton did not follow suit. Although some Scots and Corsican pines have now been planted, Ganton remains a rare example of a genuine open heathland course.

Harry S. Colt was one of the many eminent architects and players who have left their mark on the course since it came into being in 1891. Among the others were the great amateur Harold Hilton, Tom Dunn, Horace Hutchinson, and Frank Pennink, as well as all three members of the Great Triumvirate. Harry Vardon was also the club professional from 1896 until 1903. In the 1920s, Dr. Alister Mackenzie introduced the tiered greens that were his trademark. The best examples of his work are at the 3rd, 7th, and 9th holes. The course was further strengthened by Ken Cotton in preparation for the Ryder Cup match that was held at Ganton in 1949.

The Ganton course generally puts a premium on accuracy rather than length. Combined with the firmness of the turf and the splendid surroundings, this quality makes it one of the world's finest inland courses.

GLEN ABBEY

GLEN ABBEY GOLF CLUB, OAKVILLE, ONTARIO, CANADA

GLEN ABBEY WAS one of the first courses designed specifically to meet the demands of modern professional tournament golf. In the mid-1970s, Jack Nicklaus was brought in to create a permanent home for the Canadian Open on this spectacular site, with its wooded ravine carved over the centuries by Sixteen Mile Creek on its way towards Lake Ontario. Nicklaus made imaginative use of the magnificent natural terrain to create a fine championship course. Today the Golf House, once used by the Jesuit Fathers as a retreat, houses the Royal Canadian Golf Association.

15 Out of the valley
The last of Glen Abbey's par 3s, the 15th, is one of the most demanding holes, despite being only 141 yards from the back tee. The shot is to a greatly elevated green, shaped like the continent of Africa. The green, sloping sharply from back to front, has bunkers to its front and rear. Choice of club is critical. An extra club might be felt necessary to make sure of reaching the green, but putts from above the hole are difficult to stop down the slope.

The concept to which Nicklaus worked was that of a truly championship-standard course, designed for tournament play with spectators very much in mind. It became the forerunner of the current crop of so-called "stadium" courses, aimed at providing maximum viewing areas.

To assist spectators, the ground has been elevated behind the tees and gentle, grassy slopes curve behind and to the sides of the greens. The course layout means that six of the greens and five of the tees are within 100 yards of the clubhouse. This allows the spectators to see plenty of golf without moving too far.

EASY VIEWING

Wide spaces have purposely been left between the fairways to accommodate the enormous crowds attracted by the Open, and the 18th green is set in an amphitheater that provides comfortable viewing for thousands on the last day of this prestigious USPGA event.

Nicklaus did not start from scratch in designing Glen Abbey; there had been a golf course on the site since the time it was sold by the Jesuit order in the early 1960s. But Nicklaus completely rebuilt it, remodeling all 18 holes. He added fresh bunkers, trees, and lakes to produce a challenging new layout, while exploiting to the full the natural test presented by the Sixteen Mile Creek ravine. The 11th to the 15th, set in the ravine and known as the "Valley" holes, are among the toughest on the whole Glen Abbey course.

The course was opened in June, 1976 – an occasion when Nicklaus played an 18-hole exhibition match with Tom Weiskopf, who had won the 1975 Canadian Open. In 1977 Glen Abbey hosted the Open for the first time, Lee Trevino taking the title. The event has been played there every year since, with the exception of 1980 when it returned to Royal Montreal to fulfill an earlier commitment. Winners at Glen Abbey include Greg Norman and Curtis Strange.

Despite its severity for the tournament players, the course still presents an enjoyable test from the forward tees for those mortals possessed of more modest golfing ability.

GLEN ABBEY CHAMPIONSHIP COURSE

CHAMPIONSHIP LENGTHS		
OUT	3,482 YARDS	PAR 35
IN	3,620 YARDS	PAR 38
TOTAL	7,102 YARDS	PAR 73

COURSE RECORD

62 GREG NORMAN, CANADIAN OPEN 1987

12 Watch the length

The first short hole on the back nine, the 12th, is deceptive in length. It is 187 yards from the back tee, but tends to play longer. The player needs to take an extra club and favor the right. The undulating green requires careful putting.

14 Crossing the creek

The tee shot at the 14th carries Sixteen Mile Creek. The aim line of the ideal shot is between the two fairway bunkers, but a choice has to be made on how much of the dogleg is to be cut off.

Harbour Town

Harbour Town Golf Links, Hilton Head Island, South Carolina, U.S.A.

At a time when the trend in the United States was toward longer and longer courses, Pete Dye, with Jack Nicklaus as his consultant, swam against the tide in designing the famous Harbour Town links. The course is only of moderate length, and Dye made the greens small, keeping the number of bunkers to a minimum. There are only 56 bunkers on the course, and a dozen of these are hardly ever visited. The rest are relatively flat; a buried lie in the sand is almost unheard-of at Harbour Town.

Harbour Town championship course

Clubhouse
Lighthouse
Harbor
9 PAR 4 337 YARDS
18 PAR 4 478 YARDS
PAR 4 376 YARDS 16
PAR 3 192 YARDS 17
Calibogue Sound

18 Carry over the marsh
The farthest back tee at the last hole is called the "Nicklaus tee" by the members. So difficult and long is the flight across the marsh, along the shore of Calibogue Sound, that it is seldom used, even by the USPGA for the Heritage Classic event.

The Harbour Town course is only 6,912 yards long when stretched to its limit, and is virtually flat, with fairways often more than 40 yards wide. The fall between the highest and lowest points on the course is no greater than the height of the average man; consequently there are no uphill or downhill lies for those who live in fear of such features. The three par-5 holes are modest in length, and although there are some long par 4s, there are just as many on the course that are short.

So what is it that makes Harbour Town such a highly regarded course in the golf world? The answer lies in the subtlety of the design. Dye and Nicklaus hacked their way through subtropical trees and vegetation, leaving just enough trees in their wake to make Harbour Town a classic test of nerve and patience. Many of the trees were carefully left in strategic positions to confound the golfer. Wonderful live oaks festooned with Spanish moss, enormous pines, and magnificent magnolias abound in this most spectacular of settings, in the holiday playground of Hilton Head Island.

Accuracy Wins Out

Wayward shots from the tee are often punished severely at Harbour Town by water or the trees. The care required for second shots – and the variety of them needed – is phenomenal. Dye's design demands unusual accuracy, and long hitters who cannot place the ball with pinpoint precision will lose any advantage that they may generally have

Coastal splendor (below)
The lush beauty of subtropical land at the edge of the sea gives Harbour Town Golf Links an exotic backdrop. It is enhanced by the lighthouse, which is a distinctive landmark as well known as the course itself. The trees are a constant hazard.

Heritage Road

1 PAR 4 414 YARDS

2 PAR 5 505 YARDS

6 PAR 4 419 YARDS

5 PAR 5 535 YARDS

8 PAR 4 462 YARDS

7 PAR 3 180 YARDS

3 PAR 4 411 YARDS

4 PAR 3 198 YARDS

10 AR 4 36 YARDS

11 PAR 4 438 YARDS

15 PAR 5 575 YARDS

12 PAR 4 413 YARDS

Baynard Cove Road

14 PAR 3 165 YARDS

Plantation Drive

13 PAR 4 378 YARDS

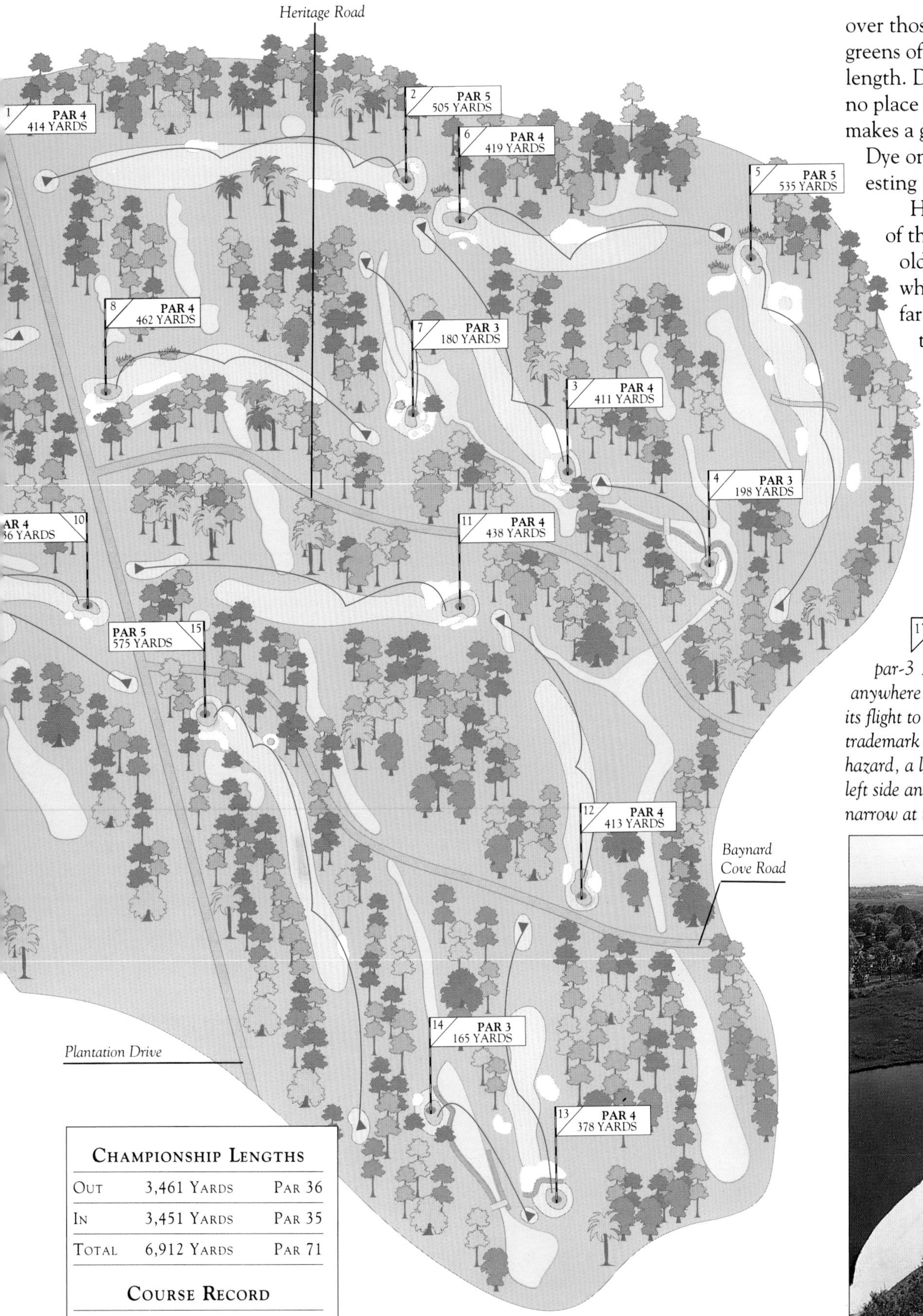

CHAMPIONSHIP LENGTHS		
OUT	3,461 YARDS	PAR 36
IN	3,451 YARDS	PAR 35
TOTAL	6,912 YARDS	PAR 71

COURSE RECORD

63 J. NICKLAUS 1975; D. WATSON 1984; J. HALLETT 1988; W. LEVI 1989

over those of more modest length. The greens offer few putts of any considerable length. Dye believes that long putting has no place in the game. "Something that makes a golfer chip with finesse," Dye once stated, "is a lot more interesting to him than a 95-foot putt."

Harbour Town is now the home of the South Carolina Golf Club, the oldest golf club in North America, which originated in Charleston as far back as 1786, just ten years after the Declaration of Independence.

In recognition of its age, the club holds the annual Heritage Classic, traditionally in the week after the U.S. Masters. Arnold Palmer, Jack Nicklaus, Bernhard Langer, and Nick Faldo are among the stars who have won the Heritage event.

17 **Flying over trouble**

The tee shot at Harbour Town's par-3 17th hole is one of the most daunting anywhere. It must carry water for two-thirds of its flight to a green propped up by railroad ties, the trademark of architect Pete Dye. As an added hazard, a long ribbon of a bunker runs down the left side and around the back of a green which is narrow at the front but widens towards the rear.

LINDRICK

LINDRICK GOLF CLUB, WORKSOP, NOTTINGHAMSHIRE, ENGLAND

THE FAMOUS COURSE *architect Dr. Alister Mackenzie, designer of Augusta National, declared that Lindrick "has the best terrain of any inland course in Britain." Such an emphatic declaration by someone with such impeccable credentials is high praise indeed, but it is no more than this fine example of heathland golf, on the border between Nottinghamshire and South Yorkshire, deserves.*

4 Over the hill
A bunker guards the left of the fairway on the 4th, a short par 5 of 480 yards. The second shot is played blind over a hill, toward a green that lies in front of a river.

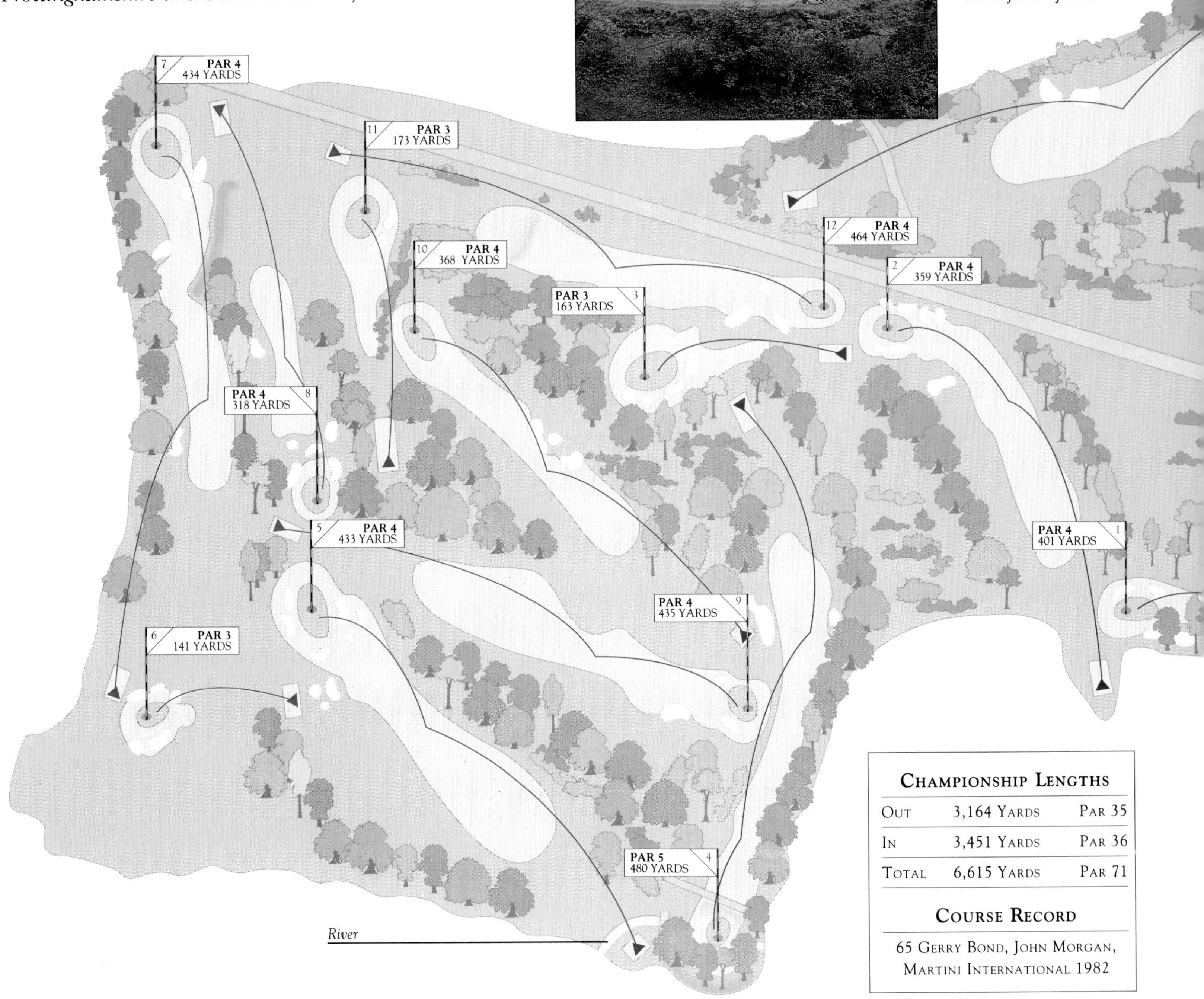

7 PAR 4 434 YARDS

11 PAR 3 173 YARDS

12 PAR 4 464 YARDS

10 PAR 4 368 YARDS

2 PAR 4 359 YARDS

PAR 3 163 YARDS 3

PAR 4 318 YARDS 8

5 PAR 4 433 YARDS

PAR 4 401 YARDS 1

PAR 4 435 YARDS 9

6 PAR 3 141 YARDS

PAR 5 480 YARDS 4

River

CHAMPIONSHIP LENGTHS

OUT	3,164 YARDS	PAR 35
IN	3,451 YARDS	PAR 36
TOTAL	6,615 YARDS	PAR 71

COURSE RECORD

65 GERRY BOND, JOHN MORGAN, MARTINI INTERNATIONAL 1982

The Lindrick club was formed in 1891 as the Sheffield and District Golf Club. Laid out on heathland overlying limestone, the course has not changed greatly over the years. Only the 2nd and 18th holes have been subject to major alterations.

Gorse is the predominant shrub at Lindrick, but birch trees have invaded the area over the years and it is no longer as open a heath as it originally was. The club has been in the vanguard of the movement to preserve traditional British golfing turf, a movement led by the late Eddie Park and his son Nicholas. They have practiced what they preach at Lindrick. Top priority is accorded to sustaining the bent and fescue grasses that provide such marvelous turf for fairways and greens. Lindrick has, in fact, some of the best putting surfaces found anywhere in the world. A great deal of care is taken to keep this fine course in the best playing condition all through the year.

Lindrick has a justifiably famous place in golfing history as the course on which Great Britain and Ireland last won the Ryder Cup against the Americans without recourse to reinforcements from Europe. It was in 1953 that Welshman Dai Rees led his team to that memorable victory. On the second day the British trailed by three matches to one, but they then won six of the eight singles to take the trophy. Even in defeat, the U.S. captain, Jackie Burke, recognized the true worth of Lindrick. "The course is a golfing paradise," Burke said. "The turf is perfect and the greens flawless."

The most famous hole at Lindrick is the 4th. This challenging hole also has a colorful history. At one time, before the county boundaries were changed, the hole straddled the borders of Nottinghamshire, Derbyshire, and Yorkshire, and so was a popular spot for such illegal activities as cockfighting. To evade the police from any one county, the participants had only to step over the border and continue.

13 PAR 4 438 YARDS

14 PAR 5 557 YARDS

15 PAR 4 362 YARDS

PAR 5 486 YARDS 16

PAR 4 397 YARDS 17

18 PAR 3 206 YARDS

Practice area

Practice area

LINDRICK CHAMPIONSHIP COURSE

Clubhouse

17 **Bunkers in range**
Bunkers cluster around the green at the 397-yard 17th hole. A hook there can be disastrous, as Greg Norman found out when he took a 14 at the hole during the Martini International in 1982.

18 **Confident approach** (below)
The 18th is the second of the Lindrick holes to have undergone a change from the original layout. It is a testing 206-yard short hole that demands a solid shot to carry across bunkers to a double-tiered green. All the greens at Lindrick are very fine putting surfaces.

MARIYA

MARIYA COUNTRY CLUB, KISARAZU, CHIBA, JAPAN

THE MAGNIFICENT COURSE of the Mariya Country Club in Japan bears the unmistakable hallmark of America's most controversial course architect, Pete Dye. One look at the rolling, hillock-strewn landscape of the course, coupled with an island green propped up by railroad ties, leaves the onlooker in no doubt that Dye has been at work. As with all of this master architect's work, there is more than enough challenge at Mariya for anyone. From the back tees the course offers a fiercely demanding test of more than 7,000 yards. Water has a part to play on nine of the course's holes.

10 Short par 5
A long drive might get a player on in two at the 10th green, which is defended by bunkers. The most dangerous is shored up by railroad ties.

12 PAR 4 365 YARDS

11 PAR 3 190 YARDS

10 PAR 5 492 YARDS

14 PAR 5 541 YARDS

16 PAR 4 423 YARDS

13 PAR 4 462 YARDS

17 PAR 3 193 YARDS

Clubhouse

18 PAR 4 369 YARDS

15 PAR 4 463 YARDS

9 PAR 4 443 YARDS

7 PAR 5 534 YARDS

8 PAR 4 454 YARDS

12 On target
Length is not the problem on the 365-yard 12th; accuracy is the key to the hole. It takes the deftest of tee shots, into a small landing area guarded by a nest of bunkers, to achieve success. The approach only requires a short iron, but much care.

CHAMPIONSHIP LENGTHS

OUT	3,513 YARDS	PAR 36
IN	3,498 YARDS	PAR 36
TOTAL	7,011 YARDS	PAR 72

COURSE RECORD

NO OFFICIAL RECORD

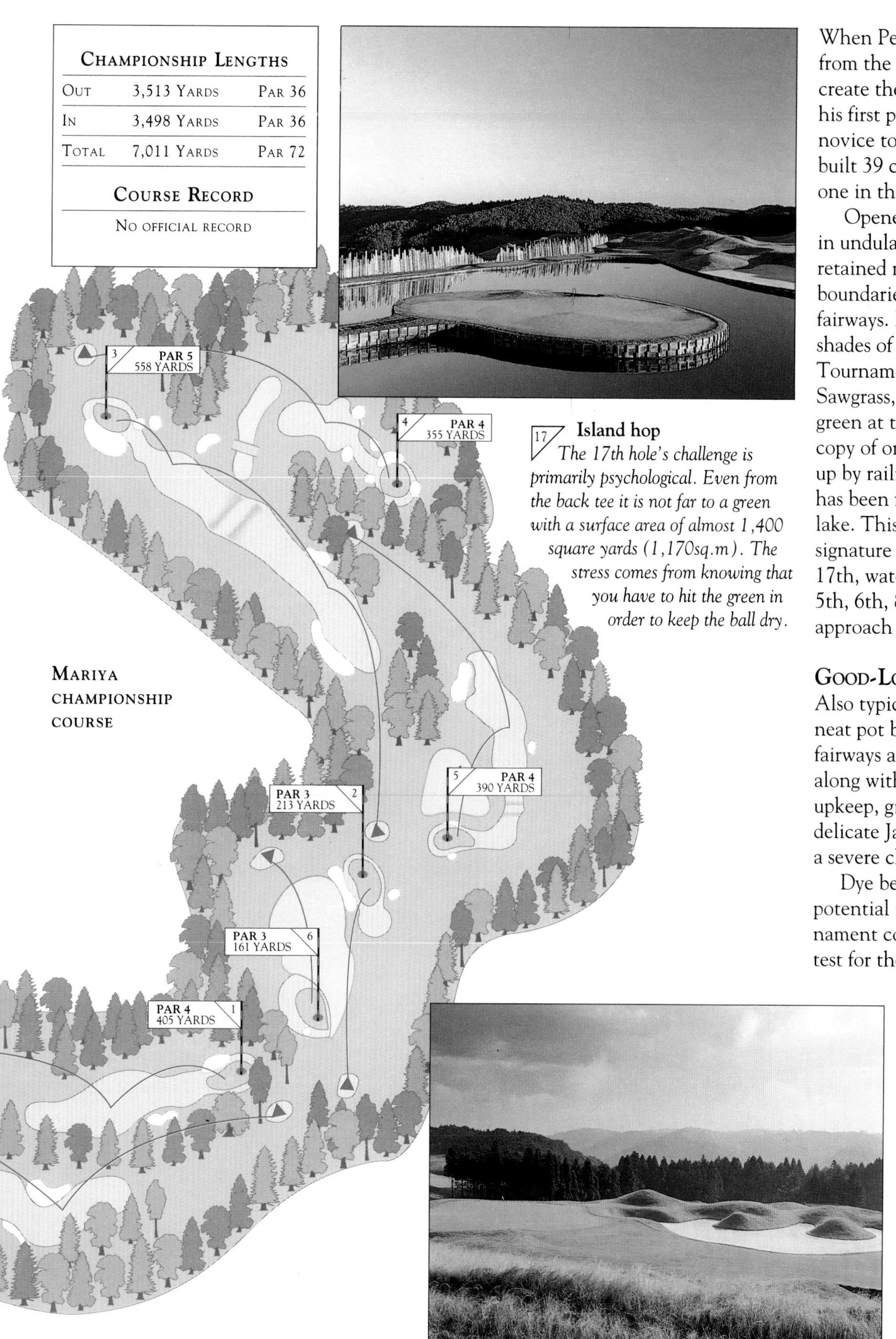

MARIYA CHAMPIONSHIP COURSE

17 **Island hop**
The 17th hole's challenge is primarily psychological. Even from the back tee it is not far to a green with a surface area of almost 1,400 square yards (1,170sq.m). The stress comes from knowing that you have to hit the green in order to keep the ball dry.

When Pete Dye accepted a commission from the giant Mariya Group of Japan to create the Country Club course, it was his first project in Japan. But he was no novice to the trade, as he had already built 39 courses in the United States and one in the Dominican Republic.

Opened in 1987, the course is set in undulating forested country. Dye has retained many of the trees, which act as boundaries to the beautifully maintained fairways. In the Mariya layout there are shades of Dye's earlier work for the Tournament Players Club course at Sawgrass, Florida. The spectacular island green at the 17th is virtually a carbon-copy of one at the Florida course. Shored up by railroad ties, the green looks as if it has been floated out into the middle of a lake. This feature has become the signature of a Dye course. As well as the 17th, water guards the greens of the 2nd, 5th, 6th, 8th, and 13th, and threatens approach shots on the 4th, 9th, and 18th.

GOOD-LOOKING BUT TOUGH

Also typical of Dye designs are Mariya's neat pot bunkers and undulations on both fairways and greens. These Dye hallmarks, along with the exquisite care taken over upkeep, give the course the feel of a delicate Japanese garden. It is nevertheless a severe challenge to the player.

Dye believes the Mariya course has the potential to become Japan's "finest tournament course," while still offering a fair test for the club's exclusive membership.

The course won instant recognition in Japan when Jack Nicklaus and Jumbo Ozaki played a televised pro-celebrity challenge match there in October, 1989.

9 **Tight landing**
The 9th hole might appear a relatively straightforward par 4, but the landing area for the drive is tight, with threatening bunkers lying along the right-hand side of the fairway. A huge bunker short and to the right of the green constitutes a major hazard and must be avoided at all costs.

MEDINAH

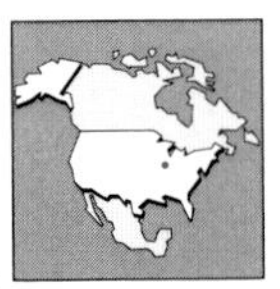

MEDINAH COUNTRY CLUB, MEDINAH, CHICAGO, ILLINOIS, U.S.A.

THE GOLF CLUB at Medinah, in the suburbs of Chicago, is an unusual place by any standards. Built in the 1920s as a private club for the Ancient Arabic Order of Nobles of the Mystic Shrine – popularly known as the Shriners – its clubhouse is a mock-Moorish, temple-like building with a huge dome. But if the clubhouse is lacking in traditional golfing atmosphere, the Number 3 course more than compensates. The course has hosted three U.S. Opens since 1949, the most recent in 1990, and many players place it at the top of the "difficulty" list for the country's foremost professional championship.

17 **Over the lake** *Like the 12th at Augusta, the par-3 17th at Medinah is a critical factor in victory or defeat. At a length of 168 yards, it is played from a raised tee down to a narrow green, mostly over water. Whereas Rae's Creek guards the 12th green at Augusta, Medinah's 17th has to carry Lake Kadijah, named after the Prophet Mohammed's wife.*

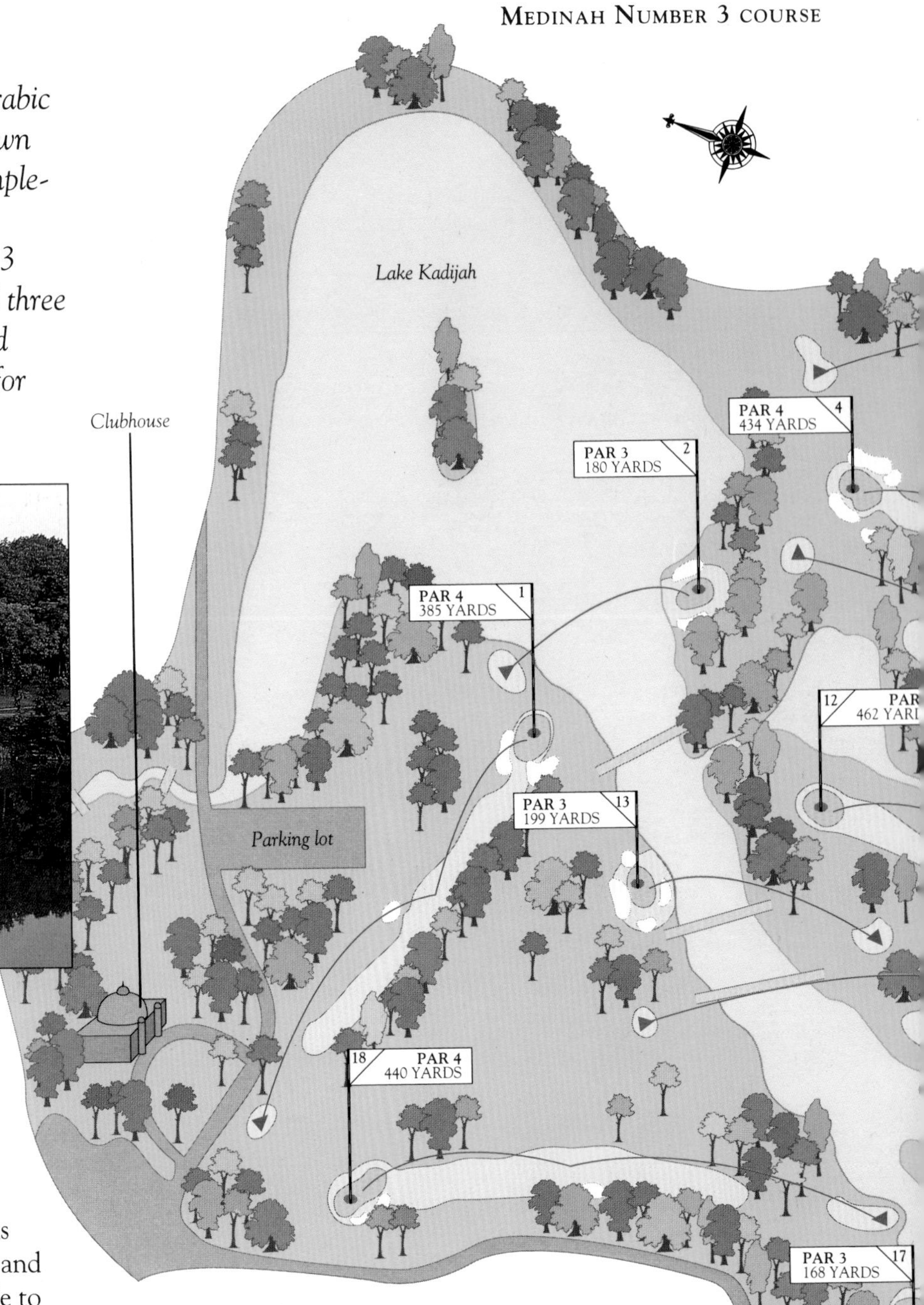

Medinah's Number 3 course was originally designed by Tom Bendelow, an expatriate Scotsman. He intended it for women's golf, but it was considered too difficult and was soon handed over to the men. Bendelow had a dubious reputation as a golf-course designer and many changes have since been made to his course to bring it up to standard.

After Harry Cooper shot 63 on his way to winning the 1930 Medinah Open, five new holes were laid out, and the course was again much altered before the U.S. Open was first played there in 1949. Cary Middlecoff won the championship that year with a score of 286.

It was not until 1975 that the U.S. Open returned to Medinah. In preparation for that championship, Tom Fazio, who a quarter of a century earlier had been beaten in a three-way play-off for the title, was called in to make changes. Par was reduced by one stroke to 71. Lou Graham beat John Mahaffey in the play-off.

MEDINAH NUMBER 3 COURSE

Lake Kadijah
Clubhouse
Parking lot
PAR 4 385 YARDS 1
PAR 3 180 YARDS 2
PAR 4 434 YARDS 4
12 PAR 462 YARDS
PAR 3 199 YARDS 13
18 PAR 4 440 YARDS
PAR 3 168 YARDS 17

16 The sharpest dogleg

Originally the 13th hole, before the USGA made various changes to the back nine prior to the 1990 U.S. Open, Medinah's 16th is a notorious dogleg left. Heavy trees on both sides of the fairway add to the other hazards, which include a very small, elevated green. Two bunkers lie in wait short of the green to the sides, with another behind.

Championship Lengths		
Out	3,582 Yards	Par 36
In	3,613 Yards	Par 36
Total	7,195 Yards	Par 72

Course Record

66 S. Simpson, T. Simpson, J. Sluman, U.S. Open 1990; R. Price 1990

U.S. Open Champions

1949 Cary Middlecoff; 1975 Lou Graham; 1990 Hale Irwin

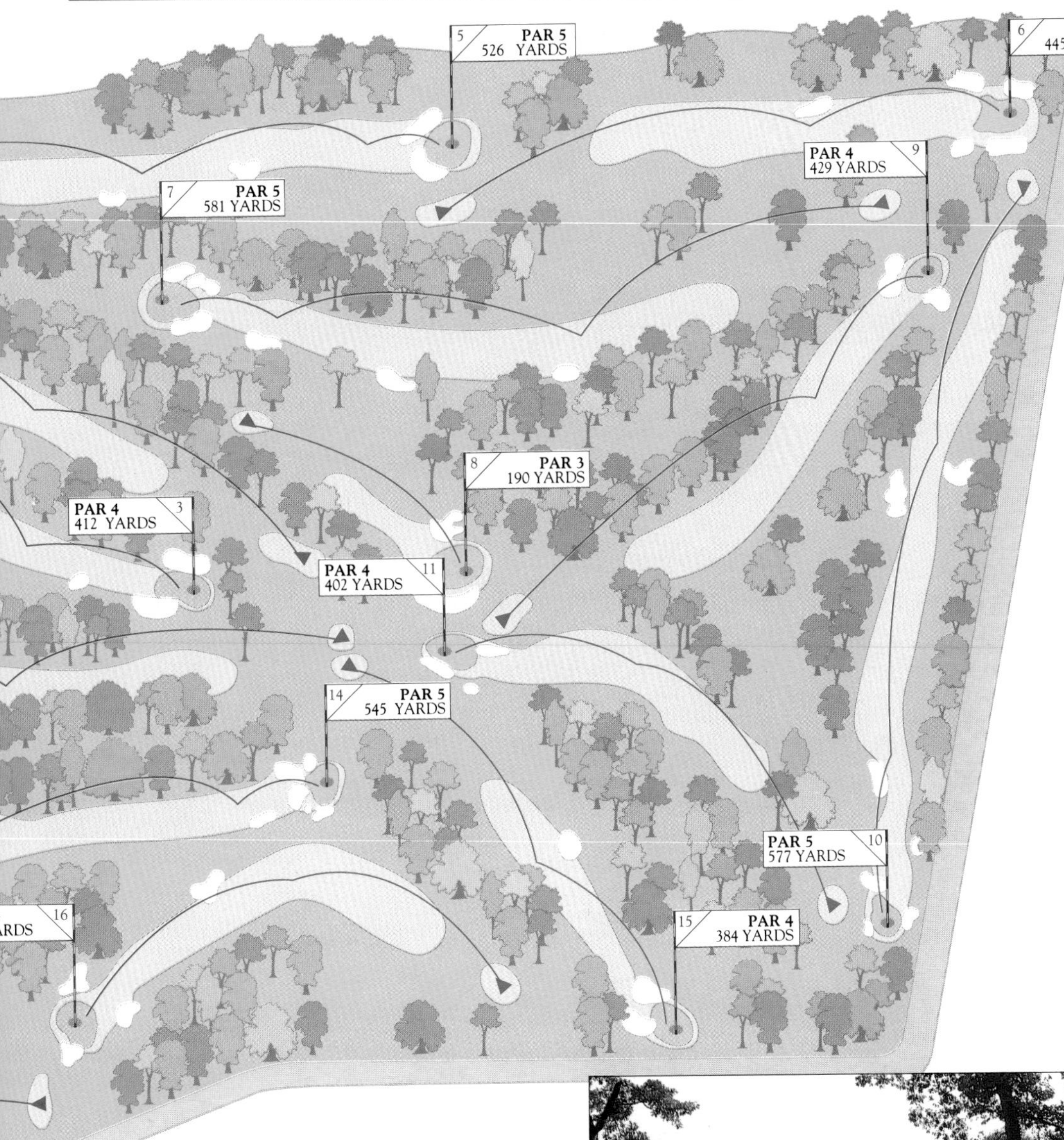

For the 1990 Open, the USGA, in collaboration with the Medinah Club, contrived to make the course even tougher. Two new holes were added to the course, another hole was lengthened, and the back nine holes were extensively rerouted. Fazio's par of 71 was raised to 72 again, and the redesigned course measured a formidable 7,195 yards, the longest ever test set for the U.S. Open.

Memorable Open

Before the 1990 championship began, the greens were honed until they were wickedly fast, like polished marble. But nobody could control the weather, and by the time the championship was under way the greens had been drenched by a thunderstorm that took much of the sting out of them. The result was a leading score of 280, seven strokes better than Lou Graham's tie with John Mahaffey in 1975 and six better than that achieved by Cary Middlecoff in 1949.

Hale Irwin carried off the title after a thrilling contest. Irwin holed a massive 45 ft. (13.5m) putt on the last green – the ball ran for seven seconds before falling into the cup – to enter a play-off with Mike Donald. The following day, he sank a 6 ft. (1.8m) birdie putt at the 16th to tie again with Donald, and then holed an 8 ft. (2.4m) putt for a birdie on the first sudden-death hole to win. At 45, Irwin became the oldest winner in U.S. Open history, and he was the first champion to have gone 91 holes for victory.

13 Lovely but deadly

The famous par-3 13th is another hole that crosses the long inlet from Lake Kadijah. The beauty of the landscape should not lure golfers into a false sense of security: the green is hard to hold and great accuracy is needed to negotiate the water and avoid the encircling bunkers.

MERION

MERION GOLF CLUB, ARDMORE, PHILADELPHIA, PENNSYLVANIA, U.S.A.

THE EAST COURSE at Merion was designed by Hugh Wilson, an expatriate Scot, despite the fact that he had never previously laid out a golf course. Wilson received his commission after revealing an unexpected grasp of the principles behind course design while acting as a member of his club committee researching championship courses.

Novel markers
The wicker baskets that are used to cap the pins at Merion are a unique feature of the course.

Golf at Merion was originally run by the Merion Cricket Club, which had been founded in 1865, just after the end of the Civil War. When golf took hold in the United States in the late nineteenth century, the club members adopted the game with relish. They leased a 100-acre plot in nearby Haverford, and here a nine-hole course was opened for play in 1896. In 1900 this was expanded to 18 holes on adjacent land loaned by Clement A. Griscomb. The club hosted the U.S. Women's Amateur Championship on the Haverford course in 1904, and again in 1909. But it was then decided that the course was too short to satisfy the growing demands of championship golf. The club acquired new land in Ardmore, a fashionable Philadelphia suburb, while Hugh Wilson and his committee set out to study classic courses. They visited The National Golf Links of America several times, and Wilson spent six months in Britain. When he returned from his fact-finding mission, he brought with him several unusual ideas for the new course at Merion. Among them was the use of wicker baskets instead of flags on the pins, which is now one of Merion's hallmarks. The baskets are supposed to have the advantage that, unlike flags, they do not reveal the wind direction.

Bobby's success
A plaque at Merion's 11th tee commemorates Bobby Jones's completion of the "Impregnable Quadrilateral" – victories in both Amateur and Open Championships on both sides of the Atlantic in one year. He then retired from competition golf.

The ground that the club had acquired for Wilson's new layout was hardly ideal. It was covered in trees and shrubs, and there was an old stone quarry, which had been out of use for many years. But Wilson clearly had a natural gift and feel for golf-course architecture – no doubt a product of his Scottish background. He transformed the unlikely property into a magnificent course: a masterpiece of parkland golf that is now recognized as one of America's finest courses. The East course was opened for play in 1912, and since then it has hosted no fewer than 13 USGA championships – more than any other course in the United States and a glowing tribute to its quality. Sadly, Wilson died at the age of 46, not long after completing the course.

White faces (right)
The bunkers at Merion were dubbed "the white faces" by Chick Evans, who won the U.S. Amateur Championship there in 1916.

Water course (above)
The narrow streams that weave their way around Merion prove an unforgiving grave for any errant shot.

UNUSUALLY SHORT

The restricted confines of the East course – a mere 110 acres – are reflected in Wilson's design, which features tight greens, a modest total of 120 bunkers, and a par-70 length of 6,482 yards. This makes it one of the shortest courses on the USGA's championship schedule. Set up at that length for the 1971 U.S. Open, it was the second-shortest course used for the event since the First World War.

But although the East course is of modest length, it does have two par 5s. These two holes, which alone account for a good percentage of the total course length, are in the first four holes. The 2nd

Hogan iron (below)
The USGA museum displays the 1-iron Ben Hogan used for his long second shot at the 18th during the 1950 Open at Merion.

is a 536-yard hole, played uphill alongside Ardmore Avenue, which runs through the course and has to be crossed twice. The second par 5 is the 4th, which stretches a massive but rather unspectacular 600 yards. A stream relieves the otherwise plain aspect of the hole. It runs in front of the green and makes it almost impossible to reach in two strokes.

The bunkers and the small fast greens are the key to the Merion defenses, and Wilson did a masterful job with both. Typical is the 8th hole, which, although only 360 yards, is one of the toughest par 4s to be found anywhere. A large bunker down the right-hand side threatens the short hitter, while the longer hitter has to watch out for a dangerous bunker that eats into the fairway on the left.

Hogan's Comeback

Merion's East course was where Ben Hogan made the most incredible comeback in golfing history. He won the 1950 U.S. Open just over a year after the terrible car crash that all but took his life. Hogan was still in great pain, and both his legs were bandaged throughout. As he started the final nine holes, he was gripped by terrible cramp in his left leg and almost had to retire. When he reached the 13th, close to the clubhouse, the pain was almost more than he could bear. Despite this he valiantly played on and fought his way into the play-off with Lloyd Mangrum and George Fazio. His second shot with a 1-iron at the last hole of the last round is still remembered, and the club is displayed in the USGA museum at Far Hills, New Jersey. Hogan won comfortably in the play-off the following day.

Another legendary player, Bobby Jones, led the field after the first round of his first U.S. Amateur Championship at Merion in 1916, at the tender age of 14. But when Jones reached the short par-3 6th hole on the West course in the second round, he was faced with a 30 ft. (10m) downhill putt from behind the pin. He putted right off the green and into the stream in front of it. Shattered, he ended the round with a score of 89. Jones went back to Merion, however, to win the first of his five Amateur titles in 1924, and six years later, returning yet again, he won a historic victory over Eugene Holmes by 8-and-7 in the final of the 1930 Amateur to complete his unrepeatable Grand Slam.

Championship Lengths

Out	3,420 Yards	Par 36
In	3,062 Yards	Par 34
Total	6,482 Yards	Par 70

Course Record

64 Lee Mackey, U.S. Open 1950

U.S. Open Champions at Merion

1934 Olin Dutra; 1950 Ben Hogan; 1971 Lee Trevino; 1981 David Graham

1 **Challenging opening** (above)
The 362-yard 1st has a dogleg to the right and severe bunkering, which makes it one of the toughest holes on the course. The second shot, although short, must be extremely accurate to a green that has a wide option of pin placements.

11 **Frustration point** (right)
In the 1934 U.S. Open, the unfortunate Bobby Cruikshank threw his iron into the air after a poor shot had landed in the stream at the 11th. The club fell and struck him on the head, knocking him to the ground. Fortunately he was not seriously hurt.

18 **Final green**
On this 463-yard finishing hole, only a good drive will carry over the crown of the hill, through an opening between trees. From there a solid shot with a long club is required to get up to and hold the green, which is trapped on both sides by bunkers.

13 **Easy three**
The view from the 13th tee is of the shortest hole and the easiest par 3. The small green is saucer-shaped, sloping toward the center. It is surrounded by five bunkers, including a dangerous, high-lipped one at the front.

MUIRFIELD

THE HONOURABLE COMPANY OF EDINBURGH GOLFERS, MUIRFIELD, GULLANE, EAST LOTHIAN, SCOTLAND

THERE ARE MANY *who believe that Muirfield is the fairest examination of golf among all Scotland's great championship courses. There are no hidden bunkers or subtle humps, no blind shots, few trees, and no water hazards. Muirfield is a scrupulously honest but demanding test where the dangers are in open view for all to see.*

Drum call
In early years, drummers announced the annual competition for the Silver Club, given by the City of Edinburgh to the Honourable Company of Edinburgh Golfers when it was founded in 1744. The first winner, John Rattray, was declared Captain of the Golf.

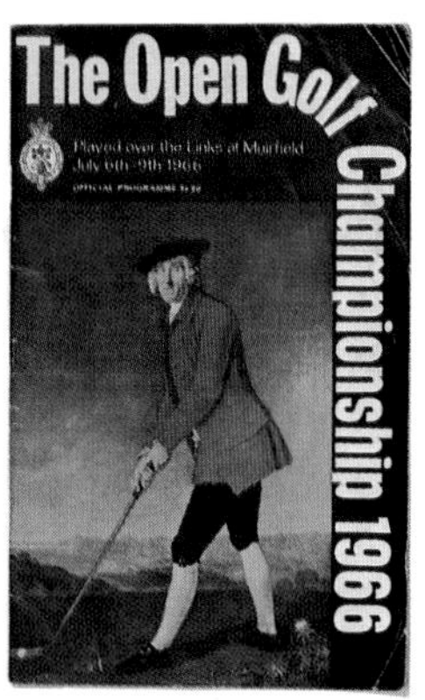

Pioneering golfer
To emphasize its long golfing traditions, the Honourable Company of Edinburgh Golfers depicted its 1771 club captain, William St. Clair of Roslin, on the program for the 1966 British Open at Muirfield.

The mighty Jack Nicklaus paid Muirfield the ultimate compliment by giving the name of Muirfield Village to his own course in Dublin, Ohio, out of respect for the golf course where he won his first British Open in 1966. He is not alone among the great players who consider Muirfield exceptional.

The course was built in 1891, which is relatively recent in comparison with the antiquity of the club itself. The Honourable Company was formed in 1744, when "several Gentlemen of Honour skilful in the ancient and healthful exercise of Golf" petitioned the Edinburgh City Council to donate a silver club for their annual competition on Leith links.

EARLIEST RULES

There were then only five holes, and the members had to share the ground with the local citizens and occasionally the military. The Company established the first rules of the game in the year of their formation, ten years before the Royal & Ancient Golf Club of St. Andrews was founded.

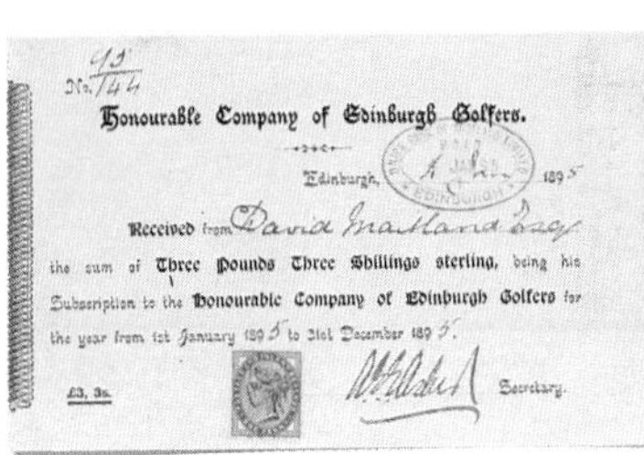
No. 93/144

Honourable Company of Edinburgh Golfers.

Edinburgh, 1895

Received from David Maitland Esq.

the sum of Three Pounds Three Shillings sterling, being his Subscription to the Honourable Company of Edinburgh Golfers for the year from 1st January 1895 to 31st December 1895.

£3, 3s. [signature] Secretary.

Golfing elite
This subscription receipt for the Honourable Company dates from 1895. Membership has always been exclusive.

In 1836, when the Leith links became too populated for the Company to continue to play there happily, it moved to Musselburgh, 6 miles (10km) east along the coast, to share the course there with the Musselburgh Golf Club.

With the passage of time, Musselburgh in turn became too crowded, so the Honourable Company made another move east – this time to Gullane, where the present course, laid out by Old Tom Morris, was opened for play in 1891. The following year, on the new course, the British Open was played over 72 holes for the first time. It was won by the English amateur Harold Hilton.

There was some resentment that the Honourable Company had taken the British Open with it when moving from Musselburgh to Gullane, and the course was also criticized by some players as being too short and too easy.

Since those days, however, Muirfield has evolved into one of the world's outstanding courses. The present layout owes much to the changes made by Harry Colt, designer of the New course at Sunningdale, and Tom Simpson in the mid-1920s.

Unlike the great links of St. Andrews and Carnoustie, Muirfield is in no way a public course. The home of the Honourable Company is a private place indeed, where the members play on uncrowded

Open vistas (right)
Lying on the southern shores of the Forth, Muirfield enjoys a fine natural setting. Not everyone appreciated the new course in the 1890s; Andrew Kirkaldy, the St. Andrews professional, even described it as "an old water meadow."

Tricky traps (below)
Muirfield has more than 160 bunkers, many of them with walls of turf sod.

Championship Lengths

Out	3,511 Yards	Par 36
In	3,415 Yards	Par 35
Total	6,926 Yards	Par 71

Course Record

64 Rodger Davies, The Open 1987

Open Champions at Muirfield

1892 Harold Hilton †; 1896 Harry Vardon; 1901 James Braid; 1906 James Braid; 1912 Ted Ray; 1929 Walter Hagen; 1935 Alf Perry; 1948 Henry Cotton; 1959 Gary Player; 1966 Jack Nicklaus; 1972 Lee Trevino; 1980 Tom Watson; 1987 Nick Faldo

17 Fearsome bunkers *The 542-yard 17th at Muirfield is one of three magnificent long holes. Guarded by a string of deep bunkers down the left side, it demands a precise drive. After the dogleg there is rough ground with five more bunkers. The green is surrounded by harsh rough.*

fairways and where the great traditions of the game are jealously guarded. It has remained a regular venue for the British Open over the years.

Of many memorable Opens at Muirfield, the 1972 confrontation between Lee Trevino and Tony Jacklin had perhaps the most dramatic finish. The two men were even when Trevino's fourth shot at the par-5 17th ran through the green and into the short rough. With Jacklin well placed for a par or birdie, Trevino thought he had lost. But when he chipped back on to the putting surface, the ball landed softly and ran into the hole. Clearly shaken, Jacklin three-putted and Trevino went on to take the title.

Muirfield Championship Course

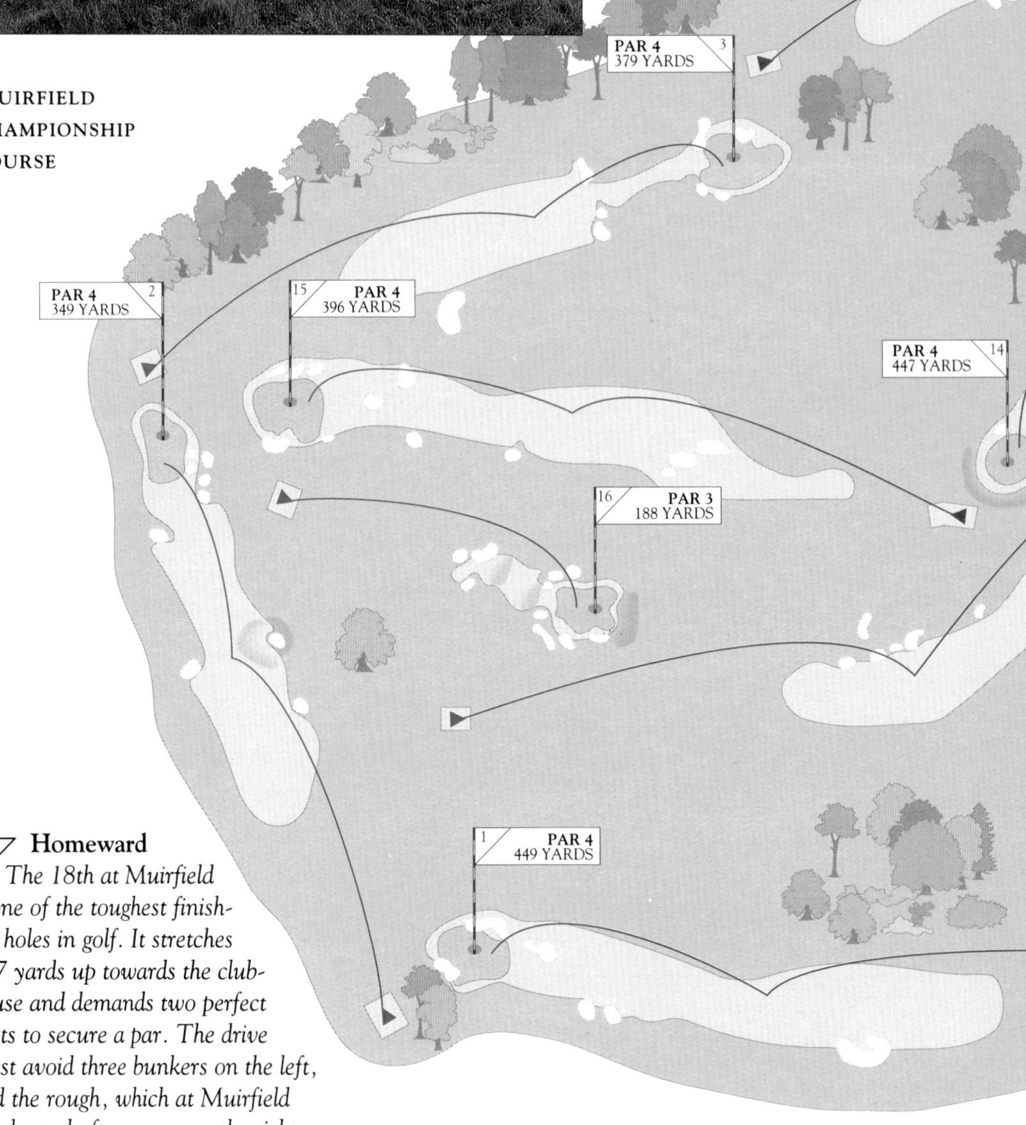

18 Homeward *The 18th at Muirfield is one of the toughest finishing holes in golf. It stretches 447 yards up towards the clubhouse and demands two perfect shots to secure a par. The drive must avoid three bunkers on the left, and the rough, which at Muirfield can be truly fearsome, on the right.*

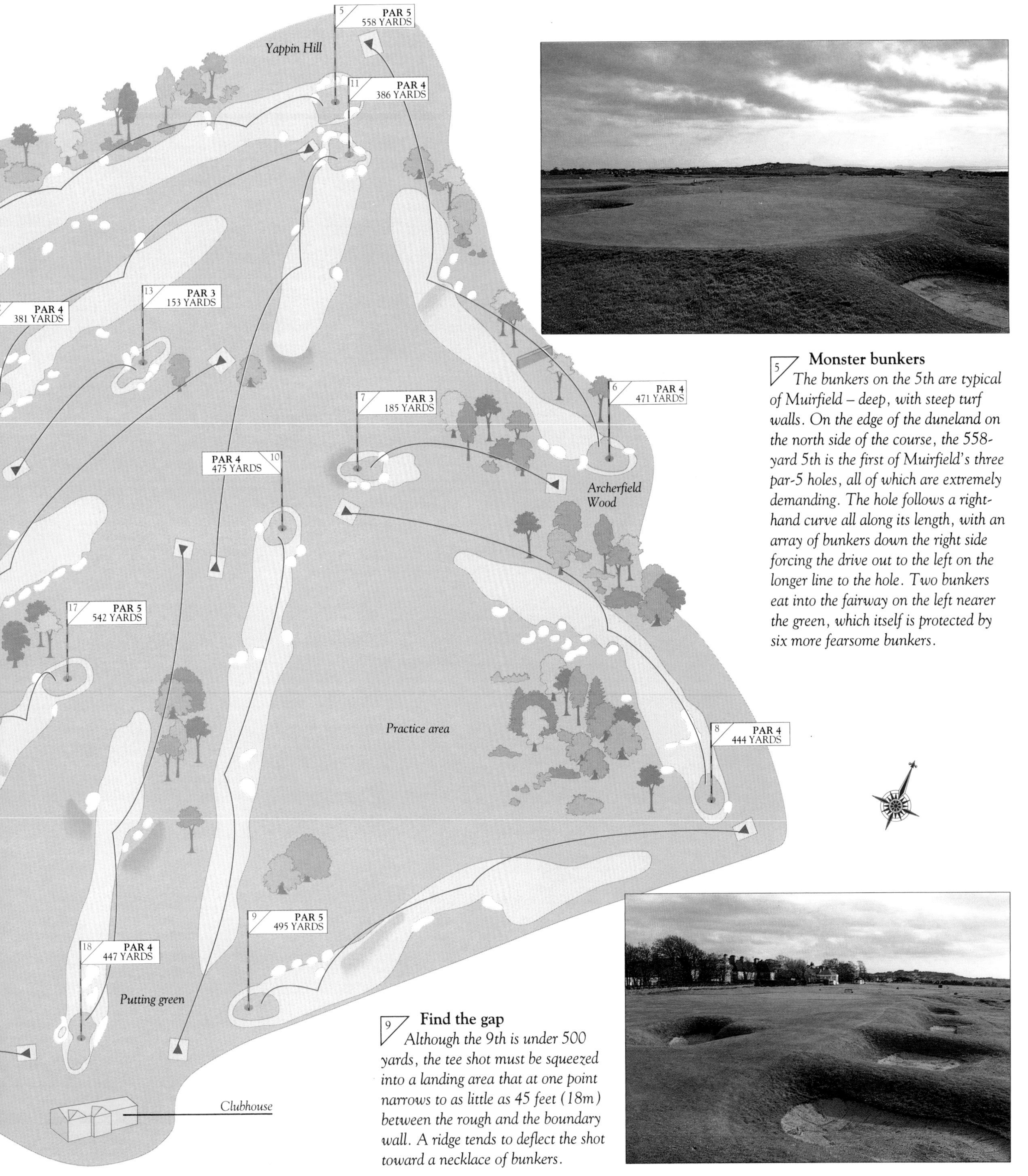

5 Monster bunkers

The bunkers on the 5th are typical of Muirfield – deep, with steep turf walls. On the edge of the duneland on the north side of the course, the 558-yard 5th is the first of Muirfield's three par-5 holes, all of which are extremely demanding. The hole follows a right-hand curve all along its length, with an array of bunkers down the right side forcing the drive out to the left on the longer line to the hole. Two bunkers eat into the fairway on the left nearer the green, which itself is protected by six more fearsome bunkers.

9 Find the gap

Although the 9th is under 500 yards, the tee shot must be squeezed into a landing area that at one point narrows to as little as 45 feet (18m) between the rough and the boundary wall. A ridge tends to deflect the shot toward a necklace of bunkers.

MUIRFIELD VILLAGE

MUIRFIELD VILLAGE GOLF CLUB, DUBLIN, COLUMBUS, OHIO, U.S.A.

WHEN JACK NICKLAUS, the greatest player in the modern game, decided he wanted to build a course of his own, he called it Muirfield Village out of nostalgia for the Scottish links where he had won the first of his three British Opens. But the seed for the idea was sown at that other shrine where he had stamped his mark in the course of his fabulous career – Augusta National.

Trophy emblem
The crest of Muirfield Village encompasses a silhouette of the claret jug that serves as the British Open trophy.

It was at Augusta in 1966, while sitting on the veranda chatting with a friend, that Nicklaus first suggested the idea of building a course in his native town of Columbus, Ohio, to the same standard as the home of the U.S. Masters. Nicklaus won the Masters that year and went on to triumph in the British Open at Muirfield three months later. The idea that he had first proposed on the veranda in Georgia was then given its name.

NO RESEMBLANCE

In fact, lest anyone should be under any misapprehension, the course that Jack Nicklaus built at Muirfield Village bears no resemblance whatsoever to the home of the Honourable Company of Edinburgh Golfers at Muirfield in Scotland. Nicklaus chose for his dream course a piece of steeply rolling ground into which he built a vast array of water hazards, in keeping with contemporary thinking in golf architecture. It could not be more different from the old links of Muirfield, where what water there is runs in the burns and even the Firth of Forth is mostly hidden from view by dunes.

Many people, including his then manager, Mark McCormack, thought Nicklaus was foolish to take his concept to unfashionable Columbus. McCormack said it would be like "standing on the street corner and burning $100 bills" and urged him to rethink the whole affair. But Jack knew exactly what he wanted. He ignored the warnings and eventually overcame the many difficulties that confronted him, including problems with obtaining the financing.

When Nicklaus had raised enough money to go ahead, he brought in fellow designers Pete Dye and Desmond Muirhead to advise him, and set about building a course that would test the best players in the world and yet be "playable" for lesser mortals. Another important consideration was to provide an element that previously had played little part in the thinking of course designers – vantage points for spectators. Muirfield Village was to be in the vanguard of the so-called

Memorial (above)
The Memorial Tournament was so named because Jack Nicklaus wanted to honor an outstanding player each year for his contribution to the game. A bronze of the player is placed in the Memorial Garden at Muirfield Village to mark the event.

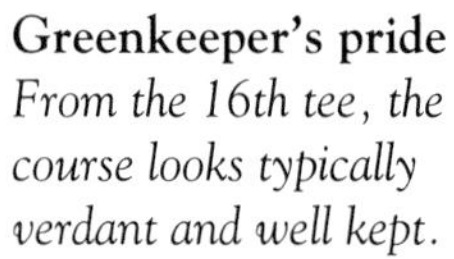

Greenkeeper's pride
From the 16th tee, the course looks typically verdant and well kept.

Good looking (right)
There is plenty of space around the lush, beautifully manicured turf of Muirfield Village. This makes the course ideal for spectators who have plenty of access and can see events well.

Jack of all trades (left)
Putter in hand, Nicklaus ponders the borrow on a green. Muirfield Village greens are famous for their speed and their superb condition.

"stadium" style of golf course, which is designed almost as much for viewing the game as for playing it.

Nicklaus has gone to immense lengths to produce a truly outstanding course. Over the years Muirfield Village has undergone more than 100 changes, some major and some a matter of detail. Money has been no object for "The Course that Jack Built."

The prestigious Memorial Tournament, Muirfield Village's annual U.S. Tour event, was first played there in 1976, when it was won by Roger Maltbie in a play-off. For that opening event the course measured 7,027 yards and it was lengthened to 7,101 for the next three years. Since then it has been consistently over 7,100 yards, making it one of the toughest tests on the Tour.

Downhill Drive

It was the late Sir Henry Cotton who once said that there was no more satisfying thing in golf than to stand on an elevated tee with a driver, surveying the fairway stretching below and into the distance. Nicklaus is clearly also a subscriber to this view. On the first five holes of the Muirfield Village course the drive is from an elevated tee, and there are several more examples on the way round the course. There are no tee shots played

11 **Splashing out**
When Nicklaus played the long par-5 11th in its original design, it had a lake in front of the green. Jack did not like the fact that the lake was invisible from the drive landing area, so he ordered a small stream to be sited in its place. Among the more expensive changes to the course, this improvement alone cost close to $250,000.

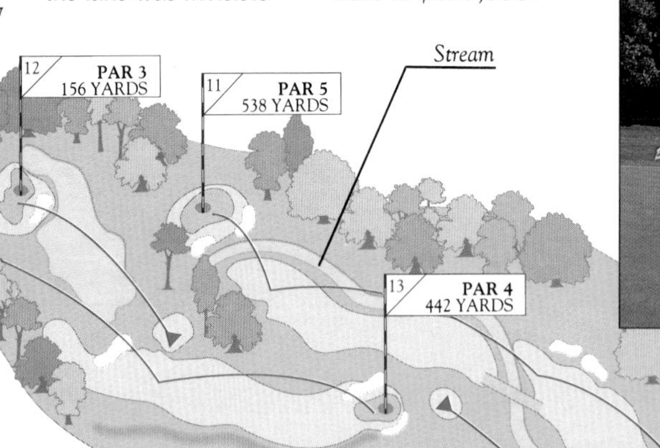

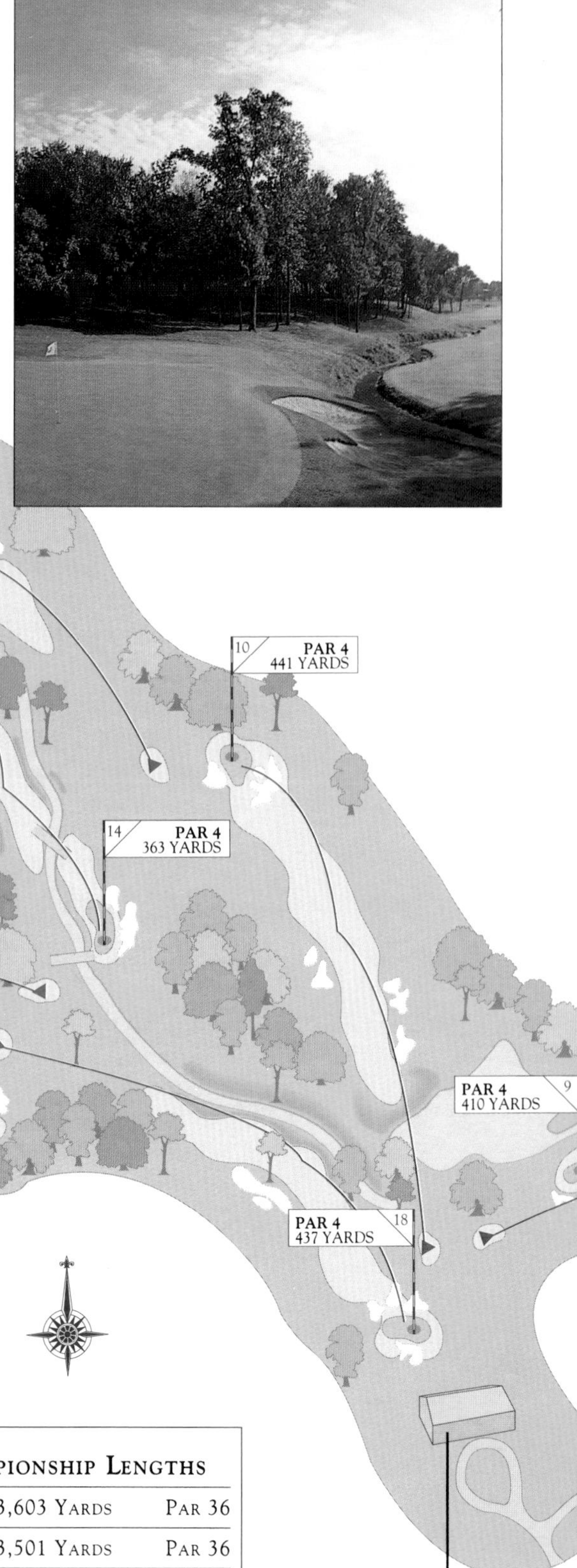

Muirfield Village championship course

12 **Water hole**
There are shades of that most magnificent of Augusta holes, the 16th, in Nicklaus's 12th hole at Muirfield Village. There is water to be carried all the way to a green that has been built into a beautiful setting in the side of a hill and is guarded both front and back by bunkers.

Championship Lengths

Out	3,603 Yards	Par 36
In	3,501 Yards	Par 36
Total	7,104 Yards	Par 72

Course Record

64 M. McCumber, C. Byrum, S. Hoch, H. Sutton, F. Couples, C. Strange

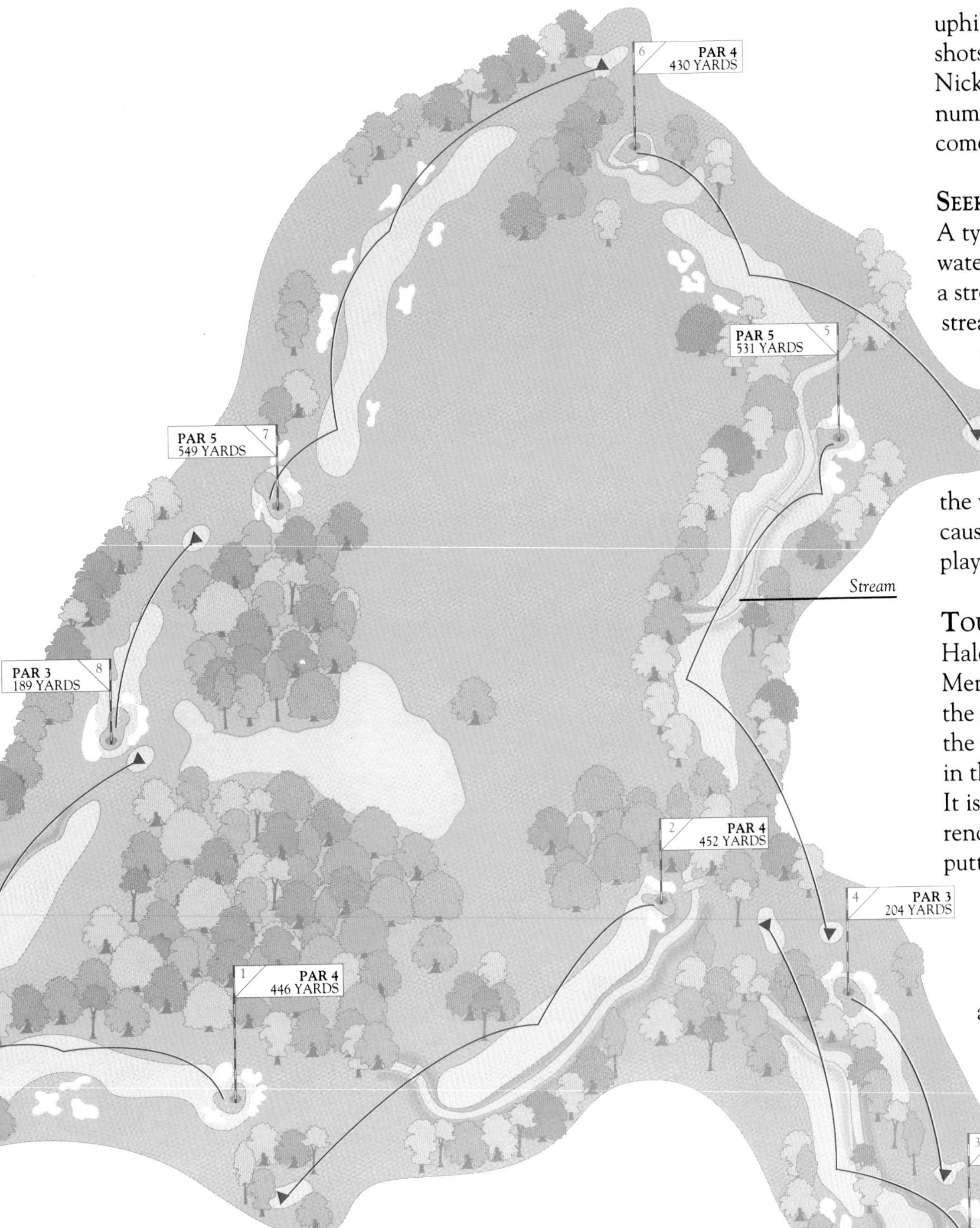

uphill. Indeed, there are only two uphill shots of any kind on the entire course. Nicklaus has confined himself to a modest number of bunkers, 70 in all, but water comes into play on 11 of the holes.

Seeking Dry Land

A typical example of Nicklaus's use of water is at the 3rd, where the drive is over a stream that crosses the fairway. The stream then runs down the entire left side of the fairway to open out into a lake immediately in front of the green. The hole is just short of 400 yards long and the second shot to a two-tier green over the water is extremely demanding. It has caused many problems both to the great players and to more humble golfers.

Tough Greens

Hale Irwin, a two-time winner of the Memorial Tournament, once described the greens at Muirfield Village as "some of the most beautiful and well-conditioned in the world – and some of the toughest." It is hardly surprising that Nicklaus, renowned as one of the game's greatest putters, should excel at green design.

Much thought has gone into the siting of the teeing areas, in line with Nicklaus's intention to create a course suitable for those of modest ability as well as for tournament players. There are three separate tees at each hole, some of them as much as 50 yards apart. This has almost the effect of creating three separate courses, with different problems set in each one. Few golfers will have the confidence to tackle the course from the back tees, as it is certainly not a circuit for the faint of heart. Yet from the members' tees there is charm and challenge for the most modest players.

With an apparently limitless budget lavished on maintenance, there are few courses in the world that are better to look at than Muirfield Village. It is a delight for spectators and players alike.

5 Stream in the center

The 5th hole is the first of four par 5s. It is a dogleg to the right with water very much in play on the second half of the hole. A stream runs up the center of the fairway, threatening the second shot, before running away close to the front left of the green. Two bunkers menace the right of the green, as does one at the back.

THE NATIONAL

THE NATIONAL GOLF CLUB, WOODBRIDGE, ONTARIO, CANADA

GIL BLECHMAN'S DISILLUSIONMENT with the atmosphere of country-club life in the suburbs of Toronto drove this soft-spoken American manufacturer, living in Canada, to form what he described as "a real golf club" in 1972. Tom Fazio was employed to realize the Blechman dream in Ontario, and today The National Golf Club is the top-rated course in Canada.

Leaf logo
The crest of The National is a simple contemporary design showing the leaf of the red maple, a tree that has been an emblem of Canada since the nineteenth century.

Blechman's concept of the new course was clear and stunningly ambitious: "What I wanted was a course you could play the U.S. Open on at a week's notice without gimmicking it up," he said.

When Blechman called designer Tom Fazio to give him the contract, his instructions were simple. He told the designer he wanted the best golf course in the world, the project was to start immediately, and money was no object. Fazio's first reaction was to dismiss it as a crank call. But in the space of a few months the Blechman dream was well on its way to becoming a reality.

THE RIGHT PLACE

The site chosen for The National was a previously existing course called Pine Valley. It bore little resemblance to its splendid namesake in New Jersey, where Fazio's uncle George, a former Canadian Open winner, had played for many years. In fact, The National might never have been built there had Fazio not discovered some additional ground bordering the course. He argued that the existing course was not worth spending a lot of money on, but that with the additional ground the site offered real possibilities. This extra land now forms a five-hole section of the course beginning at the 11th, which is acknowledged as the most difficult, and yet scenically spectacular, stretch of golf course in the country.

Blechman's golf course was built in 1973, the year after Blechman had formed The National Golf Club, and it was officially opened for play by its founder and owner in 1975. The actual construction of the course was completed in just over three months, however. The building

Fall glory (above)
In autumn, the many deciduous trees color the course a flaming red and gold. The winters can be tough in Canada, and the course is closed for five months in each year.

Wild water (right)
The view across the lake to the 18th green is typical of The National in its scenic splendor. The course abounds with wildlife; the water hazards are home to swans and geese.

New land, new holes
Five of the holes on the course, including the 11th, shown here, were built on extra land acquired by Blechman alongside the original Pine Valley golf course. Designer Tom Fazio considered this area essential to his plans for constructing the finest course in Canada.

Talented family
Tom Fazio (left), the architect of the course, is the nephew of the talented George Fazio (right), a winner of the Canadian Open. George, a prolific course designer, was a valued source of advice to his nephew during the building of The National.

schedule coincided with an early spring and 80 consecutive days of sunshine, a rare occurrence in such northern latitudes.

The National very much reflects Blechman's idea of a golf club. His antipathy to the stereotypic atmosphere of suburban country-club golf is easily felt; the emphasis is firmly on the game of golf rather than on other diversions.

Playing the National

There are 72 bunkers on the course, and water is a hazard on nine of the holes. Some of the holes can be fearsomely difficult, and even Fazio admits that the course is not meant to be played from the back tees on every hole.

The front nine is long and severely guarded by bunkers. Water comes into play on four of the holes, and because this half of the course is situated on the high ground, play is liable to be affected by the wind. There is great variety in these nine holes, with many changes in direction. The back nine is in a river valley more than 100 feet (30m) below the front nine. The holes are shorter and tighter, winding through a mass of pines.

Viewing areas for an estimated 50,000 spectators have been provided in the design, using the natural hillsides. After the official opening of The National, its quality was immediately recognized. The club's first director of golf, Al Balding, undertook an interesting exercise when an informal tournament for Toronto's top

16 **Dodge the bunkers**
Large bunkers distract the eye at the par-4 16th, but long hitters have a decided advantage from the tee. The second shot has to hold the green or it will finish in the back bunkers.

The National Championship Course

12 **Testing time**
Although not a long par 5, the 12th can be tricky. It is a narrow, snaking dogleg left, with drives hit too close to the left threatened by the stream. Drives right are menaced by a bunker. The second shot has to avoid a large bunker on the left, and the approach should clear the stream that comes around in front of the green.

amateur players was played on the new course. Balding asked all the competitors to write down what they thought was the best hole on the course, and he received 14 different answers. This great diversity of opinion was a great source of satisfaction for both the founder and the designer of The National.

But it was not all plain sailing for Blechman. He lost a considerable amount of money developing the club during the time when he was the owner. In 1987 he sold the course to the members, although he remained executive director for a further three years, responsible for supervising improvements to the course as it developed. This work has included changes to the 4th and 12th holes and a major renovation of the clubhouse.

Championship Lengths

Out	3,616 Yards	Par 36
In	3,373 Yards	Par 35
Total	6,989 Yards	Par 71

Course Record

67 Lee Trevino, Canadian PGA 1979

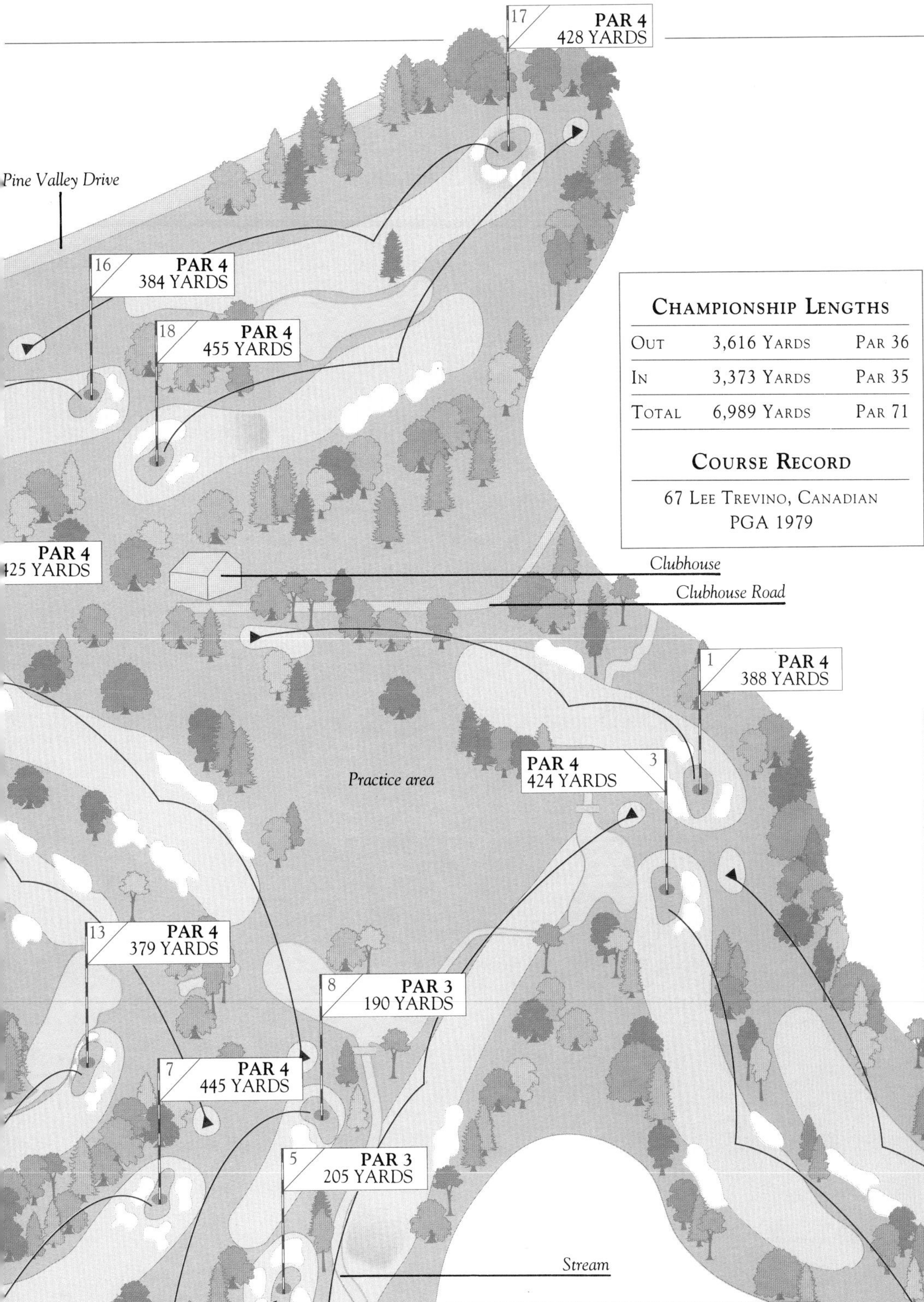

17 PAR 4 428 YARDS
Pine Valley Drive
16 PAR 4 384 YARDS
18 PAR 4 455 YARDS
PAR 4 425 YARDS
Clubhouse
Clubhouse Road
1 PAR 4 388 YARDS
Practice area
3 PAR 4 424 YARDS
13 PAR 4 379 YARDS
8 PAR 3 190 YARDS
7 PAR 4 445 YARDS
5 PAR 3 205 YARDS
2 PAR 4 427 YARDS
Stream
4 PAR 5 581 YARDS

13 **Make a splash**
Water comes into play all along the left side of the 13th hole, and any shots drifting left will end up lost in lakes or the creek that connects them. Bunkers on both sides of the green make accuracy with the second shot vital.

4 **Abundant trouble**
The green of the 4th, the longest of the par 5s, is guarded by some intricately shaped bunkers. Hazards abound: water threatens all three shots, and a large bunker lurks halfway up the fairway on the left.

OAKLAND HILLS

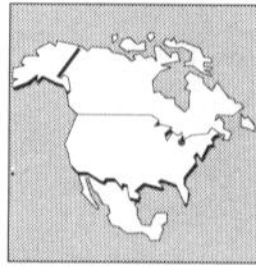

OAKLAND HILLS COUNTRY CLUB, BIRMINGHAM, MICHIGAN, U.S.A.

FOR THE 1951 U.S. Open, the USGA called in the eminent American golf-course architect Robert Trent Jones to make changes to the Oakland Hills course outside Detroit. This famous course had hosted the championship twice before, in 1924 and 1927, but it was felt that some modernization was needed to bring it into line with the developing game. Even the greatest players of the day were hardly prepared for Trent Jones's "alterations."

Oakland Hills was already a very fine course before Trent Jones started work on it. No less a personage than Donald Ross, the great pioneering course architect, had laid out the original course in 1917 on a perfect site which, he claimed, "the Lord had intended" for a golf course.

TEST FOR THE BEST

When Trent Jones presented the course for the 1951 U.S. Open, eyebrows were raised. The fairways were narrower, the rough was punishing, and there were well in excess of 100 bunkers, most of them deep and dangerous, to threaten fairway landing areas and greens alike.

The Jones strategy was to force the players to hit clearly defined but well-defended landing areas from the tee.

17 **Elevated green** (right)

After the challenge of the heavily landscaped 16th, a necklace of huge, gaping bunkers around the 17th green maintains the pressure. It makes the tee shot to this par 3 one of the most demanding at Oakland Hills. The green, which has massive undulations, is more than 30 feet (9m) above the teeing ground.

14 PAR 4 465 YARDS

5 PAR 4 457 YARDS

15 PAR 4 399 YARDS

Stream

PAR 5 560 YARDS 12

Lahser Road

13 PAR 3 172 YARDS

6 PAR 4 359 YARDS

4 PAR 4 433 YARDS

PAR 4 405 YARDS 7

PAR 5 527 YARDS 2

3 PAR 3 199 YARDS

7 **On guard**

A long, accurate drive at the par-4 7th is vital. Water threatens the tee shot on the right, while a pulled shot is punished by bunkers to the left. Trees guard the approach to the green on the right.

Championship Lengths		
Out	3,472 Yards	Par 35
In	3,524 Yards	Par 35
Total	6,996 Yards	Par 70

Course Record

65 George Archer 1964; T. Chen, A. North, D. Watson 1985

U.S. Open Champions at Oakland Hills

1924 Cyril Walker; 1937 Ralph Guldahl; 1951 Ben Hogan; 1961 Gene Littler; 1985 Andy North

USPGA Champions

1972 Gary Player; 1979 David Graham

Disaster awaited any loose approach shots to the green, in the form of deep bunkers with overhanging faces.

Ben Hogan was the defending Open champion at Oakland Hills in 1951, and his opening round of 71 proved the severity of the test set by Trent Jones and the USGA. A second round of 73 took him to within five strokes of the leader, Bobby Locke, and he went into the final round only two strokes behind Locke and Jimmy Demaret, who were joint leaders.

Slaying the Monster

It was then that Ben Hogan produced one of the greatest rounds in the history of championship golf. Playing conservatively from the tee to avoid trouble, Hogan put together a magnificent round of 67 to win comfortably from Clayton Heafner. The expression "monster" was first applied to a golf course by Hogan after that victory, when he said: "I am glad that I brought this course, this monster, to its knees."

Oakland Hills championship course

Oakland Drive
17 PAR 3 201 YARDS
10 PAR 4 454 YARDS
16 PAR 4 409 YARDS
18 PAR 4 453 YARDS
11 PAR 4 411 YARDS
8 PAR 4 439 YARDS
PAR 3 217 YARDS 9
1 PAR 4 436 YARDS
Practice area
Maple Road
Clubhouse

16 **Miracle stroke** *Trees add to the menace of the pond on the right at the 16th. In the 1972 USPGA, Gary Player cut his drive behind them, but made an impossible shot over trees and lake to the green for a birdie.*

Oakland Hills has mellowed since that memorable Open, but it remains a tough challenge. The last five holes are the peak of the test. From the 14th, the longest par-4 on the course, through to the dogleg 18th with its fiendish, narrow approach to a humpbacked green, there is unrelenting pressure on the player's nerve and skill. Trent Jones said of his own course: "The player with the best shots, swing, and nerve control has the best chance to win."

Since 1951, Oakland Hills has staged both the U.S. Open and the USPGA Championship twice, and two U.S. Senior Opens, in 1981 and in 1991.

Oakmont

Oakmont Country Club, Oakmont, Pennsylvania, U.S.A.

The memorable round that gave Johnny Miller victory in the U.S. Open at Oakmont in 1973 is one of the leading candidates for the coveted title of "best round ever played." Miller's record-breaking final 63, on rain-soaked greens, would have been remarkable anywhere, but it almost defies belief that he should have achieved it at Oakmont, on a course that has humiliated some of the greatest players. Oakmont is widely considered one of the most difficult rounds of 18 holes ever designed.

Not a prayer
The drives from the tee at the 3rd and 4th are dominated by the famous Church Pews bunker that lies between the two fairways. This massive hazard is 180 ft. (55m) long by 120 ft. (36m) wide.

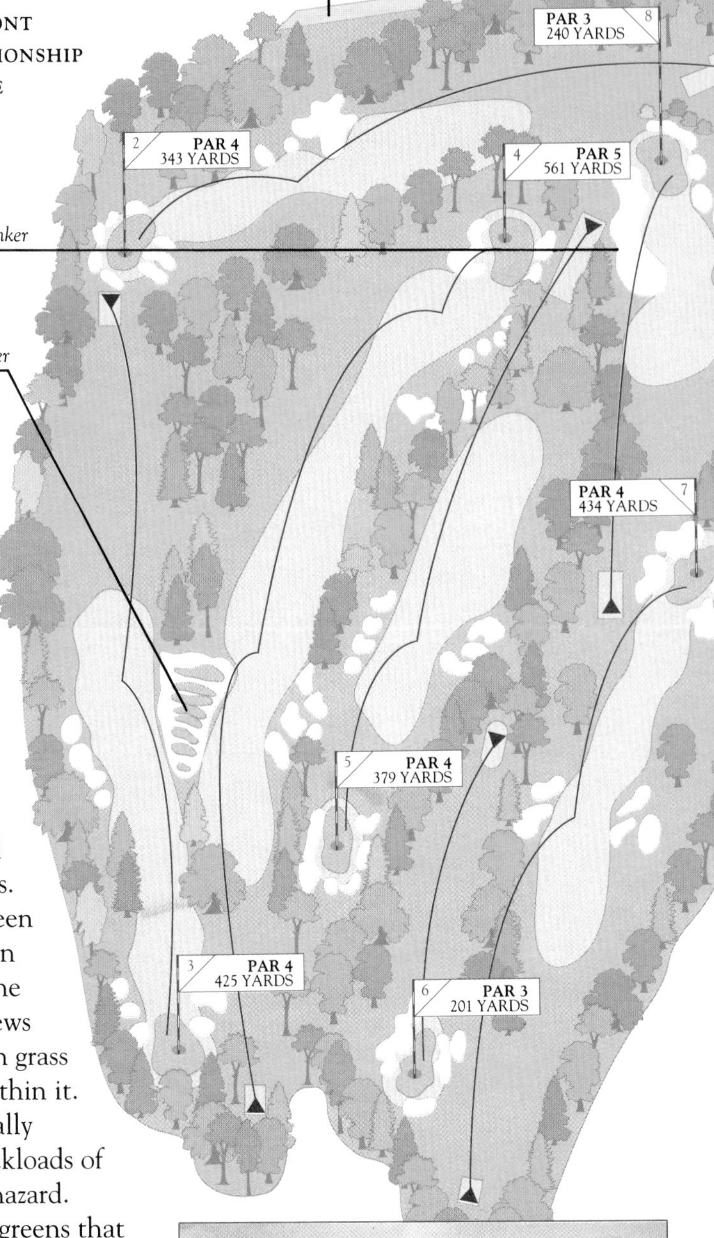

The Oakmont Country Club layout was the brainchild of the club's first president, the industrialist Henry C. Fownes, who designed and built the course in 1903–4. The Fownes philosophy of golf-course design was brutally simple: he wanted the toughest golf course possible, and he proceeded to build it.

Building Oakmont

In the autumn of 1903, using 150 men and 25 mule teams, Fownes had the first 12 holes completed in six weeks. They stopped work for the winter, but when spring returned so did Fownes's assault force, and the remaining six holes were ready for play by the following autumn.

Oakmont was constructed just as the rubber-core ball was replacing the guttie ball, but the course was able to make the transition virtually intact because it was so long and difficult. Par has been reduced to compensate for improvements in technology, but golfers today still play on the same tees, fairways, and greens that Gene Sarazen and Bobby Jones used in the 1920s.

Initially there may have been 350 bunkers at Oakmont; even today there are nearly 200. The most famous is the Church Pews bunker, named after the seven grass ridges set like church pews within it. But the Sahara bunker is equally intimidating. It is said 11 truckloads of sand were needed to fill this hazard.

However, it is Oakmont's greens that do most to make this magnificent course such a great challenge. They are said to be the fastest and most difficult in the United States. Jimmy Thomson claimed that during the 1935 U.S. Open he marked his ball with a dime at the 5th, but the green was so fast that when he went back to putt, "the dime had slid off!"

In 1987 Oakmont was designated a National Historic Landmark, the only U.S. golf course to have this distinction.

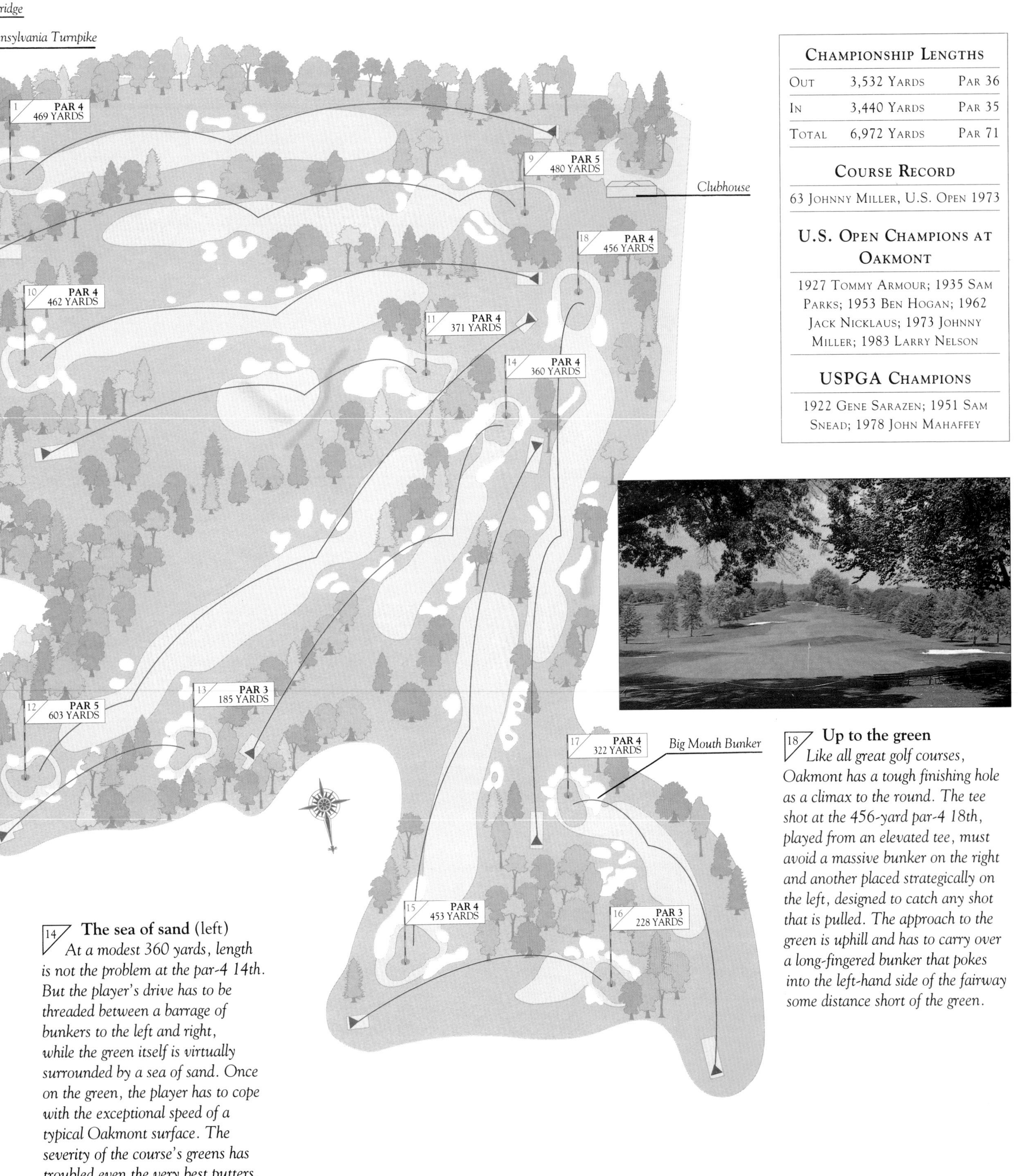

Championship Lengths

Out	3,532 Yards	Par 36
In	3,440 Yards	Par 35
Total	6,972 Yards	Par 71

Course Record

63 Johnny Miller, U.S. Open 1973

U.S. Open Champions at Oakmont

1927 Tommy Armour; 1935 Sam Parks; 1953 Ben Hogan; 1962 Jack Nicklaus; 1973 Johnny Miller; 1983 Larry Nelson

USPGA Champions

1922 Gene Sarazen; 1951 Sam Snead; 1978 John Mahaffey

18 Up to the green

Like all great golf courses, Oakmont has a tough finishing hole as a climax to the round. The tee shot at the 456-yard par-4 18th, played from an elevated tee, must avoid a massive bunker on the right and another placed strategically on the left, designed to catch any shot that is pulled. The approach to the green is uphill and has to carry over a long-fingered bunker that pokes into the left-hand side of the fairway some distance short of the green.

14 The sea of sand (left)

At a modest 360 yards, length is not the problem at the par-4 14th. But the player's drive has to be threaded between a barrage of bunkers to the left and right, while the green itself is virtually surrounded by a sea of sand. Once on the green, the player has to cope with the exceptional speed of a typical Oakmont surface. The severity of the course's greens has troubled even the very best putters.

PEBBLE BEACH

PEBBLE BEACH GOLF LINKS, PEBBLE BEACH, CALIFORNIA, U.S.A.

EACH YEAR THE Pebble Beach Golf Links is one of the hosts of the National Pro-Am – now sponsored by AT&T, but remembered as "The Crosby." Televised to a vast audience, this event has helped spread the fame of this magnificent course around the world. Between 1972 and 1982, Pebble Beach also staged three Major tournaments: the U.S. Open, twice, and the USPGA.

CHAMPIONSHIP LENGTHS		
OUT	3,274 YARDS	PAR 36
IN	3,525 YARDS	PAR 36
TOTAL	6,799 YARDS	PAR 72

COURSE RECORD

62 TOM KITE 1983

U.S. OPEN CHAMPIONS AT PEBBLE BEACH

1972 JACK NICKLAUS; 1982 TOM WATSON

USPGA CHAMPIONS

1977 LANNY WADKINS

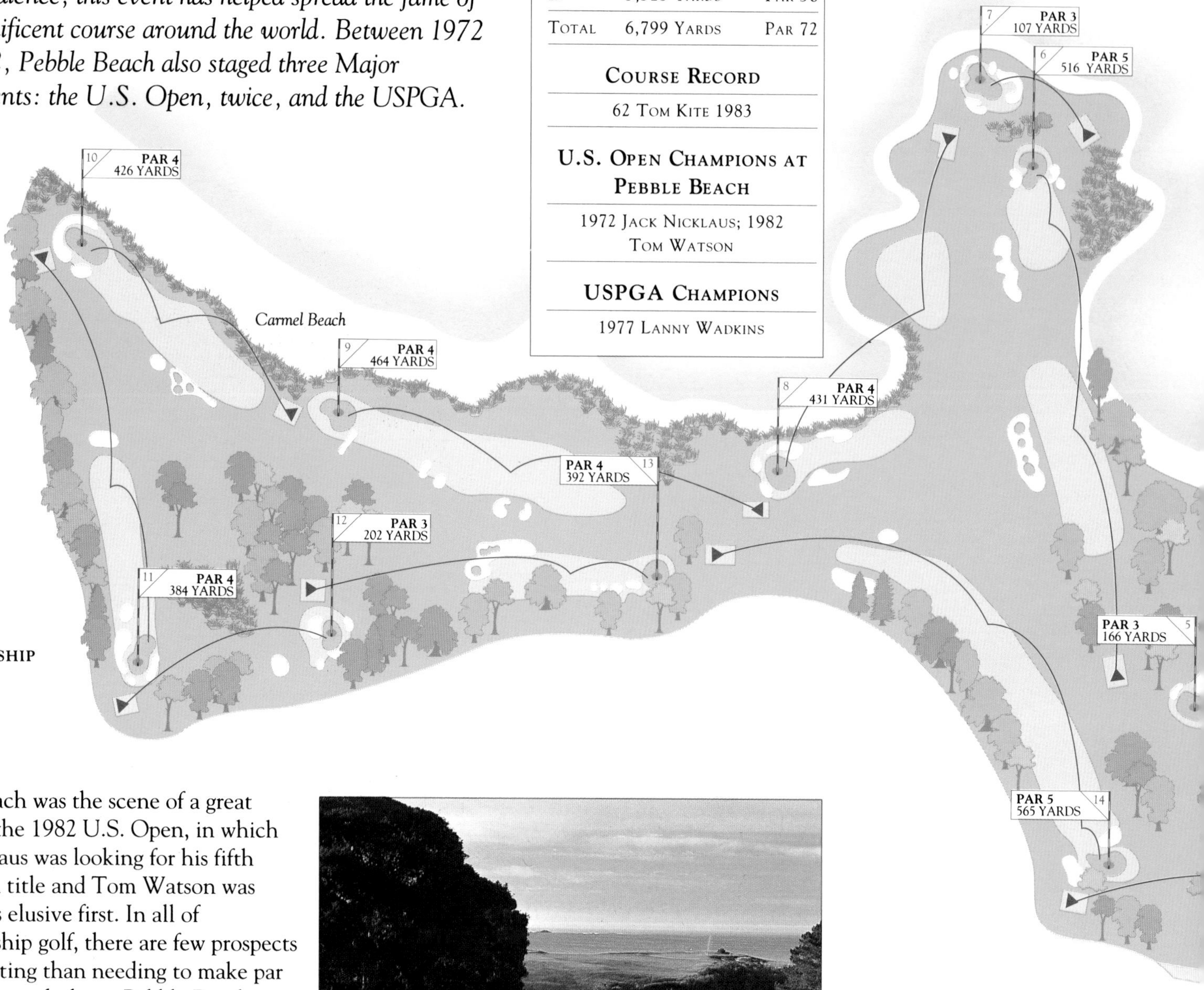

10 PAR 4 426 YARDS

Carmel Beach

9 PAR 4 464 YARDS

8 PAR 4 431 YARDS

7 PAR 3 107 YARDS

6 PAR 5 516 YARDS

13 PAR 4 392 YARDS

12 PAR 3 202 YARDS

11 PAR 4 384 YARDS

5 PAR 3 166 YARDS

14 PAR 5 565 YARDS

PEBBLE BEACH CHAMPIONSHIP COURSE

Pebble Beach was the scene of a great climax to the 1982 U.S. Open, in which Jack Nicklaus was looking for his fifth U.S. Open title and Tom Watson was seeking his elusive first. In all of championship golf, there are few prospects more daunting than needing to make par on the last two holes at Pebble Beach (which is what Watson needed for a play-off), let alone playing them under par to win. But Watson memorably birdied both holes to beat Nicklaus by two strokes.

It was only the second time the U.S. Open had been played on the magnificent Pebble Beach course on the Monterey

6 **Uphill work**
The 6th hole, the second of Pebble Beach's par 5s, starts out in a copse of trees and finishes in spectacular style on the cliffs above Stillwater Cove. The second shot, threatened by the ocean, has to be played uphill towards the green.

Peninsula in California, widely regarded as the finest "ocean" course on the American continent. The USGA has been reluctant to take the U.S. Open to Pebble Beach more often because it considers its location to be too far from a major city – it lies some 120 miles (190km) south of San Francisco. Nonetheless, the course was once more selected to host the U.S. Open for 1992, confirming its impressive worldwide reputation.

Opened for play in 1919, Pebble Beach was created through the vision of Samuel F. Morse, nephew of the inventor of Morse code and the telegraph, who bought the area from the Southern Pacific Railroad Company. To build the course, Morse recruited Jack Neville, a man who was not a golf-course architect but a real-estate salesman. What emerged from Neville's efforts was a magnificent layout, sprawling along the top of the cliffs and meandering up from the ocean to the edges of the Del Monte Forest.

The course at Pebble Beach is as tough to play as it is spectacular to look at. It remains open to all public play, although green fees are high and guests of the Lodge at Pebble Beach enjoy privileges, being able to book advance tee times.

18 Test of nerves
The final hole at Pebble Beach is one of the great finishing holes in golf. It curves left all the way, following the line of the cliffs. The tee shot is played across the corner of the cliffs, and how much of the dogleg is cut depends on the player's bravery.

18 PAR 5 548 YARDS

17 PAR 3 209 YARDS

Monterey Bay

water Cove

Pier

3 PAR 4 388 YARDS

4 PAR 4 327 YARDS

16 PAR 4 402 YARDS

The Lodge

1 PAR 4 373 YARDS

2 PAR 5 502 YARDS

15 PAR 4 397 YARDS

Palmero Road

17 Clifftop green
The longest par 3 at Pebble Beach, the 17th is played into the teeth of the wind and onto a small finger of land above the cliffs. Here Tom Watson made his famous pitch onto the green and into the hole for the birdie that won him the 1982 Open.

PEVERO

PEVERO GOLF CLUB, PORTO CERVO, COSTA SMERALDA, SARDINIA, ITALY

ROBERT TRENT JONES, a man not known for a feeble sense of the dramatic, was commissioned by the Aga Khan to build a golf course in that marvelous playground of the well-heeled, the Costa Smeralda in northeastern Sardinia. What Trent Jones produced in this natural, craggy paradise, with its temperate climate, was one of the most beautiful and spectacular courses in Europe. It is almost infinitely challenging and, from the back tees, just about impossible for all but the finest players.

4 **Careful aim** *The drive from the 4th tee down into the valley is memorable; the view across Pevero Bay and the challenge of the hole are both superb. Bunkers guard the approach and accuracy is of prime importance.*

Whatever the standard of the golfer, and no matter which tees are played from, there is great, pleasurable golf on the Pevero course, with its panoramic views and stunning, untamed beauty.

The course rises and plunges in great waves of scrub through alleys of jagged rock, some of which had to be blasted away to let Trent Jones realize his design. Despite this, the course is not artificial in any sense. Trent Jones admits openly to great affection for Pevero, rating it among the best work he has ever done.

LOST IN THE ROUGH

It is as well that the design built generous width into the fairways, for the rough is penal to play from even if the ball can be found. A firm rein on ambition and a little restraint are the qualities best suited to this marvelous layout.

The course nestles in a valley between two spectacular bays: Pevero Bay is on one side and the glorious sandy beach of Cala di Volpe (Bay of Foxes) on the other. The course rises through hills resplendent with dwarf pine, broom, and gorse, where, in spring, wild flowers and shrubs splash riotous color across the landscape.

Lush fairways run into large and, for the most part, elevated greens, but it is hard to concentrate upon them, so strong is the influence of the panoramic views. Complementing the beauty of the natural surroundings, the clubhouse and other associated facilities are equipped in suitable Mediterranean fashion, with a terrace looking out over the view and a pool for those wishing to cool down after a round in the heat of the day.

From the 3rd tee the course tracks a dangerous golfing path uphill to a green which, when reached, reveals an expansive vista of the Mediterranean fading away toward Italy. A change of direction to the 4th tee produces one of the most stunning views in European golf. Beyond the green far below and over the azure waters of Pevero Bay can be seen the snowcapped mountains of Corsica.

The first of two lakes that Trent Jones built into the design dominates the 6th and 7th holes, two of the best on the course. Played from a tee set back in a spectacular rockery garden of flowers and

4 PAR 4 351 METERS

5 PAR 3 175 METERS

7 PAR 3 166 METERS

Pevero Bay

6 PAR 4 306 METERS

1 PAR 4 376 METERS

8 PAR 4 339 METERS

CHAMPIONSHIP LENGTHS

OUT	2,999 METERS	PAR 36
IN	2,848 METERS	PAR 36
TOTAL	5,847 METERS	PAR 72

COURSE RECORD

63 H. JACKSON, SPANISH OPEN 1971

shrubs, the 6th is a short par 4 to a narrow fairway. The lake eats into the fairway on the left and only the most accurate of tee shots will survive. Even when the sanctuary of the fairway is reached, the player's troubles are not over, as the short pitch has to carry the lake to the green. A cool nerve and steady hand are needed, since the green slopes viciously toward the water. The lake dominates the 7th as well, a long par 3 of 166m. It requires a very solid blow with a long iron from the elevated tee to make the carry over the lake and reach the safety of a narrow green. The second lake influences play at the 16th and 17th, with the tee shot at the penultimate hole requiring a long carry over the water to a generous but deceptively sloping target.

This is golf in the most rarefied of sporting atmospheres, where there is no room for doubt that the hand of man has, for once, complemented the already magnificent work of Mother Nature.

15 Green with a view
The second shot at the 15th is over a hill toward a green well guarded by bunkers. The view from the green is spectacular.

16 Tricky second
One of the toughest strokes anywhere is the second shot at the 16th. A lake guards the right of the long, narrow hole and a selection of three bunkers guards the left. Mistakes are punished severely.

Pine Valley

Pine Valley Golf Club, Clementon, New Jersey, U.S.A.

George Crump, wealthy Philadelphia businessman and avid golfer, spent many years and the best part of his fortune in pursuit of his dream of building the best and hardest golf course in the world. At Pine Valley, he certainly succeeded in creating one of the world's toughest inland courses. Crump picked 184 acres of forest and marshland on the highest piece of ground in southern New Jersey, land he spotted from his railroad car while traveling from Philadelphia to Atlantic City.

10 **Devil's work**
The 10th green is surrounded by many sand traps, but this deep conical one, nicknamed the Devil's Arse, is particularly vicious. The only way out is to play away from the green because the lip is too steep.

The records of the Pine Valley Club give no insight into the reasons that might have led Crump to think this stretch of unpromising land, once the home of the Delaware Indians, suitable for fashioning into a great inland links. But he had no doubts, and in 1912, after persuading 18 friends to put up $1,000 each, he bought the ground. Sadly, Crump did not live to see the completion of his golfing dream; he died in 1918, when only 14 of the 18 holes were finished. The Pine Valley course eventually opened a year later.

What Crump created was a series of green islands in a sea of dense undergrowth, trees, water, and sand. This has given Pine Valley the reputation of being the biggest bunker in the world. There are no fairways as such. The landing areas are precisely defined and generous enough in their own way, but the penalty for missing any of them is severe, and the damage to one's score will be terminal. Many of them are encircled by steep-sided potholes.

Psychological Pressure

Pine Valley therefore presents as much a psychological challenge as a physical test. Most people who play the course for the first time are awestruck by its terrifying reputation. After a few holes, almost invariably their play becomes increasingly erratic as an irrational fear takes hold of them and reduces the quality of their play. Pine Valley members are so confident of their course's capacity that they offer a

17 **Trapped**
The 17th is a shortish par 4, but it makes up for its lack of length by being uphill all the way. By the standards of the rest of the course, the green is small and, in line with Pine Valley's vicious penal design, it is comprehensively guarded by sand traps that begin 50 yards in front of the green.

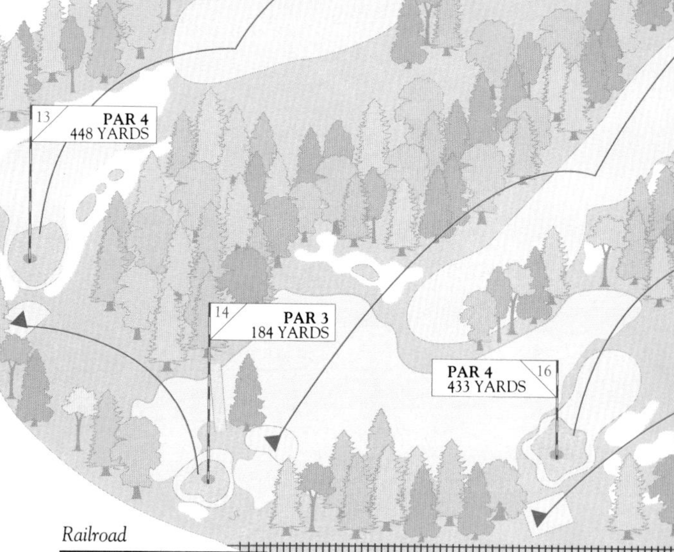

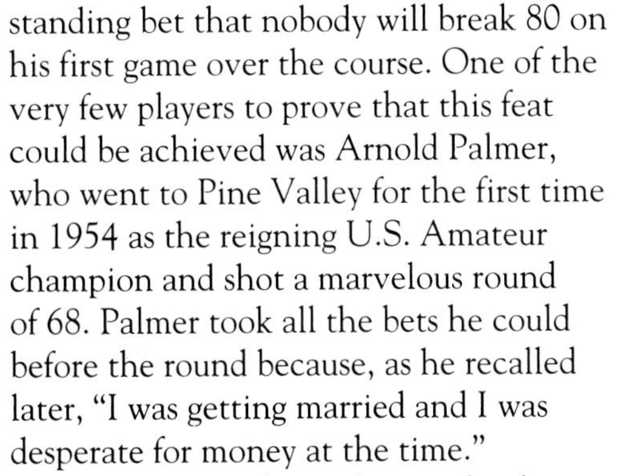

standing bet that nobody will break 80 on his first game over the course. One of the very few players to prove that this feat could be achieved was Arnold Palmer, who went to Pine Valley for the first time in 1954 as the reigning U.S. Amateur champion and shot a marvelous round of 68. Palmer took all the bets he could before the round because, as he recalled later, "I was getting married and I was desperate for money at the time."

In addition to being famous for the severity and toughness of the challenge it presents, beautiful Pine Valley is notable for its undiluted devotion to the game. Unlike many modern clubs, it remains, as it always has been, strictly a golf club, with no pretensions to being anything else.

CHAMPIONSHIP LENGTHS		
OUT	3,352 YARDS	PAR 35
IN	3,304 YARDS	PAR 35
TOTAL	6,656 YARDS	PAR 70

COURSE RECORD

64 ROBERT LEWIS, JR., LAWRENCE BATLEY INTERNATIONAL 1981

18 Dangerous waters

The 18th is played from a high tee, which makes the 185-yard carry over sand and scrub to the fairway landing area easier to achieve. The second shot has to cross water in front of the green from a downhill lie, with attendant dangers. The large green runs uphill from the front, and there is always a risk of three-putting.

PINE VALLEY CHAMPIONSHIP COURSE

Hell's Half-Acre

6 PAR 4 388 YARDS

8 PAR 4 319 YARDS

7 PAR 5 567 YARDS

3 PAR 3 181 YARDS

The Sahara

11 PAR 4 392 YARDS

15 PAR 5 591 YARDS

2 PAR 4 367 YARDS

5 PAR 3 232 YARDS

9 PAR 4 427 YARDS

4 PAR 4 444 YARDS

PAR 4 428 YARDS 18

PAR 4 338 YARDS 17

10 PAR 3 146 YARDS

1 PAR 4 427 YARDS

Clubhouse

Devil's Arse Bunkers

PINEHURST

PINEHURST RESORT & COUNTRY CLUB, PINEHURST, NORTH CAROLINA, U.S.A.

THERE IS NO golf resort in the United States with a better claim to the title of "Golf Capital of America" than Pinehurst in North Carolina, which boasts no fewer than seven golf courses. This small community of only a few thousand people has a deep respect for and understanding of golf, matched only by that of enthusiasts in Scotland, the cradle of the game. This shared feeling for golf probably reflects the community's early connections with Scotland. The main influence on Pinehurst was Donald J. Ross, a Scottish professional from Dornoch.

Telling emblem *The Pinehurst logo incorporates the Putter Boy, after the design of a sundial once found on the club's practice putting green.*

Ford's golf balls *U.S. President Gerald R. Ford, an avid golfer, has strong links with Pinehurst. He declared the World Golf Hall of Fame open a month after taking office in 1974.*

Donald Ross settled in Pinehurst, a small community situated between Raleigh and Charlotte, after emigrating from Scotland to the United States in 1898. Previously he had been an apprentice to Old Tom Morris in St. Andrews. At about the same time as Ross was making his way to a new life in America, a Boston pharmacist by the name of James W. Tufts suddenly became captivated by the new game of golf that was then growing in popularity on the East Coast. He had already bought a 5,000-acre site in Pinehurst, at a mere $1 an acre, with the grand scheme of developing a resort where New Englanders like himself could escape the ravages of the northern winters.

Tufts built a golf course at Pinehurst, primitive by present-day standards, but after Harry Vardon played four rounds there in 1900, golf took off. Tufts brought in Donald Ross as resident professional, and the man from Dornoch set about building Pinehurst Number 2, now recognized as one of the world's greatest golf courses.

The Carolina sandhills on which Ross laid out his course were perfect for the purpose. The land, barren and of little use for anything else, was similar in many ways to the seaside links of his native country. Ross made the most of it, refining it over the years into a true masterpiece. He went on to become involved in the design of many more American courses, including Broadmoor, Cedar Rapids, East Lake, Oak Hill, Oakland Hills, Scioto, and Seminole.

Although Pinehurst Number 2 can stretch to more than 7,000 yards when necessary, it is not designed to be punitively long. Ross's vision was of a challenge that requires accuracy and planning rather than strength. It puts the emphasis on a tight, short game around the slightly raised greens, as well as a fine touch with the putter on the subtle slopes of the putting surfaces.

There is a wonderful feeling of tranquillity, almost of solitude, when playing this marvelous course. The growth of the trees over the years has resulted in

Heroes' hall (above) *Pinehurst's World Golf Hall of Fame celebrates great figures in golf history, chosen by the Golf Writers of America. Henry Cotton (right) was inducted into the Hall of Fame in 1980.*

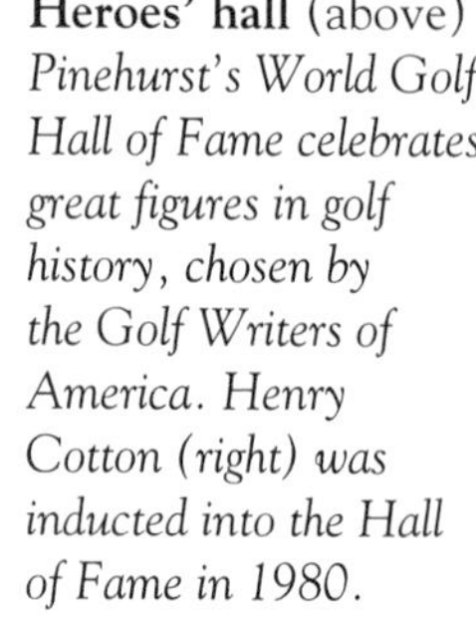

Capital house (left) *The large clubhouse complex serves five of the seven courses at the Pinehurst resort, which is widely regarded as being the "Golf Capital of America."*

Shady pines (right) *The scene around the short 9th hole is typical of the blend of turf and woodland that makes playing the Pinehurst Number 2 course such a pleasant experience.*

each hole becoming virtually a course of its own. The sandhills and mild climate are the perfect combination for developing the crisp Pinehurst turf.

This is very much a golf course for the game's "thinkers," and it will not easily surrender to a frontal assault. The great Sam Snead once warned, "You've got to hit every shot on old Number 2." For those who do not, there is humiliation in wait around every corner.

Had it been blessed with a more accessible location, there is no doubt that Donald Ross's masterpiece would have hosted many more championships than it has. Important events staged at Pinehurst over the years have, however, included the USPGA Championship in 1936, the Ryder Cup in 1951, and the U.S. Amateur Championship in 1962. Since 1901, the North and South Championship, an amateur event that ranks second only to the Amateur Championship itself, has been played regularly at Pinehurst.

Number 2 Takes Over

For the first eight years the event was played over the original Number 1 course, which was then a little short. From 1909, play was moved to the Number 2 course, where it has since remained.

Pinehurst also hosted the World Open, the inaugural event being played there in 1973; Miller Barber took the $100,000 winner's prize. The Colgate Hall of Fame Classic was staged there in 1977, and Pinehurst has been selected as the venue for the 1991 U.S. Tour Championship and the 1994 U.S. Senior Open.

The long association between Pinehurst and the Tufts family has continued over the decades. Richard S. Tufts, the grandson of the community's founding father, made a major contribution not only to Pinehurst but to the development of the game in the United States. Tufts was a leading figure in the USGA and played a major part in the standardization of the Rules of Golf between the USGA and the Royal & Ancient Golf Club in 1951 (see page 25). He was also the prime mover in the inauguration of the World Amateur Team Championship, known as the Eisenhower Trophy.

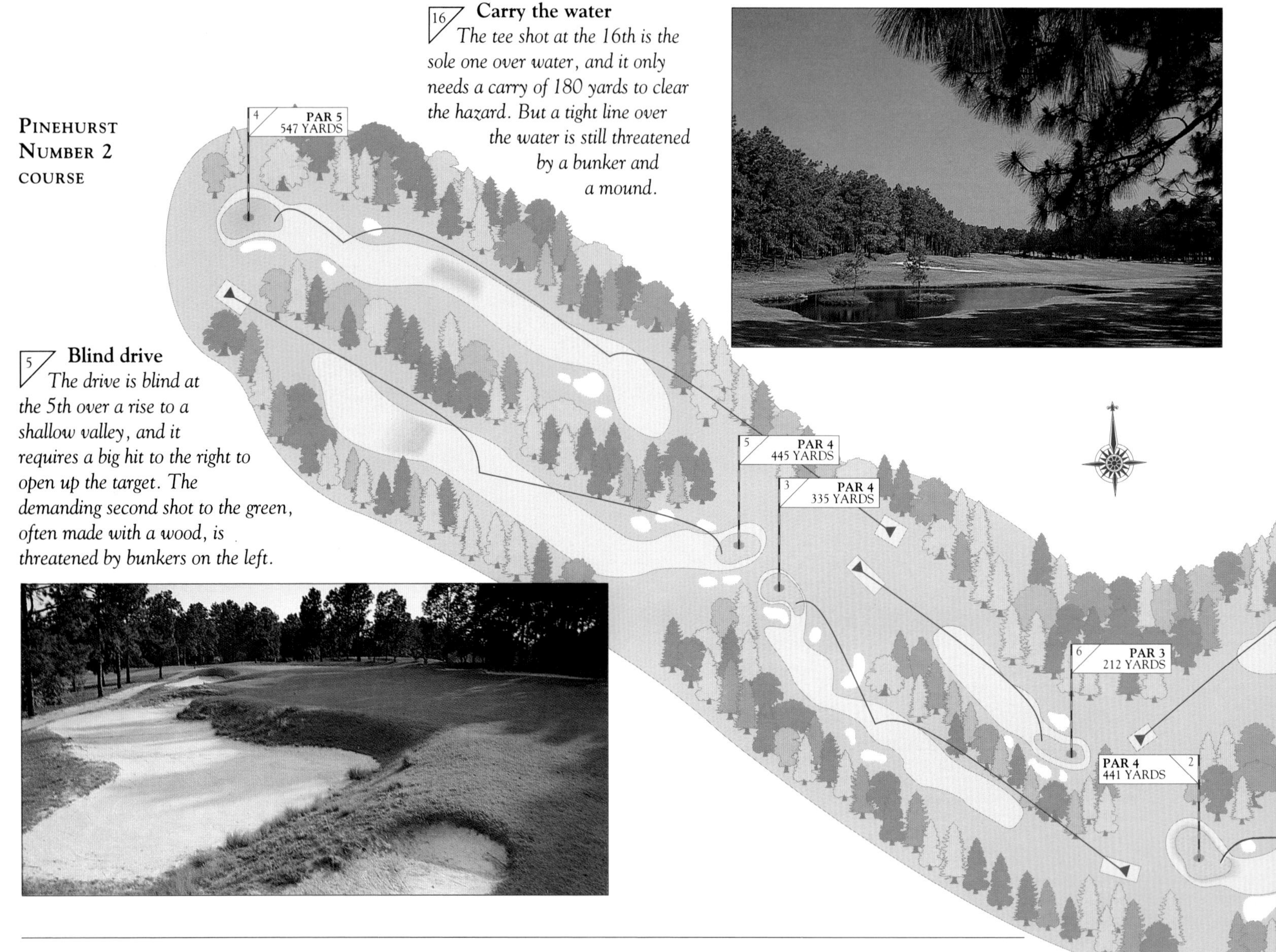

Pinehurst Number 2 course

16 **Carry the water**
The tee shot at the 16th is the sole one over water, and it only needs a carry of 180 yards to clear the hazard. But a tight line over the water is still threatened by a bunker and a mound.

5 **Blind drive**
The drive is blind at the 5th over a rise to a shallow valley, and it requires a big hit to the right to open up the target. The demanding second shot to the green, often made with a wood, is threatened by bunkers on the left.

Championship Lengths

Out	3,430 Yards	Par 36
In	3,590 Yards	Par 36
Total	7,020 Yards	Par 72

Course Record

62 Gibby Gilbert, World Open 1973

USPGA Champions at Pinehurst

1936 Densmore Shute

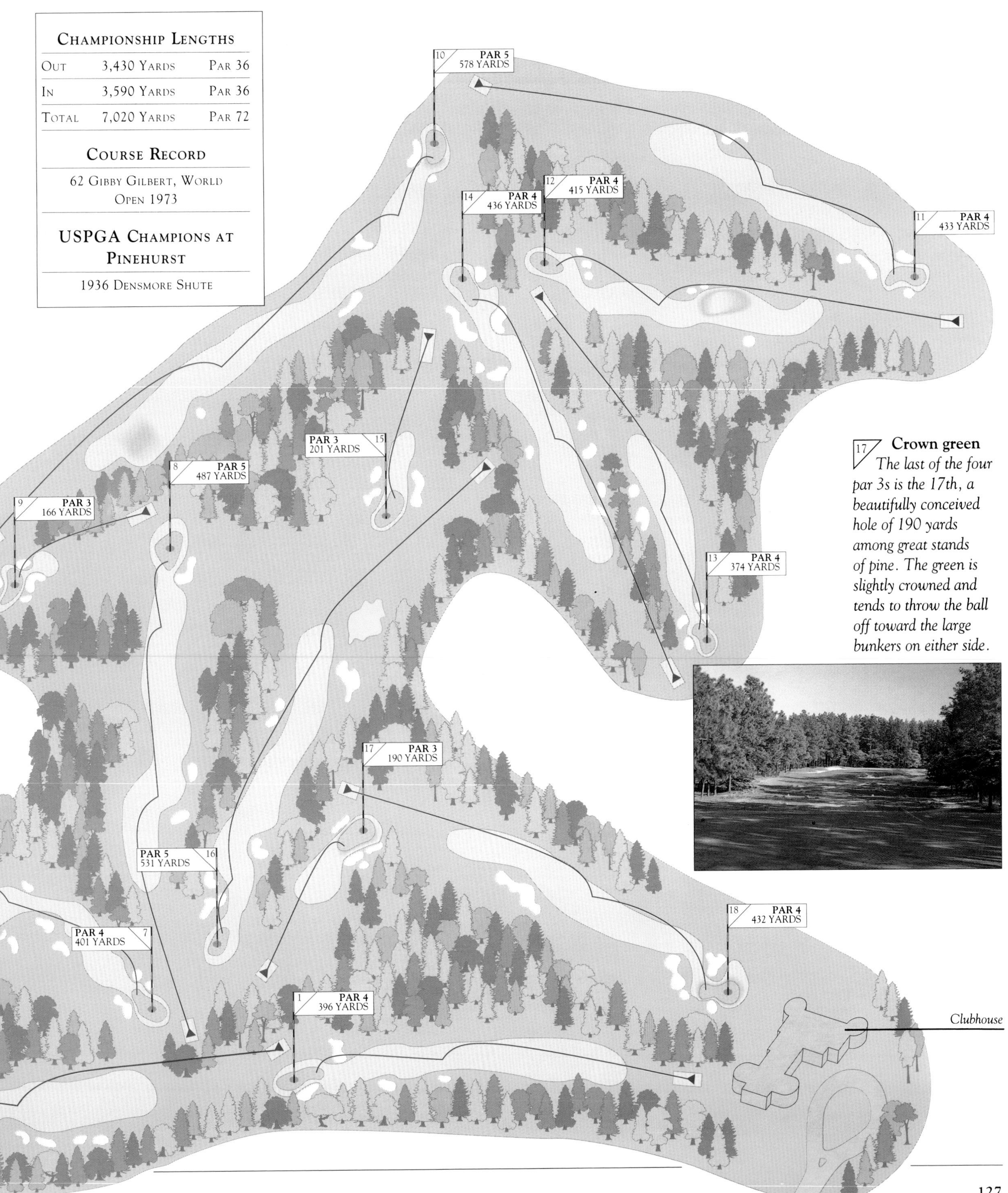

17 **Crown green**

The last of the four par 3s is the 17th, a beautifully conceived hole of 190 yards among great stands of pine. The green is slightly crowned and tends to throw the ball off toward the large bunkers on either side.

PORTMARNOCK

PORTMARNOCK GOLF CLUB, COUNTY DUBLIN, REPUBLIC OF IRELAND

THE GREAT FOUR-TIME winner of the British Open, Bobby Locke, rated the magnificent links of Portmarnock in County Dublin, Ireland, among the very finest anywhere in Europe. There are few who would argue with that judgment, for Portmarnock has all the qualities of the truly great seaside championship courses. It also offers the additional challenge of an unpredictable and capricious climate, changing swiftly from sunlight to storm.

Warm hosts (above)
The present clubhouse at Portmarnock dates from 1906, after the first, a mere shack, burned down. The club is renowned for the warmth of its welcome.

Local birdie
In the club's coat of arms there is a grey plover, a species found on the links. The shield is capped by a bishop's miter with crossed golf clubs behind.

Unlike many other courses of its caliber, Portmarnock's origins are quite well documented. It was set up by two men, W.C. Pickeman and George Ross, who rowed across the estuary from Sutton in 1894. Although only ten miles (16km) northeast of Dublin, it was a remote spot, but the two men felt it was the ideal place for a golf course. In fact, there had already been a course of sorts on the peninsula, owned by the Irish whiskey family, Jameson. Pickeman and Mungo Park designed the first nine holes of the new course, and four years later the course was extended to 18 holes by Pickeman alone. A shed was provided as basic accommodation, but it burned down early in this century. Today the clubhouse is a much more elegant affair, shining clean and white in the Irish sunshine. Fred W. Hawtree laid out a third nine holes in the 1970s. Like all the great links courses, however, Portmarnock ultimately owes far more to nature than it does to the hand of man.

Nowadays Portmarnock is accessible by road; originally, however, it could only be reached by the ferry used by Pickeman and Ross on their original voyage of discovery. There are many strange stories attached to the passage across the estuary. None is stranger, nor perhaps more apocryphal, than that concerning the club ferryman who had a disagreement with a clergyman on the crossing. The ferryman was not renowned for his tolerance, and it is said that the unfortunate cleric, apparently not of the same faith as his captain, did not make it across the water to Portmarnock.

Over the water (left)
When W.C. Pickeman and George Ross rowed across the estuary in 1894 to the peninsula on which Portmarnock now lies, they found a wilderness of sand dune and bracken, inhabited only by farmers and fishing folk.

Those who are privileged to play on this marvelous stretch of classic links will undergo an examination of the most testing nature. Like many of its contemporaries among great courses, Portmarnock is a place of moods governed by wind and weather. On a sunny and calm day looking across

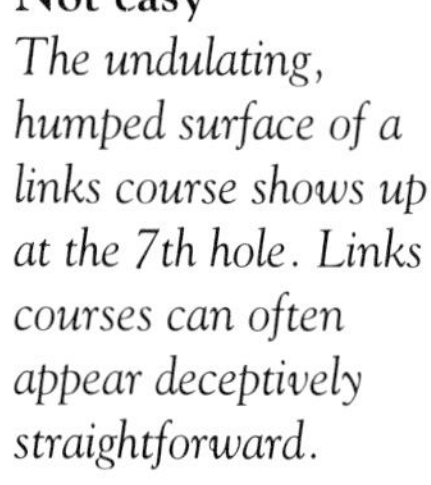

Not easy
The undulating, humped surface of a links course shows up at the 7th hole. Links courses can often appear deceptively straightforward.

Sea green (right)
The Portmarnock course is set on an exposed peninsula and playing conditions there are greatly affected by capricious changes in the wind and weather. The par-3 15th hole is typical of the short holes on this strikingly situated links course.

P.J. CARROLL

the estuary to Ireland there is a magical tranquility about the place, and yet it can transform itself rapidly, putting on a fierce and forbidding face.

There are no hidden problems on the Portmarnock course. It is a truly honest test; its inherent difficulty and the terrain are quite sufficient to provide a wonderful challenge without having recourse to modern design trickeries.

Portmarnock has hosted many fine tournaments over the years, including the Dunlop Masters, the Canada Cup (now the World Cup), and of course the Irish Open. In 1949 Portmarnock hosted the only Amateur championship to be played outside the United Kingdom. While it played host to the Carroll's Irish Open, Portmarnock was voted by the players themselves as the best PGA European Tour tournament site.

Length of the Course

When the course was originally extended to 18 holes it measured just over 5,350m. In response to improvements in equipment, and particularly in the golf ball, that length has since been extended to 6,529m for the top professional events. Of the par 4s, five are in excess of 380m in length, and two of the three par 5s measure more than 510m.

Two holes are critical to any score recorded at Portmarnock, the 14th and 15th. The 14th is less than 360m long, but it is undoubtedly one of the best holes on the course. The great Henry Cotton once took seven here to lose an Irish Open. Playing the short par-3 15th in the 1960 Canada Cup, Arnold Palmer shot through the stiff sea breeze to within a yard of the stick with a 3 iron.

Despite the length and challenge of this great links, when the wind does not blow its worst and the course has been softened by some rain, Portmarnock can offer little defense against the skill of the greatest players. When Bernhard Langer won his second Carroll's Irish Open in 1987, his worst round was 68 and his winning total of 269 was no fewer than 19 strokes under par.

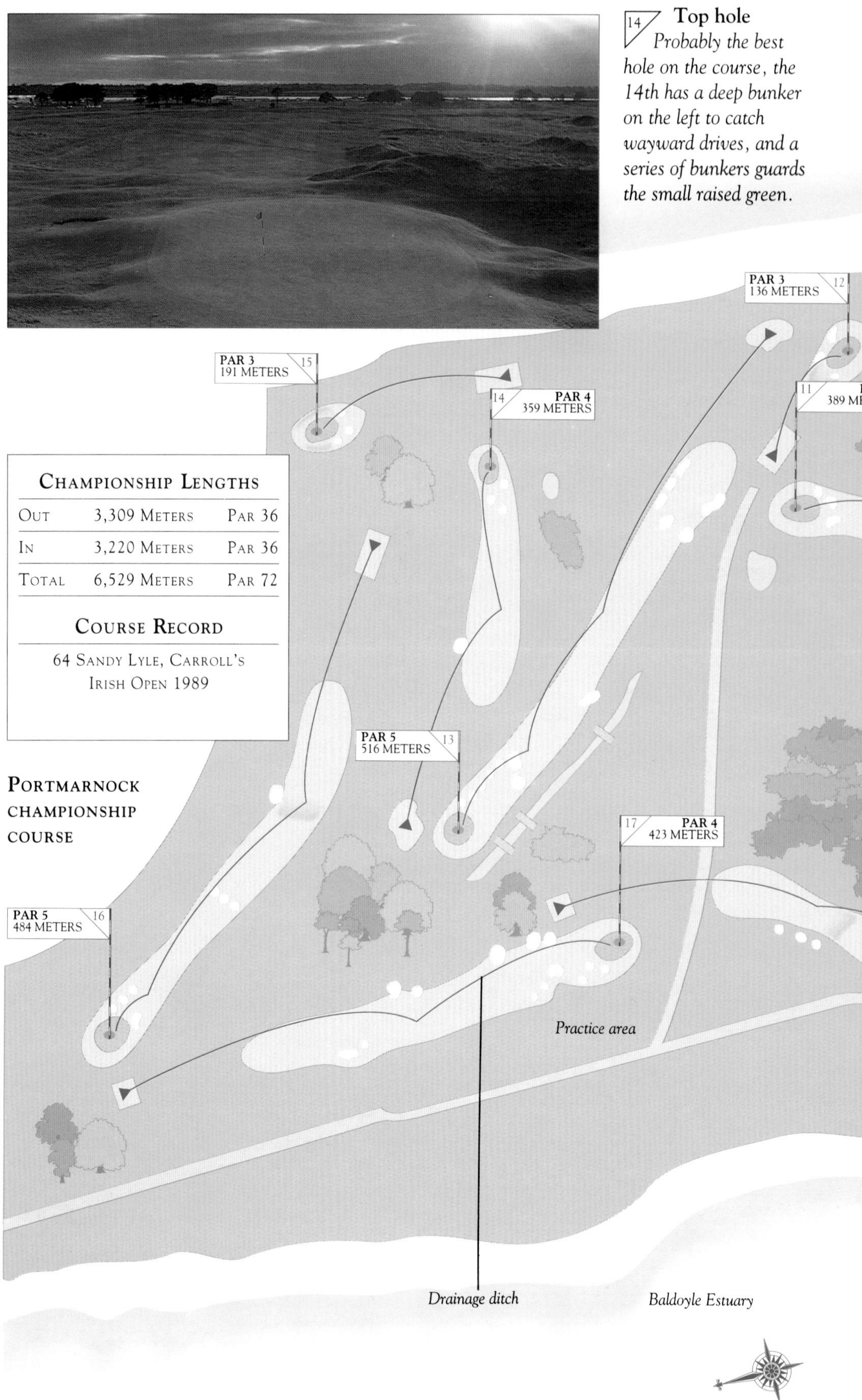

14 **Top hole**
Probably the best hole on the course, the 14th has a deep bunker on the left to catch wayward drives, and a series of bunkers guards the small raised green.

Championship Lengths

Out	3,309 Meters	Par 36
In	3,220 Meters	Par 36
Total	6,529 Meters	Par 72

Course Record

64 Sandy Lyle, Carroll's Irish Open 1989

Portmarnock Championship Course

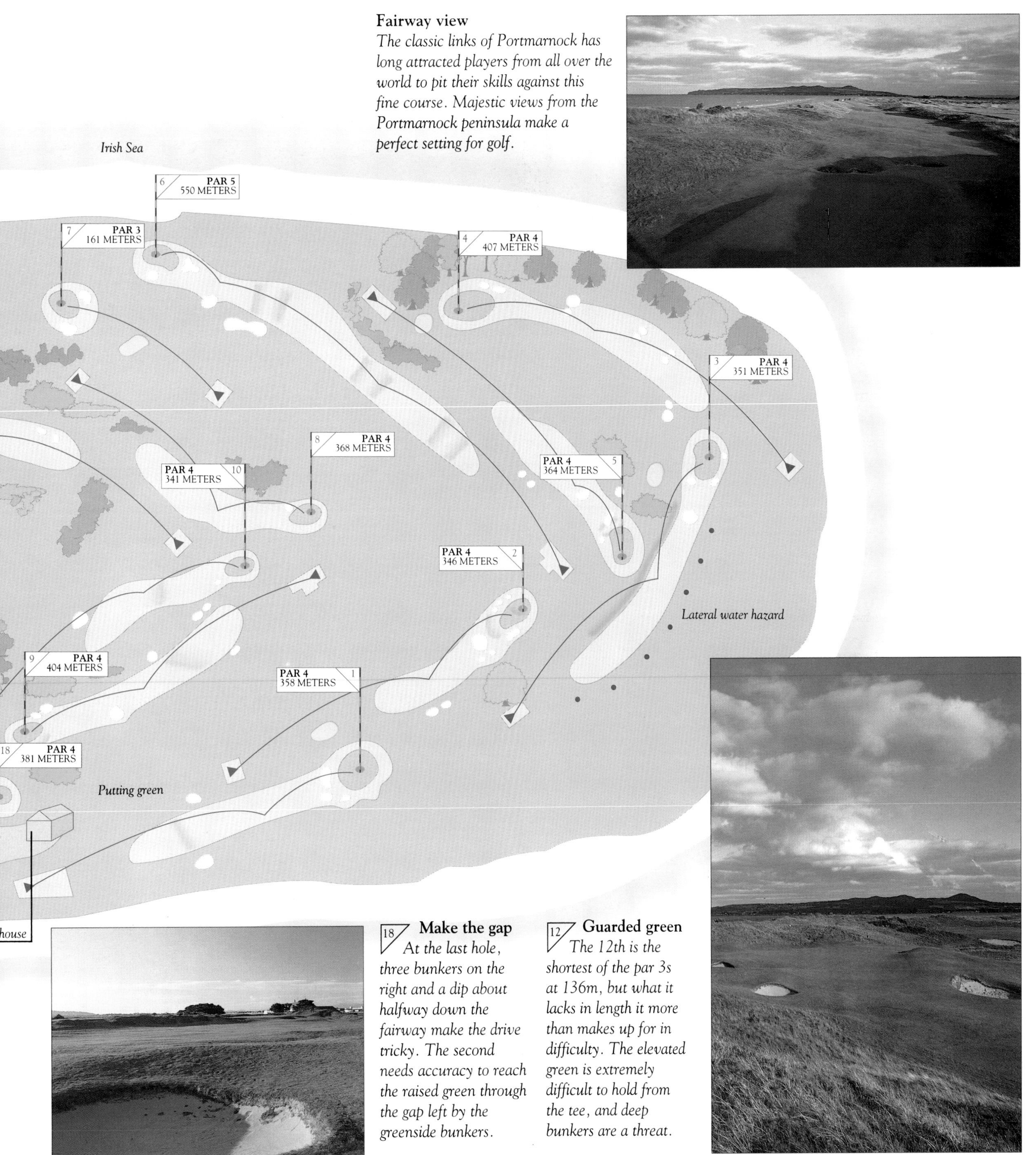

Fairway view
The classic links of Portmarnock has long attracted players from all over the world to pit their skills against this fine course. Majestic views from the Portmarnock peninsula make a perfect setting for golf.

18 Make the gap
At the last hole, three bunkers on the right and a dip about halfway down the fairway make the drive tricky. The second needs accuracy to reach the raised green through the gap left by the greenside bunkers.

12 Guarded green
The 12th is the shortest of the par 3s at 136m, but what it lacks in length it more than makes up for in difficulty. The elevated green is extremely difficult to hold from the tee, and deep bunkers are a threat.

RIVIERA

RIVIERA COUNTRY CLUB, PACIFIC PALISADES, CALIFORNIA, U.S.A.

LITTLE HAS CHANGED at the Riviera Country Club since George Thomas laid out this uncompromising course at Pacific Palisades, near Los Angeles, in 1927. Some reconstruction work was carried out half a century later, but this was merely to return the course to its pristine glory. Riviera enjoys a deserved worldwide reputation as a challenging course that demands the use of all the shots in a golfer's repertoire. Its qualities are said by some to be as solid and enduring as the quiet mountains overlooking it.

Set in the rich landscape of southern California, the Riviera course has been graphically described as "an agitated green wave rolling down historic canyons of the ancient Boca de Santa Monica ranchos." It is the golfing playground of the show-business fraternity, and for many years has been the most regular home of the Los Angeles Open, now sponsored by Nissan.

Great names who have won this event at Riviera include Byron Nelson, Tom Watson, Sam Snead, and Ben Hogan.

It was at Riviera in 1948 that Ben Hogan won his first U.S. Open, so far the only one to be played there, with a score of 276 that stood as a course record for 19 years. Two years later, Hogan made his comeback at Riviera after a car crash had almost taken his life. He entered the Los Angeles Open to test whether his mind and body could tackle an important tournament. He not only survived the four rounds but tied for first with Sam Snead. Although he lost the play-off, he had proved he could take the strain.

Riviera is a course that offers no hiding place for a player's weaknesses. In his design, George Thomas managed to

18 Looking for trouble
Many players have come unglued while being watched by thousands of spectators from the 18th green's natural amphitheater. The approach needs a firm shot with a long iron or wood.

6 Bunker in the green
A small bunker almost in the center of the green is only one of the problems at the short 6th. Another bunker lies in the center of the fairway immediately in front of the green, while yet another lurks at the back to penalize overclubbing.

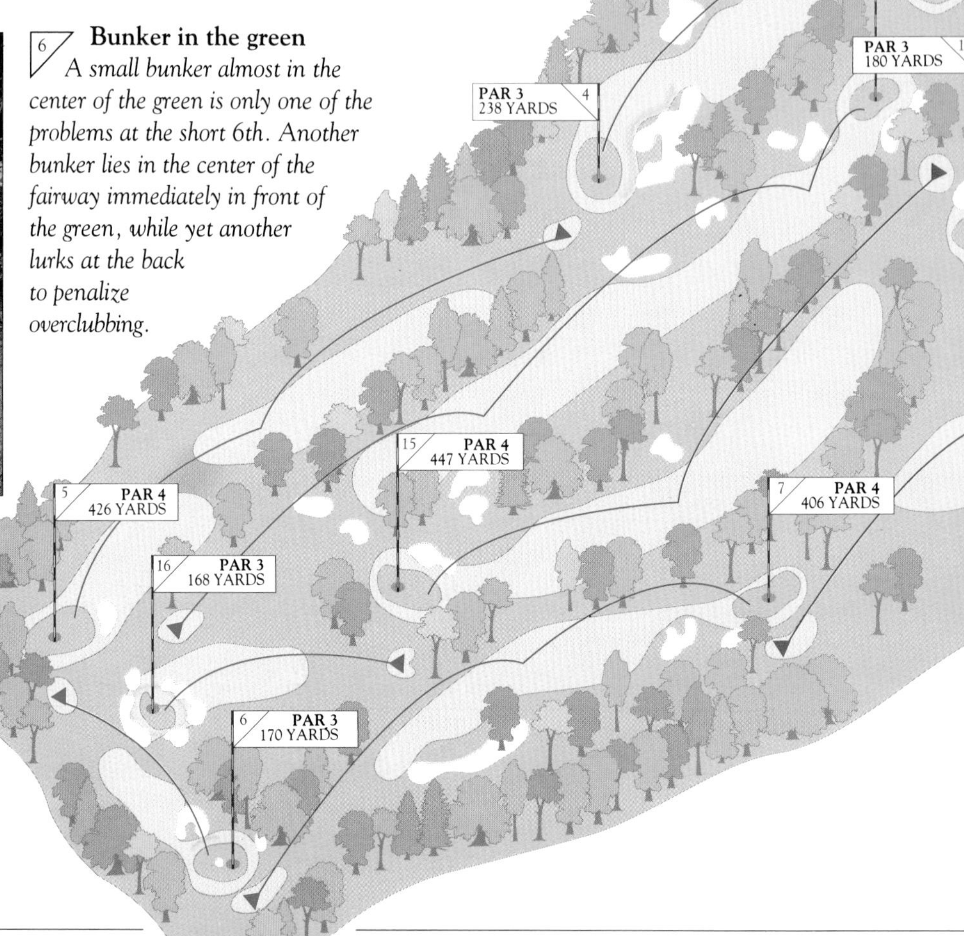

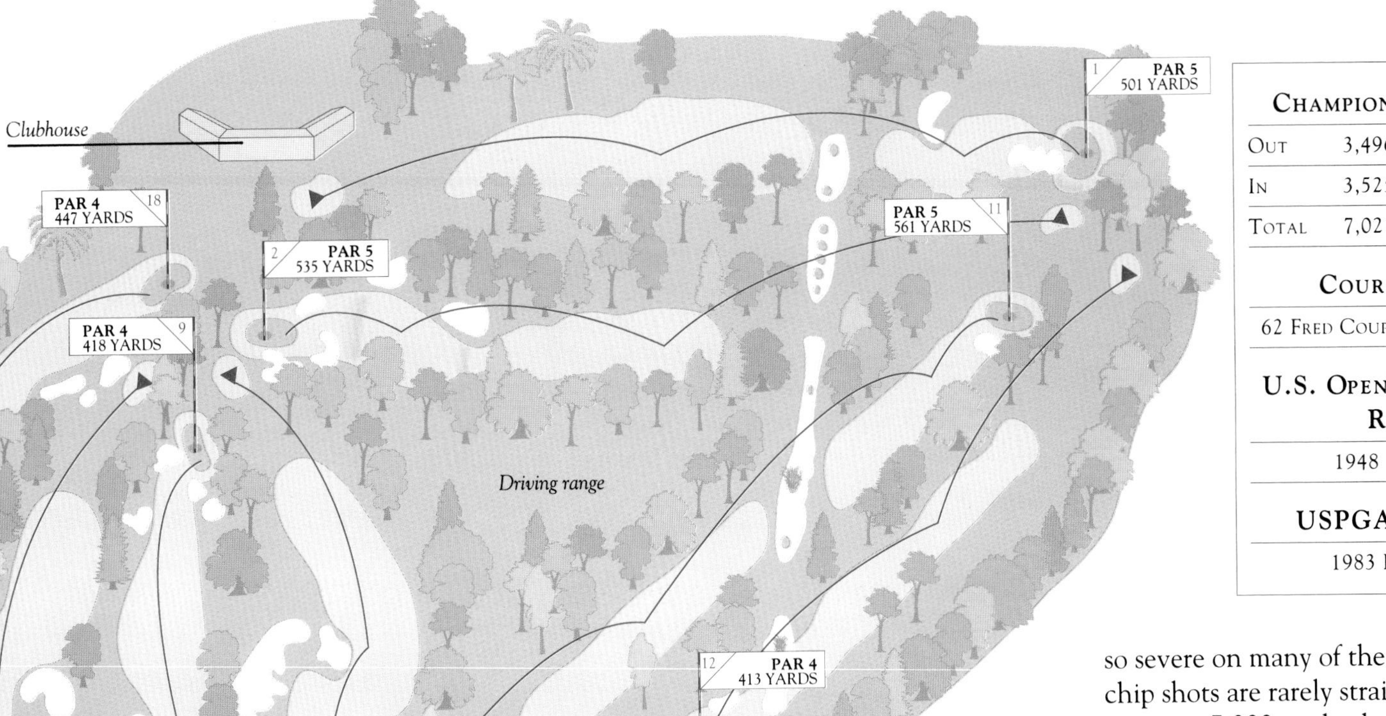

Championship Lengths		
Out	3,496 Yards	Par 36
In	3,525 Yards	Par 36
Total	7,021 Yards	Par 72

Course Record

62 Fred Couples, LA Open 1990

U.S. Open Champions at Riviera

1948 Ben Hogan

USPGA Champions

1983 Hal Sutton

Riviera championship course

combine a demand for long and accurate shots from the tee with the need for precision approach play with the irons. He built big greens for the long holes, extremely small greens for the short holes, and for the remainder allowed a happy medium. He defended all of them tenaciously with clever bunkering. The contouring around the Riviera greens is so severe on many of the holes that short chip shots are rarely straightforward. At just over 7,000 yards, the course is not long by present-day championship standards, but with its lush fairways it plays every one of those yards. The lushness leads to rather soft and spongy turf. Thus the ball does not roll, and the longer holes, especially the par 5s, are difficult; the enormously long 17th is a real trial of strength, requiring great power.

Essential Values

But sheer strength is certainly not all that is needed at Riviera. The bunkering is a constant danger and the ravine that winds around the edge of the course threatens the careless player. The trees that line the fairways – eucalyptus, redwood, sycamore, and pine – not only add to the beauty of the scene but also constitute a hazard. The course demands precision, accuracy, and ball control. Aspiring golfers who play Riviera will quickly find their true ability exposed. It is one of the world's great tests of golf.

The Riviera course was extensively reconstructed in the mid-1970s. The problem was a small stream that, over the years, had eroded itself into a deep gully. The work reclaimed 17 acres of land and restored the course to its original glory. The clubhouse, on a rise overlooking the fairways, perfectly matches the luxuriant beauty of the course.

10 **Jack's rating**
Jack Nicklaus rates the 10th as one of the great holes in golf. The landing area of this par-4 hole is extremely tight, with two looping bunkers on the right. Some players gamble and go for the green from the tee.

Royal Birkdale

The Royal Birkdale Golf Club, Southport, Lancashire, England

This superb seaside course has been by far the most important site for tournaments in England since the Second World War, hosting more than 30 championships and international matches. One of a group of fine courses set among the large sand dunes that dominate the landscape along much of the coast of Lancashire, it was once summed up by the great Australian player Peter Thomson as "man-sized but not a monster."

Short but not sweet
The 16th is a short hole for a par 4, only 414 yards, but that does not make it easy to play. As Palmer found during the 1961 British Open, any inaccuracy with the drive is threatened by heavy rough that runs right up to the edge of the fairway. The green is on a plateau that is strongly protected by bunkers.

Birkdale is a club with a long history; it celebrated its centenary in 1989. But the club does not play on its original course. The first layout of nine holes was about a mile away from the present 18. It survived for only eight years before George Low, from the neighboring course of Royal Lytham and St. Annes, was brought in to supervise the layout of the new Birkdale course.

Between the Dunes

Low threaded the fairways through the valleys between the giant sandhills rather than over the top of them, with the result that Birkdale has in many ways more of the character of an inland course than a true links. What makes it particularly formidable is the rough and scrub that grows wildly on the great dunes. There is an abundance of willow scrub, which in many ways presents a more punitive threat than heather, and is just as unyielding as gorse.

There have been many memorable tournaments at Birkdale, including the 100th British Open in 1971, when Lee Trevino triumphed over Lu Liang Huan of Taiwan. But perhaps none was more significant than the 1961 Open, won by Arnold Palmer, which restored the Championship to its full prestige.

It was during this Open that Palmer played his famous stroke out of the rough on what was then the 15th hole (now the 16th), which is commemorated by a plaque on the course. He had driven into rough under a bush 150 yards from the green and seemed ready to drop a shot. But in an astonishing display of strength he thrashed the ball with a 6 iron and forced it over cross-bunkers and onto the green.

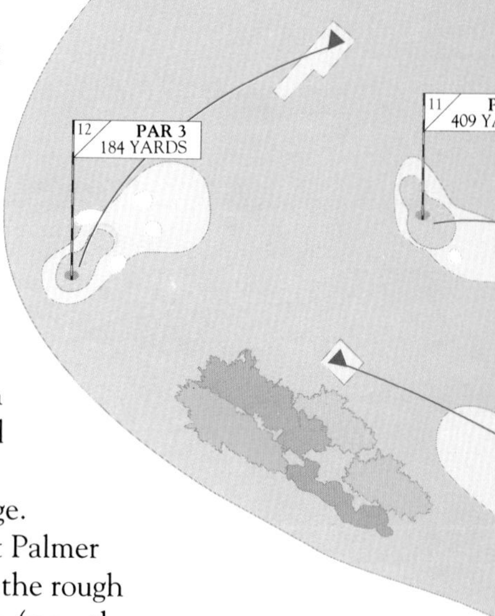

Royal Birkdale Championship Course

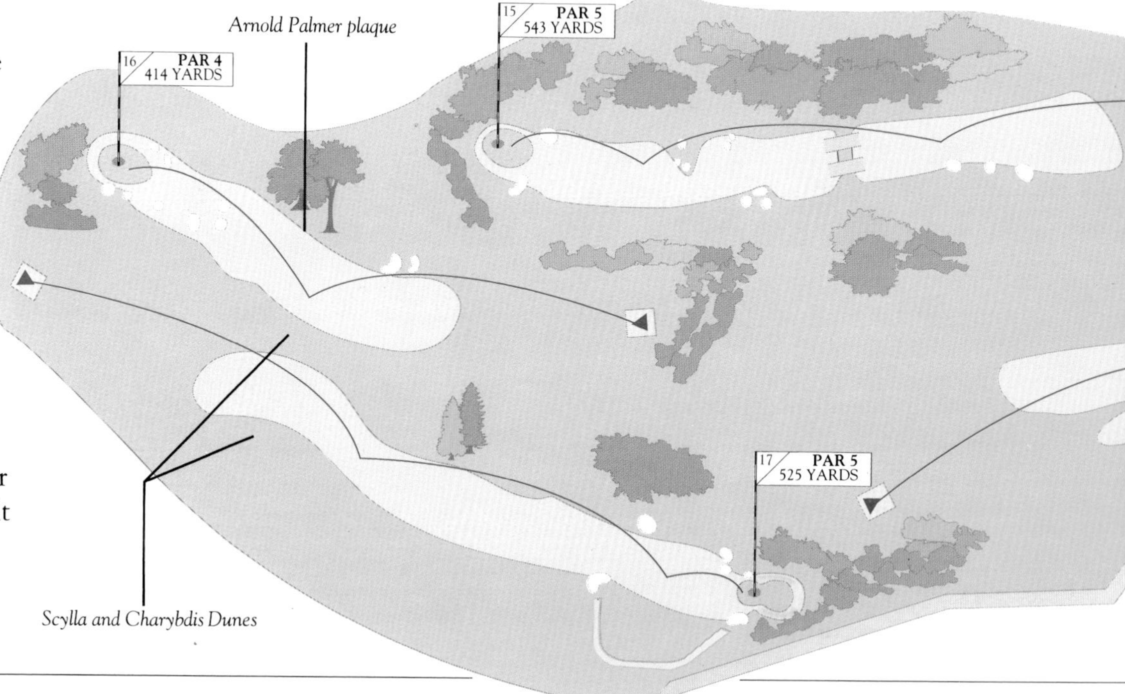

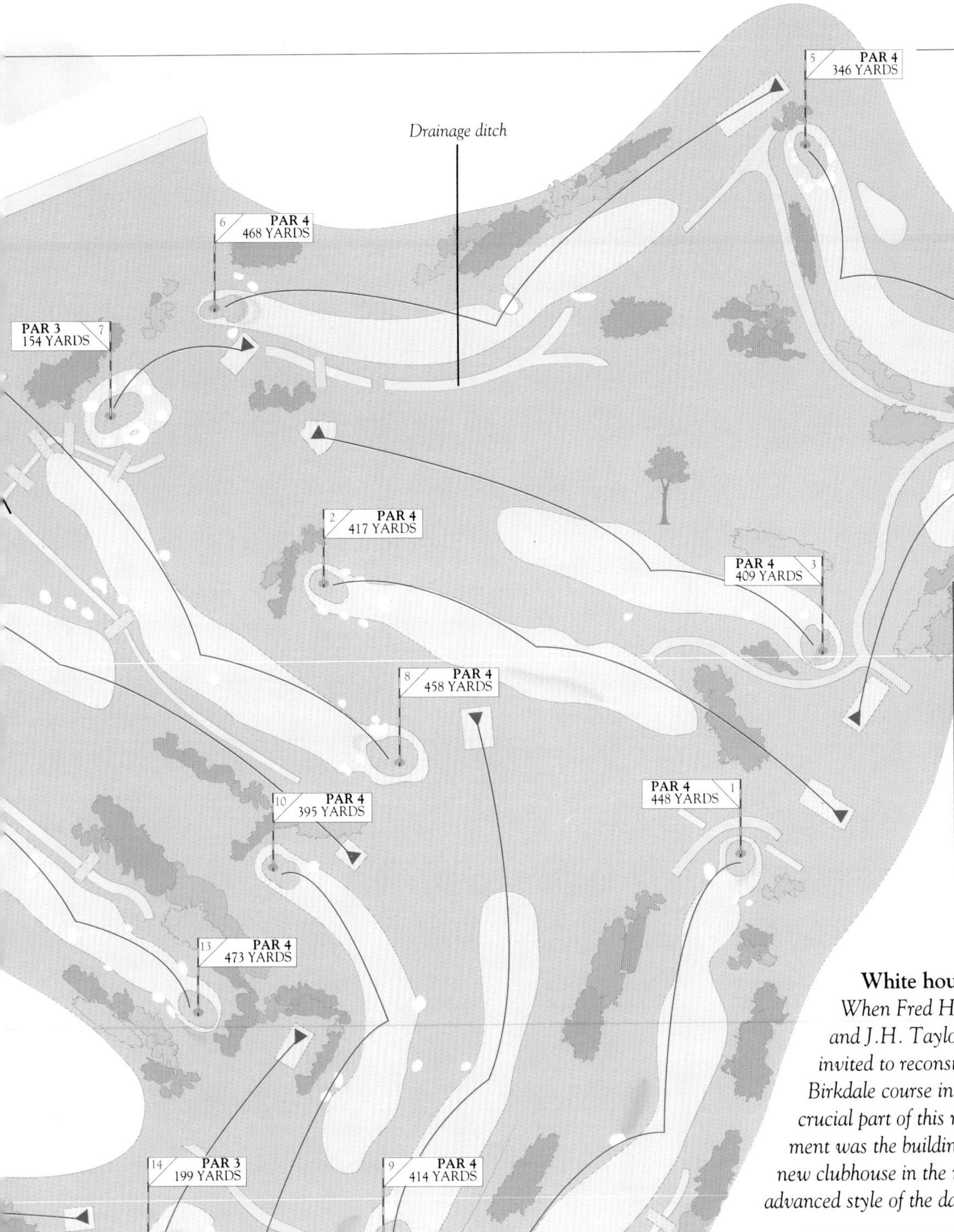

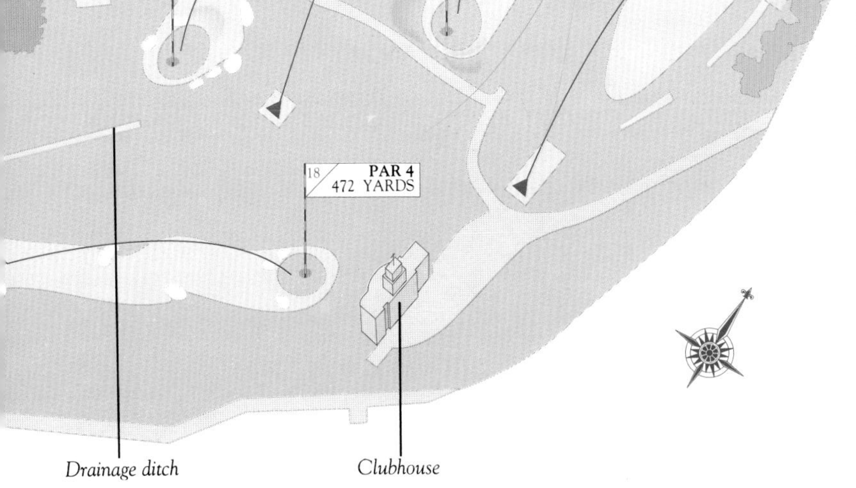

Drainage ditch

5 PAR 4 346 YARDS

6 PAR 4 468 YARDS

PAR 3 154 YARDS 7

4 PAR 3 203 YARDS

2 PAR 4 417 YARDS

PAR 4 409 YARDS 3

8 PAR 4 458 YARDS

PAR 4 448 YARDS 1

10 PAR 4 395 YARDS

13 PAR 4 473 YARDS

14 PAR 3 199 YARDS

9 PAR 4 414 YARDS

18 PAR 4 472 YARDS

Drainage ditch

Clubhouse

White house

When Fred Hawtree and J.H. Taylor were invited to reconstruct the Birkdale course in 1931, a crucial part of this redevelopment was the building of a new clubhouse in the most advanced style of the day.

8 Dead ground

Although it is played with the prevailing wind, the 458 yards of the 8th hole are demanding. There are two bunkers limiting the landing area for the drive down the right side, and a difficult hollow of dead ground in front of the green requires players to hit a bold second shot.

Championship Lengths

Out	3,317 Yards	Par 34
In	3,615 Yards	Par 36
Total	6,932 Yards	Par 70

Course Record

64 Mark O'Meara 1987

Open Champions at Royal Birkdale

1954 Peter Thomson; 1961 Arnold Palmer; 1965 Peter Thomson; 1971 Lee Trevino; 1976 Johnny Miller; 1983 Tom Watson

ROYAL CAPE

ROYAL CAPE GOLF CLUB, WYNBERG, CAPE TOWN, SOUTH AFRICA

LIEUTENANT-GENERAL SIR Henry D'Oyley Torrens, a soldier of some distinction when the British Empire was at its zenith, is the man credited with introducing golf to South Africa and also with founding what is now the Royal Cape Golf Club. Early records show the General was a fanatical enthusiast for the royal and ancient game.

16 PAR 5 489 METERS

11 PAR 5 447 METERS

15 PAR 3 148 METERS

14 PAR 4 404 METERS

13 PAR 3 170 METERS

6 PAR 4 343 METERS

Railroad

9 **Tight option**
The 9th is one of the most difficult par-4 holes at Royal Cape. Lined with trees and doglegged to the left, the hole has a ditch along the right side. The farther the tee shot is hit to the left, the tighter the hole becomes because of the trees and a bunker.

Within nine days of his arrival in South Africa, General Torrens had convened a meeting, on November 14, 1885, "for the purpose of introducing the game of golf and starting a club for same in South Africa." All those present at the meeting, with the exception of one, were military men, and most of them were Scots into the bargain. With the help of an officer of the Royal Engineers, a nine-hole course was eventually laid out on Waterloo Green, immediately in front of the Wynberg barracks. Each stage of its design had to receive the General's approval.

Since then the club has moved its location twice, in 1891 and 1905, and there have been many changes to the

1 **Keep right**
The long par-4 opening hole at Royal Cape is usually played into the prevailing southeast wind. It demands a long straight drive favoring the right of the fairway.

ROYAL CAPE CHAMPIONSHIP COURSE

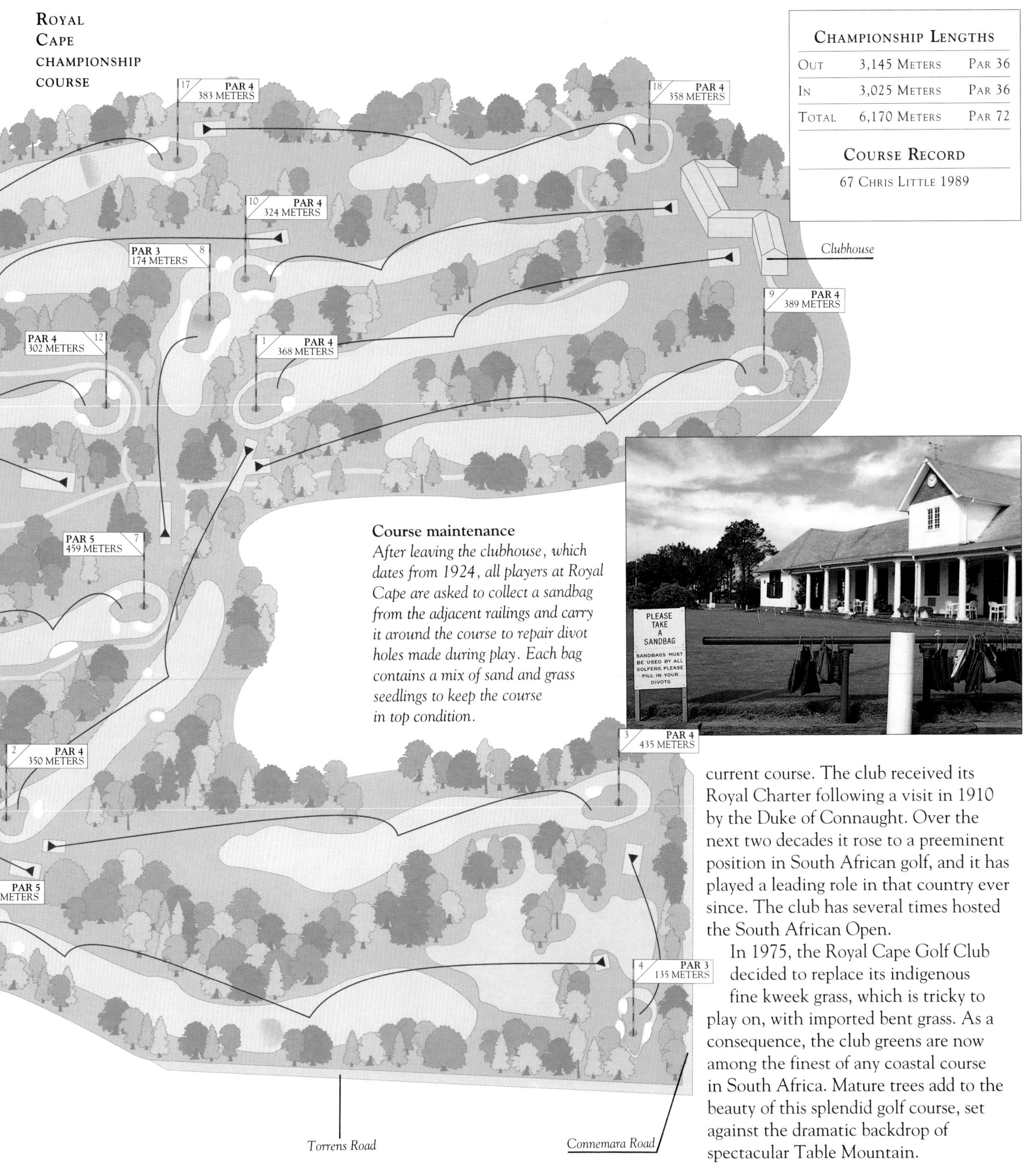

CHAMPIONSHIP LENGTHS		
OUT	3,145 METERS	PAR 36
IN	3,025 METERS	PAR 36
TOTAL	6,170 METERS	PAR 72

COURSE RECORD

67 CHRIS LITTLE 1989

Course maintenance

After leaving the clubhouse, which dates from 1924, all players at Royal Cape are asked to collect a sandbag from the adjacent railings and carry it around the course to repair divot holes made during play. Each bag contains a mix of sand and grass seedlings to keep the course in top condition.

current course. The club received its Royal Charter following a visit in 1910 by the Duke of Connaught. Over the next two decades it rose to a preeminent position in South African golf, and it has played a leading role in that country ever since. The club has several times hosted the South African Open.

In 1975, the Royal Cape Golf Club decided to replace its indigenous fine kweek grass, which is tricky to play on, with imported bent grass. As a consequence, the club greens are now among the finest of any coastal course in South Africa. Mature trees add to the beauty of this splendid golf course, set against the dramatic backdrop of spectacular Table Mountain.

ROYAL COUNTY DOWN

ROYAL COUNTY DOWN GOLF CLUB, NEWCASTLE, COUNTY DOWN, NORTHERN IRELAND

SOME SAY THAT next to Pine Valley in the United States, Royal County Down is the world's most difficult golf course. Such an assessment depends very much on personal opinion, but Welshman Dai Rees, captain of the last successful British Ryder Cup team before assistance arrived from the Continent, certainly supported such a view. Royal County Down is also one of the most beautiful courses, lying around the curve of Dundrum Bay within the shadow of the Mountains of Mourne.

5 **Blind challenge** (above)
A dogleg to the right from the 5th tee invites the player to cut off as much as he dares with a blind drive across heather. A long second shot to the green is menaced by a defensive phalanx of bunkers and sand dunes.

1 **Distracting scene**
Looking down to the first green, the scenery is fine enough to challenge the concentration of the most dedicated player, yet the first tee shot requires the closest attention. The drive to a narrow fairway in a valley, with sandhills on either side, demands a long and straight shot.

On a clear day the view from Royal County Down embraces both the peak of Slieve Donard and, 40 miles (64km) away to the east, the Isle of Man. On the other side, the hills of Ballynahinch complete a picture of breathtaking splendor.

Old Tom Morris laid out the original course for £4 in 1889, according to the minutes of the club, which was formed in March of that year. The club soon gained a reputation as having one of the finest courses in all Ireland. George Combe, the club captain in 1895–6, was largely

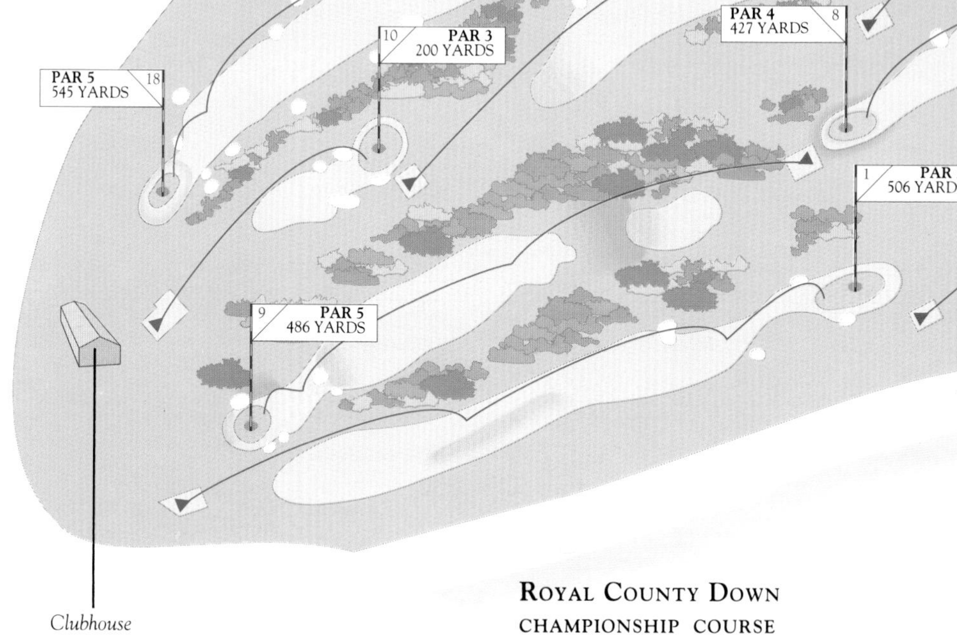

ROYAL COUNTY DOWN
CHAMPIONSHIP COURSE

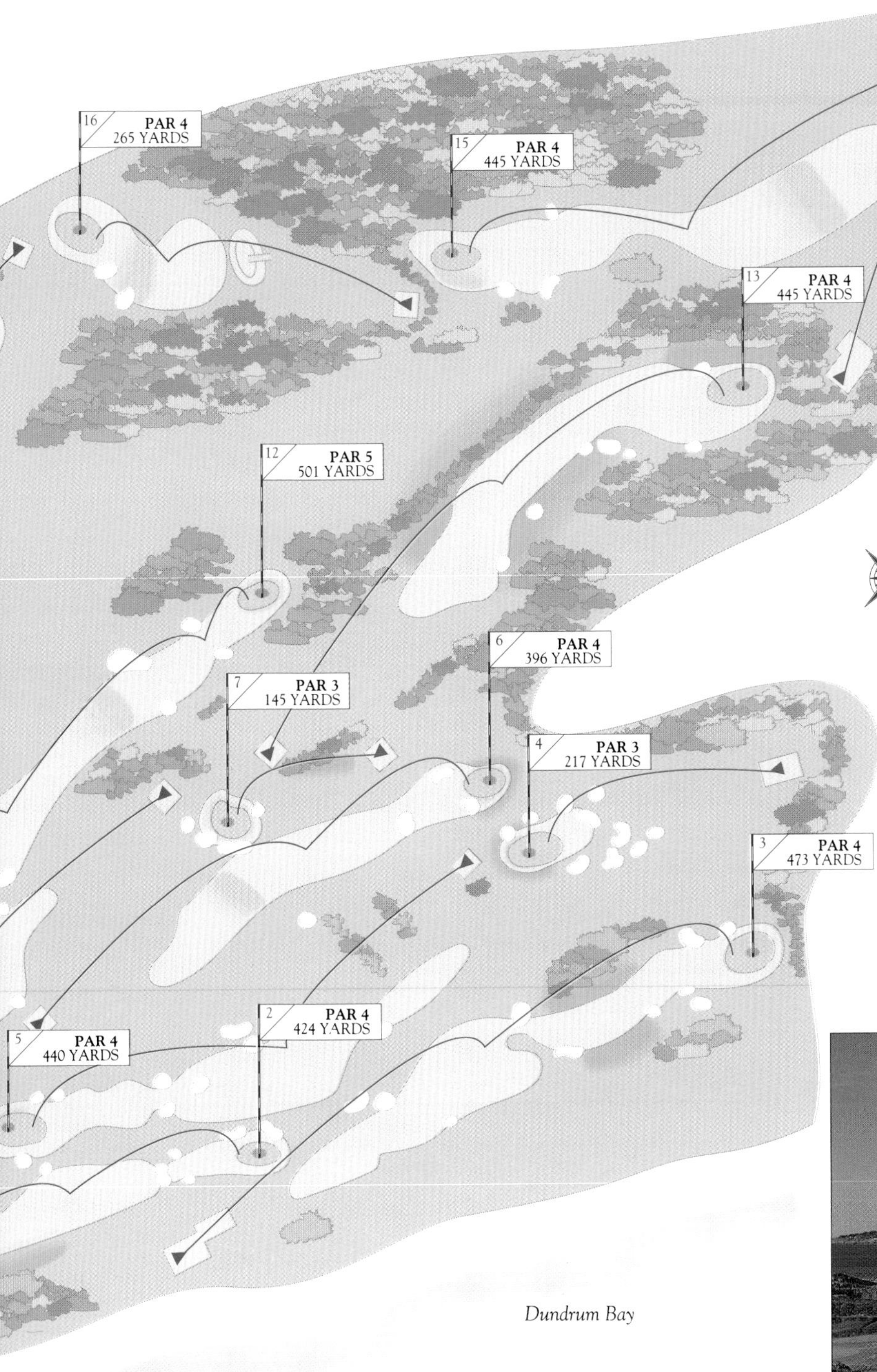

responsible for its layout then being changed to two loops of nine holes returning to the clubhouse, a revolutionary concept at the time. Later improvements to the course were influenced by the club professional Seymour Dunn in 1904, Harry Vardon in 1908, and Harry Colt in 1926. Since then the course has changed little.

Gorse and Roses

There is everything a player could wish for on this marvelous links at Newcastle, with splendid individual holes running through narrow valleys of rich, crisp turf, flanked by great swathes of gorse and wild roses. The championship course creates the most searching challenge for even the best of the world's players.

Five holes – the 2nd, 5th, 6th, 9th, and 15th – call for blind shots from the tee, and others impose blind shots to the green. Three of the par-3 holes are 200 yards or more in length and very demanding, severely punishing any mistake from the tee with threatening bunkers, gorse, and heavy rough. Only the 9th among the par-5 holes is under 500 yards, while the 18th is 545 yards. Uncompromising sand dunes add to the severity of the test.

Championship Lengths

Out	3,514 Yards	Par 36
In	3,454 Yards	Par 36
Total	6,968 Yards	Par 72

Course Record

66 James Bruen, Irish Open 1939

4 **Green in the gorse**
Spectacular scenery and a testing challenge are the hallmarks of Royal County Down. Gorse and wild flowers abound in the duneland around the curve of Dundrum Bay. All the par-3 holes on the course are magnificent, and the 4th, although not the toughest, is no exception.

ROYAL DORNOCH

ROYAL DORNOCH GOLF CLUB, DORNOCH, SUTHERLAND, SCOTLAND

IN THE FAR northeast corner of Scotland lies a golf course that is unsurpassed in its wild beauty. Royal Dornoch, a historic links where records show golf has been played since 1616, has a unique atmosphere born of its remoteness as well as the undoubted quality of its layout. It is a course for the traditionalist and the purist.

Local folk legend
On the Dornoch crest, a Sutherland wild mountain cat holds a horseshoe torn from the rear leg of an invading Norseman's mount.

To reach Royal Dornoch requires a journey through some of the finest of Scotland's landscapes. And what a joy is in store for the intrepid traveler who reaches the historic old town, with its air of peace and remoteness and the open friendliness of its population.

Only St. Andrews and Leith can claim greater antiquity than Dornoch. In 1630 Sir Robert Gordon wrote in his *History of Sutherland*: "About this toun there are the fairest and largest links of any pairt of Scotland, fit for Archery, Golfing, Ryding, and all other exercises; they doe surpasse the fields of Montrose and St. Andrews." Thus, some form of the royal and ancient game has probably been played at Dornoch for more than 350 years. Organized modern golf came to Dornoch in the autumn of 1876, when the local chief constable, Alex McHardy, who was from Fife, and Dr. Hugh Gunn, a graduate of St. Andrews University, arranged a meeting to establish the Dornoch Golf Club. The club was formed the following spring, originally with a nine-hole course. Some ten years later Old Tom Morris from St. Andrews was called in to add a further nine holes. The man who most influenced the development of Dornoch, however, was John Sutherland, in his time one of the most revered names in Scottish golf. An estate manager in the town of Dornoch, he was appointed secretary of the club in 1883, a position he was to hold for more than 50 years. He made several revisions to the course layout in collaboration with J.H. Taylor, who became a regular visitor.

Postcard home
Among the game's wealthy and famous who journeyed to Dornoch were Joyce and Roger Wethered, who were regular summer visitors and helped to spread Dornoch's fame.

Railroad town
The coming of the railroad in 1903 put Dornoch on the golfing map, and the small Scottish town soon became a popular holiday resort.

Royal links (right)
Royal Dornoch is a course that everyone who loves the game of golf should visit, simply to enjoy its unique, remote atmosphere.

Arctic winds (above)
The homeward nine is played alongside the Dornoch Firth, fully exposed to the wild moods of the weather.

John Sutherland was one of the early pioneers of greenskeeping and course maintenance. The construction of greens was his speciality, but he was also an architect in his own right and planned several northern courses. He was a fine player and unrivaled administrator.

The present course at Dornoch has four par 3s and only two par 5s. It follows a natural soft S-shape along the line of the shore, a classic "out-and-back" configuration. As in all classic links, the wind is the key factor. When it is from the prevailing west, the first eight holes may lull the player into a false sense of well-being, although if the course is fast and dry the ability to judge approaches will have been well tested by then. From the 9th tee the

Influential Scot
Donald Ross based the design of many U.S. courses on Dornoch.

battle for home is on and there is no let-up. Only the 17th reverses the direction of the homeward journey, but it allows little respite because the drive into a hidden valley is fraught with danger if too much liberty is taken with the bunkers and gorse on the left side. The pitch to the green will seldom be of much length, but it requires a deft touch over a gaggle of awkward bunkers to a plateau green which is difficult to hold.

The home hole requires two solid blows to make the open green, even in normal circumstances. When the weather boils up, as it so quickly can in this isolated corner of Sutherland in the far north of Scotland, it often requires three strokes from even the strongest player, and all must be substantially struck.

5 **High tee**
Dornoch's 357-yard par-4 5th hole is without doubt one of the most beautiful on the course. The tee is set high on the ridge of sand dunes and lost in a sea of gorse which, when in bloom, creates one of golf's most spectacular sights.

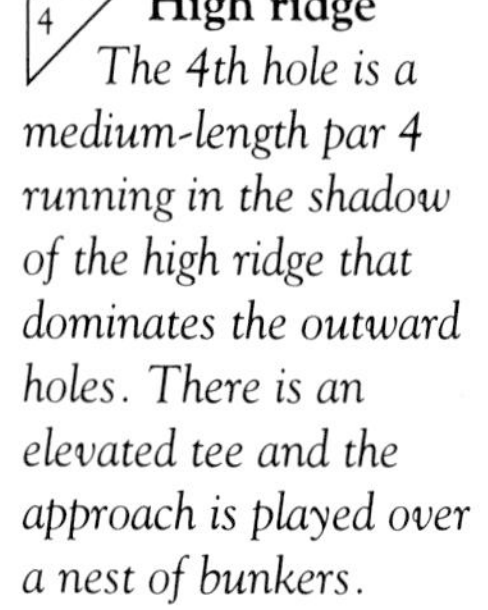

4 **High ridge**
The 4th hole is a medium-length par 4 running in the shadow of the high ridge that dominates the outward holes. There is an elevated tee and the approach is played over a nest of bunkers.

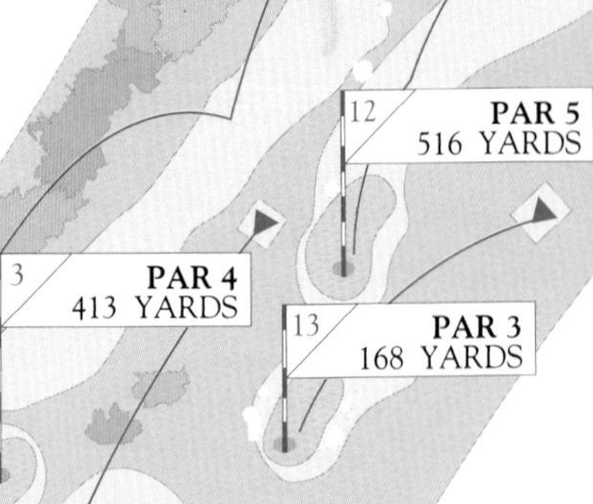

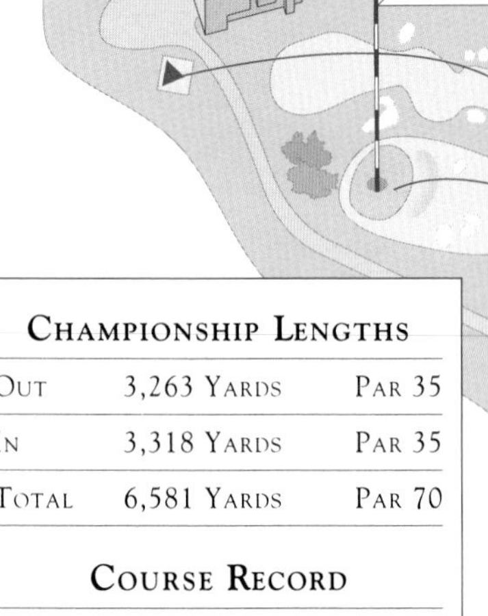

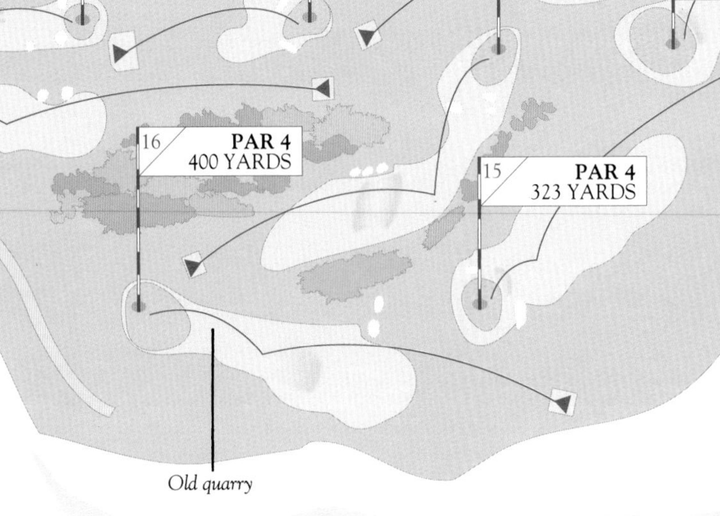

Championship Lengths

Out	3,263 Yards	Par 35
In	3,318 Yards	Par 35
Total	6,581 Yards	Par 70

Course Record

65 Jim Miller,
Fraser Shield 1971

14 **Foxy** (right)
The 14th, known as Foxy, does not possess a single bunker, and this reflects the quality of what is widely accepted as the best and most subtle of holes on this great links.

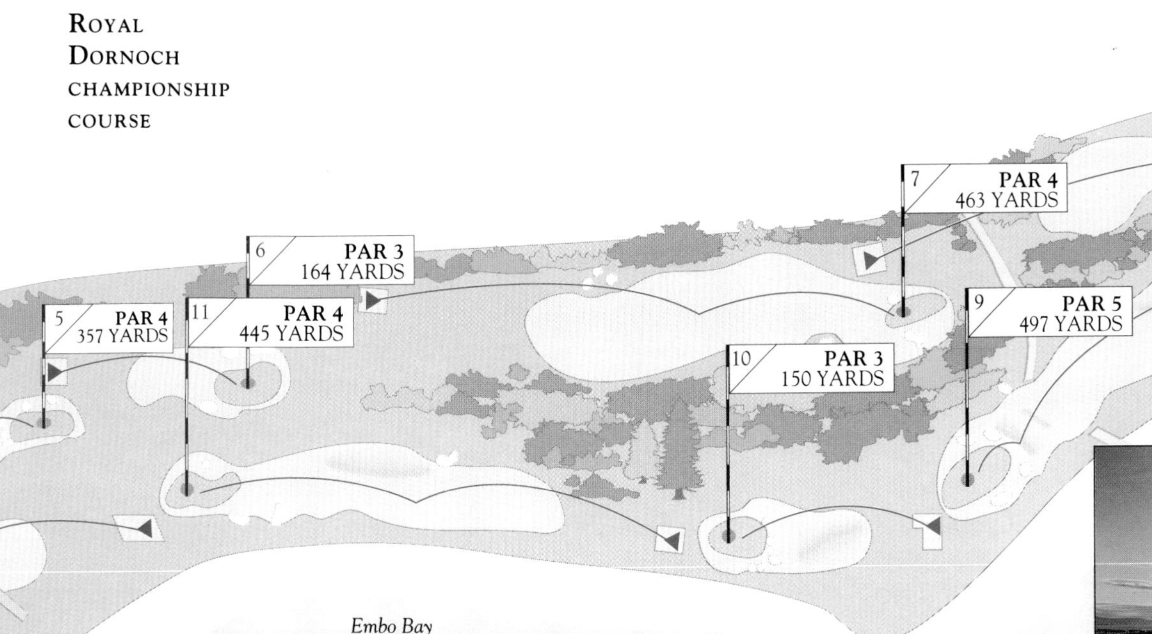

Dornoch's remoteness has mitigated against its hosting major events. The Scottish Ladies' Amateur Championship was played there in 1971, and again in 1984. The following year the Amateur Championship went to Dornoch, Garth McGimpsey emerging victorious. But unfortunately this famous links has not, on the whole, witnessed a great deal of top-flight competition.

Although Dornoch has not hosted many leading championships, it has nevertheless been the site of much first-class play. Tom Watson, five-time British Open champion, rates Dornoch as one of the great courses of the five continents. "I have played none finer," he has said; "It is a natural masterpiece."

The influence of Dornoch has been enormous, through the club's former professional and head greenskeeper, Donald Ross. Ross went to the United States at the turn of the century and became one of the game's greatest golf-course architects. Many of his courses, notably Pinehurst, are among the best in the United States.

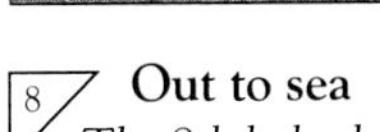

Out to sea
The 8th hole, known as Dunrobin, is a 437-yard par 4. It is played northeast toward the sea across an old quarry, the drive sailing downhill into a hidden hollow. The green is, as usual, well defended by bunkers. The course then turns back along the shore for the remaining ten holes.

The Names of Royal Dornoch

1st First	10th Fuaran
2nd Ord	11th A'chlach
3rd Earl's Cross	12th Sutherland
4th Achinchanter	13th Bents
5th Hilton	14th Foxy
6th Whinny Brae	15th Stulaig
7th Pier	16th High Hole
8th Dunrobin	17th Valley
9th Craiglaith	18th Home

The 5th hole is named for the great Hoylake amateur, Harold Hilton. Other names, such as Ord (for the Ord of Caithness) and Sutherland, relate to geographical features of the area. The 14th is called Foxy because it is considered exceptionally tricky to play.

Royal Liverpool

Royal Liverpool Golf Club, Hoylake, The Wirral, Merseyside, England

Despite its somewhat austere first appearance, the links of the Royal Liverpool Golf Club at Hoylake lies at the very heart of the history of the royal and ancient game in England, and golf owes a large debt of gratitude to the club for its pioneering spirit. The Hoylake course is without question among the toughest and most demanding of the great seaside championship courses.

Seaside memento
The Royal Liverpool Golf Club crest depicts a mythical bird holding a piece of seaweed, or "liver," in its beak.

Built in 1869 on the Warren, a racecourse owned by the Royal Liverpool Hunt Club, Hoylake is the oldest of English seaside courses, except for Westward Ho! in Devon. Robert Chambers and George Morris built the original course, which was enlarged to 18 holes in 1871.

For its first seven years, the course doubled as a racetrack, and Hoylake's racing origins are still remembered in the name of the 18th hole, known as the Stand, and in the ringing of the original saddling bell to summon members to dine.

Until 1895, Royal Liverpool's clubhouse was at the Royal Hotel, which was owned by the father of one of Hoylake's most famous players, the amateur John Ball. Hoylake was also the home of Ball's arch-rival, Harold Hilton, another great amateur of the same era.

For many decades Hoylake was recognized as the most important course in England, and it is steeped in golfing history. The British Amateur Championship, the oldest event of its kind in the world, had its origins there in 1885, and the first international match between Scotland and England was played at Hoylake in 1902. The first competition between an amateur men's team from the United States and one from Great Britain was also held there in 1921; this match was the precursor of the Walker Cup.

The Royal Liverpool Golf Club was also one of the earliest arbiters of amateur and professional status. When the club staged the first Amateur Championship, an entry was received from a Scotsman by the name of Douglas Rolland who, the previous year, had finished second in the British Open. His application was rejected, but this still left the club with the problem of how precisely an "amateur" was to be defined.

Open landscape
Hoylake's enduring quality is evident in this 1957 oil painting by Arthur Weaver, probably golf's leading contemporary artist.

Sovereign Issue

John Ball was a crucial case in point. He wished to enter the amateur event, but in 1878 he had taken money from the game. Still only 15 years old, he had finished tied for fourth place in the British Open. He lost the play-off, but there was a money prize due him.

There is some doubt as to whether the sum involved was a sovereign or half a sovereign, but young John Ball put the money in his pocket. This incident was brought up against Ball when he wanted to enter the Amateur Championship. However, a diplomatic solution was found to the problem. The age limit for receiving cash prizes was fixed at 16, and so John Ball, only 15 when he had taken the money, did not forfeit his amateur status. He went on to win the Amateur Championship eight times.

The Hoylake course is a classic links course, exposed to the vagaries of wind and weather. There is little in the way of great scenic splendor here, although the

Home player (above)
John Ball was born at Hoylake in 1862 and was always considered unbeatable on his home ground, where he had honed his golfing skills.

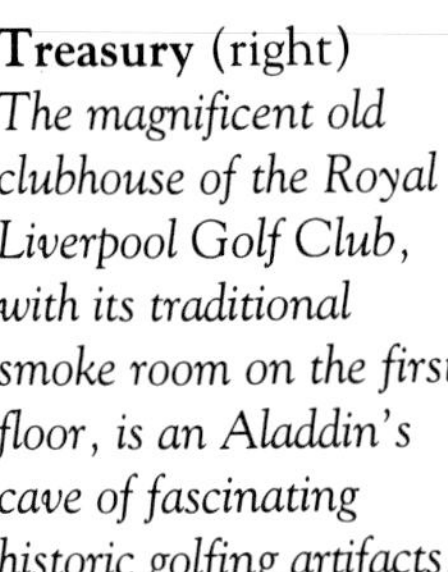

Treasury (right)
The magnificent old clubhouse of the Royal Liverpool Golf Club, with its traditional smoke room on the first floor, is an Aladdin's cave of fascinating historic golfing artifacts.

hills of North Wales come into view toward the middle of the round and Hilbre Island rises out of the vast expanse of sandbanks in majestic solitude.

The course is unique among open championship sites because a player can hit the ball out-of-bounds even within the course boundaries. It has one of the most fearsome opening shots in championship golf. The practice ground runs along the entire right side of the hole, turning sharply right in the landing area for the drive and continuing all the way to the green. It is a most unnerving start whether with or against the wind.

All the great players of the past, including Bobby Jones and Walter Hagen, have faced this particular challenge and the many others that follow. The short, controversial 7th, known as Dowie, is a fine example of Hoylake's need for accurate play. The hole is flanked on the left by a low turf wall beyond which is out-of-bounds. The drive has to carry 200 yards to the green and there is absolutely no margin for error.

The five holes to the finish are extremely long, totaling 2,349 yards, and as difficult as will be found anywhere. The 17th, a 418-yard par 4, is generally regarded as the toughest among them. The second shot here requires precision and good judgment to avoid bunkers on the left and the road to the right. If there is an adverse wind, the problems multiply.

Royal Liverpool Championship Course

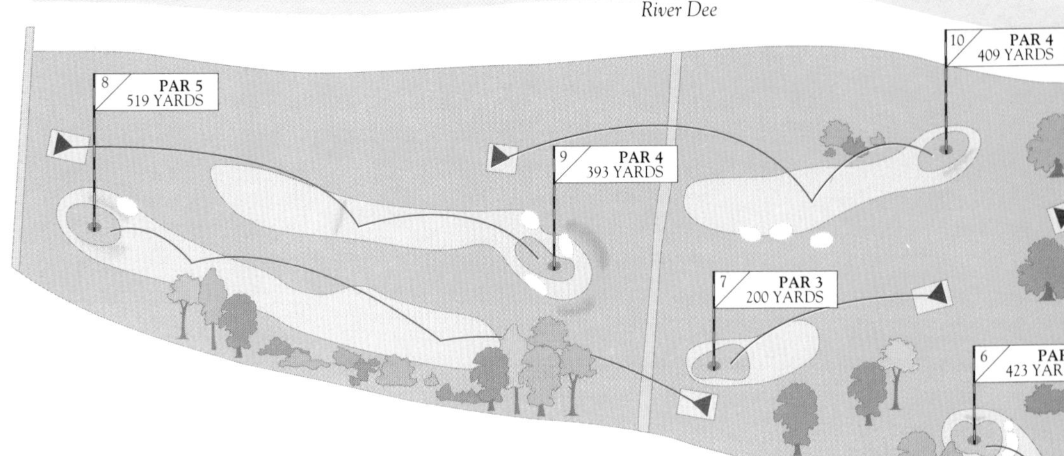

The British Open has been played at Hoylake ten times. Bobby Jones achieved the second of his four Grand Slam wins in 1930 on this course, despite taking a 7 at the 8th hole in the last round. The last occasion Royal Liverpool hosted the Open was in 1967, when the popular Argentinian Roberto de Vicenzo was the winner. With Jack Nicklaus in hot pursuit, de Vicenzo birdied the par-5 16th in the last round, after hitting a superb second shot over the out-of-bounds practice area to the middle of the green. Hoylake has since been taken off the Open Championship roster, and many people believe that the tournament is poorer as a consequence of this decision.

11 **Alpine remoteness** (above)
In among the dunes at the far end of the course from the clubhouse, the 11th – known as the Alps – is a superb one-shot hole. It demands a prodigious blow to reach the remote oblong green. Some players tackle it with a wood.

The Names of Royal Liverpool

1st Course	10th Dee
2nd Road	11th Alps
3rd Long	12th Hilbre
4th New	13th Rushes
5th Telegraph	14th Field
6th Briars	15th Lake
7th Dowie	16th Dun
8th Far	17th Royal
9th Punch Bowl	18th Stand

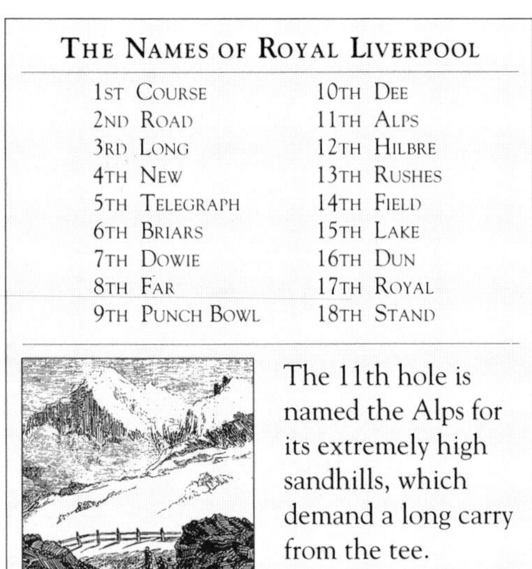

The 11th hole is named the Alps for its extremely high sandhills, which demand a long carry from the tee.

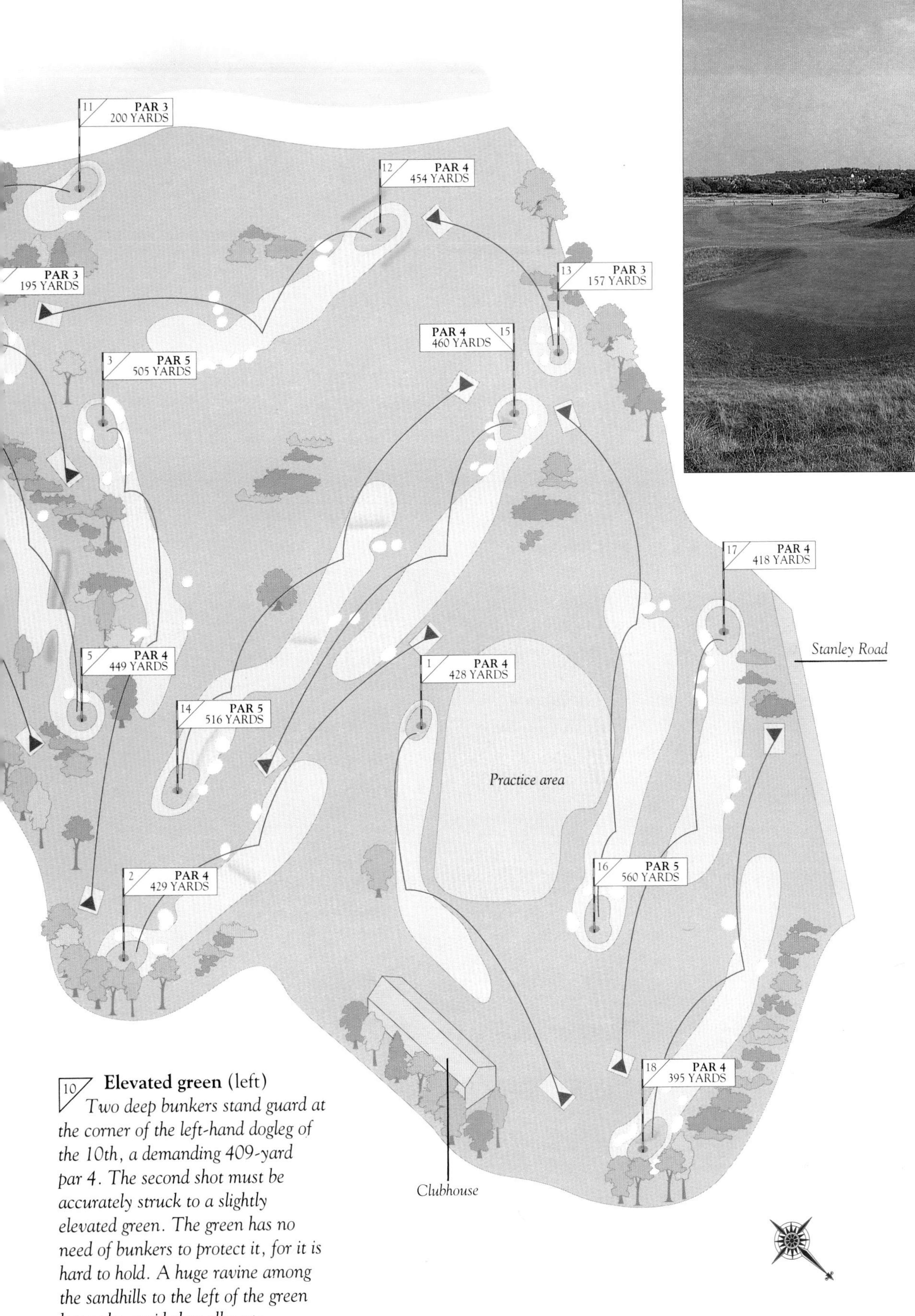

12 Accurate strokes

The dogleg 12th is a severe test of shot-making ability. It requires a long, straight drive into the neck of a tight landing area between two groups of savage bunkers, a visit to any of which virtually guarantees the loss of a stroke. The long second shot must steer well clear of a pair of bunkers set on the edge of the fairway in front of the green.

10 Elevated green (left)

Two deep bunkers stand guard at the corner of the left-hand dogleg of the 10th, a demanding 409-yard par 4. The second shot must be accurately struck to a slightly elevated green. The green has no need of bunkers to protect it, for it is hard to hold. A huge ravine among the sandhills to the left of the green has to be avoided at all costs.

Championship Lengths		
Out	3,541 Yards	Par 36
In	3,569 Yards	Par 36
Total	7,110 Yards	Par 72

Course Record

64 Brian Waites, European Open 1981

Open Champions at Royal Liverpool

1897 Harold Hilton †; 1902 Sandy Herd; 1907 Arnaud Massy; 1913 J.H. Taylor; 1924 Walter Hagen; 1930 Bobby Jones †; 1936 Alf Padgham; 1947 Fred Daly; 1956 Peter Thomson; 1967 Roberto de Vicenzo

Royal Lytham and St. Annes

Royal Lytham and St. Annes Golf Club, Lytham St. Annes, Lancashire, England

The last of the great line of golf courses along the edge of the Irish Sea, which begins at Hoylake and is strung out northward along the Lancashire coast, Royal Lytham and St. Annes is one of England's most difficult championship courses. Since the first 18 holes were laid out here in 1897, it has changed in character from a pure seaside links to a softer, lusher course. But the roll call of British Open champions at Lytham includes many of the game's finest players and is a tribute to the quality of the challenge that the course continues to present.

Changing outlook
Over the years, the Lytham course has become more hemmed in, and it now has a distinctly urban setting; three sides are overlooked by houses and the fourth runs alongside a railroad. Although it is now some way from the sea and is greener than it once was, the course still retains many of the qualities of a true links.

Championship Lengths

Out	3,302 Yards	Par 35
In	3,555 Yards	Par 36
Total	6,857 Yards	Par 71

Course Record

65 Christy O'Connor, The Open 1969; Brian Huggett, Dunlop Masters 1970; Bill Longmuir, Seve Ballesteros, The Open 1979

Open Champions at Royal Lytham and St. Annes

1926 Bobby Jones †; 1952 Bobby Locke; 1958 Peter Thomson; 1963 Bob Charles; 1969 Tony Jacklin; 1974 Gary Player; 1979, 1988 Seve Ballesteros

Alexander Doleman, a schoolteacher from Musselburgh in Scotland, was the driving force behind the formation of the Lytham and St. Annes Golf Club in 1886. Grounds were leased from the St.-Annes-on-Sea Land and Building Company and an 18-hole course was built, with an additional nine holes for ladies.

The club had negotiated only a short lease, however, and the leasing company was not eager to extend it, so in 1897 the club moved to its present location. By 1903 the club had 751 members, and nine years later the membership was able to raise £8,500 for the building of a magnificent new clubhouse, which still stands today. This sum must have seemed a king's ransom in those days.

George Lowe is credited with the design of the original course on the present site, but such notable architects as Harry Colt, Herbert Fowler, and C.K. Cotton have also left their mark at Royal Lytham and St. Annes over the years. Their course has withstood the onslaught of the modern game extremely well.

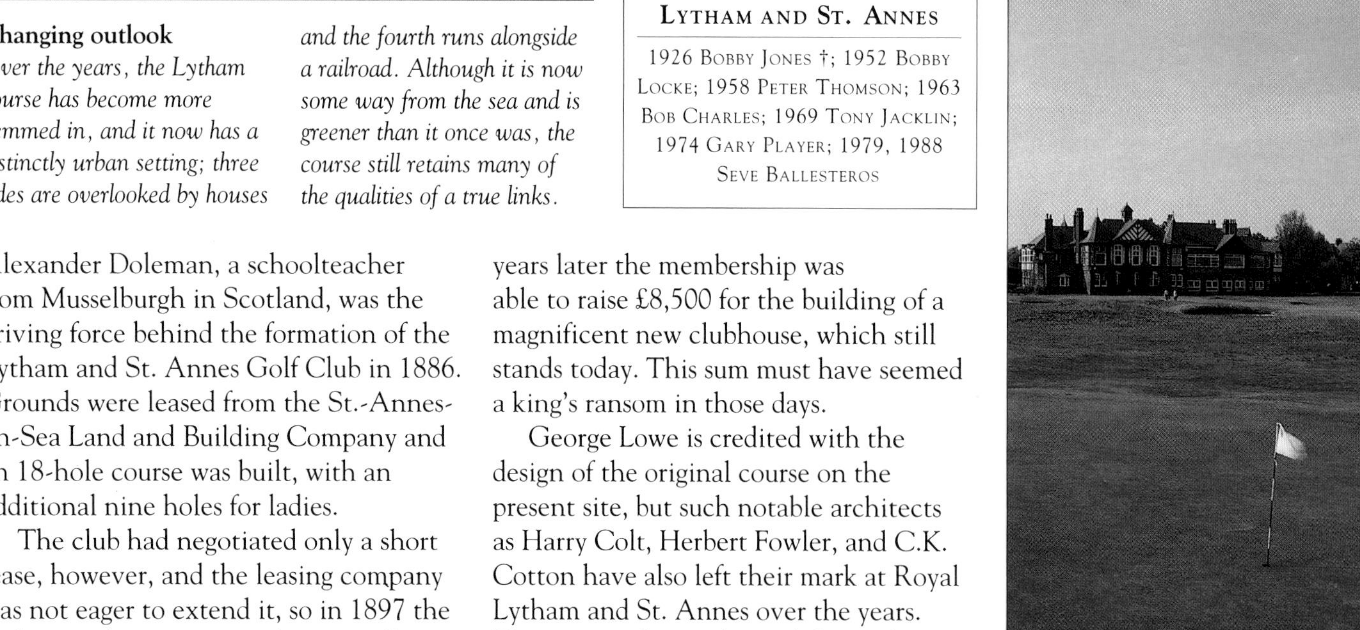

Recalling his first visit to Lytham in the 1920s, Henry Cotton likened the greens, burned by the hot summer, to "putting on ice." Anyone who has ever played on traditional British golfing turf during a drought, when no water is available to temper the speed, will know what Cotton meant. Modern watering systems have ended the days of icelike greens at Lytham, but they can still be slick in dry conditions, and they have retained the fine links grasses that many great courses have lost in recent times through overuse of the sprinkler.

The British Open was first played at Lytham in 1926, when Bobby Jones scored the first of his three British Open victories. Bobby Locke, Peter Thomson, and left-hander Bob Charles all survived dramas to win Opens there in later years.

Tight Finishes

In 1974 Gary Player made his final shot to the last green left-handed, using the back of his putter, after he had run through the green with his approach and the ball had lodged against the wall of the clubhouse. This hole was also the scene of great emotion in 1969, when Tony Jacklin became the first Briton for 18 years to win the Championship. A decade later the crowds were cheering the first Open win by Severiano Ballesteros, a victory that he was to repeat when the Championship returned to Lytham again in 1988. Curiously, the British Open has not yet been won at Lytham by an American professional, the only course on the regular Championship roster where this has not occurred.

Although Peter Thomson played the front nine in 29 strokes in the 1963 Open – amazing Henry Cotton, who said it was a "puzzle to anyone" to know just how Thomson had done it – low scores are not common at Royal Lytham unless the weather is particularly benign. There is too much impending trouble for the course to fail to extract a penalty over four rounds of championship golf.

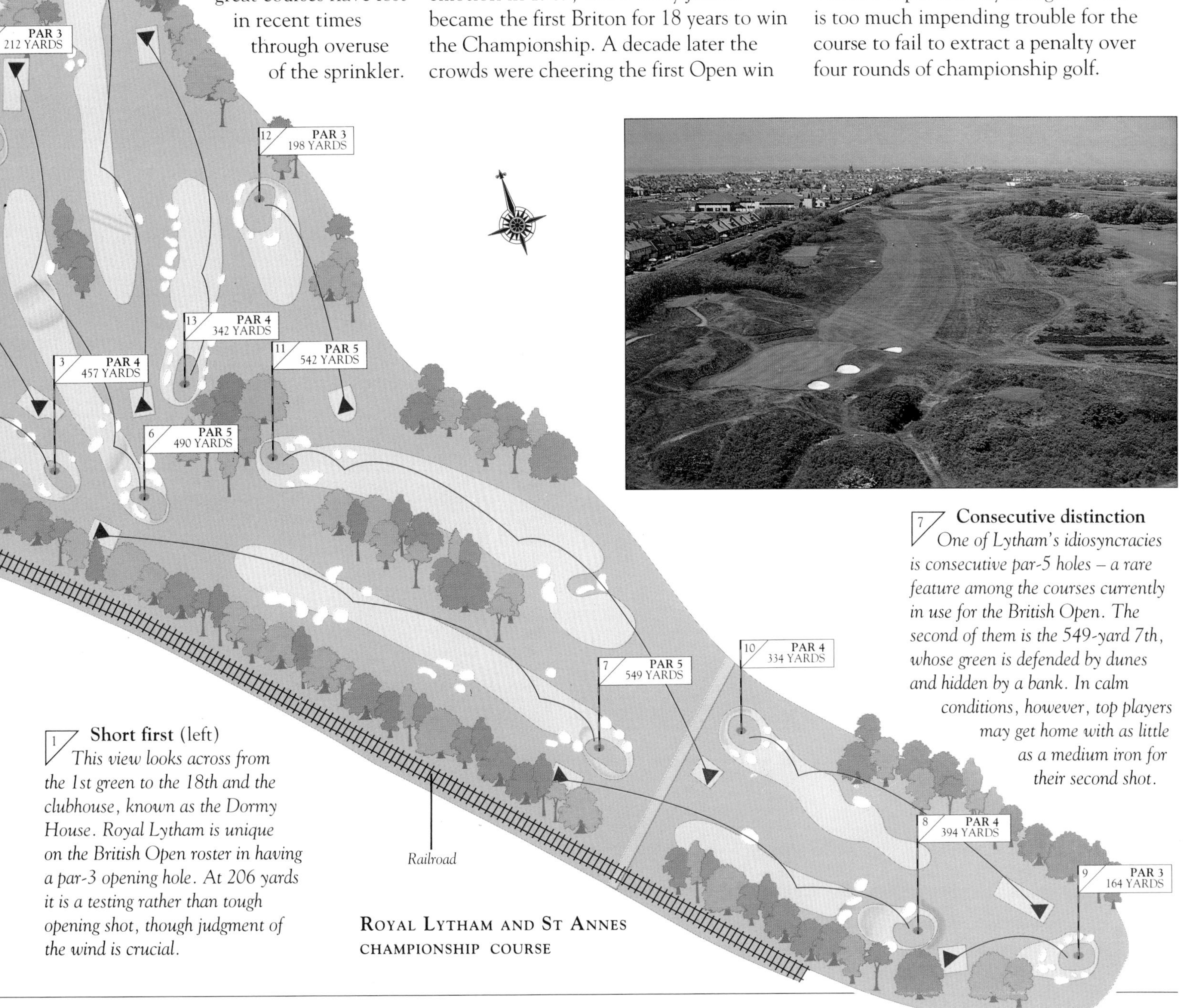

Royal Lytham and St Annes
championship course

7 **Consecutive distinction**
One of Lytham's idiosyncracies is consecutive par-5 holes – a rare feature among the courses currently in use for the British Open. The second of them is the 549-yard 7th, whose green is defended by dunes and hidden by a bank. In calm conditions, however, top players may get home with as little as a medium iron for their second shot.

1 **Short first** (left)
This view looks across from the 1st green to the 18th and the clubhouse, known as the Dormy House. Royal Lytham is unique on the British Open roster in having a par-3 opening hole. At 206 yards it is a testing rather than tough opening shot, though judgment of the wind is crucial.

Royal Melbourne

Royal Melbourne Golf Club, Black Rock, Victoria, Australia

The championship course at Royal Melbourne is an amalgamation of some of the finest work of two great golf-course designers: Alex Russell, the 1924 Australian Open champion, who was responsible for the East course, and Dr. Alister Mackenzie, architect of Augusta National, who laid out the West course. The two courses were blended at the end of the 1950s to form the finest course in Australia, and one of the world's greatest.

The enthusiastic immigrants who founded the Royal Melbourne Club in 1891 were strongly influenced by the traditions of St. Andrews, many of them having arrived in Australia from the "auld grey toon." When the club's members were seeking a new site for their course in 1924, it was natural they should be attracted by a stretch of duneland covered in heather and bracken, reminiscent of a Scottish links, and that Mackenzie, a Scotsman, should be imported as a designer.

Combining the Best

The current championship course was devised so as to avoid the busy roads that crossed the existing East and West courses and was first used for the Canada Cup (now the World Cup) in 1959. It comprises six holes from Russell's layout and 12 from Mackenzie's.

Amalgamation produced a course of outstanding quality. The short 304m par-4 3rd and the formidable 395m par-4 18th – a truly stupendous finishing hole – are among the most challenging holes anywhere in the world. But it is the Royal Melbourne greens that mark the caliber of this course. They are a joy to putt on and there are none faster or truer anywhere the game is played. To Claude Crockford, head greenskeeper at the club for many years, belongs the credit for these masterpieces, which are preserved in the finest traditions of links golf.

The rough-hewn bunkers, dug out by horse and scoop in the same manner as the rest of the course, are another remarkable feature of this outstanding layout. There is none of the sterile prissiness so evident in modern bunker design. These are genuine, gutsy hazards, often wild in appearance and most of them deadly in their severity.

5 **Slippery slope** *A steep slope in front of the 5th green ensures that any shot left short will trickle down the hill, leaving an extremely difficult chip back. The green itself slopes steeply from the back to the front, and the player requires a deft stroke with the putter to avoid three-putting.*

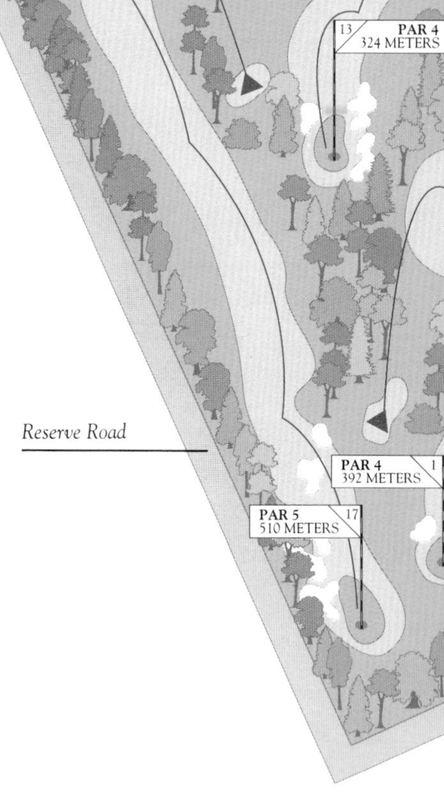

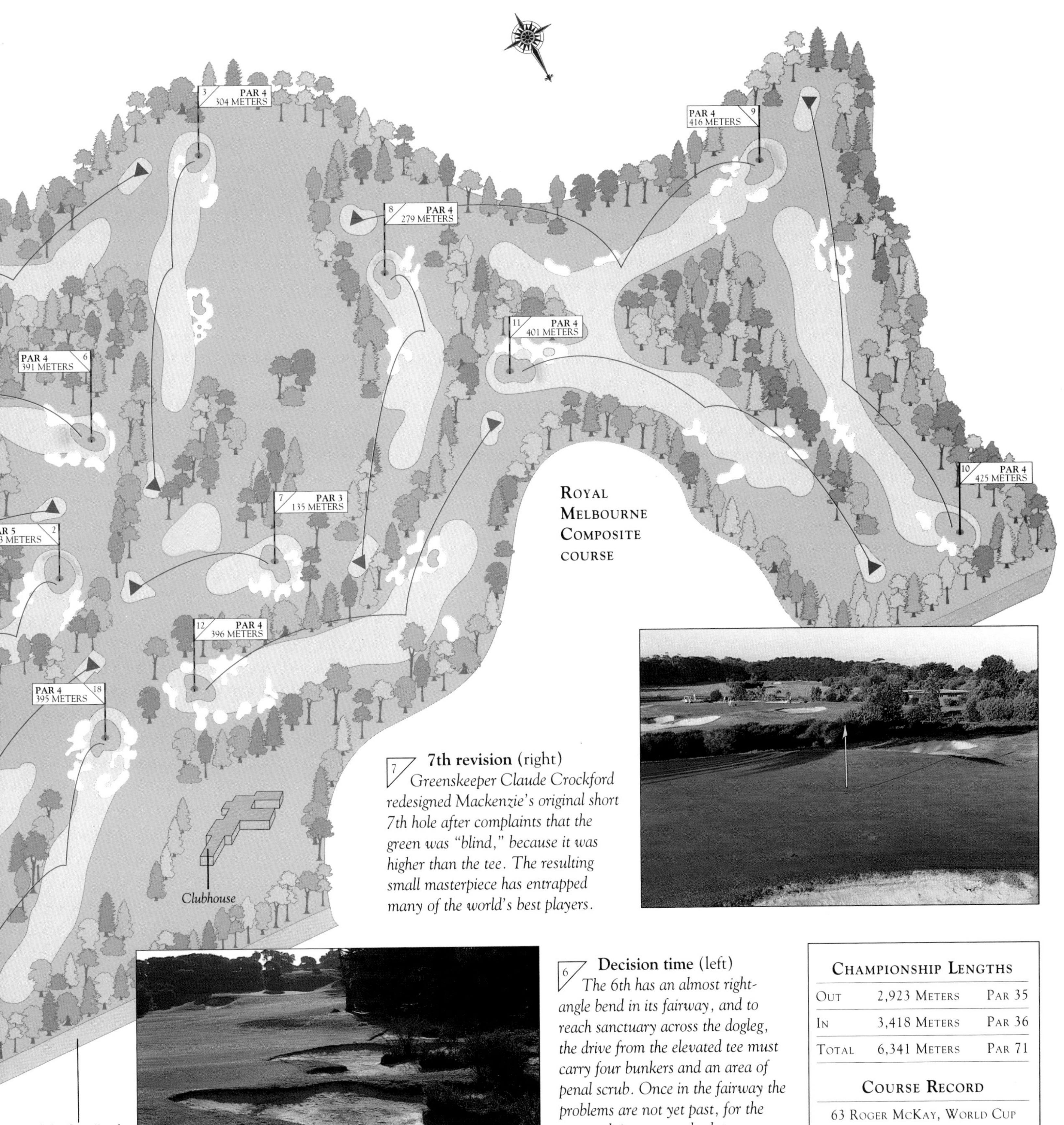

ROYAL MELBOURNE COMPOSITE COURSE

7th revision (right)
Greenskeeper Claude Crockford redesigned Mackenzie's original short 7th hole after complaints that the green was "blind," because it was higher than the tee. The resulting small masterpiece has entrapped many of the world's best players.

Decision time (left)
The 6th has an almost right-angle bend in its fairway, and to reach sanctuary across the dogleg, the drive from the elevated tee must carry four bunkers and an area of penal scrub. Once in the fairway the problems are not yet past, for the approach is up a gentle slope to a green guarded by deep bunkers.

Championship Lengths

Out	2,923 Meters	Par 35
In	3,418 Meters	Par 36
Total	6,341 Meters	Par 71

Course Record

63 Roger McKay, World Cup 1988; Ian Baker-Finch 1990

ROYAL NORTH DEVON

ROYAL NORTH DEVON GOLF CLUB, WESTWARD HO!, BIDEFORD, DEVON, ENGLAND

THE LINKS COURSE of the Royal North Devon Club at Westward Ho! is the oldest in England and a supreme example of natural seaside golf. The layout is nearly the same as it was over 80 years ago, and while some people might call it a museum piece, it is no less a challenge now than it was then. It requires dedication to make the journey to Westward Ho! because of its remoteness, but the trip is well worthwhile. Were it not so difficult to reach, the course would surely have hosted many more championships than it has in its long history.

Grazed turf (above)
The difference between the totally untended linksland and that of the course at Westward Ho! shows up clearly. The course is relatively smooth – it is grazed by livestock as well as being cared for by greenskeepers – and has become more mellow with the passage of time.

Royal plumes
The club's crest is dominated by the plumes of the Prince of Wales, later Edward VII, who awarded the North Devon Club its Charter in 1865.

Golf has been played at Westward Ho! since the early 1850s, and Old Tom Morris traveled all the way from Scotland to have a look at the first primitive layout in 1860. But it was not until 1864 that the club itself was founded. It was then called the North Devon and West of England Club, and the Rev. I.H. Gossett, vicar of the nearby village of Northam, whose family had been instrumental in developing the game there, was elected the first captain of the club.

Old Tom Morris again made the long journey from Scotland that year and laid out two courses, one of 17 holes and the other of 22. There were several alterations before the turn of the century, but the layout today is much as Herbert Fowler left it after reconstructing it in 1908. The course has always been on common land, known as the Burrows, and the commoners have rights to graze animals there. They still exercise those rights today, and sheep and horses may be encountered by the golfer, sometimes in large numbers. Westward Ho!, named after the famous novel of that name by Charles Kingsley, is characterized by several other striking features, not least of them the sea rushes that threaten not only a player's score but his physical well-being. On the inland holes these rushes form the rough and are often 6 feet (1.8m) tall. They are tipped with steel-hard spikes that have been known to impale a golf ball and would do the same to its owner were he fool enough to do battle with them.

The course is famous, too, for the many top players who have emanated from it. J.H. Taylor, one of the members of the Great Triumvirate, learned to play at Westward Ho! He became interested in the game when he caddied for the teenage Horace Hutchinson, who was later to win the Amateur Championship twice and become an eminent writer on golf. Taylor was then a houseboy in the Hutchinson household, but within a few years he

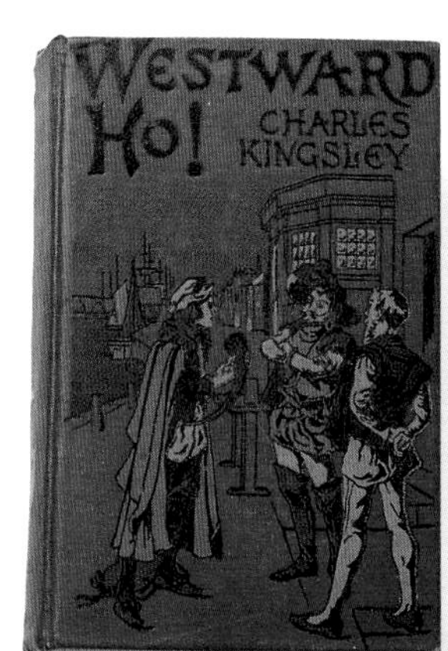

Novel name
Charles Kingsley's famous adventure novel Westward Ho!, *written in 1855, gave the course its name.*

Taylor's links with the past (left)
Royal North Devon's most famous son, J.H. Taylor, owed his Open triumphs to the lessons he learned on its fine Devon linksland.

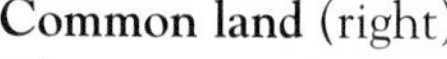

Common land (right)
There are occasional expansive views across the Bristol Channel from the links at Royal North Devon. In addition to threatening hillocks, obstacles on the course include animals that graze the common land. The course abounds with white-painted marker stones.

became the first English professional to beat the Scots at their own game, winning the Open Championship five times between 1894 and 1913. In 1957 he was elected president at North Devon, the club where he had been a caddie as a boy.

Hosting the Amateur

The course has hosted the Amateur Championship three times in its history. In 1912 John Ball from Hoylake won the last of his eight titles, beating Abe Mitchell at the 38th hole. The Amateur returned there in 1925, Robert Harris taking the honors, and Eric Martin Smith was something of a surprise winner when the Amateur Championship was last played there in 1931.

This historic links has never been easy to score on, even for the finest players. In the first 100 years of the history of Royal North Devon, only four rounds under 70 were recorded in any of the club's regular medal competitions.

In more recent years, as with so many other great links courses, the greens have become far more meadowlike in character and their slickness has been softened. In fact, there are many who feel Westward Ho! would be the finest links course in all of England were it to be returned to its original, more natural condition.

The clubhouse and other facilities are comfortable and welcoming, and the atmosphere within its walls reeks of the tradition behind this most ancient of

Royal North Devon
Championship Course

1 Happy with a par
The 1st is a par 5 of a modest 485 yards, but the player who goes to the second hole without having conceded a stroke to the course should be well pleased. The outlook from the tee may appear flat and featureless, but the course is actually full of natural hazards, including grazing livestock.

Championship Lengths

Out	3,309 Yards	Par 36
In	3,353 Yards	Par 35
Total	6,662 Yards	Par 71

Course Record

66 Kel Nagle, Martini International 1975

4 Carry the Cape
There is no other option but to hit over the massive, sleepered Cape bunker at the 4th hole with the drive.

English golf courses. The wide-open skies of a virtually treeless links give the course an almost limitless sense of freedom. In golfing terms, however, it is a freedom that allows a player to score well or else to get into deep trouble, and the course layout demands constant concentration. Westward Ho! will continue to delight golf connoisseurs for years to come.

6 **Over humps**
The 6th hole runs through humps and hollows toward the River Torridge estuary. It has an open plateau green and demands a long second shot.

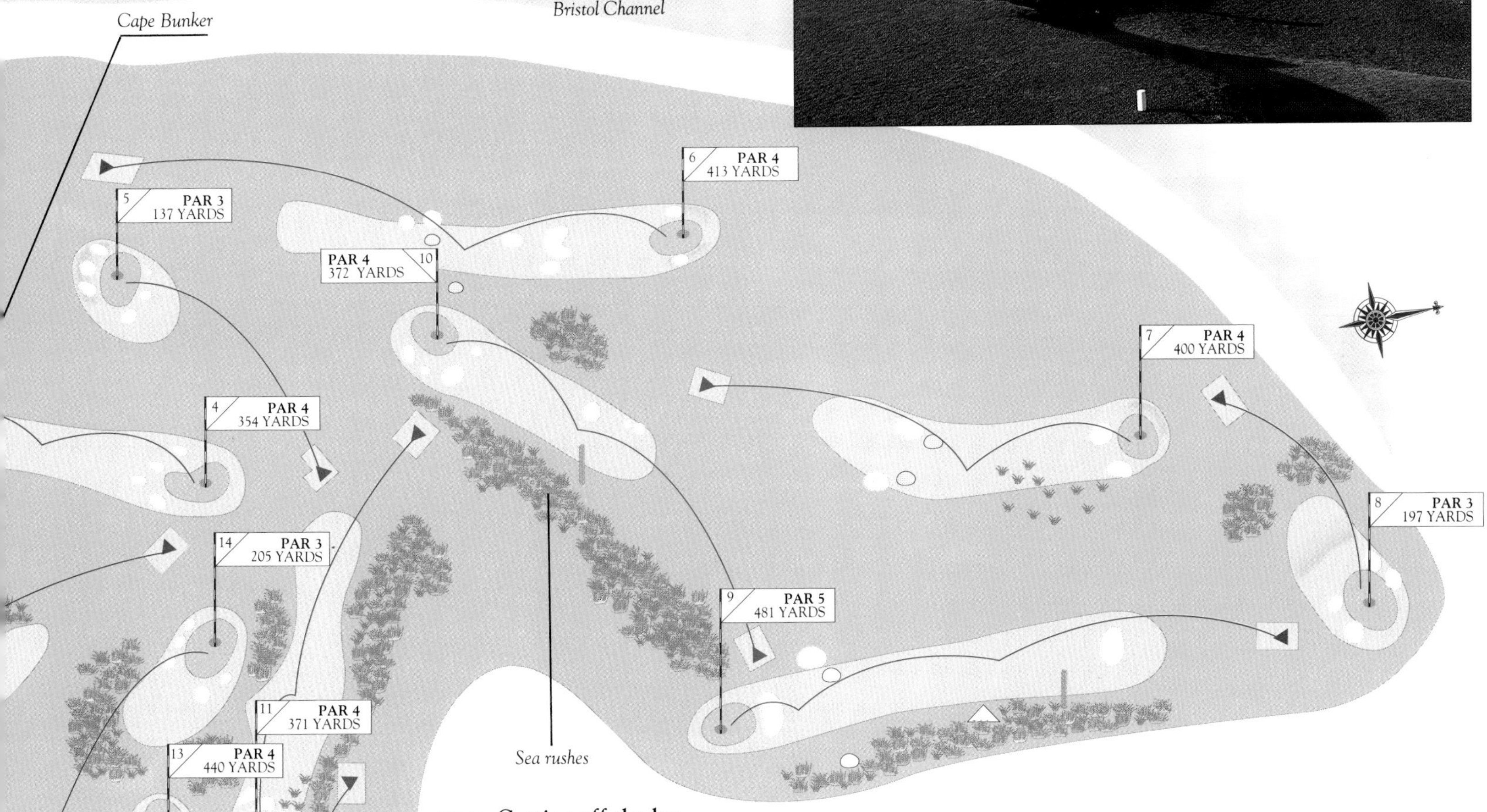

Bristol Channel

Cape Bunker

5 PAR 3 137 YARDS

6 PAR 4 413 YARDS

PAR 4 372 YARDS 10

7 PAR 4 400 YARDS

4 PAR 4 354 YARDS

8 PAR 3 197 YARDS

14 PAR 3 205 YARDS

9 PAR 5 481 YARDS

11 PAR 4 371 YARDS

13 PAR 4 440 YARDS

Sea rushes

12 PAR 4 425 YARDS

10 **Cutting off the leg**
The 10th is a testing dogleg needing a tee shot over sea rushes. It is best to cut off as much of the dogleg as possible on the way to the small green.

THE NAMES OF ROYAL NORTH DEVON

1ST BURN	10TH RUSH
2ND BAGGY	11TH APPLEDORE
3RD SANDYMERE	12TH HINDE
4TH CAPE	13TH LUNDY
5TH TABLE	14TH IRON HUT
6TH CREST	15TH CHURCH
7TH BAR	16TH PUNCH BOWL
8TH ESTUARY	17TH ROAD
9TH WESTWARD HO!	18TH HOME

The 14th hole at Westward Ho! is named Iron Hut after a strange building that served as a substitute for a clubhouse in the early days of the Royal North Devon club. Despite its primitive amenities, it did yeoman service for the members for many years.

Royal Portrush

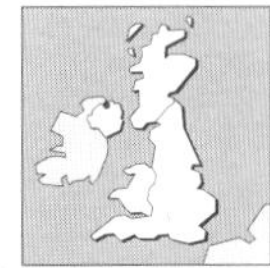

Royal Portrush Golf Club, Portrush, County Antrim, Northern Ireland

THE CHAMPIONSHIP COURSE at Portrush in Northern Ireland is one of the finest and most historic links anywhere in the British Isles. The Royal Portrush Golf Club, which was founded in 1888, actually has three courses set amid its 480 acres of duneland. Of these, the marvelous Dunluce course is rightly famous the world over. Dunluce is as stern a test of golf as any of the great links courses, and has the distinction of being the only Irish course so far to have been selected to host the British Open, which it did in 1951.

13 **Bunker danger**
Three bunkers guard the outer corner of the sharp dogleg 13th. An accurate tee shot is needed to pass them. Once on the fairway, the approach is simple, except for a fiendish bunker short of the green to the left.

14 **Calamity corner**
The 213-yard 14th on Dunluce is one of the most famous holes in Ireland. Depending on the wind, the tee shot demands anything from a medium iron to a solid blow with the driver. A chasm to the green's right leaves no margin for error and the hole is aptly named Calamity.

Royal Portrush was originally founded in May 1888 as the County Club, with Colonel J.M. McCalmont, MP, and J.S. Alexander (known as the "Admiral of Portglenone") as the founding fathers. Portraits of these pioneers still hang in the clubhouse. In 1892 the club was granted royal patronage by the Duke of York. Three years later, it became the Royal Portrush Golf Club, with the Prince of Wales, later King Edward VII, as patron.

The original layout at Portrush in 1888 was nine holes, but within a year another nine had been added. At that time eight holes were on the landward side of the coast road that runs out to the famous rock formations of the Giant's Causeway, but over the years substantial changes have resulted in the course moving farther out into the dunes. The towering sandhills provide a vast panorama. To the west are the Donegal hills, and north over the sea lie Islay and the Hebrides. The Causeway and the Skerries are to the east.

Narrow Fairways

The Dunluce fairways are narrow, and all except the 1st and the 18th dogleg one way or the other, demanding accuracy as well as length from the tee. Max Faulkner won the Open here in 1951 thanks to an extraordinary swerved second shot to the green at the last hole.

Royal Portrush also has the Valley course, a layout especially suited to the women's game, which the club has always championed. A nine-hole pitch-and-putt course lies at the end of the links nearest to the town.

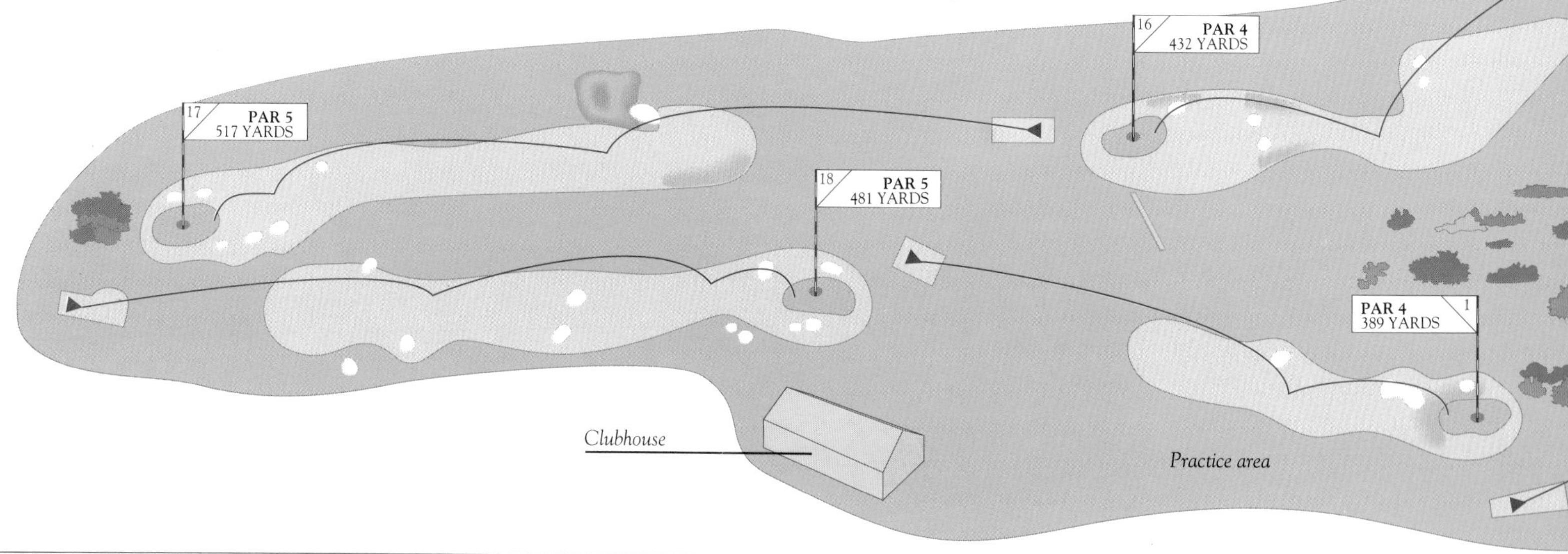

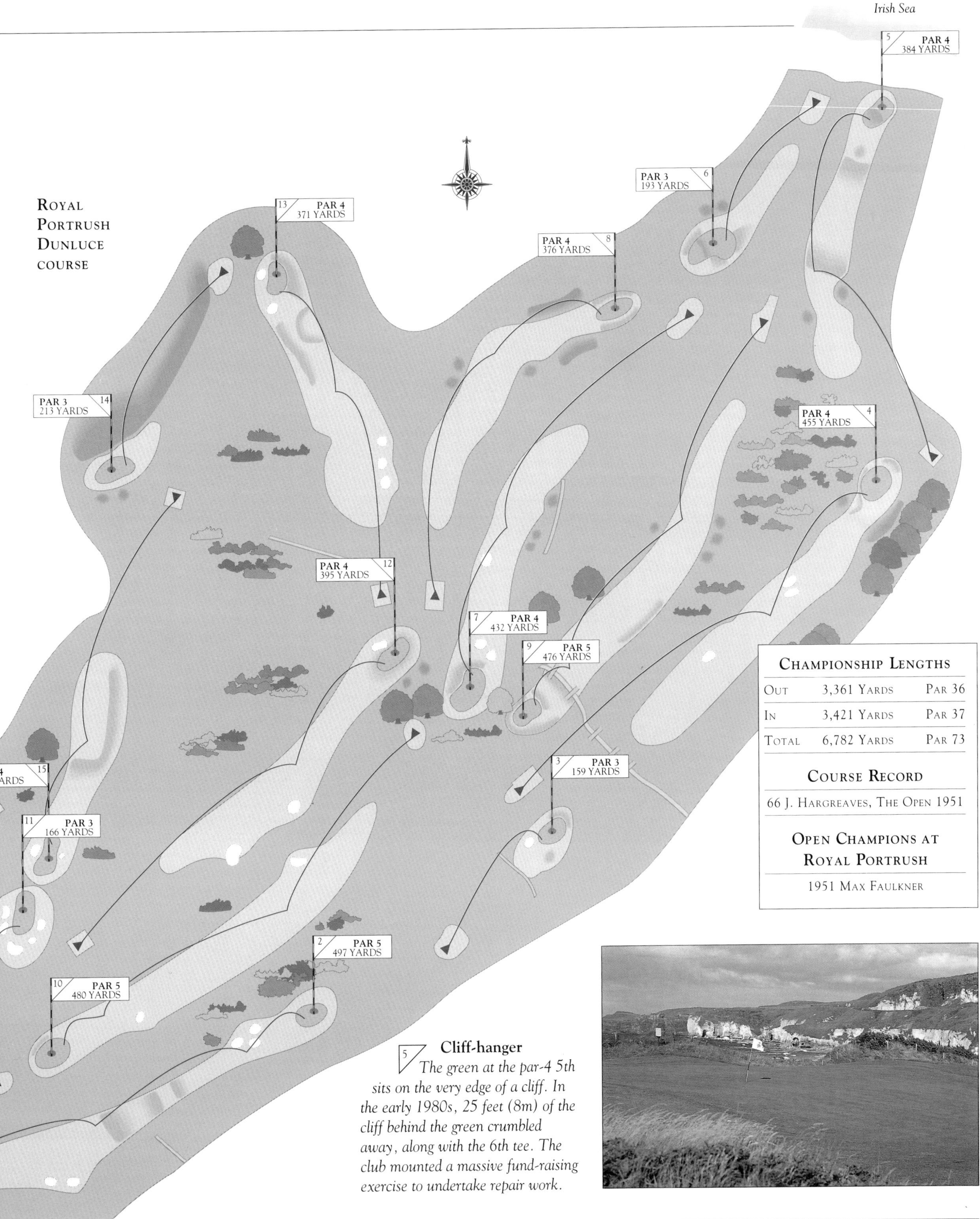

Championship Lengths

Out	3,361 Yards	Par 36
In	3,421 Yards	Par 37
Total	6,782 Yards	Par 73

Course Record

66 J. Hargreaves, The Open 1951

Open Champions at Royal Portrush

1951 Max Faulkner

5 Cliff-hanger

The green at the par-4 5th sits on the very edge of a cliff. In the early 1980s, 25 feet (8m) of the cliff behind the green crumbled away, along with the 6th tee. The club mounted a massive fund-raising exercise to undertake repair work.

ROYAL ST. GEORGE'S

ROYAL ST. GEORGE'S GOLF CLUB, SANDWICH, KENT, ENGLAND

THIS FINE LINKS, with its towering sandhills and rumpled fairways, has a long and distinguished history in English golf dating back to the mid-1880s. It began when Dr. Laidlaw Purves, a Scot who had come down from Edinburgh and who was a member at Royal Wimbledon, set out in search of a suitable seaside site for a course to serve the needs of London golfers. At that time inland courses were not highly thought of, and Dr. Purves wanted to create a links course inspired, no doubt, by the fine examples he had left behind in his native country.

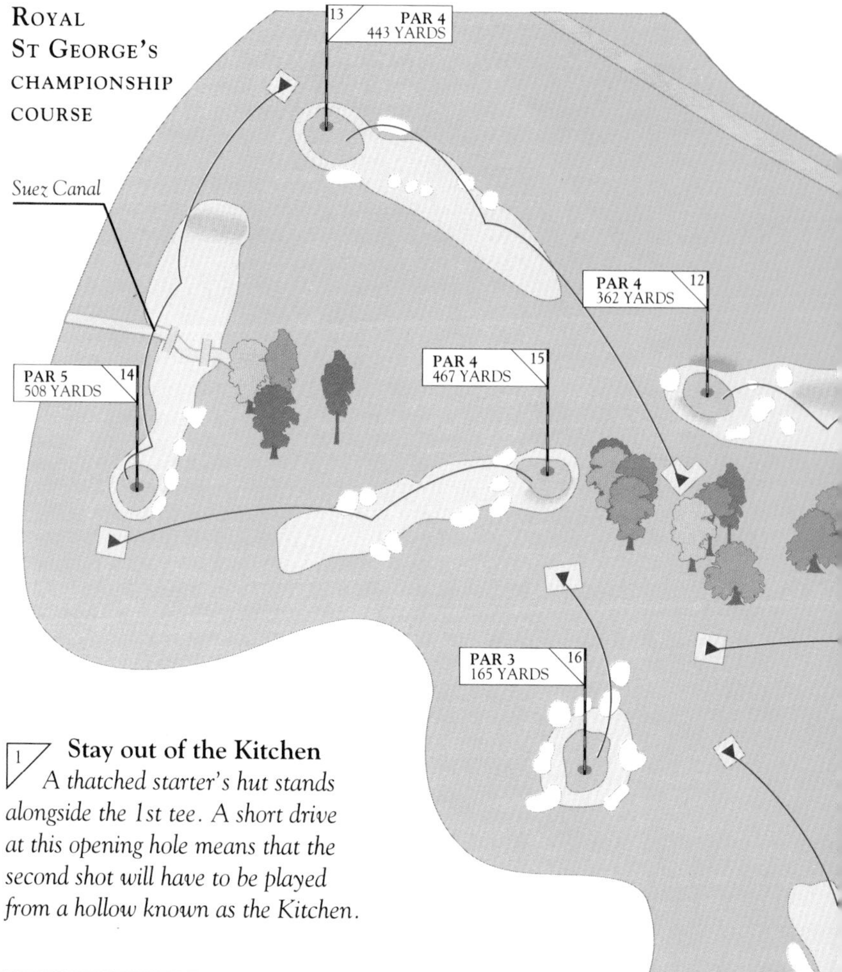

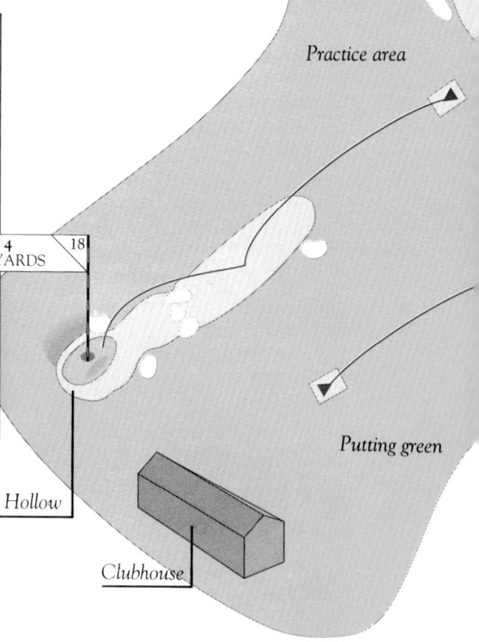

It is said the good doctor surveyed the links of Sandwich from the tower of St. Clement's church and declared it perfect. In 1887 he formed the Sandwich Golfing Association and plans were drawn up. Since then there have been changes, most recently by the respected architect Frank Pennink, but essentially the layout remains as it originally was.

Sloping lies on the fairways are a common factor on the undulating ground and have prompted several famous players to criticize the Kent links as "unfair." But this is a harsh judgment, as St. George's is certainly a classic seaside links.

The great Henry Cotton, who won his first of three British Opens at Sandwich, was a firm admirer of this famous links. He once remarked, "The turf at Sandwich

6 Against the breeze
The par-3 6th needs a tricky shot into the prevailing wind to the green, which is guarded by four bunkers. The one to the left of the green is particularly dangerous.

ROYAL ST GEORGE'S CHAMPIONSHIP COURSE

13 PAR 4 443 YARDS

12 PAR 4 362 YARDS

14 PAR 5 508 YARDS

15 PAR 4 467 YARDS

16 PAR 3 165 YARDS

18 PAR 4 458 YARDS

Suez Canal

Practice area

Putting green

Duncan's Hollow

Clubhouse

1 Stay out of the Kitchen
A thatched starter's hut stands alongside the 1st tee. A short drive at this opening hole means that the second shot will have to be played from a hollow known as the Kitchen.

5 Bottled out

In the celebrated 1949 British Open, the Irish player Harry Bradshaw was leading the field in the final round when he found his ball lying inside a broken beer bottle behind the 5th green. He elected to play the ball as it lay and smashed it out. But he scored a 6, and was eventually beaten by Bobby Locke in a play-off. It is argued that his famous "bottle shot" cost him the Open, as he was entitled to a free lift and drop. If he had taken it he would probably have had a putt for a 4.

gives lies one dreams about. The ball is always 'lying a treat,' so with larks singing and the sun shining on the waters of Pegwell, it is a golfer's heaven."

Course of Champions

In 1894 it was decided that the British Open should be moved to England for the first time, and Royal St. George's was chosen as the site. The Championship was won for the first time by an English professional, the legendary J.H. Taylor, marking the start of the domination of the event by the Great Triumvirate of Vardon, Braid, and Taylor. The course has thus had a long association with the Open, and hosted it nine times up to Bobby Locke's win there in 1949. Thereafter it fell out of favor, not because any fault could be found with the course but because the Open had become too big an event for the little town of Sandwich to handle comfortably.

Eventually, the Royal & Ancient decided to take the Open back to St. George's in 1981. The choice was such a success that it was repeated in 1985, when Sandy Lyle won the first British victory in 18 years. The course is now firmly back on the Open schedule.

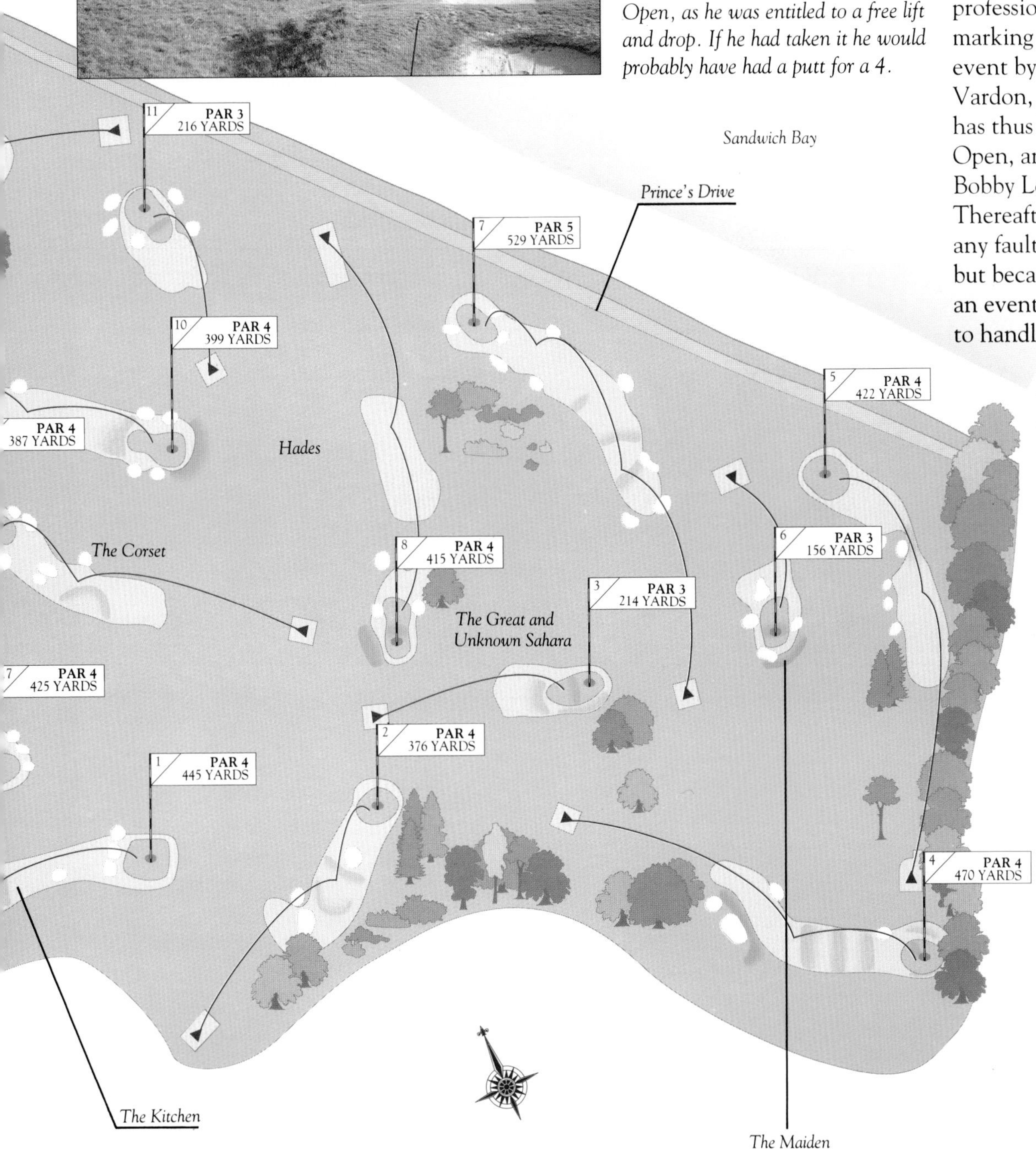

Championship Lengths

Out	3,414 Yards	Par 35
In	3,443 Yards	Par 35
Total	6,857 Yards	Par 70

Course Record

64 Tony Jacklin, Dunlop Masters 1967; Christy O'Connor, Jr., British Open 1985

Open Champions at Royal St. George's

1894 J.H. Taylor; 1899 Harry Vardon; 1904 Jack White; 1911 Harry Vardon; 1922 Walter Hagen; 1928 Walter Hagen; 1934 Henry Cotton; 1938 Reg Whitcombe; 1949 Bobby Locke; 1981 Bill Rogers; 1985 Sandy Lyle

ROYAL SYDNEY

THE ROYAL SYDNEY GOLF CLUB, ROSE BAY, NEW SOUTH WALES, AUSTRALIA

UNDULATING GREENS, NARROW fairways, and fearsome rough combine to give Royal Sydney its reputation as one of the finest courses in Australia. When the Royal Sydney Golf Club was founded in 1893, the members played on a nine-hole layout. Three years later, under the direction of the club's new professional, James Scott, the course was extended to 18 holes. These holes were built on the inside of the original nine on sandy soil, a terrain that gives Royal Sydney something of the flavor of links golf. S.J. Robbie is generally credited with the original design, but Dr. Alister Mackenzie, famous for his work at Augusta National and Royal Melbourne, stamped his unmistakable mark on the course in the 1920s.

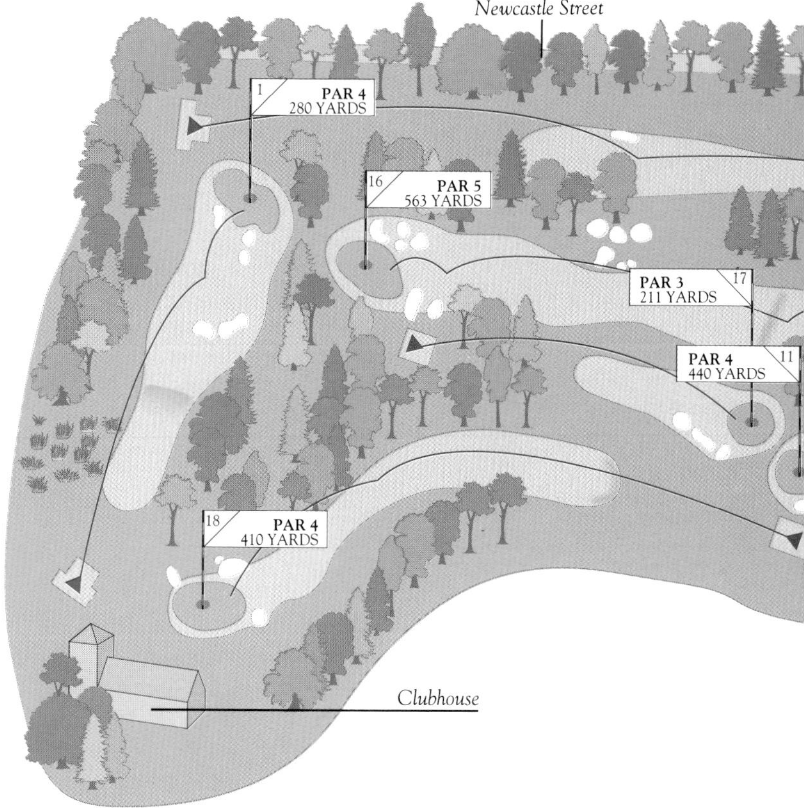

18 Drawing around the bend
The 18th is one of the best finishing holes in Australia. A stiff dogleg left of 410 yards, it needs a drive long enough to pass the elbow of the bend to leave a clear approach to the green. Shots less than 230 yards from the tee may be blocked out by trees, but big hitters who can draw the ball around the corner have a significant advantage. The green is large, but care must be taken to avoid bunkers that threaten any shots hit short and to the right.

Mackenzie concentrated on alterations to the bunkers, making them bigger and deeper, as well as adding to the number. The sand is dazzling white and soft; it is quite common to find the ball in a plugged lie in a Royal Sydney bunker.

Further alterations were made to the course during the 1980s, in preparation for Royal Sydney to host the Australian Open in 1988. In particular, the greens were enlarged significantly.

As with all courses close to the sea, the wind is a constant factor. It can change from being off the sea in the morning to off the land in the afternoon, as the land heats up relative to the sea. Generally the weather is good, as would be expected from a course sited in this clement part of the Australian continent, although the occurrence of violent thunderstorms can be a hazard for golfers in October.

SUCCESS STORY

In 1897, four years after the club was founded, it was granted royal patronage. It quickly became established as one of the best courses in Australia, and has now developed into a vast golf, tennis, and social club with over 5,000 members.

Royal Sydney lies only ten minutes away from the center of Sydney and is surrounded by the fashionable houses of the city suburbs. The course has a high proportion of elevated tees looking down to open fairways below, with greens stretching out into the distance. This attractive feature was made possible by the natural site. The ground forms a saucer shape, allowing the tees to be cut into the higher ground around the slopes.

The variable wind is the course's main defense. On those occasions when it does not blow too strongly, Royal Sydney is vulnerable to the skills of the world's top professionals. Mark Calcavecchia proved this conclusively in the 1988 Australian Open. The American's winning score was a staggering 19 under the course's par.

Royal Sydney Championship Course

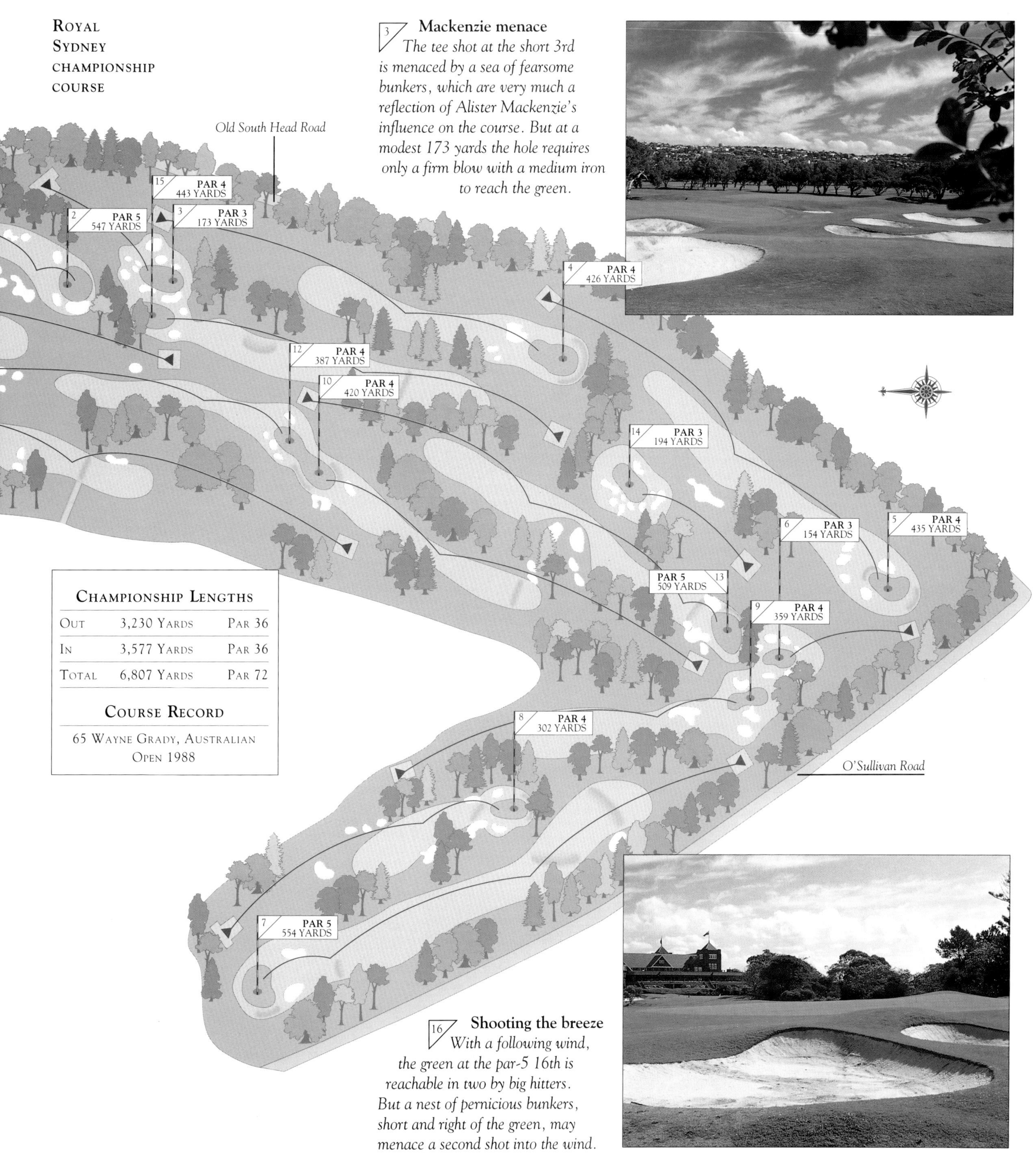

3 Mackenzie menace
The tee shot at the short 3rd is menaced by a sea of fearsome bunkers, which are very much a reflection of Alister Mackenzie's influence on the course. But at a modest 173 yards the hole requires only a firm blow with a medium iron to reach the green.

Championship Lengths

Out	3,230 Yards	Par 36
In	3,577 Yards	Par 36
Total	6,807 Yards	Par 72

Course Record

65 Wayne Grady, Australian Open 1988

16 Shooting the breeze
With a following wind, the green at the par-5 16th is reachable in two by big hitters. But a nest of pernicious bunkers, short and right of the green, may menace a second shot into the wind.

Royal Troon

Royal Troon Golf Club, Troon, Ayrshire, Scotland

The marvelous course at Royal Troon lies at the southern end of a long run of duneland stretching from Irvine to Prestwick, which is host to most of the best links courses on the west side of Scotland. Troon is an exceptionally demanding course, recognized as one of the sternest tests on the British Open schedule. The club was awarded its royal charter in 1978, its centenary year.

Troon emblem
The serpent circling the clubs is the symbol of medicine – a reference to Dr. Highet, founder of the club and its first honorary secretary and treasurer. The motto means "as much by skill as by strength."

In at the finish
Members can watch the action at the last green from the comfort of the clubhouse smoke room, out of the wind.

There are many stories of golf being played on the links at Troon long before there was a recognized golf course on this beautiful stretch of Ayrshire coastline. There is evidence in Ian Mackintosh's excellent history of the club that a "course" of four or five holes existed as early as 1870. The holes on this course were made with a knife and "were neither round nor square, but were large enough!"

James Braid
Braid helped in the design of the tricky short 8th at Troon.

Planning Troon

The club itself, however, did not come into existence until March, 1878. The prospective members met for the first time to lay their plans in a local hostelry, the Portland Arms Hotel, at the instigation of Dr. John Highet. Another of the founding fathers was James Dickie from Paisley, a town on the outskirts of Glasgow. Although he did not live in Troon, Dickie was no stranger to the area, where he had a summer house. It was Dickie who approached the 6th Duke of Portland, the owner of the Estate of Fullarton upon which he wanted to build the course.

He was granted permission for a golf club to play on the land between Craigend and the Pow Burn. Part of this ground turned out to be unsuitable, and the founding fathers of Troon Golf Club had to make do with the ground from Craigend to Gyaws Burn. Today the Craigend Burn is piped under the road in front of the clubhouse, while the Gyaws Burn is still a part of the course.

The present layout has evolved through the attentions of various notable golf-course architects, including the 1883 Open champion, Willie Fernie (who was instructed to make alterations when he was the club's professional), James Braid, Dr. Alister Mackenzie, and Frank Pennink.

Arthur Havers won the first Open played at Troon in 1923, and many illustrious names have joined him in Troon's list of Open champions since. It was 37 years after Havers's victory before the Open was back there again, when the great South African, Bobby Locke, won with a score of 279, the first time 280 had been broken in the Open.

In 1962 Arnold Palmer came to defend his Open title at Troon and won with a new record score of 276. Tom Weiskopf was a popular winner in 1973, equaling Palmer's score, and Tom Watson won the fourth of his five Open titles there in 1982. In 1989 the Open went to a four-

Holiday golf (above)
This postcard shows the clubhouse before the First World War. The combination of a railroad and a golf course led vacationing golfers to flock to Troon, to sample the delights of this west-coast links and the hospitality of the clubhouse.

Golf doctor (above)
John Highet, a local doctor, called the original small group of members together in the Portland Arms Hotel to start the club in March, 1878.

By the sea (right)
The view from the links of Troon occasionally allows gorgeous glimpses across the Firth of Clyde to the Isle of Arran.

The Names of Royal Troon

1st Seal	10th Sandhills
2nd Black Rock	11th The Railway
3rd Gyaws	12th The Fox
4th Dunure	13th Burmah
5th Greenan	14th Alton
6th Turnberry	15th Crosbie
7th Tel-El-Kebir	16th Well
8th Postage Stamp	17th Rabbit
9th The Monk	18th Craigend

The 12th is named the Fox not because it is tricky, but because there was once a grove alongside the present tee that sheltered foxes.

Tel-El-Kebir, the name of the 7th, recalls a battle fought in Egypt in 1882.

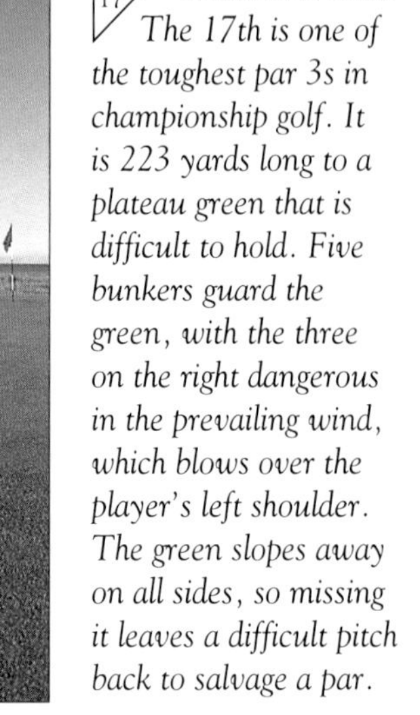

17 **Wind and sand** *The 17th is one of the toughest par 3s in championship golf. It is 223 yards long to a plateau green that is difficult to hold. Five bunkers guard the green, with the three on the right dangerous in the prevailing wind, which blows over the player's left shoulder. The green slopes away on all sides, so missing it leaves a difficult pitch back to salvage a par.*

hole play-off for the first time, with Mark Calcavecchia pitted against Greg Norman and Wayne Grady. Norman lost his chance when he took three strokes from the back of the green at the 17th, and Calcavecchia birdied the 18th to win.

The Long and the Short

There are several famous holes at Royal Troon, including both the longest and the shortest holes in British Open Championship golf. The longest, at 577 yards, is the fearsome 6th, known as Turnberry. It has a long carry into the wind off the tee to reach a narrow strip of fairway guarded by a triangle of bunkers, two to the left and one to the right. The drive is best placed just to the right of the left-hand bunkers, while the second shot must avoid a bunker on the left side of the fairway 50 yards short of the green, and a cavernously deep bunker situated on the right-hand side 20 yards farther on.

A long line of high dunes covered in impenetrable rough runs along the right side of the fairway, and the green itself sits in the lee of a massive dune. It is guarded by a wickedly deep bunker that eats into the front left of the green.

Even when conditions are favorable there are few who can reach the green in two strokes, or who are brave enough even to try, and when the wind is blowing against the player, usually with a hint of right quarter to it, the green is simply out of anyone's reach in two.

The shortest hole in Open Championship golf is Troon's 8th, known as the Postage Stamp, apparently after Willie Park, Jr. commented in 1923 that it had "a pitching surface skimmed down to the size of a postage stamp." This hole is where, in the 1950 Open, a German amateur by the name of Hermann Tissies had only one putt but needed 15 strokes for the hole – including five shots from

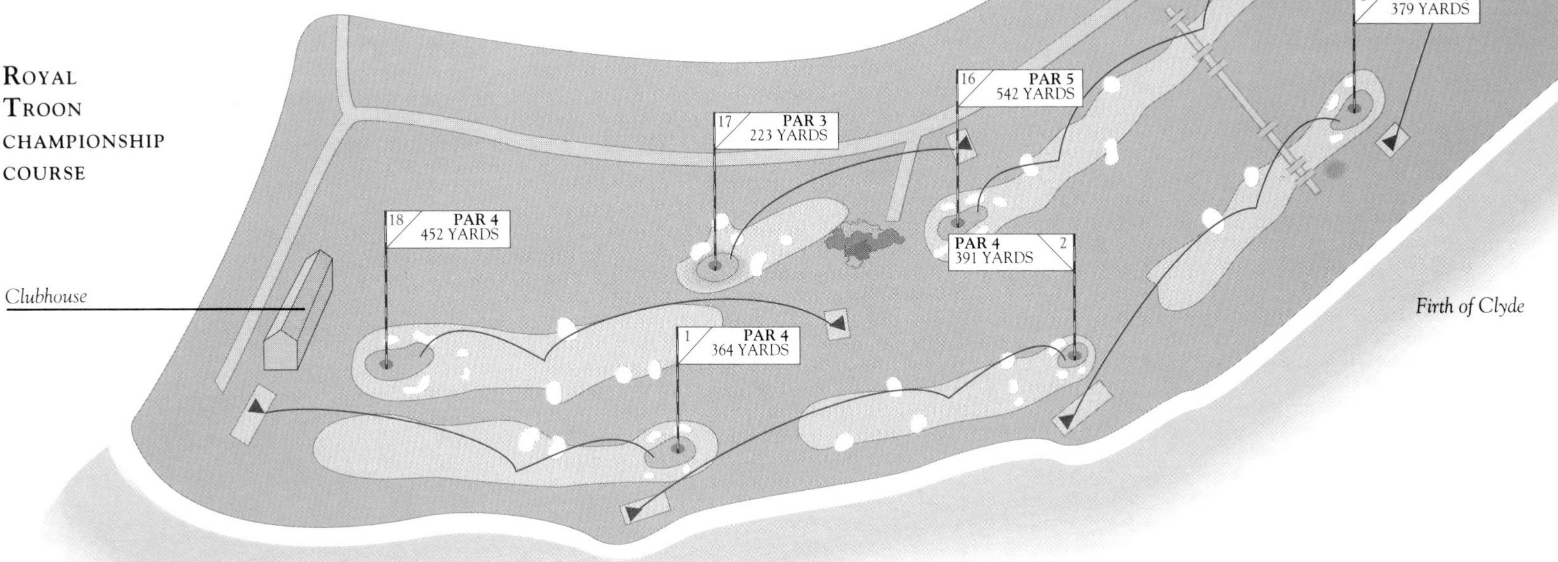

Royal Troon championship course

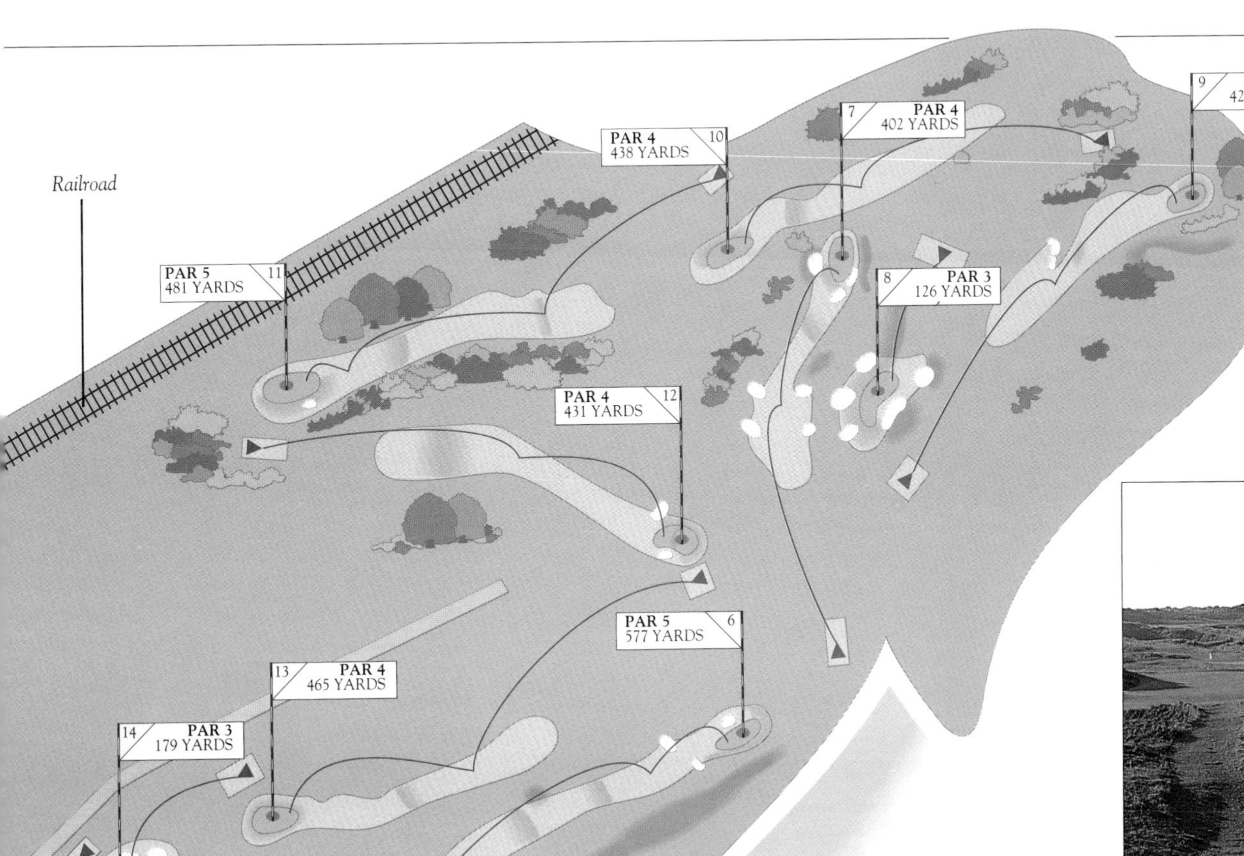

8 **Short but deadly**
The 8th at Royal Troon, famous throughout the world as the Postage Stamp, is the shortest hole in British Open golf. It is a modest 126 yards long but is, as Henry Leach once wrote, "as full of wickedness as it is of beauty."

11 **Off the rails**
The par-5 11th is not long, but it is fraught with danger. Hitting out-of-bounds over the railroad tracks is a real risk approaching the green. There is so much gorse that only one bunker is needed as an extra hazard.

a bunker on the left, another five from a bunker on the right, and three to escape from the original bunker a second time. In contrast, in 1973 the legendary Gene Sarazen, then in his seventies, came to Troon on a sentimental journey and played the 8th hole twice in a total of only three strokes (see page 293).

Tough Test of Troon

Although the 6th and 8th have been awarded special notoriety, all the holes at "Old Troon" present a test of strength, concentration, and imagination, especially when the wind blows. The prevailing south-westerly wind flies off the sea to ruin numerous golfers' scorecards, either on the front or back nine. Long carries to narrow, rolling fairways, surrounded by punishing rough, led golf writer Bernard Darwin to comment wryly that Troon was "a good and testing course well suited to the spectator."

Championship Lengths

Out	3,429 Yards	Par 36
In	3,668 Yards	Par 36
Total	7,097 Yards	Par 72

Course Record

64 Greg Norman, The Open 1989

Open Champions at Royal Troon

1923 Arthur Havers; 1950 Bobby Locke; 1962 Arnold Palmer; 1973 Tom Weiskopf; 1982 Tom Watson; 1989 Mark Calcavecchia

RYE

RYE GOLF CLUB, CAMBER, RYE, EAST SUSSEX, ENGLAND

THE ANCIENT WALLED town of Rye on the south coast of England is a place of history and tradition, and so too is the great course that bears its name. This is not the world of brash, modern commercial golf. It is a place where there is still respect for the older, and some might say better, values of the game.

New clubhouse
The Rye course suffered badly during the Second World War, and the old clubhouse was badly damaged by a flying bomb that exploded on the 15th fairway in 1944. The clubhouse was not rebuilt until 1949.

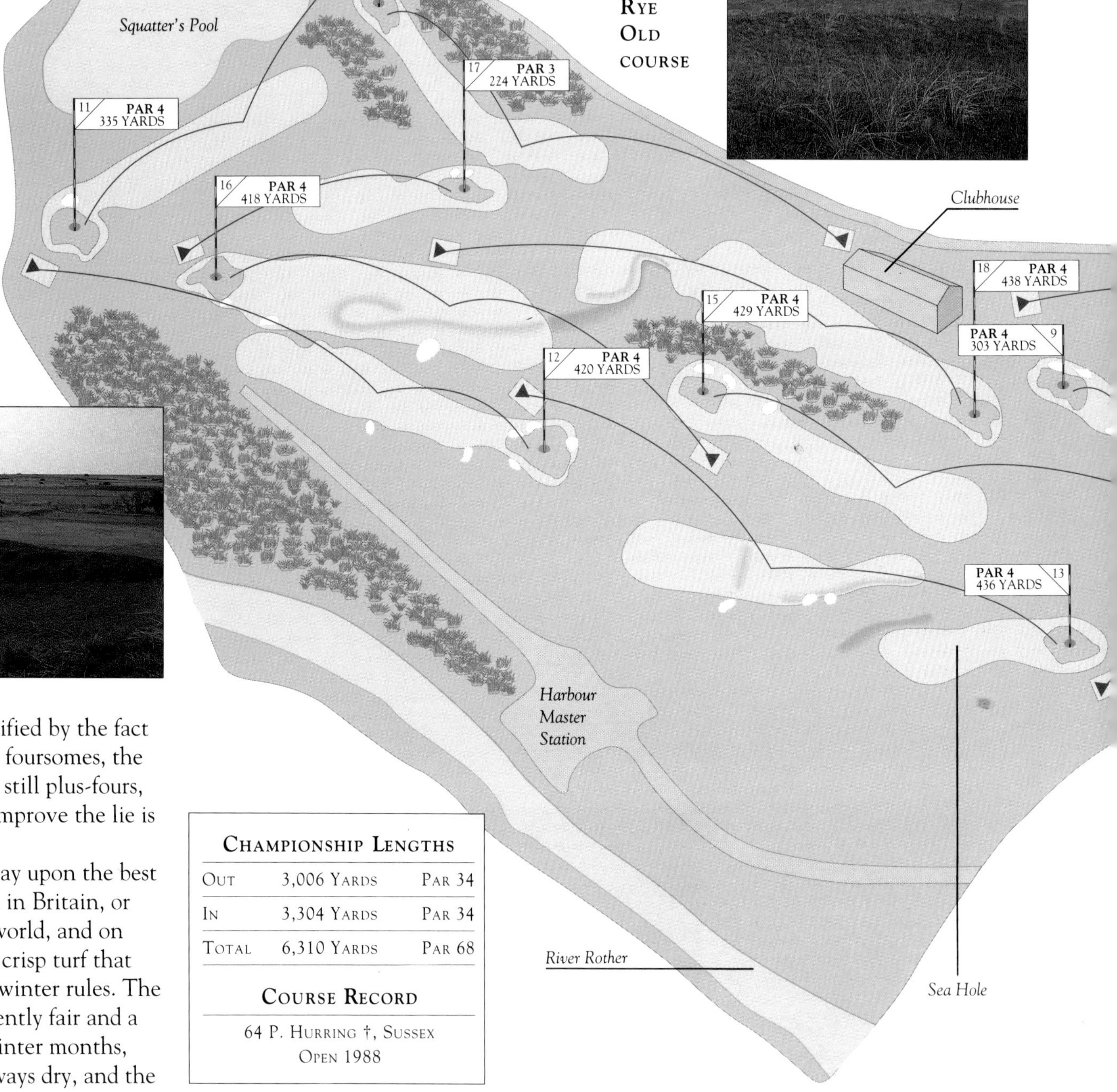

RYE OLD COURSE

13 **Go for a long drive**
The key shot in tackling the marvelous 13th at Rye, known as the Sea Hole, is the drive. It must be long enough to give a chance of carrying the great wall of sandhills that blocks the way on a journey of just under 440 yards. The green is hidden from view and needs a long approach shot.

Squatter's Pool

10 PAR 4 425 YARDS

17 PAR 3 224 YARDS

11 PAR 4 335 YARDS

16 PAR 4 418 YARDS

Clubhouse

18 PAR 4 438 YARDS

15 PAR 4 429 YARDS

9 PAR 4 303 YARDS

12 PAR 4 420 YARDS

13 PAR 4 436 YARDS

Harbour Master Station

River Rother

Sea Hole

Rye's character is exemplified by the fact that players are mostly in foursomes, the most usual golfing garb is still plus-fours, and to move the ball to improve the lie is considered uncivilized.

To play at Rye is to play upon the best fescue greens of any links in Britain, or indeed anywhere in the world, and on fairways of such splendid crisp turf that there is no such thing as winter rules. The course is tough but eminently fair and a joy to play even in the winter months, when the fairways are always dry, and the

CHAMPIONSHIP LENGTHS

OUT	3,006 YARDS	PAR 34
IN	3,304 YARDS	PAR 34
TOTAL	6,310 YARDS	PAR 68

COURSE RECORD

64 P. HURRING †, SUSSEX OPEN 1988

greens fast and true. It is a salutary reminder to others of the need to preserve traditional British golfing turf. No artificial fertilizers have been used on this land and Rye is all the better for it.

Rye is an excellent links course and many of the holes are quite deceptively difficult. The wind is a key factor when it blows, and at Rye it is usually blowing. A typical Rye hole is the par-4 16th. It needs a good drive to have any chance of a par. At 418 yards the 16th is not unduly long, but the tee shot must carry over a ridge running diagonally across the fairway. Even with the drive well placed, there is still much work to be done. The second demands a substantial blow with a long iron, or even a wood, to reach the green.

There have been many changes at Rye since the first course was built in 1894. Most of them have been brought about by the increase in traffic on the road that runs along the northern boundary. There was considerable upheaval to the course just before the start of the First World War, and more changes were made after hostilities ceased. New holes have also been built since the Second World War, with the result that the first nine holes have changed completely and retain only the 5th hole from earlier times.

Conserving Tradition

But if the layout has changed, little else has at Rye. It is a conservative place where the old corrugated pavilion might still be there, were it not for the German bomb that destroyed it in 1944. The new one is a comfortable replacement which presents the prospect of an excellent lunch and good company.

Being the home of the Oxford and Cambridge Golfing Society, Rye is the site of the Society's annual tournament for the President's Putter, always held in the month of January. The heavy snow of the winter of 1979 forced cancellation that year, but that is the only time since the first Putter was played for in 1920 that the weather prevented play. On one occasion play had to be transferred to Littlestone because of frost in the opening rounds; otherwise the Putter goes on regardless.

The putter for which contestants play was originally owned by the 1891 Open champion, Hugh Kirkaldy. The club was used by the Society's first president, John L. Low, when he was narrowly beaten by Harold Hilton in the final of the Amateur Championship at St. Andrews in 1901. Today it hangs on the clubhouse wall. Attached to it is a row of balls that commemorate the winners of the Putter.

4 **Tough going**
The 4th ranks among golf's greatest holes. The drive onto the narrow fairway is always hard enough, but when the wind blows, as it often does at Rye, it is a searching test of nerve and technique. There are rough sandhills on the left and a drop down to the plain on the other side. The 4th is not nearly the longest of the two-shot holes, but there is none harder.

Rye–Camber Road
1 PAR 5 483 YARDS
2 PAR 3 182 YARDS
3 PAR 4 437 YARDS
4 PAR 4 410 YARDS
5 PAR 3 168 YARDS
6 PAR 4 469 YARDS
7 PAR 3 161 YARDS
8 PAR 4 393 YARDS
14 PAR 3 179 YARDS

5 **Green in the hills**
The attractive 5th is a par 3 across a wide gully. The green sits high up in the sandhills and is slightly saucer-shaped. A medium iron is all that is called for under reasonable conditions for a hole of just over 160 yards, but the stroke must be truly and carefully struck if the ball is to hold the green and not run over.

St. Andrews

St. Andrews Links Management Committee, St. Andrews, Fife, Scotland

Perhaps the most thrilling sight in golf is that of the ancient buildings and dramatic spires of the town of St. Andrews standing sentinel over the most famous stretch of golf links in the world. Here lies the cradle of the game, its historical and cultural home, the Mecca to which every golfer who ever put club to ball wants to make a pilgrimage at least once during his golfing life.

Crossed clubs
The St. Andrews Links crest has an image of the saint with crossed clubs in place of the normal cross of the St. Andrews flag.

R & A trophy room
The R & A clubhouse exhibits in its trophy room the silver clubs, to which each captain adds a silver or gold ball after taking office.

It is here that great deeds have been done and rules and standards set, and it is here that the golfing world still looks today for example and guidance.

Golf has been played on the Old course itself for more than 400 years, and on the links of the town for longer still. The course is unique in that it owes little to the hand of man for its design or layout. It has evolved over the centuries at the whim of time and tide, a masterpiece that stands as a lasting tribute to the shaping power of nature itself.

All the great names in the history of the game (with the exception of Ben Hogan) have walked across the famous little stone bridge over the Swilcan Burn onto the final fairway with the most famous view in golf before them. The Royal & Ancient clubhouse, now brilliantly white following restoration of the stonework, stands guard over the vast expanse of the fairway that is shared by the first and last holes.

Crossing that antique bridge and looking toward the clubhouse, the wide stretch of the West Sands lies to the left, sweeping away towards the Eden Estuary. To the right is the ancient town itself, which is the home not only of the game of golf but also of Scotland's most ancient and respected seat of higher academic learning, the University of St. Andrews.

Early putters (above)
This engraving purports to show a group of players holing out on the 1st green in 1798. However, the clubhouse, visible in the top left of the picture, was not built until 1854.

Golfing party
On the 1st fairway golfers and their caddies contemplate the shot. Clubs used to be carried loose; the bag is a comparatively recent invention.

The Old course is a classic seaside links, although the sea is seldom in view, except on the first and last holes where the view of St. Andrews Bay is dramatic. There are none of the great dunes found, for example, at Royal Birkdale, only undulating fairways with little elevation, crossed at intervals by the huge double greens. There are only four single greens on the Old course, the 1st, the 9th, the famous 17th, and the home hole, the 18th.

The 1st tee is directly in front of the big window of the Royal & Ancient clubhouse. Before the player lies the most inviting fairway in the game. Shared with the 18th, it is more than 100 yards wide. But despite this tempting expanse, the stroke from the 1st tee on the Old course at St. Andrews remains the most nerve-racking opening one anywhere in the world.

Once across the Swilcan Burn that guards the 1st green, and where the shot is always one more club than you think, the course turns right and follows the sweep of St. Andrews Bay, sharing fairways and greens along the way until it turns right

Stone bridge (right)
The stone span of Swilcan Bridge, once the route into the ancient city from the west, has been crossed by almost all the great names in the history of the game. It shows the way to the magnificent old clubhouse that dominates the view over the links.

again at the start of what is known as the Loop. It is here, starting at the 7th and finishing at the 11th, where the fairways of these two holes cross, that game-winning scores have to be made.

Within this run of five holes, the Old course's only two short holes are found – the 8th and the wickedly difficult 11th, known as the High Hole (in). From there the course starts for home back along the path already trodden, often sharing the fairways of the journey out and playing to the other side of the huge double greens. White flags mark the pins on the outward journey, whereas red distinguish the homeward stretch. The exception is the

Rainy day (left)
This painting by J. Michael Brown (1880–1916), titled A Rainy Day at St. Andrews, *is probably of the 13th hole. It records the match between Harold Hilton and Robert Harris in the 1913 Amateur Championship. Hilton won by 6-and-5.*

THE ROYAL & ANCIENT GOLF CLUB

The Royal & Ancient Golf Club came into existence in 1754, when the first members gathered for copious eating and drinking, either at Baillie Glass's or the Black Bull Tavern. The club was known as the Society of St. Andrews Golfers until King William IV became the Society's patron in 1834 and the title of the Royal & Ancient Golf Club of St. Andrews was conferred.

Ten years after the Society was formed, it decreed that the number of holes on the Old course should be reduced from 22 to 18, the standard that has prevailed to this day. Contrary to widespread belief, the Royal & Ancient Golf Club does not own the Old course. The course is held in trust by the local government under an Act of Parliament. This ensures that the world's most famous course remains, as it has always been, a municipal links that is open to anyone to play upon payment of a greens fee.

The Royal & Ancient is the governing body of golf throughout the world, with the exception of the United States and Mexico. It sets and reviews the rules and standards of the game and is the arbiter in disputes. It also runs and administers several major events, of which the British Open is the most important. It derives considerable revenue from what has now become a large-scale commercial enterprise, and plows the money back into the development of the game, benefiting all aspects from junior golf to the training of greenskeepers.

But the Royal & Ancient is also a private golf club and is used by its members as such. There are two major meetings of the members each year, in the spring and the autumn, when the club's competitions are played – for the Silver Cross of St. Andrews in the spring and the Gold Medal in the autumn. The George Glennie Medal is awarded annually for the lowest aggregate score over the two meetings. These are also enjoyable social occasions, when members from all over the world gather to swap tales of golfing triumph and disaster.

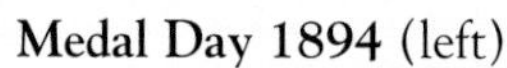

Medal Day 1894 (left)
This painting, hanging in the clubhouse of the R & A, depicts future British Prime Minister Arthur James Balfour playing as the club's captain during the Autumn Meeting of 1894. The names of all 191 figures are known. Apparently Balfour hit a fine drive.

Ticket to St. Andrews (right)
This tag shows the bearer was a guest of the Royal & Ancient Club at the 1990 Open. The annual event is run by the R & A.

Leaping the burn
In their enthusiasm to follow the action during the final round of the 1927 Open, members of the gallery hurdle the Swilcan Burn. The Open was won by the legendary Bobby Jones with a score of 285.

last hole, where tradition demands that the flag is white. The course has changed little over the years, and apart from a new tee added here and there, it was much the same for Nick Faldo when he won the 1990 British Open as it was for Tom Kidd when he won the first Open over the Old course in 1873.

Training for golf
This 1920s poster was distributed by the London and North Eastern Railway, which served St. Andrews at that time. The growth in the popularity of golf was closely tied to the spread of railroads, giving easy access to these remote locations.

Avoiding the bunkers is the key to survival on the Old course. There are dozens of them, and most are hidden from view, a result perhaps of the fact that in days past the course was played in a clockwise direction and not counter-clockwise, as it is currently.

Many of these treacherous obstacles have fascinating names. The most famous is known as Hell, a huge pit of sand that guards the 14th, the Long Hole. There are others that are less obvious but just as dangerous. In front of the 7th green, the High Hole (out), is the huge Cockle bunker, and a few yards to its left Strath bunker eats into the front of the 11th. At the 16th, the Corner of the Dyke, a group of three bunkers are known as the Principal's Nose. Only one of them is visible from the tee, and it lies in the center of the fairway. Many players have felt confident that they have driven sufficiently well to pass the Principal's Nose, only to find their ball nestling deeply in Deacon Sime, a nasty little pot bunker some 30 yards further on. The notorious Road bunker, which eats into the front of the 17th, the Road Hole, has also claimed many a victim.

One golfer who fell foul of the Road bunker was poor Tommy Nakajima. The Japanese player was well placed in the

Prewar guide
A spectators' guide to the 1939 Open, the last held for seven years. It was won by Dick Burton, breaking the run of American wins at St. Andrews. The first postwar Open was also at St. Andrews in 1946.

Faldo's triumph
Confirming his position as one of the greats, Britain's Nick Faldo won the British Open at St. Andrews in 1990. Here he holes out at the 18th in front of the huge crowds that St. Andrews now attracts during the final round.

Birdie chance (left)
The 9th is a short par 4 at 356 yards, and should leave a short chip to the flat green for big hitters. During championships, golfers look to this hole for a birdie. The bunkers can still catch the unwary, however.

Formed by nature
The Old course is on a strip of land jutting into the Eden Estuary. The land is mostly level, but has many bumps and depressions. Sea and wind have sculpted the layout, endowing it with a very different character from today's man-made courses.

St Andrews Old course

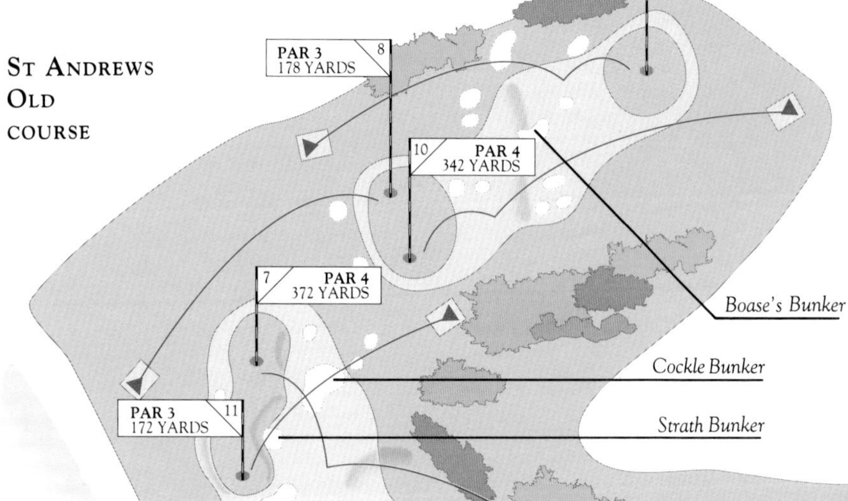

The Names of the Old course at St. Andrews

1st Burn	10th Bobby Jones
2nd Dyke	11th High (in)
3rd Cartgate (out)	12th Heathery (in)
4th Ginger Beer	13th Hole o'Cross (in)
5th Hole o'Cross (out)	14th Long
6th Heathery (out)	15th Cartgate (in)
7th High (out)	16th Corner of Dyke
8th Short	17th Road
9th End	18th Tom Morris

The 4th hole takes its name from a ginger beer stall run there by David Anderson, known as Old Da', during the last century.

Infernal hazard
The key factor in playing the notorious 14th hole is to avoid the Beardies group of bunkers down the left side. The vast, deep Hell bunker defends the Long Hole from the second shot, 100 yards from the green, at the end of the flat stretch of fairway that is known as the Elysian Fields. Many golfers who have not played safely either to the left or the right, have found themselves coming to grief in this frightening cavern.

1978 British Open until he found this bunker. He will be long remembered for the four strokes it took him to escape.

Once past the Road Hole, the Old course has no bunkers left before the player makes his way back to the haven of the home green and into the town itself. Looking from the tee, the drive at the 18th is straight at the clock on the right-hand side of the R & A clubhouse. The acres of space that were enjoyed at the 1st are there again for the finish.

Back to the Town

The final green, with its white fence on two sides, the R & A clubhouse on one side, and on the other St. Andrews golf clubs, shops, and houses, provides a characteristically magnificent finish to the world's most famous course.

Whatever the time of day, there is an inevitable knot of spectators leaning over the white fences to watch the players negotiate the approach over, or through, the Valley of Sin, and to pass judgment according to the level of failure or success.

18 **Nervous ending**
Not a hard hole, the 18th still holds a few surprises, especially the Valley of Sin, a series of depressions in front of the green. Match pressure causes many a crisis at this relatively simple last hole.

Championship Lengths

Out	3,501 Yards	Par 36
In	3,432 Yards	Par 36
Total	6,933 Yards	Par 72

Course Record

62 Curtis Strange, Dunhill Cup 1987

British Open Champions at St. Andrews

1873 Tom Kidd; 1876 Bob Martin; 1879 Jamie Anderson; 1882 Bob Ferguson; 1885 Bob Martin; 1888 Jack Burns; 1891 Hugh Kirkaldy; 1895, 1900 J.H. Taylor; 1905, 1910 James Braid; 1921 Jock Hutchison; 1927 Bobby Jones †; 1933 Densmore Shute; 1939 Dick Burton; 1946 Sam Snead; 1955 Peter Thomson; 1957 Bobby Locke; 1960 Kel Nagle; 1964 Tony Lema; 1970, 1978 Jack Nicklaus; 1984 Seve Ballesteros; 1990 Nick Faldo

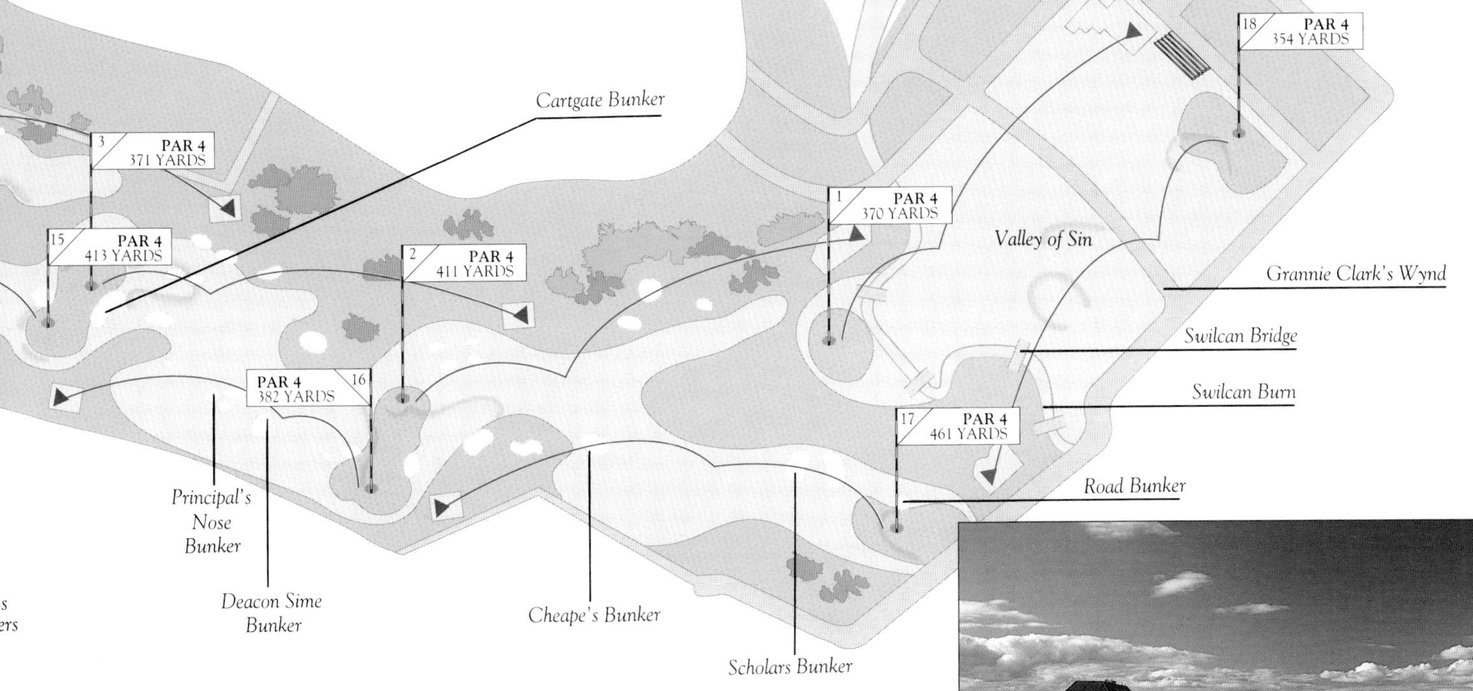

17 **Hard Road**
The famous Road Hole bunker, to the front left of the green, has probably ruined more score cards than any other hazard in the game. The road behind the green has also claimed its share of victims, including Tom Watson in 1984.

El Saler

El Saler Golf Club, El Saler, Valencia, Spain

The course designed by Javier Arana at El Saler, near Valencia on the east coast of Spain, is one of Europe's best. Indeed, El Saler has been, at one stage in its relatively short existence, rated by some players as the top course in continental Europe. The reliable climate, combined with intelligent use of the links-like terrain, make this course a true joy to play, as well as a tough challenge to match the more windblown courses of northern Europe.

There are strong grounds for rating El Saler highly. At almost 6,500m in its championship guise, it is a stern test of golfing ability. Golf writer Peter Dobereiner once commented that "if it were transplanted to the west coast of Ireland, or to Scotland, exposed to the Atlantic gales, it would be a monster." This is indeed high praise.

The creator of this fine course, Javier Arana, is perhaps more widely remembered as a player than as a course architect, but his reputation as a designer is high. He has, however, confined his work to his native Spain, and it was not until the spread of European championship golf to that country in the early 1970s that the richness of his creations gained more

El Saler Championship Course

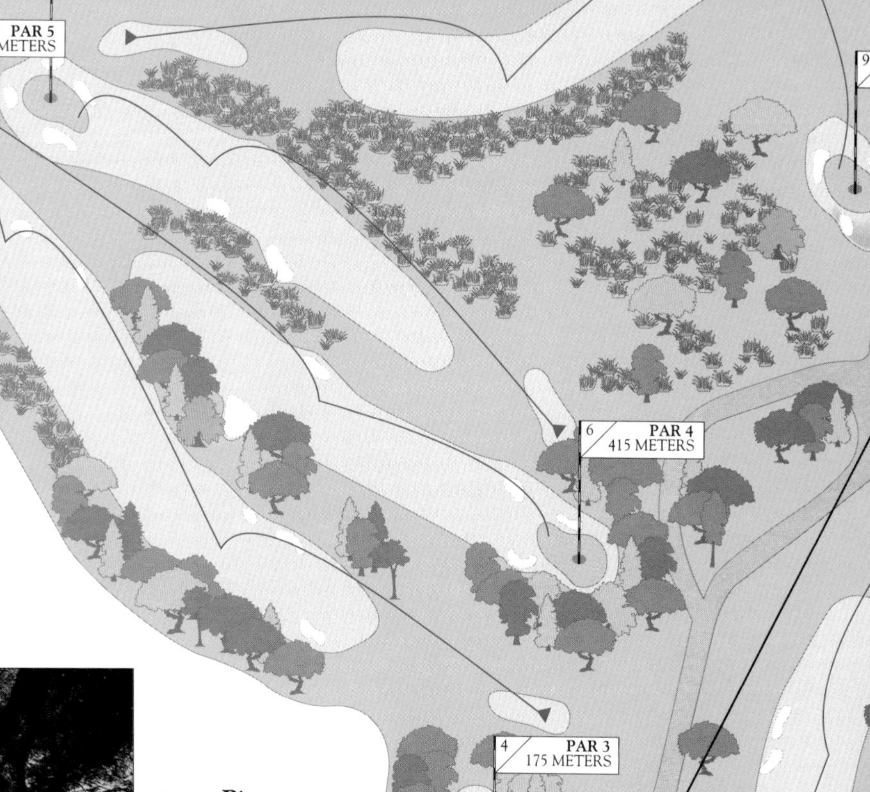

1 Pine green
Umbrella pines grace the gentle inland landscape at the 1st. A drive right opens up the dogleg, making the approach less difficult, but two greenside bunkers threaten, particularly one in the front right.

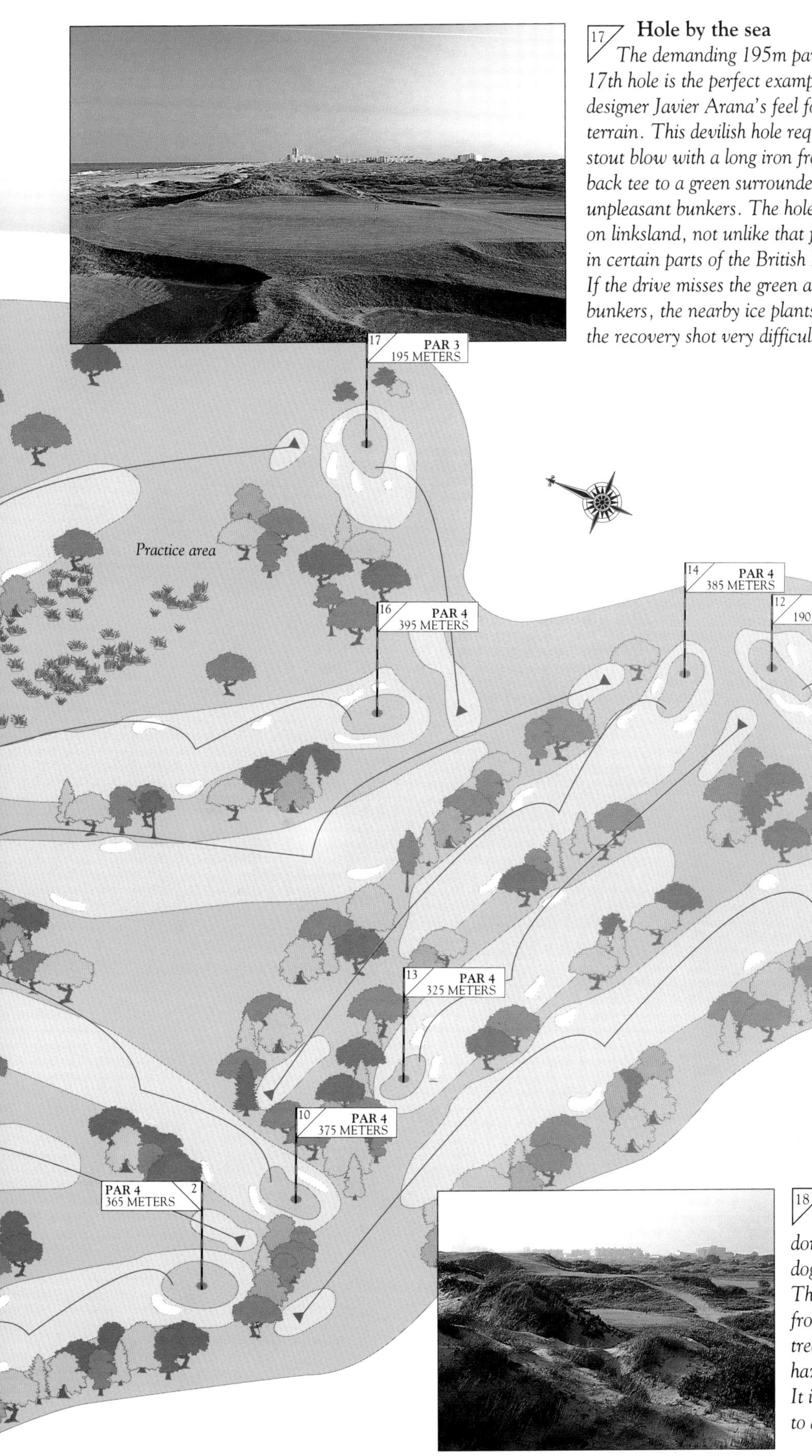

17 **Hole by the sea**

The demanding 195m par-3 17th hole is the perfect example of designer Javier Arana's feel for the terrain. This devilish hole requires a stout blow with a long iron from the back tee to a green surrounded by unpleasant bunkers. The hole is set on linksland, not unlike that found in certain parts of the British Isles. If the drive misses the green and the bunkers, the nearby ice plants make the recovery shot very difficult.

general acclaim. His Club de Campo course in Madrid and El Prat in Barcelona are highly thought of, but El Saler clearly rates as his masterpiece.

It covers an unusual combination of terrain, ranging from the umbrella pines of the farthest inland part of the course to the spectacular holes built among the sand dunes beside the Mediterranean. This is a combination that makes for a fascinating and varied challenge. Arana has made excellent use of the links environment in the seaside sections.

Langer's Hot Round

El Saler hosted a memorable Spanish Open in 1984. Bernhard Langer had to overcome the disruption of a robbery in his hotel bedroom, which relieved him of $5,000, and then a fine for slow play in the third round. On the final day he came back from seven strokes behind to win with a round of 62. The round included an amazing nine birdies in 11 holes from the 5th, and Langer, who went on to win the U.S. Masters the following year, judged it to be the best he had ever played in his life. At the time, he also rated El Saler as one of the best courses in Europe.

The weather can be hot at El Saler in summer. However, with the variation in the temperature between the sea and the land during the day, sea breezes can keep the air moving and cool things down. The clubhouse is close by one of Spain's magnificent state-run hotels, the Parador Luis Vives, with its excellent facilities.

18 **Linksland**

Wild sand dunes dominate the tee at the dogleg left par-4 18th. The fairway emerges from the links, with trees creating an added hazard near the green. It is a daunting finish to a spectacular course.

Championship Lengths

Out	3,150 Meters	Par 36
In	3,335 Meters	Par 36
Total	6,485 Meters	Par 72

Course Record

62 Bernhard Langer, Spanish Open 1984

SHINNECOCK HILLS

SHINNECOCK HILLS GOLF CLUB, SOUTHAMPTON, NEW YORK, U.S.A.

AS AMERICA'S FIRST 18-hole course, Shinnecock Hills has an important place in the history of golf in the New World. An early site of the importation of the game into the U.S., it was heavily influenced by the traditional home of golf, Scotland, both in the choice of site and in the personalities associated with the founding of the course.

Shinnecock badge
Built on an Indian burial site, the course commemorates its native American link on its official badge.

After a short spell as professional at Westward Ho!, England, and then as the professional and course designer at Biarritz in France, Scotsman Willie Dunn, Jr. was persuaded, as were many before and after him, to move to the United States.

He was tempted there by a wealthy American, William K. Vanderbilt, the son of the founder of the Vanderbilt empire, who had seen Dunn stage an exhibition of his prowess as a player in southern France during the winter of 1890. On his return to the United States, Vanderbilt immediately started discussing with his friends the possibility of building a golf course at the fashionable summer resort of Southampton on Long Island. Within a few months Willie Dunn, the former professional from Musselburgh, had left France and was looking for a site where he could build a course for Vanderbilt. He chose a spot a couple of miles from the sea among sandhills reminiscent in some ways of his native east coast of Scotland. Using the labor of Indians from a nearby reservation, and with very little equipment other than a few roadscrapers drawn by horses, he laid out the first 12 holes at Shinnecock Hills, destined to be one of the world's most exclusive golf clubs.

Rolling sandhills
Dunn and Vanderbilt chose the low-lying sandhills near the small resort of Southampton as a site for the course. Most of the work of cleaning off fairways and forming bunkers was done by hand.

These first holes were ready for play by late summer, 1891. The members brought in Stanford White, one of the top architects of the day, to design and build a suitable clubhouse in the style of the surrounding area. By the summer of the following year it was ready for occupation, with locker rooms, showers, and even a grill room. Shinnecock Hills was then by far the best-appointed golf club in the United States.

The course was extended to 18 holes the following year, and the game rapidly developed an influential following among the wealthy elite who spent their summers in fashionable Southampton. They even imported the custom of playing in red coats which had prevailed in the early days of the game in Britain.

Red coats (below)
For a while after their founding, the members of Shinnecock wore red jackets when playing, after the early British tradition that evolved to warn others on the course that golfers were coming.

Hill house (right)
The original clubhouse, opened in 1892, forms the core of the club complex today, presiding gracefully over the surrounding countryside.

INDIAN RELICS

It was not unusual for players to find some strange objects emerging when they played bunker shots on the original 12-hole layout. Old whiskey flasks and even human bones were excavated by overzealous use of a wedge. The explanation for these bizarre discoveries lies in the fact that scattered across the sandy land were some ancient Indian burial mounds, a few of which Willie Dunn shaped into bunkers.

Today the clubhouse built by Stanford White is still the heart of the rambling Shinnecock Hills Club, and though the course that Dunn laid out may have

Junior Scot (above)
Willie Dunn, Jr. was brought from Europe to design Shinnecock.

4 **Protected dogleg**
Two huge bunkers guard the corner of the 382-yard 4th, a sharp dogleg right which, though not overly long, does demand care. A drive safely to the left will leave a short iron approach to a green fearsomely defended by a group of six bunkers.

SHINNECOCK HILLS CHAMPIONSHIP COURSE

changed a great deal in the interim, the values and traditions for which it has always stood remain very much the same. The club was one of the five founding members of the USGA in 1894.

The present course mostly dates back to 1931, when Dick Wilson was called in to make changes. It had soon become clear that because of its shortness – it was under 5,000 yards for the second U.S. Open, which was played there in 1896 – the original course was not suitable for championship golf. Today it is still under 7,000 yards, not long by present-day championship standards, but it has since been picked as a Major championship venue. It was chosen to stage the 1986 U.S. Open, which was won by Ray Floyd. Three players, Chip Beck, Lanny Wadkins, and Mark Calcavecchia, broke the course

CHAMPIONSHIP LENGTHS

OUT	3,374 YARDS	PAR 35
IN	3,366 YARDS	PAR 35
TOTAL	6,740 YARDS	PAR 70

COURSE RECORD

65 C. BECK, M. CALCAVECCHIA, L. WADKINS, U.S. OPEN 1986

U.S. OPEN CHAMPIONS AT SHINNECOCK HILLS

1896 JAMES FOULIS; 1986 RAY FLOYD

9 **Good drive**
Shinnecock Hills puts a premium on good driving. Typical is the par-4, 411-yard 9th hole, where an enormous mound has to be carried by the drive. Only a well-struck shot over the mound can take some of the difficulty out of the approach shot, which is played uphill to the partially hidden green.

record of 68 that had stood for more than half a century, each scoring a round of 65. But no one found the course easy; Floyd's total was 279, only one under par.

There are only two par-5 holes on the course. Of these, the 16th demands the highest respect. At 519 yards, usually played into the wind, it requires a long drive to a landing area protected by four bunkers, followed by a second shot that must carry a minefield of bunkers in deep rough on the left. The green itself is guarded by another five bunkers. A par here always represents stalwart play.

But perhaps the best example of the tough test of Shinnecock Hills is the fine finishing hole. Its undulating fairway is reminiscent of British links golf, with rough on both sides as fearsome as can be found anywhere. The wind usually blows hard from the right, making it difficult to keep the ball in the fairway, while the long approach shot is threatened by two bunkers that protect the narrow neck of fairway in front of the green.

The Names of Shinnecock Hills

1st Westward Ho!	10th Eastward Ho!
2nd Plateau	11th Hill Head
3rd Peconic	12th Tuckahoe
4th Pump House	13th Road Side
5th Montauk	14th Thom's Elbow
6th The Pond	15th Sebonac
7th Redan	16th Shinnecock
8th Lowlands	17th Eden
9th Ben Nevis	18th Home

Some of the holes at Shinnecock are named after other courses, including Westward Ho!, where Willie Dunn, the designer of Shinnecock, had been a professional before coming to America. Other holes take names from physical features around the course.

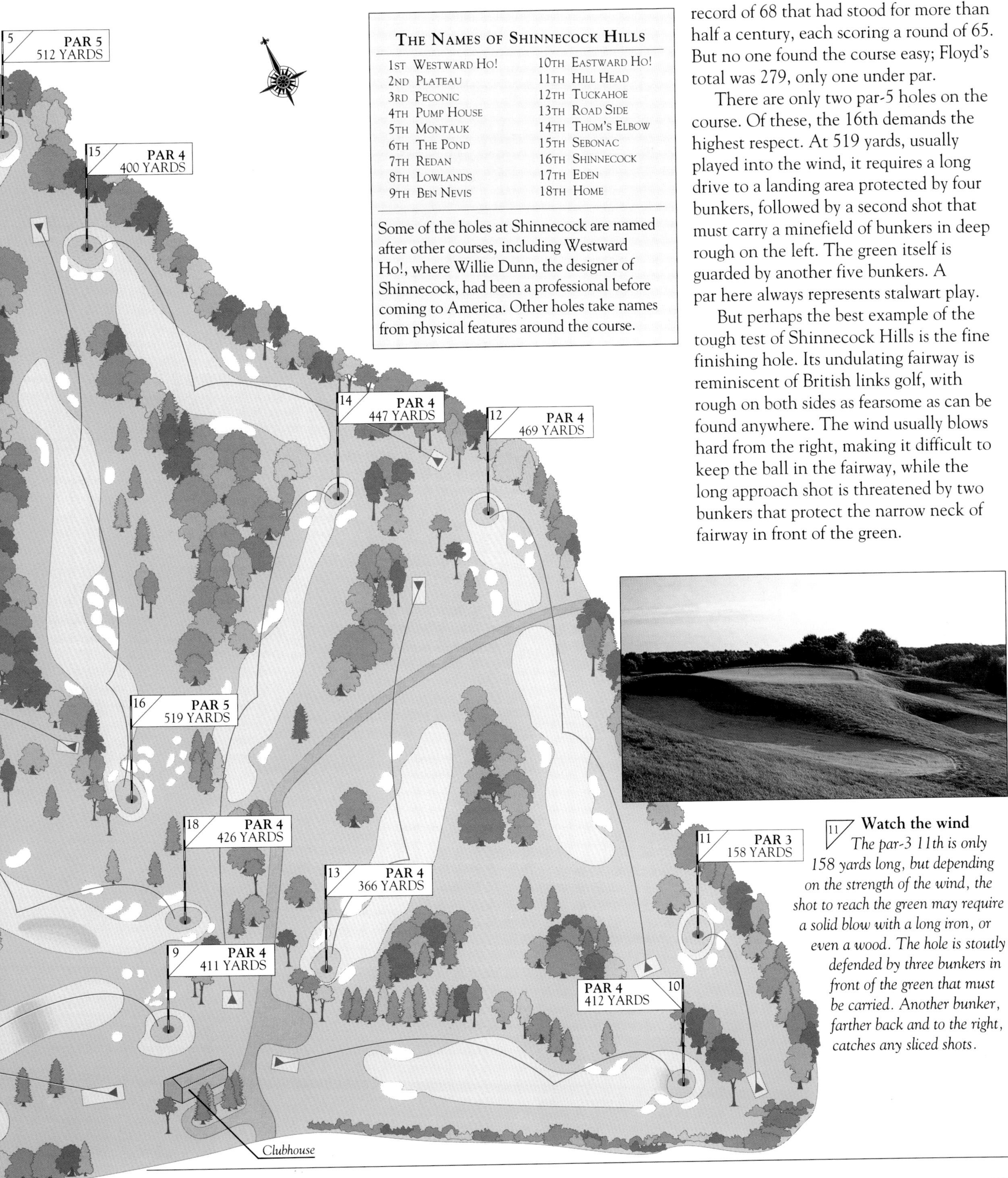

11 Watch the wind
The par-3 11th is only 158 yards long, but depending on the strength of the wind, the shot to reach the green may require a solid blow with a long iron, or even a wood. The hole is stoutly defended by three bunkers in front of the green that must be carried. Another bunker, farther back and to the right, catches any sliced shots.

SUNNINGDALE

SUNNINGDALE GOLF CLUB, SUNNINGDALE, ASCOT, BERKSHIRE, ENGLAND

MANY PUNDITS BELIEVE that the perfect round of golf was played over the Sunningdale Old course by the great Bobby Jones in 1926 during a qualifying round for the British Open, held later that year at Royal Lytham. He scored 33 on the front nine and 33 on the back for a round of 66, composed of 33 strokes and 33 putts, with not a 5 on the card. The stage upon which this magical performance was played could not have been more appropriate; the Old course at Sunningdale is a fine, traditional example of heathland golf only a few miles from the center of London.

Course symbol
A beautiful spreading oak tree makes up the crest of Sunningdale. It is a representation of the tree by the 18th green, next to the course's clubhouse.

To play at Sunningdale is to enjoy one of golf's great experiences. Jones certainly felt this to be the case, because after scoring 68 in the second qualifying round, in which his only blemish was a single 5, he declared to the world that he would "like to take the course home."

When golf moved inland, away from its original linksland environment, it soon became obvious that rough heathland with its heather, firm turf, and well-drained soil was perfect for the game. Indeed, golf played on heathland shares many of the characteristics of seaside golf.

Trees on the heath
Once Sunningdale was a comparatively bleak and treeless heath, but in the last 80 years the land has seen the growth of pine and birch trees.

The man who had the vision to create a course on the heathland at Sunningdale, west of London, was T.A. Roberts. In 1898 he built a house on the land and negotiated a lease with the owners, St. John's College, Cambridge. The lease permitted Roberts to have a course built, along with some housing. Sunningdale may have been the first property development in England linked to a golf course.

Attractive features
The natural beauty of the countryside at Sunningdale is gentle and appealing. The famous spreading oak tree by the clubhouse (right) *has provided shade for its caddies for many years, and hides a fine array of flower beds* (above).

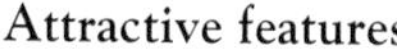

WOODED HEATHLAND

The course builder was Willie Park, Jr., son of the first Open champion and twice winner of the title himself. The land on which he laid out the original course was markedly different from what one sees today. When the course was opened for play in 1901 there were no trees to obscure the views across the heath. Since then, thousands of trees have been encouraged to grow. Today virtually every hole runs through great stands of pine and birch, creating a wonderful atmosphere of tranquillity that is hard to equal.

Golf-course architect Harry Colt, who was secretary at Sunningdale for 17 years, made some improvements to the course to compensate for the increased distances players were able to hit with the arrival of the Haskell ball (see page 48). In 1922

Willie Park, Jr.
Park built the Old course in 1900.

Colt also built the New course at Sunningdale, which is rather different in character. In many ways the New course is more demanding, although it is less intricate than its older companion, but it, too, is an excellent example of heathland golf, with rolling fairways and crisp turf. An iron shot can clip the ball off this type of turf with a satisfactory feeling rarely experienced on those modern courses that owe more to man than nature.

To putt on these splendid Sunningdale greens, so fast of pace and of such delicate texture, is heaven indeed for those who are able to understand and appreciate their difference from less subtle surfaces. Sunningdale is that rare breed of course where the playing conditions vary little with the changing of the seasons. The greens retain their speed and firmness even during the winter, making it a truly year-round course.

In common with all great courses, Sunningdale has a marvelous finishing hole, but one of the hazards at the 18th is relatively new. In 1940 a German bomb left a huge crater, providing the chance

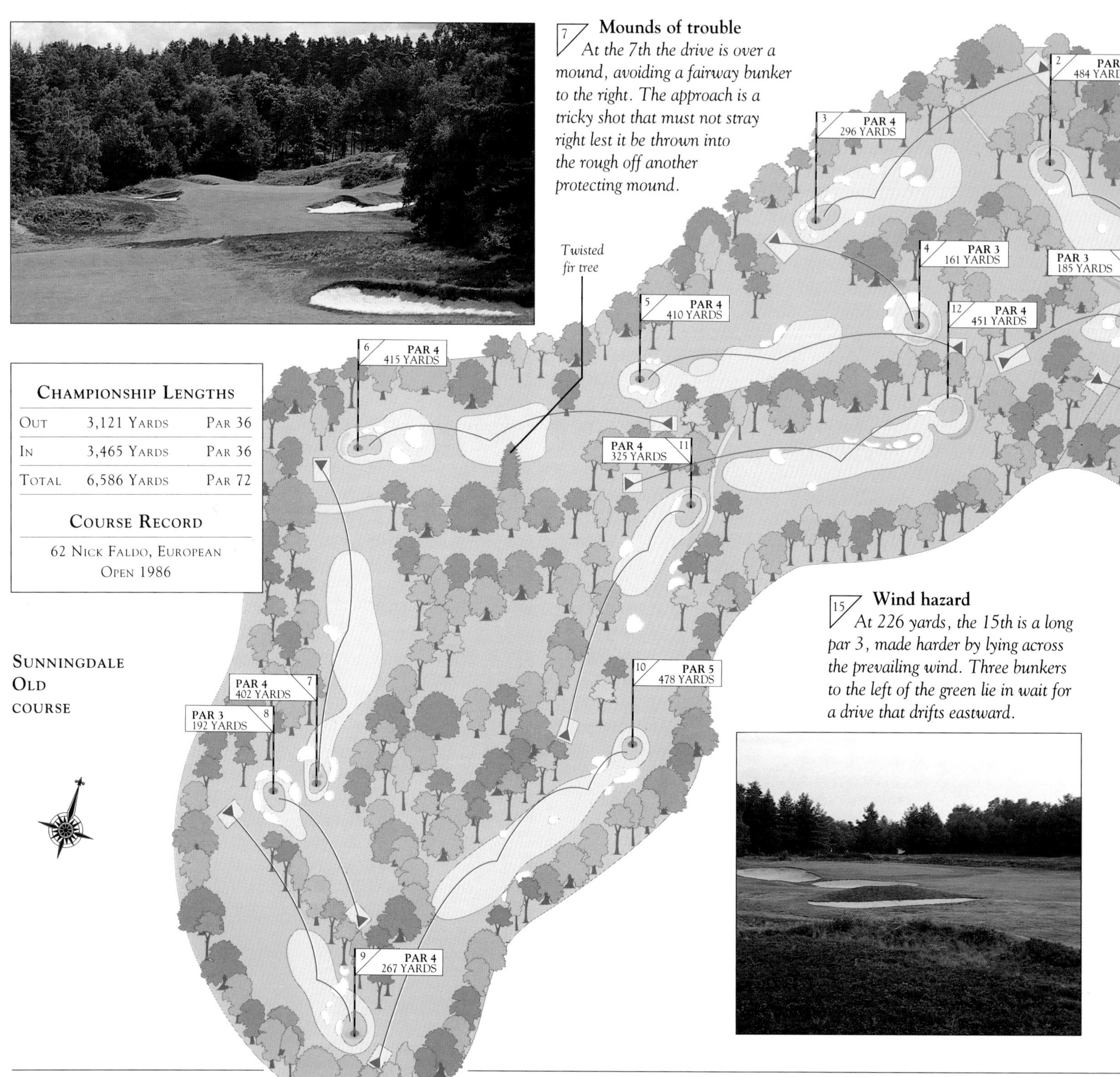

7 Mounds of trouble
At the 7th the drive is over a mound, avoiding a fairway bunker to the right. The approach is a tricky shot that must not stray right lest it be thrown into the rough off another protecting mound.

Championship Lengths

Out	3,121 Yards	Par 36
In	3,465 Yards	Par 36
Total	6,586 Yards	Par 72

Course Record

62 Nick Faldo, European Open 1986

Sunningdale Old Course

15 Wind hazard
At 226 yards, the 15th is a long par 3, made harder by lying across the prevailing wind. Three bunkers to the left of the green lie in wait for a drive that drifts eastward.

18 **Home** (right)
A long drive uphill is required at the 18th. It must avoid a deep bunker to the left and heavy rough on the right to leave any chance of getting home in two shots at this 432-yard par 4. The second shot is aimed at the big oak tree, which stands sentinel between the clubhouse and green. The shot has to carry a string of four bunkers.

17 **Green slopes** (above)
The green at the 17th has subtle slopes and is protected with four bunkers. The approach shot is fairly simple, as long as the drive has found the fairway. Missing the fairway, however, is easy to do. The drive at this hole, typical of many on the Old course, is played from an elevated tee down into a fairway that slopes gently and invitingly away. A group of trees around the driving distance menaces a shot aimed too far left, but devilish bunkers protect the right side in the corner of the slight dogleg and must be avoided at all costs.

to put in the extra bunker protection the hole now enjoys. A feature of the Old course is that the ball rolls well. In fact, despite being almost 500 yards long, the par-5 1st can often be comfortably reached in two shots when the course is fast in the summer months.

Power Play

While Sunningdale generates splendid enjoyment, and is a sufficient challenge for the amateur player, it is vulnerable to the power and strength of the modern tournament professional, particularly if the ground has been a little softened by rain. It says a lot that the professional course record, held by Nick Faldo, is as low as 62. Another example of the vulnerability of the course was given by Ian Woosnam in 1988, when the Welshman won the Panasonic European Open at Sunningdale with a remarkable score of 260, 20 strokes under par (for the European Open two tees are moved forward, which reduces the par to 70).

Even if the Sunningdale course is less menacing to great players than some of the other courses it is necessary for them to master on their Tour, it does have its own strengths. Above all, at the Old course the players enjoy a form of golf more virtuous and loyal to the game's traditional origins than is to be found at the majority of other courses on the circuit.

TRYALL

TRYALL GOLF, TENNIS AND BEACH CLUB, HANOVER, MONTEGO BAY, JAMAICA, WEST INDIES

THE BRITISH PLANTERS, many of them Scots, who ran the sugar plantations in Jamaica in the nineteenth century introduced golf to this beautiful island in the Caribbean. Many of the plantations had their own golf courses, and while most of these have since disappeared, there is a lasting legacy of fine golf on the island. Tryall, the most western of the island's courses and only half an hour from the international airport at Montego Bay, is the most famous, although it was built as recently as 1957.

Tryall is home to the Jamaica Classic, the opening event on the U.S. LPGA Tour, when the top 80 players in women's golf battle for $500,000 in prize money in the balmy warmth of a tropical January sun. The course was also chosen to stage the first Johnnie Walker World Championship in the week before Christmas, 1991.

Built by a group of Texas businessmen, the course is in an undulating lush landscape rising hundreds of feet around the historic Tryall Great House, the centerpiece of the resort and a legacy of the days of the sugar plantations. Views from the course, which is part of the Tryall Golf, Tennis and Beach Club, are breathtaking.

UPHILL STRUGGLE

The severe slopes overlooking Sandy Bay on the western tip of Jamaica were not promising material for a quality golf course, but architect Ralph Plummer managed to create sufficient flat fairway areas, even though the majority of tee shots are either uphill or downhill. This makes it possible to hit attacking shots to difficult green positions.

At only 6,654 yards, Tryall is not long by comparison with many courses, but what the course lacks in length it more than compensates for in the speed of its sloping greens and its challenging tees. For championship events the course starts at the hole that is normally the 7th for members and visitors, an alteration

CHAMPIONSHIP LENGTHS

OUT	3,107 YARDS	PAR 34
IN	3,547 YARDS	PAR 37
TOTAL	6,654 YARDS	PAR 71

COURSE RECORD

64 BETSY KING, JAMAICA CLASSIC 1990; JANE GEDDES 1991

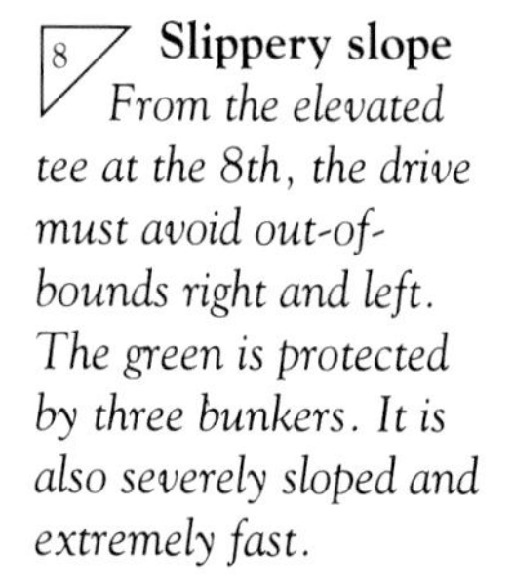

8 Slippery slope
From the elevated tee at the 8th, the drive must avoid out-of-bounds right and left. The green is protected by three bunkers. It is also severely sloped and extremely fast.

6 Sharp green
At 208 yards the championship 6th is not long, but it is one of the toughest par-3 holes to be found anywhere in the world. The green slopes sharply from left to right, and only a perfect tee shot placed below the hole will do. Four putts are not uncommon on this wickedly fast green. The ocean backdrop is a spectacular distraction.

15 **Caribbean blue**

The dazzling Caribbean laps behind the 15th green on one of the toughest holes on the championship course. A lake guards the corner of the dogleg left, and the second shot into the prevailing wind demands a long carry. The approach to the green is difficult to judge, but the ocean view is breathtaking.

Panorama in paradise

This is the view from the Tryall Great House east along the course toward the famous Round Hill Hotel in the distance. For championship events the course ends below the House.

introduced to meet the needs of television. Tryall boasts many spectacular holes, none more so than the par-3 14th on the championship layout. The tee shot must carry water all the way to the green. Thick vegetation catches anything sliced, often landing the ball in the water.

A Caribbean island such as Jamaica is always prone to catch any wind, and thus wind is a permanent factor in play at Tryall. The 1990 winner of the Jamaica Classic, Patty Sheehan, called the event "The War of the Winds."

TURNBERRY

TURNBERRY HOTEL AND GOLF COURSES, TURNBERRY, AYRSHIRE, SCOTLAND

FRANK HOLE'S NAME is not widely known in the world of international golf, but the game owes him a great debt. It was he who, in a persistent postwar campaign, managed to extract from the British government enough compensation money to attempt to recreate the Turnberry golf courses after they had been dug up to build an airfield during the Second World War.

Beacon of light
Part of the Turnberry crest is the lighthouse, which stands on the headland between the Firth of Clyde and Turnberry Bay.

Hole succeeded brilliantly, and with the help of architect Mackenzie Ross rebuilt and redesigned the courses, rescuing them from under the runways. In the process he resurrected one of the great golf resorts.

Turnberry lies at the southernmost end of a huge stretch of classic linksland along the Ayrshire coast in the west of Scotland. Its Ailsa course is by common consent one of the most beautiful and challenging golf courses in the world, set among scenery on the grand scale.

SPECTACULAR LANDSCAPE

High on the hill overlooking the links is the famous Turnberry Hotel, whose white facade and russet red roof make an attractive landmark on the skyline. Behind stretches the rich agricultural land of Ayrshire, while at sea, across the Firth of Clyde, lies the stark beauty of the Isle of Arran, with the Mull of Kintyre beyond.

To the left is the intriguing silhouette of Ailsa Craig, a great, round island of granite, which the locals call Paddy's Milestone. It towers out of the waters of the Firth close to where the great ships from the yards of Clydebank once used to run a measured mile as part of their sea trials. Today only a few still recall when the stones for another of Scotland's great sporting traditions, curling, were hewn from the granite of Ailsa Craig.

Turnberry's is not a long history by the standards of the courses that are currently on the Open rotation. All of it is contained within this century, and twice during that period the courses have been torn up to make way for military aircraft. In the First World War it was the Royal Flying Corps that built a training airfield.

Flying course
During the Second World War, Turnberry (right) *became an airfield, parts of which are still visible today. It was built for pilots being trained to fly Liberator bombers* (above), *which were used for sorties against German submarines.*

Shared glory (above)
In the 1977 Open at Turnberry, Tom Watson (right) beat Jack Nicklaus in the legendary "Duel in the Sun" *(see page 307)*.

Hilltop hotel (above)
On a rise behind the two courses is the famous hotel, part of the complex that opened in 1906. In the foreground to the right is the clubhouse.

Shortly afterward the rebuilding work of Major C.K. Hutchinson, in collaboration with James Braid, restored the courses and they were available for play for a short while until the outbreak of the Second World War. This time it was the Royal Air Force that tore up the courses to build a three-runway airfield, the crumbling remains of which can still be seen today.

Many thought the courses would never be revived after the war, but Hole took on the challenge. With the help of the hotel company's superintendent of grounds and golf courses, and of a firm of English contractors, Hole and Ross created in the design of the Ailsa course one of Britain's greatest championship links. The other Turnberry course, the Arran, is no mean

Green to blue (right)
Turnberry's lighthouse stands on a headland jutting into the Firth of Clyde. Through the haze is Ailsa Craig, known as Paddy's Milestone because it is on the way to Ireland.

course either and, were it not for its more famous sister, would be thought a worthy site for any championship.

The courses are very much part of the hotel operation at Turnberry. The two have always been linked. The 3rd Marquis of Ailsa, who was captain at Prestwick in 1899, and after whom the championship course is named, leased the land at Turnberry to the Glasgow and South Western Railway Company. Willie Fernie, the 1883 British Open champion and professional at Troon farther up the coast, had designed two 13-hole courses on the site by 1905. When, shortly afterward, the Turnberry Hotel was completed, the railway company took over the courses.

It took over 40 years for Turnberry to rise to championship standards, after its reconstruction by Hole and Ross. Since hosting the Amateur Championship in 1961, the Ailsa course has been the site for many important events. It has twice staged the British Open. The first time, in 1977, saw the great battle between Jack Nicklaus and Tom Watson which became known as "The Duel in the Sun." On the second occasion, in 1986, Greg Norman won his first Major event.

One of the toughest holes at Turnberry is the 528-yard, par-5 7th. During the

9 Over the sea
The 9th has a precipitous championship tee perching on a rocky promontory above the waters of the Firth of Clyde. A shot of more than 200 yards across the sea is required to make the carry to the safety of the fairway on the other side of a small bay. The 8th green lies to the right of the 9th tee, protected by its three bunkers.

The Names of Turnberry

1st Ailsa Craig	10th Dinna Fouter
2nd Mak Siccar	11th Maidens
3rd Blae Wearie	12th Monument
4th Woe-be-tide	13th Tickly tap
5th Fin' Me Oot	14th Risk-an-Hope
6th Tappie Toorie	15th Ca Canny
7th Roon the Ben	16th Wee Burn
8th Goat Fell	17th Lang Whang
9th Bruce's Castle	18th Ailsa Hame

Most Ailsa course names describe hole features, disguised by local Scottish dialect, but the 9th is named after the nearby remains of a castle said to have been used by the great Scottish king, Robert the Bruce.

5 In the valley
The 5th is a tough par 4 of 441 yards that lies in a sweeping valley between the dunes. Players need a good drive down the right to miss two large bunkers at the corner of the dogleg. The fairway then turns left, following the shore, to a green screened by a bunker short and left, and other bunkers eating into the surface.

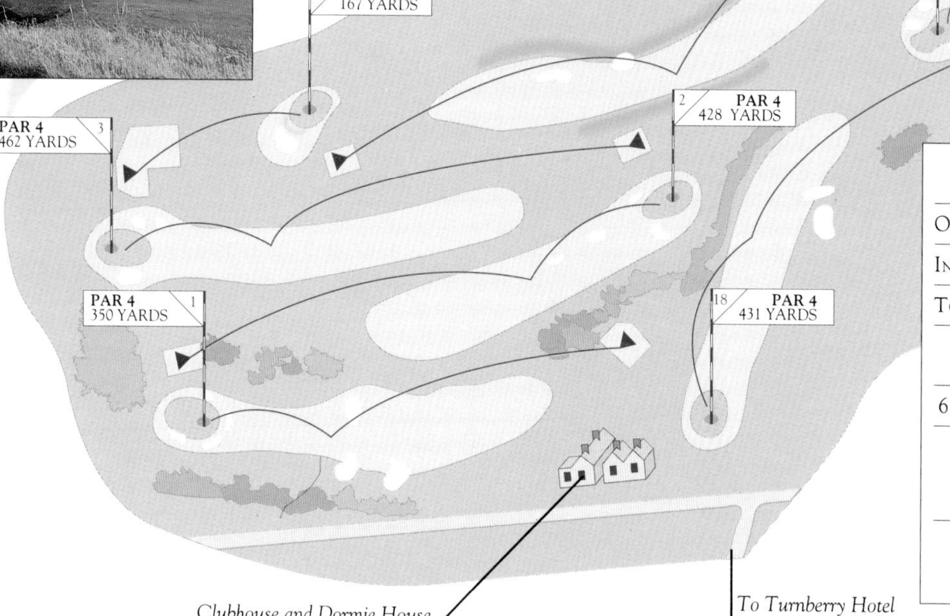

Championship Lengths

Out	3,480 Yards	Par 35
In	3,477 Yards	Par 35
Total	6,957 Yards	Par 70

Course Record

63 Greg Norman, The Open 1986

Open Champions at Turnberry

1977 Tom Watson, 1986 Greg Norman

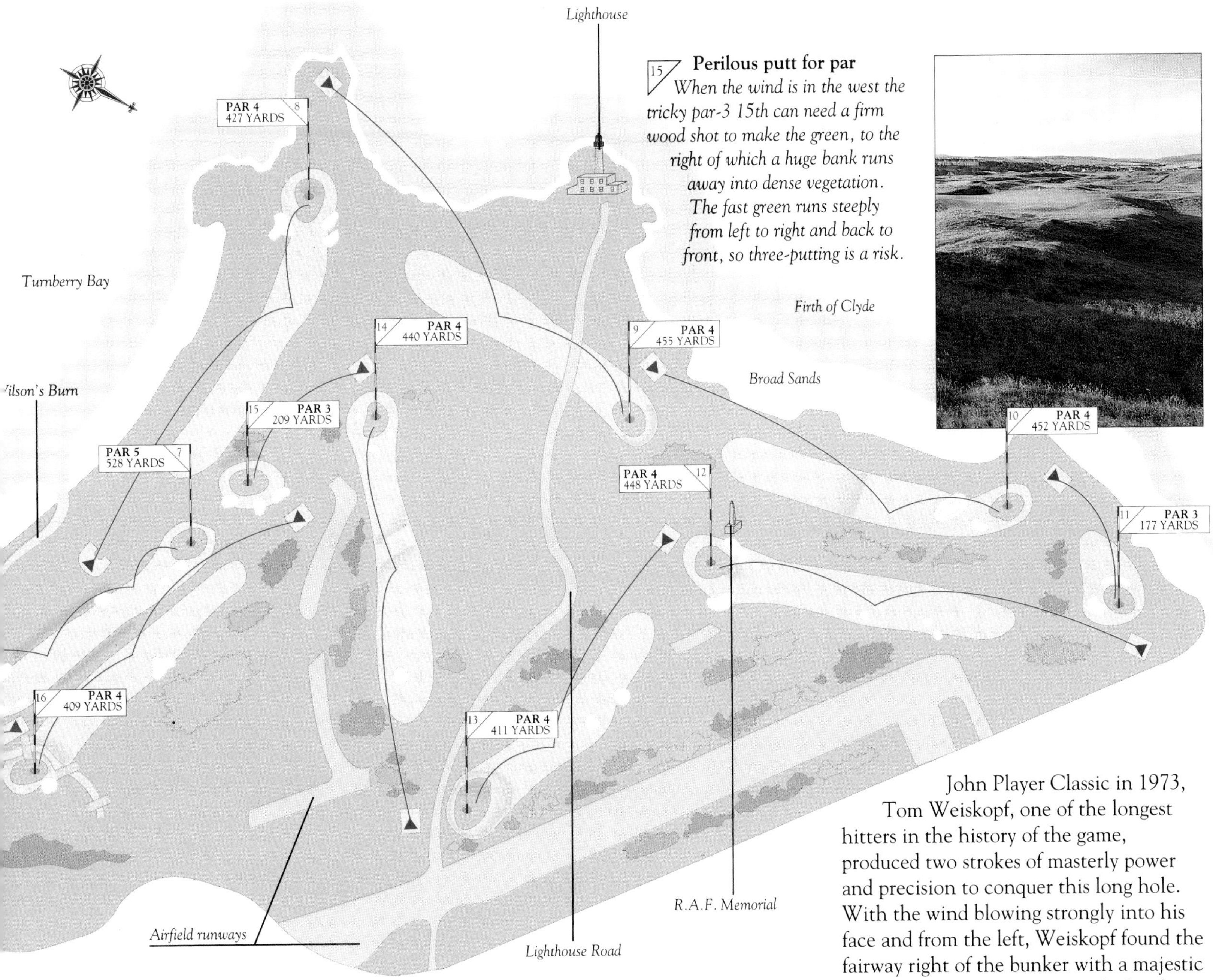

Lighthouse

Turnberry Bay

ilson's Burn

Firth of Clyde

Broad Sands

R.A.F. Memorial

Airfield runways

Lighthouse Road

PAR 4 427 YARDS 8

PAR 4 440 YARDS 14

PAR 4 455 YARDS 9

PAR 3 209 YARDS 15

PAR 5 528 YARDS 7

PAR 4 452 YARDS 10

PAR 4 448 YARDS 12

PAR 3 177 YARDS 11

PAR 4 409 YARDS 16

PAR 4 411 YARDS 13

15 Perilous putt for par

When the wind is in the west the tricky par-3 15th can need a firm wood shot to make the green, to the right of which a huge bank runs away into dense vegetation. The fast green runs steeply from left to right and back to front, so three-putting is a risk.

7 Big drive

The par-5 7th dog-legs left and runs along a shelf between the dunes with the sea hard on the left. To get to the green in two demands a huge first drive, especially to clear the lone deep bunker at the corner of the dogleg. A vast and cavernous bunker guards the left approach to the green, and two deep ones guard the front right.

John Player Classic in 1973, Tom Weiskopf, one of the longest hitters in the history of the game, produced two strokes of masterly power and precision to conquer this long hole. With the wind blowing strongly into his face and from the left, Weiskopf found the fairway right of the bunker with a majestic drive. He then struck a 3 wood of such purity that it did not waver by a yard from the line on which it was struck and flew like a bullet to the front of the green.

Lang Whang

Another notable challenge is the 500-yard, par-5 17th hole, named Lang Whang. This means "a long hit" and sums up exactly what is required. The drive is from a high tee down to the fairway, from where the hole rises to a green protected by three bunkers. Against the wind it is a formidable test, but in still conditions a strong player can usually reach the green in two strokes.

VALDERRAMA

VALDERRAMA GOLF CLUB, SOTOGRANDE, CADIZ, SPAIN

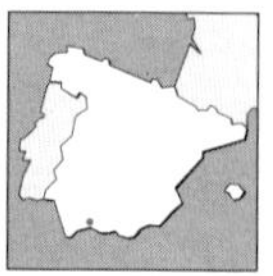

AMERICAN GOLF-COURSE architect Robert Trent Jones has long maintained that the course at Valderrama in the south of Spain is one of his finest achievements and that it truly belongs among the world's great courses. It has established itself as a challenging European Tour venue.

CHAMPIONSHIP LENGTHS		
OUT	3,048 METERS	PAR 35
IN	3,305 METERS	PAR 36
TOTAL	6,353 METERS	PAR 71

COURSE RECORD

65 JOSE RIVERO, VOLVO MASTERS 1990

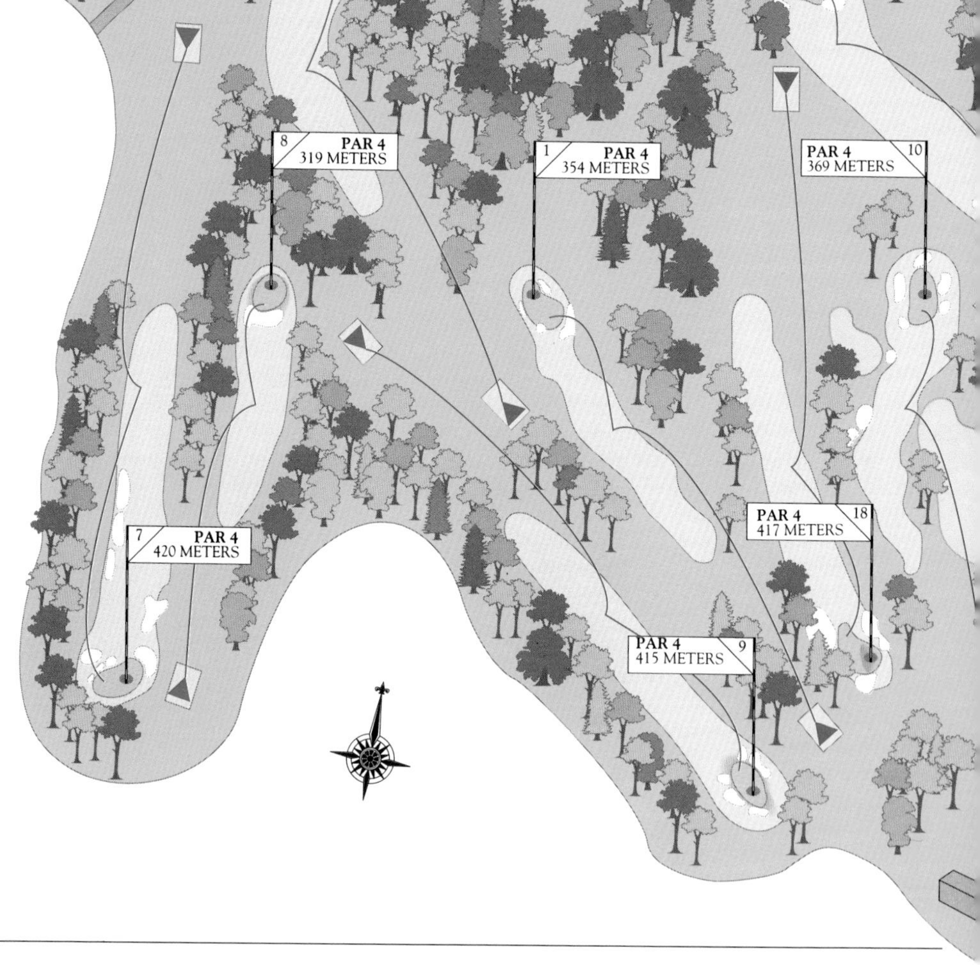

VALDERRAMA CHAMPIONSHIP COURSE

1 PAR 4 354 METERS
2 PAR 4 375 METERS
3 PAR 3 156 METERS
4 PAR 5 515 METERS
5 PAR 4 344 METERS
6 PAR 3 150 METERS
7 PAR 4 420 METERS
8 PAR 4 319 METERS
9 PAR 4 415 METERS
10 PAR 4 369 METERS
17 PAR 5 519 METERS
18 PAR 4 417 METERS
Avenida del Carmen
Calle Escorial

5 **Tree trouble**
Bunkers threaten the tee shot on both sides of the 5th fairway, which swings gently left. Uniquely, the approach shot is threatened by a cork tree, the foliage of which blocks the direct line. The safe line is to the left, away from front and back bunkers.

Trent Jones designed and built the course, originally known as Los Aves, in a fine location on a hill above the old village of Sotogrande. Sitting on the veranda at Augusta National in 1983, Severiano Ballesteros, who had just won the U.S. Masters, mentioned to Trent Jones that he attributed much of his success to two weeks' practice at Los Aves.

In 1985 industrialist Jaime Ortiz-Patino and seven of his golfing friends acquired the course and formed the Valderrama Golf Club with the aim of making it an attractive private club. Trent Jones was brought in again to remodel the course and made some subtle but significant changes, without altering the intrinsic character of the layout. He described it at the time as "polishing the diamond to improve the shot values in some areas of the course." The object was to make it a magnificent, challenging championship layout, and there is no doubt at all that he has succeeded.

Ultimate Accolade

Valderrama has been widely acclaimed as one of golf's outstanding tests when tackled from the championship tees, and this challenging course is now the host club for the Volvo Masters, the grand finale of the European Tour.

Ronan Rafferty, winner of the Volvo Masters and the Volvo Order of Merit in 1989, has described Valderrama's back nine as "probably more difficult than any other course in Europe . . . You are always looking for pars; birdies are a bonus." The final four holes are generally accepted by players as the most punishing on the European Tour. However, playing from tees farther forward, those who pursue the royal and ancient game in a less rarefied atmosphere than the touring professional still experience immense enjoyment on Robert Trent Jones's creation.

The course is situated near the Mediterranean, and sea breezes play an important part when deciding how to tackle each hole. The trees, too, are a hazard, and the spectacular panoramic views may be distracting. The club itself exudes an air of quiet elegance and charm usually encountered only in clubs of much greater antiquity. Some devotees even believe that Valderrama is rapidly becoming the Augusta of Europe.

2 **Test of accuracy** (left)
The par-4 2nd is more a test of precision than of strength. The fairway is lined by trees on both sides and the drive must find the left of the fairway to leave a clear view of the green. The approach, played to an elevated green guarded by two bunkers, demands care. The green is no safe haven, as the borrows are subtle and putts can be tricky, especially when the pin is in the center of the green.

12 **Tee up for three**
All the single-shot holes on the championship course at Valderrama are spectacular, but the 12th is by far the hardest. The tee shot is played from an elevated tee to a green set amidst cork trees. When the wind blows it is a very difficult green to hit, and anything off-target is almost sure to find one of the surrounding bunkers. The green itself is not easy, as it undulates and slopes from front to back.

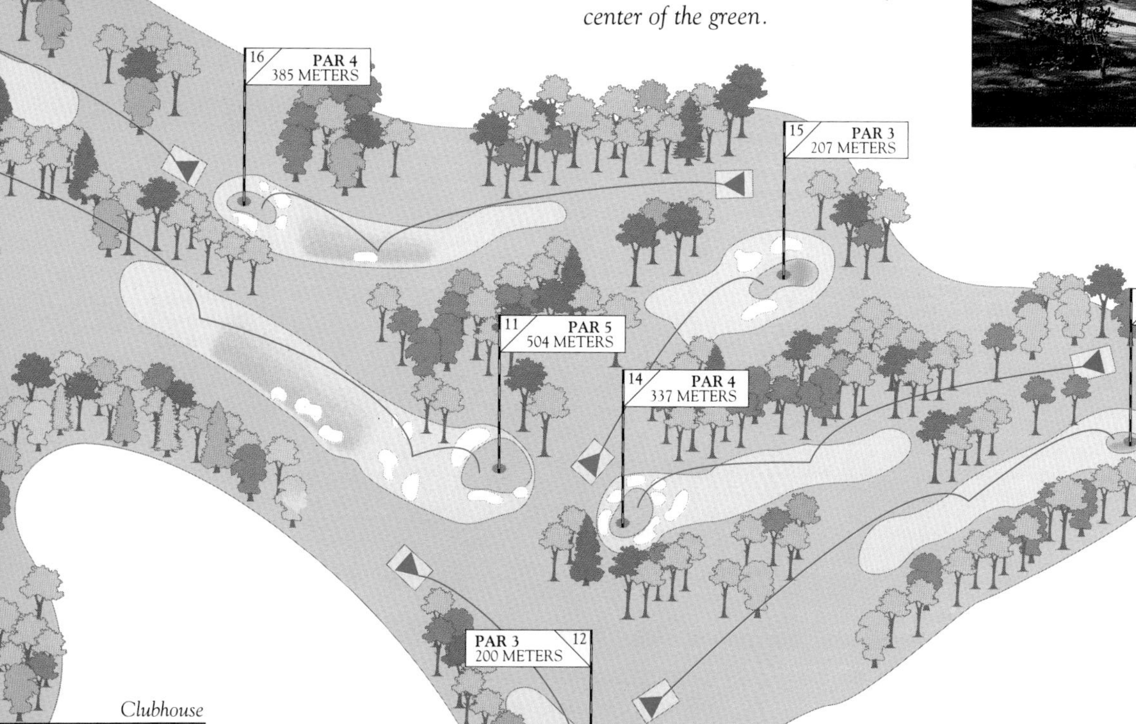

WENTWORTH

WENTWORTH CLUB, VIRGINIA WATER, SURREY, ENGLAND

THE WEST COURSE at Wentworth, home of the World Matchplay Championship, is one of the most famous of England's inland courses. Since 1964, when the World Matchplay was first played, there have been some remarkably low scores achieved, prompting Wentworth-watchers to wonder whether modern golf equipment and softer greens might have pulled the teeth of this great course. But Wentworth West, nicknamed the Burma Road, remains one of Britain's longest, toughest layouts.

Work began on Wentworth in 1923. It was one of the first developments in Britain to be based on the American country club idea, where a wide range of other leisure facilities is provided as well as golf courses.

The Wentworth project was to include within its 1,750 acres provision for large houses, each set in at least an acre of ground, close to the fairways. Two 18-hole courses and a short nine-hole layout were planned and built under the direction of respected course architect Harry S. Colt.

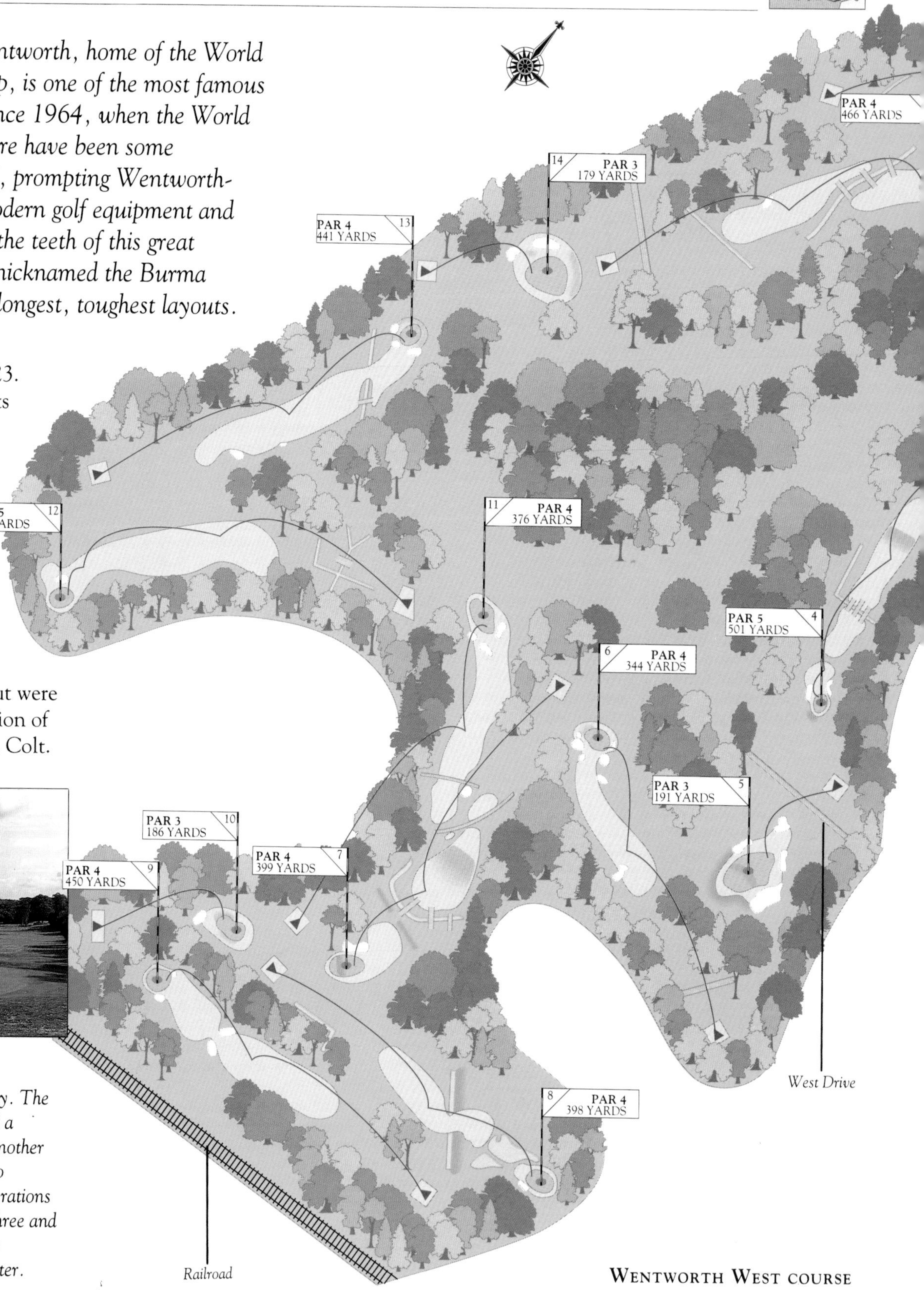

3 **Two-tiered green**

The long par-4 3rd is uphill all the way. The drive must not only be long but also avoid a dangerous bunker on the right. There is another bunker further down the fairway, and two bunkers guard the green itself. Recent alterations to the fearsome two-tiered green, where three and often four putts were once common, have been widely welcomed as being for the better.

WENTWORTH WEST COURSE

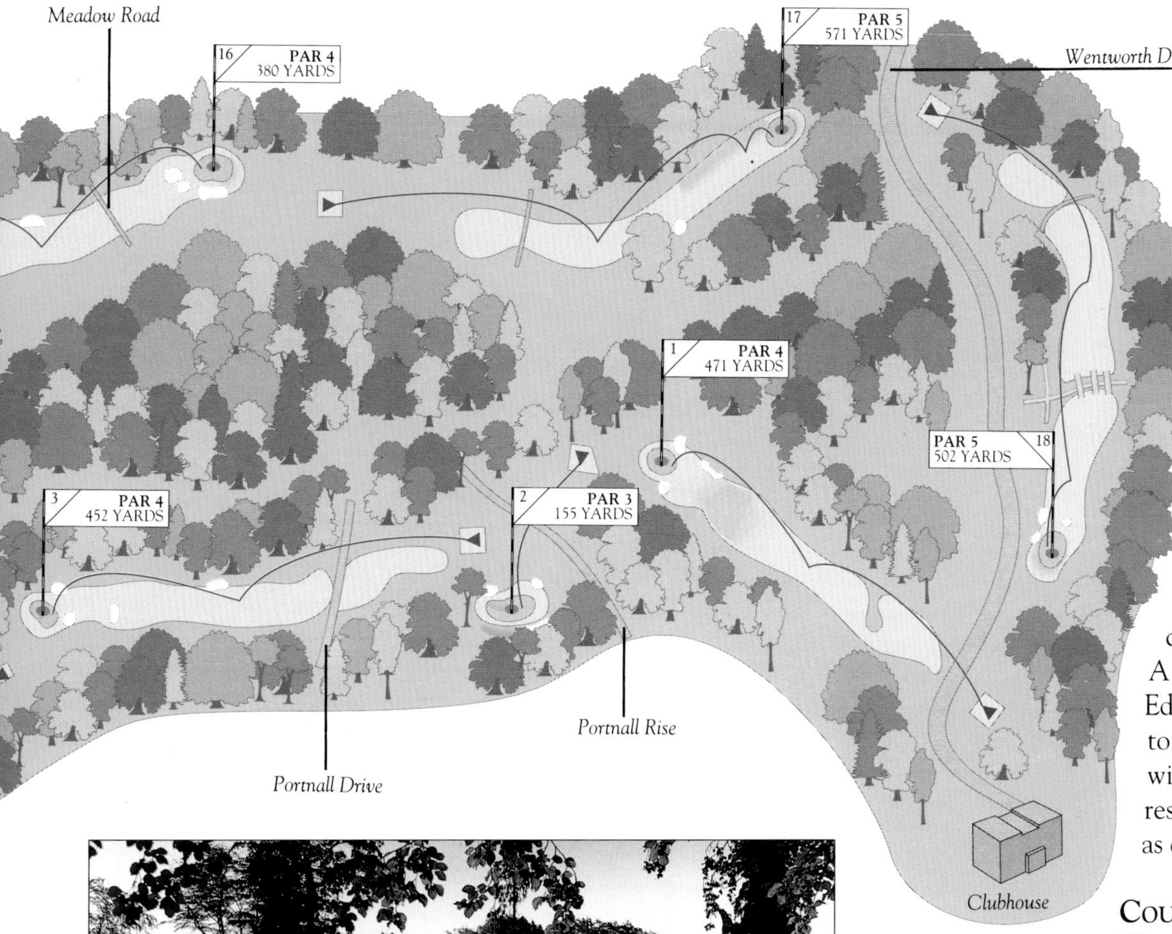

Championship Lengths		
Out	3,361 Yards	Par 35
In	3,584 Yards	Par 37
Total	6,945 Yards	Par 72

Course Record

63 Wayne Riley, PGA Championship 1991

Lying in a marvelous stretch of sandy heathland to the southwest of London, the ground Colt was given to work with was a prize indeed. What he created has stood the test of time. The East course was finished before the longer West course, which was opened in 1927. A third 18-hole course, called the Edinburgh, has been built more recently to a design by John Jacobs, together with Bernard Gallacher, Wentworth's resident professional, and Gary Player as design consultants.

18 **Drama hole**
A long, well-placed drive will open up the par-5 18th. The green can be reached in two shots, but bunkers right and left make the green difficult to hold with a long second shot. The 18th hole has been the site of much World Matchplay drama.

2 **Over the road** (right)
At 155 yards, the 2nd on the Wentworth West course is the first and the shortest of the one-shot holes. The shot is played from an elevated tee, across a road that is in a dip, up to an elevated green protected by two bunkers in front and a third at the back left. The green slopes from back to front, and care is required on the putting surface if no more than the allotted two strokes are to be taken.

Courses for the Wealthy

The courses were built in a fine setting amid woodland of fir and silver birch, and today masses of rhododendrons add to the aesthetic appeal of the estate. Henry Cotton once described the clubhouse as "one of the most beautiful in England."

There may be some truth in the suggestion that Wentworth provides "millionaires' golf," but this does not detract from the quality of the golf the courses offer. There have been many great and memorable events held there over the years. In 1926 an informal match was played between the professionals of Great Britain and America, which the British won comfortably. It was not the first match between the countries but was, in effect, the forerunner of the Ryder Cup.

In more recent times the famous Burma Road has seen some marvelous matches in the World Matchplay Championship, including five victories in nine appearances by Gary Player, two wins by Arnold Palmer, and four wins between 1981–5 by Seve Ballesteros.

WINGED FOOT

WINGED FOOT GOLF CLUB, MAMARONECK, NEW YORK, U.S.A.

WHEN THE MEMBERS of the New York Athletic Club decided they wanted a suburban golf club of their own, they asked the somewhat eccentric American course architect A.W. Tillinghast to build it for them. The architect received a less than comprehensive brief, being simply instructed by the good gentlemen of New York to "give us a man-sized course." Part of Tillinghast's response was the West course at Winged Foot, which not only met the members' requirements but may even have exceeded the brief, as it has itself proved to be one of the toughest courses in the United States.

18 **Great putt** *At the dramatic 18th, the fairway is narrow, and the green has fearsome undulations. These did not bother Greg Norman in the 1984 U.S. Open. It was here that he holed a massive putt from off the left edge for a birdie to force a play-off against Fuzzy Zoeller.*

Tillinghast built many fine courses, including Baltusrol and Quaker Ridge, but Winged Foot was probably his most ambitious undertaking. During its construction he cut down nearly 8,000 trees and removed over 7,000 tons of rock. The West course was built in 1923, along with another 18-hole layout, the East course, which some still argue is just as difficult. But the West at Winged Foot is the accepted championship course, and has been host to the U.S. Open four times.

Eight of the par 4s on the West course are more than 400 yards long and extremely demanding. Only the best amateurs can hope to reach the majority of these greens in two shots and many top professionals find it difficult. These long two-shot holes are the principal reason why Winged Foot is so difficult. There have, in fact, been many "big score" victories in the U.S. Open at Winged Foot. In 1929 Bobby Jones and Al Espinosa were both 14 over par when they tied for the championship, and 30 years later Billy Casper had to single-putt no fewer than 31 greens to win with a score of 282.

WINNING OVER PAR

In its wisdom the USGA decided to make the course even tougher before the 1974 U.S. Open. Hale Irwin's winning score of 287, seven over the par for that championship, was a reflection of just how difficult it had become. Fuzzy Zoeller and Greg Norman reduced the course to more manageable proportions in the 1984 U.S. Open, when Norman staged a remarkable last-round challenge to tie Zoeller on 276, four under the card. But the course took its revenge next day: Norman took 75 and lost the play-off to Zoeller by eight strokes.

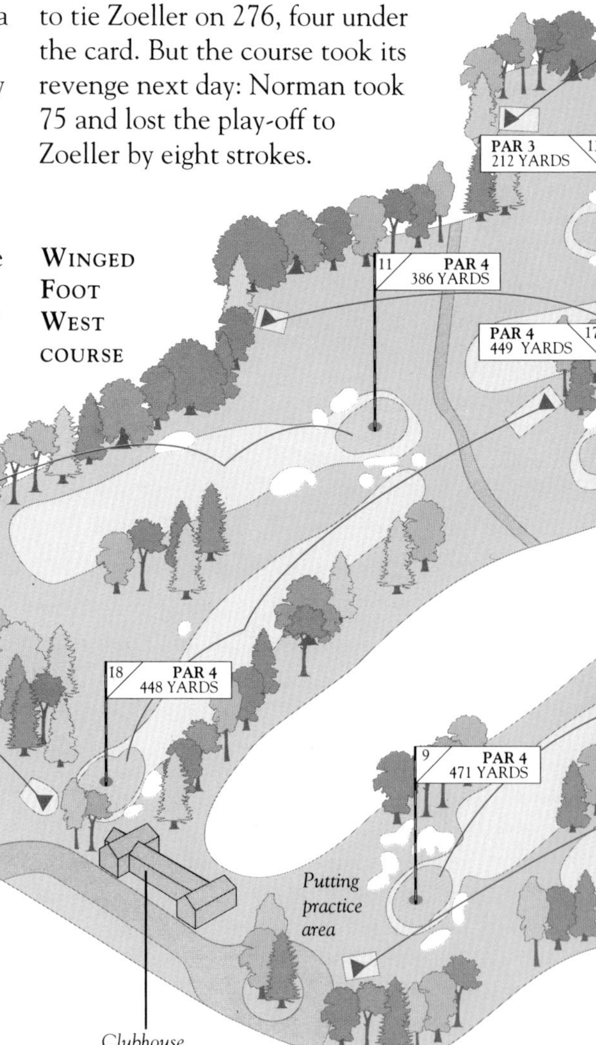

10 **Tough 10th** *The green at this par 3 is protected by two deep, kidney-shaped bunkers. Behind, a house has its yard within 30 ft. (9m) of the green, and on the left trees catch hooked or pulled shots.*

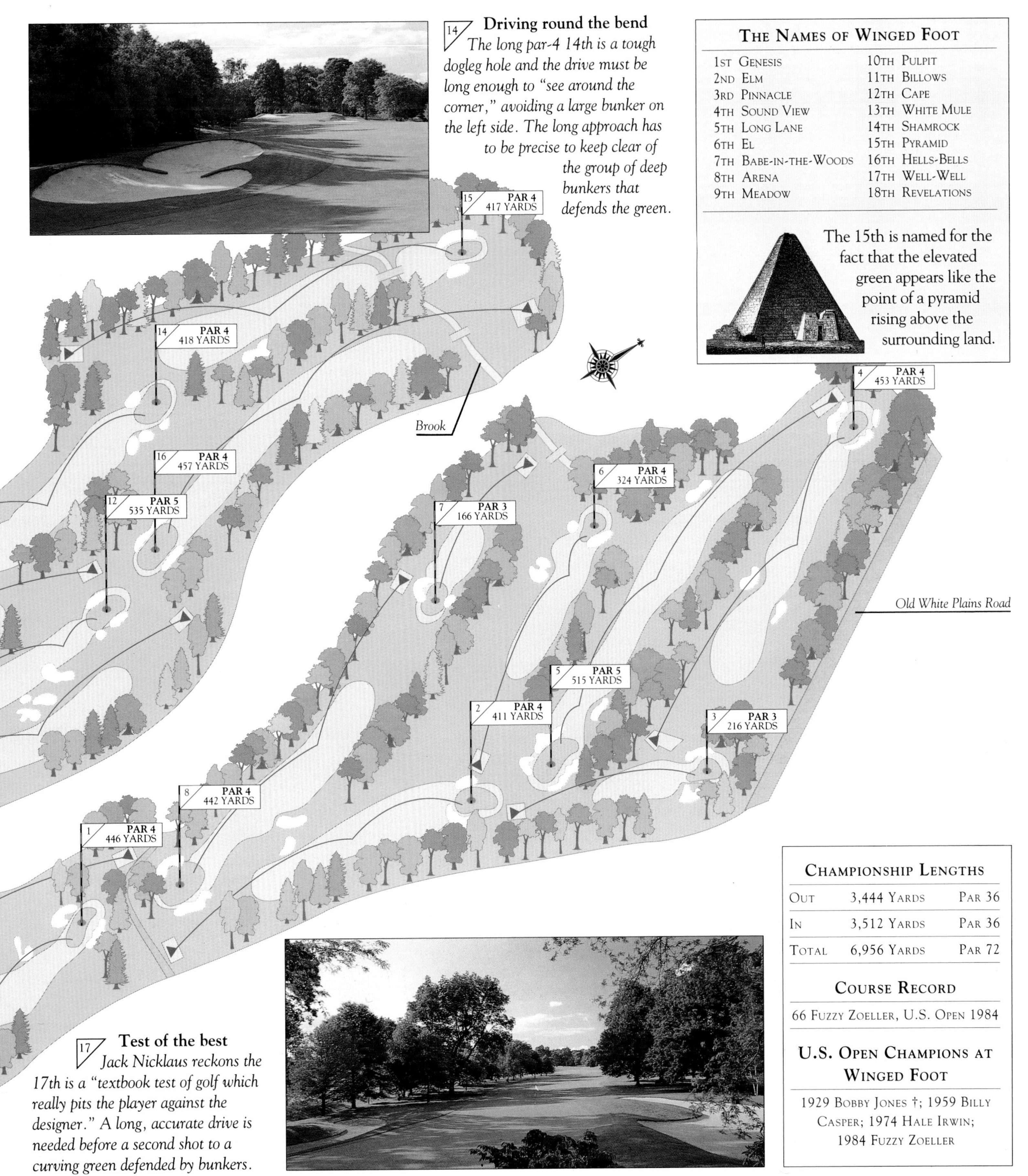

14 Driving round the bend

The long par-4 14th is a tough dogleg hole and the drive must be long enough to "see around the corner," avoiding a large bunker on the left side. The long approach has to be precise to keep clear of the group of deep bunkers that defends the green.

The Names of Winged Foot

1st	Genesis	10th	Pulpit
2nd	Elm	11th	Billows
3rd	Pinnacle	12th	Cape
4th	Sound View	13th	White Mule
5th	Long Lane	14th	Shamrock
6th	El	15th	Pyramid
7th	Babe-in-the-Woods	16th	Hells-Bells
8th	Arena	17th	Well-Well
9th	Meadow	18th	Revelations

The 15th is named for the fact that the elevated green appears like the point of a pyramid rising above the surrounding land.

Championship Lengths

Out	3,444 Yards	Par 36
In	3,512 Yards	Par 36
Total	6,956 Yards	Par 72

Course Record

66 Fuzzy Zoeller, U.S. Open 1984

U.S. Open Champions at Winged Foot

1929 Bobby Jones †; 1959 Billy Casper; 1974 Hale Irwin; 1984 Fuzzy Zoeller

17 Test of the best

Jack Nicklaus reckons the 17th is a "textbook test of golf which really pits the player against the designer." A long, accurate drive is needed before a second shot to a curving green defended by bunkers.

World Directory of Courses

In the second section of this chapter are a further 50 of the world's outstanding championship courses. The majestic layouts featured here – ancient and historic links as well as lesser-known gems tucked away in unlikely settings – present a wide array of golfing challenges.

The awesome antiquity of Prestwick, birthplace of the Open Championship and its home for its first 12 years (and 12 more times after that), contrasts with the New St. Andrews Club in Japan, for example, where an electronic trolley system transports players' clubs around the course. There is the miraculous green oasis in the desert that is the Emirates course in Dubai, and the sheer charm of Corfu. These spectacular courses complete a collection of 100 of the world's greatest courses, representing outstanding golf on an international scale. Across their fairways is written the history – and the continuing development – of a royal and ancient game whose beginnings were uncertain, but whose appeal is international and whose future is assured.

Banff

BANFF, ALBERTA, CANADA

The Canadian Pacific Railway Company built the original nine holes amidst the spectacle of the Canadian Rockies in 1911 for guests at its splendid Banff Springs Hotel. German prisoners of war built an additional nine during the First World War before Canadian architect Stanley Thompson was commissioned to redesign the course in 1927. The 8th hole, known as the Devil's Cauldron, is recognized as one of the great holes in world golf.

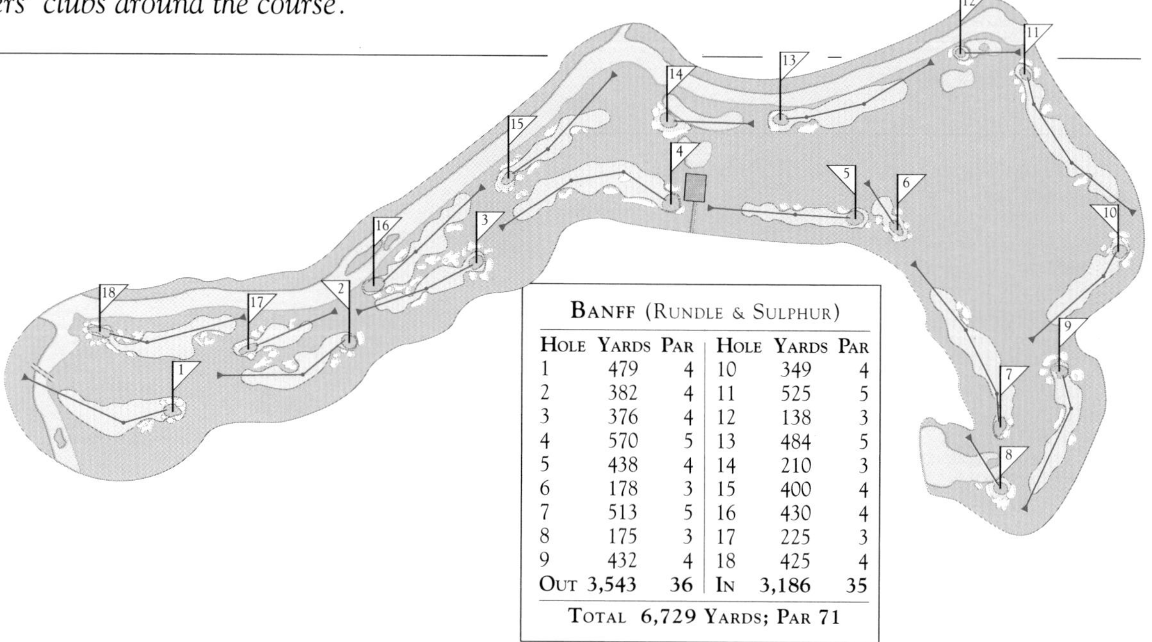

Banff (Rundle & Sulphur)

Hole	Yards	Par	Hole	Yards	Par
1	479	4	10	349	4
2	382	4	11	525	5
3	376	4	12	138	3
4	570	5	13	484	5
5	438	4	14	210	3
6	178	3	15	400	4
7	513	5	16	430	4
8	175	3	17	225	3
9	432	4	18	425	4
Out	3,543	36	In	3,186	35

Total 6,729 Yards; Par 71

The Belfry (Brabazon)

Hole	Yards	Par	Hole	Yards	Par
1	418	4	10	275	4
2	349	4	11	420	4
3	465	4	12	235	3
4	579	5	13	394	4
5	399	4	14	194	3
6	396	4	15	550	5
7	183	3	16	410	4
8	460	5	17	575	5
9	400	4	18	474	4
Out	3,649	37	In	3,527	36

Total 7,176 Yards; Par 73

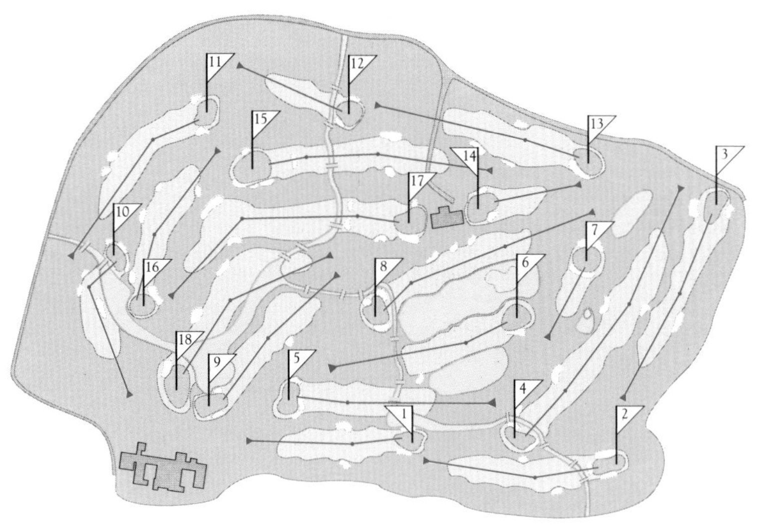

The Belfry

WISHAW, WARWICKSHIRE, ENGLAND

Two dramatic encounters between the professionals of Europe and the United States, together with a public debate over its continued use as a Ryder Cup site, have made The Belfry one of the best-known courses in Britain. Transformed by Peter Alliss and Dave Thomas from farmland into an American-style course, its showpieces are the 10th, reachable with the drive across a guarding lake by big hitters, and the 18th, which carries water twice, from the tee and again with the second shot to the three-tier green.

Las Brisas

MARBELLA, MALAGA, SPAIN

Water dominates this Robert Trent Jones layout, built in a valley beneath the Sierra Blanca. Opened in 1968, it is a sterner test than Jones's earlier work at Sotogrande. He has combined the aquatic threat on this course with some fearsome contouring of the greens. The par-3 16th rates as probably the most difficult hole, with the green sloping wickedly toward the water in front of it. Las Brisas has been a site for the Spanish Open and for the World Cup.

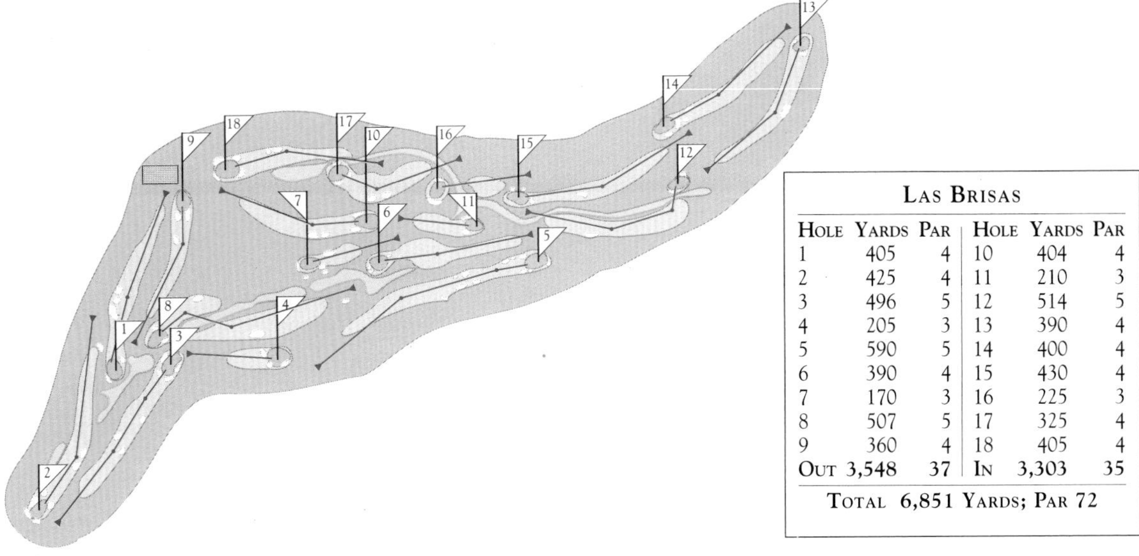

Las Brisas

Hole	Yards	Par	Hole	Yards	Par
1	405	4	10	404	4
2	425	4	11	210	3
3	496	5	12	514	5
4	205	3	13	390	4
5	590	5	14	400	4
6	390	4	15	430	4
7	170	3	16	225	3
8	507	5	17	325	4
9	360	4	18	405	4
Out	3,548	37	In	3,303	35

Total 6,851 Yards; Par 72

Butler National

OAK BROOK, CHICAGO, ILLINOIS, U.S.A.

George Fazio designed this course in Chicago's suburbs. Eleven of its 18 holes are threatened by water hazards. The lake at the par-4 14th has to be carried twice and it poses a major threat to the left of the green on the previous hole, the tough par-3 13th. The par-3 5th has a carry over water of 201 yards from the championship tee. Butler is renowned for the difficulty of its greens, which have subtle contours requiring particular care in judgment of the line.

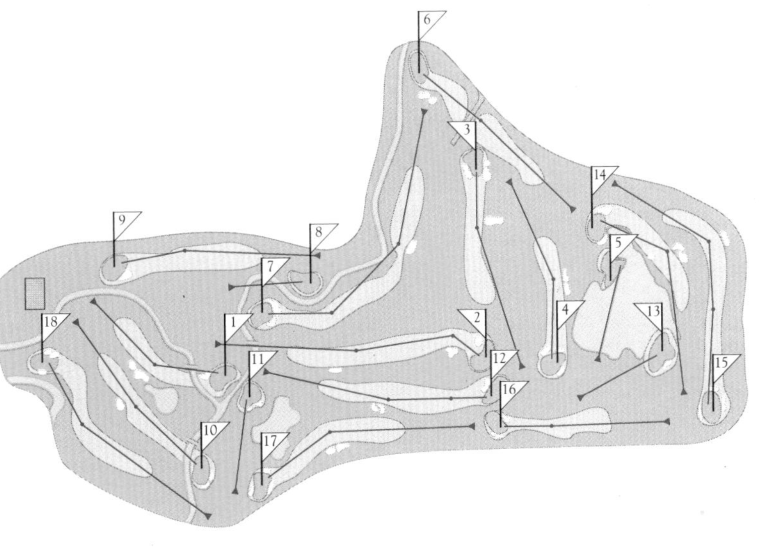

Butler National

Hole	Yards	Par	Hole	Yards	Par
1	372	4	10	446	4
2	563	5	11	193	3
3	433	4	12	482	5
4	406	4	13	197	3
5	201	3	14	430	4
6	443	4	15	583	5
7	623	5	16	385	4
8	195	3	17	459	4
9	431	4	18	464	4
Out	3,667	36	In	3,639	36

Total 7,306 Yards; Par 72

Chicago

WHEATON, ILLINOIS, U.S.A.

The Chicago Golf Club is the oldest 18-hole course in the United States. It was formed at Belmont, Illinois, in 1892 with a nine-hole course laid out by Charles Blair Macdonald, which was extended to 18 holes in 1893. In 1894, the club moved to its Wheaton site with an 18-hole layout again designed by Macdonald. That same year it was one of the five clubs that formed the United States Golf Association. Chicago has hosted the U.S. Open three times and the U.S. Amateur four times.

Chicago

Hole	Yards	Par	Hole	Yards	Par
1	450	4	10	139	3
2	440	4	11	410	4
3	219	3	12	414	4
4	536	5	13	149	3
5	320	4	14	351	4
6	395	4	15	393	4
7	207	3	16	525	5
8	413	4	17	382	4
9	406	4	18	425	4
Out	3,386	35	In	3,188	35

Total 6,574 Yards; Par 70

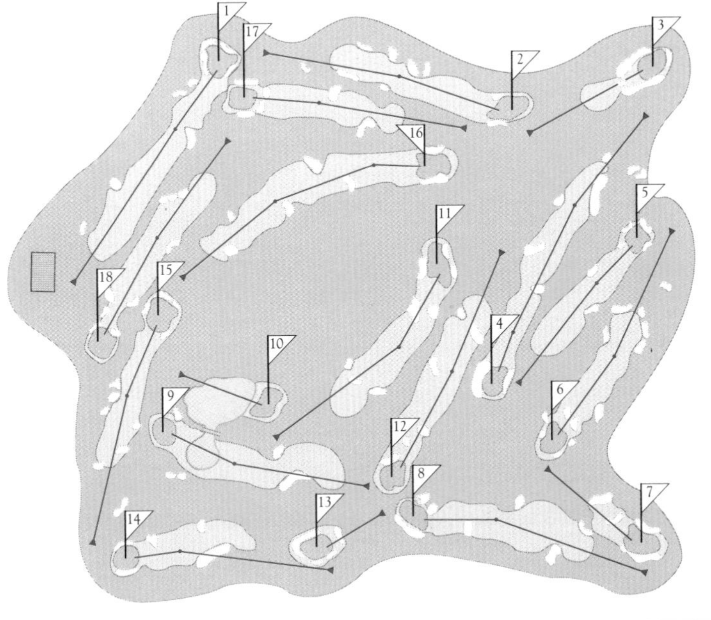

CHRISTCHURCH

SHIRLEY, CHRISTCHURCH, NEW ZEALAND

This course was established in 1873 by expatriate Scots. It moved from its original site at Hagley Park partly because of the interference of horned cattle, and it features the early Scottish practice of nine holes out and nine holes back. The 5th is a daunting par 5 of 539m that doglegs to the left in the landing area for the drive. A solitary bunker guards the green on the front left. The club has hosted the New Zealand Open Championship 13 times.

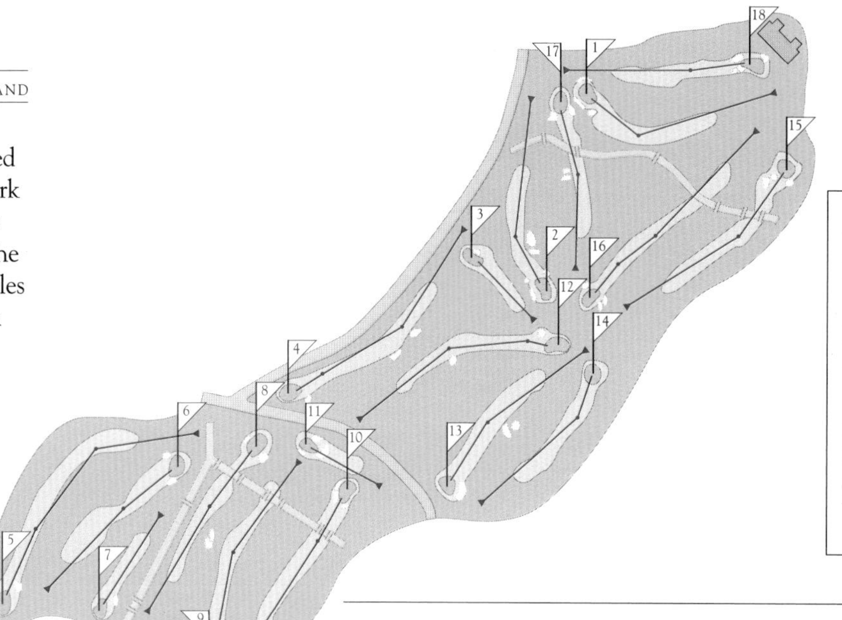

CHRISTCHURCH

Hole	Meters	Par	Hole	Meters	Par
1	330	4	10	398	4
2	302	4	11	130	3
3	133	3	12	415	5
4	489	5	13	393	4
5	539	5	14	334	4
6	366	4	15	407	4
7	183	3	16	480	5
8	389	4	17	343	4
9	439	4	18	320	4
Out	3,170	36	In	3,220	37

Total 6,390 Meters; Par 73

CORFU

CORFU, GREECE

Designed by Donald Harradine, the Corfu Golf and Country Club is one of the hidden golfing gems of Europe. It lies in the peaceful and verdant Ropa Valley on this romantic Greek island in the Ionian Sea. Although not long by the standards of some courses, Corfu nonetheless presents an exciting challenge, with several water hazards and great stands of mature cypress, pine, and eucalyptus.

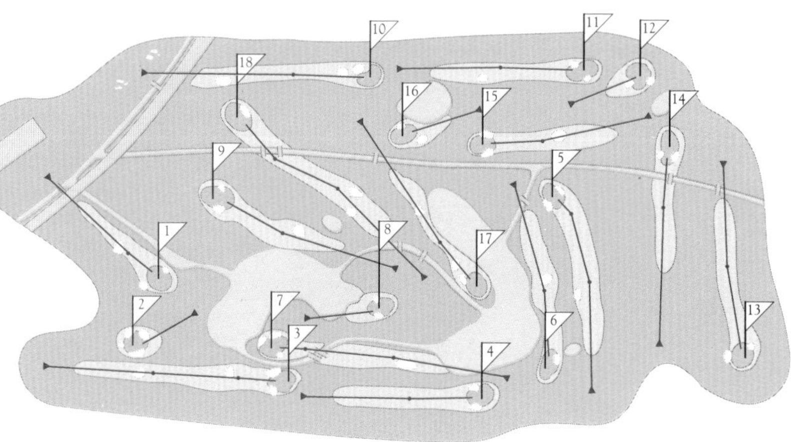

CORFU

Hole	Meters	Par	Hole	Meters	Par
1	310	4	10	430	4
2	150	3	11	380	4
3	470	5	12	160	3
4	380	4	13	370	4
5	435	5	14	305	4
6	350	4	15	345	4
7	505	5	16	205	3
8	205	3	17	405	4
9	425	4	18	470	5
Out	3,230	37	In	3,070	35

Total 6,300 Meters; Par 72

CRANS-SUR-SIERRE

MONTANA, SWITZERLAND

Founded in 1924, this golf club is set on a mountain plateau at a height of 5,000 feet (1,600m) in the Berner Alps. The 6,165m course is shortened by the greater distance the ball travels in the rarefied air. Despite being under snow during the winter, the course always returns to fine condition in time for the Swiss Open, which has been staged there since 1939. Crans-sur-Sierre is the largest club in Switzerland with some 1,500 members and enjoys a link with the Royal Hong Kong Club.

CRANS-SUR-SIERRE

Hole	Meters	Par	Hole	Meters	Par
1	490	5	10	370	4
2	395	4	11	190	3
3	165	3	12	355	4
4	460	4	13	185	3
5	315	4	14	520	5
6	295	4	15	475	5
7	275	4	16	290	4
8	160	3	17	315	4
9	565	5	18	345	4
Out	3,120	36	In	3,045	36

Total 6,165 Meters; Par 72

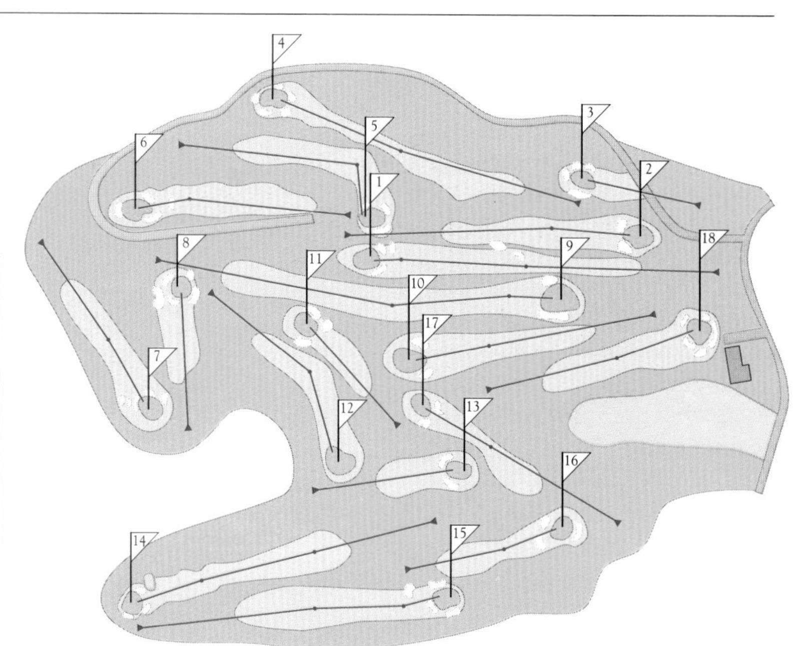

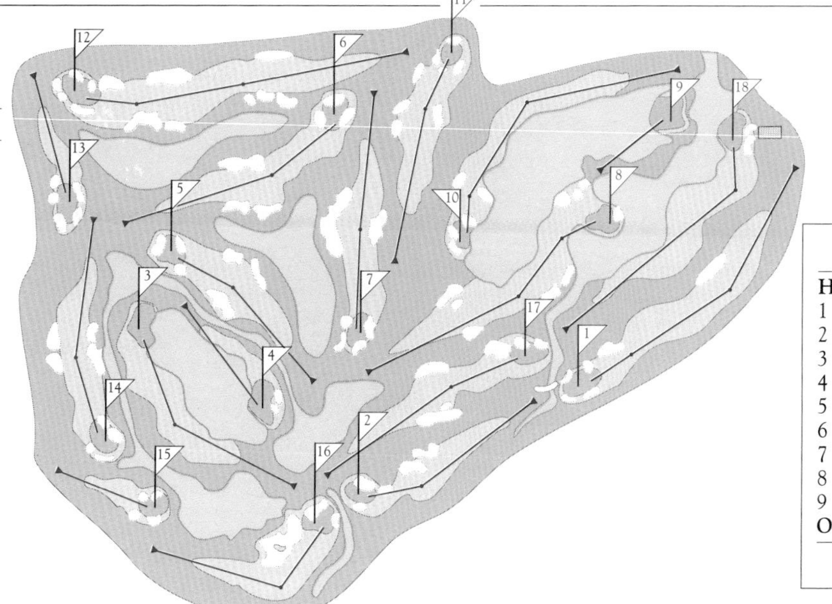

Doral

MIAMI, FLORIDA, U.S.A.

Of the four courses at this Florida resort complex, the Blue course enjoys a worldwide reputation. Known as the "Blue Monster," it is truly of championship standards and is the home of the Doral Open, a major early-season fixture on the U.S. Tour. Dick Wilson designed the course and its memorable finishing hole running alongside a lake. Close by, the 9th is similarly exacting, requiring a 163-yard carry over water all the way to the green.

Doral (Blue)

Hole	Yards	Par	Hole	Yards	Par
1	514	5	10	563	5
2	355	4	11	348	4
3	398	4	12	591	5
4	237	3	13	246	3
5	371	4	14	418	4
6	427	4	15	174	3
7	415	4	16	360	4
8	528	5	17	406	4
9	163	3	18	425	4
Out	3,408	36	In	3,531	36

Total 6,939 Yards; Par 72

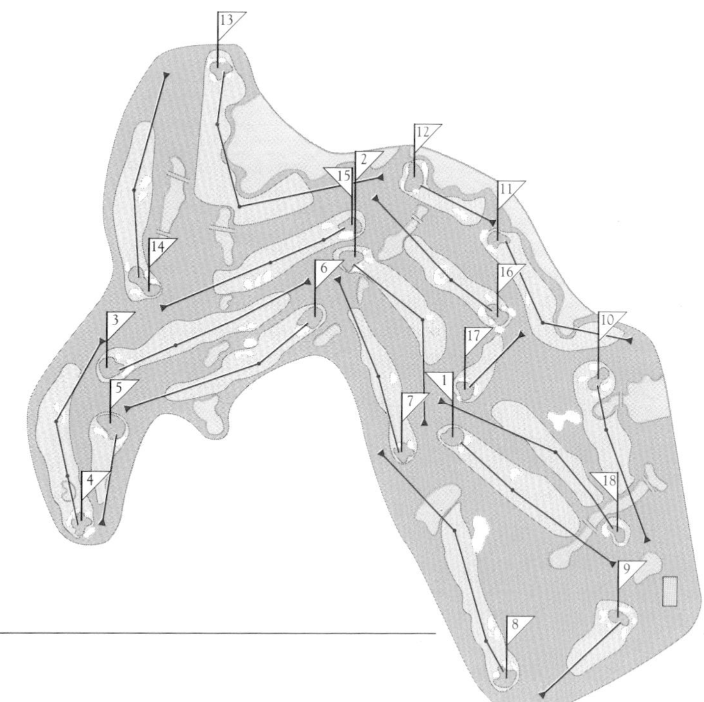

The Dunes

MYRTLE BEACH, SOUTH CAROLINA, U.S.A.

Designed in 1947 and one of Robert Trent Jones's earliest courses, The Dunes is now the center of one of the world's busiest golf resorts. Bearing all the Jones hallmarks (large teeing areas, fairway bunkers, and massive greens), the course also has water, trees, and swampland. The 576-yard 13th is the most famous hole, tracing a semicircle around a lake to a well-bunkered green. It may tempt unwary golfers to try too short a line over the water.

The Dunes

Hole	Yards	Par	Hole	Yards	Par
1	424	4	10	381	4
2	422	4	11	358	4
3	431	4	12	191	3
4	508	5	13	576	5
5	203	3	14	455	4
6	436	4	15	531	5
7	397	4	16	360	4
8	535	5	17	178	3
9	188	3	18	441	4
Out	3,544	36	In	3,471	36

Total 7,015 Yards; Par 72

Emirates

DUBAI, UNITED ARAB EMIRATES

In less than two years a barren stretch of desert scrubland was miraculously transformed into a lush, green, manicured golf course by designer Karl Litten. Daytime temperatures in Dubai range between 30–45°C (86–112°F), requiring that almost a million gallons (4.5 million liters) of water be pumped onto the course through 500 sprinkler heads every 24 hours. So successful is the course that the Karl Litten Desert Classic is now recognized as a regular part of the European Tour.

Emirates

Hole	Yards	Par	Hole	Yards	Par
1	433	4	10	549	5
2	351	4	11	169	3
3	530	5	12	467	4
4	184	3	13	550	5
5	435	4	14	434	4
6	450	4	15	177	3
7	184	3	16	392	4
8	434	4	17	351	4
9	463	4	18	547	5
Out	3,464	35	In	3,636	37

Total 7,100 Yards; Par 72

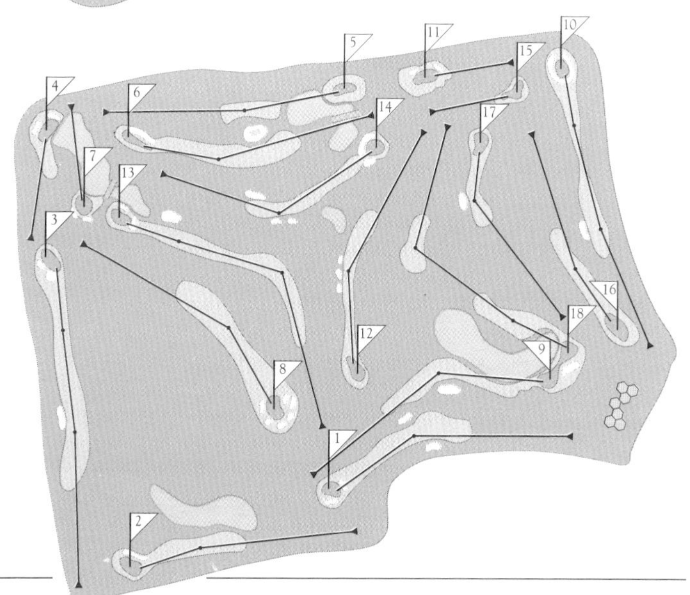

ESTELA

ESTELA, POVOA DE VARZIM, PORTUGAL

Always within sight or sound of the sea, this is a true Scottish-style links course on the north coast of Portugal. Constantly swept by breezes off the Atlantic, the often narrow fairways consist of fine, crisp turf, while the rough is a mixture of sand and ground-hugging scrub. Two lakes on both front and back nines give a special beauty to the course. Most holes run out and back along the shore, so the wind is often across the line of the shot.

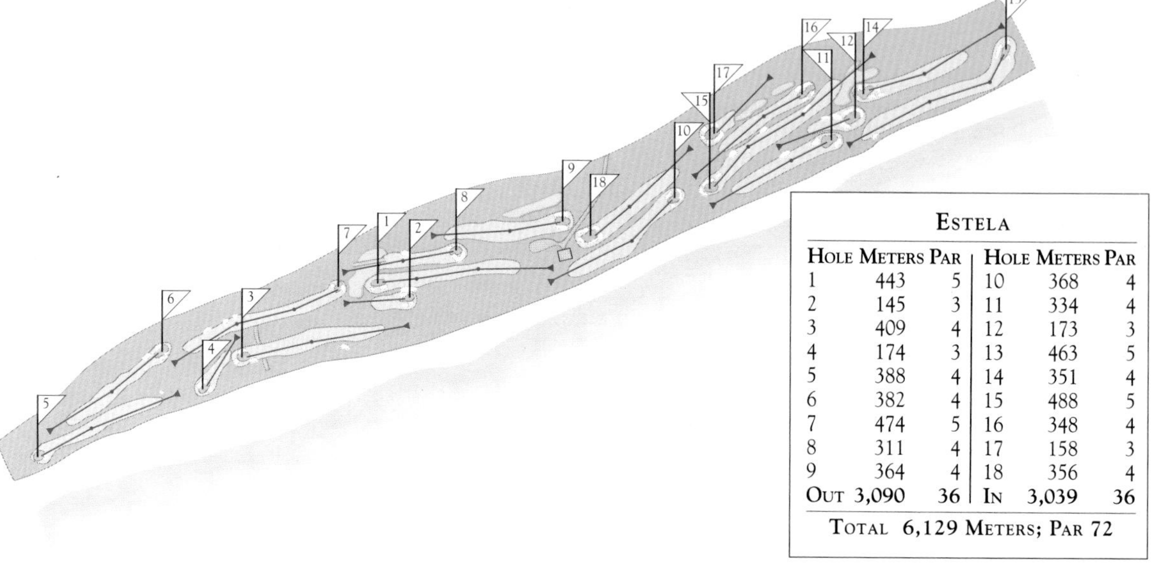

ESTELA					
HOLE	METERS	PAR	HOLE	METERS	PAR
1	443	5	10	368	4
2	145	3	11	334	4
3	409	4	12	173	3
4	174	3	13	463	5
5	388	4	14	351	4
6	382	4	15	488	5
7	474	5	16	348	4
8	311	4	17	158	3
9	364	4	18	356	4
OUT	3,090	36	IN	3,039	36
TOTAL 6,129 METERS; PAR 72					

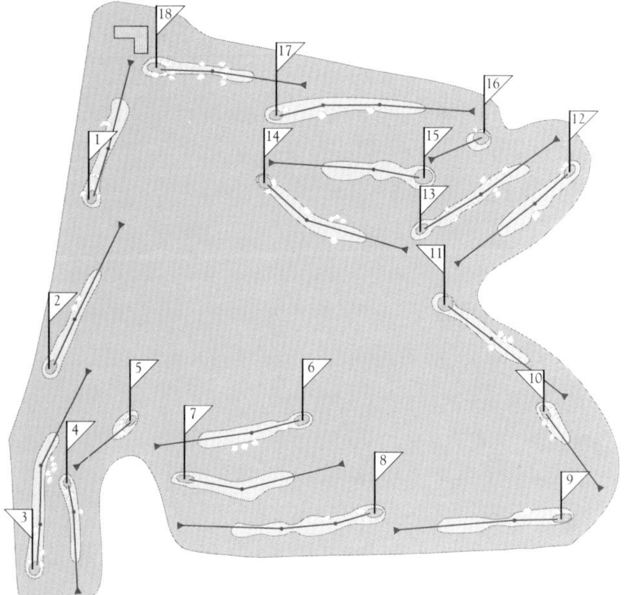

FORMBY

FORMBY, MERSEYSIDE, ENGLAND

The original nine holes of this completely natural golf course, which first came into being in 1884, were subsequently increased to a full 18 in the 1890s. The only changes to this links course since then have been necessitated by rapid erosion in the 1970s. Three new holes had to be brought into play to replace the original 8th, 9th, and 10th, but the course has nonetheless stayed true to its nature, characterized by heather and stands of pine.

FORMBY					
HOLE	YARDS	PAR	HOLE	YARDS	PAR
1	415	4	10	182	3
2	381	4	11	384	4
3	518	5	12	405	4
4	312	4	13	380	4
5	162	3	14	420	4
6	402	4	15	403	4
7	377	4	16	127	3
8	493	5	17	494	5
9	450	4	18	390	4
OUT	3,510	37	IN	3,185	35
TOTAL 6,695 YARDS; PAR 72					

GLENEAGLES

AUCHTERARDER, PERTHSHIRE, SCOTLAND

James Braid laid out the many excellent holes of the King's and Queen's courses in their spectacular setting in the Perthshire hills as the first phase of the Gleneagles development. Both of the courses were actually in play 10 years before the opening of the hotel, which was delayed until 1924 by the First World War. Braid was proudest of the challenge presented by the 13th hole, Braid's Brawest (Best), where the drive has to carry a mound defended by deep bunkers.

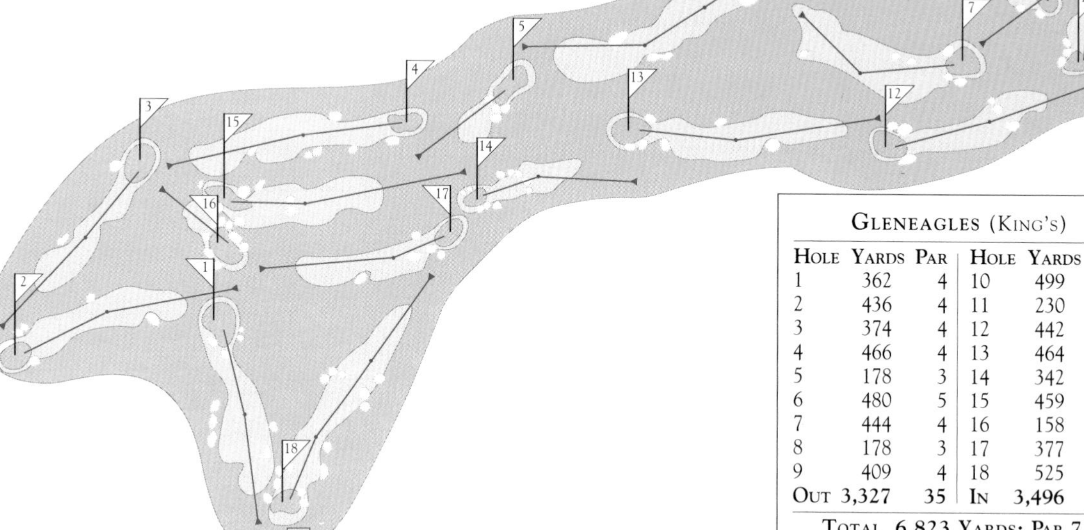

GLENEAGLES (KING'S)					
HOLE	YARDS	PAR	HOLE	YARDS	PAR
1	362	4	10	499	5
2	436	4	11	230	3
3	374	4	12	442	4
4	466	4	13	464	4
5	178	3	14	342	4
6	480	5	15	459	4
7	444	4	16	158	3
8	178	3	17	377	4
9	409	4	18	525	5
OUT	3,327	35	IN	3,496	36
TOTAL 6,823 YARDS; PAR 71					

Grand Cypress

Orlando, Florida, U.S.A.

The influence of the Old course at St. Andrews is obvious in the design of the New course at the Grand Cypress Resort. Course designer Jack Nicklaus included double greens, pot bunkers, wild rough, and even a version of the famous Swilcan Bridge over a stream at the 1st hole. The large greens allow a pitch-and-run shot to come into play. The 140 bunkers include one at the 15th reminiscent of Hell Bunker at St. Andrews.

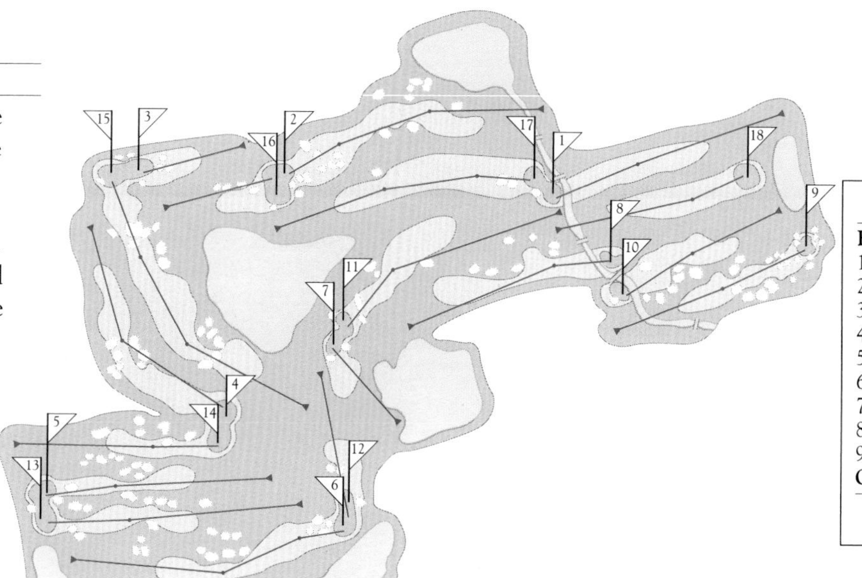

Grand Cypress (New)

Hole	Yards	Par	Hole	Yards	Par
1	362	4	10	330	4
2	514	5	11	430	4
3	179	3	12	207	3
4	440	4	13	431	4
5	393	4	14	371	4
6	496	5	15	570	5
7	182	3	16	190	3
8	440	4	17	485	5
9	382	4	18	371	4
Out	3,388	36	In	3,385	36

Total 6,773 Yards; Par 72

Gullane

Gullane, East Lothian, Scotland

There are three courses located in this small East Lothian village, but the Number 1 probably has an edge on the other two. From its lofty position, the course holds a commanding position over its more distinguished neighbor, Muirfield, and enjoys glorious views across the Firth of Forth. The greens are renowned for their quality, and share the same fine texture as the adjacent Open Championship course. The inward nine is the longer and more testing.

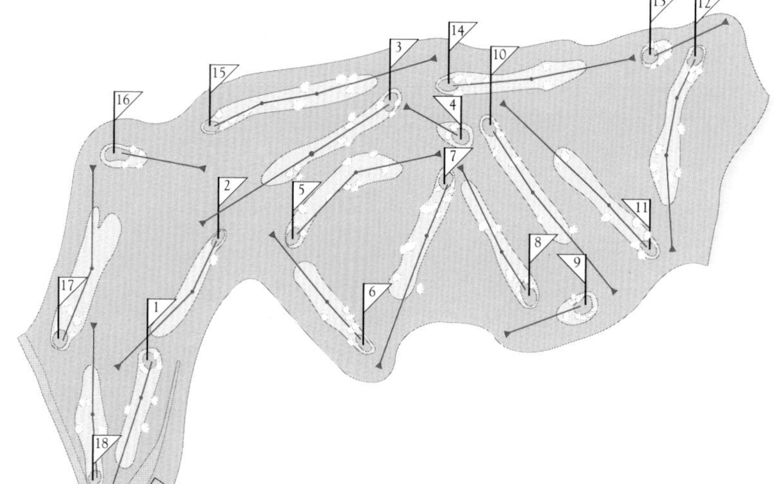

Gullane (Number 1)

Hole	Yards	Par	Hole	Yards	Par
1	302	4	10	466	4
2	379	4	11	471	4
3	496	5	12	480	5
4	144	3	13	170	3
5	450	4	14	435	4
6	324	4	15	537	5
7	398	4	16	186	3
8	332	4	17	390	4
9	151	3	18	355	4
Out	2,976	35	In	3,490	36

Total 6,466 Yards; Par 71

Hamburg-Falkenstein

Hamburg, Germany

The Falkenstein course was laid out by English architects Harry S. Colt, Charles Alison, and John Morrison between 1928 and 1930, and later modernized by Dr. Bernhard von Limburger. The course, built amid sandy terrain of heather and pine, is characterized by its narrow, tree-lined fairways and fast greens. Many of the holes are doglegs, and bunkers are used only where they will achieve a maximum effect. Bernhard Langer won his first German Open here in 1981,scoring a course-record round of 64.

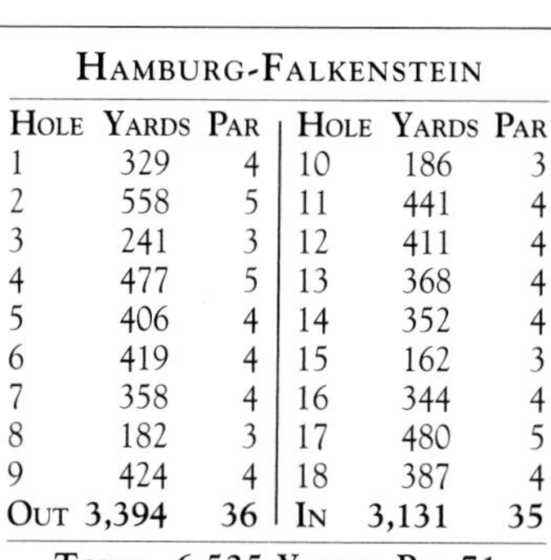

Hamburg-Falkenstein

Hole	Yards	Par	Hole	Yards	Par
1	329	4	10	186	3
2	558	5	11	441	4
3	241	3	12	411	4
4	477	5	13	368	4
5	406	4	14	352	4
6	419	4	15	162	3
7	358	4	16	344	4
8	182	3	17	480	5
9	424	4	18	387	4
Out	3,394	36	In	3,131	35

Total 6,525 Yards; Par 71

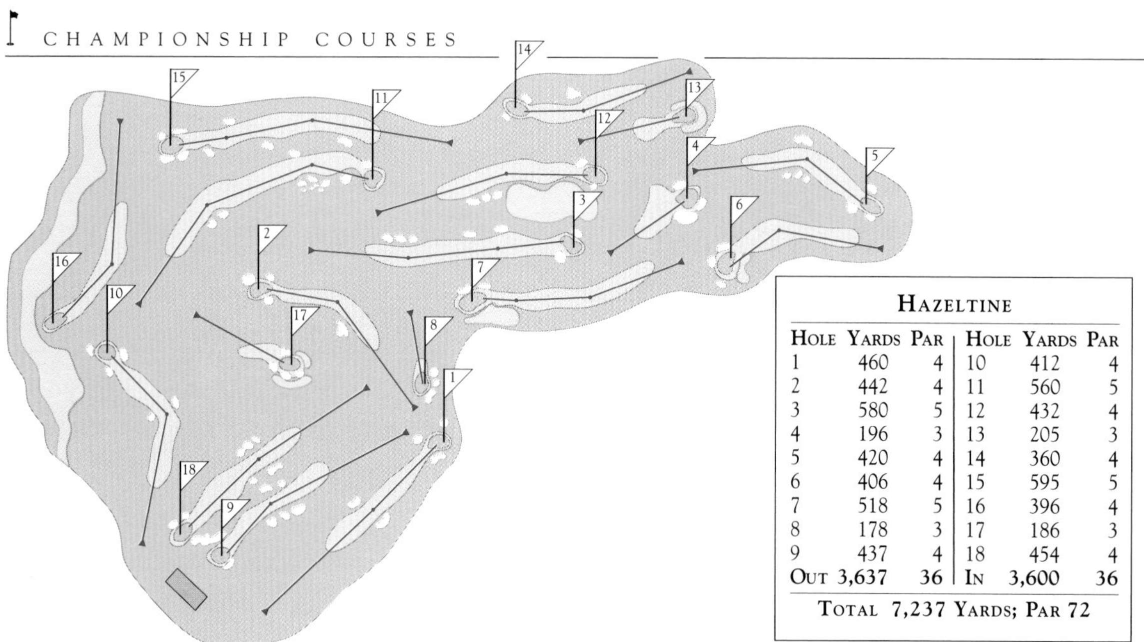

HAZELTINE

CHASKA, MINNESOTA, U.S.A.

The Hazeltine National Golf Club was the scene of Tony Jacklin's famous victory in the 1970 U.S. Open, when he became the first home-based Briton to win the U.S. title for 50 years. The club had been founded by former USGA president Totten Heffelfinger only a decade earlier, but the Robert Trent Jones layout has undergone extensive modifications since Jacklin's victory. Hazeltine hosted the U.S. Open Championship for the second time in 1991.

HAZELTINE

HOLE	YARDS	PAR	HOLE	YARDS	PAR
1	460	4	10	412	4
2	442	4	11	560	5
3	580	5	12	432	4
4	196	3	13	205	3
5	420	4	14	360	4
6	406	4	15	595	5
7	518	5	16	396	4
8	178	3	17	186	3
9	437	4	18	454	4
OUT	3,637	36	IN	3,600	36

TOTAL 7,237 YARDS; PAR 72

THE JOCKEY CLUB

SAN ISIDRO, BUENOS AIRES, ARGENTINA

Dr. Alister Mackenzie, famous for several of the world's greatest courses, took an extremely flat piece of ground at The Jockey Club and built two outstanding courses on it. Of the two, the Red course is the more famous; it features clever mounding and contouring and subtle Mackenzie bunkering. The course is short but testing, and hosted the 1970 World Cup. However, golf here is regarded merely as a subsidiary adjunct to horse-racing and polo.

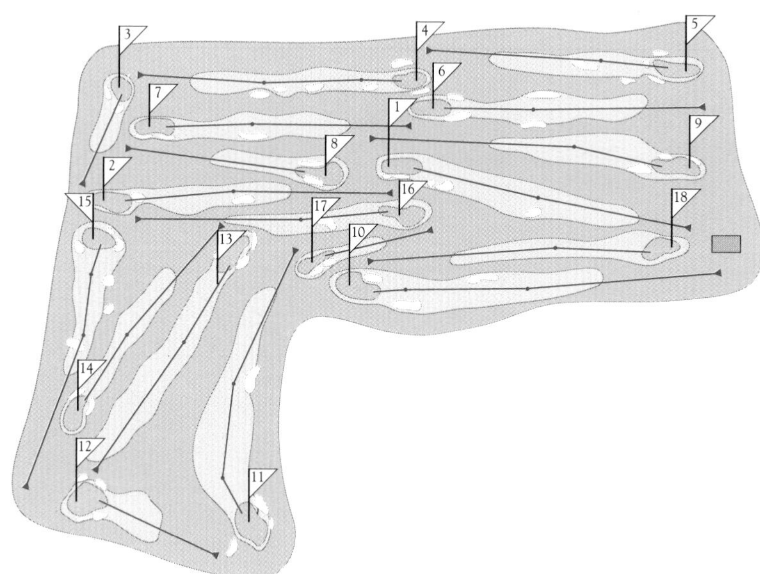

THE JOCKEY CLUB (RED)

HOLE	YARDS	PAR	HOLE	YARDS	PAR
1	425	4	10	465	5
2	354	4	11	523	5
3	145	3	12	168	3
4	483	5	13	436	4
5	340	4	14	392	4
6	367	4	15	505	5
7	418	4	16	429	4
8	208	3	17	180	3
9	442	4	18	348	4
OUT	3,182	35	IN	3,446	37

TOTAL 6,628 YARDS; PAR 72

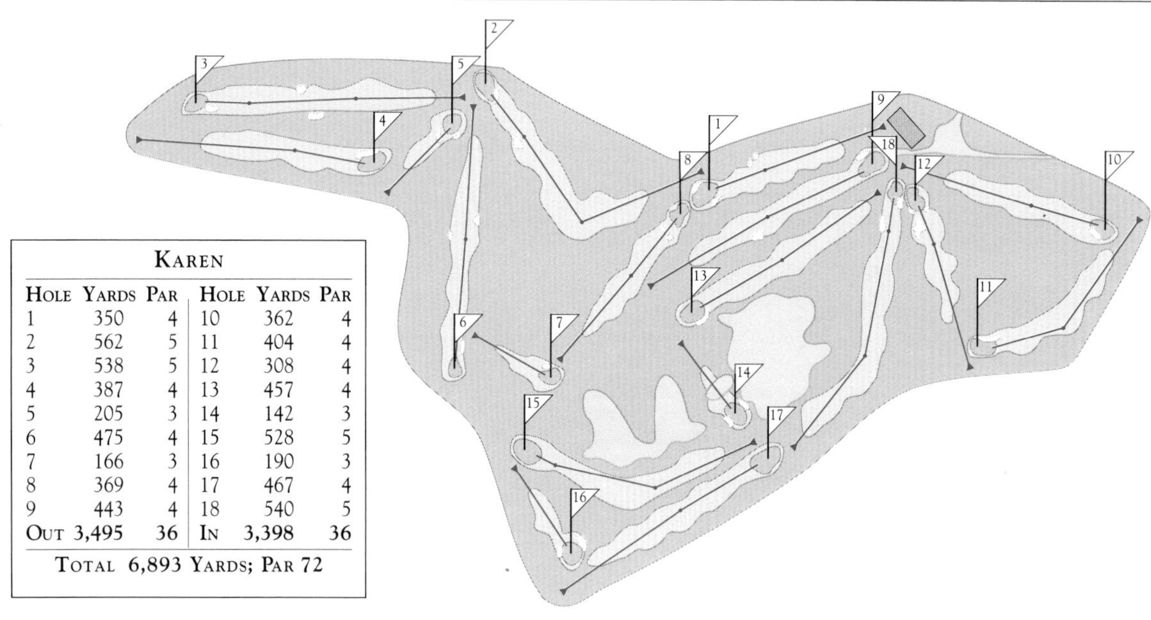

KAREN

HOLE	YARDS	PAR	HOLE	YARDS	PAR
1	350	4	10	362	4
2	562	5	11	404	4
3	538	5	12	308	4
4	387	4	13	457	4
5	205	3	14	142	3
6	475	4	15	528	5
7	166	3	16	190	3
8	369	4	17	467	4
9	443	4	18	540	5
OUT	3,495	36	IN	3,398	36

TOTAL 6,893 YARDS; PAR 72

KAREN

NAIROBI, KENYA

Baroness Karen von Blixen, author of *Out of Africa*, once owned the property on which is now laid out the beautiful Karen course. Twelve miles (19km) to the west of Nairobi, the setting is full of birdsong, botanical beauty, and challenge for the golfer. Back-to-back par 5s at the 2nd and 3rd, one a 90-degree dogleg, the other straight, give a rather unbalanced feel to the first nine. Length is not the problem at the 142-yard par-3 14th, but there is an abundance of water to add difficulty.

KASUGAI

NAGOYA, AICHIKEN, JAPAN

The "cut and fill" construction method, in which heavy equipment removes the tops of hills and deposits the earth in the valley below to build up the fairways, was used at Kasugai. Seichi Inoue designed the layouts. There are two courses, the East and West, with the East having been the site for the Japan Open in 1975. Severe slopes present an arduous test and a conifer-planting operation has given definition to the fairways on both courses.

KASUGAI (EAST)

HOLE	YARDS	PAR	HOLE	YARDS	PAR
1	415	4	10	362	4
2	395	4	11	368	4
3	498	5	12	174	3
4	199	3	13	503	5
5	416	4	14	435	4
6	460	4	15	189	3
7	182	3	16	429	4
8	511	5	17	529	5
9	407	4	18	410	4
OUT	3,483	36	IN	3,399	36

TOTAL 6,882 YARDS; PAR 72

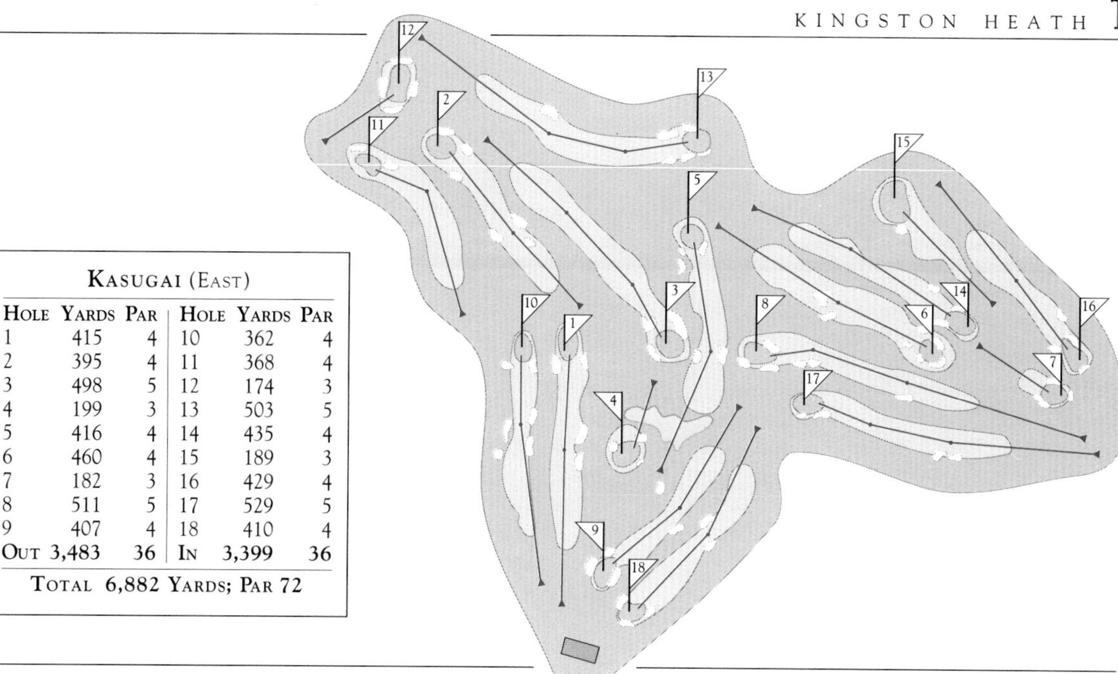

KENNEMER

KENNEMER, ZANDVOORT, NETHERLANDS

Perhaps the supreme links course on the European continent, Kennemer was designed by H.S. Colt in the late 1920s in an area of massive dunes and stands of pine trees. Kennemer has returning nines, reminiscent of Muirfield, rather than the more common out-and-back format. The imposing thatched clubhouse enjoys a perfect position on one of the highest sandhills. The design takes full advantage of elevated tees and greens, and of valley fairways.

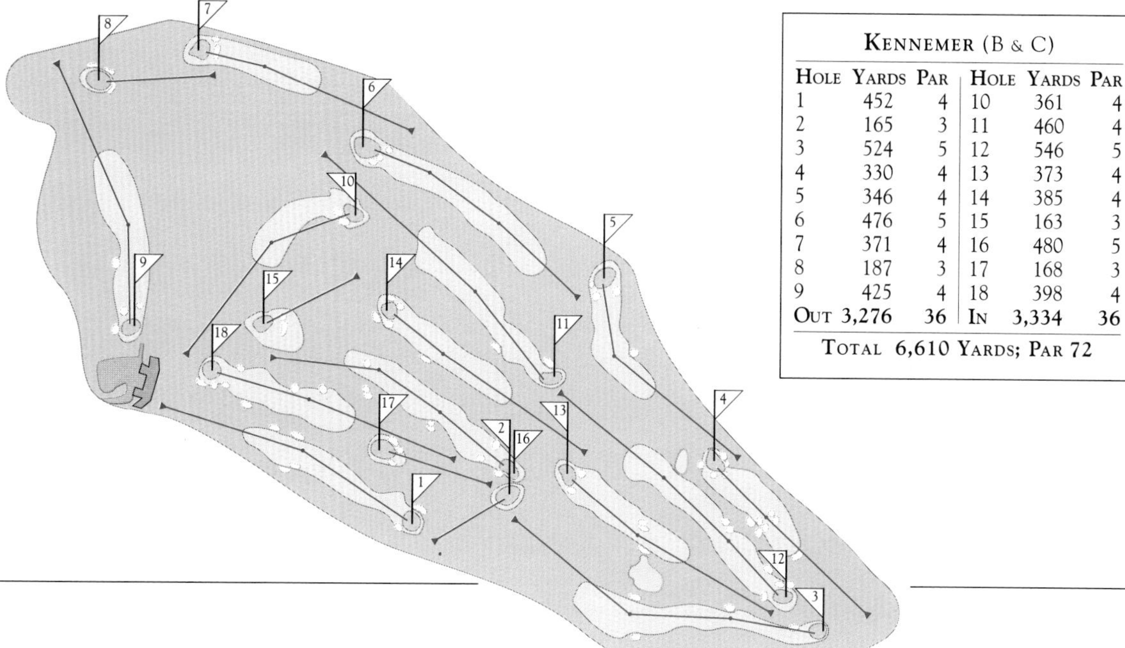

KENNEMER (B & C)

HOLE	YARDS	PAR	HOLE	YARDS	PAR
1	452	4	10	361	4
2	165	3	11	460	4
3	524	5	12	546	5
4	330	4	13	373	4
5	346	4	14	385	4
6	476	5	15	163	3
7	371	4	16	480	5
8	187	3	17	168	3
9	425	4	18	398	4
OUT	3,276	36	IN	3,334	36

TOTAL 6,610 YARDS; PAR 72

KINGSTON HEATH

CHELTENHAM, VICTORIA, AUSTRALIA

The original course was swallowed up in the expansion of Melbourne, but the new design, constructed in 1925, is on a fine area of sandy sub-soil close to Royal Melbourne Golf Club. Dr. Alister Mackenzie, of Augusta fame, introduced a new bunkering plan in 1928, when the old timber clubhouse was demolished to make way for a new brick construction. In 1944 a huge bush fire engulfed most of the course, almost reaching the clubhouse and necessitating an impressive replanting operation.

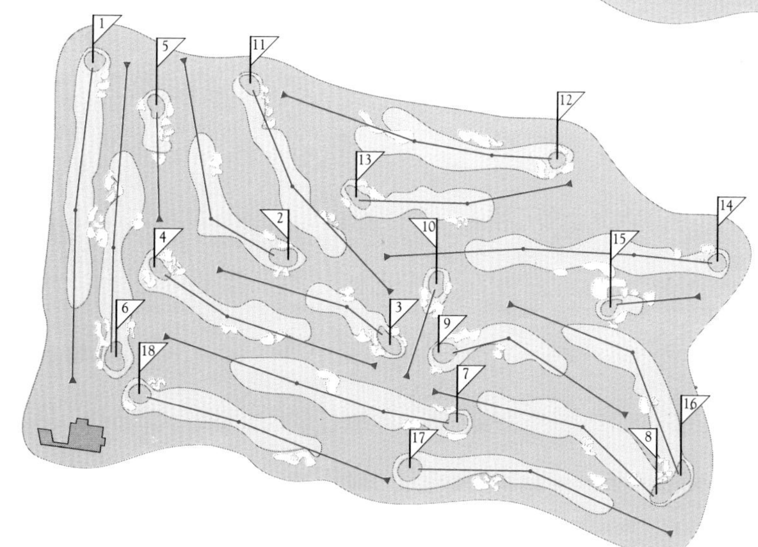

KINGSTON HEATH

HOLE	METERS	PAR	HOLE	METERS	PAR
1	419	4	10	131	3
2	334	4	11	368	4
3	271	4	12	442	5
4	356	4	13	324	4
5	173	3	14	502	5
6	397	4	15	142	3
7	459	5	16	386	4
8	394	4	17	418	4
9	324	4	18	391	4
OUT	3,127	36	IN	3,104	36

TOTAL 6,231 METERS, PAR 72

Lake Karrinyup

Karrinyup, Perth, West Australia

The main feature is the massive lake, which only comes into play on the 190m 8th, where the tee shot must be solidly struck. The fairways are wide, bunkers a prominent design feature, the greens large and subtly shaped. Wind is a constant factor on this fine course and when it is against at the long 400m 16th, two prodigious blows are required to reach the green in regulation.

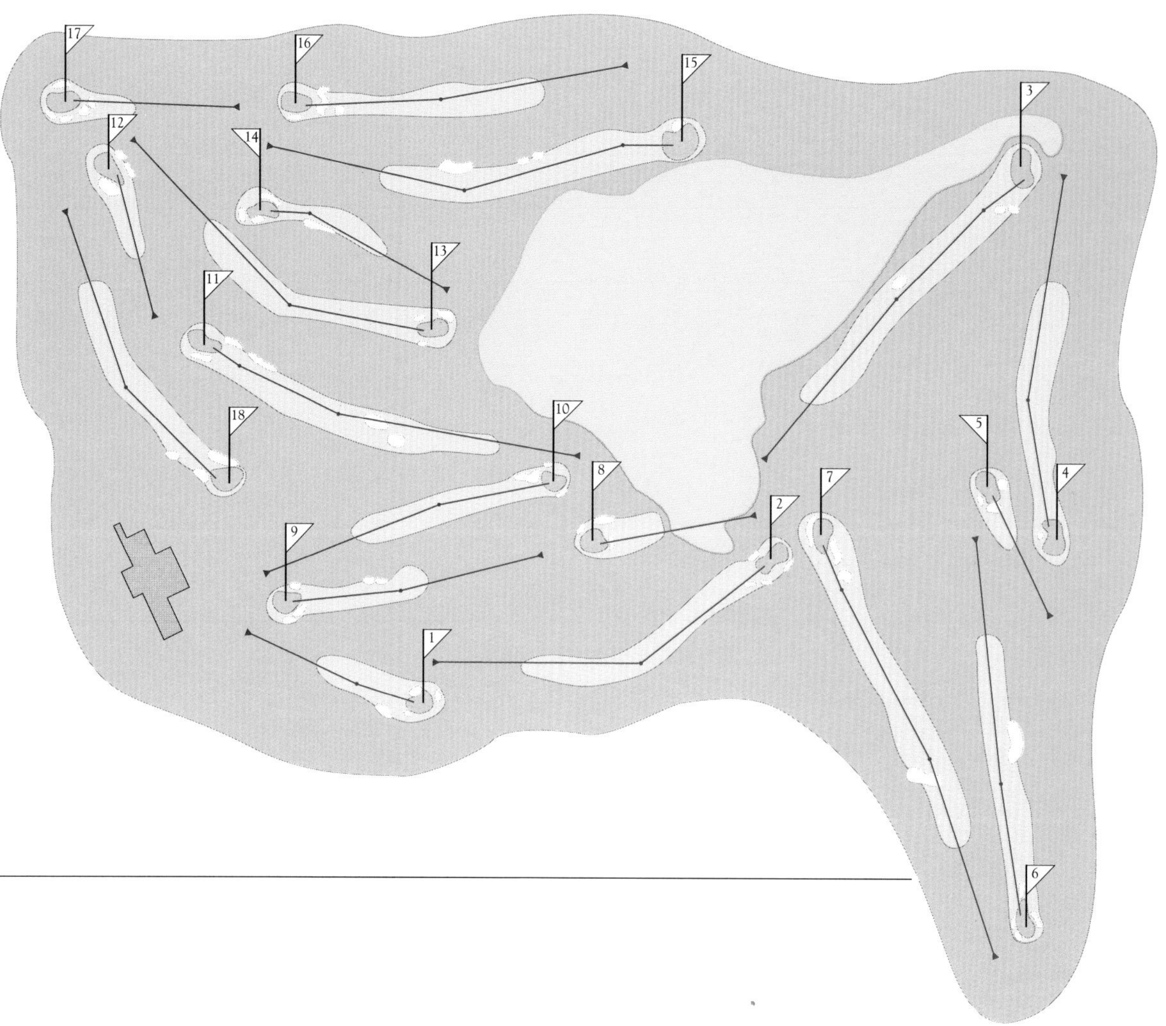

Lake Karrinyup					
Hole	Meters	Par	Hole	Meters	Par
1	220	4	10	340	4
2	430	4	11	450	5
3	455	5	12	150	3
4	390	4	13	385	4
5	150	3	14	260	4
6	390	4	15	485	5
7	500	5	16	400	4
8	190	3	17	180	3
9	330	4	18	370	4
Out	3,055	36	In	3,020	36
Total 6,075 Meters; Par 72					

La Manga

Cartagena, Murcia, Spain

Both the North and South courses at La Manga are typified by wide fairways, large, flat, white sand bunkers, and generously sized greens. There are scores of palm trees, lakes in profusion, and numerous "barrancas" – deep ravines filled with rough and rocks that can ruin a score. The South course is the longer of the two and water comes into play on more than half of the holes. The 8th and 9th holes are a stiff examination of golfing ability, especially when the wind blows.

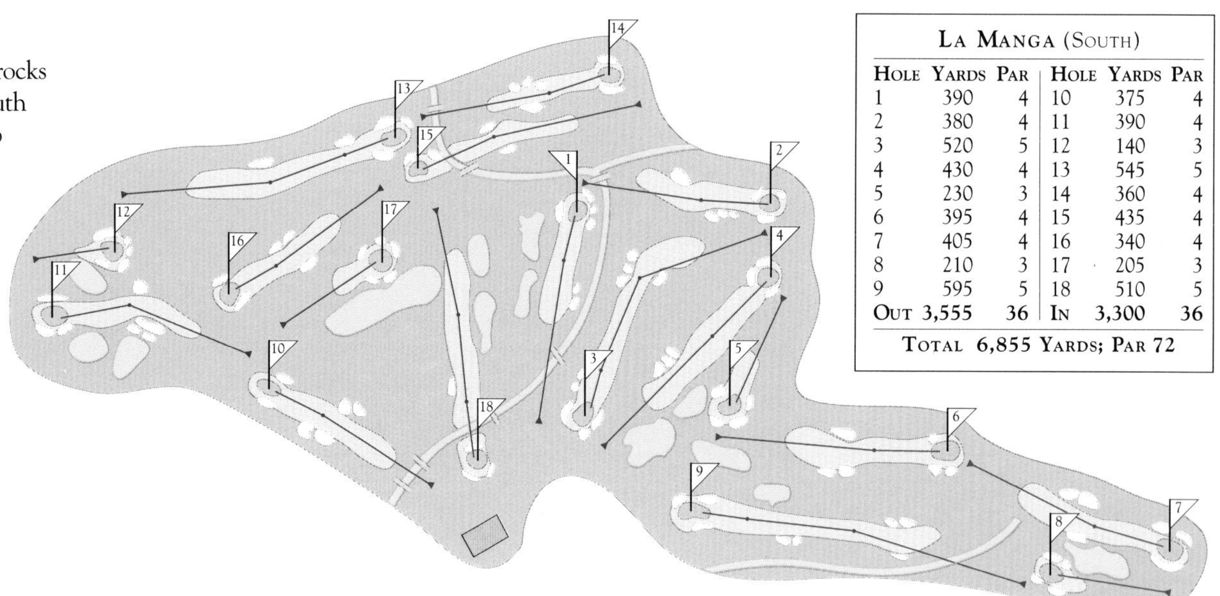

La Manga (South)					
Hole	Yards	Par	Hole	Yards	Par
1	390	4	10	375	4
2	380	4	11	390	4
3	520	5	12	140	3
4	430	4	13	545	5
5	230	3	14	360	4
6	395	4	15	435	4
7	405	4	16	340	4
8	210	3	17	205	3
9	595	5	18	510	5
Out	3,555	36	In	3,300	36
Total 6,855 Yards; Par 72					

NAIRN

NAIRN, NAIRNSHIRE, SCOTLAND

The links at Nairn on the Moray Firth is one of the most underrated courses in world golf. Archie Simpson designed the first layout of this course in 1887 but changes were made by James Braid and Old Tom Morris. Three holes (the 13th, 14th, and 15th) loop from the shore; the remainder follow the out-and-back pattern of early courses.

NAIRN					
HOLE	YARDS	PAR	HOLE	YARDS	PAR
1	400	4	10	500	5
2	499	5	11	161	3
3	400	4	12	445	4
4	145	3	13	435	4
5	378	4	14	206	3
6	183	3	15	309	4
7	507	5	16	422	4
8	330	4	17	361	4
9	359	4	18	516	5
OUT	3,201	36	IN	3,355	36
TOTAL 6,556 YARDS; PAR 72					

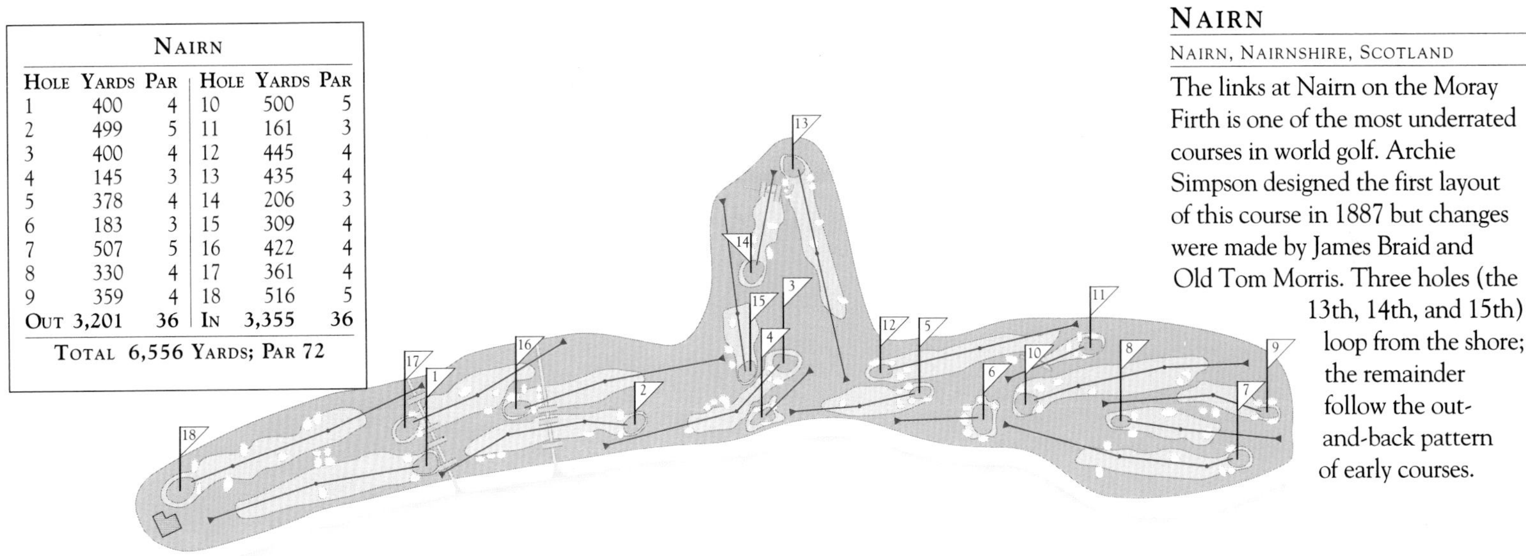

NATIONAL GOLF LINKS OF AMERICA

SOUTHAMPTON, NEW YORK, U.S.A.

Charles Blair Macdonald spent five years studying British links courses before building this one on the shores of Peconic Bay on eastern Long Island. A telescope at the clubhouse recalls the days when wealthy members arrived by private yacht. Opened in 1909, the balanced layout concentrates on strategy. Despite a well-deserved reputation, the National has hosted only one major event, the Walker Cup in 1922.

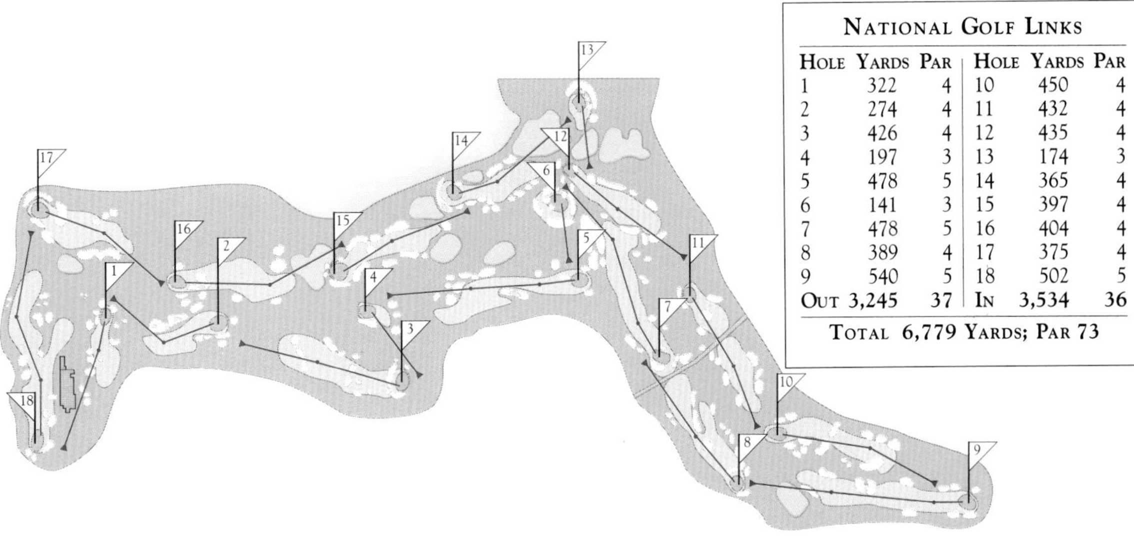

NATIONAL GOLF LINKS					
HOLE	YARDS	PAR	HOLE	YARDS	PAR
1	322	4	10	450	4
2	274	4	11	432	4
3	426	4	12	435	4
4	197	3	13	174	3
5	478	5	14	365	4
6	141	3	15	397	4
7	478	5	16	404	4
8	389	4	17	375	4
9	540	5	18	502	5
OUT	3,245	37	IN	3,534	36
TOTAL 6,779 YARDS; PAR 73					

NEW ST. ANDREWS

TOCHIGI, JAPAN

Situated outside Tokyo, this course is a monument to new technology. The 18-hole New course, designed by Jack Nicklaus and Desmond Muirhead, is a great challenge. Golf bags are carried on an electronic trolley system that is controlled by the caddies. Nine holes on the New course are floodlit for evening play. The nine-hole Old course, with its replica of the Swilcan Bridge, is modeled on the club's Scottish namesake. A monorail transports players to the course from the clubhouse.

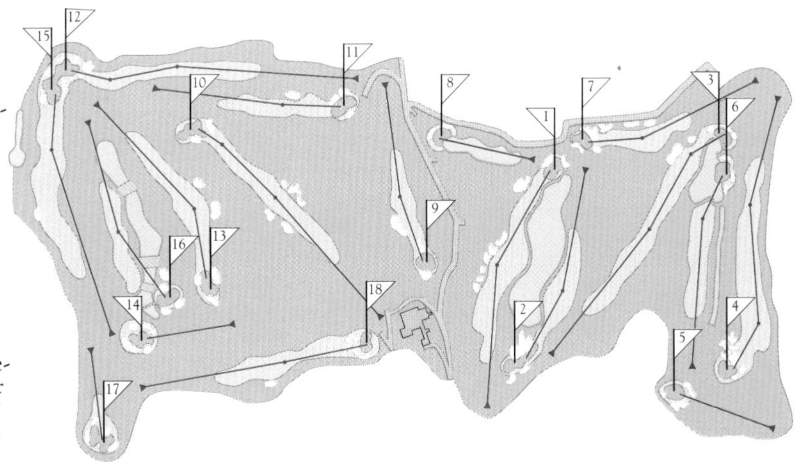

NEW ST. ANDREWS (NEW)					
HOLE	METERS	PAR	HOLE	METERS	PAR
1	410	4	10	447	5
2	349	4	11	334	4
3	494	5	12	498	5
4	487	5	13	379	4
5	194	3	14	144	3
6	339	4	15	429	4
7	318	4	16	341	4
8	169	3	17	181	3
9	320	4	18	394	4
OUT	3,080	36	IN	3,147	36
TOTAL 6,227 METERS; PAR 72					

New South Wales

Matraville, N.S.W., Australia

Built by Dr. Alister Mackenzie on a headland separating the Pacific Ocean from Botany Bay, this superb course – tight fairways, difficult rough, and strategic bunkering – is open to every bit of wind from any direction. The 181m 6th hole played over an inlet is a design feature that has since been copied all over the world. Taken over by the army in 1942, this great links required a massive restoration project to restore it to its former glory.

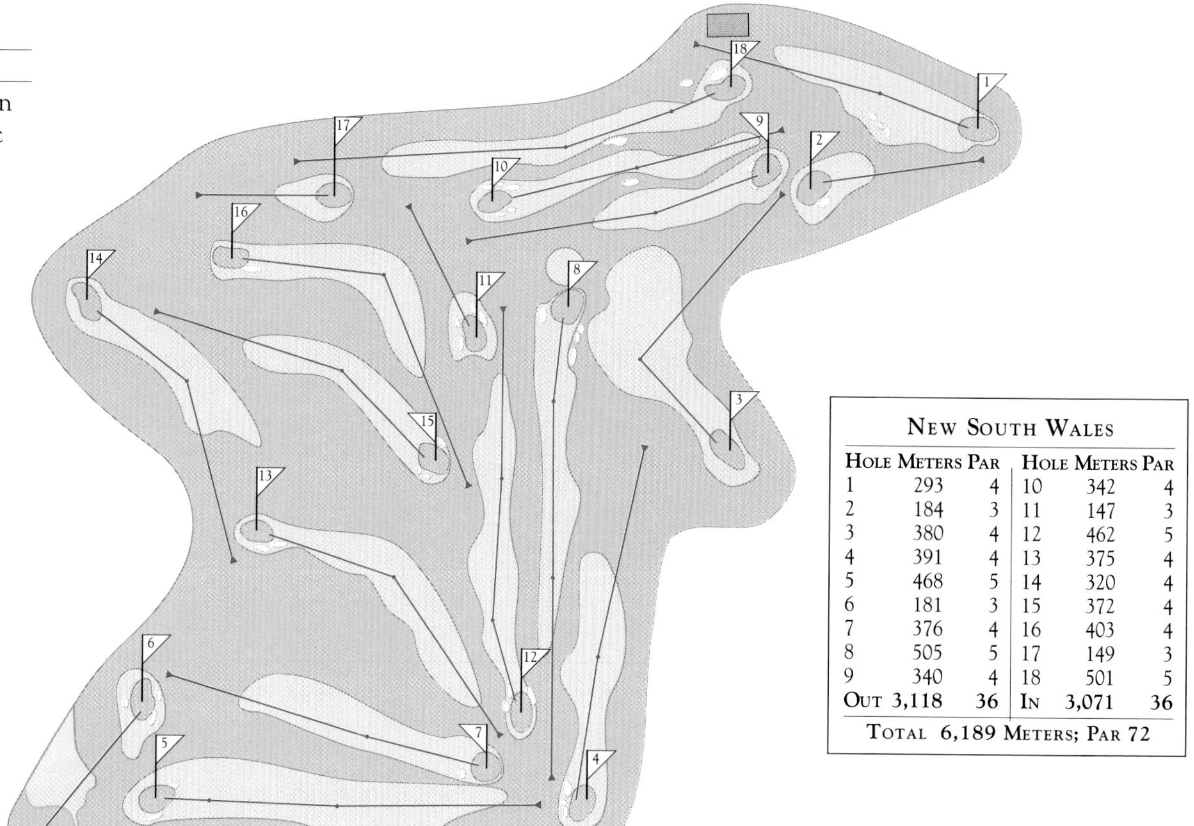

New South Wales					
Hole	Meters	Par	Hole	Meters	Par
1	293	4	10	342	4
2	184	3	11	147	3
3	380	4	12	462	5
4	391	4	13	375	4
5	468	5	14	320	4
6	181	3	15	372	4
7	376	4	16	403	4
8	505	5	17	149	3
9	340	4	18	501	5
Out	3,118	36	In	3,071	36
Total 6,189 Meters; Par 72					

Olgiata

Largo Olgiata, Rome, Italy

There was sufficient land available when Ken Cotton, a graduate of Cambridge University, England, designed this course in 1961 to allow him to create each hole in an individual setting. He took full advantage of the sweeping undulations of the site and its many mature trees to create a well-balanced layout that demands every shot in the book. When the course staged the World Cup seven years after its inauguration, Al Balding holed a bunker shot for an eagle-3 at the 17th to clinch a victory for the Canadian team.

Olgiata					
Hole	Yards	Par	Hole	Yards	Par
1	377	4	10	396	4
2	212	3	11	431	4
3	465	4	12	427	4
4	399	4	13	430	4
5	487	5	14	170	3
6	427	4	15	503	5
7	195	3	16	202	3
8	377	4	17	520	5
9	552	5	18	427	4
Out	3,491	36	In	3,506	36
Total 6,997 Yards; Par 72					

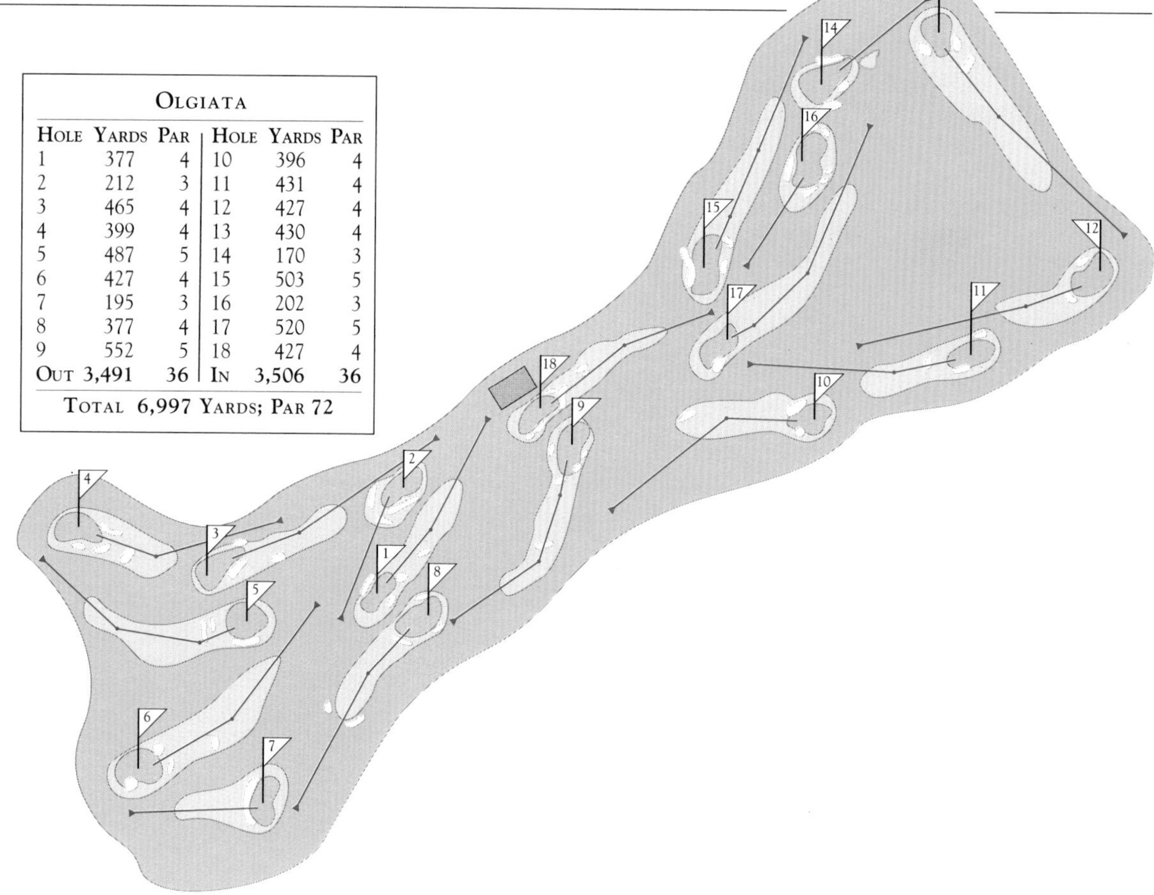

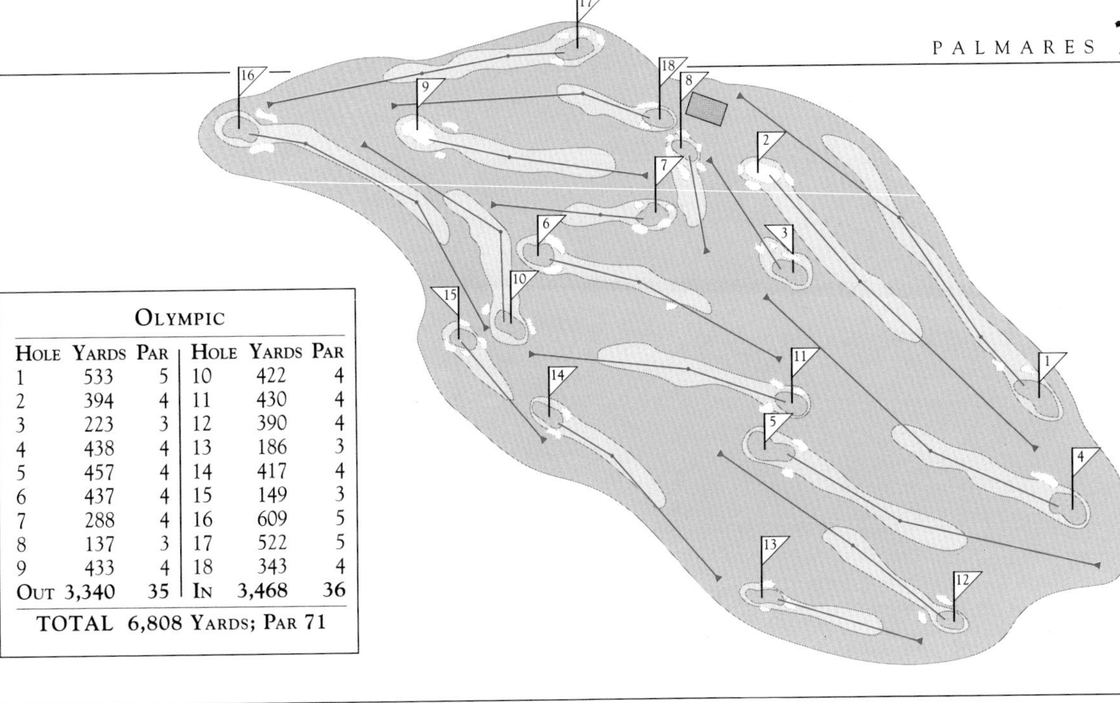

OLYMPIC

San Francisco, California, U.S.A.

This lakeside course was already in existence on the western edge of San Francisco, close to the Pacific, when the Olympic Club decided to get into golf and acquire it for their own members to use. They immediately planted the area with cypress, eucalyptus, and pine. Since that date in 1922, the trees have come to dominate the course, providing extremely tight driving lines and small target areas. The course has been used three times for the U.S. Open.

Olympic					
Hole	Yards	Par	Hole	Yards	Par
1	533	5	10	422	4
2	394	4	11	430	4
3	223	3	12	390	4
4	438	4	13	186	3
5	457	4	14	417	4
6	437	4	15	149	3
7	288	4	16	609	5
8	137	3	17	522	5
9	433	4	18	343	4
Out	3,340	35	In	3,468	36
TOTAL 6,808 Yards; Par 71					

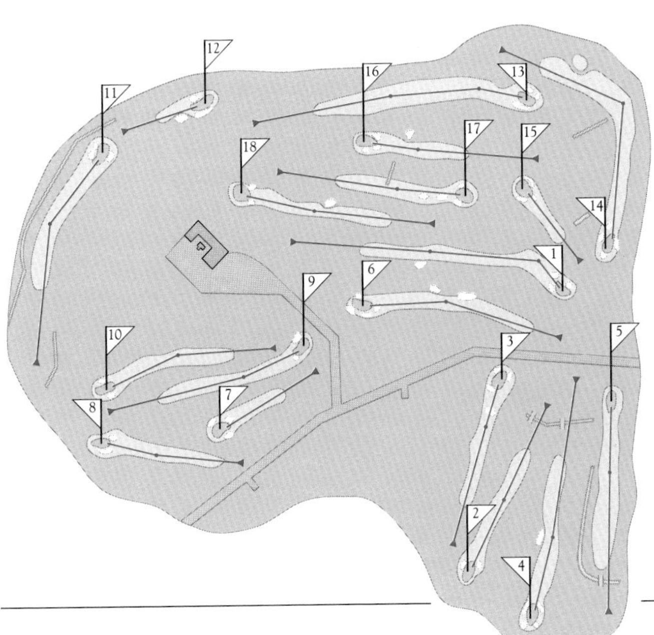

OTAGO

Maori Hill, Dunedin, New Zealand

Many times the setting for the New Zealand Amateur and Professional Open Championships, the Balmacewen course at Otago is made difficult by its hilly terrain, surrounded by native bush. The 361m par-4 11th is a classic driving hole, with a steep gradient on the right, mirrored by a creek on the opposite side. When he was once playing Bob Charles in an exhibition match here, Arnold Palmer solved the problem this hole poses by driving the green.

Otago (Balmacewen)					
Hole	Meters	Par	Hole	Meters	Par
1	533	5	10	360	4
2	297	4	11	361	4
3	284	4	12	164	3
4	367	4	13	537	5
5	374	4	14	408	4
6	346	4	15	190	3
7	165	3	16	266	4
8	280	4	17	272	4
9	374	4	18	370	4
Out	3,020	36	In	2,928	35
Total 5,948 Meters; Par 71					

PALMARES

Lagos, Algarve, Portugal

One of an expanding number of courses located on Portugal's Algarve coast, Palmares manages to combine the best of all possible worlds. The clubhouse is set on a hillside and commands superb views over the course and the coast. The 1st hole drops downhill out of the trees to a stretch of five pure links holes situated between the railroad and the shore. The course then climbs back up the slope for the remaining holes, which are played over gently undulating parkland.

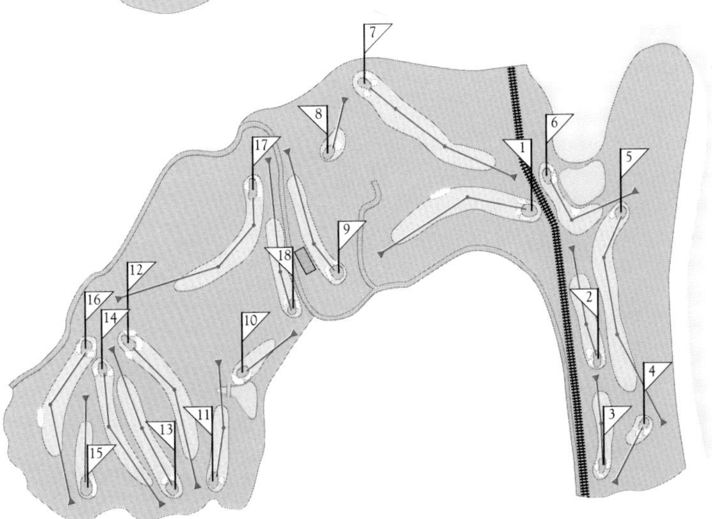

Palmares					
Hole	Meters	Par	Hole	Meters	Par
1	418	4	10	165	3
2	321	4	11	271	4
3	287	4	12	400	4
4	142	3	13	386	4
5	550	5	14	347	4
6	344	4	15	212	3
7	462	5	16	418	4
8	142	3	17	458	5
9	317	4	18	321	4
Out	2,983	36	In	2,978	35
Total 5,961 Meters; Par 71					

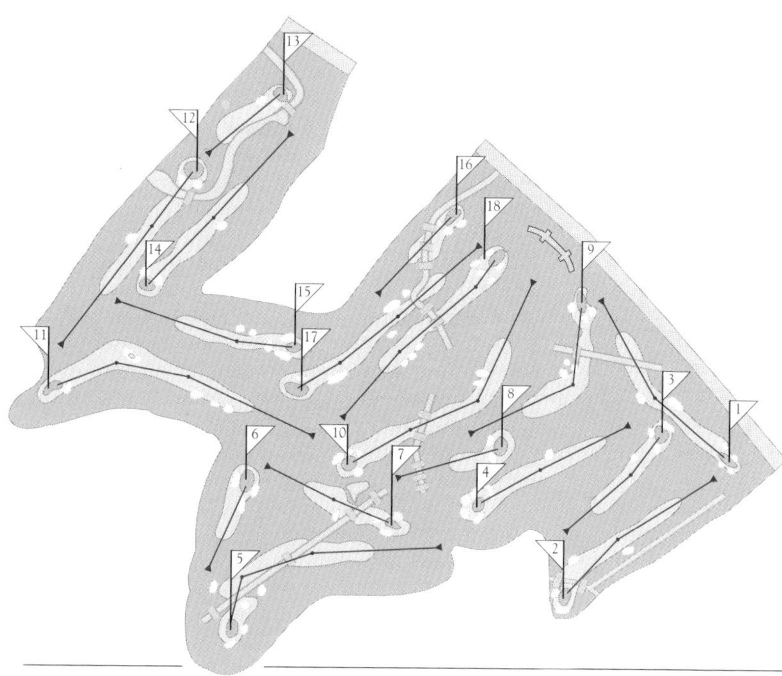

Penina

Portimão, Algarve, Portugal

Built on bare, flat ricefields, this course that Henry Cotton designed, and which he made his home for a great part of his later life, has been transformed, since it was first laid out in 1964, by more than 350,000 trees and shrubs.

Cotton visualized the effect of this planting, and his vision has become a reality. The course is monstrously long from the championship tees, and every shot has to be carefully planned – just as the maestro intended.

Penina

Hole	Meters	Par	Hole	Meters	Par
1	411	4	10	500	5
2	401	4	11	491	5
3	301	4	12	397	4
4	375	4	13	208	3
5	463	5	14	394	4
6	186	3	15	318	4
7	299	4	16	210	3
8	180	3	17	450	5
9	405	4	18	450	5
Out	3,021	35	In	3,418	38

Total 6,439 Meters; Par 73

Prestwick

Prestwick, Ayrshire, Scotland

Prestwick is the original home of the British Open; it was played here for the first 12 years of its existence, beginning in 1860. The Open returned 12 more times, but by 1924 it had outgrown the restricted area in which the course is set. Prestwick remains a monument to the early days of golf, with fast-running, bumpy fairways, deep bunkers, and many blind shots among unpredictable winds. Many of the holes remain unchanged from its early days.

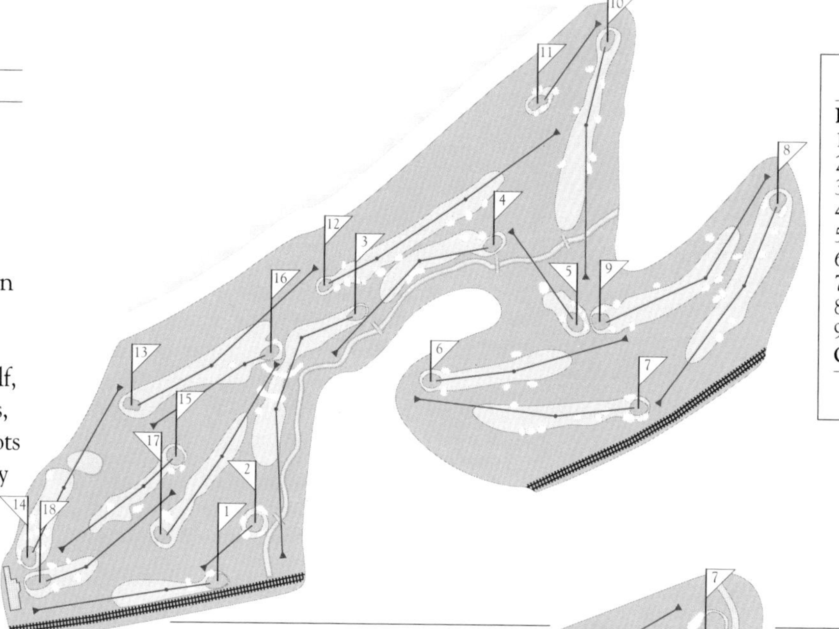

Prestwick

Hole	Yards	Par	Hole	Yards	Par
1	346	4	10	454	4
2	167	3	11	195	3
3	500	5	12	513	5
4	382	4	13	460	4
5	206	3	14	362	4
6	400	4	15	347	4
7	430	4	16	298	4
8	431	4	17	391	4
9	458	4	18	284	4
Out	3,320	35	In	3,304	36

Total 6,624 Yards; Par 71

Rome

Acquasanta, Rome, Italy

This golf course is set among the glorious relics of ancient Rome, with impressive views of aqueducts and of the Appian Way. It is situated in low, rolling hills, with well-positioned trees that provide an extra hazard on the fairways. The ground is maintained in good condition and is consistently well watered. The greens and their approaches are mainly flat, with few features to help the golfer judge distances. Although the course is not long, players find it a sufficiently tough challenge.

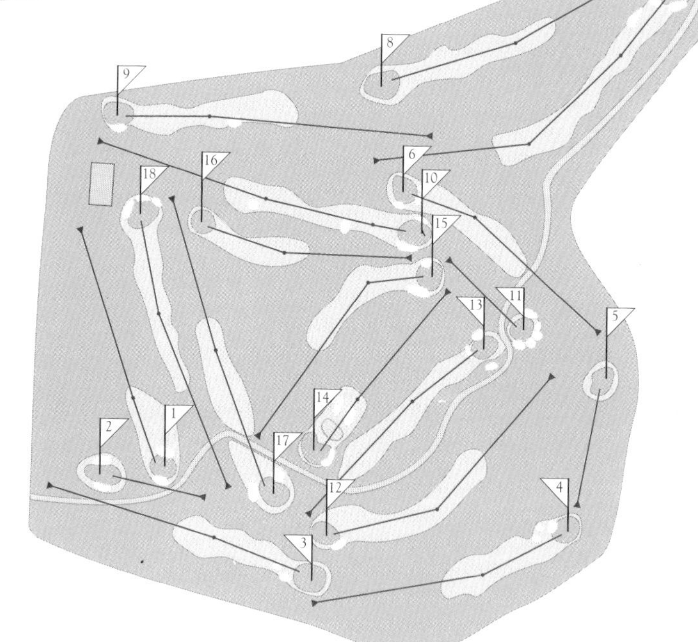

Rome

Hole	Meters	Par	Hole	Meters	Par
1	305	4	10	444	5
2	141	3	11	120	3
3	317	4	12	408	4
4	359	4	13	348	4
5	197	3	14	331	4
6	351	4	15	329	4
7	504	5	16	319	4
8	368	4	17	391	4
9	398	4	18	370	4
Out	2,940	35	In	3,060	36

Total 6,000 Meters; Par 71

Royal Aberdeen

Bridge of Don, Aberdeen, Scotland

While this club is more than 200 years old, the fine course over which members now play was built in 1866, after two earlier moves. The first hole plays down toward the sea, and then the course veers northward along the shore in true links fashion. There is great variation in the direction of play, with holes angled away from, or back toward, the shore. Subtle doglegs are created by setting tees in the dunes at an angle to the shallow valley of the fairways.

Royal Aberdeen					
Hole	Yards	Par	Hole	Yards	Par
1	409	4	10	342	4
2	530	5	11	166	3
3	223	3	12	383	4
4	423	4	13	375	4
5	326	4	14	390	4
6	486	5	15	341	4
7	375	4	16	389	4
8	147	3	17	180	3
9	453	4	18	434	4
Out	3,372	36	In	3,000	34
Total 6,372 Yards; Par 70					

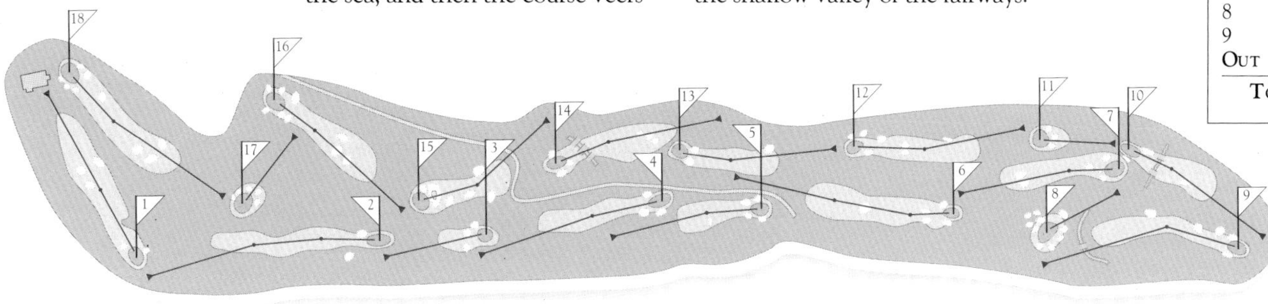

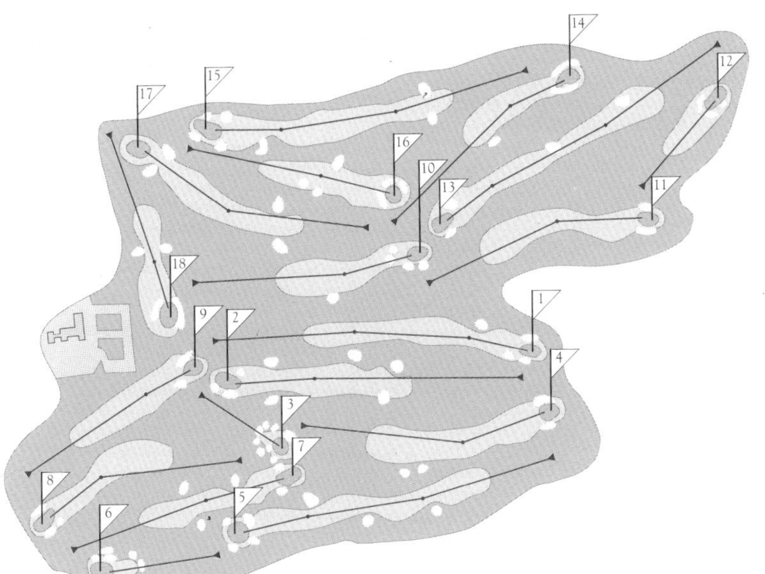

Royal Belgique

Tervuren, Belgium

This course was established by royal decree in 1904 and laid out from a design by Tom Simpson. In an area of parkland, he created a short, interesting test of golf, with eight par-4s under 380m, but still demanding thought and accuracy for the second shot through the careful use of bunkers and through tightening up the line of the tee shot. The Belgian king is honorary president, and the clubhouse, once the Château of Ravenstein, is a national monument.

Royal Belgique					
Hole	Meters	Par	Hole	Meters	Par
1	449	5	10	319	4
2	384	4	11	381	4
3	143	3	12	177	3
4	379	4	13	478	5
5	467	5	14	297	4
6	191	3	15	470	5
7	341	4	16	307	4
8	330	4	17	383	4
9	307	4	18	279	4
Out	2,991	36	In	3,091	37
Total 6,082 Meters; Par 73					

Royal Calcutta

Tollygunge, Calcutta, India

Founded in 1829, Royal Calcutta was the first golf club established outside of the British Isles. To compensate for its low-lying, flat terrain, small lakes or tanks were dug to supply the earth needed to raise tees and greens. Even so, the highest point is only 6 feet (1.8m) above the level of the River Ganges. No hole is free from watery problems, and with trees in abundance, few bunkers are required to make this long course difficult and demanding.

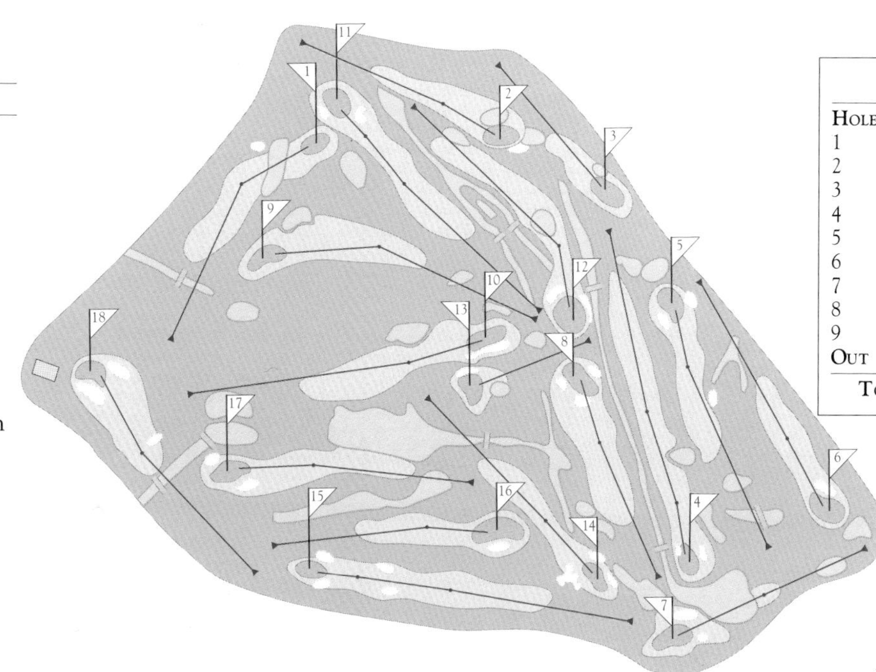

Royal Calcutta					
Hole	Yards	Par	Hole	Yards	Par
1	366	4	10	448	4
2	436	4	11	508	5
3	156	3	12	359	4
4	525	5	13	187	3
5	415	4	14	431	4
6	418	4	15	493	5
7	455	4	16	364	4
8	401	4	17	374	4
9	404	4	18	437	4
Out	3,576	36	In	3,601	37
Total 7,177 Yards; Par 73					

ROYAL HONG KONG

NEW TERRITORIES, HONG KONG

This club has come a long way since its inception at Happy Valley in 1889. At that time, it was not possible to have bunkers or holes because the ground was shared with polo players and cricketers. The club now has three 18-hole courses on the mainland at Fanling. The Old course, built in the 1900s, incorporates a picturesque loop, starting at the 10th hole, that is crucial to success on the back nine; yet all holes here require accurate driving and confident chipping.

ROYAL HONG KONG (OLD)

HOLE	YARDS	PAR	HOLE	YARDS	PAR
1	325	4	10	396	4
2	292	4	11	467	4
3	157	3	12	162	3
4	395	4	13	397	4
5	190	3	14	498	5
6	496	5	15	377	4
7	179	3	16	205	3
8	339	4	17	474	5
9	514	5	18	376	4
OUT	2,887	35	IN	3,352	36

TOTAL 6,239 YARDS; PAR 71

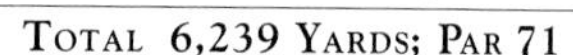

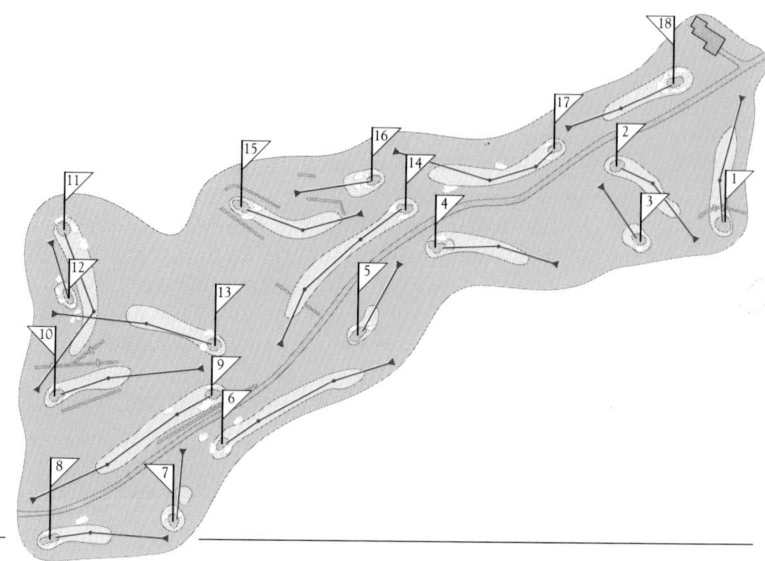

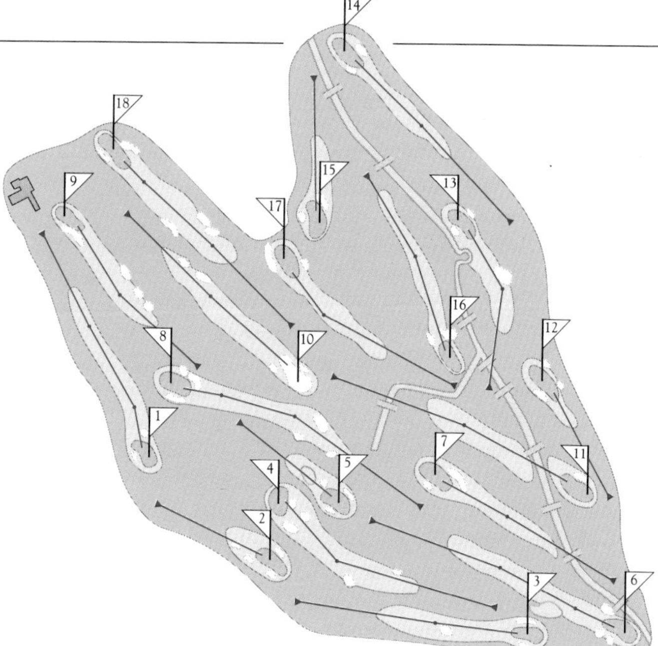

ROYAL JOHANNESBURG (EAST)

HOLE	METERS	PAR	HOLE	METERS	PAR
1	473	5	10	469	4
2	228	3	11	467	4
3	418	4	12	186	3
4	444	4	13	359	4
5	145	3	14	398	4
6	530	5	15	199	3
7	384	4	16	448	4
8	489	5	17	354	4
9	366	4	18	468	5
OUT	3,477	37	IN	3,348	35

TOTAL 6,825 METERS; PAR 72

ROYAL JOHANNESBURG

TRANSVAAL, SOUTH AFRICA

At 6,825m, the East course may seem daunting, but it is set in the high veldt country of the Rand, 6,000 feet (1,830m) above sea level, where the thin air allows golfers to hit the ball extraordinary distances. A prime location for the South African Open, the East course favors long, accurate hitters, since its driving areas are squeezed by trees or well-placed bunkers. There is a good variety of holes as the course layout dips and climbs through a wooded valley.

SAUNTON

BRAUNTON, DEVON, ENGLAND

Superbly situated on Devon's north coast, just the other side of the Taw Estuary from Westward Ho!, this old, established course has the river, the Atlantic, and golden sands as its backdrop. Used during the Second World War as a battle school, Saunton did not reopen until Herbert Fowler's original East course had been revamped and restored by Ken Cotton in 1951. At that time, three new holes were brought into play, the 1st and the last two, and the course provides a good test of shot-making ability.

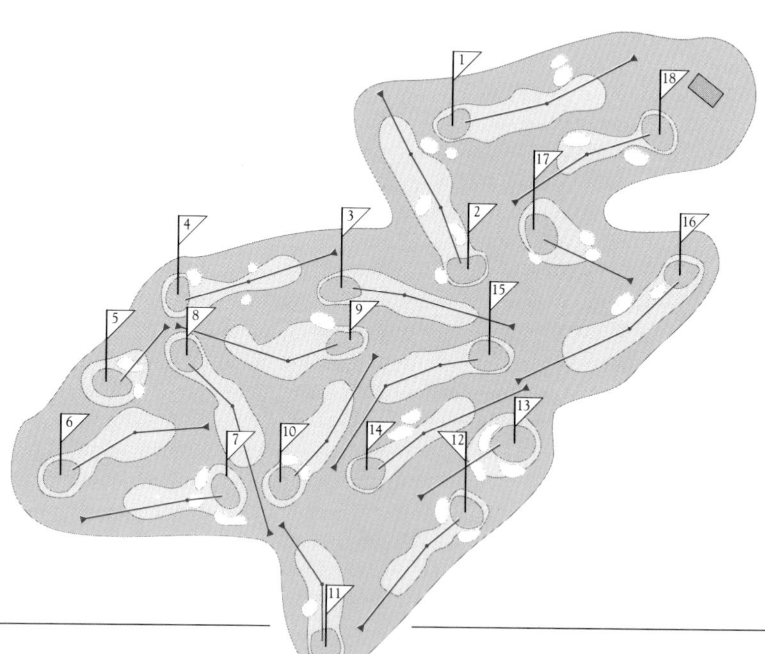

SAUNTON (EAST)

HOLE	YARDS	PAR	HOLE	YARDS	PAR
1	470	4	10	337	4
2	476	5	11	362	4
3	402	4	12	418	4
4	444	4	13	136	3
5	112	3	14	461	4
6	370	4	15	485	5
7	428	4	16	430	4
8	380	4	17	202	3
9	382	4	18	408	4
OUT	3,464	36	IN	3,239	35

TOTAL 6,703 YARDS; PAR 71

SCIOTO

COLUMBUS, OHIO, U.S.A.

Built on land once the home of Wyandotte Indians, the Scioto Country Club was laid out to a design by Donald Ross in 1912. A classic course, it is one of the best created by this architect. It is a strategic course, demanding careful assessment and shot-making, the very qualities that have made Jack Nicklaus, who learned his golf at Scioto, possibly the world's greatest player. The long 505-yard par-5 8th stands out as one of the toughest holes.

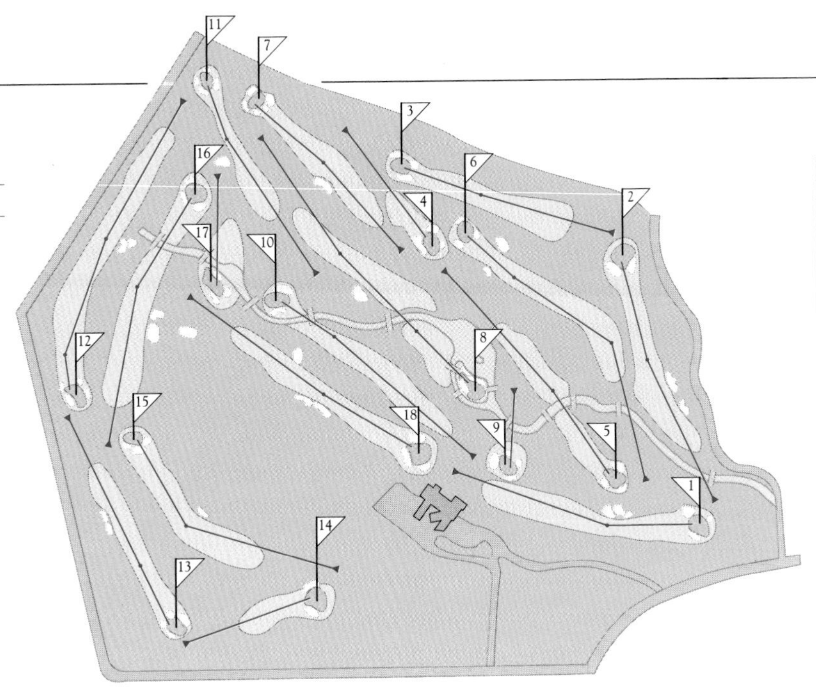

SCIOTO					
HOLE	YARDS	PAR	HOLE	YARDS	PAR
1	410	4	10	424	4
2	438	4	11	365	4
3	377	4	12	545	5
4	194	3	13	435	4
5	438	4	14	238	3
6	527	5	15	408	4
7	372	4	16	425	4
8	505	5	17	209	3
9	162	3	18	445	4
OUT	3,423	36	IN	3,494	35
TOTAL 6,917 YARDS; PAR 71					

SEEFELD-WILDMOOS

SEEFELD, TIROL, AUSTRIA

Located at 4,300 feet (1,310m), this course was designed by Donald Harradine. When it emerges from snow cover for a six-month golf season, the layout reveals itself to be extremely tight, requiring great accuracy. The mountain terrain is in places exploited to dramatic effect, as at the par-3 9th, where the tee towers 195 feet (60m) above the green. Harradine has made sparing use of bunkers, relying instead on the abundant pine and birch trees to provide hazards.

SEEFELD-WILDMOOS					
HOLE	METERS	PAR	HOLE	METERS	PAR
1	418	4	10	360	4
2	363	4	11	282	4
3	294	4	12	518	5
4	349	4	13	156	3
5	218	3	14	534	5
6	351	4	15	379	4
7	519	5	16	293	4
8	243	4	17	165	3
9	163	3	18	337	4
OUT	2,918	35	IN	3,024	36
TOTAL 5,942 METERS; PAR 71					

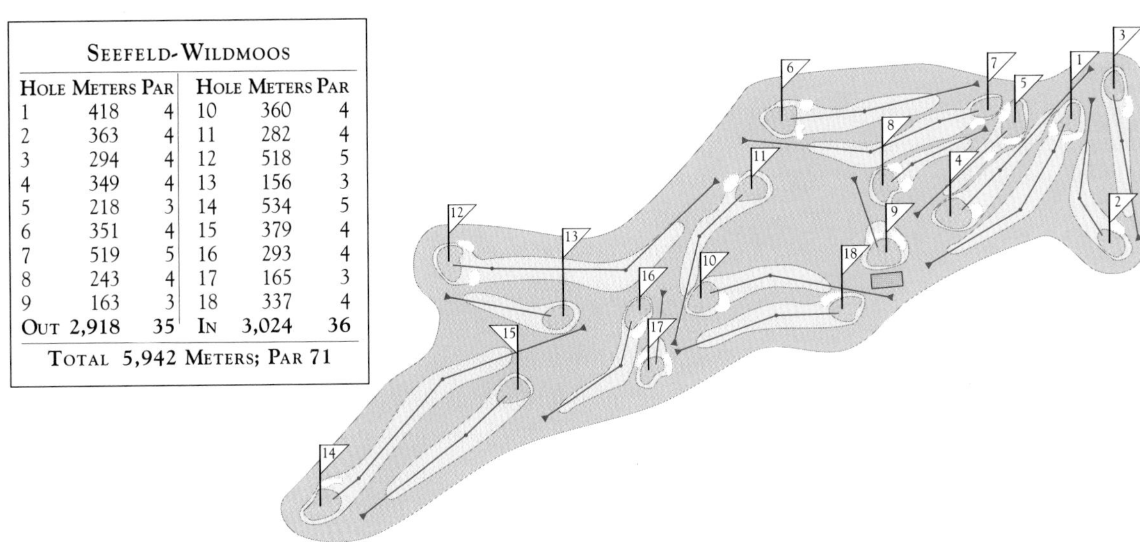

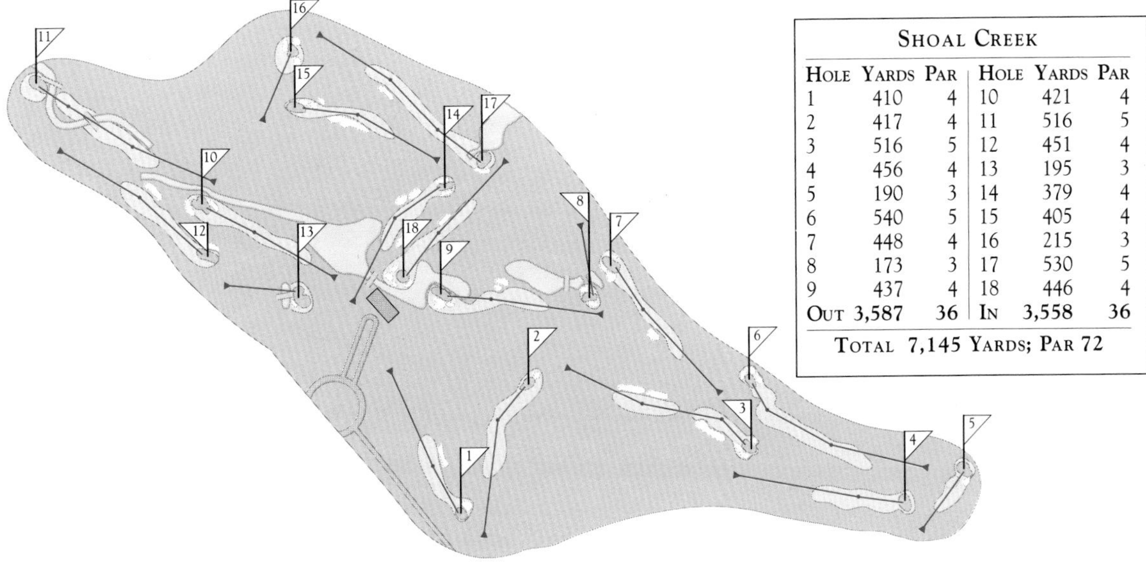

SHOAL CREEK					
HOLE	YARDS	PAR	HOLE	YARDS	PAR
1	410	4	10	421	4
2	417	4	11	516	5
3	516	5	12	451	4
4	456	4	13	195	3
5	190	3	14	379	4
6	540	5	15	405	4
7	448	4	16	215	3
8	173	3	17	530	5
9	437	4	18	446	4
OUT	3,587	36	IN	3,558	36
TOTAL 7,145 YARDS; PAR 72					

SHOAL CREEK

BIRMINGHAM, ALABAMA, U.S.A.

Originally designed by Jack Nicklaus as a members' course, Shoal Creek was torn apart by the professionals during the 1984 USPGA Championship. Before it hosted the event again in 1990, Nicklaus was called back to make it more difficult and lengthen many of the holes. With its fierce rough, the course was almost too difficult second time around. Trees, lakes, and creeks combine with both creative bunkering and large, well-contoured greens to achieve a fine test of golfing skill.

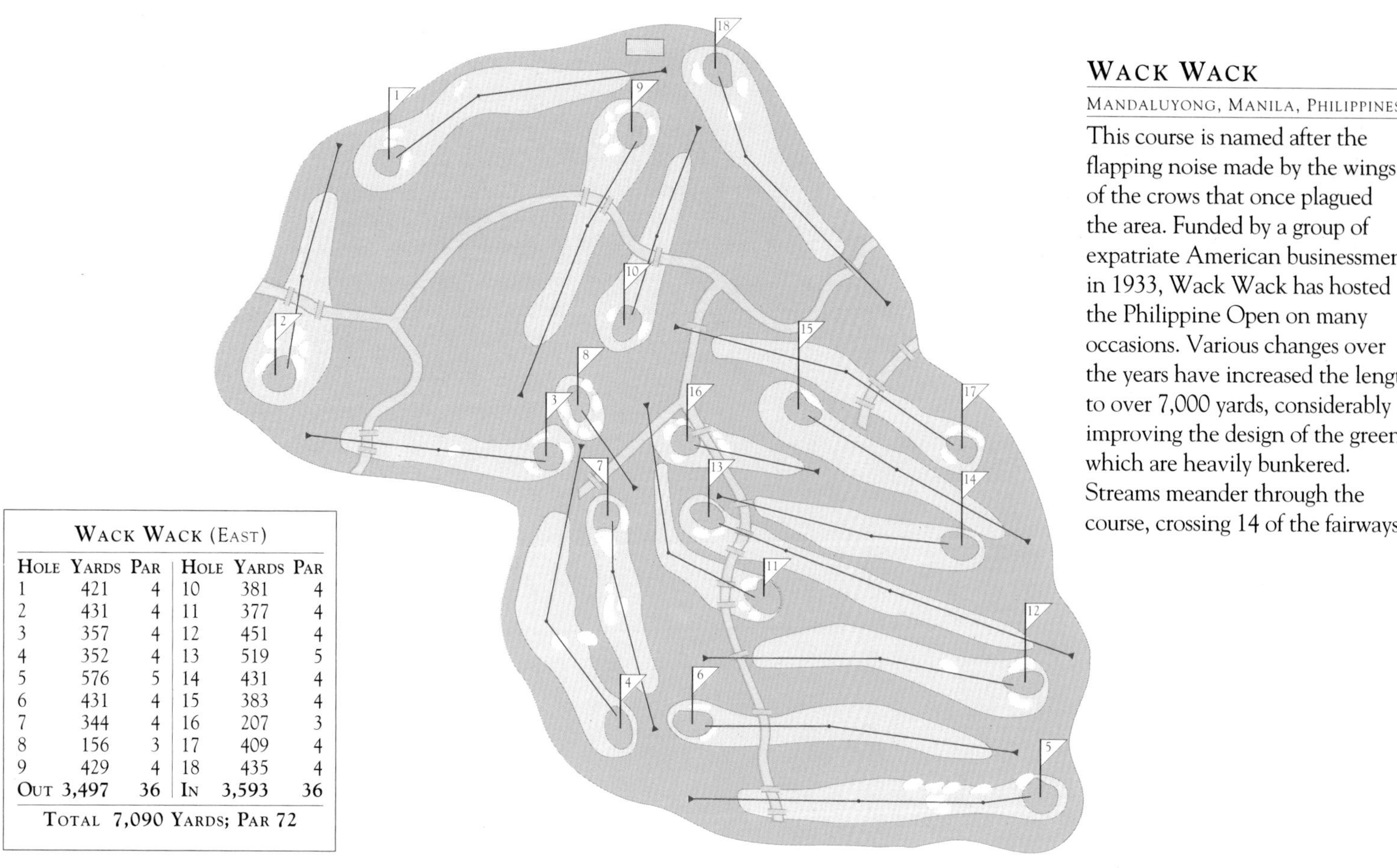

WACK WACK

MANDALUYONG, MANILA, PHILIPPINES

This course is named after the flapping noise made by the wings of the crows that once plagued the area. Funded by a group of expatriate American businessmen in 1933, Wack Wack has hosted the Philippine Open on many occasions. Various changes over the years have increased the length to over 7,000 yards, considerably improving the design of the greens, which are heavily bunkered. Streams meander through the course, crossing 14 of the fairways.

WACK WACK (EAST)

HOLE	YARDS	PAR	HOLE	YARDS	PAR
1	421	4	10	381	4
2	431	4	11	377	4
3	357	4	12	451	4
4	352	4	13	519	5
5	576	5	14	431	4
6	431	4	15	383	4
7	344	4	16	207	3
8	156	3	17	409	4
9	429	4	18	435	4
OUT	3,497	36	IN	3,593	36

TOTAL 7,090 YARDS; PAR 72

WALTON HEATH

TADWORTH, SURREY, ENGLAND

Although Walton Heath is not far from London, there is a distinct seaside quality about its short heathland turf, deep bunkers, and large, rolling greens. The Old course was for many years the home of the original Matchplay Championship. "Exposed to all the breezes that blow," according to Bernard Darwin, the course has a demanding nature, typified by the 517-yard par-5 14th with its long carry from the tee and bunker-strewn journey to the green.

WALTON HEATH (OLD)

HOLE	YARDS	PAR	HOLE	YARDS	PAR
1	442	4	10	138	3
2	289	4	11	384	4
3	441	4	12	371	4
4	391	4	13	513	5
5	427	4	14	517	5
6	174	3	15	408	4
7	494	5	16	510	5
8	400	4	17	181	3
9	399	4	18	404	4
OUT	3,457	36	IN	3,426	37

TOTAL 6,883 YARDS; PAR 73

WILD DUNES

CHARLESTON, SOUTH CAROLINA, U.S.A.

Architect Tom Fazio felt he had the perfect material to work with when he designed this course on the Isle of Palms in South Carolina. A prehistoric hurricane is believed to have created the huge ridge of dunes 50-foot (15m) high that dominate the back nine of this layout. The front nine has holes carved from the maritime forest of palmetto, loblolly pine, and magnolia. The course threads its way through marsh and sand, with two classic links holes at the finish.

WILD DUNES (LINKS)

HOLE	YARDS	PAR	HOLE	YARDS	PAR
1	501	5	10	331	4
2	370	4	11	376	4
3	420	4	12	192	3
4	170	3	13	427	4
5	505	5	14	489	5
6	421	4	15	426	4
7	359	4	16	175	3
8	203	3	17	405	4
9	451	4	18	501	5
OUT	3,400	36	IN	3,322	36

TOTAL 6,722 YARDS; PAR 72

WOODHALL SPA

LINCOLNSHIRE, ENGLAND

Harry Vardon laid out the first course at Woodhall Spa in 1905, but it was subsequently redesigned by Harry S. Colt in 1912. The outstanding present layout is that of Colonel S.V. Hotchkin. The bunkers that guard the three short holes are deep and intimidating, and the 560-yard 9th has its fairway completely blocked by bunkers, which come into play against a head wind.

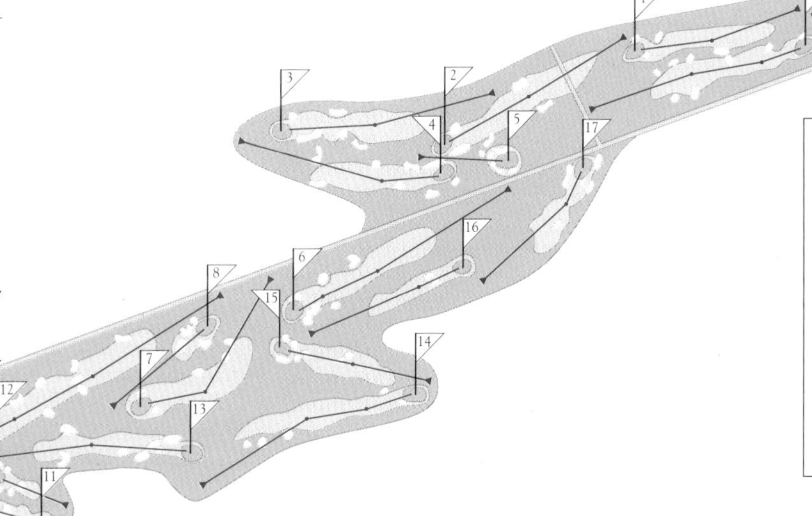

WOODHALL SPA

HOLE	YARDS	PAR	HOLE	YARDS	PAR
1	363	4	10	333	4
2	408	4	11	442	4
3	417	4	12	157	3
4	415	4	13	437	4
5	155	3	14	489	5
6	506	5	15	325	4
7	438	4	16	398	4
8	193	3	17	322	4
9	560	5	18	544	5
OUT	3,455	36	IN	3,447	37

TOTAL 6,902 YARDS; PAR 73

YOMIURI

TOKYO, JAPAN

In common with many other Japanese courses, there are two greens at every hole here – one for use in summer, the other for winter. There are times when this arrangement interferes with the best tactical bunkering for each green, but in general it works well.

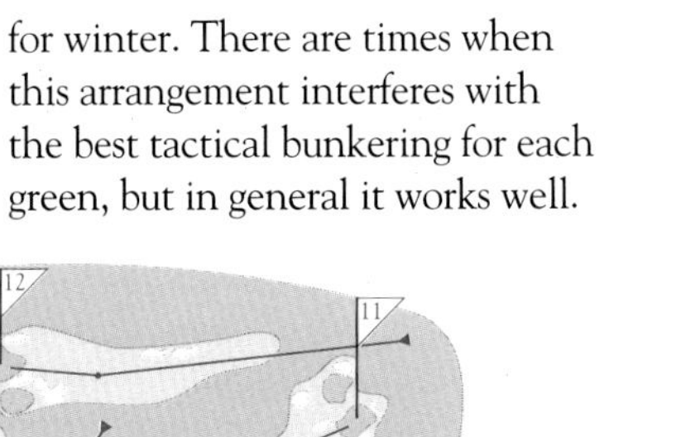

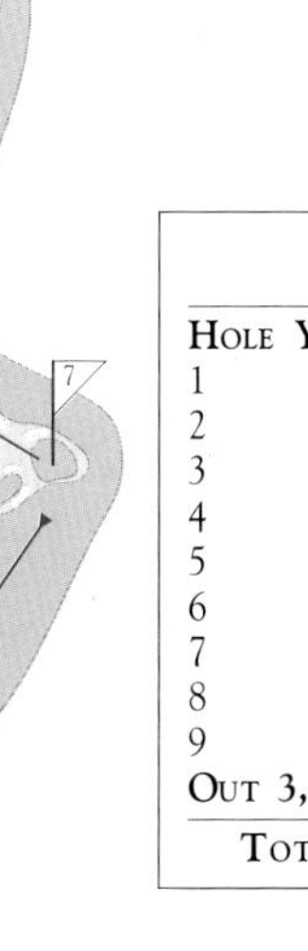

YOMIURI

HOLE	YARDS	PAR	HOLE	YARDS	PAR
1	396	4	10	425	4
2	180	3	11	507	5
3	403	4	12	432	4
4	508	5	13	450	4
5	384	4	14	364	4
6	541	5	15	194	3
7	389	4	16	410	4
8	197	3	17	510	5
9	448	4	18	224	3
OUT	3,446	36	IN	3,516	36

TOTAL 6,962 YARDS; PAR 72

CHAPTER

THE HALL OF FAME

Over the centuries, golf has thrown up an extraordinary number of outstanding characters, sportsmen and women of the most striking personality and individuality. Professional golfers are now among the highest paid of the world's athletes, but they are also among the most respected, because of their rigorous adherence to the rules of their game and their respect for its traditions.

Tobacco-tin greats: Abe Mitchell, George Duncan, Harry Vardon, James Braid

This chapter lists 100 of the outstanding men and women who have made a special individual contribution to golf. It is a list that comprises not only great champions, but also golf-course architects and administrators who have played a significant role in the history of the game.

The legendary Bobby Jones, Grand Slam winner 1930

A statistical box at the end of each player's entry records his or her selective career highlights, including any Major championship victories and participation in the most prominent international team matches.

White Shark (left)
Nicknamed "The Great White Shark," Greg Norman tees off at the 9th at Turnberry.

Amy Alcott

BORN KANSAS CITY, MISSOURI, U.S.A., FEBRUARY 22, 1956

A STEADY PLAYER *on the U.S. Women's Tour, Amy Alcott has one of the neatest swings in the game. There is power in it but no obvious force. She proves what most golfers know in their hearts, but so often forget in their play: the important thing is to hit the ball squarely, with the sweet spot, along the right line.*

Amy won the U.S. Junior Championship in 1973 when she was 16 years old. Turning professional in 1975, she won the third tournament that she entered, the Orange Blossom Classic. Up to 1990, she never fell below eighteenth in the money list.

Three times – in 1979, 1980, and 1984 – Alcott scored four tournament victories in a year. In 1980 she won the U.S. Women's Open by nine strokes. By the end of 1989 she had amassed $2,392,617 in official earnings.

Using a relatively short backswing, Amy Alcott's long- and medium-iron play is outstanding. It is this, together with her steadiness on the greens, that makes her such a consistent competitor.

Ahead of the pack
Amy Alcott putts her way to victory in the 1980 U.S. Women's Open at the Richland Country Club. Her score of 280 set a new record for the Women's Open.

Steady and willing (below)
Alcott's skill and determination have brought a stream of LPGA successes.

AMY ALCOTT

WON PETER JACKSON CLASSIC 1979; U.S. WOMEN'S OPEN 1980; DINAH SHORE INVITATIONAL 1983, 1988, 1991. ROOKIE OF THE YEAR 1975. VARE TROPHY 1980.

Peter Alliss

BORN BERLIN, GERMANY, FEBRUARY 28, 1931

SON OF THE *well-known professional Percy Alliss, Peter was born in Berlin, where his father was serving as a professional, but was brought up in England, at Ferndown in Dorset. As a boy he was seldom far from the famous courses in that area. It was obvious from the start that he was a naturally gifted player of the game.*

Iron will
Peter Alliss's strength lay in his ease with long-iron shots. In 1967 he won the Agfa-Gevaert Tournament, two years before retiring to concentrate on a career as a commentator.

Peter Alliss was selected to represent England as a Boy International in 1946, and was hailed as a future champion by such an experienced observer as Leonard Crawley. He turned professional a few weeks later, while still only 15.

Nightmare Shot

In 1953 Alliss was thrown into the deep end when he was invited to play for Great Britain in the Ryder Cup at Wentworth, at the tender age of 22. It turned out to be a harrowing experience that might have seriously damaged his career. The key event occurred at the last hole in his singles match against Jim Turnesa.

Confronting a pitch shot to the green in the tightest possible situation, Alliss hit a nightmare fluff which was to haunt him for years. It allowed Turnesa to win by one hole, and the United States to win the Cup by that one match. British team captain Henry Cotton was furious.

Alliss himself forgot that other players, including Bernard Hunt, had also failed at this last hole. He took his narrow defeat, and the overstated and absurd newspaper headlines that followed it, very badly.

It was several years before Alliss recovered from this experience, but ultimately it may have provoked him into greater efforts. In 1956 he won his first important championship, the Spanish

Fruits of success
Over the years, Peter Alliss has kept the same "Put 3" number plate on his successive cars. As his television career has grown, the cars have become grander.

Open, and in 1958, his best year, he took the Italian and Portuguese Open titles, as well as the Spanish Open for a second time. He went on to win 23 other significant tournaments up to 1969.

Peter Alliss played in eight Ryder Cup matches, as well as ten World Cup clashes for England. Yet he never won the British Open, although many supporters felt he should have done so.

When his putting – never the strongest point of his game – finally went into decline, Alliss was embraced by BBC Television. While Tony Jacklin, Sandy Lyle and Nick Faldo have won the Major titles at golf, the voice of golf in the United Kingdom for many years has been that of Peter Alliss. His background, coming up from a pro shop, has helped to form a rare personality of considerable all-round ability.

Putting trouble
Throughout his career, Alliss was plagued by erratic putting. It never quite matched the quality of the rest of his game.

There has never been any doubt of Alliss's popularity. It is little wonder that in 1987 he was made captain of the British PGA, based at The Belfry, a course that he had been in part responsible for designing.

PETER ALLISS

WON SPANISH OPEN 1956, 1958; ITALIAN OPEN 1958; PORTUGUESE OPEN 1958; BRAZILIAN OPEN 1961. RYDER CUP 1953, 1957–69. WORLD CUP 1954–55, 1957–59, 1961–62, 1964, 1966–67. HARRY VARDON TROPHY 1964, 1966. BRITISH PGA CAPTAIN 1962, 1987.

ISAO AOKI

BORN ABIKO, JAPAN, AUGUST 31, 1942

WHEN HE WAS a boy, Isao Aoki caddied at his local club at Abiko, and used to play in the early mornings and the evenings, or whenever else the course was clear. Turning professional in 1964, it was not until 1971 that he won his first tournament. After that success, he rapidly became Japan's first international star.

Aoki's victories include two Japan Opens and five Japan PGA Matchplay titles. In 1978 he won the World Matchplay at Wentworth and the following year lost by only one hole to Bill Rogers.

Gentleman golfer
Tall and good-looking, Isao Aoki is renowned for his excellent manners on the course.

In 1978 at St. Andrews, he led the field in the British Open at the end of the first round and shared the lead after two rounds, only to finish seventh, as he did in 1979. His first U.S. Tour win was the Hawaiian Open in 1983, which he achieved with a spectacular eagle at the last hole, sinking his third shot from thick rough to win by one stroke.

Isao Aoki has developed a highly individual putting style, with the toe of the putter pointing to the sky, which is recognized as his trademark worldwide.

Getting on line (right)
Aoki lines up a putt; his short game has helped make him one of the world's outstanding players.

ISAO AOKI

WON JAPAN PGA 1973, 1981, 1986; WORLD MATCHPLAY 1978; EUROPEAN OPEN 1983; JAPAN OPEN 1983, 1987; HAWAIIAN OPEN 1983. DUNHILL CUP 1985. FOUR TOURS CHAMPIONSHIP 1985, 1987–88.

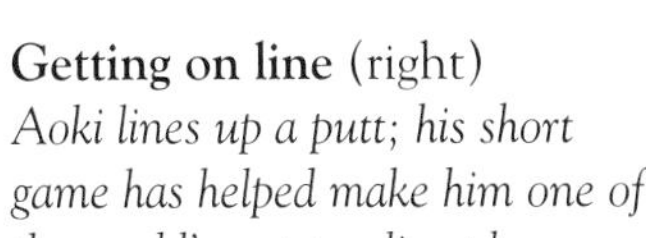
JOHN BALL, see page 220

SEVE BALLESTEROS

BORN PEDREÑA, SPAIN, APRIL 9, 1957

LONG BEFORE SEVERIANO Ballesteros beat Jack Nicklaus and Ben Crenshaw by three strokes to win the 1979 British Open at Royal Lytham and St. Annes, it was obvious that golf had a refreshingly new and precocious talent. The young man from the north coast of Spain turned professional at 17 and took the game by storm. In five years he developed from a raw youngster into one of the world's leading players.

There can be little argument that Seve Ballesteros is one of the greatest players of all time. Where precisely he is placed in the final order of merit will depend on which criteria are applied. If the yardstick is the number of Majors won, then the Spaniard will be well down the league compared with Nicklaus. But it can be safely argued that in Seve's generation Majors have been much harder to win.

Ballesteros has won just five Majors compared to Nicklaus's 20 – the British Open three times and the U.S. Masters twice. Some feel his remarkable talent should have delivered more, and it may well do so in the future.

Ballesteros is the youngest of four brothers who all became professional golfers. He taught himself to play by sneaking onto the Santander Golf Course, which was out of bounds to him, to learn under cover of dusk. The eight-year-old Seve practiced every conceivable shot with just one club – an old 3-iron – which may just possibly account for his amazing ability in later life to invent brilliant recovery shots from seemingly impossible situations.

Mastering Augusta (above)
On his way to winning the U.S. Masters for the second time, Ballesteros is watched by a tense crowd at Augusta in 1983. He has finished in the top five in the Masters no fewer than six times.

SWASHBUCKLING YOUTH

When he emerged onto the professional stage, Ballesteros brought with him a swashbuckling, go-for-everything attitude that the game had not seen since the legendary Arnold Palmer. Seve would hit it, find it, and hit it again, aiming at the pin with every shot. The crowds loved him. He tied for second place in the British Open at Royal Birkdale in 1976 at the age of only 19, and the world knew it had a superstar in the making.

When he won his first British Open title three years later he was christened the "parking-lot champion" by the

Magical touch (left)
The hallmark of the young Seve's game was his genius around the greens. Although these marvelous skills have never deserted him, his mature game lacks something of the brash self-confidence of his earlier years.

Playing for Europe (left)
Whenever he is representing Europe in the Ryder Cup, Ballesteros curbs his natural instinct for flamboyant strokes in the interests of his team.

Far and sure
One of the longest hitters on the Tour, Seve tends to miss by a lot whenever he plays a shot off line. However, since entering his 30s he has combined distance with accuracy.

Anticipation and Triumph

Ballesteros won the British Open at Royal Lytham in 1988 with a remarkable last-round 65. At the last hole, needing a par 4 to avoid a play-off with Nick Price, Seve hit his second shot into an awkward lie off the back of the green. Choosing a sand wedge, he chipped the ball onto the green; it rolled, hit the edge of the cup and stopped. As his display of elation shows, victory was secure.

American press, after he had played his second at the 16th hole from among the cars. As Ballesteros revealed later, the drive had been deliberately hit down that side of the hole because the prevailing wind made it difficult to attack the green from the left. Far from being a wild shot, it had been a calculated tactic that brought him a birdie – typical of his genius for the unexpected.

The following year he won the U.S. Masters and led the European challenge into the decade that was to see the American supremacy in world golf overturned. In the 1983 U.S. Masters he won a second Green Jacket, paving the way for European victories by Bernhard Langer, Sandy Lyle, and Nick Faldo.

After Ballesteros's second British Open victory, achieved amid memorable scenes at St. Andrews in 1984, he seemed to lose his winning touch. For a while he showed a distressing tendency to "choke" on crucial shots. But then came his triumph at the rain-interrupted Open at Royal Lytham in 1988, and Seve was back on top of the world.

Apart from his personal successes, he took particular delight in the defeat of the Americans by the European team in the Ryder Cup in 1985 and 1987. It was his presence in the European camp that gave his colleagues much of their confidence to grasp victory.

Severiano Ballesteros

Won British Open 1979, 1984, 1988; U.S. Masters 1980, 1983; World Matchplay 1981, 1982, 1984, 1985. Winner of 46 PGA European Tour events 1976–90. World Cup 1975–77. Ryder Cup 1979, 1983–89. Dunhill Cup 1985–86, 1988. Harry Vardon Trophy 1976–78, 1986, 1988.

Gracias, amigos
Seve acknowledges the tumultuous applause of the gallery after his popular victory in the British Open at St. Andrews in 1984.

JOHN BALL

BORN HOYLAKE, ENGLAND, DECEMBER 24, 1862; DIED 1940

ANY ATTEMPT TO assess John Ball's status among golfers of all time is futile; he is too remote from the modern game. But he was unquestionably the outstanding amateur of his own era, at a period when there were many top-class amateurs who were as good as most professionals. Quiet and modest, Ball shunned the limelight. Yet in his prime he drew an enormous following, particularly in his home area, where he was considered unbeatable.

Well out (right)
John Ball played his way out of bunkers with a mashie, never resorting to a niblick.

John Ball was born at Hoylake, Cheshire, where his father, a first-class golfer, owned the Royal Hotel next to land that was soon to become the links of the Royal Liverpool Golf Club. Ball was able to use the course in his youth and soon became a formidable young player.

He first played in the British Open in 1878 at the precocious age of 15; he lost the play-off for fourth place, taking a small cash prize. When some years later the question of amateur status was raised, the age limit for winning money was fixed at 16, so that Ball could avoid being classed as a professional (see page 144). In 1885 he reached the semifinal of the first Amateur Championship, going on to win the title at Prestwick in 1888 and again at Hoylake in 1890. In the latter year he also became the British Open champion. He was the first golfer from outside Scotland to win the title, and also the first player to win the Open and Amateur titles in the same year. Ball never won the Open again, but he won the Amateur eight times, the last time in 1912. He entered for the final time in 1921 when, aged 58, he still reached the fifth round.

Palm grip
As was usual in his day, Ball gripped the club in his palms.

Amateur caricature
In 1892, the year of his third Amateur Championship victory, Ball was caricatured by "Lib" – Italian artist Liberio Prosperi – in Vanity Fair.

MANUFACTURING SHOTS

Ball had a complete mastery over every club he used. He was adept at playing half and quarter shots with any club; no one was more versatile. He refused to recognize the necessity for a niblick and played from even the worst lies in bunkers with his mashie. In his young days Ball was always an immensely long hitter; as he grew older he lost some of his length, but he always retained uncanny accuracy with his irons.

JOHN BALL, JR.

WON BRITISH OPEN 1890; BRITISH AMATEUR CHAMPIONSHIP 1888, 1890, 1892, 1894, 1899, 1907, 1910, 1912.

MILLER BARBER

BORN SHREVEPORT, LOUISIANA, U.S.A., MARCH 31, 1931

KNOWN FOR MANY years as "X" because of his dislike of the limelight, Miller Barber is, nonetheless, a genial and friendly individual. He is also a fine player and always a delight to watch. It is a great source of regret to Barber that he never won a Major title in his 20 years on the U.S. Tour, but he has moved on to become an exceptionally proficient performer on the Senior Tour, accumulating prize money in excess of $2 million.

Golfing half-century
Miller Barber had more success as a 50-year-old on the Senior Tour than he had ever enjoyed previously.

After a successful career on the amateur circuit, Miller Barber turned professional in 1958. He joined the USPGA Tour the following year.

His swing was unorthodox, with a pronounced "flying" right elbow on the backswing, but it proved effective, and he became a very competitive player. After completing his apprentice years, he scored his first win on the Tour in 1964.

Seniors silver
Barber and his wife enjoy holding the USPGA Seniors trophy in 1981.

CONSISTENT VICTORIES

Barber won a U.S. Tour victory every year between 1967 and 1974, an eight-year sequence equalled by very few players. His most significant triumph came in the World Open in 1973, a marathon event played over eight rounds that carried the first $100,000 prize in golf history.

Surprisingly, in the Majors Barber was rarely in the running, though in the U.S. Open of 1969 only a disastrous last round robbed him of a chance for glory.

When Barber reached the age to qualify for the USPGA Senior Tour in March 1981, it was a different story. He won both the major events on the Senior Tour in his first two years – the USPGA Seniors in 1981 and the USGA Senior Open in 1982. Overall, 1982 was an excellent year for Barber. He started with a win in the Vintage, which had the largest winner's prize on the Senior Tour. Then, at the Suntree Classic in Florida, he had four rounds of 66 for an aggregate of 264, beating the previous Senior Tour winning score by nine strokes.

Barber has continued as one of the top Senior players. By 1990 he had won a total of 25 Senior tournaments.

MILLER WESTFORD BARBER, JR.

WON USPGA SENIORS 1981; USGA SENIOR OPEN 1982, 1984, 1985. WINNER OF 11 U.S. TOUR EVENTS 1964–78. RYDER CUP 1969–71. FIRST PLAYER TO WIN $2 MILLION ON THE SENIOR TOUR.

PATTY BERG

BORN MINNEAPOLIS, MINNESOTA, U.S.A., FEBRUARY 13, 1918

PATTY BERG IS not only one of the outstanding players of the modern women's game, but has also been among its great ambassadors. Her marvelous personality, exceptional golfing talents, and striking good looks were evident from her early days as an amateur. In 1935, aged only 17, she was narrowly defeated in the final of the U.S. Women's Amateur Championship by Glenna Collett Vare. Berg went on to win the Women's Amateur three years later, and she was twice selected to represent the United States in the Curtis Cup competition.

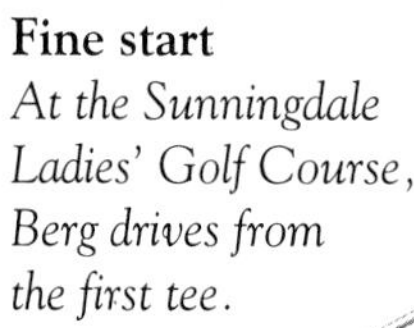

Fine start
At the Sunningdale Ladies' Golf Course, Berg drives from the first tee.

Berg's greatest contribution to the game, however, came after she joined the professional ranks in 1940. The Second World War intervened before her professional career got into its stride, but after the war her game blossomed. In her lifetime she won more than 80 tournaments, 41 of them after the U.S. LPGA was founded in 1948. She was a founding member of that association and also became its first president.

BERG IN THE MONEY

Berg won the first U.S. Women's Open Championship, and the $5,600 first prize, in 1946 at the Spokane Country Club in Washington State. The $19,700 purse was then the largest in the history of women's golf. This was the only time the Women's Open was a matchplay event. Berg's total of 145 in the medal-qualifying round was seven strokes better than her nearest rival, Babe Zaharias. Berg went on to beat Betty Jameson in the final.

Patty won the World Championship four times, and three times she was the leading money winner on the LPGA Tour, in 1954, 1955 and 1957. In 1953 she recorded six victories on the Tour and she repeated this feat two years later. She also received the Vare Trophy three times for achieving the lowest scoring average of the year.

Berg frequently proved capable of performing outstanding feats of scoring. One round of 64 stood as a record at the Richmond Club in California for well over a decade.

By the time she played in her last Women's Tour event in 1962, Patty Berg had won 57 professional tournaments. She did not retire from the game altogether, but elected to pass on her experience to others. She proved an outstanding teacher, winning worldwide acclaim for the clinics she gave in virtually every golfing country.

Early success
Two years before turning professional, Berg won this trophy at Westmoreland as the 1938 USGA Women's Amateur Champion.

PATRICIA JANE BERG

WON U.S. WOMEN'S AMATEUR 1938; WESTERN OPEN 1941, 1948, 1951, 1955, 1957, 1958; U.S. WOMEN'S OPEN 1946; TITLEHOLDERS CHAMPIONSHIP 1948, 1953, 1955, 1957. WINNER OF 29 AMATEUR EVENTS 1934–40; 57 PROFESSIONAL EVENTS 1941–62. CURTIS CUP 1936, 1938. LPGA HALL OF FAME 1951. VARE TROPHY 1953, 1955, 1956. BOB JONES AWARD 1963. WORLD GOLF HALL OF FAME 1974. BEN HOGAN AWARD 1975. OLD TOM MORRIS AWARD 1986.

Tommy Bolt

Born Haworth, Oklahoma, U.S.A., March 31, 1918

With a volcanic temperament and a smooth artistic style, Tommy "Thunderbolt" Bolt was one of the United States' longest-lasting tournament stars. He won the U.S. Open in 1958 and came close to winning the USPGA tournament at Palm Beach in 1971 while in his fifties, finishing third to Jack Nicklaus and Billy Casper.

Thunderbolt (right) *Tommy Bolt had an excellent swing that partly compensated for his shaky putting.*

Lake throw (left) *Bolt reacts to a bad shot by throwing his club into a lake during the 1960 U.S. Open.*

Most of the stories about Tommy Bolt are of his tantrums. He threw so many clubs, it is said, that once when he abused his caddie for handing him a 2-iron for a 7-iron shot, the boy explained, "It's the only iron we have left." After being beaten 4-and-3 by Eric Brown in the 1957 Ryder Cup at Lindrick, he remarked, "This isn't golf; it's war."

It was probably because of Bolt's fiery personality that he became a great shotmaker, engineering shots from strange places that few people would have considered possible. He was a truly fine swinger and, had he been blessed with a more equable temperament, he would surely have won many more tournaments.

Thomas Bolt

Won U.S. Open 1958; World Seniors 1969. Winner of 14 U.S. Tour events. Ryder Cup 1955–57.

Michael Bonallack

Born Chigwell, England, December 31, 1934

Michael Bonallack has the finest record of all modern British amateurs. Strangely, he was not a great driver of the golf ball, but he did not need to be. It was his short game that won him so many important tournaments, including the British Amateur Championship title five times between 1961 and 1970.

Keeping track *As Secretary of the Royal & Ancient Golf Club, Bonallack keeps a keen eye on the contemporary game.*

When he won the 1963 English Amateur Championship in a 36-hole final match against Alan Thirwell, Bonallack got up-and-down in two from off the greens no fewer than 22 times. In the 1970 British Amateur, he stood one down at lunch against Bill Hyndman, yet won by 8-and-7.

Bonallack's putting stance was highly individual and most unusual. He stood with his legs wide apart, his head down, his eyes almost touching what appeared to be a short-shafted putter. This style was unusually effective although few, if any, other players have ever copied it.

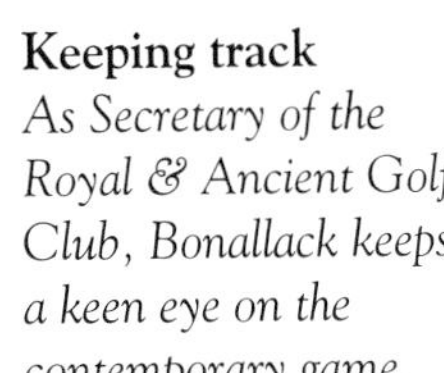

Top amateur *Bonallack's record puts him in the class of such great amateurs as John Ball and Harold Hilton.*

Michael Francis Bonallack, OBE

Won British Amateur 1961, 1965, 1968, 1969, 1970. Walker Cup 1957–73 (captain 1969–71). Eisenhower Trophy 1960–72 (captain 1968–72). Secretary R & A Golf Club.

James Braid

Born Earlsferry, Scotland, February 6, 1870; Died 1950

James Braid was the first golfer to win five British Open titles, and he did it in the short space of ten years – between 1901 and 1910. One of the greatest golfers of all time, he also won the first Matchplay professional tournament in 1903, a victory he repeated on three more occasions. He enjoyed a long career, coming in second in the 1927 Matchplay event at the age of 57.

Braid was born in Earlsferry and showed great promise as a youngster on the links at Elie. He was a carpenter and worked in St. Andrews; it was there that he had an accident with some lime, which affected his eyes, causing some difficulty with his sight. Despite this early setback, he continued to show great aptitude for golf. He was a long hitter and a master of all clubs except the putting cleek, which often let him down on the "short ones." He was so ardent that he often practiced in the evening, even though he had to walk many miles from work to the links.

Golf was in his family – he had cousins who were top-class golfers – so eventually he was persuaded to take a job in golf, against his parents' advice. Using his skill as a carpenter to become a clubmaker, he went south, starting work in the Army and Navy Stores, London, in 1893.

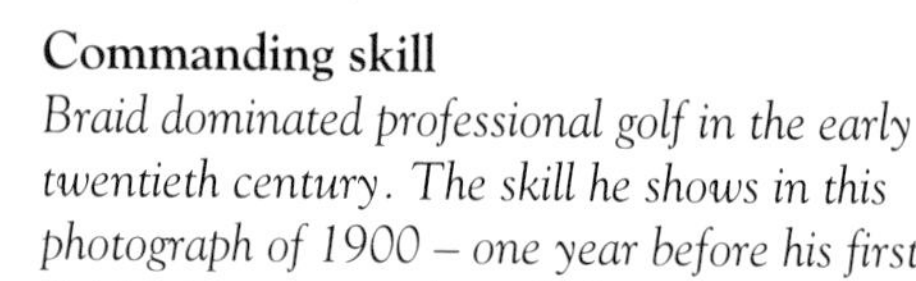

Commanding skill
Braid dominated professional golf in the early twentieth century. The skill he shows in this photograph of 1900 – one year before his first British Open win – brought him great success.

Popular player
Known affectionately as "Jimmy," as in this 1907 cartoon (above) *by "Spy" (Sir Leslie Ward), Braid was a tall, unassuming man. Despite his run of early successes, he changed little from the courteous young professional of 1900* (right).

Early Successes

Braid began golfing in London on the weekends, and soon word spread around that the young Scot was something of a player. A match was arranged between Braid and the reigning British Open champion, J.H. Taylor. Braid succeeded in halving the match after being two down with two to play, a result that secured him a job as a professional at Romford.

More successes soon followed. He had entered, from Elie, for the 1894 Open at St. George's and finished tenth. In 1896 at Muirfield he was entered from Romford, and finished sixth. A year later he was runner-up to Harold Hilton at Hoylake: his putting – still his weakness – let him down in a final round of 79 to the winner's 75. He finally achieved his first Major success in 1901, at Muirfield, when he became the British Open champion.

Championship Golf

His next Open victory was recorded at St. Andrews in 1905. He won by five strokes, in spite of trouble in the final round. He was twice on the railway, at the 15th and 16th holes; on the second occasion, he found his ball right up against the rail, but he still managed to get out in two shots, and recorded a 6, which was far from disastrous. Characteristically, he remained quite calm and deliberate, even in such high-pressure situations.

Elder statesman (above)
As one of the founders of the British PGA, Braid did much to promote the stature of the professional golfer and to advance the reputation of the game.

Braid defended his title successfully the following year at Muirfield, won again at Prestwick in 1908, and yet again at St. Andrews in 1910. By then, he had moved to Walton Heath, the club with which he would be connected for the rest of his life. It was typical of his unassuming nature that, although he was an honorary member at Walton Heath for 25 years, he always entered the clubhouse by the back door.

Putting to victory
Putting was originally a weak point in Braid's game. His breakthrough came when he changed his cleek for a putter; success soon followed in the British Open of 1901.

Braid played for Britain against the United States in 1921, and appeared eight times in the professional Scotland vs. England internationals during the period up to the First World War. A true ambassador for professional golf, he was a founding member of the PGA and later became its president, a position in which he was renowned for his wisdom and patient advocacy of moderation.

Braid's Legacy

Braid was consulted for many years about the design and layout of golf courses and he made a notable contribution; many are the courses that bear his mark. At a time when professional course design was in its infancy, he brought to the task his immense experience and much thought. Perhaps his best-known creation is the King's Course at Gleneagles, where he imaginatively used a lovely setting.

To the end of his life he remained an enthusiast for the game and there were few days on which he did not play. Respected as one of the greatest of golfers and the finest of men, he died in 1950.

James Braid

Won British Open 1901, 1905, 1906, 1908, 1910; Matchplay Tournament 1903, 1905, 1907, 1911. Great Britain vs. U.S.A. 1921. Scotland vs. England eight times 1903–12.

Eternal enthusiast
In his later years Braid could still be guaranteed to return a score less than his age. He approached each game with the same keenness he had shown as a young man, never playing carelessly.

JACK BURKE, JR.

BORN FORT WORTH, TEXAS, U.S.A., JANUARY 29, 1923

JACK BURKE HAD every encouragement to become a fine professional player. His father was a golf professional who had only just failed to win the U.S. Open in 1920, finishing one stroke behind the winner, Ted Ray. Young Jack became a professional in 1940 when he was 17, but he did not start to win tournaments until 1950. Between then and 1963, he had 15 wins on the U.S. circuit.

Burke was runner-up in the U.S. Masters of 1952, but he had to wait until 1956 to win a Major – and then he won two, in what was by far his most successful year.

In the U.S. Masters, Burke played extremely steadily in difficult conditions and came from the pack to win by one stroke from Ken Venturi, who had had an eight-stroke lead over him before the final round. Later in the year, Burke captured the USPGA Championship at Boston, in its penultimate year as a matchplay tournament. He came from behind in both the semifinal round and the final, eventually defeating Ted Kroll through a display of superior putting.

In the eight games he played in the Ryder Cup between 1951 and 1957, Burke lost only once. He is now the professional at a course that he owns in Texas.

Golf promotion
Burke was one of several players paid by the MacGregor company to advertise their clubs and balls.

JACK BURKE, JR.

WON U.S. MASTERS 1956; USPGA 1956. RYDER CUP 1951–59 (CAPTAIN 1957, NON-PLAYING CAPTAIN 1973).

SIR GUY CAMPBELL

BORN LONDON, ENGLAND, JANUARY 31, 1885; DIED 1960

BOTH A PROFICIENT amateur golfer and a respected journalist, Major Sir Guy Campbell is also remembered for his provocative golf-course designs. With J.S.F. Morrison, he restored the Prince's course at Sandwich after the Second World War.

Sir Guy's playing career was at its peak in the Edwardian era. In 1907 he reached the semi-finals of the British Amateur Championship, where he lost to the eventual winner, John Ball. He played three times for Scotland vs. England between 1909 and 1911.

In 1920 he joined the staff of *The Times* and for many years was a prolific contributor, often assisting Bernard Darwin. Sir Guy Campbell was never afraid to say what he thought, and his dry humor often tempered straightforward and sharp comment. He was a noted authority on the history of golf, his great-grandfather being Robert Chambers, an early writer about the game, from whom Sir Guy must have inherited something in the quality of his writing. His favorite course always remained the Old course at St. Andrews, where he had a hole-in-one at the 8th in 1918, during a game against the 1904 British Open champion, Jack White.

St. Andrews favorite
Sir Guy was a familiar figure at St. Andrews, where his name is kept alive by an annual foursomes trophy that he presented in 1910.

MAJOR SIR GUY COLIN CAMPBELL, 4TH BARONET

SCOTLAND VS. ENGLAND 1909–11.

JoAnne Carner

Born Kirkland, Washington, U.S.A., April 4, 1939

JOANNE CARNER HAD a glittering 14-year career as an amateur, and since 1970 has had an equally fine career as a professional. She was only 15 years old when, as JoAnne Gunderson, she took the U.S. Junior title, and 18 when she first won the U.S. Women's Amateur Championship. She won this title four more times before finally turning professional.

As a professional, Carner won a total of 42 tournament wins between 1970 and 1990. She has twice been U.S. Women's Open Champion and five times holder of the Vare Trophy, awarded for the lowest scoring average in the year's LPGA Tour.

Sam Snead, in 1984, assessed Carner as the best woman player he had ever seen, although it has been her power and her scoring ability, rather than her swing, that have impressed Snead most. An athlete with a special interest in physical training,

JoAnne and Nancy (above)
Two of the greatest American women golfers of modern times, Nancy Lopez (left) and JoAnne Carner, are joined in friendly rivalry.

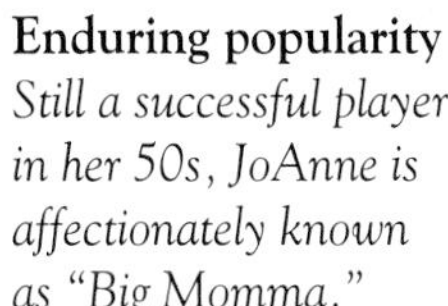

Enduring popularity
Still a successful player in her 50s, JoAnne is affectionately known as "Big Momma."

Hard graft (above)
Power play has always been Carner's natural game, but putting is relatively hard work.

JoAnne is a hitter rather than a swinger, a sturdy woman known affectionately throughout the Tour as "Big Momma." Never very keen on practicing, she believes in keeping it simple. "Turn around to the right on the backswing," she says, "then let the legs swing the club through powerfully along the right line up to a full finish. It's as simple as that."

Elusive Third Open

In 1987, at the age of 48, Carner came within a play-off of winning her third U.S. Women's Open. She was eventually beaten by Britain's Laura Davies, another power player, but much younger.

JoAnne Carner's record is a quite remarkable one. Her winnings up to 1990 totalled $2,299,699. Entering her fifties, she is still an impressive golfer and a force to be reckoned with on the LPGA Tour.

JoAnne Gunderson Carner

Won U.S. Women's Amateur 1957, 1960, 1962, 1966, 1968; U.S. Women's Open 1971, 1976. Curtis Cup 1958–64. Vare Trophy 1974, 1975, 1981, 1982, 1983. LPGA Hall of Fame 1982. World Golf Hall of Fame 1985.

JOE CARR

BORN DUBLIN, IRELAND, FEBRUARY 18, 1922

SWASHBUCKLING JOE CARR was how the popular newspapers described the Dublin amateur in the 1950s when he was, without doubt, a world-class force in golf. The exciting manner in which he won every Irish title again and again captured the public's heart and imagination.

Walker fixture
Joe Carr is here on his way to win the 1959 Berkshire Trophy, one of the official Walker Cup trials. He played in the Walker Cup ten times, but sadly, most of his performances were unimpressive.

Carr's victories in the East and West of Ireland Amateur Open Championships spanned the years from 1941 to 1969. He represented his country in every possible golf event, including the World Cup, usually reserved for professionals. At one time he held the course record at 12 clubs.

Despite his obvious qualities, Carr's record in Walker Cup matches was not impressive. Out of 20 matches played, Carr won just five. So it gave him great pleasure when his son Roddy won three out of four matches in the 1971 Walker Cup, with one match halved, and thus helped defeat the United States.

Carr was awarded the Hagen Trophy in 1967 for his contribution to Anglo–American goodwill. Six years earlier he had won the Bob Jones Award for sportsmanship given by the USGA.

So popular was he during his playing career that, two decades later, he was still an honorary member of most golf clubs in Ireland, as well as several elsewhere in the world. Joe was also an excellent storyteller and an entertainer at the 19th hole.

JOSEPH BENEDICT CARR

WON IRISH OPEN AMATEUR 1946, 1950, 1954, 1956; BRITISH AMATEUR 1953, 1958, 1960; IRISH AMATEUR 1954, 1957, 1963, 1964, 1965, 1967. WALKER CUP 1947–63, 1967 (NON-PLAYING CAPTAIN 1965, CAPTAIN 1967). BOB JONES AWARD 1961.

BILLY CASPER

BORN SAN DIEGO, CALIFORNIA, U.S.A., JUNE 24, 1931

DURING THE FINAL round of the 1966 U.S. Open at the Olympic Club in San Francisco, Billy Casper stood seven strokes behind the great Arnold Palmer with nine holes to play. Then, in one of the most remarkable comebacks in the history of golf, Casper made up the difference to tie. He went on to beat Palmer in the play-off the following day by four strokes, 69 to 73. It was the highest point of a most distinguished golfing career.

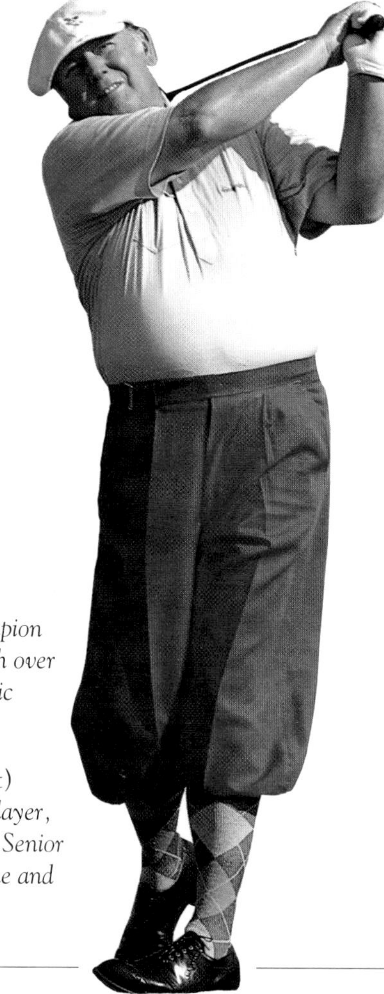

Billy Casper won two other Majors: he had become U.S. Open Champion for the first time at Winged Foot in 1959, and in 1970 he won the U.S. Masters at Augusta after a play-off with Gene Littler.

Casper is a giant of American golf in physique as well as in performance. His golfing record is outstanding, but he has also been plagued by weight problems, particularly in the latter part of his career.

WILLIAM EARL CASPER, JR.

WON U.S. OPEN 1959, 1966; U.S. MASTERS 1970; USGA SENIOR OPEN 1983. WINNER OF 51 U.S. TOUR EVENTS 1956–75. RYDER CUP 1961–75 (NON-PLAYING CAPTAIN 1979). VARDON TROPHY 1960, 1963, 1965, 1966, 1968. USPGA PLAYER OF THE YEAR 1966, 1970. WORLD GOLF HALL OF FAME 1978. USPGA HALL OF FAME 1982.

Olympic victory (above)
The 1966 U.S. Open Champion savors his memorable triumph over Arnold Palmer at the Olympic Club in San Francisco.

Eye-catching outfits (right)
Still an extremely powerful player, Billy Casper graces the U.S. Senior Tour with his marvelous game and outrageous plus-fours.

Bob Charles

Born Carterton, New Zealand, March 14, 1936

BOB CHARLES IS *the only left-handed golfer and the only New Zealander ever to have won the British Open – or indeed any one of the four Majors – and he is recognized as the finest left-hander ever to have played the game. He is also possibly the finest putter the world has ever seen. As well as winning the British Open at Royal Lytham and St. Annes in 1963, Charles was twice runner-up in that championship.*

Playing on (below)
Aged 52, Bob Charles contests the Seniors British Open in 1988.

Master of the art (above)
Possibly the finest putter the world has ever seen, left-hander Bob Charles demonstrates his great skill to spellbound spectators on the 5th green at Royal Lytham and St. Annes during the 1963 British Open, which he won.

Spectators talked about the last-green hijinks in the final round of the 1963 British Open for weeks. Was it shocking behavior or show-business fun? Little-known Phil Rodgers, from San Diego, California, was level with Bob Charles at the head of the field. The American knocked in his putt, pulled off his cap and covered the hole and ball in a comical music-hall mime of relief. Waiting, with a short putt to tie, was an unamused Bob Charles. Would this elaborate charade upset him? It did not, and his own putt went in to force a play-off.

The way in which Bob Charles putted on that occasion meant that there was never much doubt that he would win – and he did. The tall New Zealander from the North Island went on to a magnificent tournament-winning career.

Best Left-hander

Although he won the New Zealand Open as an amateur in 1954, Charles did not turn professional until 1960. He then won the New Zealand Open three more times as a professional, as well as many other New Zealand tournaments. His other successes included the 1962 and 1974 Swiss Opens, the 1968 Canadian Open, the World Matchplay in 1969, the 1972 British Masters and four U.S. tournaments. At the age of 40, Charles was thinking of retiring to his farm in New Zealand, but found he was winning too much money on the U.S. Senior Tour to retire.

With the help of modern equipment, in his fifties he hits the ball farther than he managed when younger and just as straight. There was a short spell when his magnificent touch with the putter deserted him, but wearing glasses has put him back in form.

In 1986, his first year on the Senior Tour, Charles won $570,000. He found himself playing more events for much more money than he had as a young man.

Robert J. Charles

Won New Zealand Open 1954, 1966, 1970, 1973; New Zealand Professional 1961, 1979, 1980; British Open 1963; World Matchplay 1969; British Masters 1972; Seniors British Open 1989. World Cup 1962–68, 1971–72.

Glenna Collett, see Glenna Collett Vare, page 306

HENRY COTTON

BORN HOLMES CHAPEL, ENGLAND, JANUARY 26, 1907; DIED 1987

WHEN HENRY COTTON was only 11 years old he autographed a photo of himself; he was a schoolboy playing at being a champion. It was only a youthful daydream, of course, but Henry Cotton went on to become that champion of his dreams, one of the greatest players of any era. His record of three British Open victories remains the best of any British player since the Great Triumvirate at the turn of the century.

Delicate touch (right)
Henry Cotton believed that the hands were the key to the correct execution of golf shots.

Early talent (above)
As a 20-year-old, Cotton competed in the 1927 British Open at St. Andrews, finishing ninth.

Thomas Henry Cotton was born in 1907, the son of a prosperous iron caster. His father sent him to Alleyn's private school, giving him a far more privileged start in life than that enjoyed by most other professional golfers of his day, who came from lowly backgrounds.

At school Henry was a better cricketer than golfer, but his headmaster banned him from cricket after he refused a caning. Asked what he would do when the rest of the boys were playing cricket, Cotton replied, "I'll play golf, sir." And that is what he did. Precociously talented, Cotton turned professional at the age of 16. In 1927, when he was still only 20, he finished ninth in the British Open at St. Andrews, won that year by Bobby Jones.

HEADING WESTWARD

Cotton was so impressed by the young American that he decided to cross the Atlantic "to find out what made them tick." He finished third in his first event on American soil and was well on his way to stardom. He had an obsessive drive for perfection and practiced for long and aching hours. It paid off in the British Open at Sandwich in 1934. Cotton led the field by ten strokes after three rounds, including a 65 that was to remain an Open record for the next 43 years. Despite a last round of 79, he finally ended the American supremacy in the event with a five-stroke victory.

Three years later, in the Open at Carnoustie, he was opposed by the full strength of the visiting American Ryder

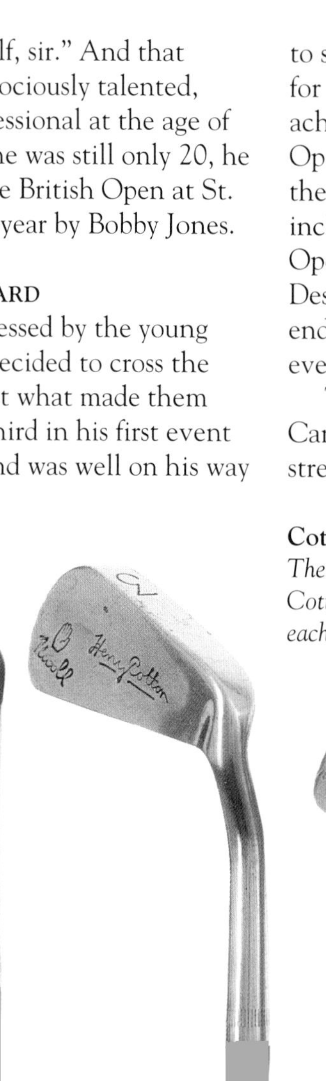

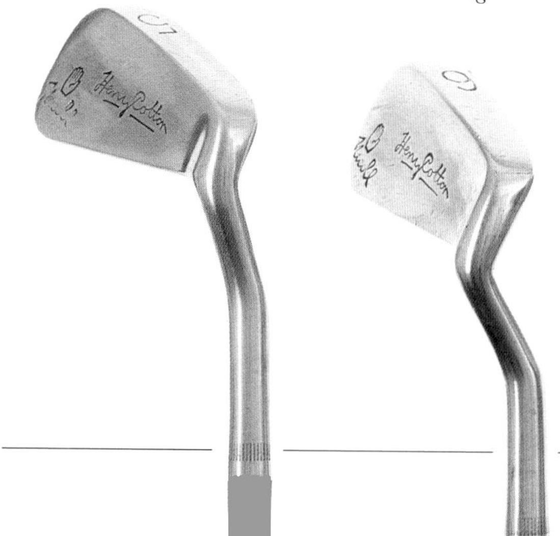

Cotton as innovator (below)
These 1939 "anti-shank" irons were designed by Cotton. A crank in the shaft leaves the face of each iron free of the bulbous joint between shaft and head that caused "shanking."

Cup team. It was during this championship that Cotton played what is still considered one of the greatest rounds ever in the competition, a 71 in torrential rain on a waterlogged course, to take the title.

Golfing Variety

The war years undoubtedly robbed Cotton of more honors, but he won the British Open for a third time in 1948, setting a record for the Muirfield course of 66. He was a member of four Ryder Cup teams, twice as captain. He wrote a weekly newspaper column on golf for more than 30 years and was the author of many excellent books on the game he did so much to popularize. Indeed, he became so popular that he even topped the bill in a variety show with a golf act.

At the end of his career he became involved in golf-course architecture; his designs included the famous Penina course in Portugal. He was knighted – very belatedly – in 1987, but died before the honor could be officially conferred.

Outstanding as his playing record was, Cotton will be remembered equally for his contribution to improving the standing of the golf professional. He took the pro out of the caddie shed and made him respectable. Cotton handed on to others his own vision of golf as a "noble occupation."

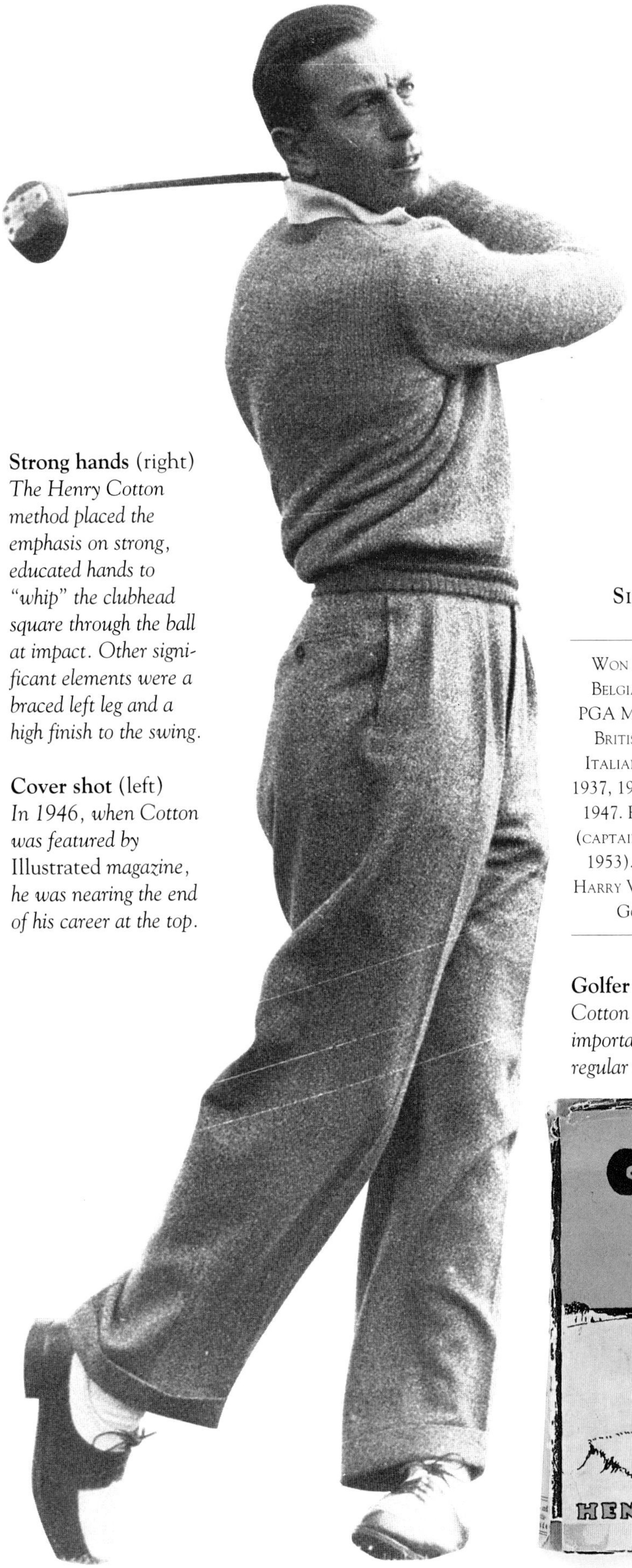

Strong hands (right)
The Henry Cotton method placed the emphasis on strong, educated hands to "whip" the clubhead square through the ball at impact. Other significant elements were a braced left leg and a high finish to the swing.

Cover shot (left)
In 1946, when Cotton was featured by Illustrated *magazine, he was nearing the end of his career at the top.*

The Dunlop 65
In 1934 Henry Cotton played a record round of 65 during his British Open victory at Sandwich. To mark this outstanding feat, Dunlop named their rubber-core ball the 65.

Sir Thomas Henry Cotton

Won Mar Del Plata Open 1930; Belgian Open 1930, 1934, 1938; PGA Matchplay 1932, 1940, 1946; British Open 1934, 1937, 1948; Italian Open 1936; German Open 1937, 1938, 1939; French Open 1946, 1947. Ryder Cup 1929, 1937, 1947 (captain 1947, non-playing captain 1953). Captain PGA 1934, 1948. Harry Vardon Trophy 1938. World Golf Hall of Fame 1980.

Golfer and author
Cotton was the author of several important golf books and wrote a regular newspaper column.

Ben Crenshaw

Born Austin, Texas, U.S.A., January 11, 1952

There is probably no player in the modern professional game who is more loved and admired by his fans and fellow players than Ben Crenshaw. Certainly, there is no other American golfer with a comparable respect for the great legends and traditions of the game. At his home in Austin, Texas, Crenshaw has a fine collection of antique clubs, golf books and memorabilia that he has lovingly acquired over the course of an impressive career.

Even before turning professional in 1973, Ben Crenshaw had proved himself an exceptionally talented golfer. He was the leading amateur in the U.S. Open at the age of 18 and winner of the Fred Haskins Trophy three years in a row as the outstanding college player.

He made his mark on the professional game with startling rapidity. His first entry brought him victory in the 1973 San Antonio Texas Open, and this win was immediately followed by a second place in the eight-round World Open. Inevitably, he was soon being tagged as the natural successor to Jack Nicklaus.

The Nearly Man

In 1975 Crenshaw came in third in the U.S. Open, hitting an iron shot into the water when he seemed set to qualify for the play-off, and the following year he was second on the U.S. money list. But he did not go on to realize the full extent of his undoubted potential. He was acclaimed as among the best putters in the history of golf, but his tee shots could be wayward. Over the years he gained an unwelcome reputation as the "nearly man."

Crenshaw finished runner-up twice in the British Open, in 1978 and 1979, twice in the U.S. Masters, in 1976 and 1983, and once in the USPGA Championship, at Oakland Hills in 1979, when he lost a sudden-death play-off to David Graham.

For America
Ben Crenshaw represented the United States in the Ryder Cup three times in the course of the 1980s.

Loose swing (above)
Ben Crenshaw has always been a great putter, but his tee shots have often had a certain tendency to waywardness.

He finally got his name on a Major title in 1984, winning the U.S. Masters in a dramatic finish at Augusta. Going into the last round, he trailed fellow Texan Tom Kite by two strokes. Kite faded, however, and Crenshaw's final-round 68 gave him a two-stroke victory over Tom Watson.

The euphoria of 1984 was followed by a slump. It was discovered that "Gentle Ben," as he is known on the Tour, had an overactive thyroid. Fortunately, he was soon returned to full health. In 1989 he came close to winning the Masters again; he had a chance for a play-off with Nick Faldo and Scott Hoch, but missed a makable putt on the last green.

Crenshaw once said: "I do not think I could go on living unless I felt that one day I might win the Open Championship at St. Andrews." This obsession shows his sense of the history of the game. He once recalled playing the last round of the 1978 Open at the "home of golf" in mystical terms. "Suddenly I felt I was walking not on the fairway at all but slightly above it,"

Crenshaw said, "and I was walking with the ghosts of the great players of the past who had trodden these famous links. I wondered how Old Tom Morris would have played the stroke I faced. It was the most eerie sensation."

In two consecutive years, 1978 and 1979, Crenshaw narrowly failed to win the British Open. If his highest ambition is ever fulfilled, and he wins the Open at St. Andrews, there will never have been a more popular victory.

Gentle Ben
Crenshaw may lack the killer instinct in the final round of an event, but his good nature and love of the game have won him many admirers.

BEN DANIEL CRENSHAW

WON IRISH OPEN 1976; MEXICAN OPEN 1982; U.S. MASTERS 1984. WINNER OF 15 U.S. TOUR EVENTS 1973–90. EISENHOWER TROPHY 1972. WORLD CUP 1972, 1987–88 (INDIVIDUAL WINNER 1988). RYDER CUP 1981–83, 1987. ROOKIE OF THE YEAR 1974. BYRON NELSON AWARD 1976. BOB JONES AWARD 1991.

BERNARD DARWIN

BORN DOWNE, ENGLAND, SEPTEMBER 7, 1876; DIED 1961

REMEMBERED AS THE best writer the golf world has ever produced, Bernard Darwin was also a fine amateur golfer. A grandson of the naturalist Charles Darwin, he played golf for Cambridge University and appeared in eight England vs. Scotland matches. He also, by accident, became Britain's first Walker Cup captain.

Foursome victory
Bernard Darwin (center) and Joyce Wethered receive congratulations and the trophy after winning the Worplesdon Mixed Foursomes in 1933.

Bernard Darwin turned to golf writing in 1908 and joined *The Times* in 1919. When the first Walker Cup match was played in the United States in 1922, Darwin naturally accompanied the Great Britain and Ireland team to cover the event for his newspaper.

After the British captain, Robert Harris, fell ill, Darwin was asked to fill in as playing captain, a task he fulfilled with great aplomb. He even beat the U.S. captain, Bill Fownes, in the singles.

As a golf writer, Darwin was greatly respected by professional golfers. The great J.H. Taylor wrote: "I want nothing more than to be remembered by posterity in the words of Bernard Darwin."

BERNARD RICHARD DARWIN, CBE

CAPTAIN CAMBRIDGE UNIVERSITY 1897. WALKER CUP 1922. CAPTAIN R & A GOLF CLUB 1934.

LAURA DAVIES

BORN COVENTRY, ENGLAND, OCTOBER 5, 1963

Driving to the top
At 5 ft. 10 in. (1.78m) and strongly built, Laura Davies hits the ball farther than most male golfers.

EARLY IN 1987, Laura Davies was invited to play in one of the early season tournaments on the U.S. Women's Tour. The American authorities refused to allow her to play, saying that European women golfers had not yet made sufficient impact in the United States. Later that year, Laura made them eat their words; in a three-way play-off, she won the U.S. Women's Open.

In 1984, at the age of 20, Laura Davies was selected for the British Curtis Cup team. The following year she turned professional, borrowing £1,000 from her mother to help her do so. After a few months she was able to pay all the money back. Later in her rookie year she won the Hennessy Cognac Ladies' Cup in France, and at the end of the year found herself at the top of the WPGA Order of Merit.

In 1986 Davies headed the money list again, winning the Women's British Open. As British Open Champion, she ventured to the United States, finishing eleventh in the U.S. Women's Open. The following year, she came back to win.

Double champion (below)
Davies shows off her trophies: the candlesticks from the British Open, the cup from the U.S. Open.

Not a winner this time
Laura Davies agonizes over a missed putt during her failed bid for the 1989 U.S. Women's Open.

In 1988 Laura won twice in the United States and three times in Europe, but by 1990 her performances had deteriorated alarmingly. As with many natural golfers – she never had a formal lesson – when things went wrong, she had no easy way of analyzing her problem.

LAURA J. DAVIES

WON WOMEN'S BRITISH OPEN 1986; U.S. WOMEN'S OPEN 1987. CURTIS CUP 1984. SOLHEIM CUP 1990.

ROBERTO DE VICENZO, see page 303

Bruce Devlin

Born Armidale, New South Wales, Australia, October 10, 1937

When golf first started to take him seriously, Bruce Devlin was a 20-year-old Australian plumber. But his smooth, well-rounded swing was just too good to let him stay long in the amateur ranks. In 1959 he won the Australian Amateur Championship and the following year, while still an amateur, the Australian Open.

On the right line
Bruce Devlin's decision to leave Australia for the big time in the United States was one he never regretted.

In 1961 Bruce turned professional and in 1962 he decided to try his luck on the American Tour. He was not immediately successful, although in 1963 he won tournaments elsewhere, notably the French and New Zealand Opens. But in 1964 he won the St. Petersburg Open and in 1966 the Colonial Invitation: his American career was well under way.

In 1966 he also triumphed in the Carling World Tournament at Royal Birkdale. In 1970, with David Graham, he carried off the World Cup for Australia.

As his earnings in the United States continued to increase, Devlin decided to settle in Texas for good. He won several more tournaments and in 1982 led the U.S. Open for the first two rounds, eventually losing to Tom Watson by six strokes. But his main interest had now turned to golf-course architecture.

In 1987 Devlin joined the U.S. Senior Tour for most of the season, and by the end of 1989 had banked another $278,000 to add to the million he had earned already. He is ranked very highly by all those who know him personally or have ever seen him on the course.

Bruce William Devlin

Won Australian Open 1960; French Open 1963. Eisenhower Trophy 1958. World Cup 1970.

Flory Van Donck

Born Tervueren, Belgium, June 23, 1912

Until the arrival on the scene of Seve Ballesteros, most followers rated the Belgian Flory Van Donck as the most impressive golfer the European mainland had ever produced. He reached his peak around 1956, when he was runner-up in the British Open at Hoylake, just three strokes behind the winner, Peter Thomson.

Ever-present
Van Donck tees off in Tokyo in the 1966 Canada Cup, where he was representing his country for the thirteenth successive year.

Flory Van Donck won five Belgian and Dutch Opens, as well as the Open championships of Italy (four times), France (three times), Switzerland (twice), Germany (twice), Portugal, Uruguay and Venezuela. He was also runner-up, behind Gary Player, in the 1959 British Open played at Muirfield.

Based at the Royal Waterloo Golf Club, Van Donck shot a course record there of 61. Spectators were always enthralled by his magnificent swing and his regal demeanor. This tall, elegant Belgian strode the fairways of the world like the champion golfer he was.

Flory Van Donck

Won Dutch Open 1936, 1937, 1946, 1951, 1953; Belgian Open 1939, 1946, 1947, 1953, 1956; French Open 1954, 1957, 1958. World Cup 1954–70, 1972, 1979. Harry Vardon Trophy 1953.

GEORGE DUNCAN

BORN METHLICK, SCOTLAND, SEPTEMBER 16, 1883; DIED 1964

GEORGE DUNCAN HAD a lovely natural swing and was always good to watch. He was a very fast player with all his strokes, including putts, and walked quickly too. He would have found the dawdling pace of the modern game very tiresome. As a golfer he commanded great respect from his fellow professionals, and whenever he played he was followed by an admiring crowd.

Hasty player
George Duncan's style matched the title of his book: Golf at a Gallop.

Duncan was born in 1883, son of the village policeman at Methlick, Aberdeen. He first played in the British Open in 1906 at Muirfield, finishing in eighth place, and he was in the top ten six times before the First World War.

The war interrupted his career, but in 1920, at Deal, he at last became British Open champion. He started with two disastrous rounds of 80, and was well behind the leader. But a 71 in the morning and a 72 in the afternoon insured him the title.

It was a source of amazement to his fellows that this was his only British Open victory, though he was runner-up in 1922 at St. George's, very nearly tying with Walter Hagen. After a magnificent final round of 69, Duncan needed to sink a putt on the last hole, but it just failed to drop. Duncan also won the PGA Matchplay Championship in 1913, and twice lost in the final of that tournament.

INTERNATIONAL SUCCESSES

Duncan played against the United States in 1921 and 1926, and in the first three Ryder Cup matches, captaining the side in 1929. He won all his singles matches in these international encounters, beating Walter Hagen twice – the second time, in 1929, by a resounding 10-and-8. Although he was quick, Duncan was never careless. He was noted for his accurate wood shots played, of course, at great speed. He was always a mercurial player, but when he was in the mood, anything was possible.

Duncan was good at diagnosing faults in others, and helped many of the top players to correct errors in their game.

GEORGE DUNCAN

WON BELGIAN OPEN 1912; PGA MATCHPLAY 1913; FRENCH OPEN 1913, 1927; BRITISH OPEN 1920; IRISH OPEN 1927. REPRESENTED G.B. VS. U.S. 1921, 1926. RYDER CUP 1927–31 (CAPTAIN 1929).

Open action (left)
George Duncan playing on the 8th green at Troon during the British Open of 1923.

High temper (right)
Duncan's impatient personality was caricatured in the "Men of the Moment in Sport" cigarette-card series of 1928.

WILLIE DUNN, JR.

BORN MUSSELBURGH, SCOTLAND, 1865; DIED 1952

WILLIE DUNN, JR. came from a famous Musselburgh golfing family. His father and uncle had played in the famous match against Allan Robertson and Tom Morris in 1849 (see page 291). "Young Willie" had pronounced views on how to play, and many of his ideas, rejected in Britain at the time, have since gained approval. He was undoubtedly well ahead of his time; as early as the turn of the century, for instance, he experimented with steel shafts and a sort of wooden tee-peg, instead of the pinch of sand that was then standard practice. He was also an innovative course designer towards the end of the nineteenth century.

Golf in the family
Willie Dunn, Jr. was born into a famous golfing family. This golfing tableau from around 1854 shows his father Willie Dunn, Sr. teeing off, while also in the foreground stand (left to right) Allan Robertson and Old Tom Morris.

Born at Musselburgh in 1865, Willie Dunn trained as a golf professional and greenskeeper. His brother Tom, 16 years his elder, was already an established pro and course designer. Willie gained much experience from him.

Willie Dunn played in the British Open from 1882 to 1886 without any great success, his best placing being ninth at Musselburgh in 1883. He later moved to Biarritz in the southwest of France as a professional and helped his brother to lay out the new course there.

After completing his work in France, Willie Dunn was persuaded to go to the United States. He crossed the Atlantic in March, 1891. Within three months of arriving in the New World, with very limited equipment and using Indians from a nearby reservation for labor, he had built a 12-hole course at Shinnecock Hills on New York's Long Island.

INNOVATIVE DESIGN

Later extended to 18 holes, Shinnecock was the first seaside course to be created in North America. It also set a trend as the first incorporated club in the United States, and it had the first American clubhouse. "Young Willie" – as he was known to distinguish him from his father – was soon much in demand for advice and practical help. He is rightly considered the first golf-course designer of the new school and had a significant effect on the future of golf.

In 1894 Dunn won the first U.S. Open – then an unofficial matchplay event – at the St. Andrew's Club in Yonkers, New York, defeating his fellow Scot, Willie Campbell, by two holes in the final.

The following year, when the U.S. Open had the official blessing of the USGA and adopted the strokeplay formula, Dunn finished as runner-up to Horace Rawlins, failing to win the championship by just two strokes.

Dunn stayed on the east coast of the United States until 1910 as professional and greenskeeper at several clubs, before moving west to Ohio and then by stages across the continent until he at last reached California.

Dunn's fortunes varied, and there were times when he was far from well-off, but the rise in the popularity of golf in the United States over this period insured he would be a well-known and respected figure in the country for many years.

His two nephews, Seymour Dunn and John Duncan Dunn, both became golf-course designers and teachers. Willie Dunn returned to Britain in 1940 and lived there until his death in 1952.

Studio portrait
Dunn's bold spirit and keen mind are clearly visible in this studio photograph.

WILLIAM DUNN, JR.

WON UNOFFICIAL U.S. OPEN 1894. NOTED GOLF-COURSE DESIGNER AND INSTRUCTOR.

NICK FALDO

BORN WELWYN GARDEN CITY, ENGLAND, JULY 18, 1957

ON A DULL, misty Sunday afternoon at Muirfield in 1987, Nick Faldo produced 18 consecutive pars in the final round of the British Open to beat American Paul Azinger in a nail-biting finish and prove himself among the great players of the modern game. That Muirfield victory came at the end of a long road for Faldo, who, after a spectacular start to his career, had lost his way and long failed to break through into the big time as so many had expected.

Watchful guru (above)
Coach David Leadbetter looks on as Faldo practices for the 1989 British Open at Troon.

Faldo took up golf in 1972, when he was 14, inspired by seeing Jack Nicklaus playing in the U.S. Masters on a new color television his parents had just bought. He was transfixed by the marvelous backdrop of the Augusta course and by watching the man he now considers to be "the greatest golfer in the history of the game." A mere three years later, after learning the game from professional Ian Connelly at Welwyn Garden City Golf Club, Nick Faldo became the youngest player ever to win the English Amateur Championship.

He turned professional in 1976, already possessing one of the most fluent and elegant golf swings in the game. He was also an extremely gifted putter from the very beginning. Tony Jacklin has expressed the view that Faldo is the best putter that the British game has ever produced.

Precocious talent (above)
As soon as he took up golf at the age of 14, Faldo showed exceptional talent. He won the English Amateur shortly after his 18th birthday.

RYDER SUCCESSES

In 1977 Faldo won his first professional victory and became the youngest player up to then ever to play in the Ryder Cup. Partnered by Peter Oosterhuis, he won his foursomes and fourball matches, including among his victims Ray Floyd and the man he had watched on television five years earlier, Jack Nicklaus. But Faldo saved his really

Delicate touch (left)
Faldo shows great assurance in his short putts. His ability on the greens made a vital contribution to his 1989 U.S. Masters win.

Mixed fortunes
Faldo has been a major factor in European Ryder Cup successes, although his record is uneven; in 1985 he even dropped himself from the team.

big moment for last, beating Tom Watson in the singles only a few weeks after Watson had won the 1977 British Open at Turnberry.

Faldo continued to dominate in Europe; in 1983 he won five tournaments and headed the money list. The following year he won in the United States for the first time at the Sea Pines Heritage Classic. But his level of success was not as great as he might have expected, and he began to feel that his swing was not consistent enough to take him to the very top.

Hard Times

After meeting David Leadbetter, an English-born coach working in the United States, Faldo decided to remodel his swing. It took two hard years to make the change, and there were times when, as Faldo admits, he was very low. In the 1985 Ryder Cup at The Belfry he dropped himself from Tony Jacklin's team when he felt the pressure had become too much. He was, however, convinced that he was doing the right thing.

In 1987 Faldo won the Spanish Open on a very tough Las Brisas course, and then went to Muirfield for the British Open, which he won with that marvelous final round of 18 consecutive pars, proof of the consistency of his new swing. In 1988 he could have been U.S. Open Champion, had his putt gone down on the final green at Brookline; he went on to lose the play-off to Curtis Strange. The following year he went to Augusta and became only the second British player to win the U.S. Masters, beating Scott Hoch in virtual darkness at the second extra hole of a cliff-hanger play-off. Faldo had established himself as almost certainly the best player in the world. Talk turned towards a possible "Grand Slam" victory in all four Majors in 1990.

In April Faldo won the Masters again, defeating veteran Ray Floyd in another play-off, again at the second extra hole. In the U.S. Open at Medinah, however, his putt went astray by a fraction of an inch on the final green, he missed the play-off, and the dream was gone.

But a few weeks later Faldo traveled to St. Andrews and became the British Open champion for the second time, in truly convincing style. His 18 under par aggregate of 270 broke the record for an Open Championship at St. Andrews by six strokes. Although Faldo may not have won the "Grand Slam," the two years he spent remodeling his swing had unquestionably been time well spent.

Nicholas Alexander Faldo, MBE

Won British PGA Championship 1978, 1980, 1981, 1989; French Open 1983, 1988, 1989; Spanish Open 1987; British Open 1987, 1990; U.S. Masters 1989, 1990; World Matchplay 1989. Ryder Cup 1977–89. World Cup 1977. Dunhill Cup 1985–88. Harry Vardon Trophy 1983.

Surrendering to joy (left)
Nick Faldo celebrates after holing the putt that brought him his first U.S. Masters victory in 1989. His dramatic play-off with Scott Hoch took place in near darkness.

Happy and successful (right)
The new British Open champion bathes in the warm glow of success with his family after his fine five-stroke victory at St. Andrews in 1990. His caddie, Fanny Sunneson, is holding the famous claret jug.

MAX FAULKNER

BORN BEXHILL, ENGLAND, JULY 29, 1916

AFTER HE WON the 1951 British Open with a last-hole trick shot at Royal Portrush, Northern Ireland, there was no stopping Max Faulkner. He could have made a fortune – on the stage. Instead he told and retold how he "swerved" his second shot to the green at the last hole, forced to do so following a wild tee shot.

Serious practice
Warming up at Wentworth for the Ryder Cup match of 1953, Faulkner draws a curious gallery, while Sam Snead looks on unconcerned.

Max the entertainer
Faulkner gives a characteristic grimace as he drives off the tee. He never missed a chance to make spectators laugh.

There was no stroke Max could not play, and no gag he was afraid to pull, turning up for big tournaments with weird putters, including one that was made of driftwood, or in garish outfits, such as purple plus-fours. But he could be a serious man too, and on tense days during a British Open he would sometimes slip away for a few hours of quiet fishing.

Max Faulkner won many professional tournaments, including the Spanish Open three times. In 1957, when he played on the winning Ryder Cup team at Lindrick, he was dropped from the singles because the British captain, Dai Rees, thought that he looked too high-strung.

MAX FAULKNER

WON BRITISH OPEN 1951; PGA MATCHPLAY 1953; SPANISH OPEN 1952, 1953, 1957. RYDER CUP 1947–53, 1957.

RAY FLOYD

BORN FORT BRAGG, NORTH CAROLINA, U.S.A., SEPTEMBER 4, 1942

APPROACHING THE AGE of 50, Ray Floyd needed only to win the British Open to join the immortals – Sarazen, Hogan, Nicklaus and Player – who had won all four Majors. And who was to say he would not do it? In 1990, aged 47, he finished the Masters tied for first place with Nick Faldo, only to lose in the play-off.

Floyd won the St. Petersburg Open when he was only 20, but he was better known at the time as the party-going manager of an all-girl rock band called "The Ladybirds." He did have another win two years later, in 1965, but it was not until 1969 that he really came to the fore as a golfer, winning three big tournaments, including the USPGA Championship. His name was made.

Then, suddenly, that name disappeared from the leader boards. For a full six years Floyd could not win again. At last, towards the end of 1975, he did take a tournament. To prove he was back on top, he then won the 1976 U.S. Masters in the most majestic style.

MASTERS TRIUMPH

In the first round he finished with a 65. In the second it was a 66. This 131 for two rounds was a record, as was his three-round total of 201. In the final round, he missed just one makable putt, which would have given him a new record for the tournament. As it was, he equalled Jack Nicklaus's existing Masters record by finishing at 271.

Also in 1976 Ray Floyd was second in the USPGA and fourth in the Open Championship in Britain. In 1978 he was second to Jack Nicklaus in the Open at St. Andrews. Then, in 1979, the wheels seemed to come off again. He failed to qualify for the U.S. Open, was thirty-sixth in the British Open,

Aging gracefully
Something of a playboy in his younger years, Ray Floyd matured into one of the most successful players ever.

seventeenth in the U.S. Masters, and only sixty-second in the USPGA Championship.

It was 1982 before the flamboyant Floyd won a significant tournament again, the USPGA at Southern Hills. He was now 40 years old, but his opening round of 63 was, by his own reckoning, the best golf he had ever played in his life. Next, in 1986, he won the U.S. Open at Shinnecock Hills with a final round of 66.

Then came the 1990 U.S. Masters. After the third round Floyd was in front with a score of 206. But victory was not to be. He shot a last round of 72 and tied with Nick Faldo. On the second hole of the play-off he dumped his ball in the water that fronts the 11th green. It was a sad end to a brilliant career. Or was it the end?

By 1990 Floyd had a state-of-the-art graphite-shafted driver given him by "Jumbo" Ozaki, which he claimed added 40 yards to his tee shots. He might manage one more Major win to cap his career.

Putting power
Floyd's putting was one of the most effective parts of his game in his Masters and USPGA wins.

RAYMOND LORAN FLOYD

WON USPGA 1969, 1982; U.S. MASTERS 1976: U.S. OPEN 1986. WINNER OF 21 U.S. EVENTS 1963–90. RYDER CUP 1969, 1975–77, 1981–85 (NON-PLAYING CAPTAIN 1989). DUNHILL CUP 1985–86. VARDON TROPHY 1983.

Popular winner
Floyd (right) receives the USPGA Trophy in 1982, his second victory in the event.

ED FURGOL

BORN NEW YORK, U.S.A., MARCH 22, 1917

AFTER ED FURGOL'S left arm was badly smashed in a childhood accident, every medical effort was made to repair the damage, but he was never able to straighten the arm again beyond 45 degrees. When the darkly good-looking Furgol decided to take up golf, most people thought he was simply wasting his time.

Yet Furgol created his own very effective swing, disproving the theory that good golf must be played with a straight left arm. He began playing sizzling shots, and in 1945 quit a dull job to turn professional.

Nine years later, in the U.S. Open of 1954, Furgol found himself needing a last-hole par at Baltusrol, New Jersey, to hold off Gene Littler and win the title.

He stood on the tee, a tall figure with a "different" stance to suit his buckled left arm, and let fly. The ball was never going to hit the fairway and ended in trouble. Yet Furgol threaded his second shot out of trouble, scored his par, and collected the trophy. That year the USPGA made him Player of the Year and, to prove it was no fluke, Furgol helped win the 1955 World Cup, taking the individual title as well.

Taking a challenge
Furgol's left arm was permanently bent, a serious disability for a golfer, but he overcame this handicap to win the U.S. Open in 1954.

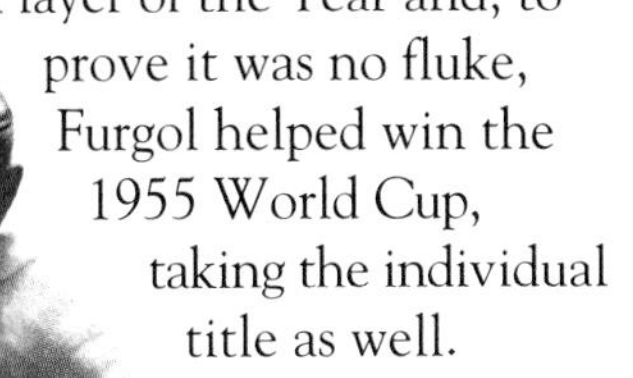

Bent-arm swing (left)
Ordinary golfers loved Ed Furgol because he showed that it was not absolutely necessary to possess a perfect swing in order to become a professional golf champion.

EDWARD FURGOL

WON U.S. OPEN 1954. WINNER OF FOUR U.S. TOUR EVENTS 1954–57. WORLD CUP 1955 (INDIVIDUAL WINNER). RYDER CUP 1957. USPGA PLAYER OF THE YEAR 1954.

DAVID GRAHAM

BORN WINDSOR, NSW, AUSTRALIA, MAY 23, 1946

DAVID GRAHAM STARTED playing with left-handed clubs as a 14-year-old, and only changed to right-handed after three years. After a spell as a club pro in Tasmania, he joined the Tour at home, late in the 1960s, and soon won the Victoria and Tasmania Opens. These victories encouraged him to go further afield, and he has since achieved success the world over, including wins in the 1979 USPGA and the 1981 U.S. Open.

In 1970 David Graham won the World Cup for Australia with Bruce Devlin, and he was twice a member of the winning team in the Dunhill Cup at St. Andrews. Also in Britain, he took the World Matchplay title in 1976, defeating Hale Irwin in the final at the 38th hole.

By 1990, Graham was living in Dallas, Texas, and playing regularly on the U.S. Tour, in which he has recorded a total of five victories besides his Major wins.

Deliberate style
A player of great determination and courage, Graham has a very accurate game; he drops few strokes through lack of care.

Shared euphoria (above)
David Graham celebrates with his wife, Maureen, after his victory in the 1981 U.S. Open at Merion, Pennsylvania. Graham won with a last round of 67, finishing three strokes clear.

ANTHONY DAVID GRAHAM

WON FRENCH OPEN 1970; WORLD MATCHPLAY 1976; AUSTRALIAN OPEN 1977; USPGA CHAMPIONSHIP 1979; U.S. OPEN 1981; LANCÔME TROPHY 1981, 1982. WORLD CUP 1970. DUNHILL CUP 1985–86, 1988.

HUBERT GREEN

BORN BIRMINGHAM, ALABAMA, U.S.A., DECEMBER 18, 1946

ALTHOUGH ALL GOOD golfers swing differently, it has often been said that they are all the same in the impact area. If this were not so, they would not hit the ball where they intend to and in the way they intend. Hubert Green's style is one of the few that makes people doubt the full truth of this law. But perhaps the story of this talented player's career finally shows that orthodox swings last longer.

Green crouches over the ball, his knees very bent. His hands at the address are well ahead of the ball. His backswing is short, his downswing fast. He seems to flick the ball away, but with great power. On the putting green this stance is further exaggerated and he uses a two-handed grip that to purists does not look correct.

Youngest of four in a family of golfers, Green joined the U.S. Tour in 1970. He won the U.S. Open in 1977 and the USPGA Championship in 1985. He also tied for second in the 1978 U.S. Masters, when Gary Player shot a final 64 to snatch the title and Hubert contrived to miss a 3 ft. (1m) putt to tie.

Players' champion
Hubert Green (right), the 1985 USPGA Champion, receives his trophy at Cherry Hills.

HUBERT MYATT GREEN

WON U.S. OPEN 1977; USPGA CHAMPIONSHIP 1985. RYDER CUP 1977–79, 1985. WORLD CUP 1977.

Ralph Guldahl

Born Dallas, Texas, U.S.A., November 22, 1912; Died 1987

Texan Ralph Guldahl was not perhaps the most popular player in the professional game, but he commanded the highest respect. Born in the same year as Sam Snead, Ben Hogan, and Byron Nelson, Guldahl had won the U.S. Open twice in succession before Nelson or Hogan had their names on the trophy; Snead never did.

Unorthodox style
Guldahl was a big man with an awkward swing; his backswing was fast. He rocked back on his heels after impact, but he developed great power and managed to control the cut shot that his swing created.

Ralph Guldahl was not a charismatic figure. He was a very careful player, always ready to take his time. He seemed almost to go into a trance over his putts and would not play until absolutely ready. The result was outstandingly steady and successful golf. Other players of the period made more impact, but Guldahl earned his place in the golfing record books.

Ralph Guldahl

Won Western Open 1936, 1937, 1938; U.S. Open 1937, 1938; U.S. Masters 1939. Ryder Cup 1937. USPGA Hall of Fame 1963. World Golf Hall of Fame 1981.

Walter Hagen, see page 244

Sandy Herd

Born St. Andrews, Scotland, April 24, 1868; Died 1944

Sandy Herd was a real St. Andrews man, born and raised within the sound of well-struck golf balls on the Old course. He stuck to the old-fashioned palm grip of the nineteenth-century Scottish golfer and to the old guttie ball until well into his thirties. He was a formidable match-player, like Walter Hagen later, but without Hagen's relaxed temperament. Herd went for everything. He was always in a hurry to win – often too much of a hurry.

Sandy Herd's name would be better known now had he not been a contemporary of the Great Triumvirate of Vardon, Braid, and Taylor. Although he had several victories over Vardon to his credit, in strokeplay he could rarely beat him or the other two great golfers. Vardon won the British Open six times, Taylor and Braid five times each, but Herd only once. That victory came at Royal Liverpool in 1902, when he beat Vardon and Braid by one stroke, 307 to their 308.

Lining up
Herd focused on the clubface and its intended line and angle at impact.

Dash and Courage

In his youth Herd was known as a "fine fighter," a man of dash, courage, and staying power, but lacking in self-restraint. His impatience seemed to be reflected in his ferocious waggle. But Bernard Darwin wrote: "The number of his waggles is only exceeded by that of his friends. I cannot conceive that Sandy ever had an enemy. If he lives to be 100 he will still be the same fine, sturdy, independent, ever-youthful creature." In fact, he was still playing an occasional tournament approaching 70.

Alexander Herd

Won British Open 1902; Professional Matchplay 1906, 1926.

Walter Hagen

Born Rochester, New York, U.S.A., December 21, 1892; Died 1969

In life, said Walter Hagen, one should always take time "to smell the flowers along the way," and he did. He said he never wanted to be a millionaire, he just wanted to live like one – and he did. He was a showman, a great golfer, and a tremendous matchplayer. He won 11 Major tournaments, including four consecutive USPGA titles from 1924 to 1927, and he completely altered the status of the golf professional in society.

When Francis Ouimet won the U.S. Open from Vardon and Ray in 1913, Walter Hagen, almost unnoticed, was in fourth place. The following year he made his mark, winning the Open at the Midlothian, Chicago, starting with a record round of 68. He won again in 1919, immediately after the First World War.

Keeping up Appearances

Hagen was ambitious to succeed on the other side of the Atlantic, however, although British snobbery did not appeal to him. When he arrived at Deal for the 1920 British Open, he was not allowed into the clubhouse. No professional was.

So Hagen hired a Daimler, a chauffeur, and a footman, parked the Daimler outside the clubhouse front door, and had his footman collect him and his gear each day as he arrived at the 18th. He finished fifty-third, but that did not worry him; he had made his point.

It was this assertive spirit that his friend Gene Sarazen was remembering when he wrote: "All the professionals who have a chance to go after the big money today should say a silent thanks to Walter each time they stretch a check between their fingers. It was Walter who made professional golf what it is."

Looking good
The stylishness of Hagen's golfing outfits, unusual at that period, contributed greatly to his popularity.

Although he won the French Open that year, Hagen returned from Europe flat broke. He borrowed the taxi fare from the docks to the Delmonico Hotel, rented the best suite, ordered a case of Scotch and $500 to be sent up, and relaxed. "A couple of tournaments and he was back in the black," Sarazen reported. Hagen simply refused to allow any worries to disturb his relaxation. In 1921 he returned to challenge for the British Open at St. Andrews, coming in sixth. In 1922 he won at Sandwich. In 1923 he lost by one stroke at Troon to Arthur Havers. In 1924 he won again at Hoylake. He did not cross the Atlantic in 1925, but in 1926 he was third behind Bobby Jones and Al Watrous at Lytham. After another year away, he was British Open champion again both at Sandwich in 1928 and at Muirfield in 1929. It was a truly remarkable record of success.

Humble roots
The poor boy from Rochester grew up to grace cigarette cards – looking every bit the debonair millionaire that he had become.

Serious Showmanship

Hagen was a showman, but he meant business. At Troon in 1923 he had whittled away at Havers's lead and arrived at the 72nd hole needing a birdie to tie. He hit his approach shot into a bunker, looked over the situation, and just failed to sink his bunker shot.

In 1926 at Lytham, needing an eagle to tie with Bobby Jones, he walked up to the green before playing his second, surveyed the green, and then asked the referee if he would kindly have the pin removed. He played a beautiful second that finished only a couple of feet from the hole. Despite his successes in the

Putting it into words
Walter Hagen gave a suitably lively account of his successes – and his failures – in a popular autobiography.

Crowd pleaser (left) *Hagen was one of the most popular sportsmen of the 1920s. In 1924, at Hoylake, the fans look on as the champion receives his wife's congratulations.*

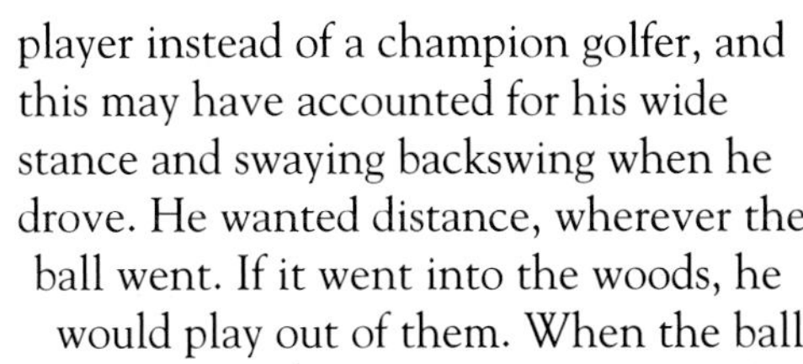

Practice style (right) *Hagen is dressed for a practice round before the 1924 Open at Hoylake. He won the championship.*

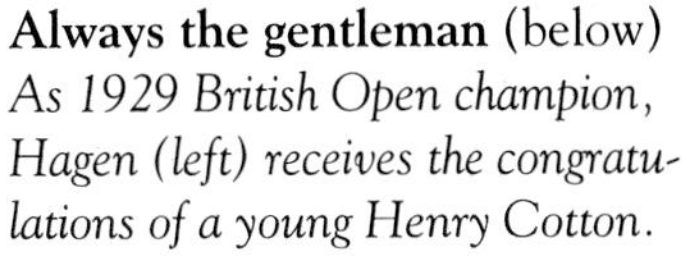

Always the gentleman (below) *As 1929 British Open champion, Hagen (left) receives the congratulations of a young Henry Cotton.*

British and U.S. Opens, however, Hagen's main strength was at matchplay. When the USPGA Championship was a matchplay event, Walter won in 1921, beating Jim Barnes 3-and-2. In the 1923 final at Pelham, he lost to Gene Sarazen at the 38th hole. Then he beat Jim Barnes again in 1924, Bill Mehlhorn in 1925, Leo Diegel in 1926, and Joe Turnesa in 1927.

Relaxed Sportsman

Hagen might have been flamboyant, but he was a true gentleman. In 1928 he was beaten 18-and-17 by Archie Compston in a 72-hole match at Moor Park. His own story of that match shows only admiration for Compston. "His every shot was masterful," he wrote later in his autobiography, *The Walter Hagen Story*. "He gave me the worst beating of my career and I had only one statement to make to the British press: 'When you are laid out good and flat, you must not squawk!'"

Hagen's golf swing reflected his attitude to life: it was totally tension-free. He might have been a first-class baseball player instead of a champion golfer, and this may have accounted for his wide stance and swaying backswing when he drove. He wanted distance, wherever the ball went. If it went into the woods, he would play out of them. When the ball was on the green, he would probably sink the putt. (It was Walter Hagen who showed the legendary Bobby Locke how to putt.) He used an extremely light grip, making a full, free swing with his arms, and he kept his head very still indeed.

Bobby Jones once said that he loved to play golf with Hagen, "He goes along chin-up, smiling away, never grousing about his luck, playing the ball as he finds it." In the 1924 British Open, Hagen started with a 77. "That would have crushed a less gallant spirit," Sarazen commented. It did not crush Hagen. He won.

Walter Charles Hagen

Won U.S. Open 1914, 1919; USPGA 1921, 1924, 1925, 1926, 1927; British Open 1922, 1924, 1928, 1929. Ryder Cup 1927–35 (captain 1927–35, non-playing captain 1937). USPGA Hall of Fame 1940. World Golf Hall of Fame 1974.

HAROLD HILTON, see page 248

Ben Hogan

Born Dublin, Texas, U.S.A., August 13, 1912

The career of Ben Hogan was slow to take off. After turning professional in 1931, he took seven years to record his first win. From 1940 onwards he dominated the U.S. money list, but he still had to wait until after the Second World War to win a Major, the USPGA Championship of 1946 at Portland. By the age of 36, however, Hogan was almost indisputably the best golfer in the world. It was at this high peak of his career that fate struck a cruel blow.

In 1948, a wonderful year for golf in the United States, Hogan won a great trio of titles: the U.S. Open, the USPGA Championship, and the Western Open. His galleries always attracted fellow professionals; they all hoped that some of the Hogan magic might rub off on them.

But on Wednesday, February 2, 1949, as Hogan and his wife Valerie were driving east of Pecos, Texas, they collided with a Greyhound bus in light fog. Hogan was critically injured. News of the accident flashed across America and there were chilling reports from the hospital that the great golfer might not survive his horrific injuries.

But Hogan survived. Very slowly and painfully he learned to walk again. Then he ventured onto a golf course on a motor scooter and built up his shattered body with exercises. By January, 1950, he was on the practice ground at Riviera in Los Angeles, ready to take on such players as Lloyd Mangrum and Jimmy Demaret.

A huge crowd gathered to see whether their sporting idol could make a comeback after such physical damage. When the starter introduced him on the first tee, the gallery roared. Hogan fired a 73; despite the painful walk, he was back.

Champion of Carnoustie (above)
Ben Hogan drives off during his assault on the British Open in 1953.

Smile of success (below)
Hogan poses in atypically relaxed style after his 1953 U.S. Open win.

American hero
One of the greatest golfers of all time, Ben Hogan dominated the American game after the Second World War.

Triumph over Injury

Three weeks later Hogan went to the Greenbrier and won the White Sulphur Springs tournament, scoring a staggering total of 259. By the time he turned up at Merion to contest the U.S. Open that June, the interest of the media and the public had been raised to fever pitch.

Although still clearly feeling the effects of his serious injury, a bandaged Hogan fought his way through two rounds on the final day to force a three-way tie with George Fazio and Lloyd Mangrum.

Comeback award
The Ben Hogan Award, a bronze sculpture of the golfer, is given every year to a golfer who has made a comeback from injury or physical disability.

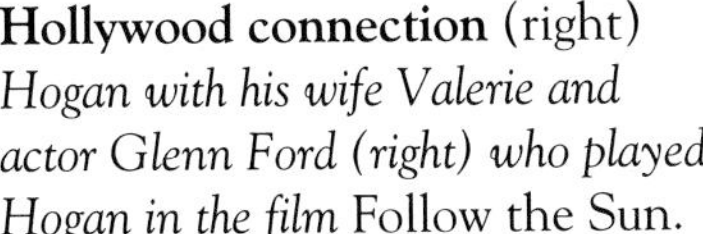

Hollywood connection (right)
Hogan with his wife Valerie and actor Glenn Ford (right) who played Hogan in the film Follow the Sun.

Somehow he found the reserves of strength he needed to score a 69 in the play-off, defeating Mangrum by four strokes and Fazio by six.

Hogan's comeback went on from success to success. In 1951 he won the Masters with a final round of 68, and kept his Open title at Oakland Hills with a last-round 67. Two years later he surpassed every previous performance by winning all three Majors in which he competed – the U.S. Open at Oakmont, the U.S. Masters, and the British Open at Carnoustie in Scotland.

Hogan hated overseas travel and had never played in the British Open. To a visiting American in 1953, Carnoustie was quite a contrast to anything in Texas. The food was different, so Hogan ate lunch in his car. The winds swept in and there was a fast-running stream of water, squirming across the finishing holes. U.S. journalists likened playing at Carnoustie to golf on the moon. But Hogan charted the course for a week and practiced hitting drives to different parts of the fairways to find the smart way into the green. The quality of his performance, once the championship began, brought tears to the eyes of spectators.

Conquering the Heights

Every round Hogan played was lower than the one before – from 73 down to a last-round 68. Despite bumpy fairways and stampeding galleries, he won the title, and returned home to a ticker-tape parade and a chat with President Dwight D. Eisenhower.

Hogan was never to reach such heights again, but he refused to retire. He was still capable of taking tenth place in the U.S. Masters in 1967, at the age of 54.

Hogan's drive for perfection did not make him popular with everyone. But it is no surprise that his life was made into a Hollywood movie. In the whole history of golf, his was the greatest story ever told.

Ben Hogan on canvas (right)
This dignified portrait of the great golfer was painted by J. Anthony Wills in 1967.

William Benjamin Hogan

Won USPGA 1946, 1948; U.S. Open 1948, 1950, 1951, 1953; U.S. Masters 1951, 1953; British Open 1953. Winner of 57 events on U.S. Tour 1938–59. Ryder Cup 1947, 1951 (captain 1947, non-playing captain 1949, 1967). World Cup 1956, 1958 (individual winner 1956). Vardon Trophy 1940, 1941, 1948. USPGA Player of the Year 1948, 1950, 1951, 1953. U.S. leading money winner 1940, 1941, 1942, 1946, 1948. Sportsman of the Decade Award 1946, 1956. Bob Jones Award 1976.

Treasured memories
Hogan is still revered by golfers worldwide, as this celebratory USGA exhibition showed.

HAROLD HILTON

BORN WEST KIRBY, ENGLAND, JANUARY 12, 1869; DIED 1942

THE GREAT AMATEUR player Harold Hilton was not the most elegant swinger of a golf club, but he was one of the outstanding players of his or any other generation. He was the only amateur player to win the Open Championship in Britain, apart from his contemporary John Ball and the immortal Bobby Jones.

Hilton learned to play golf at the Royal Liverpool Club, where John Ball was also a member, and at one time his handicap was plus 10. He was short, only 5 ft. 7 in. (1.7m) tall, but he was extremely strong for his size and powerfully built.

He won the British Open at Muirfield in 1892, the first year it was held over 72 holes, and at Hoylake in 1897. He was four times British Amateur Champion. When he won the U.S. Amateur Championship in 1911, he became the first player to hold the amateur titles on both sides of the Atlantic in the same year. Only Lawson Little, Bobby Jones, and Bob Dickson have emulated that feat.

Popular portrait
As Harold Hilton was the best amateur golfer of his era, his image was featured on cards of all kinds.

Facing front (left)
A firm believer in the follow-through, Hilton would throw his weight forward on to his left leg after every shot.

In *Golfing By-paths* (1946), Bernard Darwin described Hilton's unusual style as "a little man jumping on his toes and throwing himself and his club after the ball with almost frantic abandon." But it was a style that worked. Only John Ball and Freddie Tait posed any threat to Hilton's preeminence in the amateur game. A methodical player, Hilton was also a great student of golf and wrote sagely on the subject. In 1911 he was appointed the first editor of the publication *Golf Monthly*, the world's oldest monthly golf magazine.

HAROLD HORSFALL HILTON

WON BRITISH OPEN 1892, 1897; IRISH AMATEUR 1897, 1900, 1901, 1902; BRITISH AMATEUR 1900, 1901, 1911, 1913; U.S. AMATEUR 1911.

HORACE HUTCHINSON

BORN LONDON, ENGLAND, MAY 16, 1859; DIED 1932

AS WELL AS being a top-ranked golf player, Horace Hutchinson was one of the first people to write seriously about the game. Although himself a flamboyant player and a master of the unorthodox, in his writing he always preached orthodoxy. He was also much admired by his contemporaries as a golf administrator.

Horace's uncle was one of the founding members of the Royal North Devon Club at Westward Ho!, and by the age of 13 young Horace was playing there.

He quickly showed himself to be a fine player. When he was 16 he won the club tournament, which carried with it the club captaincy. He was soon amongst the finest amateurs of the day. He played in the first Oxford vs. Cambridge match in 1878 and took part in the first Amateur Championship in 1885, when he lost in the final to A.F. MacFie. In 1886 he won the final easily to become Amateur Champion and successfully defended his title the following year in a scintillating contest against John Ball.

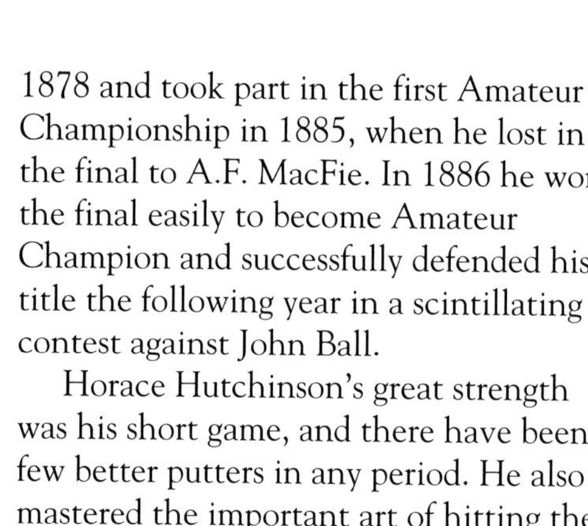

Unerring ability
Horace Hutchinson was renowned for his skill at driving and for being able to play recovery shots from every kind of bad lie.

Horace Hutchinson's great strength was his short game, and there have been few better putters in any period. He also mastered the important art of hitting the ball low into the wind.

He had great influence in the game, especially through his books and prolific magazine writing, and in 1908 he became the first English commoner to be captain of the Royal & Ancient Golf Club.

HORATIO GORDON HUTCHINSON

WON BRITISH AMATEUR 1886, 1887. LEADING AMATEUR IN BRITISH OPEN 1885. CAPTAIN ROYAL & ANCIENT GOLF CLUB 1908.

HALE IRWIN

BORN JOPLIN, MISSOURI, U.S.A., JUNE 3, 1945

TALL, STYLISH, AND powerful, Hale Irwin was one of the most consistent American golfers of the 1970s and 1980s. More athletic than he appears – he was a first-class college football player – he has built his game around control. He does not slug the ball, but keeps his rhythm, swings onplane, and stays out of trouble.

Recipe for success (above)
Competitive spirit, consistency, and all-round competence have characterized Hale Irwin's game over the 20 years that he has remained at the top of the golfing profession.

Stylish technique
With enough natural strength not to need to hit the ball really hard, Hale Irwin plays a neat and tidy game that shows great control.

Odd meal
Irwin gnaws at his club in frustration during the 1987 U.S. Open at Olympic.

When Hale Irwin came to the final green at Medinah in the 1990 U.S. Open, he hit his second shot to the edge of the sloping green 45 ft. (13.5m) from the cup. He knew he needed to get down in two more to stand any chance of winning.

Irwin struck the putt firmly and it raced in a wide curve across the green, up the slope, and around into the hole. He ran around the green doing a version of an Indian war dance. In his heart he agreed with Greg Norman, his playing partner: "You could just have seen the putt that wins the tournament." It was not quite that easy. Irwin went into an 18-hole play-off with Mike Donald that ended in a tie. But then Irwin won the 19th hole and at 45 became the oldest man ever to win the U.S. Open.

GOLDEN YEARS

Until his 1990 Open victory, Irwin's best years appeared to be behind him. A professional since 1968, he had first won the U.S. Open at Winged Foot in 1974, when the course was set up so sternly that only one of the first four finishers broke 70 in any round. He won the title again at Inverness, Ohio, in 1979, despite a last round of 75.

Between 1973 and 1981, Irwin was only twice out of the top seven on the U.S. money list. He might have taken the British Open title at Royal Birkdale in 1983, but for the 2 in. (5cm) putt that he missed at the 14th hole of the third round. Intending to tap it in, he took his eyes off the ball and missed it altogether, losing a stroke.

Hale Irwin played for the United States in four consecutive Ryder Cup matches, from 1975 to 1981, winning 11 of his 16 matches, one of the best records ever achieved by an American Ryder Cup player.

HALE S. IRWIN

WON U.S. OPEN 1974, 1979, 1990; WORLD MATCHPLAY 1974, 1975. WORLD CUP 1974, 1979 (INDIVIDUAL WINNER 1979). RYDER CUP 1975–81.

TONY JACKLIN

BORN SCUNTHORPE, ENGLAND, JULY 7, 1944

WHEN TONY JACKLIN won the U.S. Open at Hazeltine in 1970, he became the first British player for 70 years to hold both the British and U.S. Open titles at the same time. Hailed as a national hero, he was awarded an OBE and went on to become the chief inspiration for the developing European Tour. But although he continued to win tournaments all over the world, the magic of that year of Open successes gradually slipped away. Tony Jacklin's reign at the top of the game proved unhappily shorter than his numerous admirers had hoped and expected.

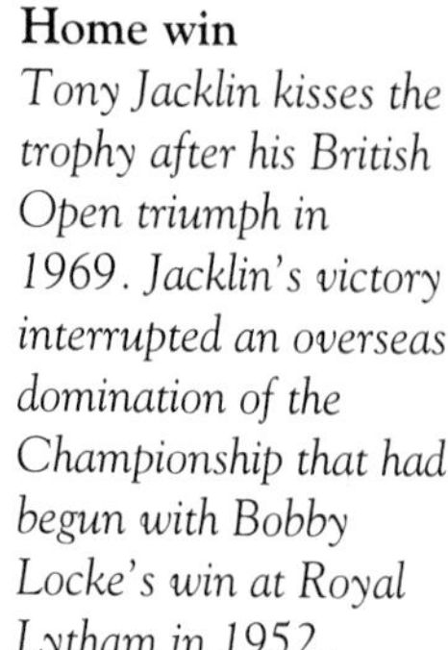

Home win
Tony Jacklin kisses the trophy after his British Open triumph in 1969. Jacklin's victory interrupted an overseas domination of the Championship that had begun with Bobby Locke's win at Royal Lytham in 1952.

Rough time (left)
Tony Jacklin fights his way out of an uncomfortable lie during the 1971 British Open at Royal Birkdale.

Balanced golf (right)
Although Jacklin had excellent balance and control, his putting could sometimes let him down under pressure.

Tony Jacklin was born the son of a truck driver in the English steel town of Scunthorpe, Lincolnshire. It was an unlikely background from which to launch a bid for fame and fortune. But soon after he was introduced to golf at the age of nine, Jacklin developed a burning ambition to become the best golfer in the world – and a millionaire to boot.

His talent was precocious. By the age of 13 he had won the Lincolnshire Boys' Championship, a title he was to hold for the next two years, and at 16 he added the Lincolnshire Open to his growing list of successes, beating the leading professional by no fewer than nine strokes.

Jacklin turned professional in 1962, and in 1963 he was named Rookie of the Year by the great Henry Cotton. The following year he won the British Assistants title.

FROM SUCCESS TO FRUSTRATION

By 1968 Jacklin had joined the U.S. Tour and won the Jacksonville Open with a record score, proving that he could take on and beat the top Americans. This was emphatically confirmed by his victory in the British Open at Royal Lytham and St. Annes in 1969, which made him the first Briton to hold the title for 18 years. The following year he took on the Americans on their home ground, winning the U.S. Open at Chaska, Minnesota, by seven strokes with a score of 281, the biggest winning margin since Jim Barnes won by nine strokes at Washington in 1921.

Tony Jacklin was the new hope of Europe. When he went to St. Andrews shortly afterwards, the galleries flocked to

Open rivals
Jacklin with Lee Trevino, who beat him in the 1972 British Open.

Big shot
With great natural ability, Jacklin was one of the best drivers in the history of the game.

see him defend his British Open crown and keep the Americans at bay. But his defense was dogged by the cruelest luck. He began by producing golf of such masterful quality that it seemed no one would be able to stop him. He went to the turn in 29 strokes and then birdied the 10th. His momentum was broken by a cloudburst, however, which put an end to play for the day. He was forced to mark his ball at the 14th and, when he returned the following day, the magic was missing. Jacklin could only manage to finish fifth.

Shattering Blow

Two years later, at Muirfield, Jacklin looked set to win the British Open again when Lee Trevino, level with Jacklin at the 17th, lay at the back of the green in four strokes. Safely on in three, Jacklin seemed almost home and dry. But Trevino then flukily holed his chip shot from off the green, and Jacklin was so shaken by this cruel turn of fate that he three-putted. Trevino went on to win a championship that he admitted later he had mentally conceded. It was a shattering blow to Jacklin. Like a boxing champion who had taken a heavy beating, Jacklin was never to be the same again.

Jacklin was never happy playing in the United States, although he knew he had to compete there to fulfill his highest ambitions. After the setbacks of the early 1970s, he left the U.S. Tour to boost the European Tour with its new crop of outstanding young players.

Captain of Europe

In the 1980s, Jacklin achieved fresh prominence as an inspirational captain of the European Ryder Cup team. He came close to guiding his team to a win at the first attempt, in Florida in 1983. Two years later, the Europeans won an emotional victory at The Belfry. Then, in 1987, Jacklin led his team to even greater glory, winning for the first time in America.

After a drawn match at The Belfry in 1989, Tony Jacklin bowed out of the captaincy, having presided over the beginning of a new era in European golf.

Anthony Jacklin, CBE

Won Dunlop Masters 1967, 1973; British Open 1969; U.S. Open 1970; Lancôme Trophy 1970; Italian Open 1973; German Open 1979; PGA Championship 1982. Ryder Cup 1967–79 (non-playing captain 1983–89). World Cup 1966, 1970–72. Honorary Life President British PGA.

Holding the cup
Ryder Cup captains Tony Jacklin and Raymond Floyd (left) of the United States display the famous trophy after the cliff-hanging drawn encounter at The Belfry in 1989.

Bobby Jones

Born Atlanta, Georgia, U.S.A., March 17, 1902; Died 1971

DURING 1936, SIX years after he had retired from championship golf with no worlds left to conquer, Bobby Jones made a sentimental return trip to St. Andrews as an ordinary holidaymaker to have a round over the famous Old course with some friends. It was not long before the word was out that Bobby Jones was back in the "home of golf"; when he arrived on the 1st tee, he found that some 2,000 of the Auld Grey Toon's inhabitants had turned out to watch him play, and the number grew as the round progressed.

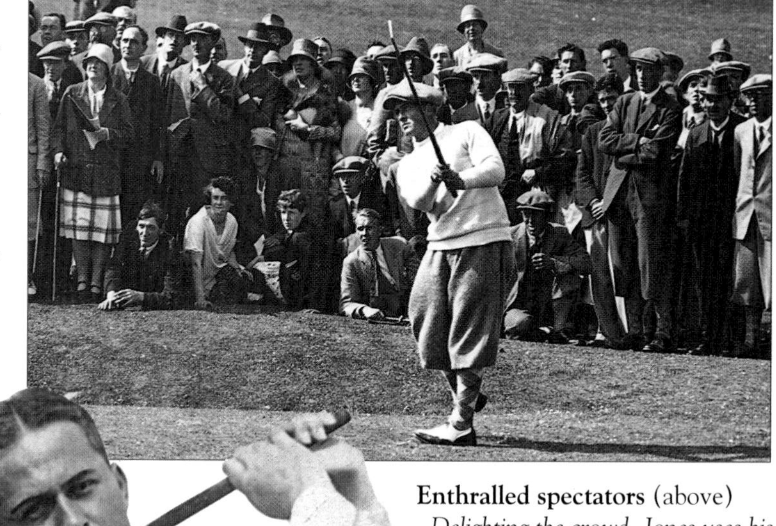

Enthralled spectators (above) *Delighting the crowd, Jones uses his mashie during the British Open at St. Andrews in 1927, in which he made a record score of 285.*

Jones recalled that day some 22 years later, when, confined to a wheelchair and in declining health, he returned to St. Andrews to be made a freeman of the city. "That spontaneous welcome was bound to be touching and it did something to me," he said. "I played golf as I had not done for more than four years or ever since." And he further added: "I could take out of my life everything except my experiences at St. Andrews and I'd still have had a rich, full life."

The son of an Atlanta attorney, Bobby Jones was a sickly child, and there was grave concern that he would not survive infancy. When he was five years old, he was introduced to golf while on holiday, and he and a friend built their own 2-hole course. A member at the nearby East Lake Country Club found an old cleek and cut it down for him.

Boy hero (left) *Bobby Jones was a precociously talented golfer. In 1916, at Merion, in his very first appearance in a U.S. Amateur Championship at the tender age of 14, he played well enough to reach the quarter-finals of the tournament.*

Flowing swing (right) *Jones's style was greatly influenced by Stewart Maiden, who was the professional at East Lake, Georgia. The young Bobby had followed the quiet Scotsman every time he played, and would mimic his flowing, rhythmical swing.*

Perseverance

It was not the ideal club for a youngster to learn to play with, but he persevered. It gives a clue as to why one of the strongest parts of Jones's game at the height of his powers was his long-iron play.

When the Jones family moved permanently to East Lake and Bobby's interest developed in what was still a relatively new game in the United States, he was greatly influenced by the East Lake Club professional, an expatriate Scot, Stewart Maiden.

Homage to greatness (left)
A Chicago Sunday Tribune *of 1928 pays tribute to Bobby Jones's position as the greatest golfer of his era.*

Crowd puller (right)
Jones won his first British Open at Royal Lytham in 1926. His swift method of play ensured him many admirers.

By the time he was 14 years old, Bobby Jones was not only good enough to play in the U.S. Amateur Championship but to get to the quarter-final. There was a lean period as he grew out of his frail early years and developed into a strong young man, but by 1923 he was the U.S. Open Champion and well on the way to becoming the greatest player of his era. In the eight-year period from that first U.S. Open victory, Jones won a total of 13 national championships, including his Grand Slam of 1930, the Open, and Amateur Championships of both Britain and the United States. He became a national hero, the most popular sportsman in American history. Thousands flocked to see him play; few realized that he did not like crowds and felt irritated, threatened, and shut in by them.

In 1930, with three legs of his Grand Slam already secure and only the U.S. Amateur at Merion standing between him and a unique sporting triumph, Bobby Jones, bothered by the crowds, suddenly lost his form. However, after a quiet final practice elsewhere, at Pine Valley, he returned to Merion for the Championship in much better heart and back to his usual form. He won comfortably in the end and, at the age of only 28, walked off the stage of competitive golf forever. Jones's retirement dream was to build his own golf course, where he and his friends could play privately, away from the attentions of well-meaning but intrusive golf fans. The result was the Augusta National Golf Club, since 1934 the permanent home of the U.S. Masters (see page 62).

True Amateur

Bobby Jones's record as a truly amateur player will live forever in the history of the game of golf. Despite many lucrative offers, he never turned professional, earning his living from his legal practice throughout his playing career.

It was not just his record that made Bobby Jones unique. His contribution to the special ethic and the great traditions of golf was as great as his remarkable achievements on the course.

Today, in the USGA museum in Far Hills, New Jersey, there is a room dedicated to the memory of Bobby Jones, where the artifacts of his incredible career are on display. Across the Atlantic, the 10th hole on the Old course at St. Andrews now bears his name, and his portrait hangs proudly in the Big Room of the Royal & Ancient Golf Club as a permanent memorial to the greatest amateur player in the game's history.

Robert Tyre Jones, Jr.

Won U.S. Open 1923, 1926, 1929, 1930; U.S. Amateur 1924, 1925, 1927, 1928, 1930; British Open 1926, 1927, 1930; British Amateur 1930. U.S.A. vs. G.B. 1921. Walker Cup 1922–30 (captain 1928, 1930). Non-playing captain Eisenhower Trophy 1958.

Ticker-tape welcome
New York mayor James J. Walker congratulates Bobby Jones on his Grand Slam wins in 1930.

Room to reflect
The Robert T. Jones, Jr. room at Far Hills is filled with memorabilia, including Jones's 32 competition medals.

ANDREW KIRKALDY

BORN DENHEAD, SCOTLAND, MARCH 18, 1860; DIED 1934

ANDREW KIRKALDY SHOWED great talent for golf at an early age, figuring as runner-up in the British Open of 1879 at the age of 19. He was a beautiful player to watch. Large, squarely built, and strong, he was noted for his long, low drives, particularly into a wind. A golfer of the top class, he was unlucky never to achieve the highest peak, a victory in the Open.

Local rivals
This early postcard in the Valentine series features Andrew Kirkaldy and Sandy Herd.

Kirkaldy was born in Denhead, outside St. Andrews, in 1860. He was the son of a miner who had been a soldier in the Crimean War. The family was very poor. After his successful appearance in the 1879 Open, he joined the Army and was in the Black Watch when they went to war in Egypt in 1882. He fought at Tel-el-Kabir, showing great dash and gallantry, always ready to be among the leaders in an attack, regardless of danger. This devil-may-care attitude was characteristic of the man and of the game of golf he played.

BACK FROM THE WARS

Kirkaldy lost many potential golfing years to soldiering, but he soon picked up the game again on his return. After a brief spell as a professional in England, at Winchester, he went back home to St. Andrews and remained at the "home of golf" for the rest of his days.

Returning to the Open in 1888, he finished sixth. The following year he tied for the Championship with Willie Park, Jr. at Musselburgh, but lost the play-off. In 1891 he was again second; this time the winner was his brother, Hugh. This was the first instance of brothers occupying the top two places in the British Open.

Clubhouse portrait
This somewhat dour portrait of Andrew Kirkaldy by W.O. Hutchison hangs in the clubhouse of the Royal & Ancient Golf Club at St. Andrews.

Although three times runner-up, three times third and twice fourth, Andrew Kirkaldy was never to win the Open. But he was involved in many big matches, usually on the winning side. In 1895, for instance, a year when the Open was held at St. Andrews, the reigning Open Champion, J.H. Taylor, issued a challenge to any golfer to play a 36-hole match over the New course. Andrew Kirkaldy picked up the gauntlet and, in a tense game, scraped out a win on the last green.

SCOTTISH HUMOUR

Kirkaldy was a person of great character, kind-hearted but prepared to express himself fluently and vividly in broad Scots. Stories abound of his humor; he was a source of enormous amusement to those able to understand him. He was quickly impatient of anyone who sought to patronize him. Few tried it twice.

After the death of Tom Morris, Kirkaldy was appointed honorary professional to the Royal & Ancient Club, a post he held from 1910 to 1933. He died in 1934 at the age of 74.

ANDREW KIRKALDY

RUNNER-UP IN THE BRITISH OPEN 1879, 1889, 1891.
HONORARY PROFESSIONAL ROYAL & ANCIENT GOLF CLUB 1910–33.

TOM KITE

BORN AUSTIN, TEXAS, U.S.A., DECEMBER 9, 1949

WINNING HAS ALWAYS been Tom Kite's problem. He was the first man to reach $5 million in earnings on the U.S. Tour. By the end of 1989 he had earned Tour prize money totalling $5,600,691, ahead even of Jack Nicklaus, who had won $5,102,420 in all his years as top man. Yet Nicklaus has 71 Tour wins to his credit, while Kite has only 13. Even allowing for the effects of inflation on prize money, the contrast is significant.

Kite had ten top-ten finishes on the U.S. Tour in each of the three years from 1987 to 1989; in 1981 he had 21. By 1990 he had secured 19 top-ten finishes in the four Majors. Yet he had never actually won a Major and had only twice won more than one Tour event in a season.

Kite's propensity for near misses started early: he came in second in the U.S. Amateur in 1970. He turned professional in 1972 and was named Rookie of the Year in 1973, his first full season on the Tour.

NEAR BUT FAR

Kite has come close to winning Majors but has never quite succeeded. In 1978 he was tied for second to Jack Nicklaus at St. Andrews in the British Open, along with Ben Crenshaw, Ray Floyd, and Simon Owen. He has been a joint second twice in the U.S. Masters. In 1983 he joined Ben Crenshaw in second place when Seve Ballesteros won after a last-round 69. In the 1986 Masters he joined Greg Norman in second place, one shot behind Jack Nicklaus. On the 72nd hole he needed to sink a 12 ft. (4m) putt to tie, but missed.

Kite has proved, however, that he can never be written off. In 1989, at the age of 39, he topped the U.S. money list with $1,395,278, won three tournaments and recorded a scoring average of 69.57.

Statistics give an insight into the strengths and weaknesses of Kite's game. In 1988 he was tied at 130th on the long-driving charts, while in 1989 he was alone at 141st. In putting he tied at forty-second in 1988, but improved to eighteenth in 1989. The plain fact is that if he drove as well as he pitched and putted, he would have won twice as many tournaments.

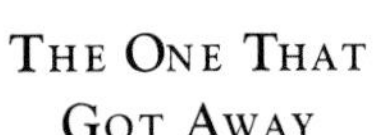

THE ONE THAT GOT AWAY

In the 1986 U.S. Masters Tom Kite came from nowhere to challenge Jack Nicklaus in the final round. On the last green he needed to sink a 12 ft. (4m) putt for a birdie to tie. But Kite never made it to the play-off with Nicklaus. Although putting was one of the strongest elements of his game, he missed the hole; his disappointment was obvious.

Top money winner
Kite has won only a modest number of U.S. Tour events, but he has accumulated more money than anyone else in the history of the game, largely through the strength of his putting.

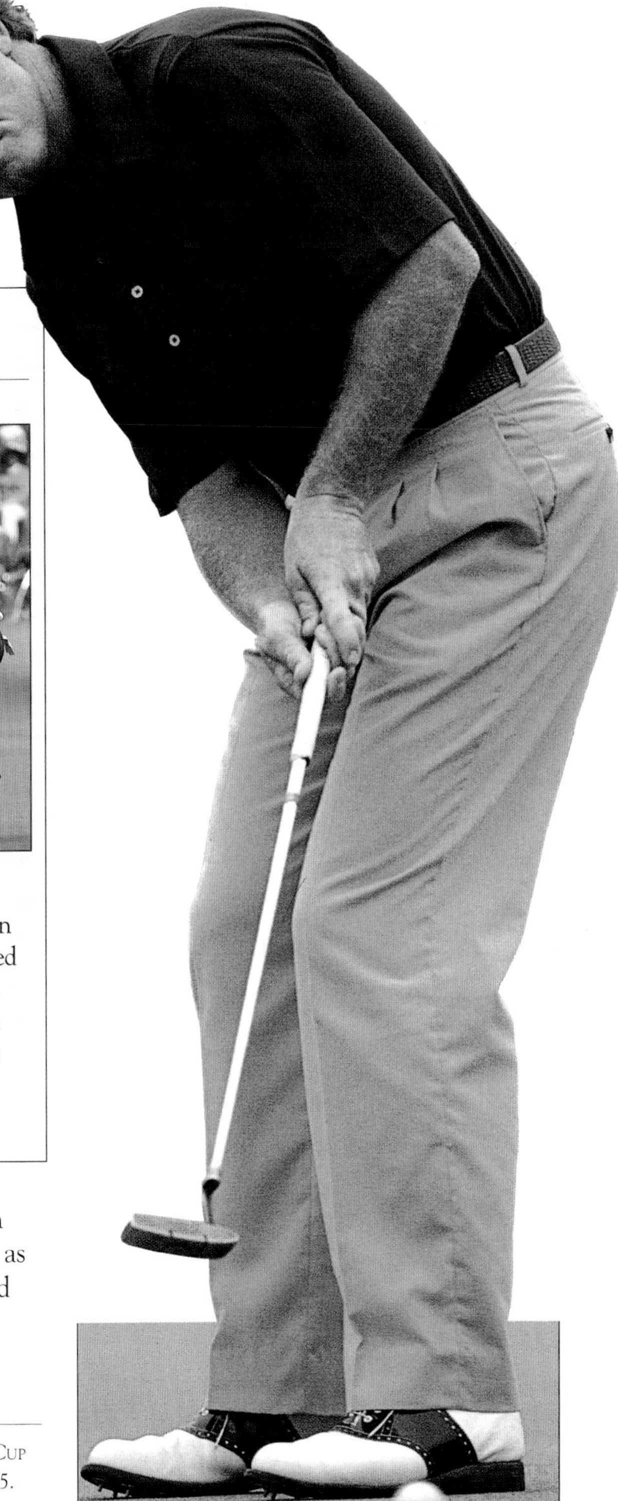

THOMAS O. KITE, JR.

WINNER 14 U.S. TOUR EVENTS 1976–90. WALKER CUP 1971. RYDER CUP 1979–89. WORLD CUP 1984–85. DUNHILL CUP 1989–90. VARDON TROPHY 1981, 1982.

JOHNNY LAIDLAY

BORN HADDINGTONSHIRE, SCOTLAND, NOVEMBER 5, 1860; DIED 1940

WHEN JOHN LAIDLAY was 12 years old, he went to Loretto School, Musselburgh, which lies just by the famous old links. Here he soon showed his great golfing skill, and by the time he was 16 he had achieved a round with a four at each hole. This was with the guttie ball, and no mean feat. Laidlay joined Luffness when he was 18 and soon won his first medal. In the 1880s and early 1890s he was the leading Scottish amateur player.

Golfing innovator
Johnny Laidlay was first to use what has become known as the Vardon Grip. He was also responsible for introducing the game to Egypt.

In the British Amateur Championship in the years from 1888 to 1894, Laidlay always reached at least the semifinal; he was in five finals, including four in a row, and won the title twice, in 1889 and 1891. He was leading amateur in the British Open on four occasions, and was runner-up in 1893. He played in the Open for the last time in 1906, but continued to enter the Amateur until 1920, when he was close to 60.

Laidlay had an unusual and individual style of play. Nearly every shot was played off a firm left side; although he broke almost every rule of style, he had great control over all his shots. His swing was often described as "peculiar" and he used a light grip, but he still developed power even off a half-swing.

Immaculate short game
Using a cleek gave Laidlay a feel for the low run-up.

JOHN ERNEST LAIDLAY

WON BRITISH AMATEUR CHAMPIONSHIP 1889, 1891.
SCOTLAND VS. ENGLAND 1902–11.

BERNHARD LANGER

BORN ANHAUSEN, GERMANY, AUGUST 27, 1957

THERE ARE FEW of the great players who have not suffered from that terrible affliction known as the "yips," which manifests itself as an involuntary lunge on short putts, reducing grown men to the consistency of jelly, with accompanying suicidal tendencies, on the green. The "yips" mostly affect top players late in their careers: Ben Hogan, Sam Snead, and Harry Vardon are classic examples of players so afflicted. In the case of the German player Bernhard Langer, however, it is not something that has crept up on him; he has suffered from this terrible burden through most of his golfing career.

It is a tribute not only to the quality of the rest of Langer's game, but also to his quite remarkable tenacity and determination, that he has at least three times been able sufficiently to overcome the problem to become one of the great players in the modern game. Indeed, he has, paradoxically, become an outstanding putter.

Rewards of victory
Bernhard Langer's international status was finally confirmed when he won the U.S. Masters in 1985. He was only the second European to wear the coveted Green Jacket.

Coming from a nation that had not even produced a good touring professional, let alone an international superstar, Langer's achievements since he turned professional in 1972 have been quite remarkable. He joined the European Tour in 1976, but made little impression until 1980. That year he found some relief from his putting problems when he came across a second-hand ladies' putter at Sunningdale during the Hennessy Cup matches. It was an Acushnet Bull's Eye, which he acquired for £5. After thickening the grip a little, Langer immediately pressed this cheap purchase into service.

The new putter worked well in the Hennessy, and Langer then reeled off a stream of rounds in the low and middle 60s, before crowning the season by

Mirror image
Bernhard Langer, in reflective mood, stands with his caddie during the 1987 U.S. Masters at Augusta, Georgia.

winning the Dunlop Masters at St. Pierre. The following year, with the "yips" at bay, he played in 17 events, finished in the top ten in 14 of them, and was runner-up six times. He won his own country's Open Championship, as well as the Bob Hope British Classic. He headed the European money list that year and played in the European Ryder Cup team for the first time. He established himself as a regular member of the team, making a major contribution to its success in the 1980s.

Return of the Jinx

The following year the old problem with short putts returned, although Langer remained an excellent putter from the longer distances. Again he sought refuge in a different putter, but he found that a change of grip had as much effect. Alternating between a conventional grip for the longer putts and a left-hand-below-the-right grip on the short ones, he was back in business again.

In 1984 Langer headed the European money list again, along with four European Tour event wins. From then on he concentrated on the U.S. Tour and shocked the Americans in 1985 by brilliantly winning the U.S. Masters. For good measure, the following week he won the Sea Pines Heritage Classic. He played much less often in Europe, but returned to carry off the British PGA Championship and the Irish Open in 1987. Despite a very limited schedule, he finished in fifth place in the European Order of Merit that year.

Alas, the "yips" came back to haunt Bernhard Langer again in 1988 and, although he won the Epson Grand Prix, he finished in his worst position in nine years in the European Order of Merit. Once again, a fresh "cure" was found, which involved gripping the putter with the left hand below the right, while the right hand clamped the upper handle to the left forearm. Such a grip sounds physically dangerous but Bernhard Langer made it work.

The rewards of success made the struggle worthwhile. In 1990, at Grand Cypress, Orlando, Langer and teammate Torsten Giedeon won Germany the World Cup for the first time.

Golfer's nightmare
Despite various determined efforts to overcome his affliction, Bernhard Langer has suffered intermittently from the "yips" throughout his career.

Bernhard Langer

Won Dunlop Masters 1980; German Open 1981, 1982, 1985, 1986; Bob Hope Classic 1981; Italian Open 1983; French Open 1984; Dutch Open 1984; Irish Open 1984, 1987; Spanish Open 1984, 1989; U.S. Masters 1985; European Open 1985; Sea Pines Heritage Classic 1985. Lancôme Trophy 1986 (tied); British PGA Championship 1987. Ryder Cup 1981–89. World Cup 1976–80, 1990. Harry Vardon Trophy 1981, 1984.

Going Stateside
Langer – here shown during the 1987 U.S. Open at Olympic, California – played much of his golf in the United States in the late 1980s.

TONY LEMA

BORN OAKLAND, CALIFORNIA, U.S.A., FEBRUARY 25, 1934; DIED 1966

IN A FATEFULLY short career, Tony Lema showed the world that he was an extraordinary golfer. He burst into the limelight by winning three tournaments in 1962 and then, in his very first appearance in the Masters at Augusta in 1963, came within one stroke of taking Jack Nicklaus into a play-off. The following year, in his first venture overseas, he won the British Open.

Easy and gifted (right)
Displaying a relaxed swing, the young Lema captivated crowds with his fluid style and easy charm.

Defending champion
Tony Lema defends his title in the British Open at Birkdale in 1965. He was beaten by Australian Peter Thomson.

Tony Lema had been a caddie, a Marine in the Korean War, and an assistant in the pro shop at the San Francisco Golf Club before he joined the U.S. Tour in 1959. Starting unpromisingly, he struggled for three years before attaining his first success.

A tall, handsome man with a good-looking, long-legged swing, Tony Lema naturally caught the eye. After his first tournament victory, at Orange County in 1962, he was nicknamed "Champagne Tony," because he had promised the press he would break open a bottle when he won. The nickname suited his style of living, which was easy and expensive.

NATURAL TALENTS

In 1963, as well as almost tying Nicklaus in the Masters, he came fourth in the U.S. money list. But it was his triumph in the British Open at St. Andrews in 1964 that made his name a legend.

Lema arrived late for the Championship, leaving himself only one day to look over the course. He had never played golf on a links before in his life, yet he won easily, by five strokes from Jack Nicklaus. Lema's opening round was a 73, but after that his scores were 68, 68 and 70. Lema gave much of the credit for his Open success to his caddie, Tip Anderson. He said he just did as Tip told him. But in fact he found, as did the St. Andrews crowds, that he was a natural links golfer. He played the chip-and-run as to the manner born. Indeed, for his second shot on the 72nd hole he played a true Scots run-up through the Valley of Sin, instead of a pitch – and naturally he got his birdie.

It looked likely that Lema would retain his Open title at Royal Birkdale in 1965, when he led after two rounds, but he eventually lost to Peter Thomson. Nevertheless, Lema had an immensely successful season in the United States in that year, coming in second to Nicklaus on the money list.

Tragically, Tony Lema never lived to complete another Tour. He was killed in a plane crash, with his wife Betty alongside him, in 1966. It was one of life's bitter ironies that the aircraft crashed on a golf course, at Lansing, Illinois. The world of golf had lost a great player.

ANTHONY DAVID LEMA

WON BRITISH OPEN 1964. RYDER CUP 1963–65. WORLD CUP 1965.

GENE LITTLER

BORN SAN DIEGO, CALIFORNIA, U.S.A., JULY 21, 1930

ANY DISCUSSION ON the great swings in the history of tournament golf must mention the skill of Gene Littler. Sportswriters christened him "Gene the Machine" because of the silky smoothness of his action. Some think he may have had the best swing of them all. Certainly, the great Gene Sarazen thought highly enough of it to comment early in Littler's career: "Here's a kid with a perfect swing like Sam Snead's – only better."

Gene the Machine
Described by sportswriters as mechanical, Gene Littler's swing was the result of hours of practice.

Littler burst on the scene by winning the U.S. Amateur in 1953, and shocked the professional game the following year by winning the San Diego Open while still an amateur. Although Littler took the glory at San Diego, runner-up Dutch Harrison took the money, which, not surprisingly, prompted Littler to turn professional the following week.

Victory meant he avoided the need to qualify as a tournament professional or for any USPGA event that year. In fact, for the rest of his career he never had to qualify for a Tour event. The following year he won four times, including the Tournament of Champions, which he successfully defended over the next two years.

EARLY PROMISE UNFULFILLED

That remarkable series of three victories in a row in such a prestigious event confirmed Littler as a major figure in world golf. When he won the 1961 U.S. Open at Oakland Hills, it seemed that many more victories would be his. But Littler lacked the fierce drive to do more than make a good living from the Tour. He preferred to spend time at home with his family and his hobby; he had a passion for classic cars.

In 1972 Littler had to undergo surgery for cancer of the lymph glands and missed almost the entire season. But he fought back and continued to earn plenty of money on the Tour well into his fifties.

EUGENE ALEX LITTLER

WON U.S. AMATEUR 1953; U.S. OPEN 1961. WINNER OF 26 U.S. TOUR EVENTS 1955–77. WALKER CUP 1953. RYDER CUP 1961–71, 1975. BOB JONES AWARD 1973. BEN HOGAN AWARD 1973. WORLD GOLF HALL OF FAME 1990.

Man of courage (right)
Littler won the Ben Hogan Award in 1973 for his comeback after illness.

Bobby Locke

Born Germiston, South Africa, November 20, 1917; Died 1987

Bobby Locke played golf from his earliest years: by the time he was eight, he had a handicap of 14, and at nine, he played in his first competition. His handicap was already down to scratch by the age of 16. He continued to make astonishing progress, winning the Transvaal Open in 1934 and soon becoming known throughout his home country, South Africa, as "the golfing robot."

Early days (right)
At the Transvaal Open in 1934, Locke was already cultivating the image that was to be his trademark, wearing full plus-fours and a white cap.

Locke soon dominated the golf scene in South Africa. In 1935 he won the South African Amateur, recovering from a dire situation in the semifinal to win at the 38th hole, and doing the same in the final, again winning at the 38th. The South African Open followed immediately, and Locke won the tournament by three strokes.

Career Moves

At this time Locke was working for the Rand Mining House, and in 1936 they sent him to work at their London office. In Britain he played often with Leonard Crawley, one of the best amateurs of the time, who helped him a great deal. He met Harry Vardon, competed for the Harry Vardon Cup, and won easily. He lost early on in the Amateur Championship, but achieved a respectable eighth place in the British Open.

Returning home in 1937, he again won both the South African Amateur and Open, and in 1938 – aged only 20 – he turned professional. Beginning his professional career in spectacular fashion, he won the South African Open and the Irish Open in 1938, and followed up with a tenth place in the British Open.

The Second World War interrupted Locke's career, although he still managed to play some golf, despite flying many hundreds of hours in the South African Air Force. Resuming his career after the war, Locke went to the United States, where his excellent results and style of play drew him a large following. In two and a half seasons he played in 59 tournaments, winning 13, finishing runner-up in ten and coming in third seven times. He was third in the U.S. Open of 1947, and won the Canadian Open. To these achievements he added the British Open title, winning at Sandwich in 1949 after a tie with Harry Bradshaw from Ireland.

Careful preparation
Always a deliberate player, Locke was particularly slow when putting, taking the care he shows here as he practices for the British Open in 1939.

As Open champion, Locke decided to stay in Britain, which started an argument in the United States, where it was said he had committed to various tournaments. His sponsors were not pleased, well aware of his crowd-drawing power. The USPGA said he had violated contracts, and Locke was barred from the U.S. Tour.

Professional Jealousy

There was more than a suspicion that his success and the jealousy of some of the Tour professionals had not helped his cause. In 1951 Locke was reinstated after opinion veered to his side and a compromise was reached, but he never played regularly in the United States again.

Despite controversies off the course, Locke meanwhile retained the British Open in 1950 at Troon, and he won it again in 1952. When he scored his fourth Open triumph at St. Andrews in 1957, he became the eighth player to have won the Championship four times or more. His career came to an abrupt end in 1959, when he was involved in a serious car accident.

Aiming right
So pronounced was the Bobby Locke hook that he aimed to the right of his target by almost 45 degrees to counteract it.

Controlled Skill

Not always a popular player, Locke was sometimes thought to be distant on a golf course. He certainly concentrated hard and had no time for unnecessary conversation. Some of his outwardly unemotional behavior stemmed from the early firmness of his father, who had threatened to take away the young Bobby's golf clubs for good if he persisted in his childish tantrums.

Locke also had an unusual style that led to his hooking nearly all his shots, even his putts. It infuriated some of his biggest critics, who failed to understand that his hook was completely under control and that the ball nearly always landed on the spot he had selected for it.

Arthur D'Arcy Locke

Won South African Open 1935, 1937, 1938, 1939, 1940, 1946, 1950, 1951, 1956; Irish Open 1938; New Zealand Open 1938; Canadian Open 1947; British Open 1949, 1950, 1952, 1957; French Open 1952, 1953. German Open 1954. World Cup 1953–56, 1960. Harry Vardon Trophy 1946, 1950, 1954.

British Open win
Runner-up Harry Bradshaw (left) congratulates Locke after the South African's victory in the 1949 Open.

Henry Longhurst

Born Bromham, England, March 18, 1909; Died 1978

Writer and talented amateur golfer Henry Longhurst decided in 1937 that there was room on the market for a book to be called simply Golf. *However, it caused a furor because it told readers how to play the game, and Longhurst, a university graduate and an amateur, was not supposed to gain financially from anything to do with a sport played solely for enjoyment.*

Despite the whisperings, Longhurst continued to turn out delightful copy, and his amateur status was not taken away by the R & A. After the Second World War he became golf writer for the *Sunday Times* and then teamed up with the BBC in its radio and television coverage of the game. His voice became equally familiar to American TV viewers.

His straightforward commentating style proved extremely popular and his delivery was much imitated. He may have been the first commentator to say, "What a dreadful shot – an awful fluff," instead of, "Bad luck!"

Public office
Longhurst had political ambitions, serving in Parliament in 1943–5.

Henry Carpenter Longhurst, CBE

Won German Amateur 1936. Runner-up Swiss Amateur 1928; French Amateur 1937. Honorary member R & A Golf Club.

Jovial figure
Longhurst was a relaxed commentator, often especially witty near the 19th hole.

NANCY LOPEZ

BORN TORRANCE, CALIFORNIA, U.S.A., JANUARY 6, 1957

NANCY LOPEZ IS not only an outstanding golfer, but also a personality with the sort of star appeal that draws new spectators to the game. During her first full year as a professional in 1978, when she won five consecutive tournaments, attendances for the U.S. LPGA Tour tripled.

Great concentration (above)
A consistent technique and a highly developed power of concentration have been the two elements at the heart of Lopez's success.

Introduced to golf by her father at the age of eight, Nancy very quickly became an exceptionally good player, winning the New Mexico Women's Amateur when she was only 12. By the time she was 15 she had won the USGA Junior Girls' title, which she successfully defended for the next two years.

AMATEUR TO PROFESSIONAL

In 1975 Lopez was runner-up in the U.S. Women's Open while still an amateur and only 18 years old. The following year she played on the winning U.S. team in the Espirito Santo and the Curtis Cup.

Clearly destined for the professional ranks, she joined the LPGA Tour in 1977 and soon hit a winning streak. Her first full season, in 1978, was outstandingly successful. She won nine tournaments, including a record five in a row, and among her victories was the LPGA title.

The whole sporting world was forced to take notice of the young lady with the rather loopy swing. Little wonder that she was named Rolex Player of the Year and Rookie of the Year. She also collected the Vare Trophy for the best tournament average and, to add to these distinctions, was named *Golf Magazine* Player of the Year.

Big swing
Nancy Lopez's unconventional swing action has always been the most controversial part of her game, but it gives her great length.

Fine putter (left)
Lopez is recognized as one of the best putters on the LPGA Tour. She has never lacked the confidence to attack the hole.

BREAKING RECORDS

Lopez's swing may have been strange to look at, but it was remarkably consistent. Eight wins in the following year led to another Rolex Player of the Year award. Her stroke average of 71.20 for 1979 set an all-time LPGA record, until she lowered it again in 1985 to 70.73. These successes put her at the top of the 1979 LPGA money list, with total winnings of nearly $200,000.

In 1982 Lopez married baseball's Ray Knight, and in the following year the couple had cause for a double celebration: their first child was born, and Nancy's total prize money rose past $1 million after only five years of play on the professional circuit. Lopez treated herself to generous time off during this period, but despite playing only a limited schedule she won the Uniden LPGA Invitational and the Chevrolet World Championship of Women's Golf in 1984.

This was a foretaste of further triumphs that lay ahead. In 1985 she took the LPGA Tour by storm, finishing in the top ten in 21 of the 25 events in which she played. She won five times, including a second LPGA Championship and the Portland Ping Championship, which was finally decided only by a tense sudden-death play-off against Lori Garbacz. Nancy's winnings for the year totalled more than $416,000, the first time that the $400,000 mark had been passed on the LPGA Tour. She set a further record in 1985 by winning the Henredon Classic with a score of 268, an extraordinary 20 under par. Her total of 25 birdies over the four rounds of the event was also a record.

In 1986 the birth of Nancy's second child again restricted her competitive appearances, but she has since returned to the top of the game. Surprisingly, by 1990 she had still never won the U.S. Women's Open, although she has been runner-up three times, in 1975, 1977, and 1989. She has three LPGA titles to her credit, however, the third of them added in 1989, and her winnings are approaching the $3 million mark.

Swinging across the Line

Although Nancy Lopez is one of the outstanding stars of women's golf and one of the most popular players in the game, her technique has always been a subject of considerable controversy.

She has an unusual swing that some purists contend has several faults. Her action takes the club very much to the outside, with a pronounced bowing of the left wrist, but she attacks the ball strongly from the inside on the downswing and hits the ball an extremely long way. This length, combined with a delicate touch, a marvelous putting stroke, and an aggressive approach to the game, has always made her a formidable player. She has a great appetite for success and can expect more of it in the years ahead.

Nancy Marie Lopez

Won LPGA Championship 1978, 1985, 1989. Winner of 42 LPGA Tour events 1978–90. Curtis Cup 1976. Espirito Santo 1976. Vare Trophy 1978, 1979, 1985. LPGA Hall of Fame 1987.

Gallery favorite (below)
Nancy has always been an immensely popular golfer in the United States. Her initial run of successes in 1978 drew a whole new public to women's golf, and she has kept her appeal over the years.

Rising standards
Lopez won 17 of her first 50 professional tournaments, and her example has since inspired other women golfers to raise their game, making victory ever more difficult to achieve. She has never lost the will to win, however.

Sandy Lyle

BORN SHREWSBURY, ENGLAND, FEBRUARY 9, 1958

ALTHOUGH BORN IN *England, Sandy Lyle adopted his father's Scottish nationality after he turned professional in 1977. When he won the British Open at Sandwich in 1985, he was the first Scot to win it for more than 60 years and the first Briton for 16 years. When he won the U.S. Masters in 1988, he was the first Briton ever to win the event. And he won both Majors in his own way – calmly, casually, and cheerfully, with the odd wayward shot only underlining the sheer brilliance of the rest of his game.*

Suspect swing
Sandy Lyle has had to work hard to correct a slight twist in his swing that for a time upset his form.

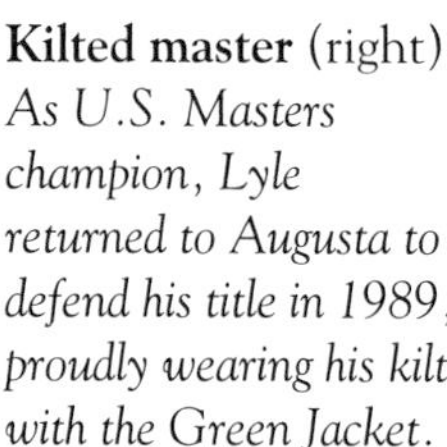

Kilted master (right)
As U.S. Masters champion, Lyle returned to Augusta to defend his title in 1989, proudly wearing his kilt with the Green Jacket.

Mild elation (below)
Lyle had an agonizing wait, while his rivals slowly finished their rounds, before he could lift the familiar claret jug trophy at the 1985 British Open at Royal St. George's, Sandwich.

Lyle is a fine, amiable man, with the best golf game Scotland has produced in over 50 years. Son of a respected teaching professional, Alex Lyle, Sandy was born at Shrewsbury, where his father was professional at the Hawkstone Park Club. It is said that he could hit a ball 80 yards when only three years old. He was a junior champion at 14 and English Amateur Strokeplay Champion at 17. He won this title again at the age of 19, played in the Walker Cup, and then turned professional. Two years later he was on the Ryder Cup team.

It was toward the end of 1977 that he joined the professional ranks, and early in 1978 he won his first tournament, the Nigerian Open, achieving a record-breaking round of 61 in the process. He went on to win all around the world, in Europe, Japan, Hawaii, and the mainland United States. In the three years after his victory in the British Open in 1985, he won five times on the U.S. Tour, including his success in the U.S. Masters at Augusta in 1988. In the autumn of that year he beat his constant rival, Nick Faldo, in the final of the World Matchplay.

Lyle started 1989 in fine style and almost immediately had four top-ten finishes in the United States. Then, inexplicably, he went into a slump. At the U.S. Masters that year he even missed the halfway cut, the Green Jacket passing to Nick Faldo.

Powerfully built and 6 ft. 1 in. (1.85m) tall, Sandy Lyle has always been a great iron player, but a great iron player with a slightly suspect swing. As Seve Ballesteros said of him, "When he is good he is the best and there is no one to touch him, but when he is bad he is almost the worst."

Ironing out his Swing

On full shots there has always been a slight twist in his backswing. His father says he often takes the club away "too much round the corner" and gets stuck halfway back. To get rid of the twist, Alex made Sandy practice his swing while standing against a brick wall, so that he had to take the club back straight and then up straight; otherwise he would damage either the club or the wall.

In the United States the famous teacher Jimmy Ballard put Sandy into a harness in order to keep his swing "connected." The harness kept his left upper arm touching the left side of his chest

Within sight of the Open (above)
Sandy Lyle won the British Open at Royal St. George's, Sandwich, in 1985 with rounds of 68, 71, 73, and 70, beating Payne Stewart of the United States by just a single stroke.

so that he had a much greater chance of swinging onplane. If the swingplane is imagined as a sheet of glass sloping down to the ball from shoulder height, Sandy would almost always shatter the glass.

Major Triumphs

Not always consistent in his play, Lyle has managed to control his game when it most mattered. Competing in the British Open at Royal St. George's in 1985, he began with an excellent 68.

In the second round he dropped three strokes in the first three holes, then in difficult conditions played the next 15 superbly for a 71. His third round was a solid 73 which left him three shots off the pace. In the final round he had a brilliant patch just when he needed it, and at the 15th shared the lead. Then Bernhard Langer and David Graham, his main rivals, fell away. He was in the lead alone. His second shot to the 18th was in a hollow, left of the green. He fluffed the chip and the ball rolled back almost to his feet, but his 5 was just good enough to win.

Dejection
Lyle's career has had its fair share of ups and downs. He depends on natural gifts, and when things go wrong he has no method to rely on.

At the U.S. Masters at Augusta in 1988, on the other hand, Lyle depended on an inspired finish to secure victory. He was in the lead at the start of the final round, but then three-putted the 11th and hit his ball into Rae's Creek at the 12th. In two holes his lead had disappeared.

Lyle eventually needed pars at the last two holes to force Mark Calcavecchia into a play-off. He got a par on the 17th, but hit his final tee shot into the left-side fairway bunker. There followed one of the greatest bunker shots ever seen at Augusta. He clipped the ball off the sand with his 7-iron, hit the ridge on the green, so that the ball rolled back down to finish 10 feet (3m) from the hole, and then sank the decisive putt for a birdie to win.

Alexander Walter Barr Lyle, MBE

Won European Open 1979; British Open 1985; U.S. Masters 1988; World Matchplay 1988. Walker Cup 1977. Ryder Cup 1979–87. World Cup 1979–80, 1987 (individual winner 1987). Dunhill Cup 1985–90. Harry Vardon Trophy 1979, 1980, 1985.

The sand holds no terrors (above)
Lyle plays his way out of a bunker during the 1988 British Open at Lytham. In difficult situations, Lyle's calmness has guaranteed success, most notably with his bunker shot on the 18th at the 1988 U.S. Masters.

Alister Mackenzie

Born Wakefield, England, August 30, 1870; Died 1934

Dr. Alister Mackenzie was one of the true giants of golf-course architecture, making his reputation in the United States after the First World War. Surprisingly, he was never a professional golf player; indeed, he was unique among the great course designers in not being a very good player at all. Yet his contribution to the game was outstanding, consisting of a number of the world's greatest courses, including Cypress Point in California and Augusta National, the home of the U.S. Masters.

Course doctor
Alister Mackenzie trained in medicine, but later changed his profession to become one of the world's top course designers.

In the second half of the nineteenth century many more people were attracted to the game of golf, partly because of the arrival of the guttie ball, which had replaced the feathery and made the game easier and less expensive (see pages 26–7). As golf spread rapidly from Scotland, where it had its natural roots, to England, and then to every corner of the world, more golf courses had to be built, and built quickly. Thus the profession of golf-course architect was born. Of the many who have been involved in this relatively young profession, few have had more influence than Dr. Alister Mackenzie.

Art of Camouflage

Although he was born in England, Alister Mackenzie was definitely a Scot by nationality, with an enthusiasm for the game of golf. Training initially as a doctor, he served as a surgeon with the Somerset Regiment in the Boer War in South Africa, but his interests were already elsewhere. He was fascinated by the art of camouflage, at which the Boers were particularly adept. It was his eye for detail and skill at disguising pitfalls that he was to put to good use on his return to Scotland, when he became increasingly involved in golf-course design.

Mackenzie's career in course design blossomed after he met Harry S. Colt, then a prominent designer, in 1907. Together they designed the course at Alwoodley, near Leeds, where Mackenzie was secretary. With the outbreak of war in 1914, he served not as a medical man, but as an expert in camouflage.

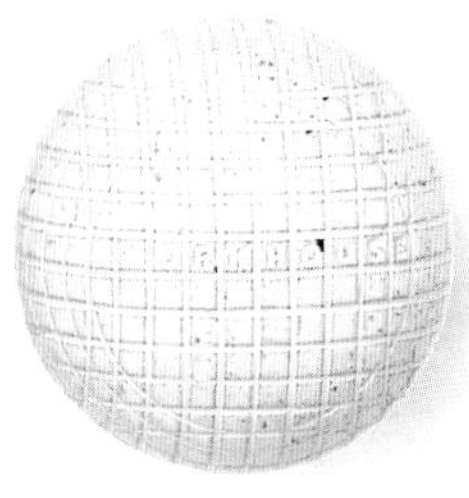

A new ball game
The introduction of the guttie ball encouraged more people to take up golf and so increased the need for courses.

Building a Reputation

After the First World War Mackenzie concentrated his energies on course design, a subject on which he had clear views. He wanted all artificial features to look natural, every hole to have its own character, and sufficient variety to require the use of every type of club. With an increasing number of courses built to his designs – especially in the north of England – his name soon spread across the world. His greatest courses include the West course at Royal Melbourne in Australia and Tiritangi in New Zealand.

His reputation was assured after he built the famous Cypress Point course on the Monterey Peninsula in California in 1928. It was after playing this marvelous Mackenzie layout that Bobby Jones invited the Doctor to help him build Augusta National. Unfortunately Mackenzie did not live to see the course completed; he was able to see the finished construction work but not the course fully covered in grass. He did not know that Augusta National, as home to the U.S. Masters, was to become one of the most famous courses in the world.

Dr. Alister Mackenzie

Designer of Augusta National, Cypress Point, Royal Melbourne, and many other courses worldwide.

Graham Marsh

Born Kalgoorlie, Western Australia, January 14, 1944

Lasting success
At the end of the 1980s, after a career that already spanned more than two decades, Marsh was still winning tournaments.

Many people are surprised when they learn that the Australian Graham Marsh, brother of the famous Test cricketer Rodney Marsh, has won nearly 40 golf tournaments worldwide, from Scotland to Thailand, from the United States to Japan, and from Australia to India. In Japan alone he had won 20 tournaments by 1990.

It was after seeing Marsh play in the Australian Amateur in 1967 that Peter Thomson urged him to turn professional. In 1970 Marsh travelled to Europe, where he won the Swiss Open. Soon after, he began his extraordinary career in Japan.

Marsh has proved he can take on the top players. In 1977 he won the World Matchplay title at Wentworth, beating Ray Floyd 5-and-3, after defeating Hale Irwin 7-and-6 in the semifinal. Never a player to produce high drama, this modest, cheerful man has shown the world the value of a simple method, consistency, and a persistent nature.

Graham Marsh, MBE

Won Swiss Open, 1970, 1972; German Open 1972; Scottish Open 1973; Lancôme Trophy 1977; World Matchplay 1977; European Open 1981; Pacific Masters 1987. Dunhill Cup 1985. Four Tours Championship 1986–88.

Gerald Micklem

Born Burgh Heath, England, August 14, 1911; Died 1988

Beating the great Ronnie White at Royal Birkdale in the final of the 1953 English Amateur Championship gave former Guards officer Gerald Micklem as much satisfaction as anything he ever achieved. Even his outstanding business success, which let him retire to a fine house near Sunningdale, could not surpass this victory.

Micklem was never a graceful swinger. He picked the club up too steeply on the backswing and one of his right-hand fingers, once injured, seemed merely a passenger. All this made his victories – President's Putter winner, twice English Amateur Champion, four times a Walker Cup player – even more outstanding.

As non-playing captain of the Walker Cup team and of the British side that played Europe, he was highly efficient.

Not a classic
Micklem never had a classic swing, but he was a successful player and administrator.

He also led the British team in the Eisenhower Trophy in 1958. But it was his role as captain of the Royal & Ancient Golf Club, leading administrator, and selector, that led the world of golf to speak of Gerald by his first name.

During the second half of the 1960s, he was successively President of the English Golf Union and President of the European Golf Association. Not always popular, he refused to tolerate ignorance of the rules and could be cutting, but seldom lost the common touch. His unusual voice and very English accent could be heard across most fairways.

Gerald Hugh Micklem, CBE

Won English Amateur 1947, 1953; President's Putter 1953. Walker Cup 1947–49, 1953–55 (non-playing captain 1957–59). England vs. France 1947–1948, 1954 (non-playing captain 1956). Non-playing captain G.B. vs. Europe 1956, 1958. Eisenhower Trophy 1958. Bob Jones Award 1969. Captain Royal & Ancient Golf Club 1968.

CARY MIDDLECOFF

BORN HALLS, TENNESSEE, U.S.A., JANUARY 6, 1921

DURING THE 1955 Masters, Dr. Cary Middlecoff rolled in an 80-foot putt on the 13th green of the final round for an eagle, then went on to win the coveted Green Jacket by a record seven strokes from Ben Hogan. It was perhaps the crowning moment of a very successful professional career for the tall dentist from Tennessee.

Middlecoff won his state Amateur four times in a row from 1940 before joining the professional ranks in 1947. Two years later he was the U.S. Open champion. From 1949 to 1956, "The Doc" was never out of the top-ten money winners on the U.S. Tour. His best year was 1955 when he won the Masters and five other Tour events.

SLOW BUT SURE

Middlecoff was noted for the slowness of his play, cautiously setting himself up for each shot. It was a style that often paid dividends. He won the U.S. Open again in 1956, and the next year narrowly lost the title to Dick Mayer in an 18-hole play-off.

This was not the only notable play-off in Middlecoff's career. In 1949, in the Motor City Open, he tied with Lloyd Mangrum at 273, and the match went to sudden death. It turned out to be the longest sudden-death play-off in USPGA history, lasting for 11 holes before play was halted because night was falling. Middlecoff and Mangrum shared the title and the $5,000 first prize.

DR. CARY MIDDLECOFF

WON U.S. OPEN 1949, 1956; U.S. MASTERS 1955. WINNER OF 37 U.S. TOUR EVENTS 1947–61. RYDER CUP 1953–55, 1959. WORLD CUP 1959. VARDON TROPHY 1956. USPGA HALL OF FAME 1974. WORLD GOLF HALL OF FAME 1986.

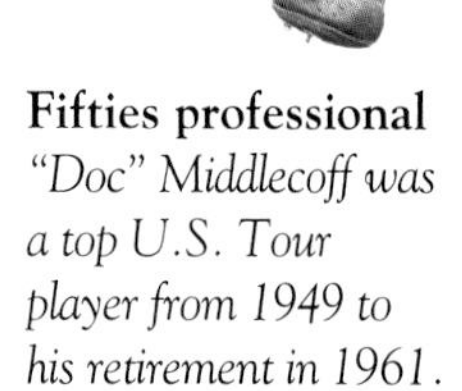

Fifties professional
"Doc" Middlecoff was a top U.S. Tour player from 1949 to his retirement in 1961.

JOHNNY MILLER

BORN SAN FRANCISCO, CALIFORNIA, U.S.A., APRIL 29, 1947

TALL, BLOND, AND handsome, Johnny Miller had the makings of a golfing superstar. In 1966 he went to San Francisco intending to be a caddie in the U.S. Open, but played instead and finished eighth. Turning professional in 1969, he was soon challenging Nicklaus for the unofficial title of the world's leading golfer, winning eight U.S. tournaments in 1974. Yet he failed to sustain his form, and by 1978 he had dropped to 111th on the U.S. money list.

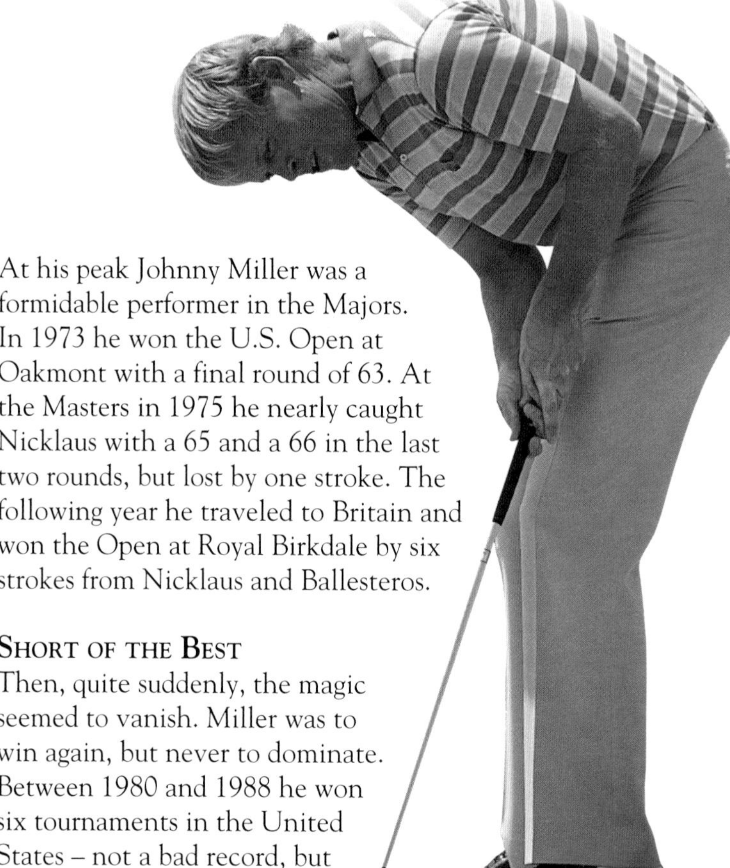

At his peak Johnny Miller was a formidable performer in the Majors. In 1973 he won the U.S. Open at Oakmont with a final round of 63. At the Masters in 1975 he nearly caught Nicklaus with a 65 and a 66 in the last two rounds, but lost by one stroke. The following year he traveled to Britain and won the Open at Royal Birkdale by six strokes from Nicklaus and Ballesteros.

SHORT OF THE BEST

Then, quite suddenly, the magic seemed to vanish. Miller was to win again, but never to dominate. Between 1980 and 1988 he won six tournaments in the United States – not a bad record, but not magnificent either. What had happened?

Quite early on in his career, Miller said, he became bored with too much golf, even when he was winning. A Mormon with deeply held beliefs, he became much more interested in his family – he has six children – than in his golf. When he lost his winning swing, he did not feel he had either the

Delicate touch
At the height of his powers in the 1970s, Johnny Miller had a magical touch with the putter that brought him the highest prizes.

Rivals at the top *Johnny Miller (left) and Jack Nicklaus were victorious partners in the 1983 Chrysler Team International. In the mid-1970s Miller was hailed as the "new Nicklaus," but his career did not sustain the same heights as his great rival.*

In control (below) *Miller combined elegance with power and control.*

time or the desire to recapture it. In his view, there were greater things in life than triumphs on the golf course. He still accumulated prize money; in 1984 his career earnings passed the $2 million mark. But money was not everything for him either.

Miller would prefer to be remembered for his 63 in the U.S. Open at Oakmont, with four straight birdies to begin with and five more later, or for his final 66 at Royal Birkdale in 1976, with its par-birdie-eagle in the middle of the round. In the turbulent world of professional golf, he is also proud of his perfect behavior on the course.

John Lawrence Miller

Won U.S. Open 1973; British Open 1976. World Cup 1973, 1975, 1980 (individual winner 1973, 1975). Ryder Cup 1975, 1981. USPGA Player of the Year 1974.

Abe Mitchell

Born East Grinstead, England, January 19, 1887; Died 1947

ABE MITCHELL HAS always been rated the best golfer never to have won the British Open. He had particularly large hands and struck the ball with great power, together with a certain elegance. Almost every amateur who saw him wanted to copy his style – including Samuel Ryder, the founder of the Ryder Cup.

Ryder hired Abe Mitchell as his private tutor, and in 1926 watched him lead a British team to victory – 13½ matches to 1½ – against a team of American professionals. Sam Ryder instantly decided to put up a solid gold trophy for future international matches.

Mitchell should have captained the first Ryder Cup team to sail for the United States in 1927, but he fell ill with appendicitis. He played in 1929, 1931, and 1933, however, winning four of his six matches in the tournaments.

Golf writer Bernard Darwin attributed Mitchell's relative lack of success to his peaceful nature, commenting, "He would rather be in his back garden."

Quiet genius *Abe was a gentle soul, but a powerful hitter.*

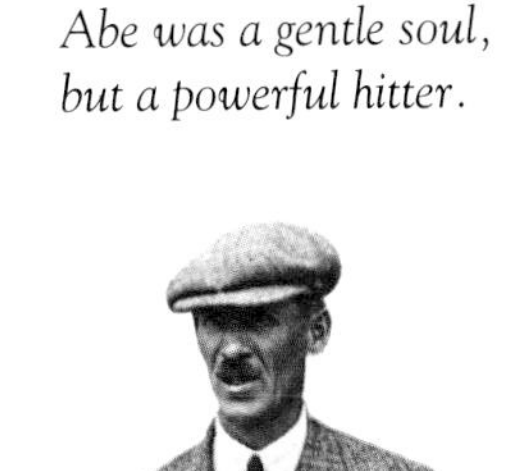

Henry Abraham Mitchell

Won Matchplay Championship 1919, 1920, 1929. Ryder Cup 1929–33.

In the English rain (below) *Mitchell plays out of a damp lie during the Amateur Championship of 1912.*

OLD TOM MORRIS

BORN ST. ANDREWS, SCOTLAND, JUNE 16, 1821; DIED 1908

OLD TOM MORRIS was, by the last two decades of the nineteenth century, the most famous golfer alive. Four times winner of the British Open, he became an institution in his home town of St. Andrews. His sound advice was much sought after, both as a player and as a designer of new courses. Even after he finally gave up competing in the Open when he was 75, he never lost his enthusiasm for the ancient game.

Sporting family (right)
As his youngest son, also called Tom, began to show exceptional golfing talent, father Tom became known as Old Tom. This postcard is just one of the hundreds of printed memorabilia that pay tribute to the outstanding family talent.

FOUNDER OF FIRM
TOM MORRIS
CHAMPION 1861-62, 64, 67

Old faithful (left)
The iron-headed putting cleek with a hickory shaft that belonged to Tom Morris.

Tom Morris played golf at St. Andrews from his early childhood. At the age of 18, he was apprenticed to Allan Robertson to make feathery balls. The two were also partners on the golf course. Their most famous victory was a dramatic win against the Dunn twins over three greens in 1849 (see page 291).

Morris and Robertson eventually quarreled over the introduction of the guttie ball, and in 1851 Tom moved to Prestwick as greenskeeper. There he played a part in arranging the first British Open in 1860 and participated in the tournament, starting as the favorite but finishing the runner-up to Willie Park, Sr. Tom Morris went on to win the Championship four times, the last in 1867 when he was 46 years old.

COMING HOME

In 1865 Old Tom was brought back to St. Andrews by the Royal & Ancient Club as greenskeeper. He subsequently became the professional at the Royal & Ancient, a post he held until his death. He was also busy as a golf-course designer.

Old Tom died in 1908 at the age of 87, never recovering after falling down the stairs at the New Golf Club in St. Andrews. At his funeral crowds gathered to mourn a man loved by all, generous by nature, and gentle in character.

TOM MORRIS, SR.

WON BRITISH OPEN 1861, 1862, 1864, 1867. HONORARY PROFESSIONAL ROYAL & ANCIENT GOLF CLUB.

Striking oils (below)
This portrait of Old Tom Morris was painted by Sir George Reid when the golfer was 81. Morris is said to have commented, when shown the finished painting, "Well, the cap's like mine."

Grand old man (above)
Old Tom Morris continued to play golf even in his eighties.

Young Tom Morris

Born St. Andrews, Scotland, April 20, 1851; Died 1875

When young Tom Morris was 13 years old he went with his famous father to a tournament on the North Inch at Perth in Scotland. Because of his background, he was not allowed to enter as an amateur, but was matched against a local youngster who was older and considered to be a coming champion. The local boy lost and Young Tom Morris was on the road to immortality.

Championship Belt (below)
In 1860 Prestwick Golf Club paid £25 for a red leather belt, decorated in silver, as a trophy for the British Open. After winning the Open three times consecutively, Young Tom Morris retained the Belt in 1870.

Young talent (above)
Young Tom was broad-shouldered, had strong hands, and played quickly and powerfully. But there was a sensitivity that gave his short game great accuracy; he was one of the best putters ever.

Handing on (below)
In a career lasting less than ten years, Young Tom Morris eclipsed his father as a golfer. Here the two men are photographed together not long before Young Tom's tragically early death in 1875.

Shortly after the match in Perth, Young Tom won a tournament at Montrose and then, at 16, tied with Willie Park, Sr., already three times Open champion, and Bob Andrew, another established player, at Carnoustie. Morris won the play-off.

In the same year of 1867, Young Tom made his second appearance in the British Open, finishing fourth. He won the tournament the following year, recording the first hole-in-one in the history of the British Open. When he repeated the victory in 1869 and again in 1870, he won the Open Championship Belt outright under the rules of the competition. With no trophy to be played for, the tournament lapsed in 1871.

Unmatched Success

When the Championship was re-introduced the following year, the present trophy, the claret jug, was put up for competition. Young Tom won again to make it four victories in a row, a feat that has never been matched since.

Young Tom was runner-up in 1874 at Musselburgh, but this was to be his last Open Championship. When his wife died in childbirth in 1875 Tom was inconsolable. He died a few months later, many believed of a broken heart. He was only 24 years old. Young Tom Morris was by far the outstanding player of his era, and one of the greatest the game has ever seen.

Tom Morris, Jr.

Won British Open 1868, 1869, 1870, 1872.

Death of a young hopeful
A memorial to Tom was erected by his parents in the grounds of St. Rule's Cathedral, St. Andrews.

KEL NAGLE

BORN SYDNEY, NEW SOUTH WALES, AUSTRALIA, DECEMBER 21, 1920

STARTING AS A professional's assistant at the age of 15, Kel Nagle had to wait until well after the Second World War to become a touring professional. This delay may have been the making of him. When young he had been a long, wild hitter, but in maturity he learned patience and calmness.

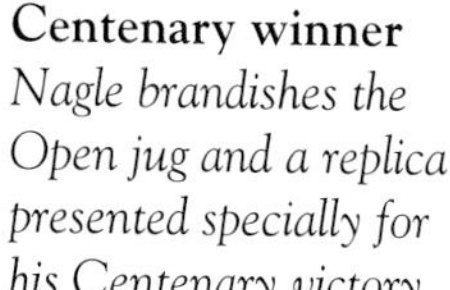

Centenary winner
Nagle brandishes the Open jug and a replica presented specially for his Centenary victory.

In his thirties Nagle built a fine winning record in New Zealand and Australia. Then he came to Britain and became internationally known by winning the Centenary Open at St. Andrews in 1960. He started with a 69 and a 67. A third round 71 put him in the lead. Arnold Palmer was four strokes behind but fought back to two behind, and then, as Nagle prepared to putt on the tricky 17th, Palmer birdied the 18th. A great cheer went up, but Nagle calmly sank a putt of 10 feet for a par 4. A safe 4 on the last hole gave him victory.

In 1965 Nagle's steadiness nearly won him the U.S. Open. He tied with Gary Player but lost the play-off. Passing 50, he won the 1971 World Seniors, a victory repeated in 1975.

Kel Nagle's record proves that good golf requires accuracy more than length, and that accuracy, once acquired, tends to last.

KELVIN DAVID GEORGE NAGLE

WON NEW ZEALAND OPEN 1957, 1958, 1962, 1964, 1967, 1968, 1969; AUSTRALIAN OPEN 1959; BRITISH OPEN 1960; FRENCH OPEN 1961; CANADIAN OPEN 1964. WORLD SENIORS 1971, 1975. WORLD CUP 1954–55, 1958–62, 1965–66.

TOMMY NAKAJIMA

BORN KIRYU CITY, JAPAN, OCTOBER 20, 1954

IT IS A HAPPY circumstance that Tsuneyuki "Tommy" Nakajima is an oriental philosopher of some experience, as well as a truly fine golfer. A successful star in his own country both as amateur and professional, by 1990 he had yet to win a top tournament abroad. He gets close, but cannot make the breakthrough.

Golf philosopher
Tommy Nakajima plays beautifully – in Japan. He was leading money winner four times, and once won nine tournaments in a year.

In 1978, at the British Open at St. Andrews, he was doing well until he putted his third shot on the 17th into the notorious Road Bunker. It took him four shots to get the ball out, and he finished the hole bravely with a 9. Many now know the bunker as "The Sands of Nakajima." At Turnberry in 1986, he was only a stroke behind Greg Norman at the start of the final round but three-putted the 1st green, then bogeyed the 3rd while Norman birdied it. Then in the World Matchplay he played superbly, only to lose to Sandy Lyle at the 38th hole. In the 1987 U.S. Open at Olympic, his ball stuck in a tree and it took him several shots to get it out. Yet Nakajima remains an excellent player.

TSUNEYUKI NAKAJIMA

WON JAPAN AMATEUR 1973; JAPAN PGA 1977, 1983, 1984; JAPAN OPEN 1985, 1986. DUNHILL CUP 1986. LEADER JAPAN MONEY LIST 1982, 1983, 1985, 1986.

BYRON NELSON

BORN FORT WORTH, TEXAS, U.S.A., FEBRUARY 4, 1912

BYRON NELSON WAS born in the same year and area as Ben Hogan, and for several years they were caddie colleagues. But Nelson found his game before Hogan and had retired by the time Ben reached his peak. At his best, in 1945, Nelson scored 11 consecutive U.S. Tour wins.

Nelson's first few years on the circuit were unsuccessful. In 1935 he finished the U.S. Open at Oakmont with an appalling total of 317. It was almost literally too much, but after many hours of practice and experimentation, Nelson discovered his own personal best swing. He won the Masters for the first time in 1937, the U.S. Open in 1939, and the USPGA in 1940.

Wartime golf
Nelson putts at Inverness, Ohio, in a War Bond Invitation event in 1944. His record would have been even better had war not disrupted his career.

He won the Masters again in 1942, just before it was halted because of the Second World War. A Tour of sorts continued, and in 1944 he won 13 out of 23 events.

After the war ended in 1945, Nelson had his greatest year. He won 18 of the 30 tournaments he entered, finishing second in seven others. His scoring average was 68.3 per round. In strokeplay tournaments, his average lead over those who came in second was 6.3 strokes, a still unbeaten record. In 1946 he won the first two tournaments and was runner-up in the U.S. Open after a play-off, but realized he was no longer in peak condition. In 1955 he won the French Open on a vacation trip to Europe, but that was the end. He returned to his Texas ranch and attended tournaments only as a TV commentator.

What was his secret? He stood close to the ball, bending to allow his arms to hang freely. He restricted his hip turn and started back with a slight lateral sway. He restricted the roll of the wrists coming into impact and kept the back of his left hand square to the arc from 30 inches before impact to 30 inches after. He also kept his left arm straight. It certainly worked for him.

In retirement
At the age of 74 Byron Nelson was still enjoying his golf, far from the pressures of top competition.

JOHN BYRON NELSON, JR.

WON U.S. MASTERS 1937, 1942; U.S. OPEN 1939; USPGA 1940, 1945. WON 54 U.S. EVENTS 1935–46. RYDER CUP 1937–39, 1947 (NON-PLAYING CAPTAIN 1965). VARDON TROPHY 1939. USPGA HALL OF FAME 1953. WORLD HALL OF FAME 1974. BOB JONES AWARD 1974.

Touring for MacGregor (below)
The MacGregor Golf Company, a leading manufacturer of clubs and balls in the United States, employed Nelson as a touring pro.

LARRY NELSON

BORN FORT PAYNE, ALABAMA, U.S.A., SEPTEMBER 10, 1947

STEADY, CONSISTENT, UNDRAMATIC, Larry Nelson is unique among top golfers in one respect: he learned his game from a book and did not even hit a golf ball until he was 21. It was a mere five years later, in 1974, that he won his way onto the American Tour, qualifying through his performance in a tournament that was only the second four-round event in which he had ever played.

A naturally self-effacing character, Nelson made only a modest impact at the top level until 1979. In that year he won two tournaments on the U.S. Tour and finished second on the U.S. money list, accumulating $281,000 in prize money.

Nelson never achieved such a high position on the money list again, but he scored some outstanding successes. He won the USPGA Championship in 1981, beating Fuzzy Zoeller by four strokes at the Atlanta Athletic Club, and two years later he achieved victory in the U.S. Open at Oakmont. Seven strokes behind after two rounds, a third-round 65 left him only one behind the leaders, Tom Watson and Seve Ballesteros. The last round developed into a straight fight between Nelson and Watson. The two men were tied when Nelson sank a 60-foot putt that settled the issue at the 16th.

Nelson won the USPGA Championship again in 1987 and registered his tenth U.S. Tour victory the following year. He has also won twice in Japan, but it is in the Ryder Cup that his record of success has been most dramatic.

Bunker sandstorm
Nelson blasts his way out of trouble, not a common experience for such a careful golfer.

FIVE STRAIGHT WINS

In 1979, at the Greenbrier Club, Nelson won all five Ryder Cup matches in which he played, beating young Seve Ballesteros by 3-and-2 in the singles. At Walton Heath in 1981 he again came through with a 100 percent record, winning all four of his games. He finally lost a Ryder Cup match for the first time at Muirfield Village in 1987. He was then 40 years old.

Larry Nelson has always been quietly efficient and has never changed his swing. He grips the club as Ben Hogan advised, stands like Hogan, concentrates on swinging onplane, and has his left wrist bowed out through impact. It is all in Hogan's *The Modern Fundamentals of Golf*.

LARRY GENE NELSON

WON USPGA 1981, 1987; U.S. OPEN 1983.
RYDER CUP 1979–81, 1987.

Ryder pals (above)
Larry Nelson (left), an outstanding Ryder Cup performer, with teammate Lanny Wadkins.

Oakmont winner
Nelson hugs the U.S. Open trophy after his 1983 win at Oakmont Country Club.

Jack Newton

Born Sydney, New South Wales, Australia, January 30, 1950

THE WORLD LOST a fine competitive golfer when Jack Newton walked into the propeller of a Cessna airplane at Sydney's Mascot airport in 1983. He lost his right arm and right eye, bringing his tournament career to an end. Newton has not abandoned the game, however, and remains an inspiration to all disabled golfers.

Crowd pleaser
Newton was a great favorite among the galleries until his tragic accident in 1983.

A fine all-around sportsman, Newton became a golf professional in 1971. Venturing to Europe, he won two tournaments in 1972. In 1975 he came close to winning the British Open at Carnoustie. He tied Tom Watson, and then lost the play-off by one stroke. The deciding strokes were a chip in from off the green by Watson on the 13th and an approach into the sand by Newton on the 18th.

Then came his tragic accident. Some 18 months later he was back on the course, determined to become the best one-armed, one-eyed golfer in the world.

Jack Newton

Won Dutch Open 1972; Benson & Hedges International 1972; PGA Matchplay 1974; Buick Open 1978; Australian Open 1979.

Jack Nicklaus, see page 276

Australian star
Jack Newton in 1980.

Norman Von Nida

Born Strathfield, Queensland, Australia, February 14, 1914

NORMAN VON NIDA is respected not only as a great Australian tournament player, but also as one of the game's most eminent teachers. He won the Australian Open three times and his country's PGA title four times.

The early progress of Von Nida's career was cruelly interrupted by the outbreak of the Second World War, just after he had begun his first assault on the U.S. Tour. After the war, in 1946, he traveled to Britain with only £17 in his pocket and a month to go before the first tournament.

But Von Nida, affectionately known as "The Von," was nothing if not resourceful. He was soon among the money winners and finished his first season in Britain in second place on the money list. The following year he created a record by winning three tournaments in a sequence of four. He also won or tied four other events to set a new money record of £3,263 for the year.

Von Nida was a colourful figure, never slow to express his views. After an incident with U.S. Ryder Cup player Henry Ransom during the Lower Rio Grande Valley Open in 1948, a fistfight developed. The press blamed Von Nida, but in fact he had been attacked first. After the local sheriff pulled them apart, Ransom was disqualified from the event.

The Von's reputation as a teacher is highly respected and he has worked with distinguished Australian players such as Greg Norman and David Graham.

"The Von" in action
Norman Von Nida tees off at Royal Lytham and St. Annes in 1947. The Australian made a major impact on the game of golf in Great Britain during the postwar period.

Norman George Von Nida

Won Australian PGA 1946, 1948, 1950, 1951; Dunlop Masters 1948; Australian Open 1950, 1952, 1953. World Cup 1956. Harry Vardon Trophy 1947.

JACK NICKLAUS

BORN COLUMBUS, OHIO, U.S.A., JANUARY 21, 1940

THERE HAS NEVER been a player quite like Jack William Nicklaus in the history of golf, and it is difficult to imagine that we will ever see his like in the future, so great has been his impact upon the game. His record is by any standards truly remarkable. Since the age of 14 he has been winning tournaments and setting records with amazing regularity. At the same time Nicklaus has followed a parallel career as a golf-course designer, a role in which he has almost equaled his influence as a player.

Golfing brain (left) *Nicklaus's exceptional power of concentration has always been one of the mainsprings of his unparalleled success.*

Cup team (above) *Nicklaus (left) and Palmer (right) won the World Cup for the United States four times in the 1960s.*

Nicklaus took up golf at the age of ten. By the time he was 19 he had won his first U.S. Amateur Championship and was on the Walker Cup team. Two years later, he won the Amateur again, after setting a record 282 for an amateur in the 1960 U.S. Open, finishing second to Arnold Palmer.

It was a meteoric start to a career that dominated golf for a quarter of a century. By 1986, when Nicklaus won the U.S. Masters for the sixth time at the age of 46, he had won 18 Major championships – seven more than any other player – and he had earned more money than anyone in the history of the game. That victory at Augusta was the highlight of the 25th season of his professional career. He had played in 100 Major championships, finishing in the top three 45 times – an achievement that no player in the game today is even remotely likely to emulate.

Evergreen Nicklaus (below) *Jack is congratulated on his 1986 U.S. Masters victory by the previous title holder, Bernhard Langer.*

Trouble spot (below) *Nicklaus under the stand at Muirfield in the 1966 British Open.*

Spanning two decades
Nicklaus contests the U.S. Open at Pebble Beach in 1982, 20 years after his first win in the championship.

Nicklaus has won every honor that it is possible to win in golf, many of them several times; only the record for the highest number of USPGA tournament wins is missing from his collection. In the process he has become one of the most popular men active in any field of sporting endeavor and is highly respected as an ambassador for the game he loves.

Winning over the Crowds

As Nicklaus's domination of the game increased over the years, so has his popularity with the galleries. As a stern, slightly overweight and crew-cut youngster, Nicklaus was not popular, particularly when he first emerged to challenge the superiority of the great Arnold Palmer. But by the beginning of the 1970s he had lost weight, grown his hair, and assumed a relaxed appearance. This did wonders for his image, although it did not affect the intense concentration behind the steely blue eyes, which could be as cold as ice one moment and then melt into a disarming smile the next.

The secret of Nicklaus's success has much to do with his capacity for intense concentration, but he was also blessed from the start with immense physical strength, especially in the legs and back. Strangely, he has very small hands and short fingers. This is why he is one of the few great champions to have used the interlocking grip, where the little finger of the right hand interlocks with the index finger of the left.

At the height of his powers, Jack's strength helped him to propel the ball colossal distances. With the possible exception of the late Sir Henry Cotton, he probably practiced more than anyone else in his formative years. He was fortunate because his father, Charlie, was wealthy enough for Jack to play as much as he liked and harden his competitive edge in amateur tournaments. He learned to play under Jack Grout, professional at the La Gorce Country Club in Miami Beach, Florida. Grout, who died in 1989, was Jack Nicklaus's only teacher and was definitely a significant influence on his career.

Unique Record

Nicklaus joined the U.S. Senior Tour in 1990 and won his first event, but the following week he was back at Augusta for the U.S. Masters, finishing sixth. Even in his fifties, he still drives almost as far as he did as a youngster, albeit aided to some extent by advances in equipment.

Jack Nicklaus's record at the top level of golf is unique. He is without a doubt the greatest player in the modern game, and, many argue, the greatest of all time.

Jack William Nicklaus

Won U.S. Amateur 1959, 1961; U.S. Open 1962, 1967, 1972, 1980; U.S. Masters 1963, 1965, 1966, 1972, 1975, 1986; USPGA 1963, 1971, 1973, 1975, 1980; British Open 1966, 1970, 1978. Winner of 71 U.S. Tour events 1962–84. Walker Cup 1959–61. Eisenhower Trophy 1960. World Cup 1963–67, 1971, 1973 (individual winner 1963, 1964, 1971). Ryder Cup 1969–77, 1981 (non-playing captain 1983, 1987). Rookie of the Year 1962. USPGA Player of the Year 1967, 1972, 1973, 1975, 1976. World Golf Hall of Fame 1974. Bob Jones Award 1975. Walter Hagen Award 1980. Honorary member R & A Golf Club.

Smiling bear
In the 1980s, Jack Nicklaus approached his golf as a pleasure rather than a job, but the will to win was still there.

First-time winner (below)
In April 1990 Nicklaus won the first Senior event he contested, the Tradition at Desert Mountain.

GREG NORMAN

BORN MOUNT ISA, QUEENSLAND, AUSTRALIA, FEBRUARY 10, 1955

GREG NORMAN WAS a latecomer to golf, taking up the game at the age of 17. Yet within two years he was a scratch player and had embarked on a meteoric career that took him to the position of the world's number-one player. He turned professional in 1976, and in only his fourth tournament, the West Lakes Classic in Australia, he led by ten strokes going into the last round; victory was a formality. Though he had played in only six professional events by the end of the season, he was selected to represent Australia in the World Cup.

Long and straight
Australian superstar Greg Norman has always been noted for the impressive power and perfect straightness of his long hitting.

THE ROUGH WITH THE SMOOTH

In the 1986 British Open at Turnberry, Greg Norman dominated the tournament with a great display of long, straight hitting on a course with wasp-waisted fairways and with severe rough waiting for those who missed them. Norman's strength, and the improvement in his short game, helped him to a second-round 63 and a 69 on the final day, to secure a comfortable victory by five strokes. Here he plays a delicate pitch from wet rough and celebrates his triumph on the last green.

At the heart of Norman's extraordinary talent is an ability to propel a golf ball vast distances. But, unlike many others who have had similar reputations, he is also a straight hitter. Tom Weiskopf, no slouch at long hitting himself, rates the Australian as the longest straight hitter he has ever seen. Norman's long game was remarkable from the very beginning, but he had to work hard on his short game. Here he was helped in no small measure by the great Australian player and teacher, Norman Von Nida. The work Greg Norman devoted to improving his putting stroke paid off handsomely, for today he is considered one of the most reliable putters in the game of golf.

WORLDWIDE VICTORIES

Since Norman's first tournament win, victories have flowed in a steady stream from all over the world. He joined the European Tour the year after he turned professional and won the Martini International on his way to finishing twentieth on the money list. By 1980 he had beaten Sandy Lyle in the final to win the first of three World Matchplay titles he would take in a seven-year period; also in 1980, he finished second on the European money list, topped the Australian Order of Merit, and won the Australian Open.

Two years later, in 1982, despite a restricted schedule, Norman emerged as the top money winner in Europe in a remarkable season that saw him, among other triumphs, become the first player to defend successfully the Dunlop Masters title. He had two closing rounds of 65 for a 17-under-par total and victory over his nearest rival by no

Studied putting
Norman is not a natural putter, but hard work and expert coaching have improved his short game.

fewer than eight strokes. Much of his success that year was due to a tremendous improvement in his putting.

Norman saw the European campaign as an apprenticeship. After reaching the top there, he felt it was time to take on the lucrative U.S. Tour. He was unsuccessful in his first attempt in 1983, but the following year he finished in ninth place on the money list.

Superstar Status

By 1986 Norman was on top of the U.S. money list with more than $650,000 and had earned himself superstar status. In that year he won twice on the U.S. Tour, was runner-up four times, and finished in the top ten in more than half of the 19 events in which he played.

More significantly, 1986 was the year when Norman joined that exclusive band of players who have won one of the game's recognized Major championships. The year had not started well, although Norman had been well placed to win both the U.S. Masters at Augusta and the U.S. Open at Shinnecock Hills. At Augusta he lost the Masters by hitting a 4-iron wildly into the crowd at the last hole, when a 4 would have given him a tie with Jack Nicklaus. At Shinnecock Hills, he was in the lead going into the final round, but then shot a disastrous 75.

It was a different story in the British Open at Turnberry. Here Greg Norman's ability as a long, straight hitter was a definite advantage on the narrow fairways. His second round of 63, including three putts on the last green, equaled the Championship record, and after coping well with the wet and windy conditions of the third round, he led by one stroke going into the final 18 holes. When he holed a 40-yard bunker shot at the 3rd for a birdie, Norman suddenly had a five-stroke lead. In the end, he won comfortably, without any pressure.

Masters miss (above)
Playing at Augusta in 1986, Norman would have tied with Nicklaus but for a wild shot at the last hole.

Tough at the Top

Despite Norman's undoubted talent, he did not follow up his British Open win with other successes. But in the big events he has perhaps suffered more at the hands of fate than most players. Bob Tway holed a bunker shot at the last hole to beat him in the 1986 USPGA at Inverness; he was beaten in a play-off for the U.S. Masters when Larry Mize chipped into the hole in 1987; and after shooting 64 in the final round of the 1989 British Open at Troon, he lost in a three-way play-off to Mark Calcavecchia. Perhaps Greg's greatest golf is yet to come.

Gregory John Norman

Won Australian Open 1980, 1985, 1987; French Open 1980; Suntory World Matchplay 1980, 1983, 1986; Australian Masters 1981, 1983, 1984, 1987, 1989, 1990; Dunlop Masters 1981, 1982; Canadian Open 1984; British Open 1986; European Open 1986. World Cup 1976, 1978. Dunhill Cup 1985–90. Harry Vardon Trophy 1982. Vardon Trophy 1989, 1990.

Suntory trophy
Greg Norman receives the Suntory World Matchplay Trophy in 1986, recording his third victory in this prestigious event.

ANDY NORTH

BORN THORP, WISCONSIN, U.S.A., MARCH 9, 1950

ANDY NORTH SUFFERED an early sporting injury that led to his having to give up football and basketball; in both games his play reached a high standard. His height of 6 ft. 4 in. (1.93m) added to his health problems. Although he did return to basketball at the college level, North had by then demonstrated his ability as a golfer.

Fine style (right) *North finishes a drive during the 1990 British Open. One of the tallest of golfers, he has had injury problems because of his height.*

Andy North joined the USPGA Tour in 1973 with a good record as an amateur. He had been an All-American choice three times, and had won the Wisconsin Amateur in 1969 and the Western Amateur two years later.

North's first professional tournament win did not come until 1977, but in the following year he leapt to prominence as winner of the 1978 U.S. Open at Cherry Hills. The victory was not achieved without some anxious moments. With five holes to play, North led by four strokes and, although he frittered shots away on the homeward stretch, he still needed only a bogey-5 at the last to win.

Narrow victory
Andy North had some anxious moments (above) *on his way to his second U.S. Open title at Oakland Hills in 1985. He finally took the trophy* (left) *with a 279 total, one stroke ahead of Denis Watson, Dave Barr, and Tze-Chung Chen.*

He made it, but with a struggle. Bunkered in three, he needed to get up and down from the sand for victory. He splashed out to leave a short putt for the title.

In 1985 he won his second U.S. Open, this time at Oakland Hills, overtaking Tze-Chung Chen of Taiwan in the last round. In both his Open victories, North beat many more fancied players, and it has been said that he was lucky. However, Majors are not won by luck; each time, North played the steadiest golf through the week, and fully deserved his success.

Andy North has continued to be beset by injuries. He has had particular problems with his knee joints and has scarcely ever completed a full season. But he is known as a man who always enjoys his golf. His strange putting style, gripping a toy-like putter and bending almost in two for the stroke, is one of the most idiosyncratic on the Tour.

ANDREW STEWART NORTH

WON U.S. OPEN 1978, 1985. WORLD CUP 1978. RYDER CUP 1985.

Christy O'Connor

Born Galway, Ireland, December 21, 1924

One of the best professionals ever to have come from Ireland, Christy O'Connor was a prominent member of the group of players who developed professional golf in the British Isles in the days before the start of the European Tour, at a time when world golf was dominated by the United States.

Last British win
At Lindrick in 1957, O'Connor helped Great Britain and Ireland win the Ryder Cup for the first time for 34 years, and for the last time ever.

Although he never achieved his ambition of winning the British Open, O'Connor nearly made it three times. He was joint-runner-up in 1965 at Birkdale and twice took third place – in 1958 at Royal Lytham and in 1961 at Birkdale.

He was, however, a prolific winner of other tournaments, and won the Irish Professional Championship ten times. He was a regular selection for the Ryder Cup team; no other player has taken part in ten Ryder Cup matches. He played in the World Cup on 15 occasions, and, with Harry Bradshaw, won it in 1958. He has been at Royal Dublin since 1959.

An Irishman with great charm, Christy O'Connor had a big following from his earliest days. The crowds flocked to see him and to enjoy his company. One of his characteristics was to improve his scores throughout a tournament and to reserve his best for the last. On many occasions, he "stole" a win after all had seemed lost. In his later years, O'Connor has remained an intuitive striker of the ball.

Always a formidable competitor, he has played the game of golf in the spirit intended, maintaining its true traditions.

Christy O'Connor

Won Dunlop Masters 1956, 1959; PGA Matchplay 1957; World Seniors 1976, 1977; PGA Seniors 1976, 1977, 1979, 1981, 1982, 1983. Ryder Cup 1955–73. World Cup 1956–64, 1966–69, 1971, 1975. Harry Vardon Trophy 1961, 1962.

Christy O'Connor, Jr.

Born Galway, Ireland, August 19, 1948

A perfectly struck 2-iron to within tap-in distance at the last hole in the 1989 Ryder Cup remains, for all who saw it, a vivid memory of a titanic struggle that resulted in the famous trophy remaining on the European side of the Atlantic. The stroke was played by Christy O'Connor, Jr., nephew of the legendary O'Connor, Sr.

Christy O'Connor, Jr. is one of the most popular players ever to grace the European golf scene. His shot at The Belfry gave him a one-hole victory over long-hitting Fred Couples of the United States. It also gained a vital point for the Europeans.

O'Connor's reaction when he arrived on the green to take the cheers of the crowd forms another indelible picture of that marvelous match. Later he sold the club to an Irish businessman for £50,000 and donated the money to a hospice in his native west of Ireland. Christy's only previous Ryder Cup outing had been in 1975, after he won the Irish Open. He also tied for third in the British Open at Royal St. George's in 1985.

Christy O'Connor, Jr.

Won Irish Open 1975. Ryder Cup 1975, 1989. World Cup 1974–75, 1978, 1985, 1989. Dunhill Cup 1985, 1989.

Steady record (right)
O'Connor has been a consistent performer on the European Tour.

Captain's thanks (left)
Captain Tony Jacklin congratulates Christy O'Connor after his historic putt that beat Fred Couples in the 1989 Ryder Cup.

AYAKO OKAMOTO

BORN HIROSHIMA, JAPAN, APRIL 2, 1951

THERE CAN BE no doubt at all who is the best woman golfer yet to have emerged from Japan: she is Ayako Okamoto. Indeed, she is one of the best international golfers regardless of gender. At a mere 5 ft. 5 in. (1.65m), Okamoto depends on the precision of her swing to give her tee shots enough distance, allowing her to keep up with all but the longest of hitters. Both her pitching and her putting are immaculate.

Ayako had won 20 tournaments in Japan – eight in the single year of 1981 – before she decided to find out what impression she could make on the American Women's Tour. In her first nine years on the U.S. golf circuit, she was victorious in 18 tournaments. When she visited Britain for the first time in 1984, she won the Women's British Open at Woburn Country Club by 11 strokes.

VICTORY IN GERMANY

In 1990, at the age of 39, Ayako took the Ladies' German Open title. In the final round she came home in 32 for a pace-setting 67. Cindy Rarick and Laurette Maritz both came to the 72nd hole needing a birdie to win, but neither could manage better than par. In a sudden-death play-off both Rarick and Okamoto made birdies at the first extra hole, and then tied on the next two. Finally Okamoto won with a steady par at the fourth extra hole.

During the German Open, Britain's Laura Davies commented, "Anyone who finishes ahead of Ayako Okamoto is going to win." That sums up Okamoto's standing in women's international golf.

Winning ways
In 1989 and 1990, Ayako Okamoto won four U.S. tournaments, and was runner-up in four more, confirming her status as the leading Japanese woman golfer.

AYAKO OKAMOTO

WON WOMEN'S BRITISH OPEN 1984; LADIES' GERMAN OPEN 1990. WINNER OF 18 U.S. LPGA EVENTS 1982–90. ROLEX PLAYER OF THE YEAR 1987.

FRANCIS OUIMET

BORN BROOKLINE, MASSACHUSETTS, U.S.A., MAY 8, 1893; DIED 1967

THE TRIUMPH OF 20-year-old amateur Francis Ouimet in the 1913 U.S. Open Championship was a turning point in the history of American golf. Until that moment, the game had been perceived as the preserve of the rich, but this marvelous victory by a young man from an ordinary American family fired the imagination of the whole country and set in motion the steady rise of the game's popularity in the United States.

Francis Ouimet (pronounced "Wimmet") did not come from a wealthy background, but fortunately when he was a youngster his family, who lived in Brookline, moved to a house near the Country Club, and he was allowed to play on the course.

He was a caddie from the age of 11, although he had to give up this job at 16 to avoid losing his amateur status. By the time he was 19, he was an accomplished player and won the Massachusetts State Championship. He took time off work to play in the U.S. Amateur in 1913, but thought he would not get leave to play in the U.S. Open later in the same year, even though it was being held at Brookline, his local course.

Ouimet's boss, however, saw to it that he played. By the time Ouimet stood on the 13th tee in the final round, Harry

People's champion
A stamp was issued in the United States in 1988 to celebrate the 75th anniversary of Ouimet's famous win in the 1913 U.S. Open.

Vardon and Ted Ray, the two leading British professionals, seemed to have the Open sewn up. They had already finished and had tied, well ahead of the American field. Yet Ouimet completed the last six holes in two under par to tie with the British pair, and then, contrary to all expectations, went on to win the play-off.

Amateur rivals
As the non-playing captain of the U.S. Walker Cup team in 1947, Ouimet (left) ties an armband on the opposing captain, John Beck.

High Regard

After this remarkable victory, the rest of Ouimet's career was something of an anti-climax. The following year he won the U.S. Amateur and the French Amateur, and was fifth in the U.S. Open. He won the U.S. Amateur again in 1931. He played in the first Anglo–American match in 1921 and participated in every Walker Cup from 1922 to 1949.

He was a modest, sincere individual with a delightful character, and was held in the highest regard by his fellow golfers. In 1951 he became the first American golfer to be elected captain of the prestigious Royal & Ancient Golf Club.

R & A captain
Ouimet is resplendent in his red coat as the first American captain of the Royal & Ancient Golf Club in 1951.

Francis de Sales Ouimet

Won U.S. Open 1913; French Amateur 1914; U.S. Amateur 1914, 1931. Walker Cup 1922–34 (captain 1932–34, non-playing captain 1936–49). PGA Hall of Fame 1940. Captain R & A Golf Club 1951. World Golf Hall of Fame 1974.

Alf Padgham

Born Caterham, England, July 2, 1906; Died 1966

Alf Padgham was a tall, slim man who had a lovely natural swing reminiscent of Harry Vardon. His long game was always immaculate, but his putting was variable. Padgham was one of the group of British players who upheld the professional flag during the 1930s. His great year was 1936, when he carried all before him, ending the season as British Open champion.

Padgham had been threatening to win the British Open for some time before his 1936 victory at Hoylake. He came in third in 1934, was runner-up in 1935, and was never out of the top seven from 1932 to 1938.

A member of the British team that played in South Africa in 1936–7, he started with a victory, but then seemed to lose his touch and was never quite able to regain it. He was one of several fine players who missed productive years because of the Second World War.

Alf Padgham was not a charismatic figure. He dressed somberly, usually in a waterproof jacket, and although he had a great sense of humor it often revealed itself only to his friends. In public he was shy and could appear somewhat taciturn.

Card player (above)
A 1930s cigarette card bears witness to Alf Padgham's fame.

Alfred Harry Padgham

Won PGA Matchplay 1931, 1935; Irish Open 1932; German Open 1934; British Open 1936; Dutch Open 1938. Ryder Cup 1933–37. Captain British PGA 1936.

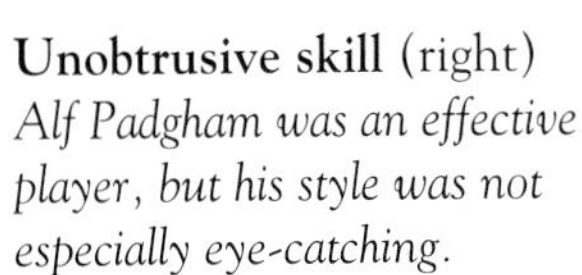

Unobtrusive skill (right)
Alf Padgham was an effective player, but his style was not especially eye-catching.

Arnold Palmer

Born Latrobe, Pennsylvania, U.S.A., September 10, 1929

The popularity of golf today, as both a spectator and a participant sport, probably owes more to the influence of Arnold Palmer than to anyone else who has ever played the game. The arrival of Palmer on the golf scene, coinciding as it did with the explosion of television as the medium for the masses, brought the game to the attention of millions. When the business acumen of American lawyer Mark McCormack was added to this potent combination, professional golf hit the big time.

Change of champions (left)
Kel Nagle congratulates Palmer on his 1961 British Open win at Birkdale.

Legendary strength (below)
Palmer has always been a marvelous athlete, immensely strong, with huge shoulders and hands.

A shot at success (above)
A good approach shot to the 18th green at Wentworth helps Palmer to victory in the Piccadilly World Matchplay in 1964.

Arnold Palmer brought something new and different to the game: excitement and naked aggression. When Palmer hit a golf ball, the crowds came out in the thousands to cheer and join what became known as "Arnie's Army."

Palmer, the son of a professional, took to the game at a very young age. He had plenty of natural ability, but an early incident helped turn a young man with considerable talent into one of the greatest names in the history of sport. Playing in a junior match while still at school, the young Arnold Palmer, furious at duffing a shot, threw his club over some trees in a fit of temper. On the way home his father, Deacon, turned on him. "Pap told me," Palmer recalled, "that this is a gentleman's game and he was ashamed of me. If I ever did such a thing again he was through with me as a golfer."

Early Tragedy

A little later in Palmer's youth, another incident occurred that deeply affected his life. A new-found friend, Buddy Worsham, was killed in an auto accident; Palmer was so shaken by this tragedy that he dropped out of the education system and enlisted in the U.S. Coast Guard for three years.

However, he won the Ohio State Amateur while on leave, and in 1954, after his discharge from the Coast Guard, also won the U.S. Amateur Championship. He then turned professional and met Mark McCormack. The professional game was never the same again.

With McCormack handling the business side, Palmer was able to concentrate on what he did best – playing golf. He had a superb putting touch, immense physical strength, fierce determination to go for everything, and an uncanny ability to power his way out of trouble when things went wrong. Palmer's motto was, "If you can see it, you can hole it." It was a philosophy that made him the most exciting player in the game's history. He was always pure theater, and his swashbuckling style helped to make him the people's hero.

Palmer's all-or-nothing attitude dazzled the British golfing public when he first crossed the Atlantic in the early 1960s to breathe new life into the British Open, which was flagging slightly as it moved into its second century. He single-handedly revived the fortunes of the Championship. When he kept coming back to the event, the other top American players followed him, thus restoring the tournament to its premier position in world golf.

Palmer's record is perhaps not as great as his enormous talents suggest it should have been. Apart from his two British Open victories, he won the U.S. Masters four times and finished second twice. He won only one U.S. Open, although he was runner-up four times, and he was never better than second in the USPGA. His victories in the Majors all occurred between 1958 and 1964.

However, Palmer won a host of important championships all over the world, and later played a leading part in establishing the immense popularity that the U.S. Senior Tour now enjoys.

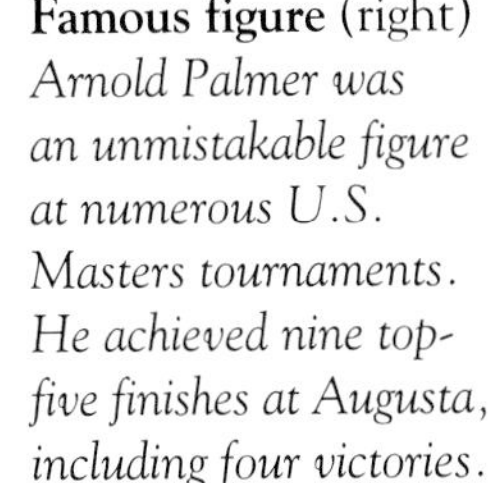

Famous figure (right)
Arnold Palmer was an unmistakable figure at numerous U.S. Masters tournaments. He achieved nine top-five finishes at Augusta, including four victories.

Palmer power (left)
Palmer fights his way out of trouble in the 1982 U.S. Open.

Precision putter (right)
A marvelous putting touch was responsible for many of Palmer's spectacular successes.

Arnold Daniel Palmer

Won U.S. Masters 1958, 1960, 1962, 1964; U.S. Open 1960; British Open 1961, 1962; World Matchplay 1964, 1967; USPGA Seniors 1980; USGA Senior Open 1981. Winner of 61 U.S. Tour events 1956–73. Ryder Cup 1961–67, 1971–73 (non-playing captain 1975). World Cup 1960, 1962–64, 1966–67 (individual winner 1967). USPGA Player of the Year 1960, 1962. Vardon Trophy 1961, 1962, 1964, 1967. World Golf Hall of Fame 1974. USPGA Hall of Fame 1980.

A winning smile
Approaching 60 but still winning on the Senior Tour, Palmer holds up the 1988 Crestar Classic trophy.

WILLIE PARK, JR.

BORN MUSSELBURGH, SCOTLAND, FEBRUARY 4, 1864; DIED 1925

WILLIE PARK'S FATHER was the first British Open champion, and won the Championship four times. From him Willie learned to love the game, and it was natural that he should inherit much of his father's skill. An exceptional golfer, he was also a successful businessman, expanding his father's club- and ball-making business, was the designer of approximately 170 courses, and the inventor of several new golf clubs.

Famous putter
Park regarded putting as the most important aspect of his game. He used a special putting cleek, with a goose-neck, offset head.

Park was tall and had an easy and unhurried swing that developed great power. He seemed to strike the ball quite effortlessly. His putting was magnificent, and at times almost uncannily accurate. With his famous putter "Old Pawky," he was hard to beat.

Park won the British Open twice, at Prestwick in 1887 and at Musselburgh in 1889, after a tie with Andrew Kirkaldy. At Prestwick in 1898 he decided to play safe at the last hole for the 4 he thought he needed to tie with Vardon, only to find that Vardon had made a 3, and that he was thus only the runner-up. At that time there were no scoreboards around the course and a player had to rely on reports from spectators to keep track of competitors' scores.

Willie Park was a great player of challenge matches. His most famous encounter was a two-course contest with Harry Vardon in 1899 at North Berwick and Ganton. Special trains were run, and the crowd at North Berwick was estimated to be 10,000. Vardon won easily. Park was active in golf all his life. His 1896 book, *The Game of Golf*, was the first complete book on golf by a professional.

Park Royal
This 56-sided ball, the Royal, was invented by Willie Park, Jr. in 1896. Park claimed the hexagonal panels slowed the ball on the green.

WILLIAM PARK, JR.

WON BRITISH OPEN 1887, 1889.

GARY PLAYER

BORN JOHANNESBURG, SOUTH AFRICA, NOVEMBER 1, 1935

MOST COMMENTATORS PUT Gary Player's success down to his determination, his muscle-building exercises, his diet, his unrelenting practice, or his positive thinking – anything, it seems, but his golf game. Yet any golfer who wins more than 100 tournaments worldwide, including the U.S. Open, the British Open (three times), the U.S. Masters (three times), and the USPGA (twice), must surely be able to play the game rather well.

First win
The 20-year-old Gary Player receives a check for £500 after winning his first important event, the Dunlop Masters at Sunningdale in 1956.

It is true that when Player first came to Britain from South Africa at the age of 19, the advice given to him by more than one top professional was to return home and take up some other game. His hooker's grip offended them, and possibly his eager confidence. But it is also true that he won the Dunlop Masters at Sunningdale the very next year. In his winning total of 270 he had two 64s – not bad for somebody who was alleged to have a "poor swing."

Player weakened his grip on the advice of the Welsh wizard, Dai Rees. His Dunlop win gained him an invitation to the U.S. Masters, and in the United States he studied the teachings of Ben Hogan. These he practiced as diligently as Hogan himself. He put on plenty of muscle too. In 1956 he won the first of his 13 South African Open titles, and in 1958 recorded the first of seven wins in the Australian

Open. In 1959 he opened his account in the Majors, winning the British Open at Muirfield. In 1965, when he took the U.S. Open title at St. Louis after a tie with Kel Nagle, he became one of only four golfers to win all four Majors.

Gary Player's second British Open win in 1968 – a tense struggle with Jack Nicklaus in foul weather at Carnoustie – and his second USPGA Championship at Oakland Hills in 1972 held out the prospect of winning all four Majors twice.

Round under 60

In 1974 Player not only won the U.S. Masters and the British Open at Royal Lytham – four shots ahead of Peter Oosterhuis – but shot one round of 59 in the Brazilian Open. His final victory in the U.S. Masters, in 1978 at the age of 42, was his ninth Major win, but he never won a second U.S. Open.

Player was also the king of matchplay. In 1965 he had his first and most dramatic win in the World Matchplay. Seven down to Tony Lema after 19 holes, he clawed back to win at the 37th; in the final he beat Peter Thomson. He beat Nicklaus in the same competition by 6-and-4 in 1966, and again by 5-and-4 in 1971.

Concentrated golf
Few players in golf have better concentration than Gary Player.

Gary Jim Player

Won British Open 1959, 1968, 1974; U.S. Masters 1961, 1974, 1978; USPGA 1962, 1972; U.S. Open 1965; World Matchplay 1965, 1966, 1968, 1971, 1973. Winner 21 U.S. Tour events 1958–78. World Cup 1956–60, 1962–68, 1971–73, 1977 (individual winner 1965, 1977). Bob Jones Award 1966. World Golf Hall of Fame 1974.

Bunker king (above)
Recognized as a great bunker player, Gary blasts from the sand during the U.S. Masters in 1985.

Man in black (left)
In his early days Player always wore black; it became his trademark. He claimed that black made him stronger by absorbing sunlight.

TED RAY

BORN JERSEY, CHANNEL ISLANDS, MARCH 28, 1877; DIED 1943

LIKE THE GREAT *Harry Vardon, Ted Ray was born in Jersey and as a young player had high hopes of following in the footsteps of his famous Channel Island contemporary. It was cruel fortune that he arrived on the professional golf scene just when the Great Triumvirate of Harry Vardon, James Braid, and J.H. Taylor was at its peak, leaving little but leftovers for other golfers. Nonetheless, there was inspiration to be found from their lead, and Ray learned much from playing with and against them.*

Ambassadors of golf
Ray (left) visited New York with Vardon in 1913. Their tour attracted huge public interest.

Ted Ray played his first British Open in 1899 and made the top ten in 1902. From 1906 onward he was always in the leading group and came in third in 1908. But it was not until 1912 that he finally won his first British Open title.

Ray reached the first Matchplay final in 1903, losing to James Braid. Although he never won this tournament, he reached the final in both 1911 and 1912.

Second best
Ted Ray had a fine swing and was a great player, but lived in the shadow of the legendary Vardon.

In 1913, Ray accompanied Harry Vardon on a record-breaking trip to the United States, playing a series of matches and exhibitions. The high point of the tour was the U.S. Open at Brookline, when both of them tied with the unknown American youngster Francis Ouimet; it was Ouimet who won the play-off.

Ray returned with Vardon to the United States in 1920 for another very successful tour. At Inverness he won the U.S. Open, becoming one of only three British players to win both the British and U.S. Opens. He twice played for Great Britain against the United States, and was in the first Ryder Cup match.

RICH CAREER

Ted Ray had a long and successful career. He continued to play in the British Open until 1932, coming close to winning the championship at Prestwick in 1925, when he finished runner-up to Jim Barnes by a single stroke.

A professional at Ganton for some years, following Harry Vardon, Ted Ray moved to the Oxhey club in Hertfordshire where he served from 1912 until his retirement in 1941.

EDWARD RAY

WON BRITISH OPEN 1912; U.S. OPEN 1920. G.B. VS. U.S.A. 1921, 1926. RYDER CUP 1927 (CAPTAIN).

Vintage player
Ted Ray continued to play championship golf well into his fifties. The familiar plus-foured figure was seldom seen on the course without his pipe.

DAI REES

BORN BARRY, WALES, MARCH 31, 1913; DIED 1983

*W*ELSHMAN DAI REES *was an incredible dynamo of a man. He won his first British PGA Matchplay Championship at the age of 23, defeating Ernest Whitcombe in 1936. A year later, he beat the legendary Byron Nelson in a Ryder Cup clash. And at the end of his career, at the age of 60, he finished second in the Martini Tournament after younger men had suggested he really ought to quit.*

Unorthodox grip
Rees used the "baseball" grip, with the two hands independent of each other.

Winning the Ryder Cup
Rees captained the 1957 team that won the Ryder Cup for Britain for the first time in 24 years.

Rees's energetic life included military service in Africa in the Second World War, when he kept his two-handed swing together by hitting shoe-polish cans with an old club he had found. One of the many highlights of his postwar career was a game with King George VI, whom he helped reach the turn in 38 in foursomes, much to the delight of both players.

Dai Rees had an extremely successful international career. He played in nine Ryder Cup matches between 1937 and 1961, and he was captain of the 1957 British team that defeated the United States at Lindrick, Yorkshire – the last time that Great Britain and Ireland won before the event was broadened to bring in European players in 1979.

As an individual player, Rees won four British Matchplay titles and was considered by most players of his day as the best golfer never to win the British Open. But he should have won in 1961 at rain-lashed Royal Birkdale. He took seven strokes at the first hole in the last round, but ended with a remarkable 72, thanks to three birdies in the last four holes. However, he was still one vital stroke behind the winner, Arnold Palmer.

CHAMPION RUNNER-UP

Since Rees had also tied for second behind Ben Hogan at Carnoustie in 1953, and tied for second behind Peter Thomson at Birkdale the following year, people began to say that he had replaced Jimmy Adams as "champion runner-up."

One journalist, who played with Rees in a pro-am on a windswept Castle Harbour course in Bermuda, tried to find out just how he played such a brilliant variety of shots. "The answer is in the mind and the hands," said Dai. "Either you have it, or you haven't. . ."

DAVID JAMES REES, CBE

WON PGA MATCHPLAY 1936, 1938, 1949, 1950; IRISH OPEN 1948; DUNLOP MASTERS 1950, 1962. RYDER CUP 1937, 1947–61 (CAPTAIN 1955–61, NON-PLAYING CAPTAIN 1967). WORLD CUP 1954, 1956–62, 1964. G.B. VS. COMMONWEALTH 1956 (CAPTAIN). G.B. VS. EUROPE 1958 (CAPTAIN). HARRY VARDON TROPHY 1955, 1959. BRITISH PGA CAPTAIN 1967, 1976.

ALLAN ROBERTSON

BORN ST. ANDREWS, SCOTLAND, SEPTEMBER 11, 1815; DIED 1859

ALLAN ROBERTSON WAS the first professional golfer to gain real public recognition, and the outstanding player of his day. He was a great ambassador for the game, a highly respected individual who could associate comfortably with everyone, lord or laborer. When he died at the age of 44 in 1859, the year before the Open Championship was first contested, a member of the Royal & Ancient Club intoned, "They may shut up their shops and toll their bells, for the greatest among them is gone."

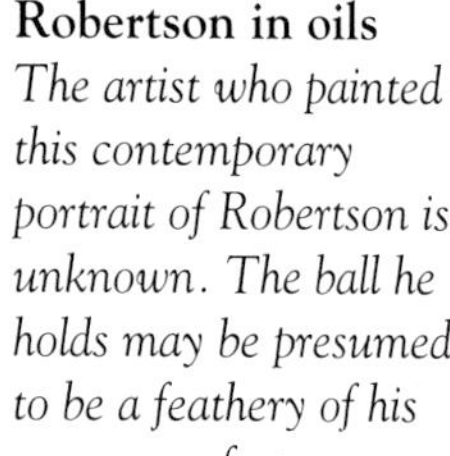

Robertson in oils
The artist who painted this contemporary portrait of Robertson is unknown. The ball he holds may be presumed to be a feathery of his own manufacture.

Allan Robertson's family had lived in St. Andrews for generations. His grandfather, Peter Robertson, had been a ball-maker and professional golfer, and his father, David, was also a ball-maker and an accomplished golfer. It was not surprising that Allan followed the family tradition.

His earliest playthings were small clubs, and he was seldom off the links. When he became a working man, he would go down to play at first light before anyone else was around and while the dew was still on the ground. He was out on the course again after work if it was still light enough. As a young man he swept the board among all other players and was recognized as the undisputed champion golfer of his age.

Winning partnership
Allan Robertson (right) and Old Tom Morris are said never to have lost when playing together.

During his lifetime the town of St. Andrews was resurrected by Sir Hugh Lyon Playfair. Allan Robertson did for golf at St. Andrews what Provost Playfair did for the town. His own keenness and dedication, both to the game and to St. Andrews Links, helped popularize golf and drew people to the town to play.

Robertson was not only a brilliant player, but also a man of great honor on and off the course. He wore a habitually droll expression; nothing ever disturbed him when he was playing.

Tom Morris – "Old" Tom Morris, as he would later be known – was apprenticed to Robertson as a ball-maker. At that time only two or three featheries could be turned out by one man in a day's work; consequently they were expensive. In addition to supplying local demand, balls were exported all over Britain and even to the colonies. In Robertson's best year some 2,500 balls were produced.

RIFT OVER RUBBER

When the use of gutta percha made much cheaper balls possible, Robertson was dismayed because he thought his business would be ruined. Later, in 1852, he would relent, but at first he refused to have anything to do with the new rubber substance. This caused a rift with Tom Morris, who left to set up on his own.

Although Robertson quarreled with Morris in business, he continued to play with him as a partner at golf. It was said of Robertson that he never lost a match, but this hardly seems possible. However, he did lose very few, though in his later years he apparently tended to avoid head-on singles confrontations with some of the better players of the day. It is almost certainly true that he was never defeated when he was playing with Old Tom Morris as a partner.

There were many famous matches. One of the earliest was in 1840 when Robertson defeated Tom Alexander, a ball-maker from Musselburgh, and one of the best players of the day. There was also a series of singles against Willie Dunn from Musselburgh. But perhaps the most famous match of all was when Robertson and Morris took on Willie and his twin brother, Jamie Dunn, in 1849 in a contest over three courses. The stake was £400, an enormous sum of money at the time.

Battle of Giants

In the first match, at Musselburgh, the Dunns won easily over the 36 holes. At St. Andrews the home pair won, everything then resting on the final match at North Berwick. Rival crowds turned up to support each pair, and the referee had considerable difficulty in keeping order as the excitement mounted.

With eight holes of the 36 left to play, the Dunns were four up. Odds of 20 to one were being offered against the Dunn brothers losing, but a storming finish by Robertson and Morris saw them all square with two to go, and the St. Andrews pair went on to win both final holes to record a truly remarkable victory.

Allan Robertson was a short man, but he was of robust stature, with a thick neck and a stoop. He was noted for his long, cool swing. If his driving was attractive to watch, his short game was exquisite. He was at his best with his half and quarter shots to the flag.

Robertson was the first to play the Old course at St. Andrews in under 80 strokes, a remarkable feat that he accomplished playing with Mr. Bethune of Blebo in 1858, the year before his death. His score was an outward nine of 40 and a homeward one of 39, a total achieved on a course that was much rougher than it is today.

Dressed in his red jacket and with his customary cap, he was almost part of the scenery at St. Andrews. He enjoyed the best of health until the very year he died. He never recovered from an attack of jaundice in the spring of 1859, and he died early in the following September.

The Royal & Ancient Club passed a resolution: "This meeting has heard with deep regret of the death of Allan Robertson, and they desire to record on their minutes the opinion, universally entertained, of the almost unrivalled skill with which he played the game of golf, combining a ready and correct judgement with most accurate execution. They desire also to express the sense of propriety of his whole conduct, and unvarying civility. . ."

Robertson's club and ball
With this playclub and guttie ball, preserved in the Royal & Ancient Golf Club collection, Allan Robertson recorded a round of 79 on the Old course at St. Andrews in 1858, becoming the first player to complete the course in under 80. He died the following year.

Allan Robertson

A renowned golfer and maker of clubs and balls.

Links with the past
Allan Robertson stands third from the right in this photograph taken around 1850. Teeing-up is R & A captain Frank Wemyss; second from the left is Old Tom Morris.

DOUG SANDERS

BORN CEDARTOWN, GEORGIA, U.S.A., JULY 24, 1933

ALTHOUGH A FINE player, Doug Sanders failed to achieve the success and acclaim commensurate with his undoubted skill. Never winning a Major title, Sanders nevertheless built up an impressive record. Between 1955 and 1972 he won a total of 20 U.S. Tour events and was regularly among the top 60 money winners.

Avoiding trouble
Sanders plays out of the rough at Hoylake in 1968.

Sanders was runner-up in the USPGA Championship in 1959, runner-up in the U.S. Open in 1961, and fourth in the U.S. Masters in 1966. He was also twice runner-up in the British Open, in 1966 and in 1970. On the second occasion, in 1970, Sanders had a short putt on the last green at St. Andrews to win, but after agonizing over the shot for some time, he missed. The following day he lost the play-off to Jack Nicklaus.

Sanders's technique was unusual: he used a short backswing that, it was once said, could be completed in a phone-booth. However, his great strength ensured that he played all shots well. An entertaining golfer on the course, Doug Sanders had a serious side too, preferring to put much of the money that he earned from golf back into the game to encourage youngsters.

DOUGLAS GEORGE SANDERS

WON CANADIAN OPEN 1956. WINNER OF 20 U.S. TOUR EVENTS 1956–72. RYDER CUP 1967.

Colorful character
Sanders always cut a flamboyant figure on the course and had an extensive collection of garish clothes.

GENE SARAZEN

BORN HARRISON, NEW YORK, U.S.A., FEBRUARY 27, 1902

LIKE MANY PLAYERS of his era, Gene Sarazen (born Eugene Saraceni) began his golf career as a caddie. He left school early to help his father as a carpenter, but for health reasons he was advised to find an outdoor job. As a caddie he played regularly and made spectacular progress. By the age of 21 he had won three Major events.

When the young Sarazen was appointed as an assistant pro in Fort Wayne, club members there helped him to enter the 1920 U.S. Open. He finished far down the order, but he could clearly live in the big time and his confidence grew.

In 1921 he again fared poorly in the Open, but he knocked reigning champion Jock Hutchison out of the USPGA Championship, then a matchplay event. In 1922 he won the U.S. Open at Skokie and the USPGA at Oakmont, becoming the first player to win both events in the same year. This was an extraordinary feat for a player who was only 20 years old.

At this time Sarazen became firm friends with Walter Hagen, a golfer ten years his senior. Hagen had missed the USPGA that year, so a 72-hole match was arranged between the two – the "World Championship" – and Sarazen

Gum card king
Sarazen was featured as a sporting hero on this gum card in 1933, the year of his third USPGA victory.

Custom built
In the early 1930s, Sarazen designed the first sand iron. With its straight face and heavy sole, it transformed bunker shots.

Natural talent
Sarazen had a lovely natural swing, and although only 5 ft. 4 in. (1.63m) tall, he was always ready to attack.

won. He went on to defend his USPGA title successfully at Pelham in 1923, increasing his victories in the Majors to three by the time he was 21.

Gene Sarazen played a good deal of exhibition golf in the following years and experimented with changes in his swing. But it was not a success and he failed to make much impact at the top level for some years. It was not until 1930 that he again did well in a Major, finishing as runner-up in the USPGA Championship.

Major Successes

After several attempts, Sarazen finally won the British Open at Prince's in 1932, and later that year he became the U.S. Open champion at Fresh Meadow. In 1933 Sarazen came close to successfully defending his British Open title at St. Andrews, and he also won the USPGA Championship for the third time at Blue Mound, Milwaukee.

Sarazen missed the first U.S. Masters in 1934 because he was playing exhibition golf in Australia, but he won the following year, when he produced one of the most famous strokes in the history of the game. At the par-5 15th hole, in the last round, he holed a two-wood shot over the water for a double eagle which enabled him to tie Craig Wood after 72 holes. He then won the play-off. This victory gave Sarazen the distinction of being the first player to win all four of the current Majors. As late as 1940 he lost a play-off for the U.S. Open title.

Twice winner of the USPGA Seniors Championship, in 1954 and 1958, Sarazen never lost his love of the game. In 1973, at the age of 71, he went to the British Open at Troon on a sentimental journey 50 years after he had failed to qualify there despite being the reigning USPGA and U.S. Open champion. Sarazen celebrated his return to Troon by making a hole-in-one with a 5 iron at the famous 8th hole. The following day, at the same hole, he found a greenside bunker with his tee shot, and then holed the shot from the sand with his sand iron for an almost unbelievable 2; thus he did not need to use his putter on the 8th hole at all.

Life at the top (above)
A relaxed and confident Sarazen sailed to England with his wife in 1924. Only 22, he had already won three Major championships.

In retirement (right)
Known affectionately as "The Squire," because of his interest in farming, Sarazen continued to enjoy the game of golf and outdoor life way past normal retirement age.

Eugene Sarazen

Won U.S. Open 1922, 1932; USPGA 1922, 1923, 1933; British Open 1932; U.S. Masters 1935; USPGA Seniors 1954, 1958. Winner of 18 U.S. Tour events 1922–41. Ryder Cup 1927–37. USPGA Hall of Fame 1940. World Golf Hall of Fame 1974.

SAM SNEAD

BORN ASHWOOD, VIRGINIA, U.S.A., MAY 27, 1912

SAM SNEAD FINISHED *in third place in the USPGA Championship in August, 1974, behind Lee Trevino and Jack Nicklaus and ahead of Gary Player; a few months before, he had been runnerup in the Los Angeles Open. He was 62 years old. It was hard to detect much difference between the quality of his play then and nearly 40 years earlier, when he had made his first appearance as a rookie touring professional on the U.S. Ryder Cup team. Snead, it seemed, could go on for ever.*

Slammin' Sam (above)
Part of the Ryder Cup team in 1953, Snead drives into the distance at Wentworth.

Serious business
Sam Snead walks from the clubhouse at St. Andrews on his way to winning the British Open in 1946, the first Open to be played after the Second World War.

Natural ability (right)
If a poll was ever taken to determine the player from any generation who had the best swing, Sam Snead would have to figure prominently among the leaders.

The secret of Snead's golfing longevity, apart from an unbounded enthusiasm for the game, has much to do with his swing. Although he was self-taught, he developed one of the most elegant swings in the history of the game.

Legend has it that Snead climbed down from the trees and, on his way down, broke off a limb that he fashioned into a golf club. He then went on to win golf tournaments barefooted. The truth is not as harsh.

TALENTED FAMILY

Sam Snead, the youngest son of five, did grow up in the backwoods and did carve out clubs from the limbs of swamp maple. The family was not welloff, although there was enough for them to foster their talents in sports and music.

The young Sam started hitting a ball around with pieces of stick cut to shape, but as the distinguished American golf writer, Dick Aultman, pointed out, "There were far more amateur whiskey distillers than professional golf instructors around Ashwood, Virginia, during the 1920s." Sam, in fact, learned to play by watching his oldest brother, Homer, hit massive drives across the fields on their cow and chicken farm. Young Sam soon graduated to cast-off clubs and became a caddie at The Homestead, a club near his home. Caddying at Hot Springs and later Cascade led eventually to an assistant's post at the Greenbrier at White Sulphur Springs, West Virginia. It was there one day that he made up a foursome with Lawson Little, for two consecutive years the British and U.S. Amateur champion, and with past U.S. Open champions John Goodman and Billy Burke. Sam's round of 61 startled and impressed the others and led to his receiving some support from his club members to try his hand at playing on the professional circuit.

He went to California for the start of the 1937 season, and in his third outing won the Oakland Open with four sub-par rounds for a total of 270. During the season he won five times and was also runner-up in the U.S. Open, a position he was destined to hold four times.

The hillbilly mountain boy from Virginia was a charismatic figure. The American public had not had a golfing

Elegant style (above)
At the age of 57, Snead relies on his idiosyncratic playing style to dig his way successfully out of a sand trap at Las Vegas, Nevada.

The sidewinder (below)
Plagued by putting problems in later life, Sam Snead uses his famous "sidewinder" technique, which is a variation of the banned "croquet" style. He faces the hole, standing to one side of the ball, and swings the putter with his right hand low down the shaft.

star to idolize since Bobby Jones. With Fred Corcoran, the Tour controller, to manage him, Sam at once became a household name. His white shirt, neat trousers, and pork-pie hat with the brim down were as well known as his laconic manner and dry humor.

He had eight tournament wins in 1938, including the Canadian Open. He was also the leading money winner and took the Vardon Trophy for the lowest score average on the Tour. In 1942, he captured his first Major, winning the USPGA title in Atlantic City.

Fighting for Success

In 1946, after the Second World War, Snead entered the British Open at St. Andrews. His final-day rounds of 74 and 75 gave him a comfortable victory by four strokes. In 1949 he won both the U.S. Masters and the USPGA Championship at Richmond, Virginia, and the Vardon Trophy again. He was also the leading money winner for the second time and Player of the Year. In all, Snead won the Vardon Trophy four times and was leading money winner three times in the course of his career.

"Slammin' Sam," as he became known, was a founder of the U.S. Senior Tour. He won the USPGA Seniors title six times, the World Seniors five times, and altogether has more Senior tournament wins to his credit than anyone else.

Although Sam Snead cultivated a hillbilly image, he has been astute in managing his affairs and is an entertaining speaker when persuaded to talk. He has passed on his golfing knowledge in many books and articles.

Samuel Jackson Snead

Won USPGA 1942, 1949, 1951; British Open 1946; U.S. Masters 1949, 1952, 1954; USPGA Seniors 1964, 1965, 1967, 1970, 1972, 1973. Winner of 84 U.S. Tour events 1936–65. Ryder Cup 1937, 1947–55, 1959 (captain 1951, 1959, non-playing captain 1969). World Cup 1954, 1956–62 (individual winner 1961). Vardon Trophy 1938, 1949, 1950, 1955.

Prize catch
Having teed off first – as is traditional – at the U.S. Masters, the three-time Masters champion, still a country boy at heart, stops off along the course for a quiet bit of fishing.

CRAIG STADLER

BORN SAN DIEGO, CALIFORNIA, U.S.A., JUNE 2, 1953

CRAIG STADLER IS a formidable golfer, although his form has been variable over the years. Not a man to dissemble, when his game is going badly he often finds difficulty in hiding his annoyance with himself. But Stadler is a good-hearted and genuine person, instantly recognizable from his bushy moustache and known, inevitably, as "The Walrus."

Stadler had a distinguished career as an amateur before turning professional in 1975 at the age of 22. He won the World Junior in 1971, the U.S. Amateur in 1973, and was an All-America university player in 1974 and 1975. He represented the United States in the Walker Cup of 1975.

In his first few years as a professional Stadler made only a moderate living. His breakthrough came with his first two wins on the Tour in 1980, a year in which he finished eighth in the U.S. money list. His big year, however, was 1982, when he won the U.S. Masters and three other tournaments – the Tucson Open, the Kemper Open and the World Series. He ended the season by taking the Arnold Palmer Award as the leading money winner on the Tour.

Stadler has twice played in the Ryder Cup and his record also includes victories in the 1985 European Masters and the 1990 Scandinavian Enterprise Open.

He is a big man and has had to fight a weight problem, but the power of his hitting more than makes up for the jibes he has to suffer from the press and from his fellow professionals.

Gentle approach
For such a bulky man, Stadler has great delicacy of touch around the green.

CRAIG ROBERT STADLER

WON U.S. AMATEUR 1973; U.S. MASTERS 1982. WALKER CUP 1975. RYDER CUP 1983–85. ARNOLD PALMER AWARD 1982.

JAN STEPHENSON

BORN SYDNEY, NEW SOUTH WALES, AUSTRALIA, DECEMBER 22, 1951

FROM HER EARLIEST days as an Australian schoolgirl champion, Jan Stephenson has been a supremely talented golfer. She is one of the outstanding players in women's golf, and since 1976 has consistently been in the top 15 money winners on the U.S. LPGA list.

Jan Stephenson won her first New South Wales Girls' title when just 13 years old, and went on to win it five times in succession. Four times she won the State Junior title and twice the State Amateur.

She turned professional in 1973 and joined the U.S. LPGA the following year. Jan made her mark immediately and was named Rookie of the Year. Her 17 LPGA victories have included the U.S. Women's Open in 1983 and the LPGA Championship in 1982.

Often admired for her good looks as much as for her play, Jan commented after winning the U.S. Women's Open, "Perhaps people will now watch me as a golfer."

JAN STEPHENSON

WON AUSTRALIAN LADIES' OPEN 1973, 1977; PETER JACKSON CLASSIC 1981; LPGA CHAMPIONSHIP 1982; U.S. WOMEN'S OPEN 1983; LADIES' FRENCH OPEN 1985.

In the pink (left)
Jan Stephenson has had many commercial interests in the fashion world. She is also the first female player to take a professional interest in golf-course design.

Center of attention (above)
Stephenson is a supremely competitive player and almost never allows the eager following that she attracts to interfere with her application and concentration.

CURTIS STRANGE

BORN NORFOLK, VIRGINIA, U.S.A., JANUARY 20, 1955

CONSISTENCY HAS BEEN the hallmark of Curtis Strange's success. His secret lies in hitting greens with uncanny regularity and holing a significant number of putts. In 1988, Strange became the first player to earn more than $1 million in one season on the U.S. Tour, but his finest triumph was winning consecutive U.S. Open Championships in 1988 and 1989.

By the time he was eight years old, Curtis Strange was playing golf every day. He was the son of a golf professional in Norfolk, Virginia, and the game has always been part of his life. As an amateur he developed into a long hitter. When he was 19, Strange was selected for the Eisenhower Trophy team, and the following year he played in the U.S. Walker Cup victory over Great Britain and Ireland.

Curtis Strange turned professional in 1976 and qualified for the U.S. Tour the following year, but he finished well down the money list in both 1977 and 1978. Strange knew that he had to make his swing more reliable and consistent. This he achieved through much hard work and at the expense of some length.

It was hard work well rewarded, for Strange soon emerged as a major force in world golf, winning his first U.S. Tour event in 1979, and the next year finishing third on the U.S. money list. Since then he has won regularly and extensively. He was runner-up in the U.S. Masters in 1985 and in the USPGA Championship at Kemper Lakes in 1989.

Strange's first U.S. Open win, at Brookline in 1988, came after a play-off with Nick Faldo that Strange won by 71 to 75. His successful defense of the title the following year, at Oak Hill, made him the first winner of consecutive Opens since Ben Hogan. Known as "The Grinder," he is a master of the art of winning at golf.

Roughing it (above)
It is rare to see Strange playing from ankle-deep rough. He is one of the game's straightest hitters.

Alone with his thoughts (right)
Strange is an introspective individual, occasionally abrupt in his dealings with other people, notably the press.

In the creek (below)
Strange's hopes of winning the 1985 U.S. Masters sank when he found the water of Rae's Creek at the 13th hole.

CURTIS NORTHRUP STRANGE

WON CANADIAN OPEN 1985, 1987; U.S. OPEN 1988, 1989. WINNER OF 17 U.S .TOUR EVENTS 1979–90. EISENHOWER TROPHY 1974. WALKER CUP 1975. RYDER CUP 1983–89. DUNHILL CUP 1985, 1987–90. ARNOLD PALMER AWARD 1985, 1987, 1988.

FREDDIE TAIT

BORN EDINBURGH, SCOTLAND, JANUARY 11, 1870; DIED 1900

WHEN FREDDIE TAIT was killed leading his men into battle in the Boer War at Koodoosberg Drift, the game of golf lost a great player. He was much loved and admired as a kind and courteous man, and his death cast a great shadow across Scotland. Although he shunned the limelight and tried various subterfuges to avoid publicity, he collected a following wherever he went.

Mark of respect
Lieutenant Tait of the Black Watch was greatly admired by his fellow soldiers.

A man and his dog
A posthumous portrait of Tait by J.H. Lorimer includes his terrier.

The young Freddie took to the links at the age of five. He soon displayed remarkable ability, and by the age of 12 he had played the Old course at St. Andrews in fewer than 100 strokes, a marked achievement in those days for one so young. At this stage he hit the ball as hard as he could, but he soon developed an unhurried and comfortable swing, displaying both power and control.

In 1890 Tait joined the Royal & Ancient Club, and that same year lowered the Old course record to 77 in a match against the former Amateur Champion, A.F. MacFie. Four years later he reduced it again to 72.

Freddie Tait first played in the British Open in 1891 and was three times leading amateur in the event. In 1896 he won the Amateur Championship at Sandwich, trouncing Harold Hilton 8-and-7 in the final. After winning the Amateur title again in 1898 at Hoylake, he lost to John Ball at the 37th hole in an epic final at Prestwick in 1899.

Today he is remembered through the Freddie Tait Medal, which is played for annually in St. Andrews.

FREDERICK GUTHRIE TAIT

WON BRITISH AMATEUR CHAMPIONSHIP 1896, 1898; ST. GEORGE'S CHALLENGE TROPHY 1896, 1898, 1899.

J.H. TAYLOR

BORN NORTHAM, ENGLAND, MARCH 19, 1871; DIED 1963

JOHN HENRY TAYLOR, known throughout his career as "J.H.," was the first to come to prominence of the immortal Triumvirate – Vardon, Braid, and Taylor – who dominated golf in the latter part of the nineteenth and early part of the twentieth centuries. Between them they won no fewer than 16 British Opens, Taylor winning five and finishing runner-up in six others.

J.H. Taylor was born close to the famous links of Westward Ho! where he worked as a youngster. His father had died when J.H. was an infant, and J.H. left school at the age of 11. By the age of 20, he had matured into a fine player and went to Burnham and Berrow as greenskeeper and professional, first making his mark by beating Andrew Kirkaldy. Shortly afterwards, he took over from Andrew Kirkaldy as professional at Winchester and later moved to Royal Mid-Surrey, where he was the resident professional for 47 years, until he retired in 1946.

Side line
An official picture of J.H. Taylor taken as he prepared to leave for Egypt, where he was to design a new golf links in partnership with Fred Hawtree.

THE ROAD TO FAME

He first played in the British Open in 1893 and led at one stage, but it was the following year that was to put J.H. Taylor on the road to becoming the greatest name in the land. The 1894 Open was played at Sandwich, the first time it had been played outside of Scotland, and after 36 holes J.H. was in the lead. He went on to win by five strokes and broke the domination the Scots had exercised over the Open from its beginnings in 1860.

In 1895 he took on the Scots again in their own heartland at St. Andrews, and despite an opening round of 86 he won by a clear four strokes. This established him as the dominant player in the game. The following year he suffered something of a setback when he was beaten in a challenge match by the up-and-coming Harry Vardon. Nor did he win at the Open one month later. With a three-stroke lead going into the final round, Taylor could only tie with Vardon, and then lost the 36-hole play-off.

He had his revenge in 1900 at St. Andrews, when he won with a score of 309, becoming only the fifth man in the history of the event to break 80 in each round, and beating Vardon by eight strokes. James Braid finished third.

In a brilliant career, Taylor also won the French Open in 1908 and 1909, the German Open in 1912, and was runner-up to Vardon in the 1900 U.S. Open at Wheaton, Illinois. He was regarded as the pioneer of professional golf, and was instrumental in the formation of the Professional Golfers' Association in Britain, doing much to elevate the status of the game. Referring to his contribution to the status of golfers, Bernard Darwin wrote that J.H. Taylor had "turned a feckless company into a self-respecting and respected body of men."

Despite his lack of early formal education, J.H. was a public speaker of rare charm. He realized early in his career that this was necessary if he was to speak for his word-shy fellow professionals. He was honored many times in his career, including honorary membership in the Royal & Ancient Golf Club in 1949. The Royal North Devon Golf Club bestowed on him their highest honor by electing him President in 1957.

J. H. Taylor was the last survivor of the Triumvirate. He was a month short of his 92nd birthday when he died in 1963.

Postcard fame (below)
J.H. enjoyed the great prestige he earned as a successful golfer and its accompanying spin-offs, such as opportunities for advertising.

Opening shot (above)
J.H. drives during the opening of St. George's Golf Club, Weybridge.

Stylish play (right)
Taylor's distinctive style is captured on this cigarette card.

Useful tips (right)
Taylor often gave displays of golfing technique on private and public courses, as well as in famous stores such as Harrods.

JOHN HENRY TAYLOR

WON BRITISH OPEN 1894, 1895, 1900, 1909, 1913; PGA MATCHPLAY 1908; FRENCH OPEN 1908, 1909; GERMAN OPEN 1912. NON-PLAYING CAPTAIN RYDER CUP 1933. HONORARY MEMBER R & A GOLF CLUB.

PETER THOMSON, see page 302

LEE TREVINO

BORN DALLAS, TEXAS, U.S.A., DECEMBER 1, 1939

LOOKING BACK ON the career of Lee Buck Trevino, Mexican-American school dropout, ex-Marine sergeant, and allround golfing hustler, golf history will probably have to rank him among the greatest ten players the world has ever seen. In the summer of 1971 "the Merry Mex" won three Open Championships – of the United States, Britain, and Canada – within the space of one month. He is unquestionably one of the most entertaining golfers in the professional game.

Down the line (above)
Trevino's swing keeps the club traveling down the line longer than that of any other player.

The illegitimate son of an immigrant Mexican gravedigger, Lee Trevino came from the humblest of backgrounds. "Rich people like to talk about their backgrounds," Trevino recalls today. "We were too poor to care. We just managed to exist." Their four-room plank house had neither electricity nor running water.

The only reason young Lee began playing golf was that his home stood in a hayfield next to the Glen Lakes Country Club. "In those days I used to practice golf shots off the mud. Today I put a new ball on pegs with my own name on them. Sure, I've come a long way."

Super Mex
Trevino's attitudes stem from a tough childhood in Texas as a Mexican immigrant. On his cap he sports the Mexican sombrero that has become his emblem.

EARLY DAYS

Trevino left school early and became a local greenskeeper. He caddied when he could, played a few holes at dusk, but took a serious interest in golf only after he joined the Marines at 17. Asked if he played any sport, he casually mentioned golf; the Marines gave him a try and he shot a round of 66. When his unit transferred to the Far East, he played in Japan, Taiwan, and the Philippines.

Returning home to Texas after his discharge in 1961, Trevino found plenty of filled wallets waiting to be tapped by a golfing hustler in local money matches. At this stage of his game, he would often play with just one club, a rusty but trusty 3-iron, and would give his opponent handicap shots just to increase the wager.

While working in the evenings, Trevino would attract a crowd by playing with a Dr. Pepper bottle at Hardy's Pitch-n-Putt. The bottle, wrapped in adhesive tape, could hit the ball a good, solid blow and Trevino, hustling against wealthy opponents using conventional clubs, would make around $200 a week. He also developed a patter that could get laughs and perhaps be distracting. Trevino later described this experience as a good grounding for success on the glamorous international scene, "Pressure is when you've got $3 in your pocket and you're playing for $10."

PROFESSIONAL SUCCESS

Although he turned professional in 1960, it was a long time before Trevino made any impact on the U.S. Tour. In 1967 he earned a respectable fifth place in the U.S. Open and was named Rookie of the Year – enough to persuade him to join the Tour full-time. But he was still a complete outsider when he came to the 1968 Open at Oak Hill, Rochester, and won in a spectacular manner, defeating the legendary Jack Nicklaus by four strokes and becoming the first player to break 70 in all four rounds of the Championship. The golfing world greeted this unorthodox character, with his inimitable style of play, as a major new superstar.

On Top of the World

Trevino reached his peak in the early 1970s. He was the leading money winner on the U.S. Tour at the start of the decade, and then came his extraordinary winning streak in 1971 when he won three Opens. He went on to retain the British Open title at Muirfield the next year, holing four pitch shots in the week to snatch the Championship from Tony Jacklin. "God is a Mexican" was Trevino's comment.

After this streak Trevino was never quite as successful again, although his further victories included two USPGA Championships and the British Masters title. He has never won the U.S. Masters, apparently finding difficulty with the course – and sometimes also with the attitudes he perceives at Augusta.

Trevino's swing has a very individual style. He lines his body up to the left of the target and swings back outside the line, returning the clubhead straight down the line into the ball. His accuracy is such that it has been said that the only time he leaves the fairway is to make a telephone call. He is also one of the most brilliant golf-course strategists.

Master putter
Trevino is known for his control and his swing, but it is often overlooked how good a putter he is.

Wit and wisdom
In the 1980s, Trevino applied his gift for witty commentary, which had often annoyed his fellow players on the course, to television coverage.

Almost as striking as his golf, however, is his behavior on the course. When he took his clubs to the British Isles, it was as though a circus act had arrived. At Muirfield, Neil Coles, a serious English professional, asked the R & A if they minded if he played with someone other than Trevino, as the Mexican's "chat" distracted him so much. At Wentworth, Tony Jacklin asked if their match could possibly be played with a certain degree of silence so that he could concentrate. "Sure," said Trevino, "you don't have to say a word; you just have to listen!"

Snake in the Grass

Other antics included producing a rubber snake on the first tee before the 1971 U.S. Open play-off against Jack Nicklaus, which Trevino won. But although the stars did not always approve of Trevino's nonstop jokes or his running patter, they respected his courage, his magical skills, and the way he brought in the spectators. Despite all his wins and the wealth they have brought, Lee Trevino has never lost sight of his poor beginnings. "A lot of guys on the Tour gripe about the travel and the food, and losing their laundry," says Trevino. "But no matter how bad the food is, I've eaten worse. And I couldn't care less about the dry cleaning because I remember when I only had one shirt."

He is proud that his children will not have to start life as laborers, as he did. Success has not been smooth; after winning a million, he lost it in a failed business venture. But Lee picked himself up and won several million more, ending up as a celebrity on the U.S. Senior Tour, where he took more money in 1990 than the winner of the regular U.S. Tour.

Lee Buck Trevino

Won U.S. Open 1968, 1971; British Open 1971, 1972; Canadian Open 1971, 1977, 1979; USPGA 1974, 1984; Lancôme Trophy 1978, 1980; Dunhill British Masters 1985. Winner of 27 U.S. Tour events 1968–89. Ryder Cup 1969–75, 1979–81 (non-playing captain 1985). World Cup 1968–71, 1974 (individual winner 1969). Vardon Trophy 1970, 1971, 1972, 1974, 1980. World Golf Hall of Fame 1981.

Low scorer (below)
Trevino won the Vardon Trophy five times. The Trophy is awarded to the player with the lowest scoring average on the USPGA Tour.

PETER THOMSON

BORN MELBOURNE, AUSTRALIA, AUGUST 23, 1929

PETER THOMSON, WINNER of five Open Championships in Britain, is the greatest golfer to emerge from Australia. His last Open victory, at Royal Birkdale in 1965, proved to be the finest of his career. He beat a field including Tony Lema, Jack Nicklaus, and Arnold Palmer, finally quashing the suggestion that he owed his spectacular record of success in Europe and Australia to weak opposition.

Talking with Thomson, one gets the strong impression that he would have been a success at anything to which he turned his hand. Intelligent and well-read, he claims that you can tell a top player simply by meeting him and seeing him under pressure. "The superplayer has one vital quality – calmness," he says.

Nowhere is that quality needed more than on the inward nine holes of an Open Championship on the last day, and that was often when Thomson showed his class as a player. A man blessed with outstanding confidence, he burst into British golf in the 1950s and took it apart, beating such fine players as Christy O'Connor, Sr., Dai Rees, and Max Faulkner. Only Bobby Locke, from South Africa, proved a match for Thomson. The two players dominated the British Open for many years. As well as winning five times, Thomson was runner-up on three occasions.

He would often start a tournament quietly with a couple of ordinary rounds, but finish strongly. His famous victory in the 1965 Open was a classic example. In the last round, playing with the defending champion Tony Lema in a wind that swirled across the Royal Birkdale links, Thomson put on a superb show. A perfect drive at the last hole set him up. He then swept a 3-iron onto the green, and his 4 gave him the title by two strokes.

When he retired from the young men's world circuit, Peter Thomson took on the Americans again, winning 10 times on the U.S. Senior Tour in 1985.

First touch (right)
Thomson receives the claret jug in 1954 after the first of his five British Open victories.

St. Andrews revisited
Thomson plays a quiet round at St. Andrews, the scene of his second Open win in 1955.

Strong nerves under pressure
Thomson had the quality he himself identified as the mark of a top player – calmness under stress.

PETER WILLIAM THOMSON, CBE

WON NEW ZEALAND OPEN 1950, 1951, 1953, 1955, 1959, 1960, 1961, 1965, 1971; AUSTRALIAN OPEN 1951, 1967, 1972; BRITISH OPEN 1954, 1955, 1956, 1958, 1965; ITALIAN OPEN 1959; SPANISH OPEN 1959; GERMAN OPEN 1960; DUNLOP MASTERS 1961, 1968. WORLD CUP 1953–57, 1959–62, 1965, 1969. HONORARY MEMBER R & A GOLF CLUB.

Jessie Valentine

Born Perth, Scotland, March 18, 1915

Born during the First World War, Janet (Jessie) Valentine was the daughter of a noted golf and cricket professional. She was only 5 ft. 1 in. (1.55m) tall, but from the beginning of her career she had a neat and compact swing that gave her great control for such a slight person. Always ready to accept a challenge, she was an attacking player with a strong competitive streak.

Leading Scot
Jessie Valentine was a formidable competitor, winning three British Ladies' and six Scottish Ladies' Championships over two decades.

Valentine came to prominence in 1936. Selected for the Curtis Cup, she sank a famous long putt on the last green to win her final singles and square the match. In the same year, she beat Pam Barton on the 37th hole of the French Ladies' final.

Jessie Valentine went on to win a hatful of other championships, and was an almost automatic choice for British international teams until the late 1950s.

Janet Valentine, MBE

Won French Ladies' Amateur 1936; British Ladies' Amateur 1937, 1955, 1958; Scottish Ladies' Amateur 1938, 1939, 1951, 1953, 1955, 1956; Worplesdon Mixed Foursomes 1963–65. Curtis Cup 1936–38, 1950–58. G.B. vs. Commonwealth 1953, 1955 (non-playing captain 1959).

Harry Vardon, see page 304

Roberto de Vicenzo

Born Buenos Aires, Argentina, April 14, 1923

Late riser
De Vicenzo rose to his greatest heights after reaching the age of 40.

Argentinian golfer Roberto de Vicenzo will always be remembered for his victory in the British Open at Hoylake in 1967 at the age of 44, the oldest winner since Old Tom Morris. A frank, wholehearted person, he always enjoyed great popularity.

Son of a poor family in Buenos Aires, Roberto de Vicenzo turned professional in 1938. Six years later he first won the Argentinian Open and established himself as the leading South American player for the next three decades.

He won six tournaments on the U.S. circuit and national opens in Belgium, the Netherlands, Spain, Germany, and France, but he struggled to reach his main goal of winning the British Open. He was runner-up in 1950 and third no fewer than six times before he was finally successful at Hoylake on his nineteenth attempt. A last round of 70 kept him two strokes ahead of runner-up Jack Nicklaus. It was an emotional occasion, and de Vicenzo's victory was one of the most popular in the history of the event.

The Argentinian might have won another Major in 1968 but for an error in marking his card. He would have forced a play-off with Bob Goalby for the U.S. Masters title had he not signed for a 4 at the 17th instead of the birdie 3 he had played. The score had to stand.

Roberto de Vicenzo

Won British Open 1967; USPGA Seniors 1974; USGA Senior Open 1980. Winner of more than 40 national tournaments worldwide 1944–74. World Cup (representing Argentina) 1953–55, 1962–66, 1968–74, (representing Mexico) 1956, 1959, 1960–61 (individual winner 1962, 1970). Bob Jones Award 1970. Honorary member R & A Golf Club.

HARRY VARDON

BORN JERSEY, CHANNEL ISLANDS, MAY 9, 1870; DIED 1937

HARRY VARDON WAS one of the greatest players ever to grace the game of golf. He may well have been the purest striker of a golf ball who has ever lived. As the leading member of the Great Triumvirate, with his colleagues James Braid and J.H. Taylor, Vardon dominated golf around the beginning of the twentieth century, winning a record total of six British Opens.

Double image (above)
Vardon's style of play was presented as a model for aspiring golfers in this 1910 stereoscopic photo.

Escape (left)
Stymied by his opponent, Vardon chips a shot over the obstructing ball.

Ace of clubs (right)
Harry Vardon was a supremely successful competitive golfer and did much to increase the popularity of the game. At his best, around the turn of the century, he was virtually invincible.

Postcard hero
One of Vardon's strengths was his ability with the driver, shown in a postcard of the time.

Harry Vardon was born at Grouville on Jersey, where there was little opportunity for him to play, but his interest in golf awoke early, and he was acting as a caddie by the age of seven. When his brother Tom went to England and found that he could make money as a professional, Harry soon decided to follow in his footsteps.

He took a job at a nine-hole course at Ripon in Yorkshire, despite having only played a few dozen games in his life. He soon moved on to Bury St. Edmunds and then to Ganton, back in Yorkshire. It was from here that he established his fame as not only the best player of his time, but also as a leading popularizer of the game.

SIX OPEN TRIUMPHS

Between them the Great Triumvirate won 16 British Opens. Vardon won six of them, a record that still stands today. His first appearance in the Open Championship was at Prestwick in 1893, but he made little impression. The following year he finished fifth at Sandwich, the first time the Open was played in England and the first time J.H. Taylor won it.

In 1895 Vardon came to prominence when he led the Open after the first round at St. Andrews, only to finish in ninth place; Taylor won again to establish himself as the leading player of the day. But the members at Ganton were so confident of the ability of their own professional that they raised the money for a

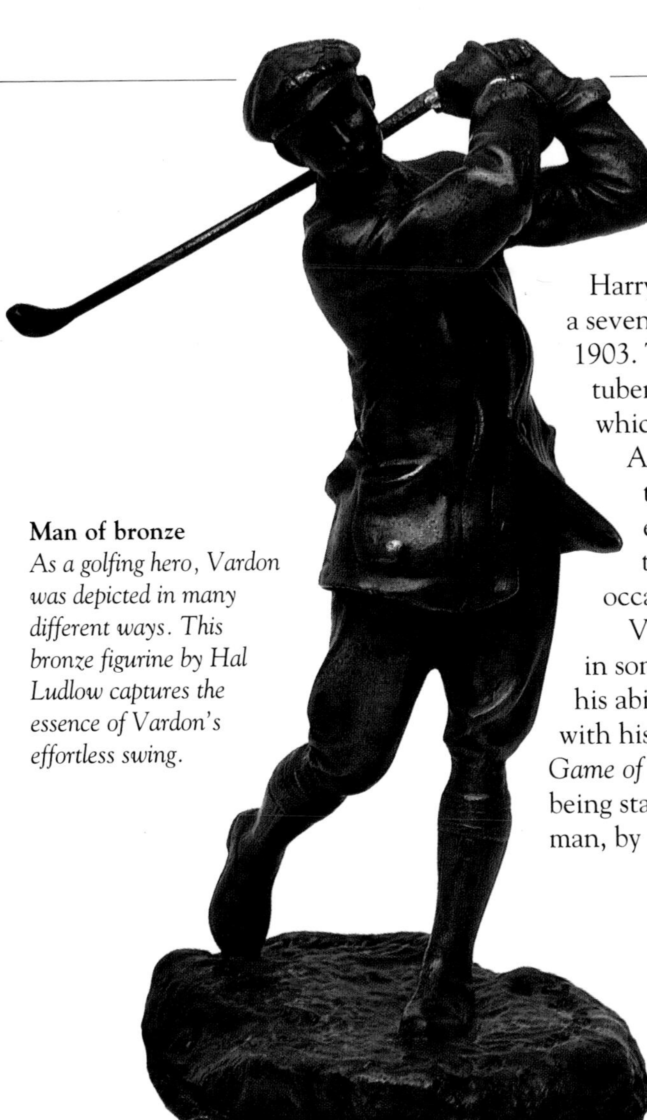

Man of bronze
As a golfing hero, Vardon was depicted in many different ways. This bronze figurine by Hal Ludlow captures the essence of Vardon's effortless swing.

twice in all the matches he played. He also won the U.S. Open at Wheaton, Illinois.

Harry Vardon was at his greatest over a seven-year period between 1896 and 1903. Then he was struck down with tuberculosis, a serious illness from which he never completely recovered. Although he could not again attain the dominance that he had once enjoyed, he still went on to win the British Open on two more occasions, in 1911 and 1914.

Vardon's illness was later blamed in some quarters for a tragic decline in his ability with the putter, particularly with his short putts. In his book, *This Game of Golf*, Henry Cotton recalled being startled by the putting of the great man, by then well past his best. Cotton

about the stiff left arm, the great man replied simply, "I like playing against people with stiff left arms." Vardon was rare among the great players in not taking a divot with any of his shots. So accurate was he with all his clubs that he could always sweep the ball off the turf cleanly, hardly disturbing the surface at all.

The Vardon Grip

Harry Vardon popularized the overlapping grip, in which the little finger of the right hand overlaps the index finger of the left in the right-handed grip. It became known as the Vardon Grip, although he did not in fact invent it. The great amateur player Johnny Laidlay is thought to have been the first to use this style of grip, which is still the most popular among today's top professionals.

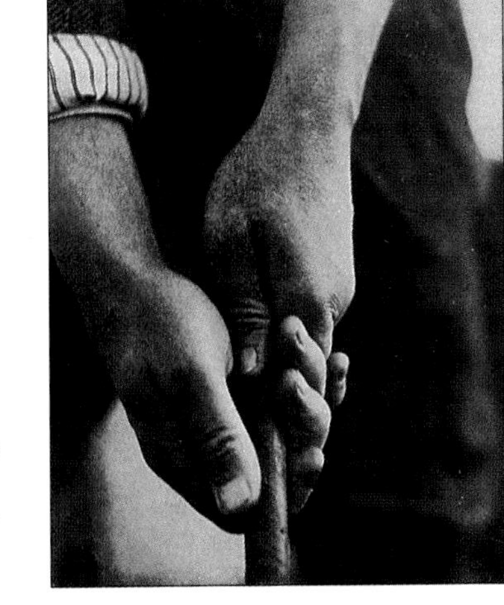

Getting a grip
Vardon shows his grip, the little finger of the right hand overlapping the index of the left.

Harry Vardon

Won British Open 1896, 1898, 1899, 1903, 1911, 1914; U.S. Open 1900. Leading member of the Great Triumvirate of Vardon, Braid, and Taylor. Winner of many exhibition and challenge matches.

challenge match between Vardon and Taylor. Vardon won decisively by 8-and-6. A month later the Open was played at Muirfield, and Harry Vardon found himself in another battle with Taylor. With one round still to play, Vardon was three behind, but he fought his way back and finished in a tie. In the play-off, which in those days was over 36 holes, Vardon won by four strokes. With Braid and Taylor, he was to dominate the Championship for the next two decades.

At a time when there were very few tournaments in Britain or America other than the Open Championships, competition play for professionals was largely confined to money matches, challenges, and exhibitions. When he was at the height of his powers around the turn of the century, Vardon spent almost a year touring the United States and playing exhibitions. He was beaten only

described "the unbelievable jerking of the clubhead, in an effort to make contact with the ball from two feet or less from the hole." This was an affliction that had affected Vardon to some degree throughout his career, but was more than compensated for by his uncanny accuracy, elegance, and purity of stroke.

His swing was much more upright than was the vogue of the time, and he played with a slightly bent left arm and a flying right elbow when the fashion was for a rigid left arm. Asked once what he thought

Vardon versus Ray (below)
Ted Ray watches the flight of the ball as Vardon tees off at the 6th during the British Open at Muirfield in 1912. Ray beat Vardon, who placed second that year.

GLENNA COLLETT VARE

BORN NEW HAVEN, CONNECTICUT, U.S.A., JUNE 20, 1903; DIED 1989

GLENNA COLLETT VARE dominated ladies' golf in the United States for many years during the 1920s and 1930s. One of the first women to hit the ball freely, she could drive great distances. She played with extreme concentration, but at the same time with a bubbling, infectious enthusiasm.

Glenna Collett did not take up golf until she was 14, but by 19 she had defeated Cecil Leitch, the British Ladies' Champion, three times. She won her first U.S. Ladies' title in 1922 and her last in 1935. Her total of six wins was a record for USGA events. From 1928–31 she won 19 consecutive matches, also a record.

She never won the British Ladies', although she twice reached the final, in 1929 and 1930. The 1929 final against Joyce Wethered at St. Andrews was one of the best ever seen. After playing the first nine holes in 34 strokes to go five up, the American player could not withstand Wethered's comeback and lost at the 35th.

Glenna Collett was certainly the finest American woman golfer of her time. She married businessman Edwin Vare in 1931.

GLENNA COLLETT VARE

WON U.S. LADIES' AMATEUR 1922, 1925, 1928, 1929, 1930, 1935; CANADIAN LADIES' 1923, 1924. CURTIS CUP 1932–38, 1948 (CAPTAIN 1934, 1936, 1948, NON-PLAYING CAPTAIN 1950). BOB JONES AWARD 1965. WORLD GOLF HALL OF FAME 1975.

Title shot (above) *Glenna playing in the 1925 Ladies' Amateur Championship at Troon.*

Off duty (below) *Glenna Collett Vare relaxes during her first appearance in the Curtis Cup in 1932.*

TOM WATSON

BORN KANSAS CITY, MISSOURI, U.S.A., SEPTEMBER 4, 1949

TOM WATSON IS rare among his generation of American professionals in being a devotee of traditional British links golf. Most of his compatriots would prefer the element of chance, so much part of seaside links golf, to be eliminated. But at his best, Watson has thrived on the unpredictable British courses.

Watson's first British Open victory was a memorable occasion. Coming to the final hole in the play-off against Jack Newton at Carnoustie in 1975, he faced a tough 2-iron shot over the burn in front of the green. Newton was in a greenside bunker and a 4 would be good enough for Watson to win. The young man from Kansas City, who had only been a professional for four years, struck a majestic shot to the heart of the green for a memorable victory that catapulted him into golf's major league.

Watson's guru
Byron Nelson (left) was Tom Watson's mentor, helping perfect his game in the 1970s.

GOLFING PSYCHOLOGIST

Watson was the top player on the Stanford University golf team, but he was not one of the golf-scholarship students that American universities were turning out tailormade for the professional Tour. He went to Stanford to study and graduated in psychology.

The following year he joined the USPGA Tour, but success was slow in coming. Although there was no doubting his rare talent, Watson was reputed to be frightened of winning. American sports journalists were keen to write off a player they christened "Huckleberry Finn."

But Watson was not frightened to win; he had simply not learned how. In 1974 he found out, winning the Western Open. The same year he led the U.S. Open by a stroke going into the last

Happy Tom (below)
Watson rejoices at winning the 1982 U.S. Open at Pebble Beach.

round, only to tie for fifth. Then came that dramatic play-off against the luckless Australian, Jack Newton, the last time the British Open was played over the great links of Carnoustie.

This first British Open victory initiated a golden age for Watson. As well as four more British Opens, he won the U.S. Masters twice, in 1977 and 1981. He also topped the U.S. money list for four consecutive years between 1977 and 1980.

Duel in the Sun

Tom Watson's greatest single triumph was the British Open of 1977 at Turnberry. In a week of high sunshine and even higher drama, Watson and Jack Nicklaus fought out one of the most dramatic matches in the history of golf. The two players were so far ahead of the field that it became a head-to-head battle – a battle that will be forever remembered as "The Duel in the Sun." For 70 holes Watson never held the lead, but going to the last hole he was one

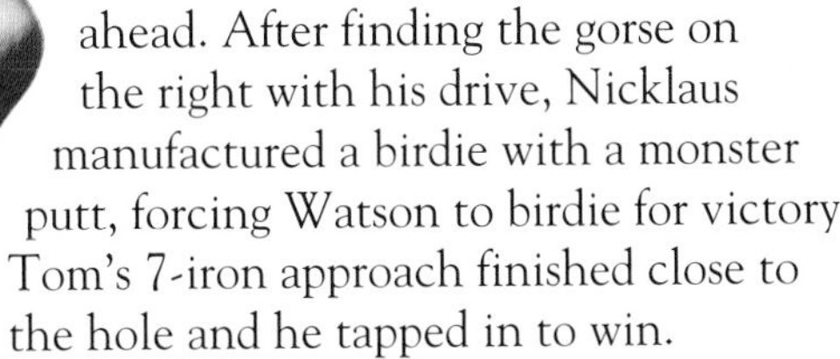

ahead. After finding the gorse on the right with his drive, Nicklaus manufactured a birdie with a monster putt, forcing Watson to birdie for victory. Tom's 7-iron approach finished close to the hole and he tapped in to win.

Double Open

Watson went on to score many further triumphs. In 1982 he won both the British Open and the U.S. Open, which had eluded him for so long (see page 118), and in 1984 he topped the U.S. money list for the fifth time.

At St. Andrews in 1984 he might easily have equaled the legendary Harry Vardon's total of six Open victories had he not fallen victim to the notorious 17th Road Hole in the final round. This failure was a turning point in his career.

Like so many great players before him, Watson suddenly suffered problems with his putter. At the top of his career he was one of the best putters the game has ever witnessed. Had the short ones not become a problem, Watson would undoubtedly have scaled even greater heights.

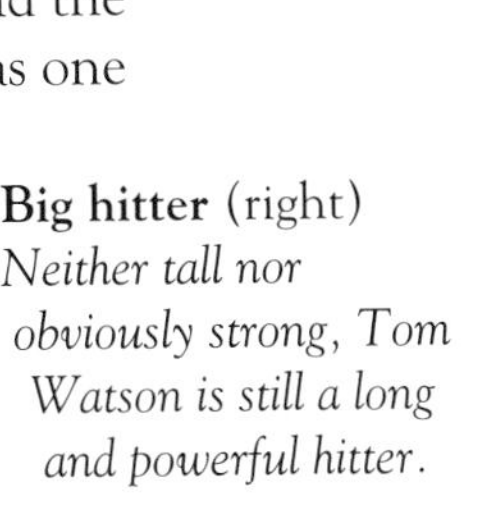

Big hitter (right)
Neither tall nor obviously strong, Tom Watson is still a long and powerful hitter.

Thomas Sturges Watson

Won British Open 1975, 1977, 1980, 1982, 1983; U.S. Masters 1977, 1981; U.S. Open 1982. Winner of 32 U.S. Tour events 1974–87. Ryder Cup 1977, 1981–83, 1989. Vardon Trophy 1977, 1978, 1979. USPGA Player of the Year 1977, 1978, 1979, 1980, 1984.

Bent jug (left)
Watson holds a damaged trophy after winning at Royal Birkdale in 1983; it had been dropped and was bent as a result.

Road victim (right)
Close to retaining the British Open at St.Andrews in 1984, Watson hit his second shot against the wall at the notorious 17th hole and never recovered.

TOM WEISKOPF

BORN MASSILLON, OHIO, U.S.A., NOVEMBER 9, 1942

LOOKING AT THE record of Tom Weiskopf, there are many who will conclude that he has done less than justice to an exceptional talent. He has one of the great golf swings of the modern game; "majestic" is the word most frequently used to describe it. Yet despite one of the best careers ever on the U.S. Tour, he has won only one Major. In truth, he should have won many more.

Triumph at Troon
Weiskopf sinks a putt during the 1973 British Open. His Open victory was the summit of his career, and earned him the durable respect of the British golfing public.

Weiskopf took up golf at the age of 15 and within a few months was a low-handicap player. After he joined the U.S. Tour in 1964, it quickly became apparent that golf had found a new and remarkable talent. "Long Tom" Weiskopf was one of the longest hitters the game had ever seen. Added to a delicate touch with the putter, this made him a formidable force.

Elegance and power
Weiskopf's long smooth swing had an elegance unusual for a tall man.

Matchplay (above)
Tom Weiskopf mounts a vigorous defense of his World Matchplay title at Wentworth in September, 1973.

Throughout his career, however, Weiskopf has also had a reputation for unpredictable temperament and motivation. He once turned down a place on the American Ryder Cup team because he preferred to go on a hunting trip. If he applied himself he could be almost unbeatable. Following the death of his father in 1973, when Weiskopf was apparently motivated to make amends for a partially squandered talent, he won five tournaments in the space of eight weeks, including the British Open at Troon. But before long he was back in his old routine, preferring hunting to the grind of playing golf on the professional Tour.

NEAR TO VICTORY

Although Tom Weiskopf won only one Major championship, it has to be remembered that he came close on many other occasions. He was runner-up in the U.S. Open once, at Atlanta in 1976, and finished third in that championship twice. He was also four times runner-up in the U.S. Masters.

THOMAS DANIEL WEISKOPF

WON WORLD MATCHPLAY CHAMPIONSHIP 1972; BRITISH OPEN 1973; CANADIAN OPEN 1973, 1975. WINNER OF 15 U.S. TOUR EVENTS 1968–82. WORLD CUP 1972. RYDER CUP 1973–75.

JOYCE WETHERED

BORN LONDON, ENGLAND, NOVEMBER 17, 1901

THE GREAT AMATEUR Bobby Jones once stated that in his opinion Joyce Wethered (Lady Heathcoat-Amory) had "the best swing of either man or woman" that he had ever seen. She was undoubtedly one of the supreme woman golfers of all time.

As a child Joyce Wethered lived in the south of England, but her parents had a holiday home next to the links at Dornoch in Sutherland, Scotland. She and her elder brother, Roger, used to play golf every day when they were there.

Roger became a first-class player and his sister was able to play against him and his friends. This helped her game immensely. She developed into an exceptional player, noted for her magnificent swing and her accuracy.

Wethered's record in competitive golf was outstanding. She played five times in the English Ladies' Amateur Championship and won each time. In all she played 33 matches in the event, winning every one. It was a similar story in the British Ladies' Amateur Championship. She won the title four times and lost only two matches.

Enjoying the game
Joyce Wethered played most of her golf purely for pleasure. She first retired from serious competition at the remarkably early age of 24.

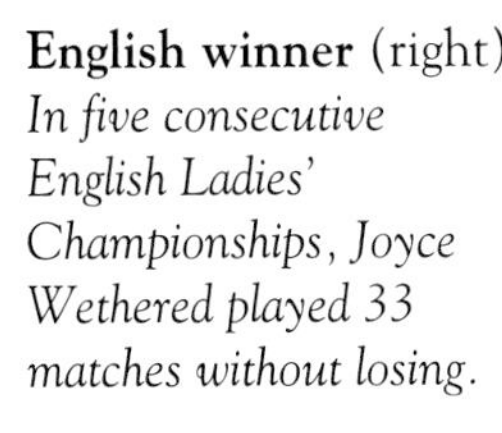

English winner (right)
In five consecutive English Ladies' Championships, Joyce Wethered played 33 matches without losing.

Lady rivals (left)
Joyce Wethered (left) and Cecil Leitch line up to contest the British Ladies' Championship at Troon in 1925.

In her first English Ladies' final, played at Sheringham in 1920, Wethered met the title holder, Cecil Leitch. A cult figure with a large following, Leitch was expected to win easily, but Wethered achieved a victory by 2-and-1, recording one of the biggest upsets in the history of the event.

FAMOUS VICTORY

Joyce Wethered returned from four years' retirement to score a memorable victory over the U.S. Ladies' Champion, Glenna Collett, in the final of the British Ladies' at St. Andrews in 1929. Wethered was five down after nine holes as Collett went to the turn in 34. But Wethered played the next 18 holes superbly for a 73, and won on the penultimate green by 3-and-1.

Wethered played in the first Curtis Cup match in 1932, but thereafter appeared only in the Worplesdon Mixed Foursomes, which she won eight times.

JOYCE WETHERED (LADY HEATHCOAT-AMORY)

WON BRITISH LADIES' 1922, 1924, 1925, 1929; ENGLISH LADIES' 1920, 1921, 1922, 1923, 1924; WORPLESDON MIXED FOURSOMES 1922, 1923, 1927, 1928, 1931, 1932, 1933, 1936. CURTIS CUP 1932 (CAPTAIN). WORLD GOLF HALL OF FAME 1975.

KATHY WHITWORTH

BORN MONAHANS, TEXAS, U.S.A., SEPTEMBER 27, 1939

KATHY WHITWORTH IS not only the most successful player ever in women's golf, but is also the most prolific winner, male or female, in the history of the professional game. In a remarkable career that has spanned more than 30 years, Whitworth has won 88 U.S. LPGA Tour events. Of all the major women's championships, only the U.S. Women's Open eludes her.

High accuracy (right) *Never a classic swinger, Whitworth's strength is her ability to keep the ball in play.*

Kathy Whitworth took up golf at the age of 15 but made little impression as an amateur, winning only a couple of state titles before she joined the professional ranks in December, 1958. She was into her fourth season on the LPGA Tour before she won a tournament, the 1962 Kelly Girl Open, but once she made the breakthrough she just kept on winning. For a 17-year spell she won at least one event each year, and at her peak in 1968 she won no fewer than ten that season.

AMBASSADOR FOR GOLF

As one of the great ambassadors for women's professional golf, Whitworth has won numerous awards, including being inducted into the LPGA Hall of Fame in 1975. She was honored by being appointed the non-playing captain of the U.S. team in the inaugural Solheim Cup – the women's equivalent of the Ryder Cup – in 1990. In the first of these biennial matches, Whitworth led the U.S. LPGA to victory against the Women Professional Golfers' European Tour.

Hard-earned riches
A career that is a model of consistency has brought high financial rewards; Kathy Whitworth was the first player to win $1 million on the LPGA Tour, and remains one of the world's top money winners.

KATHRYNNE ANN WHITWORTH

WON WESTERN OPEN 1967; LPGA CHAMPIONSHIP 1967, 1971, 1975. WINNER OF 88 LPGA EVENTS 1962–85. SOLHEIM CUP 1990 (NON-PLAYING CAPTAIN). VARE TROPHY 1965, 1966, 1967, 1969, 1970, 1971, 1972. LPGA HALL OF FAME 1975. WORLD GOLF HALL OF FAME 1982.

Ian Woosnam

Born Oswestry, England, March 2, 1958

A LTHOUGH BORN ON the English side of the border, Ian Woosnam considers himself a Welshman. He is only 5 ft. 4 in. (1.63m) tall but is one of the longest hitters in the modern game. He is also one of the most successful, and early in 1991 he hit the top spot in the world rankings. The only prize to elude him was a win in one of the Majors. But that was before the 1991 U.S. Masters.

Fight back (right)
Renowned for his tenacity and his determination to win, Ian Woosnam fought his way to fourth place in the 1990 British Open at St. Andrews.

Woosnam turned professional in 1976, but it was some time before his quality showed. In 1982 he finished eighth on the European money list, and in 1985 he played on the triumphant European Ryder Cup team. But 1987 was his first big year.

It began with a victory at the Hong Kong Open, followed by five wins on the European Tour, which made him the leading money winner. He became the first British player to win the World Matchplay title, beating Sandy Lyle in the final.

Winning millions
In 1987, repeated successes worldwide brought Woosnam over £1 million in prize money. He headed the European money list.

International Success

The Ryder Cup was next; Woosnam played in the team that recorded the first European win on American soil. He added a victory for Wales in the World Cup, taking the individual title.

Although a lean period followed, his list of successes grew each year. He was third in the British Open in 1986 and second in the 1989 U.S. Open at Oak Hill. In 1990 Woosnam had his best year since 1987 and topped the Volvo Order of Merit. Early-season victories in 1991 made him number one in the Sony World Rankings.

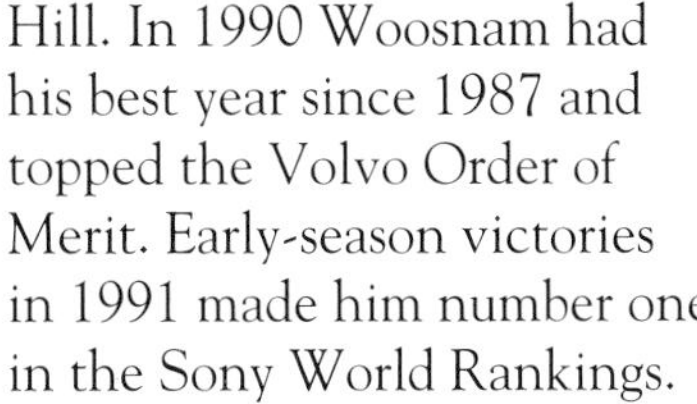

Then came the U.S. Masters at Augusta. He arrived on the last tee tied with Tom Watson and Jose-Maria Olazabal on 11 under par. His rivals found trouble and Woosnam needed a par 4 to win. He hit the ball hard with his driver but hooked it on to the members' practice ground leaving an 8-iron to the green. He came up short, but putted to within 6 feet of the pin. It all hung on this last putt. "Woosie" kept his nerve and rolled in the putt to win.

Top form (left)
As part of the winning European team in the Ryder Cup of 1985, Ian Woosnam enjoyed the taste of success, if somewhat dangerously, with his young team-mate, Paul Way.

Ian Woosnam

Won Scottish Open 1987, 1990; World Matchplay 1987, 1990; Irish Open 1988, 1989; PGA Championship 1988; European Open 1988; U.S. Masters 1991. World Cup 1980, 1982–85, 1987, 1990 (individual winner 1987). Ryder Cup 1983–89. Dunhill Cup 1985–86, 1988–90. Harry Vardon Trophy 1987, 1990.

MICKEY WRIGHT

BORN SAN DIEGO, CALIFORNIA, U.S.A., FEBRUARY 14, 1935

MICKEY WRIGHT MUST rank as one of the all-time great woman golfers. Her 82 victories on the U.S. LPGA Tour included four LPGA Championships and four U.S. Women's Opens, and for six years she recorded most victories in a season. Her extraordinary 13 wins out of 32 starts in 1963 is a record that is unlikely to be overtaken.

Glittering career
Wright's success at both junior and then professional level owed much to her powerful game, hard work, and faultless swing.

Wright was encouraged to play golf by her father, himself a keen player. At 19 she was the leading amateur in the U.S. Women's Open and decided to turn professional. Her first tournament win followed in 1956. After a great career at the top, an injury to her wrist and a painful foot forced her to leave the circuit in 1969.

MARY KATHRYN WRIGHT

WON U.S. WOMEN'S OPEN 1958, 1959, 1961, 1964; LPGA CHAMPIONSHIP 1958, 1960, 1961, 1963; WESTERN OPEN 1962, 1963, 1966. WINNER OF 82 LPGA EVENTS 1956–73. VARE TROPHY 1960, 1961, 1962, 1963, 1964. LPGA HALL OF FAME 1964. WORLD GOLF HALL OF FAME 1976.

CHARLIE YATES

BORN ATLANTA, GEORGIA, U.S.A., SEPTEMBER 9, 1913

NOT ONE OF the classic swingers to have come out of the great golfing city of Atlanta, Charlie Yates was nonetheless a formidable amateur player in his day. He was the leading amateur in the inaugural U.S. Masters at Augusta National in 1934, a club and an event with which he had a distinguished association for many years, but he made little impact on the U.S. Open.

Bringing the crowds
The ever-popular American golfer Charlie Yates engages in an unsuccessful defense of his British Amateur Championship title at the Royal Liverpool Golf Club in 1939.

Yates won the Georgia State Open in 1931 and 1932, the Intercollegiate Championship in 1934, and the Western Amateur Championship in 1935, but his best showing in the U.S. Amateur Championship was to reach the last 16 in 1932 and 1933. In 1936 he was on the Walker Cup team that trounced Great Britain at Pine Valley – the only occasion on which Britain failed to win a match.

Crossing the Atlantic in 1938 to play in the next Walker Cup at St. Andrews, he started by winning the British Amateur Championship at Troon, although he beat the former U.S. Amateur Champion Johnny Fischer only by a stymie at the 19th hole. Thereafter Yates's passage was majestic. Although unable to defeat the British team in the Walker Cup, he recorded 11 straight wins in Scotland. Few American players have found as swift and lasting a fondness among Scottish golfing galleries as the exuberant Yates.

In later years, still fully committed to the game, Charlie Yates became press officer of the U.S. Masters at Augusta.

CHARLES RICHARD YATES

WON WESTERN AMATEUR 1935; BRITISH AMATEUR 1938. LEADING AMATEUR U.S. MASTERS 1934, 1939, 1940. WALKER CUP 1936–38 (NON-PLAYING CAPTAIN 1953).

BABE ZAHARIAS, see page 314

FUZZY ZOELLER

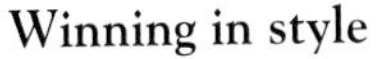

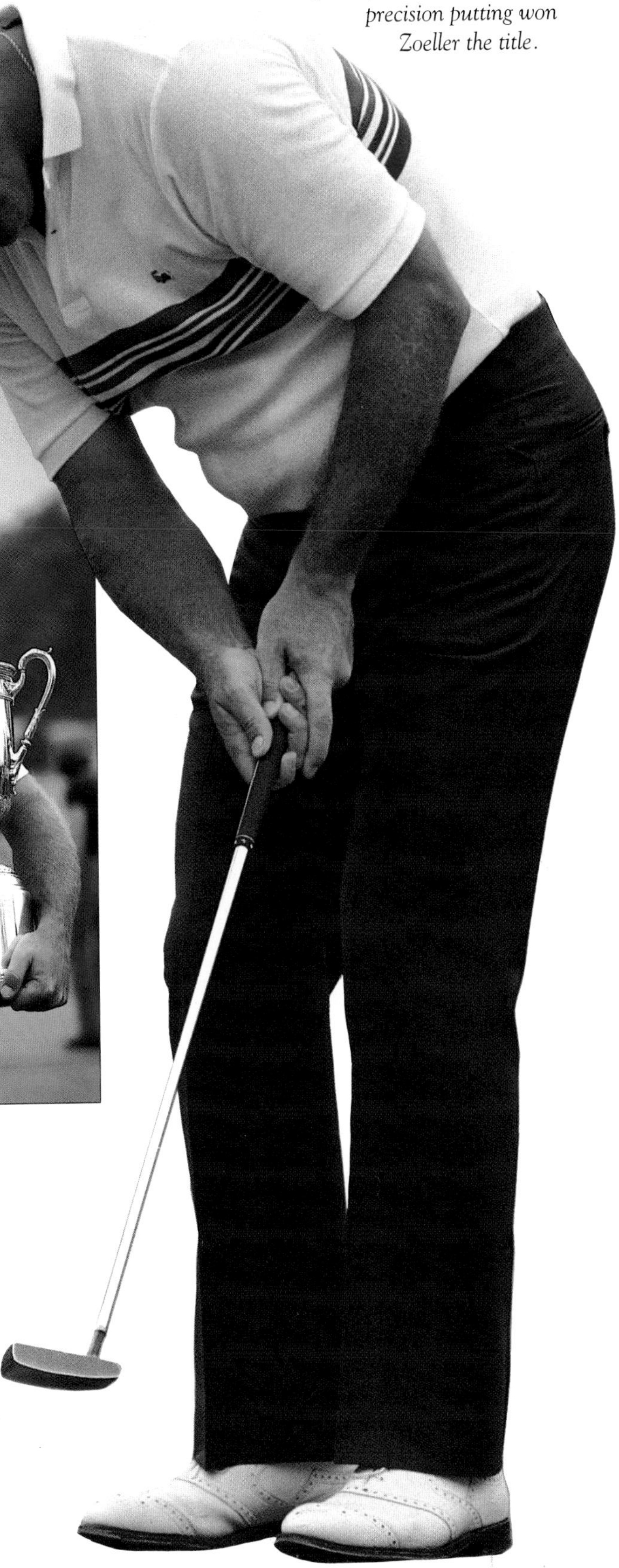

Winning in style
During the play-off with Greg Norman at the 1984 U.S. Open, powerful driving along with precision putting won Zoeller the title.

BORN NEW ALBANY, INDIANA, U.S.A., NOVEMBER 11, 1951

FUZZY ZOELLER NOT only brings a lighter side to the game of golf but also a standard of play that at times can challenge the very best. Indeed, if Zoeller had not been troubled by back problems throughout his career, he might well have won more than the two Major championships he already has to his credit.

Fuzzy Zoeller joined the U.S. Tour in 1975 after a modest career in the amateur ranks. He was soon among the money winners, and by 1978 he had topped the $100,000 mark in earnings for the season.

He arrived at the U.S. Masters in 1979 lying third in the U.S. money list for the year. After a three-way play-off with Ed Sneed and Tom Watson, he won with a birdie 3 at the second extra hole.

Five years later, in the U.S. Open, he was in another play-off. This time it was against Greg Norman, who had holed a massive 40-foot (12m) putt on the last hole to salvage par. Fuzzy waved a white towel in mock surrender, but parred the hole to finish in a tie. Winning the play-off brought him his second Major title.

FRANK URBAN ZOELLER

WON U.S. MASTERS 1979; U.S. OPEN 1984. WINNER OF 10 U.S. TOUR EVENTS 1979–86. RYDER CUP 1979, 1983–85.

Major touch (above)
Zoeller's 1984 victory in the U.S. Open was his second win in a Major event despite the pressure of injury.

Funny man (left)
Zoeller always combines skill with entertainment, and attracts a large, enthusiastic following on the course.

Babe Zaharias

BORN PORT ARTHUR, TEXAS, U.S.A., JUNE 26, 1914; DIED 1956

ONE OF THE most gifted all-around athletes in sporting history, Babe Zaharias astonished the world with her ability in every sport she chose to play. She originally made her living as a baseball and basketball player, and went on to win gold medals in the 1932 Olympic Games in field and track events. As a woman golfer she was supreme in the period after the Second World War, heading the U.S. money list every year from 1948 to 1951.

The professional way (right) *Babe Zaharias drives during an open tournament at Wentworth between professional American golfers and English amateurs in 1951.*

All-around Athlete

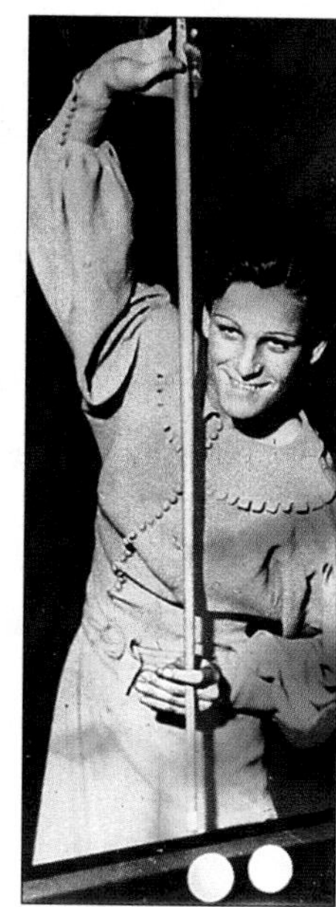

Babe Zaharias was not only an outstanding golfer, but also an enormously successful all-around athlete, whether winning a javelin event or relaxing with a game of billiards. She also excelled at baseball, basketball, tennis, hurdling, the high jump, diving, roller-skating, and bowling. No other woman has matched her range of skills.

Born Mildred Didriksen (later changed to Didrikson), it was through her prowess at baseball that she earned her nickname "The Babe" – after the legendary baseball player Babe Ruth – when she hit five home runs in one game. In 1932 she entered eight events in the National Track and Field Championships and won six of them, setting four world records in the process. At the Los Angeles Olympic Games that year, she won the javelin, the 80-meter hurdles, and the high jump; her victories in all three made her world-famous. However, the celebrations were slightly marred when, after setting a new world record, she was disqualified from the high jump for using the revolutionary Western Roll technique of jumping, which was judged "unladylike."

Turning Point

It was during those Olympic Games that the famous American sportswriter Grantland Rice persuaded 18-year-old Babe to turn her athletic prowess to the royal and ancient game of golf. She was a natural and delighted everyone with the distance she could hit the ball – hardly surprising for a woman who could generate sufficient speed and power with her right arm to win an Olympic gold medal in the javelin. Although her amazing power was her principal golfing asset, she was sufficiently adroit in the other aspects of the game eventually to become one of the great players.

Amateur Disqualification

Just as some of the gilt had been rubbed off her incredible success in the Los Angeles Olympics, so she had to face disappointment in the early stages of her golf career. She won the 1935 Texas Amateur Women's Invitational, the second event she ever contested, but two weeks later the USGA ruled that she was a professional because of her baseball and basketball earnings, and she was barred from amateur competition.

In 1938 Babe married a wrestler, George Zaharias, giving her financial security, and five years later she regained

Victorious fling
Semifinalists Babe Zaharias (left) and Jean Donald celebrate Babe's progression to the final of the 1947 British Ladies' Amateur at Gullane.

her amateur status in golf. She went on to win 17 tournaments in a row in 1946–7, including the 1946 U.S. Women's Amateur and the 1947 British Ladies' Amateur, becoming the first American ever to win this British title since its inception in 1893. In the six rounds of the competition, she lost only four holes.

In August, 1947, Zaharias joined the professional ranks through choice, and became a key figure in the evolution of women's professional golf in the United States. "The Babe" became a founder and charter member of the LPGA. She was the leading money winner on the professional Tour for four consecutive years

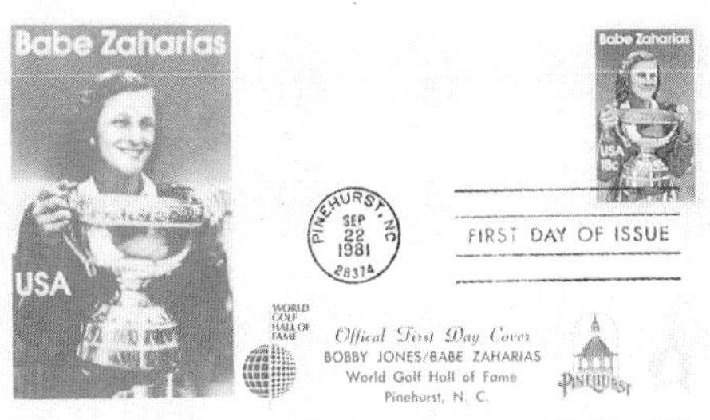

Stamp of history
An official first-day cover of 1981, issued from the World Golf Hall of Fame, commemorates Babe Zaharias's remarkable contribution to golf.

from 1948 onward, and won 31 U.S. professional events in an illustrious career, including the Titleholders Championship three times and the Western Open Championship four times.

Zaharias was the most graceful of athletes, and yet she could strike a golf ball as powerfully as any man. Stories of her hitting power are legion, including the claim that at the Gullane course on the east coast of Scotland, she once landed on the back of the green at the 540-yard 15th with a drive and a 4 iron.

She once shocked officials at the same course by appearing in red-and-white checkered shorts, and was asked to change. Her influence on women's golf was immense; she brought the crowds flocking in by the thousands to see her play.

Zaharias took a team of American women players to Britain in 1951. In a match against a team of scratch London amateurs, including the former English Champion Leonard Crawley, Babe's team won all their singles, playing the men even. In her match against Crawley, Zaharias not only won, but added insult to injury by having earlier rejected his chivalrous offer of the ladies' tees!

Tragically, Babe Zaharias contracted cancer and underwent major surgery in 1953. Such was her determination that she fought back, and the following year won an astonishing five events, including her third U.S. Women's Open by a clear 12 strokes. She won two more tournaments in 1955, but there was a recurrence of the cancer and she died shortly after.

Mildred Ella Didrikson Zaharias

Won Western Open 1940, 1944, 1945, 1950; U.S. Women's Amateur 1946; British Ladies' Amateur 1947; Titleholders Championship 1947, 1950, 1952; U.S. Women's Open 1948, 1950, 1954. LPGA Hall of Fame 1951. Bob Jones Award 1957. World Golf Hall of Fame 1974. USPGA Hall of Fame 1976.

American breakthrough
In 1947 Zaharias became the first American to win the British Ladies' Amateur, a title that had eluded her great predecessor Glenna Collett Vare.

CHAPTER

Records and Reference

The first British Open was played in 1860 over the 12-hole course at Prestwick. Only eight players took part over three rounds on a wild October day. It was an inauspicious start to the most venerable of the great golfing events, but the roll of winners in the world's oldest championship now provides a perfect mirror to reflect the development of the game and the fluctuation in fortunes from one country to another. Although the British Open led the way, other great events soon followed. Today, there are many championships and tournaments played around the world, but only four are recognized as golf's Majors: the Open Championships of Britain and the United States, the U.S. Masters Tournament played at Augusta National, and the USPGA Championship. This chapter lists the winners of these four Majors, along with the leading amateur and women's championships and the world's principal team events.

Program for the 1965 U.S. Open at Bellerive

A commemorative plate for the 1989 Ryder Cup, tied between Europe and the United States

Faldo and the jug (left)
Britain's Nick Faldo kisses the Open trophy, the historic claret jug, after his 1987 win at Muirfield.

THE BRITISH OPEN CHAMPIONSHIP

ROYAL & ANCIENT GOLF CLUB

Golf's oldest and most prestigious championship was first proposed at the October meeting of the Prestwick Golf Club in 1856, but it was 1860 before it was played. The eight entrants played three rounds of the 12 holes of the Prestwick links. Willie Park, Sr. from Musselburgh won the original trophy, the Championship Belt, with a score of 174.

***The old claret jug** (left), **golf's most famous trophy. The buckle from the Championship Belt** (right).*

Winners G.B., except where stated

Year	Course	Winner	Score	Entrants
1860	Prestwick	Willie Park, Sr. (Musselburgh)	174	8
1861	Prestwick	Tom Morris, Sr. (Prestwick)	163	12
1862	Prestwick	Tom Morris, Sr. (Prestwick)	163	6
1863	Prestwick	Willie Park, Sr. (Musselburgh)	168	14
1864	Prestwick	Tom Morris, Sr. (Prestwick)	167	6
1865	Prestwick	Andrew Strath (St. Andrews)	162	10
1866	Prestwick	Willie Park, Sr. (Musselburgh)	169	12
1867	Prestwick	Tom Morris, Sr. (St. Andrews)	170	10
1868	Prestwick	Tom Morris, Jr. (St. Andrews)	157	10
1869	Prestwick	Tom Morris, Jr. (St. Andrews)	154	8
1870	Prestwick	Tom Morris, Jr. (St. Andrews)	149	17

Young Tom Morris won the original trophy, the Championship Belt, outright after three consecutive wins, and the Open lapsed for one year. It resumed in 1872 with a new trophy, the famous claret jug, donated by the R & A, the Prestwick Club, and the Honourable Company of Edinburgh Golfers.

Year	Course	Winner	Score	Entrants
1872	Prestwick	Tom Morris, Jr. (St. Andrews)	166	8
1873	St. Andrews	Tom Kidd (St. Andrews)	179	26
1874	Musselburgh	Mungo Park (Musselburgh)	159	32
1875	Prestwick	Willie Park, Sr. (Musselburgh)	166	18
1876	St. Andrews	Bob Martin (St. Andrews)	176	34
1877	Royal Musselburgh	Jamie Anderson (St. Andrews)	160	24
1878	Prestwick	Jamie Anderson (St. Andrews)	157	26
1879	St. Andrews	Jamie Anderson (St. Andrews)	169	46
1880	Royal Musselburgh	Bob Ferguson (Royal Musselburgh)	162	30
1881	Prestwick	Bob Ferguson (Royal Musselburgh)	170	22
1882	St. Andrews	Bob Ferguson (Royal Musselburgh)	171	40
1883	Royal Musselburgh	Willie Fernie (Dumfries)	159*	41
1884	Prestwick	Jack Simpson (Carnoustie)	160	30
1885	St. Andrews	Bob Martin (St. Andrews)	171	51
1886	Royal Musselburgh	David Brown (Royal Musselburgh)	157	46
1887	Prestwick	Willie Park, Jr. (Royal Musselburgh)	161	36
1888	St. Andrews	Jack Burns (Warwick)	171	53
1889	Royal Musselburgh	Willie Park, Jr. (Royal Musselburgh)	155*	42
1890	Prestwick	John Ball † (Royal Liverpool)	164	40
1891	St. Andrews	Hugh Kirkaldy (St. Andrews)	166	82

Competition thereafter extended from 36 to 72 holes

Year	Course	Winner	Score	Entrants
1892	Muirfield	Harold Hilton † (Royal Liverpool)	305	66
1893	Prestwick	William Auchterlonie (St. Andrews)	322	72
1894	St. George's (Sandwich)	J.H. Taylor (Winchester)	326	94
1895	St. Andrews	J.H. Taylor (Winchester)	322	73
1896	Muirfield	Harry Vardon (Ganton)	316*	64
1897	Royal Liverpool (Hoylake)	Harold Hilton † (Royal Liverpool)	314	86
1898	Prestwick	Harry Vardon (Ganton)	307	78
1899	St. George's (Sandwich)	Harry Vardon (Ganton)	310	98
1900	St. Andrews	J.H. Taylor (Mid-Surrey)	309	81
1901	Muirfield	James Braid (Romford)	309	101
1902	Royal Liverpool (Hoylake)	Sandy Herd (Huddersfield)	307	112
1903	Prestwick	Harry Vardon (South Herts)	300	127
1904	Royal St. George's (Sandwich)	Jack White (Sunningdale)	296	144
1905	St. Andrews	James Braid (Walton Heath)	318	152
1906	Muirfield	James Braid (Walton Heath)	300	183
1907	Royal Liverpool (Hoylake)	Arnaud Massy (Fr.)	312	193
1908	Prestwick	James Braid (Walton Heath)	291	180
1909	Cinque Ports (Deal)	J.H. Taylor (Mid-Surrey)	295	203
1910	St. Andrews	James Braid (Walton Heath)	299	210
1911	Royal St. George's (Sandwich)	Harry Vardon (South Herts)	303	226
1912	Muirfield	Ted Ray (Oxhey)	295	215
1913	Royal Liverpool (Hoylake)	J.H. Taylor (Mid-Surrey)	304	268
1914	Prestwick	Harry Vardon (South Herts)	306	191
1920	Cinque Ports (Deal)	George Duncan (Hanger Hill)	303	190
1921	St. Andrews	Jock Hutchison (U.S.)	296*	158
1922	Royal St. George's (Sandwich)	Walter Hagen (U.S.)	300	225
1923	Troon	Arthur Havers (Coombe Hill)	295	222
1924	Royal Liverpool (Hoylake)	Walter Hagen (U.S.)	301	277
1925	Prestwick	Jim Barnes † (U.S.)	300	200
1926	Royal Lytham & St. Annes	Bobby Jones † (U.S.)	291	293
1927	St. Andrews	Bobby Jones † (U.S.)	285	207
1928	Royal St. George's (Sandwich)	Walter Hagen (U.S.)	292	271
1929	Muirfield	Walter Hagen (U.S.)	292	242
1930	Royal Liverpool (Hoylake)	Bobby Jones † (U.S.)	291	296
1931	Carnoustie	Tommy Armour (U.S.)	296	215
1932	Prince's (Sandwich)	Gene Sarazen (U.S.)	283	224
1933	St. Andrews	Densmore Shute (U.S.)	292*	287
1934	Royal St. George's (Sandwich)	Henry Cotton (Waterloo)	283	312
1935	Muirfield	Alf Perry (Leatherhead)	283	264
1936	Royal Liverpool (Hoylake)	Alf Padgham (Sundridge Park)	287	286
1937	Carnoustie	Henry Cotton (Ashridge)	290	258

Year	Course	Winner	Score	Entrants
1938	Royal St. George's (Sandwich)	Reg Whitcombe (Parkstone)	295	268
1939	St. Andrews	Dick Burton (Sale)	290	254
1946	St. Andrews	Sam Snead (U.S.)	290	225
1947	Royal Liverpool (Hoylake)	Fred Daly (Balmoral, Ire.)	293	263
1948	Muirfield	Henry Cotton (Royal Mid-Surrey)	284	272
1949	Royal St. George's (Sandwich)	Bobby Locke (S. Africa)	283*	224
1950	Troon	Bobby Locke (S. Africa)	279	262
1951	Royal Portrush	Max Faulkner	285	180
1952	Royal Lytham & St. Annes	Bobby Locke (S. Africa)	287	275
1953	Carnoustie	Ben Hogan (U.S.)	282	196
1954	Royal Birkdale	Peter Thomson (Aus.)	283	349
1955	St. Andrews	Peter Thomson (Aus.)	281	301
1956	Royal Liverpool (Hoylake)	Peter Thomson (Aus.)	286	360
1957	St. Andrews	Bobby Locke (S. Africa)	279	282
1958	Royal Lytham & St. Annes	Peter Thomson (Aus.)	278*	362
1959	Muirfield	Gary Player (S. Africa)	284	285
1960	St. Andrews	Kel Nagle (Aus.)	278	410
1961	Royal Birkdale	Arnold Palmer (U.S.)	284	364
1962	Troon	Arnold Palmer (U.S.)	276	379
1963	Royal Lytham & St. Annes	Bob Charles (N.Z.)	277*	261
1964	St. Andrews	Tony Lema (U.S.)	279	327
1965	Royal Birkdale	Peter Thomson (Aus.)	285	372
1966	Muirfield	Jack Nicklaus (U.S.)	282	310
1967	Royal Liverpool (Hoylake)	Roberto de Vicenzo (Arg.)	278	326
1968	Carnoustie	Gary Player (S. Africa)	289	309
1969	Royal Lytham & St. Annes	Tony Jacklin (Potters Bar)	280	424
1970	St. Andrews	Jack Nicklaus (U.S.)	283*	468
1971	Royal Birkdale	Lee Trevino (U.S.)	278	528
1972	Muirfield	Lee Trevino (U.S.)	278	570
1973	Troon	Tom Weiskopf (U.S.)	276	569
1974	Royal Lytham & St. Annes	Gary Player (S. Africa)	282	679
1975	Carnoustie	Tom Watson (U.S.)	279*	629
1976	Royal Birkdale	Johnny Miller (U.S.)	279	719
1977	Turnberry	Tom Watson (U.S.)	268	730
1978	St. Andrews	Jack Nicklaus (U.S.)	281	788
1979	Royal Lytham & St. Annes	Seve Ballesteros (Sp.)	283	885
1980	Muirfield	Tom Watson (U.S.)	271	994
1981	Royal St. George's (Sandwich)	Bill Rogers (U.S.)	276	971
1982	Royal Troon	Tom Watson (U.S.)	284	1,121
1983	Royal Birkdale	Tom Watson (U.S.)	275	1,107
1984	St. Andrews	Seve Ballesteros (Sp.)	276	1,413
1985	Royal St. George's (Sandwich)	Sandy Lyle	282	1,361
1986	Turnberry	Greg Norman (Aus.)	280	1,347
1987	Muirfield	Nick Faldo	279	1,407
1988	Royal Lytham & St. Annes	Seve Ballesteros (Sp.)	273	1,393
1989	Royal Troon	Mark Calcavecchia (U.S.)	275*	1,481
1990	St. Andrews	Nick Faldo	270	1,707

* *play-off* † *amateur*

THE U.S. OPEN CHAMPIONSHIP

UNITED STATES GOLF ASSOCIATION

A young English-born player, Horace Rawlins, was the first winner of the U.S. Open over a nine-hole course at Newport, Rhode Island, in 1895, the year after the formation of the USGA. His winning score of 173 for 36 holes, two better than Willie Dunn, won him a check for $150 out of the grand total of $335 that was played for. The championship was extended to 72 holes in 1898, when eight rounds of the nine-hole course at Myopia Hunt Club, Hamilton, Massachusetts, were played. Needless to say, the prize money has risen over the years: in 1990 it was $1,000,000.

The present-day U.S. Open trophy** (left) **is an exact replica of the original, which was destroyed in a fire in 1946.

Winners U.S., except where stated

Year	Course	Winner	Score
1895	Newport (RI)	Horace Rawlins	173
1896	Shinnecock Hills (NY)	James Foulis	152
1897	Chicago (IL)	Joe Lloyd	162
Competition thereafter extended from 36 to 72 holes			
1898	Myopia Hunt (MA)	Fred Herd	328
1899	Baltimore (MD)	Willie Smith	315
1900	Chicago (IL)	Harry Vardon (G.B.)	313
1901	Myopia Hunt (MA)	Willie Anderson	331*
1902	Garden City (NY)	Laurie Auchterlonie	307
1903	Baltusrol (NJ)	Willie Anderson	307*
1904	Glen View (IL)	Willie Anderson	303
1905	Myopia Hunt (MA)	Willie Anderson	314
1906	Onwentsia (IL)	Alex Smith	295
1907	Philadelphia (PA)	Alex Ross	302
1908	Myopia Hunt (MA)	Fred McLeod	322*
1909	Englewood (NJ)	George Sargent	290
1910	Philadelphia (PA)	Alex Smith	298*
1911	Chicago (IL)	John McDermott	307*
1912	Buffalo (NY)	John McDermott	294
1913	Brookline (MA)	Francis Ouimet †	304*
1914	Midlothian (IL)	Walter Hagen	290
1915	Baltusrol (NJ)	Jerome Travers †	297
1916	Minikahda (MN)	Chick Evans †	286
1919	Brae Burn (MA)	Walter Hagen	301*
1920	Inverness (OH)	Ted Ray (G.B.)	295
1921	Columbia (MD)	Jim Barnes	289

Year	Course	Winner	Score
1922	Skokie (IL)	Gene Sarazen	288
1923	Inwood (NY)	Bobby Jones †	296*
1924	Oakland Hills (MI)	Cyril Walker	297
1925	Worcester (MA)	Willie MacFarlane	291*
1926	Scioto (OH)	Bobby Jones †	293
1927	Oakmont (PA)	Tommy Armour	301*
1928	Olympia Fields (IL)	Johnny Farrell	294*
1929	Winged Foot (NY)	Bobby Jones †	294*
1930	Interlachen (MN)	Bobby Jones †	287
1931	Inverness (OH)	Billy Burke	292*
1932	Fresh Meadow (NY)	Gene Sarazen	286
1933	North Shore (IL)	Johnny Goodman †	287
1934	Merion (PA)	Olin Dutra	293
1935	Oakmont (PA)	Sam Parks	299
1936	Baltusrol (NJ)	Tony Manero	282
1937	Oakland Hills (MI)	Ralph Guldahl	281
1938	Cherry Hills (CO)	Ralph Guldahl	284
1939	Philadelphia (PA)	Byron Nelson	284*
1940	Canterbury (OH)	Lawson Little	287*
1941	Colonial (TX)	Craig Wood	284
1946	Canterbury (OH)	Lloyd Mangrum	284*
1947	St. Louis (MO)	Lew Worsham	282*
1948	Riviera (CA)	Ben Hogan	276
1949	Medinah (IL)	Cary Middlecoff	286
1950	Merion (PA)	Ben Hogan	287*
1951	Oakland Hills (MI)	Ben Hogan	287
1952	Northwood (TX)	Julius Boros	281
1953	Oakmont (PA)	Ben Hogan	283
1954	Baltusrol (NJ)	Ed Furgol	284
1955	Olympic (CA)	Jack Fleck	287*
1956	Oak Hill (NY)	Cary Middlecoff	281
1957	Inverness (OH)	Dick Mayer	282*
1958	Southern Hills (OK)	Tommy Bolt	283
1959	Winged Foot (NY)	Billy Casper	282
1960	Cherry Hills (CO)	Arnold Palmer	280
1961	Oakland Hills (MI)	Gene Littler	281
1962	Oakmont (PA)	Jack Nicklaus	283*
1963	Brookline (MA)	Julius Boros	293*
1964	Congressional (DC)	Ken Venturi	278
1965	Bellerive (MO)	Gary Player (S. Africa)	282*
1966	Olympic (CA)	Billy Casper	278*
1967	Baltusrol (NJ)	Jack Nicklaus	275
1968	Oak Hill (NY)	Lee Trevino	275
1969	Champions (TX)	Orville Moody	281
1970	Hazeltine (MN)	Tony Jacklin (G.B.)	281
1971	Merion (CA)	Lee Trevino	280*
1972	Pebble Beach (CA)	Jack Nicklaus	290
1973	Oakmont (PA)	Johnny Miller	279
1974	Winged Foot (NY)	Hale Irwin	287
1975	Medinah (IL)	Lou Graham	287*
1976	Atlanta (GA)	Jerry Pate	277
1977	Southern Hills (OK)	Hubert Green	278
1978	Cherry Hills (CO)	Andy North	285
1979	Inverness (OH)	Hale Irwin	284
1980	Baltusrol (NJ)	Jack Nicklaus	272
1981	Merion (PA)	David Graham (Aus.)	273
1982	Pebble Beach (CA)	Tom Watson	282
1983	Oakmont (PA)	Larry Nelson	280
1984	Winged Foot (NY)	Fuzzy Zoeller	276*
1985	Oakland Hills (MI)	Andy North	279
1986	Shinnecock Hills (NY)	Ray Floyd	279
1987	Olympic (CA)	Scott Simpson	277
1988	Brookline (MA)	Curtis Strange	278*
1989	Oak Hill (NY)	Curtis Strange	278
1990	Medinah (IL)	Hale Irwin	280*

** play-off † amateur*

THE USPGA CHAMPIONSHIP

UNITED STATES PROFESSIONAL GOLFERS' ASSOCIATION

The USPGA Championship was first played in 1916 at Siwanoy, New York. It was a matchplay event until it moved to a 72-hole strokeplay format in 1958. The founding of the event was one of the first actions of the newly formed Professional Golfers' Association of America in 1916. It is recognized as one of golf's four Major championships, and performance in the USPGA Tour determines which players can enter. The great Walter Hagen holds the record for the most wins with five.

The USPGA Championship trophy** (left) **was presented to the Association by Rodman Wanamaker, the Philadelphia millionaire who first conceived of the event.

Winners U.S., except where stated

Year	Course	Winner	Margin
1916	Siwanoy (NY)	Jim Barnes	1 up
1919	Engineers (NY)	Jim Barnes	6 & 5
1920	Flossmoor (IL)	Jock Hutchison	1 up
1921	Inwood (NY)	Walter Hagen	3 & 2
1922	Oakmont (PA)	Gene Sarazen	4 & 3
1923	Pelham (NY)	Gene Sarazen	at 38th
1924	French Lick (IN)	Walter Hagen	2 up
1925	Olympia Fields (IL)	Walter Hagen	6 & 5
1926	Salisbury (NY)	Walter Hagen	5 & 3
1927	Cedar Crest (TX)	Walter Hagen	1 up
1928	Five Farms (MD)	Leo Diegel	6 & 5
1929	Hillcrest (CA)	Leo Diegel	6 & 4
1930	Fresh Meadow (NY)	Tommy Armour	1 up
1931	Wannamoisett (RI)	Tom Creavy	2 & 1
1932	Keller (MN)	Olin Dutra	4 & 3
1933	Blue Mound (WI)	Gene Sarazen	5 & 4
1934	Park (NY)	Paul Runyan	at 38th
1935	Twin Hills (OK)	Johnny Revolta	5 & 4

Year	Course	Winner	Score
1936	Pinehurst (NC)	Densmore Shute	3 & 2
1937	Pittsburgh (PA)	Densmore Shute	at 37th
1938	Shawnee (PA)	Paul Runyan	8 & 7
1939	Pomonok (NY)	Henry Picard	at 37th
1940	Hershey (PA)	Byron Nelson	1 up
1941	Cherry Hills (CO)	Vic Ghezzi	at 38th
1942	Seaview (NJ)	Sam Snead	2 & 1
1944	Manito (WA)	Bob Hamilton	1 up
1945	Morraine (OH)	Byron Nelson	4 & 3
1946	Portland (OR)	Ben Hogan	6 & 4
1947	Plum Hollow (MI)	Jim Ferrier	2 & 1
1948	Norwood Hills (MO)	Ben Hogan	7 & 6
1949	Hermitage (VA)	Sam Snead	3 & 2
1950	Scioto (OH)	Chandler Harper	4 & 3
1951	Oakmont (PA)	Sam Snead	7 & 6
1952	Big Spring (KY)	Jim Turnesa	1 up
1953	Birmingham (MI)	Walter Burkemo	2 & 1
1954	Keller (MN)	Chick Harbert	4 & 3
1955	Meadowbrook (MI)	Doug Ford	4 & 3
1956	Blue Hill (MA)	Jack Burke, Jr.	3 & 2
1957	Miami Valley (OH)	Lionel Hebert	2 & 1
Competition thereafter changed from matchplay to strokeplay			Score
1958	Llanerch (PA)	Dow Finsterwald	276
1959	Minneapolis (MN)	Bob Rosburg	277
1960	Firestone (OH)	Jay Hebert	281
1961	Olympia Fields (IL)	Jerry Barber	277*
1962	Aronimink (PA)	Gary Player (S. Africa)	278
1963	Dallas (TX)	Jack Nicklaus	279
1964	Columbus (OH)	Bobby Nichols	271
1965	Laurel Valley (PA)	Dave Marr	280
1966	Firestone (OH)	Al Geiberger	280
1967	Columbine (CO)	Don January	281*
1968	Pecan Valley (TX)	Julius Boros	281
1969	NCR (Dayton, OH)	Ray Floyd	276
1970	Southern Hills (OK)	Dave Stockton	279
1971	PGA National (Palm Beach, FL)	Jack Nicklaus	281
1972	Oakland Hills (MI)	Gary Player (S. Africa)	281
1973	Canterbury (OH)	Jack Nicklaus	277
1974	Tanglewood (NC)	Lee Trevino	276
1975	Firestone (OH)	Jack Nicklaus	276
1976	Congressional (DC)	Dave Stockton	281
1977	Pebble Beach (CA)	Lanny Wadkins	282*
1978	Oakmont (PA)	John Mahaffey	276*
1979	Oakland Hills (MI)	David Graham (Aus.)	272*
1980	Oak Hill (NY)	Jack Nicklaus	274
1981	Atlanta (GA)	Larry Nelson	273
1982	Southern Hills (OK)	Ray Floyd	272
1983	Riviera (CA)	Hal Sutton	274
1984	Shoal Creek (AL)	Lee Trevino	273
1985	Cherry Hills (CO)	Hubert Green	278
1986	Inverness (OH)	Bob Tway	276
1987	PGA National (Palm Beach, FL)	Larry Nelson	287*
1988	Oak Tree (OK)	Jeff Sluman	272
1989	Kemper Lakes (IL)	Payne Stewart	276
1990	Shoal Creek (AL)	Wayne Grady (Aus)	282

* *play-off*

THE MASTERS TOURNAMENT

AUGUSTA NATIONAL GOLF CLUB

The Masters Tournament, held annually at the Augusta National Golf Club, is an invitation event with strict qualifying conditions. It was first played in 1934 as the Augusta National Invitation Tournament after Bobby Jones decided that the suggested name, The Masters Tournament, was "too presumptuous." Eventually he relented, and the Masters name was officially adopted in 1938.

A silver plaque** (left) **is presented to the Masters champion each year. The permanent trophy is kept at Augusta ***(see page 62).***

Winners U.S., except where stated

Year	Winner	Score	Year	Winner	Score
1934	Horton Smith	284	1965	Jack Nicklaus	271
1935	Gene Sarazen	282*	1966	Jack Nicklaus	288*
1936	Horton Smith	285	1967	Gay Brewer	280
1937	Byron Nelson	283	1968	Bob Goalby	277
1938	Henry Picard	285	1969	George Archer	281
1939	Ralph Guldahl	279	1970	Billy Casper	279*
1940	Jimmy Demaret	280	1971	Charles Coody	279
1941	Craig Wood	280	1972	Jack Nicklaus	286
1942	Byron Nelson	280*	1973	Tommy Aaron	283
1946	Herman Keiser	282	1974	Gary Player (S. Africa)	278
1947	Jimmy Demaret	281	1975	Jack Nicklaus	276
1948	Claude Harmon	279	1976	Ray Floyd	271
1949	Sam Snead	282	1977	Tom Watson	276
1950	Jimmy Demaret	283	1978	Gary Player (S. Africa)	277
1951	Ben Hogan	280	1979	Fuzzy Zoeller	280*
1952	Sam Snead	286	1980	Seve Ballesteros (Sp.)	275
1953	Ben Hogan	274	1981	Tom Watson	280
1954	Sam Snead	289*	1982	Craig Stadler	284*
1955	Cary Middlecoff	279	1983	Seve Ballesteros (Sp.)	280
1956	Jack Burke	289	1984	Ben Crenshaw	277
1957	Doug Ford	283	1985	Bernhard Langer (W. Ger.)	282
1958	Arnold Palmer	284	1986	Jack Nicklaus	279
1959	Art Wall	284	1987	Larry Mize	285*
1960	Arnold Palmer	282	1988	Sandy Lyle (G.B.)	281
1961	Gary Player (S. Africa)	280	1989	Nick Faldo (G.B.)	283*
1962	Arnold Palmer	280*	1990	Nick Faldo (G.B.)	278*
1963	Jack Nicklaus	286	1991	Ian Woosnam (G.B.)	277
1964	Arnold Palmer	276	* *play-off*		

THE U.S. WOMEN'S OPEN CHAMPIONSHIP

UNITED STATES GOLF ASSOCIATION

The U.S. Women's Open dates back to 1946, when Patty Berg, then a professional for six years, defeated Betty Jameson by 5-and-4 at Spokane after a 36-hole qualifying event. The following year the championship was altered to a 72-hole strokeplay format. The event is primarily for women professionals, but amateurs can compete. Unsurprisingly, the event has been dominated by American players. The only other parts of the world to produce winners have been Europe, with three victors, and Australia, with one.

Winners U.S., except where stated

Year	Course	Winner	Margin
1946	Spokane (WA)	Patty Berg	5 & 4
Competition thereafter changed from matchplay to strokeplay			Score
1947	Greensboro (NC)	Betty Jameson	295
1948	Atlantic City (NJ)	Babe Zaharias	300
1949	Landover (MD)	Louise Suggs	291
1950	Wichita (KS)	Babe Zaharias	291
1951	Atlanta (GA)	Betsy Rawls	293
1952	Bala (PA)	Louise Suggs	284
1953	Rochester (NY)	Betsy Rawls	302*
1954	Salem (MA)	Babe Zaharias	291
1955	Wichita (KS)	Fay Crocker	299
1956	Duluth (MN)	Kathy Cornelius	302*
1957	Winged Foot (NY)	Betsy Rawls	299
1958	Bloomfield Hills (MI)	Mickey Wright	290
1959	Pittsburgh (PA)	Mickey Wright	287
1960	Worcester (MA)	Betsy Rawls	292
1961	Baltusrol (NJ)	Mickey Wright	293
1962	Myrtle Beach (SC)	Murle Lindstrom	301
1963	Kenwood (OH)	Mary Mills	289
1964	San Diego (CA)	Mickey Wright	290*
1965	Atlantic City (NJ)	Carol Mann	290
1966	Hazeltine National (MN)	Sandra Spuzich	297
1967	Hot Springs (VA)	Catherine Lacoste † (Fr.)	294
1968	Moselem Springs (PA)	Susie Berning	289
1969	Scenic Hills (FL)	Donna Caponi	294
1970	Muskogee (OK)	Donna Caponi	287
1971	Erie (PA)	JoAnne Gunderson Carner	288
1972	Winged Foot (NY)	Susie Berning	299
1973	Rochester (NY)	Susie Berning	290
1974	La Grange (IL)	Sandra Haynie	295
1975	Atlantic City (NJ)	Sandra Palmer	295
1976	Springfield (PA)	JoAnne Gunderson Carner	292*
1977	Hazeltine National (MN)	Hollis Stacy	292
1978	Indianapolis (IN)	Hollis Stacy	289
1979	Brooklawn (CT)	Jerilyn Britz	284
1980	Richland (TN)	Amy Alcott	280
1981	La Grange (IL)	Pat Bradley	279
1982	Del Paso (CA)	Janet Alex	283
1983	Cedar Ridge (OK)	Jan Stephenson (Aus.)	290
1984	Salem (MA)	Hollis Stacy	290
1985	Baltusrol (NJ)	Kathy Baker	280
1986	NCR (Dayton, OH)	Jane Geddes	287*
1987	Plainfield (NJ)	Laura Davies (G.B.)	285*
1988	Baltimore (MD)	Liselotte Neumann (Swe.)	277
1989	Indianwood (MI)	Betsy King	278
1990	Duluth (MN)	Betsy King	284

* *play-off* † *amateur*

THE WOMEN'S BRITISH OPEN CHAMPIONSHIP

LADIES' GOLF UNION

The Women's British Open Championship was instituted in 1976 and first played at Fulford, when Jenny Lee Smith won with a total of 299. Players from outside Britain have dominated the championship since 1979, with the exception of the victories of Laura Davies in 1986 at Royal Birkdale and Alison Nicholas in 1987 at St. Mellion. In the mid-1980s the event attracted sponsorship from Hitachi and Burberrys, and since 1987 it has been sponsored by Nabisco, in the name of their most famous product, Weetabix.

Winners G.B., except where stated

Year	Sponsor	Course	Winner	Score
1976		Fulford	Jennifer Lee Smith † (Gosforth Park)	299
1977		Lindrick	Vivien Saunders (Tyrrells Wood)	306
1978		Foxhills	Janet Melville † (Furness)	310
1979		Southport & Ainsdale	Alison Shead (S. Africa)	301
1980		Wentworth	Debbie Massey (U.S.)	294
1981		Northumberland	Debbie Massey (U.S.)	295
1982		Royal Birkdale	Marta Figueras-Dotti † (Sp.)	296
1984	Hitachi	Woburn	Ayako Okamoto (Jap.)	289
1985	Burberrys	Moor Park	Betsy King (U.S.)	300
1986		Royal Birkdale	Laura Davies (West Byfleet)	283
1987	Nabisco	St. Mellion	Alison Nicholas	296
1988	Nabisco	Lindrick	Corinne Dibnah (Aus.)	295*
1989	Nabisco	Ferndown	Jane Geddes (U.S.)	274
1990	Nabisco	Woburn	Helen Alfredsson (Swe.)	288*

* *play-off* † *amateur*

THE BRITISH AMATEUR CHAMPIONSHIP

ROYAL & ANCIENT GOLF CLUB

The British Amateur Championship was officially inaugurated in 1886, but it is accepted that the first one was actually played the year before. The Royal Liverpool Club issued invitations in 1885 for an Open Amateur Tournament to be played during the club's spring meeting. Allan MacFie beat 43 others to win.

Winners and runners-up G.B., except where stated

Year	Course	Winner	Runner-up	Margin
1885	Royal Liverpool (Hoylake)	Allan MacFie	Horace Hutchinson	7 & 6
1886	St. Andrews	Horace Hutchinson	Henry Lamb	7 & 6
1887	Royal Liverpool (Hoylake)	Horace Hutchinson	John Ball	1 up

Year	Course	Winner	Runner-up	Margin
1888	Prestwick	John Ball	Johnny Laidlay	5 & 4
1889	St. Andrews	Johnny Laidlay	Leslie Balfour Melville	2 & 1
1890	Royal Liverpool (Hoylake)	John Ball	Johnny Laidlay	4 & 3
1891	St. Andrews	Johnny Laidlay	Harold Hilton	at 20th
1892	St. George's (Sandwich)	John Ball	Harold Hilton	3 & 1
1893	Prestwick	Peter Anderson	Johnny Laidlay	1 up
1894	Royal Liverpool (Hoylake)	John Ball	Mure Fergusson	1 up
1895	St. Andrews	Leslie Balfour Melville	John Ball	at 19th
1896	St. George's (Sandwich)	Freddie Tait	Harold Hilton	8 & 7
1897	Muirfield	Jack Allan	James Robb	4 & 2
1898	Royal Liverpool (Hoylake)	Freddie Tait	Mure Fergusson	7 & 5
1899	Prestwick	John Ball	Freddie Tait	at 37th
1900	St. George's (Sandwich)	Harold Hilton	James Robb	8 & 7
1901	St. Andrews	Harold Hilton	John Low	1 up
1902	Royal Liverpool (Hoylake)	Charles Hutchings	Sidney Fry	1 up
1903	Muirfield	Robert Maxwell	Horace Hutchinson	7 & 5
1904	Royal St. George's (Sandwich)	Walter Travis (U.S.)	Edward Blackwell	4 & 3
1905	Prestwick	Gordon Barry	Hon. Osmund Scott	3 & 2
1906	Royal Liverpool (Hoylake)	James Robb	C.C. Lingen	4 & 3
1907	St. Andrews	John Ball	C.A. Palmer	6 & 4
1908	Royal St. George's (Sandwich)	E.A. Lassen	H.E. Taylor	7 & 6
1909	Muirfield	Robert Maxwell	Cecil Hutchison	1 up
1910	Royal Liverpool (Hoylake)	John Ball	Colin Aylmer	10 & 9
1911	Prestwick	Harold Hilton	E.A. Lassen	4 & 3
1912	Royal North Devon (Westward Ho!)	John Ball	Abe Mitchell	at 38th
1913	St. Andrews	Harold Hilton	Robert Harris	6 & 5
1914	Royal St. George's (Sandwich)	J.L.C. Jenkins	Charles Hezlet (Ire.)	3 & 2
1920	Muirfield	Cyril Tolley	Robert A. Gardner (U.S.)	at 37th
1921	Royal Liverpool (Hoylake)	Willie Hunter	A.J. Graham	12 & 11
1922	Prestwick	Ernest Holderness	John Caven	1 up
1923	Cinque Ports (Deal)	Roger Wethered	Robert Harris	7 & 6
1924	St. Andrews	Ernest Holderness	Eustace Storey	3 & 2
1925	Royal North Devon (Westward Ho!)	Robert Harris	Kenneth Fradgley	13 & 12
1926	Muirfield	Jess Sweetser (U.S.)	A.F. Simpson	6 & 5
1927	Royal Liverpool (Hoylake)	William Tweddell	D.E. Landale	7 & 6
1928	Prestwick	Philip Perkins	Roger Wethered	6 & 4
1929	Royal St. George's (Sandwich)	Cyril Tolley	J.N. Smith	4 & 3
1930	St. Andrews	Bobby Jones (U.S.)	Roger Wethered	7 & 6
1931	Royal North Devon (Westward Ho!)	Eric Martin Smith	John de Forest	1 up
1932	Muirfield	John de Forest	Eric Fiddian	3 & 1
1933	Royal Liverpool (Hoylake)	Hon. Michael Scott	Dale Bourn	4 & 3
1934	Prestwick	Lawson Little (U.S.)	James Wallace	14 & 13
1935	Royal Lytham & St. Annes	Lawson Little (U.S.)	William Tweddell	1 up
1936	St. Andrews	Hector Thomson	James Ferrier (Aus.)	2 up
1937	Royal St. George's (Sandwich)	Robert Sweeny (U.S.)	Lionel Munn (Ire.)	3 & 2
1938	Troon	Charlie Yates (U.S.)	Cecil Ewing (Ire.)	3 & 2
1939	Royal Liverpool (Hoylake)	Alex Kyle	Tony Duncan	2 & 1
1946	Birkdale	James Bruen (Ire.)	Robert Sweeny (U.S.)	4 & 3
1947	Carnoustie	William Turnesa (U.S.)	Richard Chapman (U.S.)	3 & 2
1948	Royal St. George's (Sandwich)	Frank Stranahan (U.S.)	Charles Stowe	5 & 4
1949	Portmarnock	Max McCready (Ire.)	William Turnesa (U.S.)	2 & 1
1950	St. Andrews	Frank Stranahan (U.S.)	Richard Chapman (U.S.)	8 & 6
1951	Royal Porthcawl	Richard Chapman (U.S.)	Charles Coe (U.S.)	5 & 4
1952	Prestwick	Harvie Ward (U.S.)	Frank Stranahan (U.S.)	6 & 5
1953	Royal Liverpool (Hoylake)	Joe Carr (Ire.)	Harvie Ward (U.S.)	2 up
1954	Muirfield	Douglas Bachli (Aus.)	William C. Campbell (U.S.)	2 & 1
1955	Royal Lytham & St. Annes	Joseph Conrad (U.S.)	Alan Slater	3 & 2
1956	Troon	John Beharrell	L.G. Taylor	5 & 4
1957	Formby	Reid Jack	Harold Ridgley (U.S.)	2 & 1
1958	St. Andrews	Joe Carr (Ire.)	Alan Thirlwell	3 & 2
1959	Royal St. George's (Sandwich)	Deane Beman (U.S.)	Bill Hyndman (U.S.)	3 & 2
1960	Royal Portrush	Joe Carr (Ire.)	R. Cochran (U.S.)	8 & 7
1961	Turnberry	Michael Bonallack	James Walker	6 & 4
1962	Royal Liverpool (Hoylake)	Richard Davies (U.S.)	John Povall	1 up
1963	St. Andrews	Michael Lunt	J.G. Blackwell	2 & 1
1964	Ganton	Gordon Clark	Michael Lunt	at 39th
1965	Royal Porthcawl	Michael Bonallack	Clive Clark	2 & 1
1966	Carnoustie	Bobby Cole (S. Africa)	Ronnie Shade	3 & 2
1967	Formby	Robert Dickson (U.S.)	Ron Cerrudo (U.S.)	2 & 1
1968	Troon	Michael Bonallack	Joe Carr (Ire.)	7 & 6
1969	Royal Liverpool (Hoylake)	Michael Bonallack	Bill Hyndman (U.S.)	3 & 2
1970	Royal County Down (Newcastle)	Michael Bonallack	Bill Hyndman (U.S.)	8 & 7
1971	Carnoustie	Steve Melnyk (U.S.)	James Simons (U.S.)	3 & 2
1972	Royal St. George's (Sandwich)	Trevor Homer	Alan Thirlwell	4 & 3

Year	Course	Winner	Runner-up	Margin
1973	Royal Porthcawl	Dick Siderowf (U.S.)	Peter Moody	5 & 3
1974	Muirfield	Trevor Homer	Jim Gabrielsen (U.S.)	2 up
1975	Royal Liverpool (Hoylake)	Vinny Giles (U.S.)	Mark James	8 & 7
1976	St. Andrews	Dick Siderowf (U.S.)	John Davies	at 37th
1977	Ganton	Peter McEvoy	H.M. Campbell	5 & 4
1978	Troon	Peter McEvoy	Paul McKellar	4 & 3
1979	Hillside	Jay Sigel (U.S.)	Scott Hoch (U.S.)	3 & 2
1980	Royal Porthcawl	Duncan Evans	D.R. Suddards (S. Africa)	4 & 3
1981	St. Andrews	Philippe Ploujoux (Fr.)	Joel Hirsch (U.S.)	4 & 2
1982	Royal Cinque Ports (Deal)	Martyn Thompson	A.K. Stubbs	4 & 3
1983	Turnberry	Philip Parkin	Jim Holtgrieve (U.S.)	5 & 4
1984	Formby	Jose-Maria Olazabal (Sp.)	Colin Montgomerie	5 & 4
1985	Royal Dornoch	Garth McGimpsey	G. Homewood	8 & 7
1986	Royal Lytham & St. Annes	David Curry	S.G. Birtwell	11 & 9
1987	Prestwick	Paul Mayo	Peter McEvoy	3 & 1
1988	Royal Porthcawl	Christian Hardin (Swe.)	B. Fouchee (S. Africa)	1 up
1989	Royal Birkdale	Stephen Dodd	Craig Cassells	5 & 3
1990	Muirfield	Rolf Muntz (Neth.)	Michael Macara	7 & 6

THE U.S. AMATEUR CHAMPIONSHIP

UNITED STATES GOLF ASSOCIATION

The Newport Club, Rhode Island, was the site of the first U.S. Amateur Championship in 1895. It was won by Charles Blair Macdonald, a pioneer of golf in America. There were only 32 entries and matches were played over 18 holes, with a 36-hole final. The championship continued under matchplay rules until 1965 when it became a 72-hole strokeplay event. The event was changed yet again in 1973, when it reverted to matchplay. The only player to have won the event five times was the legendary Bobby Jones, whose dominance of the amateur game during the 1920s was indisputable. He won in 1924, 1925, 1927, 1928, and 1930. In that last year he also won the British Open at Royal Liverpool, the U.S. Open at Interlachen, and the British Amateur Championship at St. Andrews, an astounding series of victories known as the Impregnable Quadrilateral.

Winners U.S., except where stated

Year	Course	Winner	Runner-up	Margin
1895	Newport (RI)	Charles Macdonald	Charles Sands	12 & 11
1896	Shinnecock Hills (NY)	H.J. Whigham	J.G. Thorp	8 & 7
1897	Chicago (IL)	H.J. Whigham	Rossiter Betts	8 & 6
1898	Morris County (NJ)	Findlay Douglas	Walter Smith	5 & 3
1899	Onwentsia (IL)	Herbert Harriman	Findlay Douglas	3 & 2
1900	Garden City (NY)	Walter Travis	Findlay Douglas	2 up
1901	Atlantic City (NJ)	Walter Travis	W.E. Egan	5 & 4
1902	Glen View (IL)	Louis James	Eben Byers	4 & 2
1903	Nassau (NY)	Walter Travis	Eben Byers	5 & 4
1904	Baltusrol (NJ)	Chandler Egan	Fred Herreshoff	8 & 6
1905	Chicago (IL)	Chandler Egan	D.E. Sawyer	6 & 5
1906	Englewood (NJ)	Eben Byers	George Lyon (Can.)	2 up
1907	Euclid (OH)	Jerome Travers	Archibald Graham	6 & 5

Year	Course	Winner	Runner-up	Margin
1908	Garden City (NY)	Jerome Travers	Max Behr	8 & 7
1909	Chicago (IL)	Robert A. Gardner	Chandler Egan	4 & 3
1910	Brookline (MA)	William Fownes	Warren Wood	4 & 3
1911	Apawamis (NY)	Harold Hilton (G.B.)	Fred Herreshoff	at 37th
1912	Chicago (IL)	Jerome Travers	Chick Evans	7 & 6
1913	Garden City (NY)	Jerome Travers	John Anderson	5 & 4
1914	Ekwanok (VT)	Francis Ouimet	Jerome Travers	6 & 5
1915	Detroit (MI)	Robert A. Gardner	John Anderson	5 & 4
1916	Merion (PA)	Chick Evans	Robert A. Gardner	4 & 3
1919	Oakmont (PA)	Davidson Herron	Bobby Jones	5 & 4
1920	Engineers (NY)	Chick Evans	Francis Ouimet	7 & 6
1921	St. Louis (MO)	Jesse Guilford	Robert A. Gardner	7 & 6
1922	Brookline (MA)	Jess Sweetser	Chick Evans	3 & 2
1923	Flossmoor (IL)	Max Marston	Jess Sweetser	at 38th
1924	Merion (PA)	Bobby Jones	George Von Elm	9 & 8
1925	Oakmont (PA)	Bobby Jones	Watts Gunn	8 & 7
1926	Baltusrol (NJ)	George Von Elm	Bobby Jones	2 & 1
1927	Minikahda (MN)	Bobby Jones	Chick Evans	8 & 7
1928	Brae Burn (MA)	Bobby Jones	Philip Perkins (G.B.)	10 & 9
1929	Del Monte (CA)	Harrison Johnston	Oscar Willing	4 & 3
1930	Merion (PA)	Bobby Jones	Eugene Homans	8 & 7
1931	Beverly (IL)	Francis Ouimet	Jack Westland	6 & 5
1932	Baltimore (MD)	Ross Somerville (Can.)	Johnny Goodman	2 & 1
1933	Kenwood (OH)	George Dunlap	Max Marston	6 & 5
1934	Brookline (MA)	Lawson Little	David Goldman	8 & 7
1935	Cleveland (OH)	Lawson Little	Walter Emery	4 & 2
1936	Garden City (NY)	Johnny Fischer	Jack McLean (G.B.)	at 37th
1937	Alderwood (OR)	Johnny Goodman	Ray Billows	2 up
1938	Oakmont (PA)	William Turnesa	Patrick Abbott	8 & 7
1939	North Shore (IL)	Marvin Ward	Ray Billows	7 & 5
1940	Winged Foot (NY)	Richard Chapman	W.B. McCullough	11 & 9
1941	Omaha Field (NB)	Marvin Ward	Patrick Abbott	4 & 3
1946	Baltusrol (NJ)	Stanley Bishop	Smiley Quick	at 37th
1947	Pebble Beach (CA)	Robert Riegel	John Dawson	2 & 1
1948	Memphis (TN)	William Turnesa	Ray Billows	2 & 1
1949	Oak Hill (NY)	Charles Coe	Rufus King	11 & 10
1950	Minneapolis (M N)	Sam Urzetta	Frank Stranahan	at 39th
1951	Saucon Valley (PA)	Billy Maxwell	Joseph Gagliardi	4 & 3
1952	Seattle (WA)	Jack Westland	Al Mengert	3 & 2
1953	Oklahoma City (OK)	Gene Littler	Dale Morey	1 up
1954	Detroit (MI)	Arnold Palmer	Robert Sweeny	1 up
1955	Virginia (VA)	Harvie Ward	Bill Hyndman	9 & 8
1956	Knollwood (IL)	Harvie Ward	Charles Kocsis	5 & 4
1957	Brookline (MA)	Hillman Robbins	Frank Taylor	5 & 4
1958	Olympic (CA)	Charles Coe	Tommy Aaron	5 & 4
1959	Broadmoor (CO)	Jack Nicklaus	Charles Coe	1 up
1960	St. Louis (MO)	Deane Beman	Robert W. Gardner	6 & 4
1961	Pebble Beach (CA)	Jack Nicklaus	Dudley Wysong	8 & 6

Year	Course	Winner	Runner-up	Margin
1962	Pinehurst (NC)	Labron Harris	Downing Gray	1 up
1963	Wakonda (IA)	Deane Beman	Richard Sikes	2 & 1
1964	Canterbury (OH)	William C. Campbell	Edward Tutwiler	1 up
Competition changed from matchplay to strokeplay				**Score**
1965	Southern Hills (OK)	Robert Murphy		291
1966	Merion (PA)	Gary Cowan (Can.)		285*
1967	Broadmoor (CO)	Robert Dickson		285
1968	Scioto (OH)	Bruce Fleisher		284
1969	Oakmont (PA)	Steve Melnyk		286
1970	Waverley (OR)	Lanny Wadkins		279
1971	Wilmington (DE)	Gary Cowan (Can.)		280
1972	Charlotte (NC)	Vinny Giles		285
Reverted to matchplay				**Margin**
1973	Inverness (IL)	Craig Stadler	D. Strawn	6 & 5
1974	Ridgewood (NJ)	Jerry Pate	John Grace	2 & 1
1975	Virginia (Richmond, VA)	Fred Ridley	Keith Fergus	2 up
1976	Bel-Air (CA)	Bill Sander	Parker Moore	8 & 6
1977	Aronimink (PA)	John Fought	Doug Fischesser	9 & 8
1978	Plainfield (NJ)	John Cook	Scott Hoch	5 & 4
1979	Canterbury (OH)	Mark O'Meara	John Cook	8 & 7
1980	Pinehurst (NC)	Hal Sutton	Bob Lewis	9 & 8
1981	Olympic (CA)	Nathaniel Crosby	Brian Lindley	at 37th
1982	Brookline (MA)	Jay Sigel	David Tolley	8 & 7
1983	North Shore (IL)	Jay Sigel	Chris Perry	8 & 7
1984	Oak Tree (OK)	Scott Verplank	Sam Randolph	4 & 3
1985	Montclair (NJ)	Sam Randolph	Peter Persons	1 up
1986	Shoal Creek (AL)	Buddy Alexander	Chris Kite	5 & 3
1987	Jupiter Hill (FL)	Billy Mayfair	Eric Rebmann	4 & 3
1988	Hot Springs (VI)	Eddie Meeks	D. Yates	7 & 6
1989	Merion (PA)	Chris Patton	D. Green	3 & 1
1990	Englewood (NJ)	Phil Mickelson	M. Zerman	5 & 4

* *play-off*

THE LADIES' BRITISH OPEN AMATEUR CHAMPIONSHIP

LADIES' GOLF UNION

The Ladies' British Amateur Championship was inaugurated in June, 1893 at the nine-hole ladies' course at Lytham and St. Annes. Two clubs, Lytham and Wimbledon, each announced an open event at almost the same time. However, the newly formed Ladies' Golf Union took over the event and has administered it ever since. During the 1920s, there was great rivalry between two players, Cecil Leitch and Joyce Wethered (Lady Heathcoat-Amory), both of whom share the record for the championship with a total of four wins each. Leitch won a victory in each of the four countries hosting the championship. She also appeared in two other finals, in 1922 and 1925, in which she finished runner-up, both times to her rival Joyce Wethered. Their 1922 final had the championship's biggest winning margin when Wethered beat Leitch by 9-and-7.

Winners G.B., unless otherwise stated

Year	Course	Winner	Runner-up	Margin
1893	Royal Lytham & St. Annes	Lady Margaret Scott	Issette Pearson	7 & 5
1894	Littlestone	Lady Margaret Scott	Issette Pearson	3 & 2
1895	Royal Portrush	Lady Margaret Scott	E. Lythgoe	3 & 2
1896	Royal Liverpool (Hoylake)	Amy Pascoe	Lena Thomson	3 & 2
1897	Gullane	Edith Orr	Miss Orr	4 & 2
1898	Yarmouth	Lena Thomson	Elinor Nevile	7 & 5
1899	County Down (Newcastle)	May Hezlet (Ire.)	J. Magill (Ire.)	2 & 1
1900	Royal North Devon (Westward Ho!)	Rhona Adair	Elinor Nevile	6 & 5
1901	Aberdovey	Miss Graham	Rhona Adair	3 & 1
1902	Cinque Ports (Deal)	May Hezlet (Ire.)	Elinor Nevile	at 19th
1903	Royal Portrush	Rhona Adair	F. Walker-Leigh	4 & 3
1904	Troon	Lottie Dod	May Hezlet (Ire.)	1 up
1905	Cromer	Bertha Thompson	M.E. Stuart	3 & 2
1906	Burnham	Mrs Kennion	Bertha Thompson	4 & 3
1907	County Down (Newcastle)	May Hezlet (Ire.)	Florence Hezlet (Ire.)	2 & 1
1908	St. Andrews	Maud Titterton	Dorothy Campbell	at 19th
1909	Birkdale	Dorothy Campbell	Florence Hezlet (Ire.)	4 & 3
1910	Royal North Devon (Westward Ho!)	Grant Suttie	L. Moore	6 & 4
1911	Royal Portrush	Dorothy Campbell	Violet Hezlet (Ire.)	3 & 2
1912	Turnberry	Gladys Ravenscroft	S. Temple	3 & 2
1913	Royal Lytham & St. Annes	Muriel Dodd	Miss Chubb	8 & 6
1914	Hunstanton	Cecil Leitch	Gladys Ravenscroft	2 & 1
1920	Royal County Down (Newcastle)	Cecil Leitch	Molly Griffiths	7 & 6
1921	Turnberry	Cecil Leitch	Joyce Wethered	4 & 3
1922	Prince's (Sandwich)	Joyce Wethered	Cecil Leitch	9 & 7
1923	Burnham	Doris Chambers	A. Macbeth	2 up
1924	Royal Portrush	Joyce Wethered	Mrs. Cautley	7 & 6
1925	Troon	Joyce Wethered	Cecil Leitch	at 37th
1926	Royal St. David's (Harlech)	Cecil Leitch	Mrs. Percy Garon	8 & 7
1927	Royal County Down (Newcastle)	Simone Thion de la Chaume (Fr.)	Dorothy Pearson	5 & 4
1928	Hunstanton	Nanette Le Blan (Fr.)	S. Marshall	3 & 2
1929	St. Andrews	Joyce Wethered	Glenna Collett (U.S.)	3 & 1
1930	Formby	Diana Fishwick	Glenna Collett (U.S.)	4 & 3
1931	Portmarnock	Enid Wilson	Wanda Morgan	7 & 6
1932	Saunton	Enid Wilson	Clementine Montgomery	7 & 6
1933	Gleneagles	Enid Wilson	Diana Plumpton	5 & 4
1934	Royal Porthcawl	Helen Holm	Pam Barton	6 & 5
1935	Royal County Down (Newcastle)	Wanda Morgan	Pam Barton	3 & 2
1936	Southport & Ainsdale	Pam Barton	Bridget Newell	5 & 3
1937	Turnberry	Jessie Anderson	Doris Park	6 & 4
1938	Burnham	Helen Holm	Elsie Corlett	4 & 3
1939	Royal Portrush	Pam Barton	Mrs. T. Marks	2 & 1
1946	Hunstanton	Jean Hetherington	Philomena Garvey (Ire.)	1 up

Year	Course	Winner	Runner-up	Margin
1947	Gullane	Babe Zaharias (U.S.)	Jacqueline Gordon (U.S.)	5 & 4
1948	Royal Lytham & St. Annes	Louise Suggs (U.S.)	Jean Donald	1up
1949	Royal St. David's (Harlech)	Frances Stephens	Val Reddan	5 & 4
1950	Royal County Down (Newcastle)	Vicomtesse de Saint Sauveur (Fr.)	Jessie Valentine	3 & 2
1951	Broadstone	Kitty MacCann (Ire.)	Frances Stephens	4 & 3
1952	Troon	Moira Paterson	Frances Stephens	at 39th
1953	Royal Porthcawl	Marlene Stewart (Can.)	Philomena Garvey (Ire.)	7 & 6
1954	Ganton	Frances Stephens	Elizabeth Price	4 & 3
1955	Royal Portrush	Jessie Valentine	Barbara Romack (U.S.)	7 & 6
1956	Sunningdale	Margaret Smith	Mary Janssen	8 & 7
1957	Gleneagles	Philomena Garvey (Ire.)	Jessie Valentine	4 & 3
1958	Hunstanton	Jessie Valentine	Elizabeth Price	1 up
1959	Ascot	Elizabeth Price	Belle McCorkindale	at 37th
1960	Royal St. David's (Harlech)	Barbara McIntire (U.S.)	Philomena Garvey (Ire.)	4 & 2
1961	Carnoustie	Marley Spearman	Diane Robb	7 & 6
1962	Royal Birkdale	Marley Spearman	Angela Bonallack	1 up
1963	Royal County Down (Newcastle)	Brigitte Varangot (Fr.)	Philomena Garvey (Ire.)	3 & 1
1964	Prince's (Sandwich)	Carol Sorenson (U.S.)	Bridget Jackson	at 37th
1965	St. Andrews	Brigitte Varangot (Fr.)	Belle Robertson	4 & 3
1966	Ganton	Elizabeth Chadwick	Vivien Saunders	3 & 2
1967	Royal St. David's (Harlech)	Elizabeth Chadwick	Mary Everard	1 up
1968	Walton Heath	Brigitte Varangot (Fr.)	Claudine Rubin (Fr.)	at 20th
1969	Royal Portrush	Catherine Lacoste (Fr.)	Ann Irvin	1 up
1970	Gullane	Dinah Oxley	Belle Robertson	1 up
1971	Alwoodley	Michelle Walker	Beverley Huke	3 & 1
1972	Hunstanton	Michelle Walker	Claudine Rubin (Fr.)	2 up
1973	Carnoustie	Ann Irvin	Michelle Walker	3 & 2
1974	Royal Porthcawl	Carol Semple (U.S.)	Angela Bonallack	2 & 1
1975	St. Andrews	Nancy Syms (U.S.)	Suzanne Cadden	3 & 2
1976	Silloth	Cathy Panton	Alison Sheard (S.Africa)	1 up
1977	Hillside	Angela Uzielli	Vanessa Marvin	6 & 5
1978	Notts	Edwina Kennedy (Aus.)	Julia Greenhalgh	1 up
1979	Nairn	Maureen Madill (Ire.)	Jane Lock (Aus.)	2 & 1
1980	Woodhall Spa	Anne Sander (U.S.)	Liv Wollin (Swe.)	3 & 1
1981	Caernarvonshire	Belle Robertson	Wilma Aitken	at 20th
1982	Walton Heath	Kitrina Douglas	Gillian Stewart	4 & 2
1983	Silloth	Jill Thornhill	Regine Lautens (Swi.)	4 & 2
1984	Royal Troon	Jody Rosenthal (U.S.)	Julie Brown	4 & 3
1985	Ganton	Lilian Behan (Ire.)	Claire Waite	1 up
1986	West Sussex	Marnie McGuire (N.Z.)	Louise Briers (Aus.)	2 & 1
1987	Royal St. David's (Harlech)	Janet Collingham	Susan Shapcott	at 19th
1988	Royal Cinque Ports (Deal)	Joanne Furby	Julie Wade	4 & 3
1989	Royal Liverpool (Hoylake)	Helen Dobson	Elaine Farquharson	6 & 5
1990	Dunbar	Julie Hall	Helen Wadsworth	3 & 2

THE U.S. WOMEN'S AMATEUR CHAMPIONSHIP

UNITED STATES GOLF ASSOCIATION

There were only 13 entries for the first U.S. Women's Amateur Championship when it was played as a strokeplay event at the Meadowbrook Club, Hempstead, New York, in 1895. The following year it became a matchplay event and has remained so ever since. Among the early champions were Harriot and Margaret Curtis, the two sisters who donated the Curtis Cup. The trophy competed for in the first year of the U.S. Women's Amateur Championship was a pitcher made of silver, but the next year Robert Cox donated an attractive silver loving cup, topped with a delicate thistle decoration. This trophy is still competed for today. The event was dominated in the 1920s and 1930s by Glenna Collett Vare, who appeared in eight finals between 1922 and 1935. She won it six times, in 1922, 1925, 1928, 1929, 1930, and 1935, and was twice runner-up.

Winners U.S., unless otherwise stated

Year	Course	Winner	Runner-up	Score
1895	Meadowbrook (NY)	Mrs. Charles Brown	N.C. Sargeant	132
Competition changed from strokeplay to matchplay				**Margin**
1896	Morris County (NY)	Beatrix Hoyt	Mrs. Arthur Turnure	2 & 1
1897	Essex (MA)	Beatrix Hoyt	N.C. Sargeant	5 & 4
1898	Ardsley (NY)	Beatrix Hoyt	Maude Wetmore	5 & 3
1899	Philadelphia (PA)	Ruth Underhill	Mrs. Caleb Fox	2 & 1
1900	Shinnecock Hills (NY)	Frances Griscom	Margaret Curtis	6 & 5
1901	Baltusrol (NJ)	Genevieve Hecker	Lucy Herron	5 & 3
1902	Brookline (MA)	Genevieve Hecker	Louisa Wells	4 & 3
1903	Chicago (IL)	Bessie Anthony	J.A. Carpenter	7 & 6
1904	Merion (PA)	Georgianna Bishop	Mrs. E.F. Sanford	5 & 3
1905	Morris County (NJ)	Pauline Mackay	Margaret Curtis	1 up
1906	Brae Burn (MA)	Harriot Curtis	Mary Adams	2 & 1
1907	Midlothian (IL)	Margaret Curtis	Harriot Curtis	7 & 6
1908	Chevy Chase (MD)	Katherine Harley	Mrs. T.H. Polhemus	6 & 5
1909	Merion (PA)	Dorothy Campbell (G.B.)	Mrs. R.H. Barlow	3 & 2
1910	Homewood (IL)	Dorothy Campbell (G.B.)	Mrs. G.M. Martin	2 & 1
1911	Baltusrol (NJ)	Margaret Curtis	Lillian Hyde	5 & 3
1912	Essex (MA)	Margaret Curtis	Mrs. R.H. Barlow	3 & 2
1913	Wilmington (DE)	Gladys Ravenscroft (G.B.)	Marion Hollins	2 up
1914	Glen Cove (NY)	Mrs. Arnold Jackson	Elaine Rosenthal	1 up
1915	Onwentsia (IL)	Mrs. C.H. Vanderbeck	Mrs. W.A. Gavin	3 & 2
1916	Belmont Springs (MA)	Alexa Stirling	Mildred Caverly	2 & 1
1919	Shawnee (PA)	Alexa Stirling	Mrs. W.A. Gavin	6 & 5
1920	Mayfield (OH)	Alexa Stirling	Dorothy Campbell Hurd (G.B.)	5 & 4

Year	Course	Winner	Runner-up	Score
1921	Hollywood (NJ)	Marion Hollins	Alexa Stirling	5 & 4
1922	Greenbrier (WV)	Glenna Collett	Mrs. W.A. Gavin	5 & 4
1923	Westchester-Biltmore (NY)	Edith Cummings	Alexa Stirling	3 & 2
1924	Rhode Island (RI)	Dorothy Campbell Hurd (G.B.)	Mary Browne	7 & 6
1925	St. Louis (MO)	Glenna Collett	Alexa Stirling Fraser	9 & 8
1926	Merion (PA)	Helen Stetson	Mrs. W.D. Goss	3 & 1
1927	Cherry Valley (NY)	Miriam Burns Horn	Maureen Orcutt	5 & 4
1928	Hot Springs (WV)	Glenna Collett	Virginia Van Wie	13 & 12
1929	Oakland Hills (MI)	Glenna Collett	Leona Pressler	4 & 3
1930	Los Angeles (CA)	Glenna Collett	Virginia Van Wie	6 & 5
1931	Buffalo (NY)	Helen Hicks	Glenna Collett Vare	2 & 1
1932	Salem (MA)	Virginia Van Wie	Glenna Collett Vare	10 & 8
1933	Exmore (IL)	Virginia Van Wie	Helen Hicks	4 & 3
1934	Whitemarsh Valley (PA)	Virginia Van Wie	Dorothy Traung	2 & 1
1935	Interlachen (MN)	Glenna Collett Vare	Patty Berg	3 & 2
1936	Canoe Brook (NJ)	Pam Barton (G.B.)	Maureen Orcutt	4 & 3
1937	Memphis (TN)	Mrs. Julius Page	Patty Berg	7 & 6
1938	Westmoreland (IL)	Patty Berg	Mrs. Julius Page	6 & 5
1939	Wee Burn (CT)	Betty Jameson	Dorothy Kirby	3 & 2
1940	Del Monte (CA)	Betty Jameson	Jane Cothran	6 & 5
1941	Brookline (MA)	Betty Hicks Newell	Helen Sigel	5 & 3
1946	Southern Hills (OK)	Babe Zaharias	Clara Sherman	11 & 9
1947	Franklin Hills (MI)	Louise Suggs	Dorothy Kirby	2 up
1948	Del Monte (CA)	Grace Lenczyk	Helen Sigel	4 & 3
1949	Merion (PA)	Dorothy Porter	Dorothy Kielty	3 & 2
1950	Atlanta (GA)	Beverly Hanson	Mae Murray	6 & 4
1951	St. Paul (MN)	Dorothy Kirby	Claire Doran	2 & 1
1952	Waverley (OR)	Jacqueline Pung	Shirley McFedters	2 & 1
1953	Rhode Island (RI)	Mary Lena Faulk	Polly Riley	3 & 2
1954	Allegheny (PA)	Barbara Romack	Mickey Wright	4 & 2
1955	Myers Park (NC)	Patricia Lesser	Jane Nelson	7 & 6
1956	Meridian Hills (IN)	Marlene Stewart (Can.)	JoAnne Gunderson	2 & 1
1957	Del Paso (CA)	JoAnne Gunderson	Anne Casey Johnstone	8 & 6
1958	Wee Burn (CT)	Anne Quast	Barbara Romack	3 & 2
1959	Congressional (DC)	Barbara McIntire	Joanne Goodwin	4 & 3
1960	Tulsa (OK)	JoAnne Gunderson	Jean Ashley	6 & 5
1961	Tacoma (WA)	Anne Decker	Phyllis Preuss	14 & 13
1962	Rochester (NY)	JoAnne Gunderson	Ann Baker	9 & 8
1963	Taconic (MA)	Anne Welts	Peggy Conley	2 & 1
1964	Prairie Dunes (KS)	Barbara McIntire	JoAnne Gunderson	3 & 2
1965	Lakewood (CO)	Jean Ashley	Anne Welts	5 & 4
1966	Sewickley Heights (PA)	JoAnne Gunderson Carner	Marlene Stewart Streit (Can.)	at 41st
1967	Annandale (CA)	Mary Lou Dill	Jean Ashley	5 & 4
1968	Birmingham (MI)	JoAnne Gunderson Carner	Anne Welts	5 & 4
1969	Las Colinas (TX)	Catherine Lacoste (Fr.)	Shelley Hamlin	3 & 2
1970	Wee Burn (CT)	Martha Wilkinson	Cynthia Hill	3 & 2
1971	Atlanta (GA)	Laura Baugh	Beth Barry	1 up
1972	St. Louis (MO)	Mary Anne Budke	Cynthia Hill	5 & 4
1973	Rochester (NY)	Carol Semple	Anne Welts	1 up
1974	Broadmoor (Seattle, WA)	Cynthia Hill	Carol Semple	5 & 4
1975	Brae Burn (MA)	Beth Daniel	Donna Horton	3 & 2
1976	Del Paso (CA)	Donna Horton	Marianne Bretton	2 & 1
1977	Cincinnati (OH)	Beth Daniel	Cathy Sherk (Can.)	3 & 1
1978	Sunnybrook (PA)	Cathy Sherk (Can.)	Judith Oliver	4 & 3
1979	Memphis (TN)	Carolyn Hill	Patty Sheehan	7 & 6
1980	Prairie Dunes (KS)	Juli Inkster	Patti Rizzo	2 up
1981	Waverley (OR)	Juli Inkster	Lindy Goggin	1 up
1982	Broadmoor (Colorado Springs, CO)	Juli Inkster	Cathy Hanlon	4 & 3
1983	Canoe Brook (NJ)	Joanne Pacillo	Sally Quinlan	2 & 1
1984	Broadmoor (Seattle, WA)	Deb Richard	Kimberly Williams	1 up
1985	Fox Chapel (PA)	Michiko Hattori (Jap.)	Cheryl Stacy	5 & 4
1986	Pasatiempo (CA)	Kay Cockerill	Kathleen McCarthy	9 & 7
1987	Barrington (RI)	Kay Cockerill	Tracy Kerdyk	3 & 2
1988	Minikahda (MN)	Pearl Sinn	Karen Robb	6 & 5
1989	Pinehurst (NC)	Vicki Goetze	Brandie Burton	4 & 3
1990	Canoe Brook (NJ)	Pat Hurst	Stephanie Davis	at 37th

THE RYDER CUP

PROFESSIONAL GOLF ASSOCIATION/ PGA EUROPEAN TOUR/ UNITED STATES PROFESSIONAL GOLF ASSOCIATION

A match between the professional golfers of Britain and the United States at Wentworth in 1926 was the forerunner of the Ryder Cup. The first official match was played the next year after Samuel Ryder, a seed merchant from St. Albans, England, offered a gold cup for a biennial match between teams representing Great Britain and Ireland and the United States. In 22 matches between 1927 and 1977, Great Britain and Ireland won only three times. The match had become so one-sided that, in 1977, it was decided to include European players in the team from the rapidly developing European Tour. This change led to the end of the Americans' long dominance of the event.

The famous trophy** (left)**, given by Samuel Ryder, cost £750 in 1927.

Year	Course	Winners/Captain	Opponents/Captain	Margin
1927	Worcester (MA)	U.S. Walter Hagen	G.B. Ted Ray	9½–2½
1929	Moortown	G.B. George Duncan	U.S. Walter Hagen	7–5
1931	Scioto (OH)	U.S. Walter Hagen	G.B. Charles Whitcombe	9–3
1933	Southport & Ainsdale	G.B. J. H. Taylor*	U.S. Walter Hagen	6½–5½
1935	Ridgewood (NJ)	U.S. Walter Hagen	G.B. Charles Whitcombe	9–3
1937	Southport & Ainsdale	U.S. Walter Hagen*	G.B. Charles Whitcombe	8–4
1947	Portland (OR)	U.S. Ben Hogan	G.B. Henry Cotton	11–1
1949	Ganton	U.S. Ben Hogan*	G.B. Charles Whitcombe	7–5

* *non-playing captain*

Year	Course	Winners/Captain	Opponents/Captain	Margin
1951	Pinehurst (NJ)	U.S. Sam Snead	G.B. Arthur Lacey*	9½–2½
1953	Wentworth	U.S. Lloyd Mangrum	G.B. Henry Cotton*	6½–5½
1955	Thunderbird (Palm Springs, CA)	U.S. Chick Harbert	G.B. Dai Rees	8–4
1957	Lindrick	G.B. Dai Rees	U.S. Jack Burke	7½–4½
1959	Eldorado (Palm Desert, CA)	U.S. Sam Snead	G.B. Dai Rees	8½–3½
1961	Royal Lytham & St. Annes	U.S. Jerry Barber	G.B. Dai Rees	14½–9½
1963	East Lake (GA)	U.S. Arnold Palmer	G.B. Johnny Fallon*	23–9
1965	Royal Birkdale	U.S. Byron Nelson*	G.B. Harry Weetman*	19½–12½
1967	Champions (Houston, TX)	U.S. Ben Hogan*	G.B. Dai Rees*	23½–8½
1969	Royal Birkdale ***tied***	U.S. Sam Snead* ***and***	G.B. Eric Brown*	16–16
1971	Old Warson (St. Louis, MO)	U.S. Jay Hebert*	G.B. Eric Brown*	18½–13½
1973	Muirfield (Scotland)	U.S. Jack Burke*	G.B. & Ire. Bernard Hunt*	19–13
1975	Laurel Valley (PA)	U.S. Arnold Palmer*	G.B. & Ire. Bernard Hunt*	21–11
1977	Royal Lytham & St. Annes	U.S. Dow Finsterwald*	G.B. & Ire. Brian Huggett*	12½–7½
1979	Greenbrier (WV)	U.S. Billy Casper*	Eur. John Jacobs*	17–11
1981	Walton Heath	U.S. Dave Marr*	Eur. John Jacobs*	18½–9½
1983	PGA National (Palm Beach, FL)	U.S. Jack Nicklaus*	Eur. Tony Jacklin*	14½–13½
1985	The Belfry	Eur. Tony Jacklin*	U.S. Lee Trevino*	16½–11½
1987	Muirfield Village (OH)	Eur. Tony Jacklin*	U.S. Jack Nicklaus*	15–13
1989	The Belfry ***tied***	Eur. Tony Jacklin* ***and***	U.S. Ray Floyd*	14–14

* *non-playing captain*

THE WALKER CUP

ROYAL & ANCIENT GOLF CLUB/ UNITED STATES GOLF ASSOCIATION

Like the Ryder Cup, the Walker Cup began as an unofficial match between players from Britain and the United States, this time amateurs rather than professionals. It was played as an annual event for three years before becoming a biennial match from 1926 onwards. Great Britain has managed only three wins and one tie in the history of the event so far.

The impressive Walker Cup trophy** (left) **was named after the man who donated it, George H. Walker, the president of the USGA.

Year	Course	Winners/Captain	Opponents/Captain	Margin
1922	National Golf Links	U.S. William Fownes	G.B. Robert Harris	8-4
1923	St. Andrews	U.S. Robert A. Gardner	G.B. Robert Harris	6½–5½
1924	Garden City (NY)	U.S. Robert A. Gardner	G.B. Cyril Tolley	9–3
1926	St. Andrews	U.S. Robert A. Gardner	G.B. Robert Harris	6½–5½
1928	Chicago (IL)	U.S. Bobby Jones	G.B. William Tweddell	11–1
1930	Royal St. George's (Sandwich)	U.S. Bobby Jones	G.B. Roger Wethered	10–2
1932	Brookline (MA)	U.S. Francis Ouimet	G.B. Tony Torrance	9½–2½
1934	St. Andrews	U.S. Francis Ouimet	G.B. Hon. Michael Scott	9½–2½
1936	Pine Valley (NJ)	U.S. Francis Ouimet*	G.B. William Tweddell	10½–1½
1938	St. Andrews	G.B. John Beck*	U.S. Francis Ouimet*	7½–4½
1947	St. Andrews	U.S. Francis Ouimet*	G.B. John Beck*	8–4
1949	Winged Foot (NY)	U.S. Francis Ouimet*	G.B. Laddie Lucas	10–2
1951	Royal Birkdale	U.S. William Turnesa	G.B. Raymond Oppenheimer*	7½–4½
1953	Kittansett (MA)	U.S. Charlie Yates*	G.B. Tony Duncan*	9–3
1955	St. Andrews	U.S. William C. Campbell*	G.B. Alec Hill*	10–2
1957	Minikahda (MN)	U.S. Charles Coe*	G.B. Gerald Micklem*	8½–3½
1959	Muirfield (Scotland)	U.S. Charles Coe	G.B. Gerald Micklem*	9–3
1961	Seattle (WA)	U.S. Jack Westland*	G.B. Charles Lawrie*	11–1
1963	Turnberry	U.S. Richard Tufts*	G.B. Charles Lawrie*	14–10
1965	Baltimore (MD) ***tied***	U.S. John Fischer* ***and***	G.B. Joe Carr*	12–12
1967	Royal St. George's (Sandwich)	U.S. Jess Sweetser*	G.B. Joe Carr	15–9
1969	Milwaukee (WI)	U.S. Billy Joe Patton*	G.B. Michael Bonallack	13–11
1971	St. Andrews	G.B. Michael Bonallack	U.S. John Winters*	13–11
1973	Brookline (MA)	U.S. Jess Sweetser*	G.B. David Marsh*	14–10
1975	St. Andrews	U.S. Ed Updegraff*	G.B. David Marsh*	15½–8½
1977	Shinnecock Hills (NY)	U.S. Lou Oehmig*	G.B. Sandy Saddler*	16–8
1979	Muirfield (Scotland)	U.S. Dick Siderowf*	G.B. Rodney Foster*	15½–8½
1981	Cypress Point (CA)	U.S. Jim Gabrielsen*	G.B. & Ire. Rodney Foster*	15–9
1983	Royal Liverpool (Hoylake)	U.S. Jay Sigel	G.B. & Ire. Charlie Green*	13½–10½
1985	Pine Valley (NJ)	U.S. Jay Sigel	G.B. & Ire. Charlie Green*	13–11
1987	Sunningdale	U.S. Fred Ridley*	G.B. & Ire. Geoffrey Marks*	16½–7½
1989	Peachtree (GA)	G.B. & Ire. Geoffrey Marks*	U.S. Fred Ridley*	12½–11½

* *non-playing captain*

THE CURTIS CUP

LADIES' GOLF UNION/ UNITED STATES GOLF ASSOCIATION

The first Curtis Cup match between the amateur women of Britain and America took place in 1932, but unofficial matches between the two countries had been played from 1905. The Cup was donated by the Curtis sisters, both winners of the U.S. Women's Amateur Championship.

Harriot and Margaret Curtis gave the trophy** (left) **for a biennial match between amateur women of the United States and the British Isles.

Year	Course	Winners/Captain	Opponents/Captain	Score
1932	Wentworth	U.S. Marion Hollins*	British Isles Joyce Wethered	5½–3½
1934	Chevy Chase (MD)	U.S. Glenna Collett Vare	British Isles Doris Chambers*	6½–2½
1936	Gleneagles ***tied***	U.S. Glenna Collett Vare ***and***	British Isles Doris Chambers*	4½–4½
1938	Essex (MA)	U.S. Frances Stebbins*	British Isles Kathleen Wallace-Williamson*	5½–3½
1948	Birkdale	U.S. Glenna Collett Vare	British Isles Doris Chambers*	6½–2½

Year	Course	Winners/Captain	Opponents/Captain	Score
1950	Buffalo (NY)	U.S. Glenna Collett Vare*	British Isles Diana Critchley*	7½–1½
1952	Muirfield (Scotland)	British Isles Lady Katherine Cairns*	U.S. Aniela Goldthwaite*	5–4
1954	Merion (PA)	U.S. Edith Flippin*	British Isles Baba Beck*	6–3
1956	Prince's (Sandwich)	British Isles Zara Bolton*	U.S. Edith Flippin*	5–4
1958	Brae Burn (MA) *tied*	U.S. Virginia Dennehy * *and*	British Isles Daisy Ferguson*	4½–4½
1960	Lindrick	U.S. Mildred Prunaret*	British Isles Maureen Garrett*	6½–2½
1962	Broadmoor (CO)	U.S. Polly Riley*	British Isles Frances Smith*	8–1
1964	Royal Porthcawl	U.S. Helen Hawes*	British Isles Elsie Corlett*	10½–7½
1966	Hot Springs (VA)	U.S. Dorothy Porter*	British Isles Zara Bolton*	13–5
1968	Royal County Down (Newcastle)	U.S. Evelyn Monsted*	G.B. & Ire. Zara Bolton*	10½–7½
1970	Brae Burn (MA)	U.S. Carol Cudone*	G.B. & Ire. Jeanne Bisgood*	11½–6½
1972	Western Gailes	U.S. Jean Crawford*	G.B. & Ire. Frances Smith*	10–8
1974	San Francisco (CA)	U.S. Allison Choate*	G.B. & Ire. Belle Robertson*	13–5
1976	Royal Lytham & St. Annes	U.S. Barbara McIntire*	G.B. & Ire. Belle Robertson*	11½–6½
1978	Apawamis (NY)	U.S. Helen Sigel Wilson*	G.B. & Ire. Carol Comboy*	12–6
1980	St. Pierre	U.S. Nancy Syms*	G.B. & Ire. Carol Comboy*	13–5
1982	Denver (CO)	U.S. Betty Probasco*	G.B. & Ire. Maire O'Donnell*	14½–3½
1984	Muirfield (Scotland)	U.S. Phyllis Preuss*	G.B. & Ire. Diane Bailey*	9½–8½
1986	Prairie Dunes (KS)	G.B. & Ire. Diane Bailey*	U.S. Judy Bell*	13–5
1988	Royal St. George's (Sandwich)	G.B. & Ire. Diane Bailey*	U.S. Judy Bell*	11–7
1990	Somerset Hills (NJ)	U.S. Lesley Shannon*	G.B. & Ire. Jill Thornhill	14–4

** non-playing captain*

WORLD CUP GOLF

INTERNATIONAL GOLF ASSOCIATION

The World Cup, founded in 1953 as the Canada Cup by Canadian businessman John Jay Hopkins, is an international team tournament for professionals, with each country represented by two players. As well as the team trophy there is an individual award for the lowest score. The tournament was not played in 1981 or 1986.

(until 1966, Canada Cup)

Year	Course	Winners	Score	Leading Individual(s)	Score
1953	Montreal	Argentina (Roberto de Vicenzo, Antonio Cerda)	287*	Antonio Cerda (Arg.)	140*
1954	Laval-sur-Lac	Australia (Peter Thomson, Kel Nagle)	556	Stan Leonard (Can.)	275
1955	Washington	U.S. (Ed Furgol, Chick Harbert)	560	Ed Furgol (U.S.)	279
1956	Wentworth	U.S. (Ben Hogan, Sam Snead)	567	Ben Hogan (U.S.)	277
1957	Tokyo	Japan (Torakichi Nakamura, Koichi Ono)	557	Torakichi Nakamura (Jap.)	274
1958	Mexico City	Ireland (Harry Bradshaw, Christy O'Connor, Sr.)	579	Angel Miguel (Sp.)	286
1959	Melbourne	Australia (Kel Nagle, Peter Thomson)	563	Stan Leonard (Can.)	
1960	Portmarnock	U.S. (Arnold Palmer, Sam Snead)	565	Flory van Donck (Bel.)	279
1961	Puerto Rico	U.S. (Jimmy Demaret, Sam Snead)	560	Sam Snead (U.S.)	272
1962	Buenos Aires	U.S. (Arnold Palmer, Sam Snead)	557	Roberto de Vicenzo (Arg.)	276
1963	St. Nom-La-Breteche	U.S. (Jack Nicklaus, Arnold Palmer)	482*	Jack Nicklaus (U.S.)	237*
1964	Maui (HI)	U.S. (Jack Nicklaus, Arnold Palmer)	554	Jack Nicklaus (U.S.)	276
1965	Madrid	South Africa (Harold Henning, Gary Player)	571	Gary Player (S. Africa)	281
1966	Tokyo	U.S. (Jack Nicklaus, Arnold Palmer)	548	George Knudson (Can.)	272
1967	Mexico City	U.S. (Jack Nicklaus, Arnold Palmer)	557	Arnold Palmer (U.S.)	276
1968	Olgiata (Rome)	Canada (Al Balding, George Knudson)	569	Al Balding (Can.)	274
1969	Singapore	U.S. (Orville Moody, Lee Trevino)	552	Lee Trevino (U.S.)	275
1970	Buenos Aires	Australia (Bruce Devlin, David Graham)	544	Roberto de Vicenzo (Arg.)	269
1971	Palm Beach (FL)	U.S. (Jack Nicklaus, Lee Trevino)	555	Jack Nicklaus (U.S.)	271
1972	Melbourne	Taiwan (Hsieh Min-nan, Lu Liang-huan)	438*	Hsieh Min-nan (Tai.)	217*
1973	Marbella	U.S. (Johnny Miller, Jack Nicklaus)	558	Johnny Miller (U.S.)	277
1974	Caracas	South Africa (Bobby Cole, Dale Hayes)	554	Bobby Cole (S. Africa)	271
1975	Bangkok	U.S. (Lou Graham, Johnny Miller)	554	Johnny Miller (U.S.)	275
1976	Palm Springs (CA)	Spain (Seve Ballesteros, Manuel Pinero)	574	Ernesto Acosta (Mex.)	282
1977	Manila	Spain (Seve Ballesteros, Antonio Garrido)	591	Gary Player (S. Africa)	289
1978	Hawaii	U.S. (John Mahaffey, Andy North)	564	John Mahaffey (U.S.)	281
1979	Glyfada	U.S. (John Mahaffey, Hale Irwin)	575	Hale Irwin (U.S.)	285
1980	Bogota	Canada (Dan Halldorson, Jim Helford)	572	Sandy Lyle (Scot.)	282
1982	Acapulco	Spain (Jose-Maria Canizares, Manuel Pinero)	563	Manuel Pinero (Sp.)	281
1983	Pondok Inah (Jakarta)	U.S. (Rex Caldwell, John Cook)	565	Dave Barr (Can.)	276
1984	Olgiata (Rome)	Spain (Jose-Maria Canizares, Jose Rivero)	414*	Jose-Maria Canizares (Sp.)	205*
1985	La Quinta	Canada (Dan Halldorson, Dave Barr)	559	Howard Clark (Eng.)	272
1987	Kapalua (HI)	Wales (Ian Woosnam, David Llewellyn)	574	Ian Woosnam (Wal.)	274
1988	Royal Melbourne	U.S. (Ben Crenshaw, Mark McCumber)	560	Ben Crenshaw (U.S.)	275
1989	Las Brisas	Australia (Peter Fowler, Wayne Grady)	278*	Peter Fowler (Aus.)	137*
1990	Grand Cypress (Orlando, FL)	Germany (Bernhard Langer, Torsten Giedeon)	556	Bernhard Langer, Torsten Giedeon (Ger.)	278

** played over 36 holes in 1953 and 1989, 63 holes in 1963, 54 holes in 1972 and 1984*

GLOSSARY

Albatross Term used in Britain for a score of three under the **par** for a **hole**. In the United States this score is known as a **double eagle**.

Anti-shank Club design that attempts to eliminate the possibility of striking the ball with the **hosel**.

Approach Shot played to the **green** from the **fairway** or **rough**.

Back nine Second set of nine **holes** on an 18-hole golf course.

Baffy Sturdy wooden club, now obsolete, similar to the modern 3- or 4-wood. It replaced the earlier "baffing spoon" and had a lofted face for high shots from the **fairway**.

Balata Natural or synthetic compound used to make the cover for high-quality golf balls. Its soft, elastic qualities produce a high spin rate, and it is favored by tournament players.

Bent grass Type of fine-leafed grass that produces an ideal surface for putting greens. It is, however, difficult to maintain in hot climates.

Birdie Term used for a score of one under the **par** for a **hole**.

Bogey Term used for a score of one over the **par** for a **hole**.

Boron A strong metal powder often added during the construction of **graphite** shafts to provide added strength at the **hosel** end.

Borrow British term for the amount a putt will deviate from a straight line due to the slope of the **green**.

Brassie A wooden fairway club with a protective brass sole-plate, the equivalent of the modern 2-wood.

Break American term for the amount that a putt will deviate from a straight line due to the slope of the **green**. The term in Britain is **borrow**.

Bulger driver Designed to reduce the chances of striking the ball on the heel or toe of the club, the bulger had a convex face. Popular in the late nineteenth century, it is now obsolete.

Carry Distance between the point from which a ball is played to the point where it lands. When the ball is hit over water or a bunker, it is said to "carry" the hazard.

Chip Low running shot normally played from near the edge of the **green** toward the **hole**.

Chipper Club with a relatively straight face used for playing a low **chip** from just off the **green**.

Cleek Term of Scottish origin to describe an iron club roughly the equivalent of a modern 2-iron, although there were variations, including short cleeks, long cleeks, driving cleeks, and putting cleeks.

Couch grass Grass often regarded as a weed, with long, creeping roots. Also known as "crab grass."

Cross bunker Bunker lying across the line of the **fairway**.

Cut To miss the cut is to fail to score low enough, usually over the first 36 holes of a 72-hole tournament, to qualify for the final two rounds.

Cut shot Shot that makes the ball spin in a clockwise direction, resulting in a left-to-right bending flight. It can either be deliberate or a mistake.

Divot Piece of turf removed by the clubhead when a shot is played.

Dogleg **Hole** that sharply changes direction midway, normally in the landing area for the tee shot. It can be a turn either to left or right.

Dormie Term used in **matchplay** for the situation when a player is leading by as many holes as are left to play and therefore cannot be beaten.

Double eagle Term used in the United States for three under the par for a **hole**. In Britain this score is known as an **albatross**.

Double green Single putting surface shared by two **holes**, usually coming from opposite directions. These are a relic of the early days of golf, when courses were played out and back over the same ground.

Driver Club with a long shaft and little **loft** used for driving the ball the maximum distance from the **tee**.

Eagle Term that denotes a score of two under the **par** for a **hole**.

Fairway Area of closely mown turf between **tee** and **green**, which has as its boundary either longer grass, known as semi-rough, or completely uncut grass, called **rough**.

Feathery An early golf ball made by filling a leather pouch with boiled feathers. It was highly susceptible to damage and began to go out of use in the mid-1880s after the introduction of the cheaper **guttie** ball.

Fescue A fine-leafed, deep-rooted species of grass common on seaside links and heathland courses in the British Isles, tolerant to drought conditions and providing an ideal surface for putting greens.

Flat swing Backswing in which the club is more horizontal than vertical. This is often regarded as a fault, but many fine players have had flat swings, including Ben Hogan.

Fourball A match involving four players in teams of two, in which each player plays his own ball.

Foursome A match involving four players in teams of two, in which each team plays one ball on alternate strokes. At the start of play each team decides which player will play the first tee shot, after which they alternate the tee shot on each hole.

Free drop Ball dropped without penalty away from an immovable obstruction, or in other circumstances in accordance with the *Rules of Golf*.

Front nine First nine **holes** on an 18-hole golf course. The second nine holes are known as the **back nine**.

Graphite (carbon fiber) Carbon-based substance that when bonded in layers produces an exceptionally strong but very light material ideal for golf-club shafts. It is also increasingly employed in the manufacture of clubheads.

Great Triumvirate Name given collectively to three outstanding British professionals who were active before the First World War: James Braid, J.H. Taylor, and Harry Vardon.

Green Area of closely mown grass specially prepared for putting, into which the **hole** is cut. It is separated from the fairway by the "apron," a fringe of grass longer than the green but shorter than the fairway. Originally the term "green" was used for a whole course; hence a "three-green" tournament was one played over three courses.

Guttie Ball introduced in 1848, made of gutta percha, a rubber-like substance obtained from the latex of a species of Malaysian tree.

Handicap System that subtracts strokes from the scores of weaker players to enable people of varying abilities to play against each other on theoretically equal terms. The handicap is usually based on the average scores of a player compared to a course standard.

Haskell ball Name of the first **rubber-core ball**, which was invented in 1898 by Coburn Haskell.

Hole General term for the whole region between **tee** and **green**, but also the specific target in the ground of a standard $4^1/_4$ in. (108mm) diameter.

Hook Stroke that bends sharply to the left, caused by the application of counter-clockwise spin, either deliberately or unintentionally.

Hosel Socket on an iron-headed club that serves to connect the iron clubhead to the shaft.

Interlocking grip Method of gripping the handle of the club in which the little finger of the right hand intertwines with the forefinger of the left hand. It is usually favored by players with small hands or short fingers to maintain a firm grip.

Kweek grass Fine species of grass indigenous to South Africa. It is less than ideal for golf courses because it is extremely difficult to play on.

Lie Situation in which the ball rests after completion of a stroke. The lie can vary from good to bad, depending on how far the ball has settled down in the grass or, in the case of a bunker, in the sand.

Links Stretch of ground beside the sea upon which golf is played. Linksland is usually low-lying, with sand dunes supporting fine, salt-resistant grasses. The word probably derives from the fact that linksland *links* the foreshore and agricultural land farther inland.

Loft Angle of slope of the face of a club away from the vertical. The loft increases with the number of the iron, giving a higher flight trajectory and less distance.

Lofter Early club with a loft equivalent to a modern 5- or 6-iron and used to strike the ball on a high trajectory. Also called a lofting iron, it superseded the wooden **baffy** for **approach** shots to the **green**.

Long iron Modern iron club with minimum degree of **loft**, designed for performing long and accurate shots from the **fairway**.

LPGA Acronym for Ladies' Professional Golf Association.

Mashie Iron club that made its appearance in the late 1880s. It had a loft equivalent to the modern 5-iron. J.H. Taylor was the first acknowledged master of the mashie.

Matchplay Form of competition in which the number of **holes** won or lost, rather than the number of strokes taken, determines the winner. The alternative is **strokeplay**.

Medium iron Modern iron club used for **approach** shots to the green, combining a medium length of flight with considerable accuracy.

Mixed foursome **Foursome** in which each team is made up of one male and one female player.

Niblick Early lofted iron, now obsolete, that was roughly equivalent to the modern 9-iron. It had a heavy head and a wide face and was used for extricating the ball from difficult **lies** or for lofting it over hazards.

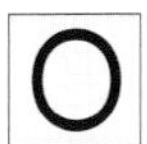

Off the pace American expression to describe the number of strokes or the position of a player behind the leader of a tournament – e.g. "two strokes off the pace."

Overclubbing Error caused by selecting a club that sends the ball farther than the intended distance.

Par Estimated standard score for a hole, based on the length of the hole and on the number of strokes a first-class player would expect to take to complete it in normal conditions.

PGA Acronym for Professional Golfers' Association.

Pitch Lofted shot to a **green** with little run at the end of its flight.

Playclub Old term for a driving club that was in common use up to the latter part of the nineteenth century, roughly equivalent to the modern driver or 2-wood.

Pot bunker Small, round, deep bunker commonly found on traditional British links courses, such as the Old course at St. Andrews.

Pro-Am Form of the game in which a professional player forms a team with amateur players.

R & A The Royal & Ancient Golf Club of St. Andrews.

Rookie A newcomer to one of the professional golf tours.

Rough Area of unmown grass alongside the **fairway** that punishes an inaccurate shot.

Rubber-core ball The golf ball, invented by Coburn Haskell in 1898, that revolutionized the game at the turn of the century. Also known as the **Haskell ball**, it was composed of a solid rubber center around which was wound many yards of elastic thread under tension. It was then covered in gutta percha. The rubber-core ball superseded the **guttie**.

Sand wedge Extremely lofted club, also known as a "sand iron," with a wide flange designed for playing from bunkers. The wide flange "bounces" the clubhead through the sand. The American player Gene Sarazen is credited with its invention.

Scoop Horse-drawn vehicle that was used to move earth in the early days of golf-course construction.

Short game Play within 100 yards of the **green**, especially chipping, bunker shots, and putting.

Short iron Lofted iron club used for short **approaches** to the **green** or for carrying over obstacles or hazards.

Slice Shot carrying considerable clockwise spin that consequently curves violently to the right.

Spoon The traditional name for a lofted **fairway** wood, the equivalent of the modern 3-wood.

Strokeplay Form of competition in which the number of strokes a player takes to complete a round is compared with the other players' scores for a round. Strokeplay has largely supplanted **matchplay** in professional tournament golf.

Stymie Situation in which one player's ball blocked another player's ball's route to the hole. The stymied player was required to play over the top of the offending ball. The stymie was outlawed in 1951 by the **USGA** and the Royal & Ancient Golf Club.

Surlyn® Trademark of a thermoplastic resin similar to natural balata, used in ball manufacture. It is an extremely resilient material and is virtually indestructible by clubs.

Sweet spot Precise point on the face of a golf club, usually in the center, that will deliver the maximum possible mass behind the ball. A ball struck at this point will travel farther than one struck on any other part of the face.

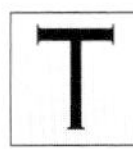

Tee Closely mown area from which the first stroke on a hole is played. The term is also used to refer to the tee peg.

USGA Acronym for the United States Golf Association.

USPGA United States Professional Golfers' Association.

Vardon grip Method of holding the handle of the club in which the little finger of the right hand overlaps the forefinger of the left. Popularized, but not invented, by Harry Vardon.

Whipping Waxed thread used to bind the area where the shaft meets the clubhead. Modern techniques have made this practice obsolete.

Yips Attack of nerves that can destroy the ability to putt, turning the stroke into a twitch or a jerk.

INDEX

accessories 30–1, 55
Aga Khan 120
Ailsa course, Turnberry 186–9
Alcott, Amy 216
Alexander, J.S. 156
Alexander, Tom 291
Alfredsson, Helen 47
Alison, Charles 56, 201
Alliss, Percy 216
Alliss, Peter 57, 196, 216–17
aluminium-headed clubs 7, 29, 50
amateurs 41, 45, 144
  matchplay 42
  women 47
Amen Corner, Augusta 64–5
Anderson, James 23
Anderson, Tip 258
Anderson, Willie 68, 69
Andrew, Bob 271
Aoki, Isao 217
Apple Tree Gang 32, 34
Arana, Javier 174–5
Argentina, The Jockey Club 202
Arran course, Turnberry 188–9
"Articles & Laws in Playing at Golf" 25
Augusta National 44, 56, 62–5
Aultman, Dick 294
Australia
  golf expansion 35
  Kingston Heath 203
  Lake Karrinyup 204
  New South Wales 206
  Royal Melbourne 150–1
  Royal Sydney 160–1
Austria, Seefeld-Wildmoos 211
"The Automaton" club carrier 31
Azinger, Paul 238

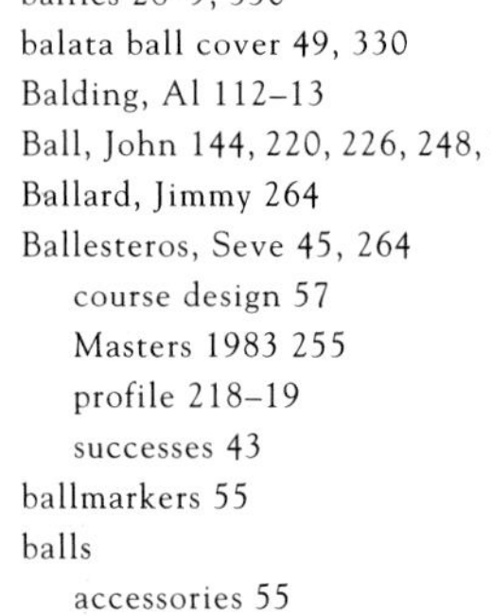

baffies 28–9, 330
balata ball cover 49, 330
Balding, Al 112–13
Ball, John 144, 220, 226, 248, 298
Ballard, Jimmy 264
Ballesteros, Seve 45, 264
  course design 57
  Masters 1983 255
  profile 218–19
  successes 43
ballmarkers 55
balls
  accessories 55
  covers 48, 49
  early designs 10–13
  dimple pattern 49
  featheries 26–7
  gutta percha 24, 27, 266
  modern types 48–9
  rubber-core 27, 39, 48–9, 331
  size rule 25, 49
Ballybunion 18, 66–7
Balmacewen *see* Otago
Baltusrol 34, 56, 68–9
Banff 196
Barber, Miller 221
Barnes, Jim 245, 288
Barr, Dave 280
Barry Burn, Carnoustie 70–3
Barry links 70
Bartholomew, Colonel 66
Barton, Pam 303
Bauer, Gunnar 84
Beck, John 283
Beijing, China 37
Belfry, The 196
Belgium
  golf expansion 36
  golf origins 12
  Royal Belgique 209
Ben Hogan Bridge 62
Bendelow, Tom 96
Berg, Patty 47, 222, 322
Berkshire, The 56, 74
Bethune, Mr. 291
Bing Crosby Pro-Am 43
Blechman, Gil 110
Blixen, Baroness Karen von 202
"Blue Monster" course, Doral 199
Bolt, Tommy 223
Bonallack, Michael 45, 223
Bradshaw, Harry 260, 261, 281
Braid, James 40, 215, 299
  Carnoustie 72
  course architect 56
  Gleneagles 200, 225
  Nairn 205
  profile 224–5
  Royal Troon 162
  Turnberry 186
brassies 28–9, 330
Bredemus, John 78
Brisas, Las 179
Britain
  growth of clubs 24–5
  U.S. dominance 42–3
British Amateur Championship 41, 322–4
  origins 25, 144
British Open Championship 41
  administration 170
  origins 208, 317, 318
  Scottish dominance 25
  trophy 44
  winners list 318–19
British Professional Golfers' Association 44
Broadmoor 124
Brodie, Robert 23
brooch, silver 59
Brookline, Country Club of 34
Brown, Eric 223
Brown, Michael J. 170
Bruntsfield 17
Bulawayo 36
bulgers 28–9, 330
bunkers
  origin 15–16
  St. Andrews 171, 173
Burke, Billy 294
Burke, Jack 226
Burma 35
Burma Road *see* Wentworth
"The Bussey" club carrier 31
Butler National 197

caddie cars 55
caddies 19, 31
Calamity hole, Royal Portrush 156
Calcavecchia, Mark 265, 279
cambuca (cambuta) 11
Campbell, Sir Guy 226
Campbell, Willie 237
Canada
  Banff 196
  Glen Abbey 88–9
  golf expansion 35
  The National 110–13
Canadian Open, Glen Abbey 88
Cape bunker, Royal North Devon 154
carbon-fibre clubs 39, 51–3, 330
Carner, JoAnne 227
Carnoustie 70–3
Carr, Joe 228
Carr, Roddy 228
Carrick family 23
Carroll's Irish Open 130
Casper, Billy 228
Cedar Rapids 124
Centenary British Open Championship 42
Chambers, Robert 144, 226
championships
  courses of the world 58–213
  development 40–5
  winners (tables) 316–29
Chantilly 74–5
Charles, Bob 229
Chicago 197
  origins 33, 35
China, golf expansion 37
chole 12
Christchurch 198
Church Pews bunker, Oakmont 116
church protests 16, 33
claret jug 19, 44, 239, 302, 318
cleekmakers 23
cleeks 28–9, 330
clothing 54–5
  plus-fours 54, 166, 260
  red coats 54, 176
Club zur Vahr 76–7
clubmakers 22–3, 52
clubs
  accessories 55
  aluminium-headed 7, 29, 50
  antique 20–1
  carbon-fibre 39, 51–3, 330
  carriers 31
  development 7, 28–9
  early 10–14, 17
  irons 21, 23, 29
  modern 50–1
  sand wedges 50–1, 53, 331
  sets 52–3
  shafts 21, 28–9, 50–1
  silver 19, 102
  wooden 20–1, 52–3
Coles, Neil 57, 77, 301
Collett, Glenna *see* Vare
Collins, Richard 21
Colonial 78–9
Colt, Harry S. 56, 266
  County Down 139
  Falkenstein 201
  Ganton 87
  Kennemer 203
  Muirfield 102
  Royal Lytham and St. Annes 148
  Sunningdale 180, 182
  Wentworth 193
  Woodhall Spa 213
Combe, George 138–9
Compston, Archie 245
Connachan, Jane 47
Connelly, Ian 238
Corcoran, Fred 295
Corfu 198
Cossar, Simon 20–1, 23
Cotton, Sir Henry 6, 41, 245
  course architect 57
  Penina 208, 231
  profile 230–1
Cotton, Ken 57, 148
  Ganton 87
  Olgiata 206
  Saunton 210
Country Club of Brookline 34
Couples, Fred 281
course architecture 40, 56–7
Cove Fields 35
Crans-sur-Sierre 198
Crawley, Leonard 216, 260, 315
Crenshaw, Ben 232, 255
Crockford, Claude 150–1
"The Crosby" 43, 118
crosse 12–13
Crump, George 56, 122
Curtis Cup 46–7, 328–9
Curtis, Harriot and Margaret 46, 326, 328
Cypress Point 80–1
Czechoslovakia, golf expansion 36

Darwin, Bernard (writer)
  on Abe Mitchell 269
  on Harold Hilton 248
  on J.H. Taylor 299
  profile 233
  on Royal Troon 165
  on Sandy Herd 243
Davies, Laura 227, 282
  profile 234
  on Women's Tour 46, 47
Decisions on the Rules 25
Desert Highlands 57, 82–3
Devil's Arse, Pine Valley 122
Devil's Cauldron, Banff 196
Devlin, Bruce 235, 242
Dickie, James 162
Dickson family 23
Diegel, Leo 245
Doleman, Alexander 148
Donald Duck figurine 35
Donald, Jean 315
Donald, Mike 249
Doral 199
Dormy House clubhouse 149
Douglas, Kitrina 47
drivers 330
  construction 52
  development 28–9
  early types 20
  modern 50–1
driving ranges, Japan 37
Duncan, George 215, 236
The Dunes 199
Dunhill Cup 42
Dunlop Masters 286
Dunluce course, Royal Portrush 156
Dunn, Jamie 291
Dunn, John Duncan 237
Dunn, Seymour 139, 237
Dunn, Tom 87, 237
Dunn, Willie, Jr. 22, 50, 237
  Shinnecock Hills 176
  U.S. Open 319
Dunn, Willie, Sr. 237, 291
Dye, Pete 57
  Harbour Town 90–1
  Mariya 94–5
  Muirfield Village 106

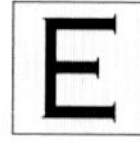

East Lake 124
Eastwood, Clint 43
Edinburgh course, Wentworth 193
Emirates 199
England
 The Belfry 196
 golf expansion 25
 Formby 200
 Ganton 86–7
 Lindrick 92–3
 Royal Birkdale 134–5
 Royal Liverpool 144–7
 Royal Lytham and St. Annes 148–9
 Royal North Devon 152–5
 Royal St. George's 158–9
 Rye 166–7
 Saunton 210
 Sunningdale 180–3
 Walton Heath 212
 Wentworth 192–3
 Woodhall Spa 213
Estela 200
Europe
 golf expansion 36
 revival 43–5
expansion
 England 24–5
 Scotland 17, 19
 World 32–7

fairways 330
 origins 18
Faldo, Nick
 at Augusta 62, 264
 Masters 1989 232
 Open Championship 1987 317
 profile 238–9
 successes 44, 45
 U.S. Open 1988 297
Falsterbo 18, 84–5
Faulkner, Max 240–1
Fazio, George 110, 197, 246
Fazio, Tom
 Medinah 96
 The National 110
 Wild Dunes 213
featheries 26, 330
Fernie, Willie 162, 188
Fischer, Johnny 312
Flower, Clement 40
Floyd, Ray 238, 255
 profile 240–1
 Ryder Cup draw 1989 251
Forbes, Duncan 25
Ford, Gerald R. 43, 124
Ford, Glenn 247
Forgan, Robert 21
Formby, England 200
Forsbrand, Anders 43
Fowler, Herbert 56
 Royal Lytham and St. Annes 148
 Royal North Devon 152
 Saunton 210
Fownes, Bill 233
Fownes, Henry C. 116
Fox hole, Royal Troon 164
Foxy hole, Royal Dornoch 142–3
France
 Chantilly 74–5
 golf expansion 36
 golf origins 11–12
French Open, Chantilly 74
Furgol, Ed 241

Gallacher, Bernard 193
The Game of Golf (Park) 286
Ganton 86–7
Garbacz, Lori 263
Garlstedter Heide course, Club zur Vahr 76–7
Gentlemen Golfers of Leith 19
George Glennie Medal 170
George VI, King 289
Germany
 Club zur Vahr 76–7
 Hamburg-Falkenstein 201
Giedeon, Torsten 257
Glen Abbey 88–9
Gleneagles 56, 200
Goalby, Bob 303
Gold Medal 170
golf bags 31, 55
golf cart (trolley) 55
Goodman, John 294
Gossett, Rev. I.H. 152
Gourlay family 27
Graham, David 232, 242
Graham, Maureen 242
Grand Cypress 201
Grand Slam events 41
graphite clubs 51–3, 330
grasses 93, 166
 green management 56–7
Gray, John 23
Great Triumvirate 40, 288, 330
Great White Shark *see* Norman, Greg
Greece, Corfu 198
"green card" system, Sweden 36
Green, Charlie 45
Green, Hubert 242
Green Jacket tradition 62
greenskeeping 56–7
greens, origins 18–19, 330
Greenwich 34
Grey Oaks 32
Griscomb, Clement A. 98
Groome, Arthur 37
Grout, Jack 277
Guldahl, Ralph 243
Gullane 201
Gunderson, JoAnne *see* Carner
Gunn, Dr. Hugh 140
guttie balls 24, 26–7, 330

Hagen, Walter 236, 243, 292
 profile 244–5
 successes 40, 41, 320
Hamburg-Falkenstein 201
Harbour Town 57, 90–1
Harradine, Donald 198, 211
Harris, John 57
Harrison, Dutch 259
Harvard University Golf Cup 34
Haskell ball 48–9, 330
Haskell, Coburn 48
Havermeyer, Theodore 34
Havers, Arthur 244
Hawtree, Fred W. 57, 128, 298
 Royal Birkdale 135
Hazeltine National 202
Heffelfinger, Totten 202
Herd, Sandy 243, 254
Heritage Classic 91
Hewson, Lionel 66
Highet, Dr. John 162
Hilton, Harold 143, 144
 British Amateur 1896 298
 British Open win 1892 102
 designer at Ganton 87
 profile 248
history 14–25, 32–5
Hoch, Scott 232, 239
Hogan, Ben 41, 42
 1-iron exhibit 98
 profile 246–7
 "yips" sufferer 256
Hogan, Valerie 246, 247
Hogan's Alley, Carnoustie 70, 73
Holbrook, Harry 33
hole cutter 56
Hole, Frank 186, 188
Holland 36
 golf origins 9–10, 13–14
Hollins, Marion 80
Holy Island links 24
Hong Kong, Royal Hong Kong 210
Honourable Company of Edinburgh Golfers 19, 25, 102
Hopkins, John Jay 329
Horsburgh, Thomas 50
Hotchkin, Colonel S.V. 213
Hourigan, Jackie 67
Hoylake *see* Royal Liverpool
Huggett, Brian 57
Huis Ten Bosch 57
Hungary, golf expansion 36
Hunt, Bernard 216
Hutchinson, Major C.K. 186
Hutchinson, Horace 87, 152, 248
Hutchison, Jock 292
Hyndman, Bill 223

I

India 35
 Royal Calcutta 209
 Western India Open Amateur 7
Inoue, Seichi 203
Ireland, Republic of
 Ballybunion 66–7
 Portmarnock 128–31
irons
 development 23, 29, 50
 hand-forged 21, 23
 modern 50–1, 52–3
irrigation 57, 82
Irwin, Hale 249, 267
Italy
 Olgiata 206
 Pevero 120–1
 Rome 208

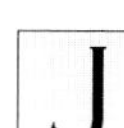

Jacklin, Tony
 course architect 57
 British Open 1971 251, 301
 profile 250–1
 Ryder Cup captain 44, 281
Jacobs, John 193
Jamaica, Tryall 184–5
Jameson, Betty 222
Japan
 driving ranges 37
 golf expansion 37
 golf fans 45
 Kasugai 203
 Mariya 94–5
 New St. Andrews 205
 Yomiuri 213
Japan Open Championship 203
jeu de mail 9, 11–12
Jockey Club, The 202
Jockie's Burn, Carnoustie 70
Johnnie Walker World Championship 184
Joint Decisions Committee 25
Jones, Bobby 215, 230, 244, 266
 championship record 41
 course architect 56
 creator of Augusta 62
 "Impregnable Quadrilateral" 324
 Merion plaque 98
 profile 252–3
 on Walter Hagen 245
Jones, Robert Trent *see* Trent

Karen 202
Kasugai 203
Keller, Louis 68
Kennemer 203
Kenya, Karen 202
Kingsley, Charles 152
Kingston Heath 203
Kinnan, Alexander P.W. 33
Kirkaldy, Andrew 298
 British Open 1889 286
 on Muirfield 102
 profile 254
Kirkaldy, Hugh 167, 254
Kitchen, The, Royal St. George's 158
"Kite" (Haskell-type ball) 48
Kite, Tom 232, 255
Knight, Ray 262
Kobe 37
kolven (kolf) 9, 11, 13–14
Kroll, Ted 226

Lacoste, Catherine 36, 47
Ladies' British Open Amateur Championship 46, 325–6
Ladies' Golf Union 46, 325
Ladies' Professional Golf Association 47, 331
Laidlay, John 256, 305
Lake Kadijah, Medinah 96–7
Lake Karrinyup 204
Lakewood 34
Lang Whang hole, Turnberry 189
Langer, Bernhard 43, 265, 276
 course architect 57
 profile 256–7
Laure de Lorenzi, Marie 47
Lawrie, Charles 57
Leadbetter, David 238, 239
Leitch, Cecil 46, 306, 309
Leith 17, 19, 25
Lema, Tony 258, 287, 302
Leonard, Marvin 78
Limburger, Dr. Bernhard von 76, 201
Lindrick 92–3
links 331
 nature 18
Litten, Karl 199
Little, Lawson 294
Littler, Gene 241, 259
Locke, Bobby 250, 302
 British Open wins 42
 profile 260–1
Lockhart, Robert 32–3
London Scottish Club 25
Longhurst, Henry 261
Lopez, Nancy 46, 47, 227
 profile 262–3
Los Angeles Open 132
Los Aves *see* Valderrama
Low, George 134
Low, John L. 167
Lowe, George 148
Lu Liang Huan 37
Lyle, Alex 264
Lyle, Sandy 278, 311
 British Open win 1985 43
 Green Jacket 62
 profile 264–5

McCalmont, Colonel J.M. 156
McCormack, Mark 42, 45, 284
 on Muirfield Village 106

McDermott, Johnny 40
Macdonald, Charles Blair 33, 324
  Chicago 197
  course architect 56
  National Golf Links of America 205
  U.S. pioneer 34–5
McEwan, Peter 21
MacFie, A.F. 248, 298, 322
MacGregor Company 226, 273
McHardy, Alex 140
Mackenzie, Dr. Alister 56
  Augusta 62, 266
  Cypress Point 80–1, 266
  Ganton 87
  The Jockey Club 202
  Kingston Heath 203
  Lindrick 92
  New South Wales 206
  profile 266
  Royal Melbourne 150
  Royal Sydney 160–1
  Royal Troon 162
Mackintosh, Ian 162
Maiden, Stewart 252
Manga, La 204
Mangrum, Lloyd 246–7, 268
Maritz, Laurette 282
Mariya 94–5
Marsh, Graham 267
mashies 28, 29, 331
Masters Tournament winners 321
matchplay disappearance 42
Maule, Sir Robert 70
Mauritius, golf expansion 35
Maxwell, Perry 78
Mayer, Dick 268
Meadow Brook 34
Medinah 96–7
Mehlhorn, Bill 245
Memorial Tournament 108
Merion 56, 98–101
Micklem, Gerald 267
Middlecoff, Cary 268
Miller, Johnny 268–9
Mitchell, Abe 215, 269
Mize, Larry 279
The Modern Fundamentals of Golf (Hogan) 274
"Modern Triumvirate" 43
money, impact 41–2, 45
Montclair 34
Morris, George 144
Morris, Old Tom 237, 254
  Carnoustie 72
  clubmaker 22, 28
  course architect 56
  Lockhart's order 1887 32
  Muirfield 102
  Nairn 205
  profile 270
  Robertson's apprentice 290
  Royal County Down 138
  Royal Dornoch 140
  Royal North Devon 25, 152
Morris, Young Tom 72, 270, 271
Morrison, J.S.F. 226
Morrison, John 201
Morristown Ladies' Club 46
Morse, Samuel F. 119
mowers 56–7
Mrs. Simpson bunker, Ballybunion 67
Muirfield 102–5
Muirfield Village 102, 106–9
Muirhead, Desmond 106, 205
Musselburgh 17
Myopia Hunt 319

N

Nagle, Kel 272, 284, 287
Nairn 205
Nakajima, Tommy 272
National, The 110–13
National Golf Links of America 56, 205
National Inter-club Championship 25
National Invitation Tournament 79
National Pro-Am 118
Nelson, Byron 273, 289, 306
Nelson, Larry 274
Netherlands, Kennemer 203
Neville, Jack 119
New Brunswick 34
New St. Andrews 205
New South Wales 206
New Zealand
  Christchurch 198
  golf expansion 35
  Otago 207
Newport 34
Newton, Jack 275, 306–7
niblick 20, 28, 331
Nicholas, Alison 47
Nicklaus, Jack
  course architect 56, 57
  Desert Highlands 57, 82–3
  earnings 255
  Faldo's inspiration 238
  Glen Abbey 88
  Grand Cypress 201
  Harbour Town 90
  Huis Ten Bosch 57
  Major wins 43, 44
  Mariya Pro-Celebrity match 1989 95
  Muirfield 102
  Muirfield Village 106, 108
  New St. Andrews 205
  British Open 1968 287
  British Open 1970 292
  British Open 1977 307
  profile 276–7
  Shoal Creek 211
  U.S. Open 1968 301
Nida, Norman Von 275, 278
Norman, Greg 215
  profile 278–9
  British Open 1986 272
  U.S. Open 1984 313
North, Andy 280
North Devon and West of England *see* Royal North Devon
Northern Ireland
  Royal County Down 138–9
  Royal Portrush 156–7

O

Oak Hill 124
Oakland Hills 56, 114–15, 124
Oakmont 116–17
O'Connor, Christy, Jr./Sr. 281
Okamoto, Ayako 282
Olazabal, Jose-Maria 36, 44, 45, 311
Old Manchester 24
Old Tom Morris *see* Morris, Old Tom
Olgiata 206
Olympic Club 207
Oosterhuis, Peter 75, 238, 287
origins of golf 9–19
Ortiz-Patino, Jaime 191
"The Osmond" club-carrier 31
Otago 35, 207
Ouimet, Francis 41, 288
  profile 282–3
Owen, Simon 255
Oxford and Cambridge Golfing Society 167
Ozaki, "Jumbo" 241

P

Padgham, Alf 283
paganica 9, 10–11
Palmares 207
Palmer, Arnold 228, 277
  Beijing 37
  Centenary British Open 43, 272
  course architect 57
  British Open 1961 289
  profile 284–5
  successes 42, 43
  U.S. Open 1960 276
Palmer, Deacon 284
Panks, Gary 83
Panton, Cathy 47
Park, Mungo 128
Park, Willie, Jr. 254
  inland courses 56
  profile 286
  Sunningdale 180
Park, Willie, Sr. 270, 286, 318
  clubmaker 20–1, 22
Paterson 34
Patrick family 23
Pau 36
Pearson, Issette 46
Pebble Beach 118–19
pell mell 11, 14
Penina 208
Pennink, Frank 57
  Ganton 87
  Royal St. George's 158
  Royal Troon 162
Persson, Magnus 43
Pevero 120–1
Philippines, Wack Wack 212
Philp, Hugh 23
Pickeman, W.C. 128
Pine Valley, Canada *see* The National
Pine Valley 56, 122–3
Pinehurst Club 35, 124–7
playclubs 20–1, 331
Player, Gary 43, 57
  profile 286–7
  U.S. Masters 1978 242
  U.S. Open 1965 272, 287
  World Matchplay Championship 193, 287
Playfair, Sir Hugh Lyon 290
Plummer, Ralph 184
plus-fours tradition 54, 166
Portmarnock 18, 128–31
Portugal
  Estela 200
  golf expansion 36
  Palmares 207
  Penina 208
Post, Sandra 47
Postage Stamp hole, Royal Troon 164–5
Premier Golf Company 23
President's Putter 167
Prestwick 208
  Open Championship origin 317, 318
professional golfers 22–3, 39–41
  women 46–7
Professional Golfers' Association 40
  European/American tours 44
Purves, Dr. Laidlaw 158–9
Putman, Kingman H. 33
putters 20, 21
  development 29
  modern 50–1, 52
putting greens, origin 18
Pyramid hole, Winged Foot 195

R

Rae's Creek, Augusta 65
ranges, Japan 37
Ransom, Henry 275
Rarick, Cindy 282
Rattray, John 102
Rawlins, Horace 237, 319
Ray, Ted 244, 305
  profile 288
  U.S. Open 1913 41, 283
Raynor, Seth 80
red coats tradition 54, 176
Rees, Dai 240, 286, 289
Reid, Dale 47
Reid, John, U.S. pioneer 32–4
Richmond 34
Riviera 37, 132–3
Road Hole bunker, St. Andrews 171, 173
Robbie, S.J. 160
Roberts, Clifford 62
Roberts, T.A. 180
Robertson, Allan 25, 237, 270
  ballmaker 26, 27
  Carnoustie 70
  profile 290–1
Robertson, David 290
Robertson, Peter 290
Rodgers, Phil 229
Rogers, Bill 217
Rolland, Douglas 144
Roman origins 9–11
Romania, golf expansion 36
Rome 208
Rosendaelsche 36
Ross, Donald J. 56
  Oakland Hills 114
  Pinehurst 124
  Royal Dornoch 140, 143
  Scioto 211
Ross, George 128
Ross, Mackenzie 186, 188
Royal Aberdeen 209
Royal Adelaide 35
Royal and Ancient Golf Club
  clubhouse 7, 169
  origins 19, 170
Royal Antwerp 36
Royal Belgique 209
Royal Birkdale 134–5
Royal Blackheath 19, 24
Royal Bombay 35
Royal Burgess 19
Royal Calcutta 35, 209
Royal Cape 35, 136–7
Royal Christchurch 35
Royal County Down 138–9
Royal Dornoch 18, 140–3
Royal Hong Kong 35, 210
Royal Johannesburg 36, 210
Royal Liverpool 25, 144–7
Royal Lytham and St. Annes 43, 148–9
Royal Melbourne 35, 150–1
Royal Montreal 35
Royal North Devon 24, 25, 152–5
royal patronage 16–17
Royal Portrush 18, 156–7
Royal Quebec 35
Royal St. George's 18, 158–9
Royal Sydney 35, 160–1
Royal Troon 162–5
Royal Wimbledon 25
rubber-core ball 27, 48–9, 331
rules
  ball size 49
  club sets 52–3
  establishment 102
  origins 9, 19, 25
  standardization 25, 126
Russell, Alex 150
Ryder Cup 317
  European revival 43–4
  winners list 327–8
Ryder, Samuel 269, 327
Rye 166–7

Sahara, Ballybunion 66
Sahara bunker, Oakmont 116
Sahara Desert, Baltusrol 68
St. Andrews 59, 168–73
  British Centenary Open 42
  history 15–16, 18
  rules development 25
St. Andrew's 33–4
St. Clair, William of Roslin 102
St. George's Hill 56
Saler, El 174–5
sand irons (wedges) 50, 51, 331
Sanders, Doug 292
Sandwich Golfing Association 158
Sarazen, Gene 40, 41
  on Gene Littler 259
  profile 292–3
  on Walter Hagen 244, 245
Saunton 19, 210
Savannah 34
Scioto 124, 211
scorecards 55, 61
Scotland 24–5
  Carnoustie 70–3
  Gleneagles 200
  golf origins 9–19
  Gullane 201
  Muirfield 102–5
  Nairn 205
  Prestwick 208
  Royal Aberdeen 209
  Royal Dornoch 140–3
  Royal Troon 162–5
  St. Andrews 7, 59, 168–73
  Turnberry 186–9
Scott, James 160
Scott, Lady Margaret 46
Seefeld-Wildmoos 211
Sellberg, Ove 43
Seminole 124
shafts
  modern 50–3
  wooden 21, 28–9
Sheffield and District *see* Lindrick
Shepard, Alan B. Jnr 43
Shiba Park 37
Shinnecock Hills 34, 176–9, 237
  aerial view 59
  ladies' course 46
Shoal Creek 211
Shotts, John C. 33
Shute, Densmore 41
Sigel, Jay 45
silver clubs 19, 102
Silver Cross of St. Andrews 170
Simpson, Archie 205
Simpson, Tom 56
  Ballybunion 67
  Chantilly 74
  Royal Belgique 209
Singapore 35
Siwanoy 320
Sixteen Mile Creek, Glen Abbey 88–9
Smith, Jenny Lee 322
Snead, Homer 294
Snead, Sam 240
  on JoAnne Carner 227
  profile 294–5
  "yips" sufferer 256
Sneed, Ed 313
Society of St. Andrews Golfers 19, 170
Solheim Cup 47
Sony World Rankings 44
South Africa
  golf expansion 35
  Royal Cape 136–7
  Royal Johannesburg 210
South Carolina Golf Club 34, 91
Southampton 34
Spain
  Brisas, Las 197
  golf expansion 36, 45
  Manga, La 204
  Saler, El 174–5
  Valderrama 190–1
Spalding 29
spoons (scrapers) 20–1, 28, 331
Sri Lanka 35
Stadler, Craig 296
Stephenson, Jan 296
Stewart, Payne 265
Strange, Curtis 239, 297, 311
Strath, Andrew 23
strokeplay 42, 331
Sunneson, Fanny 45, 239
Sunningdale 56, 180–3
Surlyn ball cover 49, 331
Sutherland, John 140
Sweden
  Falsterbo 84–5
  golf expansion 36
Swilcan Bridge, St. Andrews 168–9
  replicas 201, 205
Switzerland, Crans-sur-Sierre 198

Tait, Freddie 248, 298
Taiwan, golf expansion 37
Tallmadge, Henry O. 32, 33, 34
Taylor, J.H. 25, 40, 243
  on Bernard Darwin 233
  Kirkaldy challenge 1895 254
  profile 298–9
  Royal Birkdale 135
  Royal Dornoch 140
  Royal North Devon 152–4
  Vardon challenge 1895 304–5
tees 30, 331
  origins 18
television impact 42
Thirwell, Alan 223
This Game of Golf (Cotton) 305
Thomas, Dave 57, 196
Thomas, George 132
Thomson, Peter 235, 258, 267
  British Open wins 42
  course architect 57
  profile 302
  World Matchplay 1965 287
Thompson, Stanley 196
Tillinghast, A.W. 56, 68–9, 194
Tissies, Hermann 164
Torrens, Lt-Gen. Sir Henry D'Oyley Torrens 136
track iron 21
Trent Jones, Robert 56
  Baltusrol 69
  Brisas, Las 197
  The Dunes 199
  Hazeltine 202
  Oakland Hills 114–15
  Pevero 120
  Valderrama 190–1
Trevino, Lee 43, 251, 300–1
trolleys 55
trophies 41
  Masters trophy 62
  President's Putter 167
Tryall 184–5
Tufts, James W. 124–6
Turnberry 42, 186–9
Turnbull, Robert 84
Turnesa, Jim 216, 245
Tway, Bob 279
Tze-Chung Chen 280

United Arab Emirates, Emirates, Dubai 199
Upham, John B. 33, 34
Urquhart family 29
U.S. Amateur Championship 41, 324–5
  inception 34
U.S. Masters tournament 41, 62–4
  winners list 321
U.S. Open Championship 39, 41
  inception 34
  winners list 319–20
U.S. Women's Amateur Championship 326–7
U.S. Women's Open Championship 47
  winners list 322
U.S.A.
  Augusta National 62–5
  Baltustrol 68–9
  Butler National 197
  Chicago 197
  Colonial 78–9
  Cypress Point 80–1
  Desert Highlands 82–3
  dominance 41–4
  Doral 199
  The Dunes 199
  expansion 25, 32–8
  Grand Cypress 201
  Harbour Town 90–1
  Hazeltine 202
  Medinah 96–7
  Merion 98–101
  Muirfield Village 106–9
  National Golf Links of America 205
  Oakland Hills 114–15
  Oakmont 116–17
  Olympic 207
  Pebble Beach 118–19
  Pine Valley 122–3
  Pinehurst 124–7
  Riviera 132–3
  Scioto 211
  Shinnecock Hills 176–9, 237
  Shoal Creek 211
  Wild Dunes 213
  Winged Foot 194–5
USGA 25, 331
  origins 34
USPGA 41, 44–5, 331
  Championship winners 320–1

Valderrama 190–1
Vale do Lobo 37
Valentine, Jessie 303
Valley course, Royal Portrush 156
Valley holes, Glen Abbey 88
Valley of Sin, St. Andrews 173
Van Donck, Flory 235
Vanderbilt, William K. 176
Vardon, Harry
  at Ganton 87
  Great Triumvirate member 40
  grip 305, 331
  British Open 1896 299
  Park Challenge 1899 286
  profile 215, 304–5
  Royal County Down 139
  U.S. challenge 41
  U.S. Open 1913 244, 282–3
  U.S. Tour 288
  Woodhall Spa 213
  "yips" sufferer 256
Vare, Glenna Collett 46, 47, 309
  profile 306
  U.S. Women's Amateur 326
Venturi, Ken 226
Vicenzo, Roberto de 303
Volvo Masters 191
Von Nida *see* Nida, Norman Von

Wack Wack 212
Wadkins, Larry 274
Walker Cup winners 328
Walker, George H. 328
The Walter Hagen Story 244, 245
Walton Heath 212
Watrous, Al 244
Watson, Denis 280
Watson, Tom 6, 43
  British Open 1975 275
  British Open 1977 186, 307
  profile 306–7
  U.S. Masters 1984 232
Way, Paul 311
Weaver, Arthur 144
wedges 50–1, 53
Weiskopf, Tom 278, 308–9
Wemyss, Frank 291
Wentworth 56, 192–3
Western India Open Amateur 7
Westward Ho! *see* Royal North Devon
Wethered, Joyce (Lady Heathcoat-Amory) 140
  profile 309
  British Ladies' Championship 1929 306
  successes 46, 325
Wethered, Roger 140, 309
Weyhausen, August 76
Wheaton *see* Chicago
Whitcombe, Ernest 289
White Plains 34
White, Robert 23
White, Stanford 176
Whitworth, Kathy 47, 310
Wild Dunes 213
Wilson, Dick 178, 199
Wilson, Hugh 56, 98
Wilson, Robert 23
Wimbledon Common 24
Winged Foot 194–5
women 46–7
  clothing fashions 54
  Jamaica Classic 184
  Medinah design 96
Women's British Open Championship 322
Woodhall Spa 213
Woodhouse, P.G. 47
woods 20–1, 51, 53
  construction 52
Woosnam, Ian 44, 311
Work, Bertram 48
World Cup Golf winners 329
World Golf Hall of Fame 124
World Matchplay Championship 42, 192–3
world expansion 32–7
Worsham, Buddy 284
Wright, Mickey 47, 312

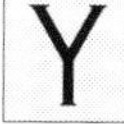

Yates, Charlie 312
"yips" disorder 256–7, 331
Yokohama 37
Yomiuri 213
Young Tom Morris *see* Morris, Young Tom
Yugoslavia, golf expansion 36

Zaharias, Babe 47, 222, 314–15
Zimbabwe, golf expansion 36
Zoeller, Fuzzy 274, 313

Acknowledgments

Golfing ephemera from:

Sarah Baddiel
The Golf Gallery
B12, Grays Antique Market
Davies Mews
London W1Y 1AR
Tel. 071–408 1239

Course map reference from:

Birdie Golf Ltd
15 Market Place
Warminster
Wiltshire BA12 9AY
Tel. 0985 216011

Dorlings Signs Ltd
235/7 Wood Street
London E17 3NT
Tel. 081–520 1056

Golfplans International
The Clubhouse
Taggs Island
Hampton
Middlesex TW12 2HA
Tel. 081–941 4078

Graphic Ideas Ltd
135/9 Curtain Road
London EC2A 3BX
Tel. 071–739 9313

Strokesport
Abbey Mill Business Centre
Seedhill
Paisley PA1 1JN
Tel. 041–848 1199

Antique golf equipment from:

Phillips Auctioneers
New House
150 Christleton Road
Chester
Cheshire CH3 5TD
Tel. 0244 313936

Alick A. Watt
6 Musgrove Gardens
Alton
Hampshire GU34 2EQ
Tel. 0420 84763

Modern golf equipment from:

American Golf Discount Ltd
Unit 4, Centre 21
Bridge Lane
Woolston
Warrington
Cheshire WA1 4AW
Tel. 0925 823299

Neil Jordan's Pro Shop
Sudbury Golf Club
Bridgewater Road
Wembley
London HA10 1AL
Tel. 081–902 7910

Lillywhites Ltd
24/36 Regent Street
Piccadilly Circus
London SW1Y 4QF
Tel. 071–930 3181

Nevada Bob's
Staples Corner
Retail & Leisure Park
Edgware Road
London NW2
Tel. 081–450 4550

Author's acknowledgments

It may be, as Dante Gabriel Rossetti averred around the time of the arrival of the guttie ball, that the worst of all worlds is to be really thankful and, as in the case of the atheist, have no one to thank. I have no such worries, for I have much to be thankful for and many people to be thankful to.

I am very grateful to Editorial Director David Lamb, for his encouragement from the beginning and for his support and understanding during the sometimes difficult early stages of this project. To Roger Smoothy, who has been an outstanding and diligent editor and a good friend throughout, I extend my sincere thanks. Carolyn King and Nick Harris have provided marvelous and vital support, and to them I also extend my warmest thanks.

Brian Rust and Caroline Murray have done valiant work on the design and have had excellent backing from the editorial and design teams at Dorling Kindersley, which have a seemingly endless capacity for hard work. My grateful thanks go to them all.

I am also extremely grateful to the R & A Historian, Bobby Burnet, for his invaluable help and research on the history of the game, and to Alick A. Watt, Alan Elliott, John Allan May, John Ingham, and Keith Mackie for their contributions. I have had outstanding cooperation and help from photographer Brian D. Morgan and the staff at Golf Photography International, Glasgow.

Finally, I owe a special debt of gratitude to my family and close friends, who have supported me so stoically throughout this project and kept me going when dark clouds crossed the horizon.

Publisher's acknowledgments

Dorling Kindersley would like to thank the club secretaries, general managers, golf professionals, tournament officers, administrative staff, and members at the featured clubs for all their cooperation and goodwill. For providing valuable reference and information and verifying accuracy, special thanks are due to Donald E. Aitken, David C. Allen, Robert Alonzi, James H. Armstrong, Jr., Christian Barras, Dorothy Bell, Marshal Bereton, A. Beveridge, Stan Bishop, Gil Blechman, Cam Boatwright, Rod Bogg, Commander J.M. Bradley, Peter Burford, Gerry Bywater, Cary Corbitt, Nancy Van Cott, Major A.S. Craven, N.T. Crewe, E.J. Davies, Chris Davis, Danette Dearborn, David E. Donaldson, Richard Doyle-Davidson, Gilberto Duavit, Jean Duysters, H.R. Ebrecht, Bud Erickson, Wilma Erskine, Eric Filfinger, Michael C. Franck, Brian Franke, William John Dennis Garvey, W.E. Geddes, R.J. Harper, C.L. Hart, Donald T. Hayes, Dr. T.M. Healy, A. Heron, Captain R.J. Hitchen, Danna Holck, W.M. Hopley, Rick Jacobson, Ben Kern, Pasquale J. LaRocca, Nelson Long, Jr., F.J. Longden, Michael Lovett, Jim Lucius, Cliffe Mann, E.P. van Marken, Jim McPhilomy, J.D. Montgomerie, Robert Nelson, Sandra Nicolson, Mark De Noble, Jeanne Poepl, D. Patrick, Stefano Pilato, Air Vice-Marshal R.G. Price, Group Captain J.A. Prideaux, Antonio Ribeiro, Dennis Roberson, C.J. Rouse, J. Rutherford, Fernando Sagnier, Werner Seelos, S.R. Sharp, Douglas La Rue Smith, E.J.C. Smith, Masuo Someya, Diane Stracuzzi, Timothy K. Surlas, Margaret Swindell, A.J.B. Taylor, A. Thirlwell, Leon M. Thompson, Rodolfo B. Valdez, Major J.G. Vanreenen, Alfredo Vercelli, Ian C.R. Walker, Sean Walsh, G.E. Watts, Barry Weickel, John Weir, Robin H. White, R. Widuhrt, Ingrid Willstrand, E. Wilson, Jim Wisler, Christina Witchell, and Allan Wood.

Thanks to the following people and organizations for their help during the creation of this book: Eunice Paterson for production; Josephine Buchanan, Joanna Chisholm, Corinne Hall, Stephanie Jackson, Andrew Mikolajski, Caroline Ollard, Deborah Rhodes, and Susannah Tapper for editorial assistance; John W.L. Adams, Sharon Clapson, Richard Dyson, Rhonda Jenkins at the USGA, David H. Linton, and John T. Milton for research and fact-checking; Indexing Specialists (Hove, East Sussex) for compiling the index; Joanna Figg-Latham, Bob Gordon, Neville Graham, Lee Griffiths, Vanessa Hamilton, Clair Lidzey, Gurinder Purewall, and Alistair Wardle for design assistance; Boyd Annison, Mark Annison, and Keith Errington at Icon Associates and Salvatore Tomaselli for computer artworks; Rowan Clifford, Andy Farmer, and Janos Marffy for illustrations; Penelope Chaplin and Pamela Thomas at DK Inc., A. Davis de Montluzin at Jack Nicklaus Golf Services, Tom Fazio at Fazio Golf Course Designers Inc., Michael Gedye, Joe Hackler, Stuart MacPherson, and J.P. Richardson of Ordnance Survey (Air Photo Sales) for assistance with artwork reference; Karen Bednarski at the USGA Museum (Far Hills, New Jersey), Bob Gowland at Phillips, Mark Kiemele at Public Image, Katherine McCudden at Christies, James T. Strachan, and James Watt (Dirleton) for providing photographs; Tim Ridley and Barnabus Kindersley for studio photography; Sean Arnold at Golf and Polo Antiques (Grays Antique Market), James Horsfield at Auchterlonie's, Leonard Jowett at John White & Sons, and Mike Mander at The Royal Botanic Gardens (Kew) for providing materials for photography; Deborah Pownall for picture research.

Picture credits

All the photographs were taken by Brian D. Morgan, except those from the following, whom Dorling Kindersley would like to thank for kind permission to reproduce their photographs:

(Abbreviations: b=below, c=center, l=left, r=right, t=top)
Allsport/David Cannon 234c, Allsport/Rick Stewart 234r. Associated Press 41tr, 222t, 228b, 246bl, 312b, 315b. Belga, Brussels 235b. Bridgeman Art Library 13br. British Library, London 10b. British Museum, London 17t. Brown Brothers, Sterling PA 34t, 47tl, 252cr, 253bl, 273l. Malcolm Campbell 56cr, 124tr. Chicot Agency, Paris 120, 121. Frank Christian Photostudio, Augusta 266. Christies, Scotland 170tl. E.T. Archive 168tr. Mary Evans Picture Library 18bl. Giraudon/Musée Condée, Chantilly 12b. Golden Bear International Inc. 57tr. Golf World 223tr, 241cr and b, 256cl, 259l, 260b, 261bl, 283tl, 288l and r, 310l, 314l. Sonia Halliday 11tr. Mathew Harris Golf Picture Library 96, 97. The Michael Hobbs Golf Collection 15b, 17b, 19b, 30t, 31c, 40bl, 223tl, 226t, 237b, 247tr and c, 252bl, 260t, 270bl, 273br, 283bl, 290b, 298tl and b. Hulton-Deutsch 13bl, 18tr, 32tl (Bettman Archive), 40br, 46br, 144tr, 216br, 217bl, 220c, 224c and t, 225 all, 230l and t, 231c, 233cr, 236t and b, 240t and bl, 243br, 244bl, 245 all, 250l and tr, 252tr, 253tr, 258 all, 267b, 268l, 269rt and b, 270br, 275b, 276tr and br, 281t, 282br, 283br, 284cl and tr, 286r, 288t, 289 all, 292tl, 293tr and c, 294l and tr, 295tl, 298r, 299c and tr, 302c and tr, 304c, 305br, 306tl and bl, 308l and tr, 309 all, 314r. LeRoy Neiman, Inc. All rights reserved/ Knoedler Publications, New York 43t. Mansell Collection 11br, 46tr. Minneapolis Institute of Arts 12t. National Gallery, London 8. National Portrait Gallery, London 16c and br. National Railway Museum, York 140bl. Bert Neale Collection/Bob Thomas Sports Photography 229t, 246c, 261br, 272t, 303b. Popperfoto 228t, 246tr, 261tl, 315tl. Ransomes Sims & Jeffries Ltd 56br. Ronan Picture Library 27r. Courtesy of the Royal & Ancient Golf Club of St. Andrews 9b, 11l, 13t, 16cl, 25cr, 26cr, 170bl, 171tl, 237t, 254b, 271l, 286l, 290r, 291b. Phil Sheldon Photography 234bl, 282l. James T. Strachan 23cr. USGA, Far Hills NJ 23tl, 32r, 43c, 98tl, 98bl, 222b, 243tr, 247tl, 253br, 312t. University of St. Andrews Library 226b, 303t. Venture Prints (Studios) Ltd 144bl. Yonex Ltd 52br, 53cl.

Every effort has been made to trace the copyright holders of photographs and illustrations. Dorling Kindersley apologizes for any unintentional omissions and would be pleased to add an acknowledgment in future editions.